Rover Metro & 100 series Service and Repair Manual

Jeremy Churchill and Christopher Rogers

Models covered
Rover Metro & 100 series models with 1118cc and 1397cc "K-series" engines, manual and automatic gearboxes.
Includes 16-valve and special/limited editions

Does not cover Diesel engined models

(1711 - 280 - 11Y3)

A book in the **Haynes Service and Repair Manual Series**

ISBN **1 85960 165 0**

British Library Cataloguing in Publication Data
A catalogue record for this book is available from the British Library.

A

Printed by **J H Haynes & Co Ltd, Sparkford, Nr Yeovil, Somerset BA22 7JJ, England**

Haynes Publishing
Sparkford, Nr Yeovil, Somerset BA22 7JJ, England

Haynes North America, Inc
861 Lawrence Drive, Newbury Park, California 91320, USA

Editions Haynes S.A.
Tour Aurore - La Défense 2, 18 Place des Reflets,
92975 PARIS LA DEFENSE Cedex, France

Haynes Publishing Nordiska AB
Box 1504, 751 45 UPPSALA, Sweden

Contents

Contents

The Rover Metro and 100 Series covered in this Manual is a much-developed version of the original Austin Metro first launched in October 1980. These models are all fitted with the new "K" series engine in either 1.1 or 1.4 litre sizes, with either SU KIF carburettors, Rover/Motorola Modular Engine Management System single-point fuel-injection (MEMS-SPi) or Rover/Motorola Modular Engine Management System multi-point fuel-injection (MEMS-MPi). The engine is able to accept a full range of emission control systems, up to and including a three-way regulated catalytic converter, and is designed to require the minimum of servicing.

The transmission, a joint development by Rover and Peugeot engineers, is of Peugeot design and produced by Rover in manual 4 and 5-speed or automatic continuously variable (CVT) forms. It is fitted to the left-hand end of the engine. The complete engine/transmission assembly is mounted transversely across the front of the car and drives the front wheels through unequal length driveshafts.

The suspension is by the Hydragas system, with the units being linked front-to-rear on each side, and is heavily revised with wishbone-type lower arms. The suspension components at front and rear are rubber-mounted on separate subframes.

Braking is by discs at the front and drums at the rear, with a dual-circuit hydraulic system.

The body is available in three or five-door Hatchback versions, with a wide range of fittings and interior trim depending on the model's specification.

Rover 114GTa

Your Rover Metro/100 series Manual

The aim of this manual is to help you get the best value from your vehicle. It can do so in several ways. It can help you decide what work must be done (even should you choose to get it done by a garage), provide information on routine maintenance and servicing, and give a logical course of action and diagnosis when random faults occur. However, it is hoped that you will use the manual by tackling the work yourself. On simpler jobs it may even be quicker than booking the car into a garage and going there twice, to leave and collect it. Perhaps most important, a lot of money can be saved by avoiding the costs a garage must charge to cover its labour and overheads.

The manual has drawings and descriptions to show the function of the various components so that their layout can be understood. Then the tasks are described and photographed in a clear step-by-step sequence.

Rover Metro 1.1S

Acknowledgements

Thanks are due to Champion Spark Plug who supplied the illustrations showing spark plug conditions. Thanks are also due to Sykes-Pickavant Limited, who supplied some of the workshop tools, and to all those people at Sparkford who helped in the production of this Manual.

We take great pride in the accuracy of information given in this manual, but vehicle manufacturers make alterations and design changes during the production run of a particular vehicle of which they do not inform us. No liability can be accepted by the authors or publishers for loss, damage or injury caused by errors in, or omissions from, the information given.

Working on your car can be dangerous. This page shows just some of the potential risks and hazards, with the aim of creating a safety-conscious attitude.

General hazards

Scalding

• Don't remove the radiator or expansion tank cap while the engine is hot.
• Engine oil, automatic transmission fluid or power steering fluid may also be dangerously hot if the engine has recently been running.

Burning

• Beware of burns from the exhaust system and from any part of the engine. Brake discs and drums can also be extremely hot immediately after use.

Crushing

• When working under or near a raised vehicle, always supplement the jack with axle stands, or use drive-on ramps. ***Never venture under a car which is only supported by a jack.***

• Take care if loosening or tightening high-torque nuts when the vehicle is on stands. Initial loosening and final tightening should be done with the wheels on the ground.

Fire

• Fuel is highly flammable; fuel vapour is explosive.
• Don't let fuel spill onto a hot engine.
• Do not smoke or allow naked lights (including pilot lights) anywhere near a vehicle being worked on. Also beware of creating sparks (electrically or by use of tools).
• Fuel vapour is heavier than air, so don't work on the fuel system with the vehicle over an inspection pit.
• Another cause of fire is an electrical overload or short-circuit. Take care when repairing or modifying the vehicle wiring.
• Keep a fire extinguisher handy, of a type suitable for use on fuel and electrical fires.

Electric shock

• Ignition HT voltage can be dangerous, especially to people with heart problems or a pacemaker. Don't work on or near the ignition system with the engine running or the ignition switched on.

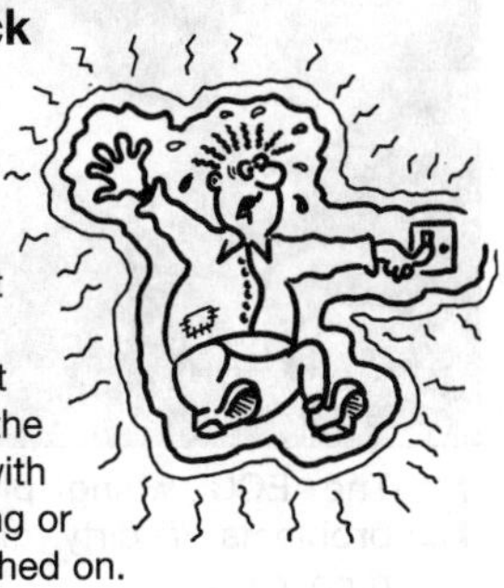

• Mains voltage is also dangerous. Make sure that any mains-operated equipment is correctly earthed. Mains power points should be protected by a residual current device (RCD) circuit breaker.

Fume or gas intoxication

• Exhaust fumes are poisonous; they often contain carbon monoxide, which is rapidly fatal if inhaled. Never run the engine in a confined space such as a garage with the doors shut.

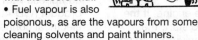

• Fuel vapour is also poisonous, as are the vapours from some cleaning solvents and paint thinners.

Poisonous or irritant substances

• Avoid skin contact with battery acid and with any fuel, fluid or lubricant, especially antifreeze, brake hydraulic fluid and Diesel fuel. Don't syphon them by mouth. If such a substance is swallowed or gets into the eyes, seek medical advice.
• Prolonged contact with used engine oil can cause skin cancer. Wear gloves or use a barrier cream if necessary. Change out of oil-soaked clothes and do not keep oily rags in your pocket.
• Air conditioning refrigerant forms a poisonous gas if exposed to a naked flame (including a cigarette). It can also cause skin burns on contact.

Asbestos

• Asbestos dust can cause cancer if inhaled or swallowed. Asbestos may be found in gaskets and in brake and clutch linings. When dealing with such components it is safest to assume that they contain asbestos.

Special hazards

Hydrofluoric acid

• This extremely corrosive acid is formed when certain types of synthetic rubber, found in some O-rings, oil seals, fuel hoses etc, are exposed to temperatures above 400ºC. The rubber changes into a charred or sticky substance containing the acid. *Once formed, the acid remains dangerous for years. If it gets onto the skin, it may be necessary to amputate the limb concerned.*
• When dealing with a vehicle which has suffered a fire, or with components salvaged from such a vehicle, wear protective gloves and discard them after use.

The battery

• Batteries contain sulphuric acid, which attacks clothing, eyes and skin. Take care when topping-up or carrying the battery.
• The hydrogen gas given off by the battery is highly explosive. Never cause a spark or allow a naked light nearby. Be careful when connecting and disconnecting battery chargers or jump leads.

Air bags

• Air bags can cause injury if they go off accidentally. Take care when removing the steering wheel and/or facia. Special storage instructions may apply.

Diesel injection equipment

• Diesel injection pumps supply fuel at very high pressure. Take care when working on the fuel injectors and fuel pipes.

Warning: Never expose the hands, face or any other part of the body to injector spray; the fuel can penetrate the skin with potentially fatal results.

Remember...

DO

• Do use eye protection when using power tools, and when working under the vehicle.

• Do wear gloves or use barrier cream to protect your hands when necessary.

• Do get someone to check periodically that all is well when working alone on the vehicle.

• Do keep loose clothing and long hair well out of the way of moving mechanical parts.

• Do remove rings, wristwatch etc, before working on the vehicle – especially the electrical system.

• Do ensure that any lifting or jacking equipment has a safe working load rating adequate for the job.

DON'T

• Don't attempt to lift a heavy component which may be beyond your capability – get assistance.

• Don't rush to finish a job, or take unverified short cuts.

• Don't use ill-fitting tools which may slip and cause injury.

• Don't leave tools or parts lying around where someone can trip over them. Mop up oil and fuel spills at once.

• Don't allow children or pets to play in or near a vehicle being worked on.

The following pages are intended to help in dealing with common roadside emergencies and breakdowns. You will find more detailed fault finding information at the back of the manual, and repair information in the main chapters.

If your car won't start and the starter motor doesn't turn

- ☐ If it's a model with automatic transmission, make sure the selector is in 'P' or 'N'.
- ☐ Open the bonnet and make sure that the battery terminals are clean and tight.
- ☐ Switch on the headlights and try to start the engine. If the headlights go very dim when you're trying to start, the battery is probably flat. Get out of trouble by jump starting (see next page) using a friend's car.

If your car won't start even though the starter motor turns as normal

- ☐ Is there fuel in the tank?
- ☐ Is there moisture on electrical components under the bonnet? Switch off the ignition, then wipe off any obvious dampness with a dry cloth. Spray a water-repellent aerosol product (WD-40 or equivalent) on ignition and fuel system electrical connectors like those shown in the photos. Pay special attention to the ignition coil wiring connector and HT leads. (Note that Diesel engines don't normally suffer from damp.)

A Check that the HT lead connections at the distributor are clean and secure.

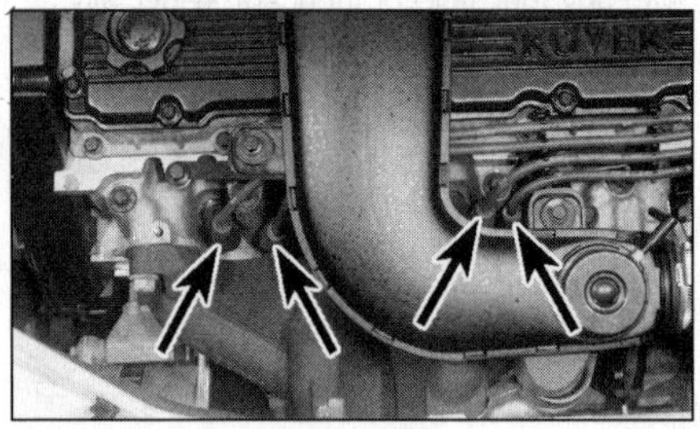

B Check that the HT lead connections at the spark plugs (arrowed) are clean and secure.

C Remove the ignition coil cover and check that the HT and LT lead connections are clean and secure.

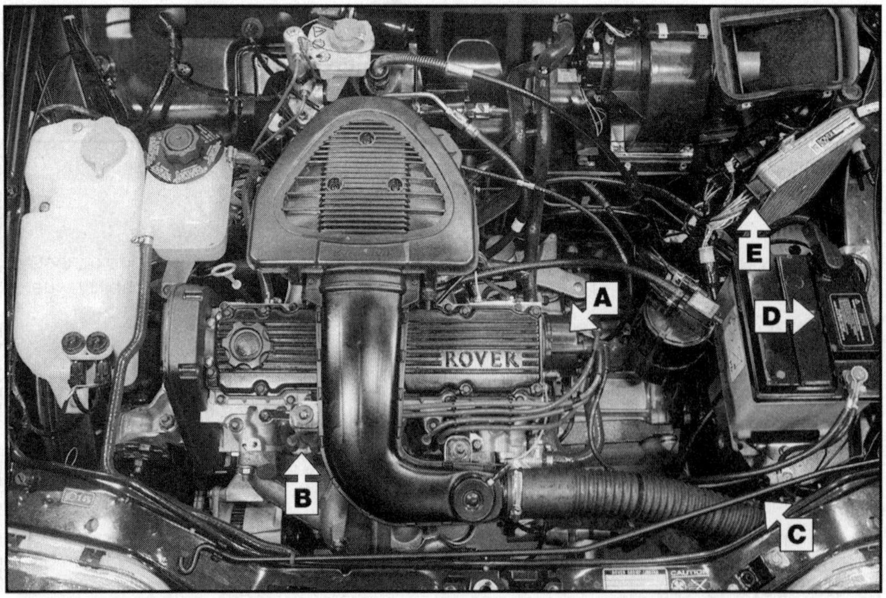

Check that electrical connections are secure (with the ignition off) and spray them with a water-dispersing spray like WD40 if you suspect a problem due to damp.

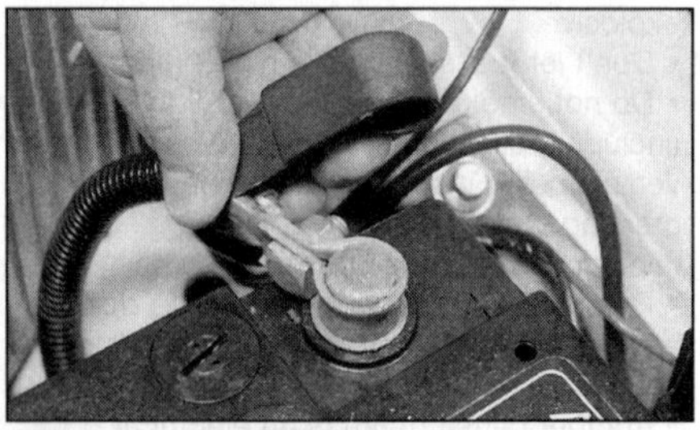

D Check the security and condition of the battery connections.

E The ECU wiring plugs may cause problems if dirty or not connected properly.

Jump starting

HAYNES HiNT ***Jump starting will get you out of trouble, but you must correct whatever made the battery go flat in the first place. There are three possibilities:***

***1** The battery has been drained by repeated attempts to start, or by leaving the lights on.*

***2** The charging system is not working properly (alternator drivebelt slack or broken, alternator wiring fault or alternator itself faulty).*

***3** The battery itself is at fault (electrolyte low, or battery worn out).*

When jump-starting a car using a booster battery, observe the following precautions:

- ✔ Before connecting the booster battery, make sure that the ignition is switched off.
- ✔ Ensure that all electrical equipment (lights, heater, wipers, etc) is switched off.
- ✔ Make sure that the booster battery is the same voltage as the discharged one in the vehicle.
- ✔ If the battery is being jump-started from the battery in another vehicle, the two vehicles MUST NOT TOUCH each other.
- ✔ Make sure that the transmission is in neutral (or PARK, in the case of automatic transmission).

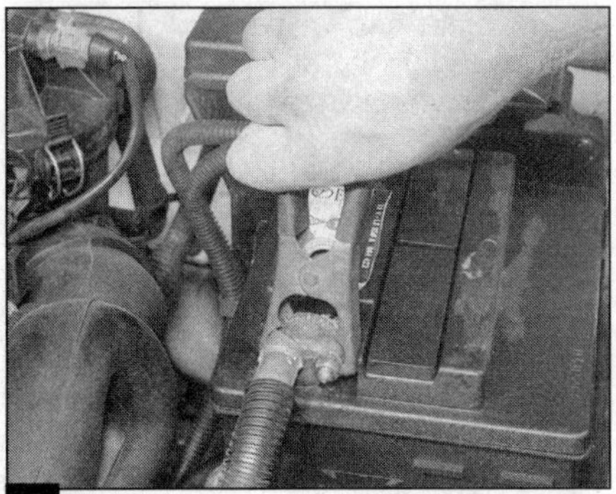

1 Connect one end of the red jump lead to the positive (+) terminal of the flat battery

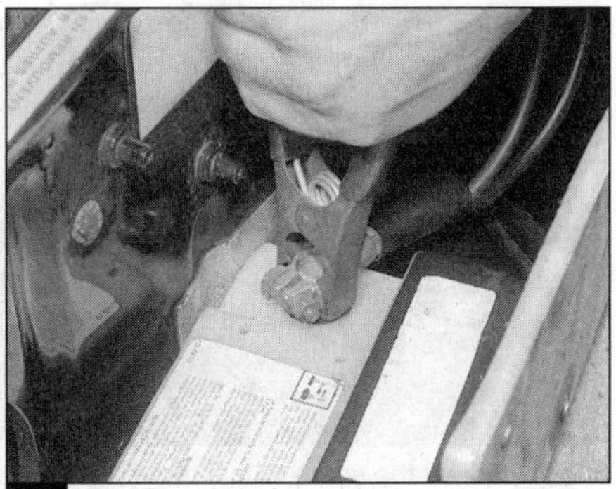

2 Connect the other end of the red lead to the positive (+) terminal of the booster battery.

3 Connect one end of the black jump lead to the negative (-) terminal of the booster battery

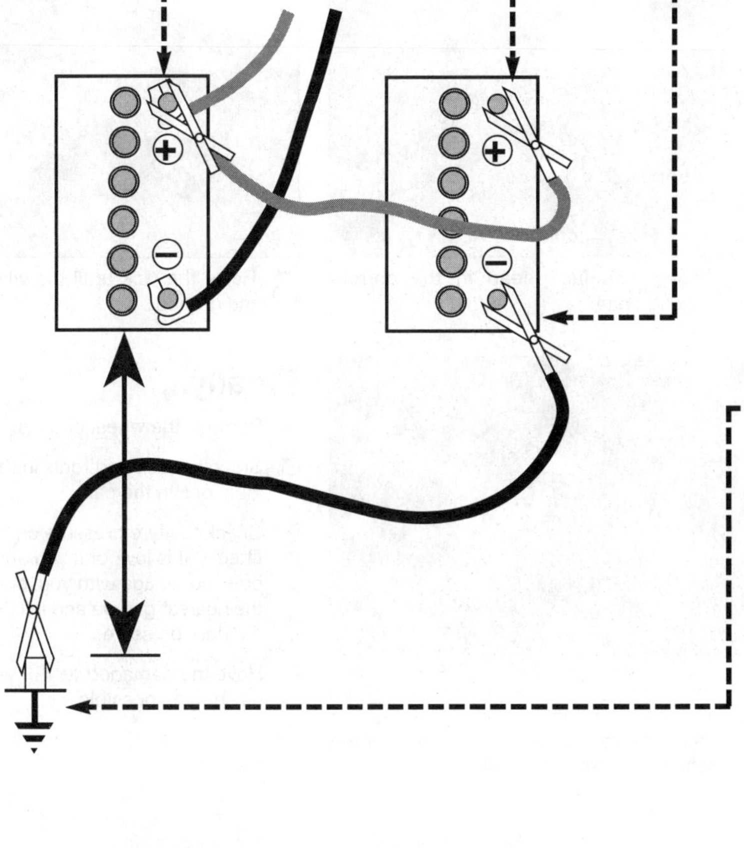

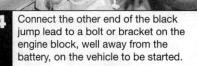

4 Connect the other end of the black jump lead to a bolt or bracket on the engine block, well away from the battery, on the vehicle to be started.

5 Make sure that the jump leads will not come into contact with the fan, drive-belts or other moving parts of the engine.

6 Start the engine using the booster battery, then with the engine running at idle speed, disconnect the jump leads in the reverse order of connection.

Wheel changing

Some of the details shown here will vary according to model. For instance, the location of the spare wheel and jack is not the same on all cars. However, the basic principles apply to all vehicles.

Warning: Do not change a wheel in a situation where you risk being hit by other traffic. On busy roads, try to stop in a lay-by or a gateway. Be wary of passing traffic while changing the wheel - it is easy to become distracted by the job in hand.

Preparation

- ☐ When a puncture occurs, stop as soon as it is safe to do so.
- ☐ Park on firm level ground, if possible, and well out of the way of other traffic.
- ☐ Use hazard warning lights if necessary.
- ☐ If you have one, use a warning triangle to alert other drivers of your presence.
- ☐ Apply the handbrake and engage first or reverse gear (or Park on models with automatic transmission).
- ☐ Chock the wheel diagonally opposite the one being removed – a couple of large stones will do for this.
- ☐ If the ground is soft, use a flat piece of wood to spread the load under the jack.

Changing the wheel

1 The spare wheel and tools are located in the boot, beneath the trim panel and spare tyre cover.

2 Unscrew the spare wheel retaining cap.

3 Use the wheel brace to prise off the wheel trim and remove trim to expose the wheel nuts.

4 Use the wheel brace to slightly loosen the wheelnuts.

5 Locate the jack head in the correct jacking point.

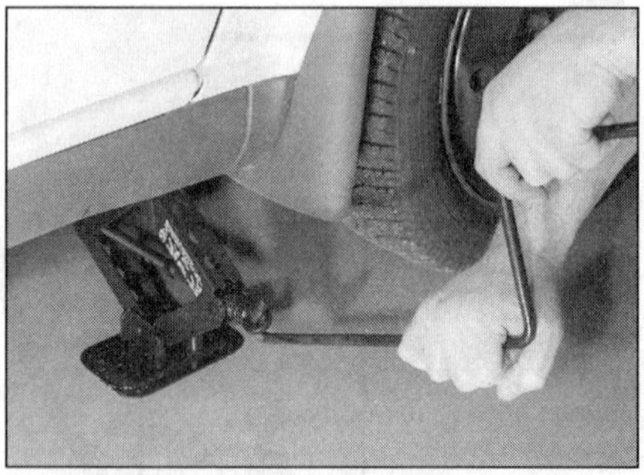

6 Raise the jack until the wheel is clear of the ground.

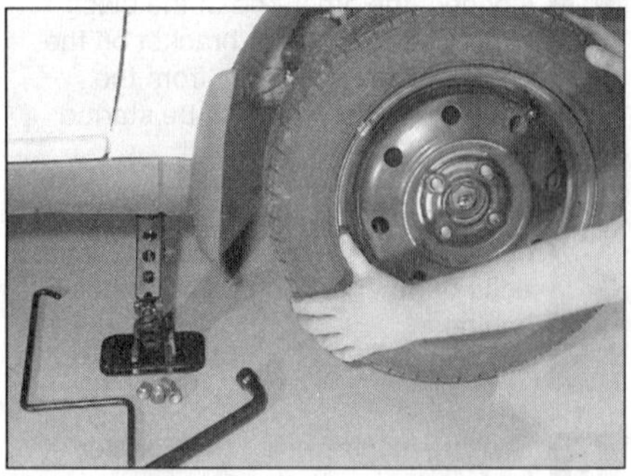

7 Remove the wheel nuts and lift off the wheel. Fit the new wheel and tighten the nuts finger-tight only at this stage.

8 Lower the car to the ground and tighten the nuts using the wheel brace. Tighten the nuts to the correct torque setting when it is convenient to do so.

Finally...

- ☐ Remove the wheel chocks.
- ☐ Stow the jack and tools in the correct locations in the car.
- ☐ Check the tyre pressure on the wheel just fitted. If it is low, or if you don't have a pressure gauge with you, drive slowly to the nearest garage and inflate the tyre to the right pressure.
- ☐ Have the damaged tyre or wheel repaired as soon as possible.

Identifying leaks

Puddles on the garage floor or drive, or obvious wetness under the bonnet or underneath the car, suggest a leak that needs investigating. It can sometimes be difficult to decide where the leak is coming from, especially if the engine bay is very dirty already. Leaking oil or fluid can also be blown rearwards by the passage of air under the car, giving a false impression of where the problem lies.

Warning: Most automotive oils and fluids are poisonous. Wash them off skin, and change out of contaminated clothing, without delay.

HAYNES HiNT *The smell of a fluid leaking from the car may provide a clue to what's leaking. Some fluids are distinctively coloured. It may help to clean the car carefully and to park it over some clean paper overnight as an aid to locating the source of the leak.*

Remember that some leaks may only occur while the engine is running.

Sump oil

Engine oil may leak from the drain plug...

Oil from filter

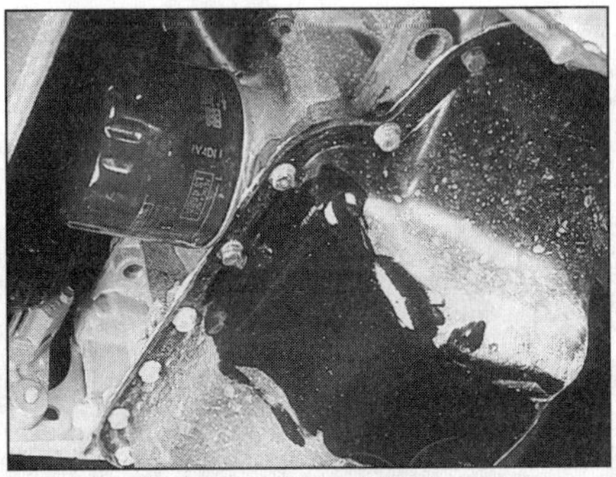

...or from the base of the oil filter.

Gearbox oil

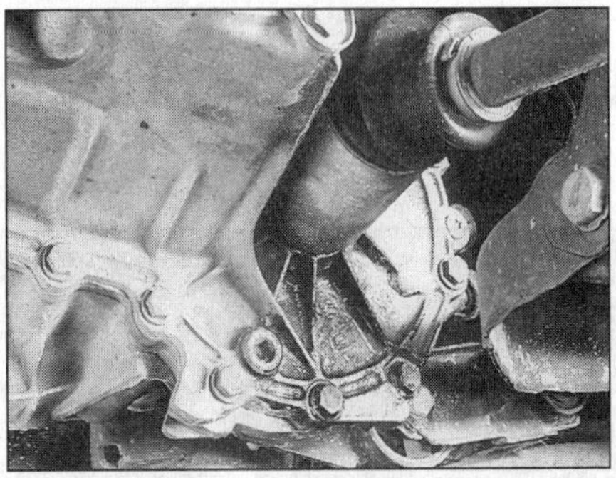

Gearbox oil can leak from the seals at the inboard ends of the driveshafts.

Antifreeze

Leaking antifreeze often leaves a crystalline deposit like this.

Brake fluid

A leak occurring at a wheel is almost certainly brake fluid.

Power steering fluid

Power steering fluid may leak from the pipe connectors on the steering rack.

Towing

When all else fails, you may find yourself having to get a tow home – or of course you may be helping somebody else. Long-distance recovery should only be done by a garage or breakdown service. For shorter distances, DIY towing using another car is easy enough, but observe the following points:

☐ Use a proper tow-rope – they are not expensive. The vehicle being towed must display an 'ON TOW' sign in its rear window.

☐ Always turn the ignition key to the 'on' position when the vehicle is being towed, so that the steering lock is released, and that the direction indicator and brake lights will work.

☐ Only attach the tow-rope to the towing eyes provided.

☐ Before being towed, release the handbrake and select neutral on the transmission.

☐ Note that greater-than-usual pedal pressure will be required to operate the brakes, since the vacuum servo unit is only operational with the engine running.

☐ On models with power steering, greater-than-usual steering effort will also be required.

☐ The driver of the car being towed must keep the tow-rope taut at all times to avoid snatching.

☐ Make sure that both drivers know the route before setting off.

☐ Only drive at moderate speeds and keep the distance towed to a minimum. Drive smoothly and allow plenty of time for slowing down at junctions.

☐ On models with automatic transmission, special precautions apply. If in doubt, do not tow, or transmission damage may result.

Introduction

There are some very simple checks which need only take a few minutes to carry out, but which could save you a lot of inconvenience and expense.

These "Weekly checks" require no great skill or special tools, and the small amount of time they take to perform could prove to be very well spent, for example;

☐ Keeping an eye on tyre condition and pressures, will not only help to stop them wearing out prematurely, but could also save your life.

☐ Many breakdowns are caused by electrical problems. Battery-related faults are particularly common, and a quick check on a regular basis will often prevent the majority of these.

☐ If your car develops a brake fluid leak, the first time you might know about it is when your brakes don't work properly. Checking the level regularly will give advance warning of this kind of problem.

☐ If the oil or coolant levels run low, the cost of repairing any engine damage will be far greater than fixing the leak, for example.

Underbonnet check points

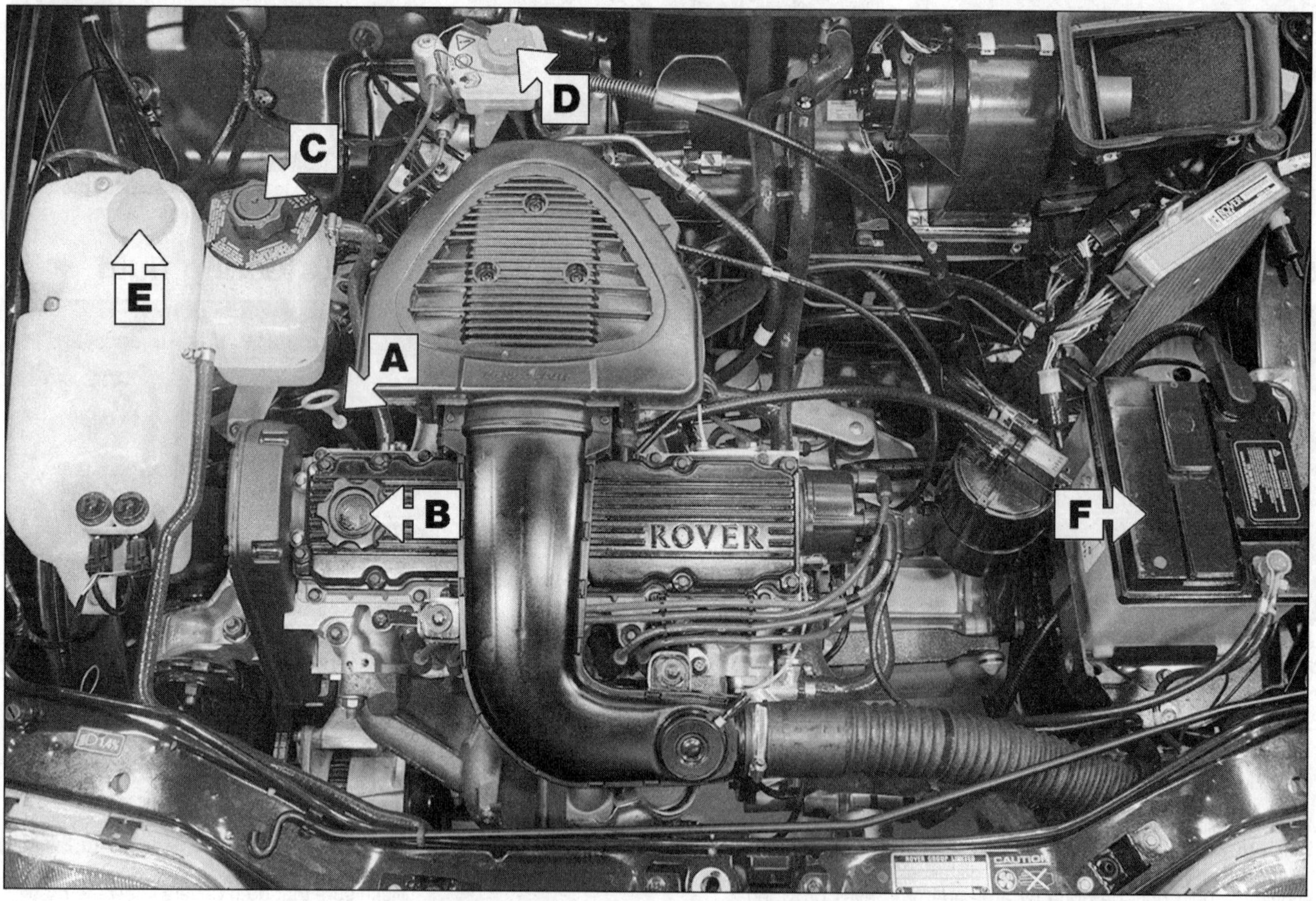

K8 fuel injection engine

A *Engine oil level dipstick*
B *Engine oil filler cap**
C *Coolant expansion tank*
D *Hydraulic fluid reservoir*
E *Screen washer fluid reservoir*
F *Battery*

* **Note:** *Item B (Engine oil filler cap) is on the opposite end of the valve cover on K16 (16-Valve) engines*

Engine oil level

Before you start

✔ Make sure that your car is on level ground.
✔ Check the oil level before the car is driven, or at least 5 minutes after the engine has been switched off.

> **HAYNES HiNT** ***If the oil is checked immediately after driving the vehicle, some of the oil will remain in the upper engine components, resulting in an inaccurate reading on the dipstick!***

The correct oil

Modern engines place great demands on their oil. It is very important that the correct oil for your car is used (See "Lubricants and Fluids" ath the end of this Chapter).

Car Care

● If you have to add oil frequently, you should check whether you have any oil leaks. Place some clean paper under the car overnight, and check for stains in the morning. If there are no leaks, the engine may be burning oil *(see "Fault Finding").*

● Always maintain the level between the upper and lower dipstick marks (see photo 3). If the level is too low severe engine damage may occur. Oil seal failure may result if the engine is overfilled by adding too much oil.

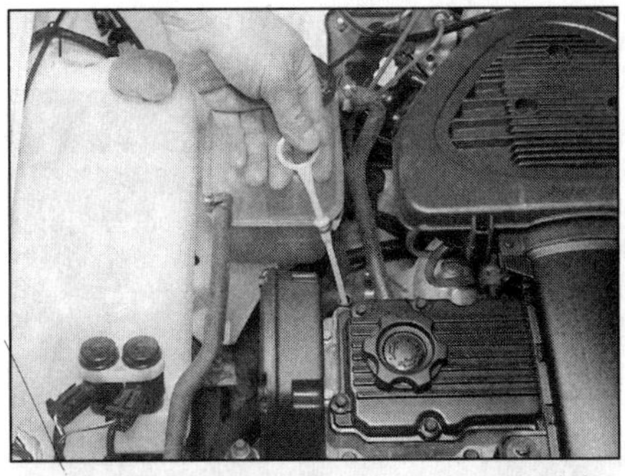

1 The dipstick is located at the rear right-hand end of the engine (see "Underbonnet Check Points" on page 0-10 for exact location). Withdraw the dipstick.

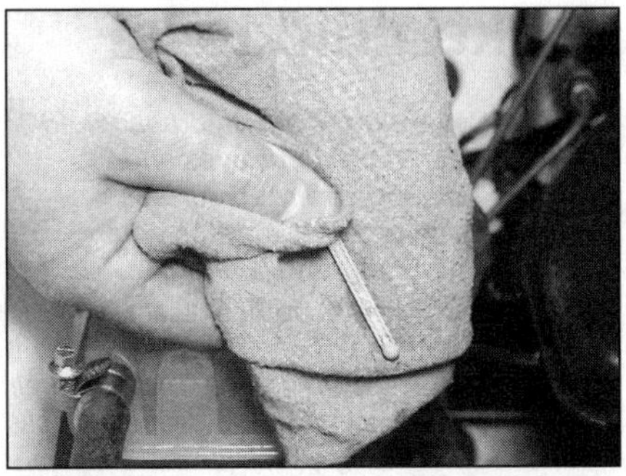

2 Using a clean rag or paper towel remove all oil from the dipstick. Insert the clean dipstick into the tube as far as it will go, then withdraw it again.

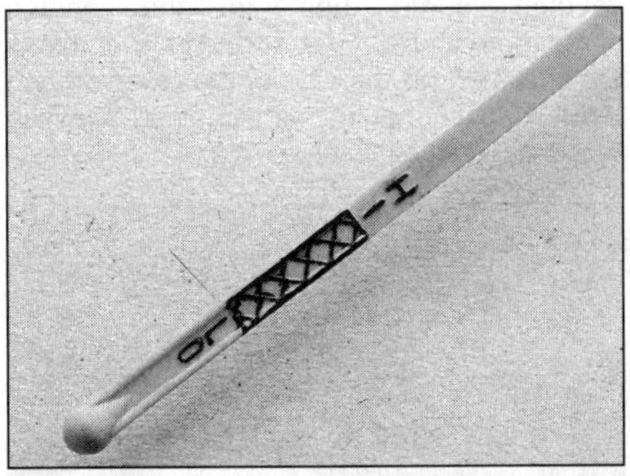

3 Note the oil level on the end of the dipstick, which should be between the upper ("HI") mark and lower ("LO") mark. Approximately 1.0 litre of oil will raise the level from the lower mark to the upper mark.

4 Oil is added through the filler cap. Rotate the cap through a quarter-turn anti-clockwise and withdraw it. Top-up the level. A funnel may help to reduce spillage. Add the oil slowly, checking the level on the dipstick often. Do not overfill.

Coolant level

> ***Warning: DO NOT attempt to remove the expansion tank pressure cap when the engine is hot, as there is a very great risk of scalding. Do not leave open containers of coolant about, as it is poisonous.***

Car Care

● With a sealed-type cooling system, adding coolant should not be necessary on a regular basis. If frequent topping-up is required, it is likely there is a leak. Check the radiator, all hoses and joint faces for signs of staining or wetness, and rectify as necessary.

● It is important that antifreeze is used in the cooling system all year round, not just during the winter months. Don't top-up with water alone, as the antifreeze will become too diluted.

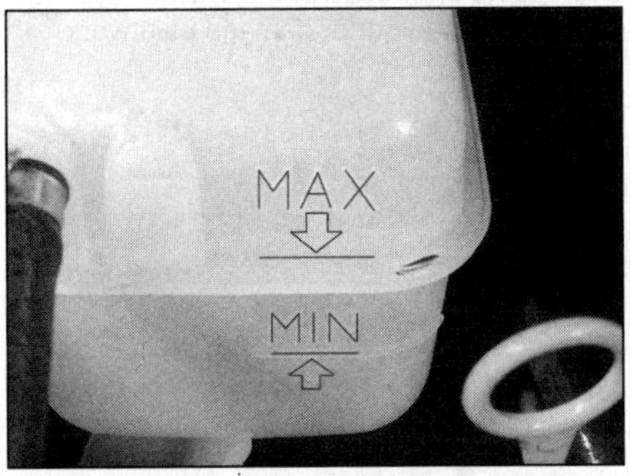

1 The coolant level varies with the temperature of the engine. When the engine is cold, the coolant level should be between the MAX and MIN marks on the side of the expansion tank. When the engine is hot, the level may rise slightly.

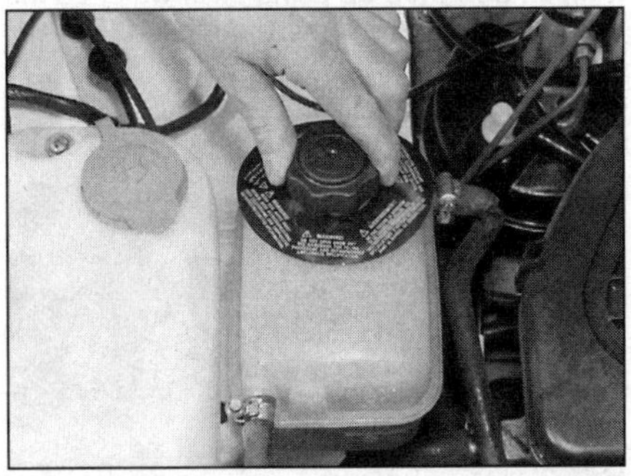

2 If topping-up is necessary, **wait until the engine is cold**. Slowly turn the expansion tank cap anti-clockwise to relieve the system pressure. Once any pressure is released, turn the cap anti-clockwise until it can be lifted off.

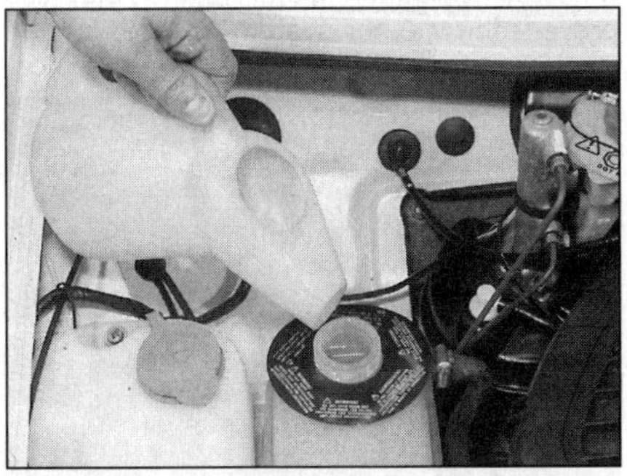

3 Add a mixture of water and antifreeze through the expansion tank filler neck until the coolant reaches the "MAXI" level mark. Refit the cap, turning it clockwise as far as it will go until it is secure.

Brake fluid level

Warning: Brake hydraulic fluid can harm your eyes and damage painted surfaces, so use extreme caution when handling and pouring it.

- *Do not use fluid that has been standing open for some time, as it absorbs moisture from the air which can cause a dangerous loss of braking effectiveness.*

HAYNES HiNT

• Make sure that your car is on level ground.
• The fluid level in the master cylinder reservoir will drop slightly as the brake pads wear down, but the fluid level must never be allowed to drop below the 'MIN' mark.

Safety first

- If the reservoir requires repeated topping-up this is an indication of a fluid leak somewhere in the system, which should be investigated immediately.

- If a leak is suspected, the car should not be driven until the braking system has been checked. Never take any risks where brakes are concerned.

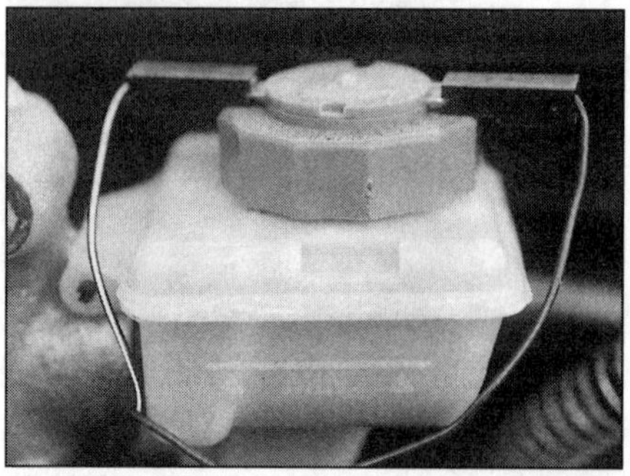

1 The brake master cylinder and fluid reservoir is mounted on top of the vacuum servo unit in the engine compartment. The MAX and MIN level marks are indicated on the side of the reservoir and the fluid level should be maintained between these marks at all times.

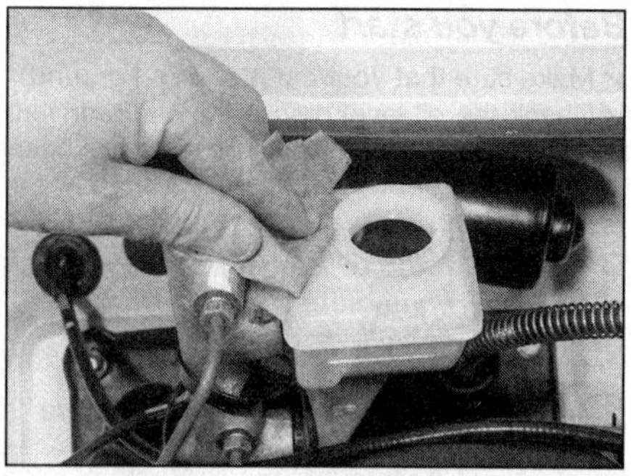

2 If topping-up is necessary, first wipe the area around the filler cap with a clean rag before removing the cap. Hold the cap's centre terminal block stationary to prevent damage to the electrical connections.

3 Before adding fluid, it's a good idea to inspect the reservoir. The system should be drained and refilled if dirt is seen in the fluid (see Chapter 9 for details).

4 Carefully add fluid avoiding spilling it on surrounding paintwork. Use only the specified fluid; mixing different types can cause damage to the system. After filling to the correct level, refit the cap securely, to prevent leaks and the entry of foreign matter. Ensure that the fluid level switch plunger is free to move. Wipe off any spilt fluid.

Screen washer fluid level

Screenwash additives not only keep the winscreen clean during foul weather, they also prevent the washer system freezing in cold weather - which is when you are likely to need it most. Don't top up using plain water as the screenwash will become too diluted, and will freeze during cold weather. On no account use engine antifreeze in the washer system - this could discolour or damage paintwork.

1 The reservoir for the windscreen and rear window (if fitted) washer systems is on the right-hand side of the engine compartment.

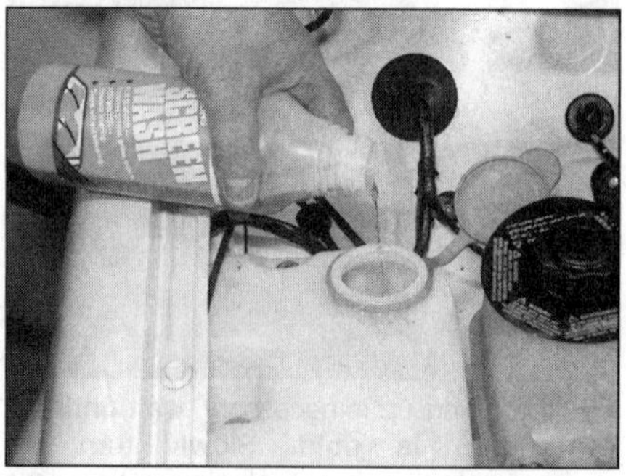

2 When topping-up the reservoir(s) a screenwash additive should be added in the quantities recommended on the bottle.

3 Check the operation of the windscreen and rear window washers. Adjust the nozzles using a pin if necessary, aiming the spray to a point slightly above the centre of the swept area.

Tyre condition and pressure

It is very important that tyres are in good condition, and at the correct pressure - having a tyre failure at any speed is highly dangerous. Tyre wear is influenced by driving style - harsh braking and acceleration, or fast cornering, will all produce more rapid tyre wear. As a general rule, the front tyres wear out faster than the rears. Interchanging the tyres from front to rear ("rotating" the tyres) may result in more even wear. However, if this is completely effective, you may have the expense of replacing all four tyres at once!

Remove any nails or stones embedded in the tread before they penetrate the tyre to cause deflation. If removal of a nail does reveal that the tyre has been punctured, refit the nail so that its point of penetration is marked. Then immediately change the wheel, and have the tyre repaired by a tyre dealer.

Regularly check the tyres for damage in the form of cuts or bulges, especially in the sidewalls. Periodically remove the wheels, and clean any dirt or mud from the inside and outside surfaces. Examine the wheel rims for signs of rusting, corrosion or other damage. Light alloy wheels are easily damaged by "kerbing" whilst parking; steel wheels may also become dented or buckled. A new wheel is very often the only way to overcome severe damage.

New tyres should be balanced when they are fitted, but it may become necessary to re-balance them as they wear, or if the balance weights fitted to the wheel rim should fall off. Unbalanced tyres will wear more quickly, as will the steering and suspension components. Wheel imbalance is normally signified by vibration, particularly at a certain speed (typically around 50 mph). If this vibration is felt only through the steering, then it is likely that just the front wheels need balancing. If, however, the vibration is felt through the whole car, the rear wheels could be out of balance. Wheel balancing should be carried out by a tyre dealer or garage.

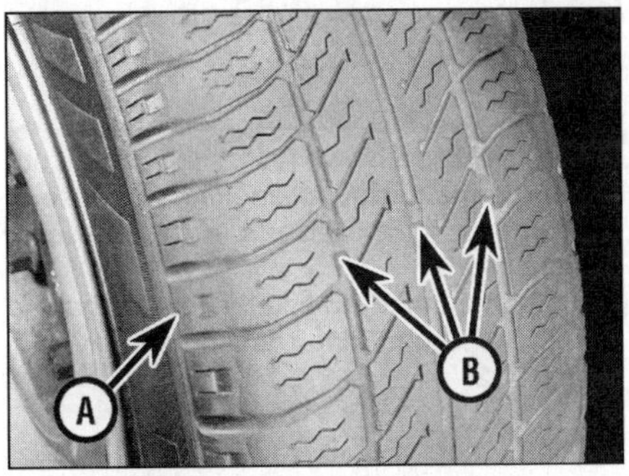

Tread Depth - visual check

1 The original tyres have tread wear safety bands (B), which will appear when the tread depth reaches approximately 1.6 mm. The band positions are indicated by a triangular mark on the tyre sidewall (A).

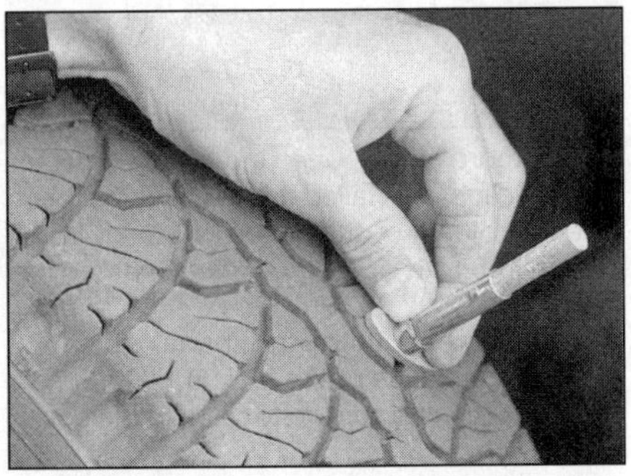

Tread Depth - manual check

2 Alternatively tread wear can be monitored with a simple, inexpensive device known as a tread depth indicator gauge.

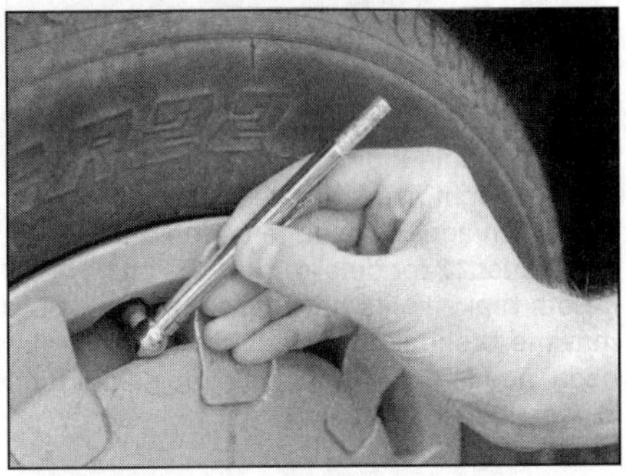

Tyre Pressure Check

3 Check the tyre pressures regularly with the tyres cold. Do not adjust the tyre pressures immediately after the vehicle has been used, or an inaccurate setting will result. Tyre pressures are shown on page 0•16

4 Tyre tread wear patterns

Shoulder Wear

Underinflation (wear on both sides)
Under-inflation will cause overheating of the tyre, because the tyre will flex too much, and the tread will not sit correctly on the road surface. This will cause a loss of grip and excessive wear, not to mention the danger of sudden tyre failure due to heat build-up.
Check and adjust pressures
Incorrect wheel camber (wear on one side)
Repair or renew suspension parts
Hard cornering
Reduce speed!

Centre Wear

Overinflation
Over-inflation will cause rapid wear of the centre part of the tyre tread, coupled with reduced grip, harsher ride, and the danger of shock damage occurring in the tyre casing.
Check and adjust pressures

If you sometimes have to inflate your car's tyres to the higher pressures specified for maximum load or sustained high speed, don't forget to reduce the pressures to normal afterwards.

Uneven Wear

Front tyres may wear unevenly as a result of wheel misalignment. Most tyre dealers and garages can check and adjust the wheel alignment (or "tracking") for a modest charge.
Incorrect camber or castor
Repair or renew suspension parts
Malfunctioning suspension
Repair or renew suspension parts
Unbalanced wheel
Balance tyres
Incorrect toe setting
Adjust front wheel alignment
Note: *The feathered edge of the tread which typifies toe wear is best checked by feel.*

Electrical system

✔ Check all external lights and the horn. Refer to the appropriate Sections of Chapter 12 for details if any of the circuits are found to be inoperative.

✔ Visually check all wiring connectors, harnesses and retaining clips for security, and for signs of chafing or damage.

HAYNES HiNT ***If you need to check your brake lights and indicators unaided, back up to a wall or garage door and operate the lights. The reflected light should show if they are working properly.***

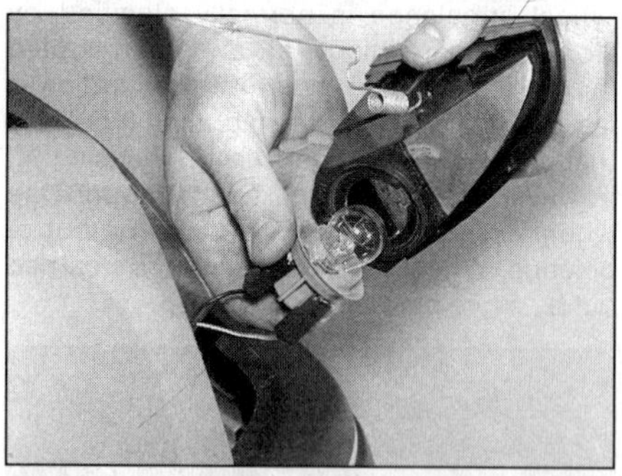

1 If a single indicator light, brake light or headlight has failed it is likely that a bulb has blown and will need to be replaced. Refer to Chapter 12 for details.

If both brake lights have failed, it is possible that the brake light switch above the brake pedal needs adjusting. This simple operation is described in Chapter 9.

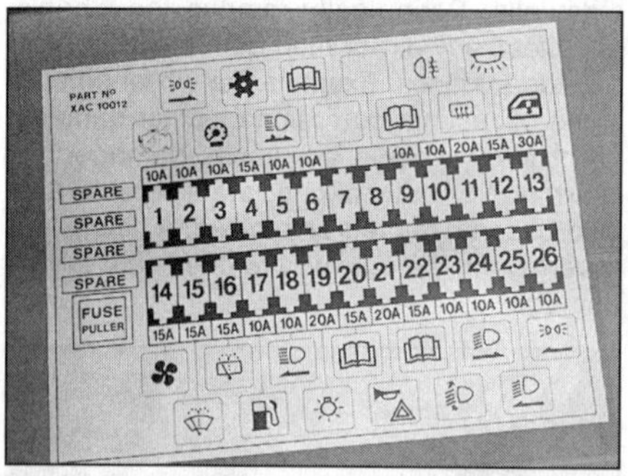

2 If more than one indicator light or headlight has failed it is likely that either a fuse has blown or that there is a fault in the circuit (refer to *"Electrical fault-finding"* in Chapter 12).

The fuses are mounted in a panel located at the right-hand side of the facia under a cover. Turn the retaining screws to release the cover.

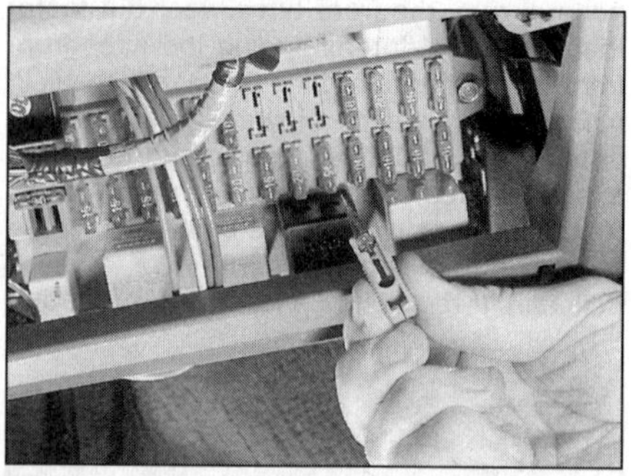

3 To replace a blown fuse, simply pull it out using the tool supplied. Fit a new fuse of the same rating, available from car accessory shops.

It is important that you find the reason that the fuse blew - a checking procedure is given in Chapter 12.

Wiper blades

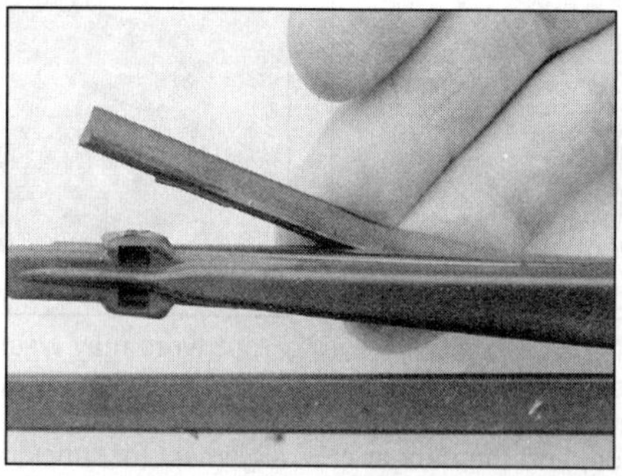

1 Check the condition of the wiper blades; if they are cracked or show any signs of deterioration, or if the glass swept area is smeared, renew them. For maximum clarity of vision, wiper blades should be renewed annually, as a matter of course.

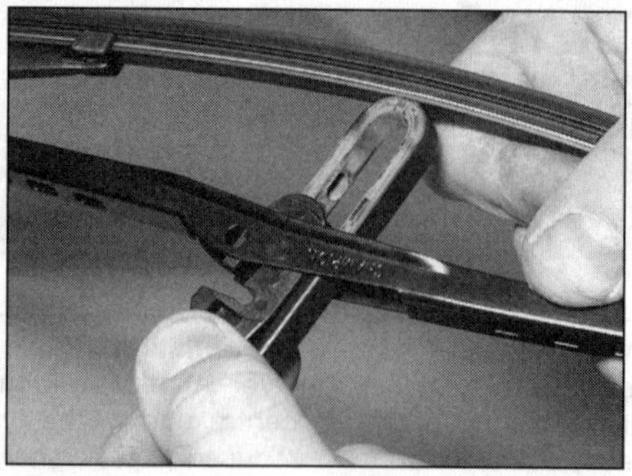

2 To remove a wiper blade, pull the arm fully away from the glass until it locks. Swivel the blade through 90°, press the locking tab(s) with your fingers, and slide the blade out of the arm's hooked end. On refitting, ensure that the blade locks securely into the arm.

Battery

Caution: *Before carrying out any work on the vehicle battery, read the precautions given in "Safety first" at the start of this manual.*

✔ Make sure that the battery tray is in good condition, and that the clamp is tight. Corrosion on the tray, retaining clamp and the battery itself can be removed with a solution of water and baking soda. Thoroughly rinse all cleaned areas with water. Any metal parts damaged by corrosion should be covered with a zinc-based primer, then painted.

✔ Periodically (approximately every three months), check the charge condition of the battery as described in Chapter 5A.

✔ If the battery is flat, and you need to jump start your vehicle, see *"Roadside Repairs"*.

HAYNES HiNT

Battery corrosion can be kept to a minimum by applying a layer of petroleum jelly to the clamps and terminals after they are reconnected.

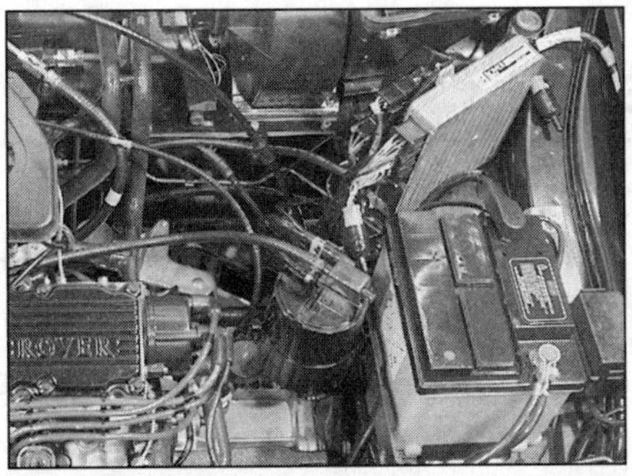

1 The battery is located on the left-hand side of the engine compartment. The exterior of the battery should be inspected periodically for damage such as a cracked case or cover.

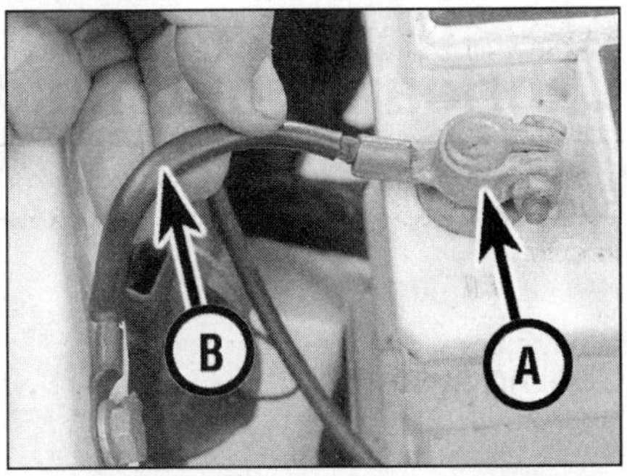

2 Check the tightness of battery clamps (A) to ensure good electrical connections. You should not be able to move them. Also check each cable (B) for cracks and frayed conductors.

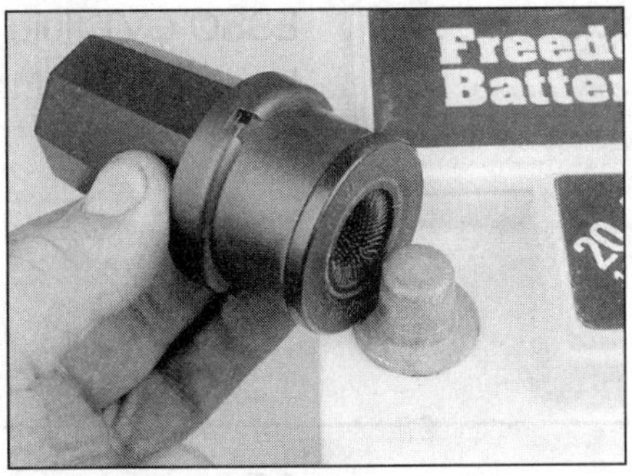

3 If corrosion (white, fluffy deposits) is evident, remove the cables from the battery terminals, clean them with a small wire brush, then refit them. Accessory stores sell a useful tool for cleaning the battery post ...

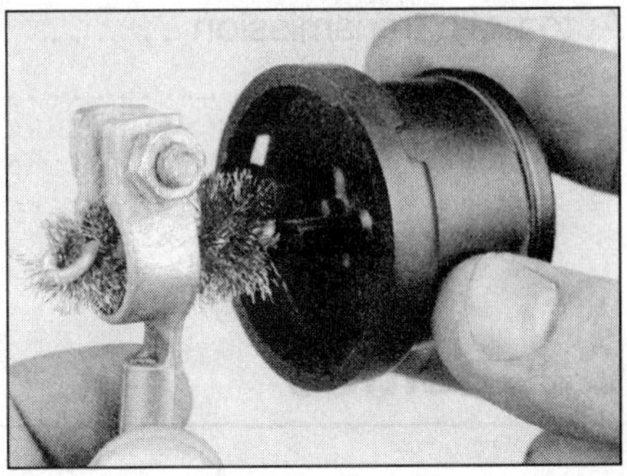

4 ... as well as the battery cable clamps

Lubricants and fluids

Engine	Multigrade engine oil, viscosity SAE10W/40 to spec. API-SG or SG/CD, CCMC G4, or RES.22.OL.G
Cooling system	Antifreeze to spec. BS 6580 and BS 5117. Ethylene - glycol based with non-phosphate corrosion inhibitors, containing no methanol. Mixture 50% by volume
Manual gearbox	ESSO Gear oil, BV 75w/80w
Gearchange linkage	Rover grease - AFU 1500 1509
Automatic transmission	ESSO CVT fluid - EZL 799
Braking system	Hydraulic fluid to SAE J1703 or DOT 4

Capacities

Engine	4.5 litres
Cooling system	4.5 litres
Manual gearbox	2.0 litres
Automatic transmission	4.5 litres
Fuel tank	30.5 litres

Tyre pressures (cold)

	Front	Rear
1.1C, 1.1L, 1.1S, 1.4SL, 1.4GS		
Up to and including four persons	2.1 bar (31 psi)	2.1 bar (31 psi)
Four persons up to maximum vehicle weight	2.1 bar (31 psi)	2.2 bar (32 psi)
GTa, GTi 16v		
All loads - up to 100 mph	2.0 bar (29 psi)	2.0 bar (29 psi)
All loads - over 100 mph	2.3 bar (33 psi)	2.3 bar (33 psi)

Note: *Pressures apply only to original equipment tyres and may vary if any other make or type is fitted. Check with the tyre manufacturer or supplier for correct pressures if necessary*

Chapter 1
Routine maintenance and servicing

Contents

Degrees of difficulty

Easy, suitable for novice with little experience	**Fairly easy,** suitable for beginner with some experience	**Fairly difficult,** suitable for competent DIY mechanic	**Difficult,** suitable for experienced DIY mechanic	**Very difficult,** suitable for expert DIY or professional

Servicing Specifications

Lubricants, fluids and capacities

Refer to the end of "Weekly checks"

Engine

Oil filter type	Champion B104

Cooling system

Antifreeze properties - 50 % antifreeze (by volume):	
Commences freezing	- 36°C
Frozen solid	- 48°C

Fuel system

Air cleaner filter element:	
Carburettor engines	Champion W218
Fuel-injected engines	Champion W221
Idle speed:	
Carburettor engines	850 ± 50 rpm
Fuel-injected engines	See text
CO level at idle speed (engine at normal operating temperature):	
Carburettor engines without catalytic converter - at exhaust tailpipe	2.0 to 3.0 %
Carburettor engines with catalytic converter - at gas-sampling pipe	1.0 to 3.0 %
Fuel-injected engines	See text
Recommended fuel:	
Vehicles without catalytic converter	95 RON unleaded (ie unleaded Premium) or 97 RON leaded (ie 4-star)
Vehicles with catalytic converter	95 RON unleaded (ie unleaded Premium) only

Ignition system

Firing order	1-3-4-2 (No 1 cylinder at timing belt end)
Direction of crankshaft rotation	Clockwise (viewed from right-hand side of vehicle)
Direction of distributor rotor arm rotation	Anti-clockwise (viewed from left-hand side of vehicle)
Ignition timing - carburettor engines (vacuum pipe disconnected):	
1.1 models:	
carburettor number MAC 10003 or MAC 10010	8° ± 1° BTDC @ 1500 rpm
carburettor number MAC 10043	10° ± 1° BTDC @ 1500 rpm
1.4 models	9° ± 1° BTDC @ 1500 rpm
Ignition timing - fuel-injected engines	See text
Spark plugs:	
Type	Champion RC9YCC
Electrode gap	0.8 mm
Spark plug (HT) lead resistance	25 K ohms per lead, maximum

Braking system

Front brake pad friction material minimum thickness	3.0 mm
Rear brake shoe friction material minimum thickness	1.5 mm
Handbrake adjustment:	
Roadwheels bind at:	
Up to VIN 661301	2 to 3 notches
VIN 661301 on	1 notch
Roadwheels lock at:	
Up to VIN 661301	3 to 4 notches
VIN 661301 on	1 to 2 notches

Tyre pressures

Refer to the end of "Weekly checks"

Electrical system

Alternator drivebelt deflection	6 to 8 mm @ 10 kg pressure
Wiper blades - front and rear	Champion X-4103

Torque wrench settings

	Nm	lbf ft
Air inlet duct-to-cylinder head support bracket screws - K16 engine	8	6
Spark plug cover screws - K16 engine	2	1.5
Spark plugs	25	18
Timing belt cover fasteners:		
Upper right-hand/outer cover	4	3
Lower and upper left-hand inner covers	9	6.5
Distributor cap screws	2	1.5
Distributor rotor arm (hex-head) screw - fuel-injected engines	10	7.5
Distributor mounting bolts - carburettor engines	25	18
Alternator pivot and clamp bolts:		
10 mm	45	33
8 mm	25	18
Engine oil drain plug	42	31
Manual gearbox oil filler/level and drain plugs	25	18
Automatic transmission drain plug	30	22
Fuel system pressure release bolt - at fuel filter	12	9
Fuel filter inlet union	40	30
Fuel filter outlet union	35	26
Front brake caliper guide pin bolts	30	22
Rear brake drum securing screws	7	5
Roadwheel nuts	70	51
Seat belt top mounting bolt	25	19

Rover Metro and 100 series - maintenance schedule

The maintenance intervals in this manual are provided with the assumption that you will be carrying out the work yourself. These are the minimum maintenance intervals recommended by the manufacturer for vehicles driven daily. If you wish to keep your vehicle in peak condition at all times, you may wish to perform some of these procedures more often. We encourage frequent maintenance, because it enhances the efficiency, performance and resale value of your vehicle.

If the vehicle is driven in dusty areas, used to tow a trailer, or driven frequently at slow speeds (idling in traffic) or on short journeys, more frequent maintenance intervals are recommended.

When the vehicle is new, it should be serviced by a factory-authorised dealer service department, in order to preserve the factory warranty.

Every 250 miles (400 km) or weekly

- ☐ Refer to "Weekly Checks"

Every 1 000 miles (1500 km) or monthly - whichever comes first

- ☐ Check the operation of all locks, hinges and latch mechanisms (Section 3)
- ☐ Check the operation of the seat belts (Section 4)
- ☐ Check the operation of the brakes (Section 5)
- ☐ Check for signs of fluid leakage (Section 6)
- ☐ Check the battery electrolyte level (Section 7)

Every 6 000 miles (10 000 km) or 6 months

- ☐ Renew the engine oil and filter (Section 8)

Note: *The manufacturer has from approximately mid.1991 extended the service schedule so that this task need no longer be carried out at this interval, except for the First Lubrication Service, carried out when the vehicle is new. Owners of high-mileage vehicles, or those who do a lot of stop-start driving, may prefer to adhere to the original recommendation, changing the oil and filter in-between the major services described in the following Section:*

Every 12 000 miles (20 000 km) or 12 months

- ☐ Renew the engine oil and filter (Section 9)
- ☐ Check the operation of the clutch (Section 10)
- ☐ Check the transmission oil level (Section 11)
- ☐ Check the tightness of the roadwheel nuts (Section 12)
- ☐ Check the exterior paintwork, the body panels and the underbody sealer (Section 13)
- ☐ Check and lubricate all locks, hinges, latch mechanisms and the sunroof (Section 14)
- ☐ Check the fuel system components and throttle linkage (Section 15)
- ☐ Check the exhaust system (Section 16)
- ☐ Check the driveshaft gaiters and CV joints (Section 17)
- ☐ Check the front brake pads, calipers and discs (Section 18)
- ☐ Check and adjust the rear brake shoes, check the wheel cylinders and drums (Section 19)
- ☐ Check the braking system master cylinder, flexible hoses and metal pipes (Section 20)
- ☐ Adjust and lubricate the handbrake (Section 21)
- ☐ Check the front suspension and lubricate the upper arm pivot bearings (Section 22)

Every 12 000 miles (20 000 km) or 12 months (continued)

- ☐ Check the steering gear, the rubber gaiters and the track rod balljoints (Section 23)
- ☐ Check the rear suspension and lubricate the trailing arm pivot bearings (Section 24)
- ☐ Check the cooling system hoses and connections (Section 25)
- ☐ Check the operation of the radiator electric cooling fan (Section 26)
- ☐ Top-up the carburettor piston damper (Section 27)
- ☐ Check, where possible, the idle speed and mixture (Section 28)
- ☐ Check the operation of the lambda sensor - where fitted (Chapter 4 and Section 29)
- ☐ Check the distributor cap and the spark plug (HT) leads (Section 30)
- ☐ Check and adjust the alternator drivebelt (Section 31)

Every 24 000 miles (40 000 km) or 2 years

- ☐ Drain, flush and refill the cooling system, renewing the antifreeze (Section 32)
- ☐ Renew the braking system hydraulic fluid (Section 33)
- ☐ Renew the air cleaner filter element (Section 34)
- ☐ Renew the fuel filter (Section 35)
- ☐ Check the crankcase breather hoses (Section 36)
- ☐ Renew the spark plugs (Section 37)
- ☐ Check and adjust the ignition timing - where possible (Section 38)

Every 48 000 miles (80 000 km) or 4 years

- ☐ Check the timing belt (Section 39)

Every 60 000 miles (100 000 km) or 5 years

- ☐ Overhaul the braking system master cylinder, the front brake calipers and the rear brake wheel cylinders and renew their seals (Chapter 9)

Every 96 000 miles (160 000 km) or 8 years

- ☐ Renew the timing belt (Chapter 2)

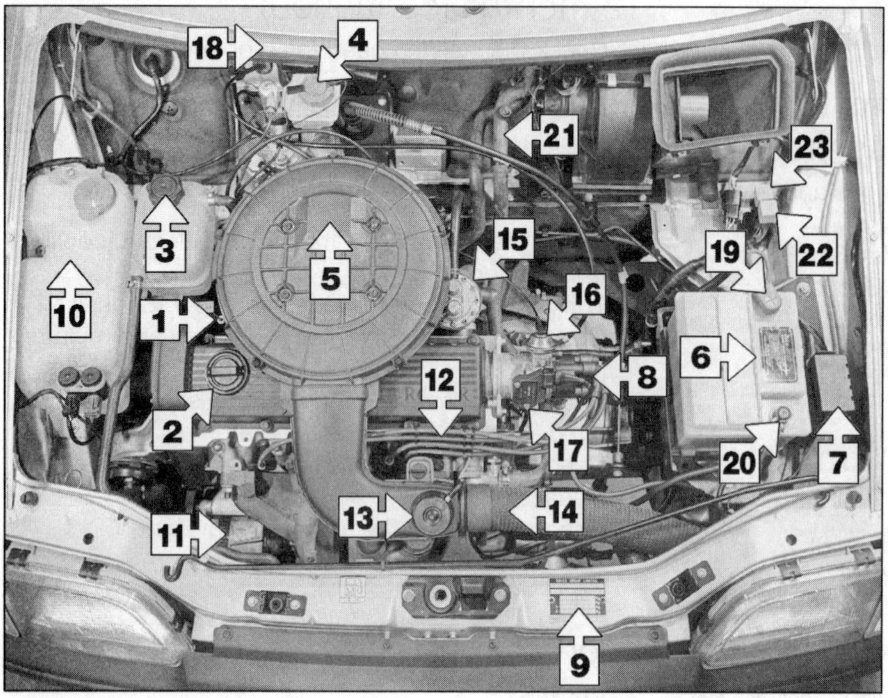

Underbonnet view of a Rover Metro with K8 carburettor engine

1 *Engine oil level dipstick*
2 *Engine oil filler cap*
3 *Cooling system expansion tank and filler cap*
4 *Braking system fluid reservoir filler cap*
5 *Air cleaner assembly*
6 *Battery*
7 *Fusible link box*
8 *Distributor*
9 *VIN plate*
10 *Washer system reservoir*
11 *Alternator*
12 *Spark plug (HT) leads*
13 *Intake air temperature control valve*
14 *Cold air intake duct*
15 *Fuel pump*
16 *Vacuum capsule*
17 *Amplifier module*
18 *Vehicle identification number*
19 *Battery positive terminal*
20 *Battery negative terminal*
21 *Coolant hose - heater feed*
22 *Starter relay*
23 *Inlet manifold heater relay*

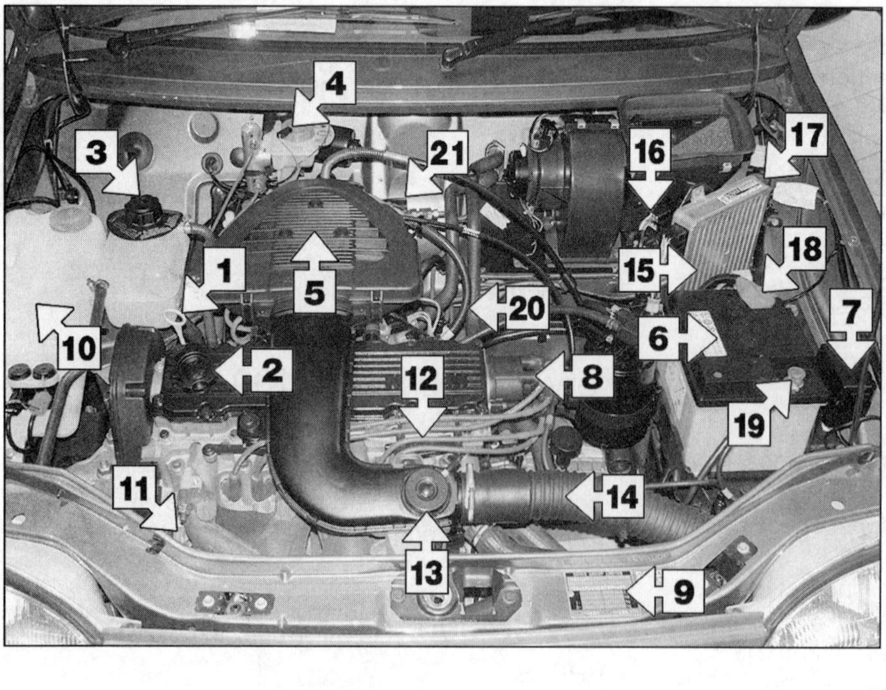

Underbonnet view of a Rover 100 series with K8 SPi engine

1 *Engine oil level dipstick*
2 *Engine oil filler cap*
3 *Cooling system expansion tank and filler cap*
4 *Braking system fluid reservoir filler cap*
5 *Air cleaner assembly*
6 *Battery*
7 *Fusible link box*
8 *Distributor*
9 *VIN plate*
10 *Washer system reservoir*
11 *Alternator*
12 *Spark plug (HT) leads*
13 *Intake air temperature control valve*
14 *Cold air intake duct*
15 *Fuel injection/ignition system ECU*
16 *Relay module*
17 *Fuel cut-off inertia switch*
18 *Battery positive terminal*
19 *Battery negative terminal*
20 *Coolant hose - heater feed*
21 *Fuel filter*

Underbonnet view of a Rover Metro with K16 SPi engine

1 Engine oil level dipstick
2 Engine oil filler cap
3 Cooling system expansion tank and filler cap
4 Braking system fluid reservoir filler cap
5 Air cleaner assembly
6 Battery
7 Fusible link box
8 Distributor
9 VIN plate
10 Washer system reservoir
11 Alternator
12 Spark plug (HT) leads
13 Intake air temperature control valve
14 Cold air intake duct
15 Fuel injection/ignition system ECU
16 Relay module
17 Fuel cut-off inertia switch
18 Vehicle identification number
19 Battery positive terminal
20 Battery negative terminal
21 Coolant hose - heater feed
22 Fuel filter
23 Fuel system pressure release bolt

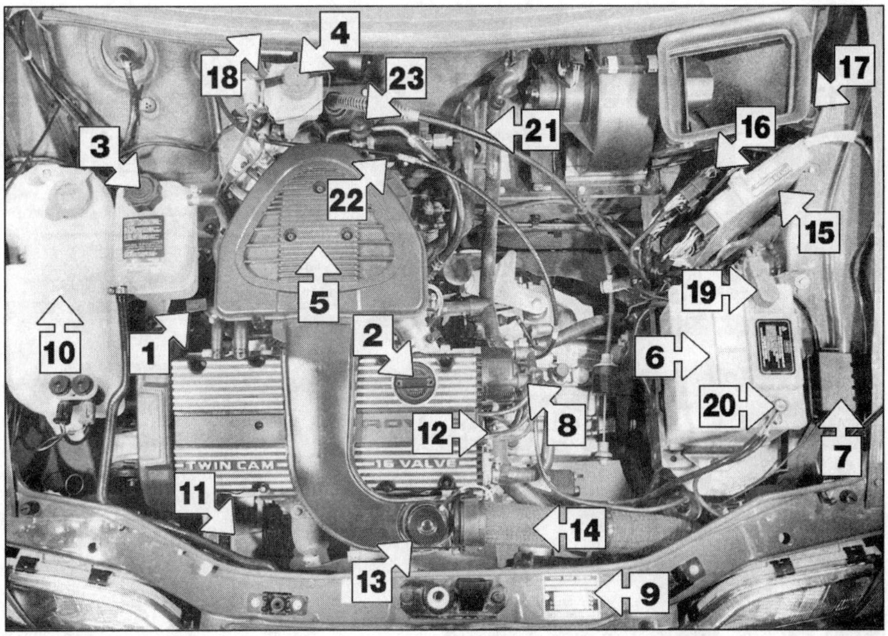

Underbonnet view of a Rover Metro with K16 MPi engine

1 Engine oil level dipstick
2 Engine oil filler cap
3 Cooling system expansion tank and filler cap
4 Braking system fluid reservoir filler cap
5 Air cleaner assembly
6 Battery
7 Fusible link box
8 Distributor
9 VIN plate
10 Washer system reservoir
11 Alternator
12 Spark plug (HT) leads
13 Throttle housing assembly
14 Cold air intake duct
15 Fuel injection/ignition system ECU
16 Relay module
17 Battery positive terminal
18 Battery negative terminal
19 Coolant hose - heater feed
20 Fuel filter
21 Injector rail

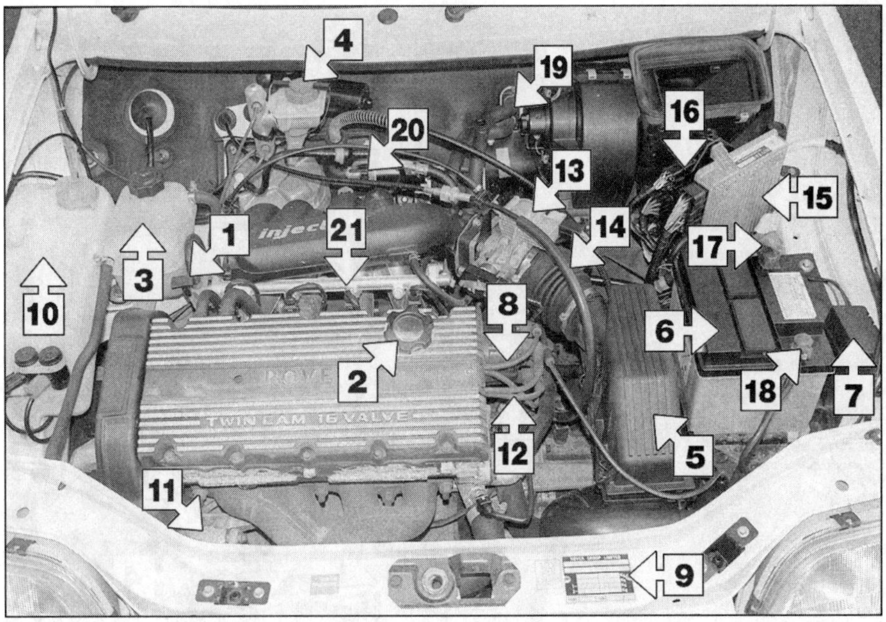

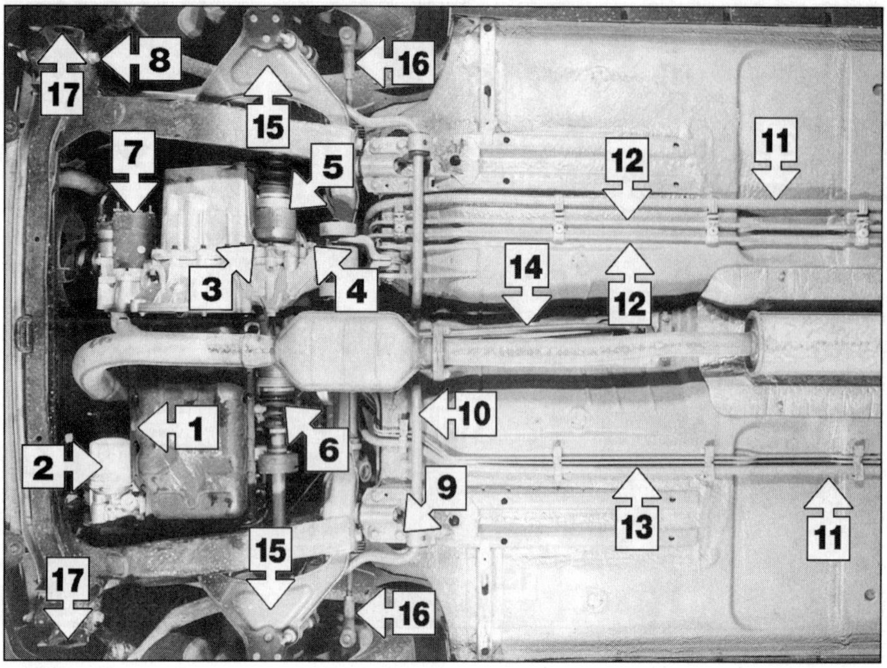

Front underbody view (typical)

1 Engine oil drain plug
2 Oil filter
3 Transmission oil drain plug
4 Transmission oil filler/level plug
5 Left-hand driveshaft inboard constant velocity joint
6 Right-hand driveshaft inboard constant velocity joint
7 Starter motor
8 Front suspension subframe front mountings
9 Front suspension subframe rear mountings
10 Anti-roll bar
11 Hydragas suspension system connecting pipe
12 Fuel feed and return pipes
13 Brake pipes
14 Gearchange linkage
15 Front suspension lower arms
16 Steering gear track rods
17 Front towing eyes

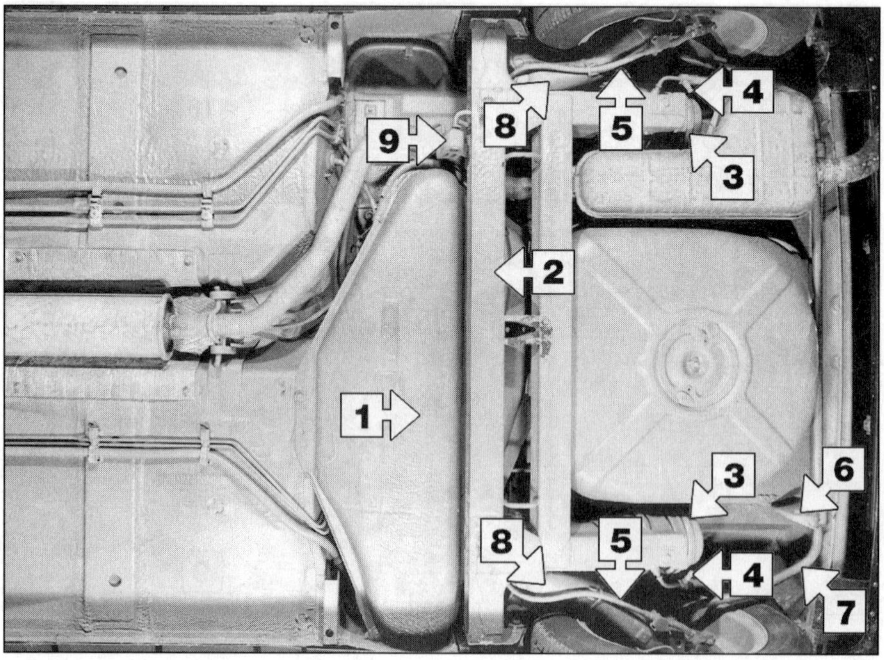

Rear underbody view (typical)

1 Fuel tank
2 Rear suspension subframe
3 Rear suspension Hydragas units
4 Hydragas suspension system ride height adjustment valves
5 Handbrake cable
6 Rear towing eye
7 Anti-roll bar
8 Rear suspension trailing arms
9 Exhaust system rubber mounting

1 Introduction

This Chapter is designed to help the home mechanic maintain his/her vehicle for safety, economy, long life and peak performance.

The Chapter contains a master maintenance schedule, followed by Sections dealing specifically with each task in the schedule. Visual checks, adjustments, component renewal and other helpful items are included. Refer to the accompanying illustrations of the engine compartment and the underside of the vehicle for the locations of the various components.

Servicing your vehicle in accordance with the mileage/time maintenance schedule and the following Sections will provide a planned maintenance programme, which should result in a long and reliable service life. This is a comprehensive plan, so maintaining some items but not others at the specified service intervals, will not produce the same results.

As you service your vehicle, you will discover that many of the procedures can - and should - be grouped together, because of the particular procedure being performed, or because of the close proximity of two otherwise-unrelated components to one another. For example, if the vehicle is raised for any reason, the exhaust can be inspected at the same time as the suspension and steering components.

The first step in this maintenance programme is to prepare yourself before the actual work begins. Read through all the Sections relevant to the work to be carried out, then make a list and gather together all the parts and tools required. If a problem is encountered, seek advice from a parts specialist, or a dealer service department.

2 Intensive maintenance

If, from the time the vehicle is new, the routine maintenance schedule is followed closely, and frequent checks are made of fluid levels and high-wear items, as suggested throughout this Manual, the engine will be kept in relatively good running condition, and the need for additional work will be minimised.

It is possible that there will be times when the engine is running poorly due to the lack of regular maintenance. This is even more likely if a used vehicle, which has not received regular and frequent maintenance checks, is purchased. In such cases, additional work may need to be carried out, outside of the regular maintenance intervals.

If engine wear is suspected, a compression test will provide valuable information regarding the overall performance of the main internal components. Such a test can be used as a basis to decide on the extent of the work to be carried out. If, for example, a compression test indicates serious internal engine wear, conventional maintenance as described in this Chapter will not greatly improve the performance of the engine, and may prove a waste of time and money, unless extensive overhaul work is carried out first.

The following series of operations are those most often required to improve the performance of a generally poor-running engine:

Primary operations

a) Clean, inspect and test the battery
b) Check all the engine-related fluids
c) Check the condition and tension of the auxiliary drivebelt
d) Renew the spark plugs
e) Inspect the distributor cap and HT leads - as applicable
f) Check the condition of the air cleaner filter element, and renew if necessary
g) Renew the fuel filter (if fitted)
h) Check the condition of all hoses, and check for fluid leaks
i) Check the idle speed and mixture settings - as applicable

5 If the above operations do not prove fully effective, carry out the following secondary operations:

Secondary operations

a) Check the charging system
b) Check the ignition system
c) Check the fuel system
d) Renew the distributor cap and rotor arm - as applicable
e) Renew the ignition HT leads - as applicable

1000 mile/1500 km or every Month

3 Lock, hinge and latch mechanism check

1 Check the security and operation of all hinges, latches and locks, adjusting them where required.

2 Check the condition and operation of the tailgate struts, renewing them if either is leaking or is no longer able to support the tailgate securely when raised.

4 Seat belt check

1 All models are fitted with three-point lap and diagonal inertia reel seat belts at both front and the rear outer seats. The rear centre seat has a two-point lap-type belt which is fixed (ie. not inertia reel).

2 Each front seat belt has two threaded holes provided in the door pillar to permit the top anchorage to be positioned (as closely as possible) so that the belt crosses the mid-point of the wearer's shoulder, rather than rest on his/her neck. If this adjustment is made, ensure that the mounting bolt is tightened to the specified torque wrench setting and that the blanking plug is refitted in the unused hole.

3 Belt maintenance is limited to regular inspection. Check the webbing for signs of fraying, cuts or other damage, pulling the belt out to its full extent to check its entire length. Check the operation of the buckles by fitting the belt tongue plate and pulling hard to ensure that it remains locked, then check the retractor mechanism (inertia reel only) by pulling out the belt to the halfway point and jerking hard. The mechanism must lock immediately to prevent any further unreeling but must allow free movement during normal driving. Finally, ensure that all mounting bolts are securely tightened. Note that the bolts are shouldered so that the belt anchor points are free to rotate.

4 If there is any sign of damage, or any doubt about a belt's condition, it must be renewed. If the vehicle has been involved in a collision any belts in use at the time must be renewed as a matter of course and all other belts should be checked carefully.

5 Use only warm water and non-detergent soap to clean the belts. Never use any chemical cleaners, strong detergents, dyes or bleaches. Keep the belts fully extended until they have dried naturally; do not apply heat to dry them.

5 Brake check

1 Make sure that the vehicle does not pull to one side when braking and that the wheels do not lock prematurely when braking hard.

2 Check that there is no vibration through the steering when braking.

3 Check that the handbrake operates correctly without excessive movement of the lever and that it holds the vehicle stationary on a slope.

6 Fluid leakage check

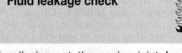

1 Visually inspect the engine joint faces, gaskets and seals for any signs of water or oil leaks. Pay particular attention to the areas around the rocker cover, cylinder head, oil filter and sump joint faces. Bear in mind that over a period of time some very slight seepage from these areas is to be expected but what you are really looking for is any indication of a serious leak. Should a leak be found, renew the offending gasket or oil seal by referring to the appropriate Chapter(s) of this Manual.
2 Similarly, check the transmission for oil leaks, and investigate and rectify and problems found.
3 Check the security and condition of all the engine related pipes and hoses. Ensure that all cable-ties or securing clips are in place and in good condition. Clips which are broken or missing can lead to chafing of the hoses, pipes or wiring which could cause more serious problems in the future.
4 Carefully check the condition of all coolant, fuel, power steering and brake hoses. Renew any hose which is cracked, swollen or deteriorated. Cracks will show up better if the hose is squeezed. Pay close attention to the hose clips that secure the hoses to the system components. Hose clips can pinch and puncture hoses, resulting in leaks. If wire type hose clips are used, it may be a good idea to replace them with screw-type clips.
5 With the vehicle raised, inspect the fuel tank and filler neck for punctures, cracks and other damage. The connection between the filler neck and tank is especially critical. Sometimes a rubber filler neck or connecting hose will leak due to loose retaining clamps or deteriorated rubber.

HAYNES HINT

Leaks in the cooling system will usually show up as white or rust- coloured deposits around the area adjoining the leak.

6 Similarly, inspect all brake hoses and metal pipes. If any damage or deterioration is discovered, do not drive the vehicle until the necessary repair work has been carried out. Renew any damaged sections of hose or pipe.
7 Carefully check all rubber hoses and metal fuel lines leading away from the petrol tank. Check for loose connections, deteriorated hoses, crimped lines and other damage. Pay particular attention to the vent pipes and hoses which often loop up around the filler neck and can become blocked or crimped. Follow the lines to the front of the vehicle carefully inspecting them all the way. Renew damaged sections as necessary.
8 From within the engine compartment, check the security of all fuel hose attachments and pipe unions, and inspect the fuel hoses and vacuum hoses for kinks, chafing and deterioration.
9 Check the condition of all exposed wiring harnesses.

7 Battery electrolyte level check

HAYNES HINT

Persistent need for topping-up the battery electrolyte suggests that alternator output is excessive or the battery is approaching the end of its life.

1 A "maintenance-free" (sealed for life) battery is standard equipment on all vehicles covered by this Manual. Although this type of battery has many advantages over the older refillable type and should never require the addition of distilled water, it should still be routinely checked. The electrolyte level can be seen through the battery's translucent case. Although it should not alter in normal use, if the level has lowered (for example, due to electrolyte having boiled away as a result of overcharging) it is permissible to gently prise up the cell cover(s) and to top-up the level.
2 If a conventional battery has been fitted as a replacement, the electrolyte level of each cell should be checked and, if necessary, topped up until the separators are just covered. On some batteries the case is translucent and incorporates MINIMUM and MAXIMUM level marks. The check should be made more often if the vehicle is operated in high ambient temperature conditions.
3 Top-up the electrolyte level using distilled or de-ionised water. This should not be necessary often under normal operating conditions. If regular topping-up becomes necessary and the battery case is not fractured, the battery is being over-charged and the voltage regulator will have to be checked.

6000 mile/10 000 km or 6 Months

8 Engine oil and filter renewal

Note: *The manufacturer has from mid.1991, approximately, extended the service schedule so that this task need no longer be carried out at this interval, except for the First Lubrication Service, carried out when the vehicle is new. Owners of high-mileage vehicles, or those who do a lot of stop-start driving, may prefer to adhere to the original recommendation, changing the oil and filter in-between the major services described in the following Section:*

12 000 mile/20 000 km or 12 Months

9 Engine oil and filter renewal

Note: *Refer to the note in Section 8 before proceeding.*

1 Frequent oil and filter changes are the most important preventative maintenance procedures that can be undertaken by the DIY owner. As engine oil ages, it becomes diluted and contaminated, which leads to premature engine wear.
2 Before starting this procedure, gather together all the necessary tools and materials **(see illustration)**. Also make sure that you have plenty of clean rags and newspapers handy to mop up any spills. Ideally, the engine oil should be warm as it will drain better and more built-up sludge will be removed with it. Take care however, not to touch the exhaust or any other hot parts of the engine when working under the vehicle. To avoid any possibility of scalding and to protect yourself

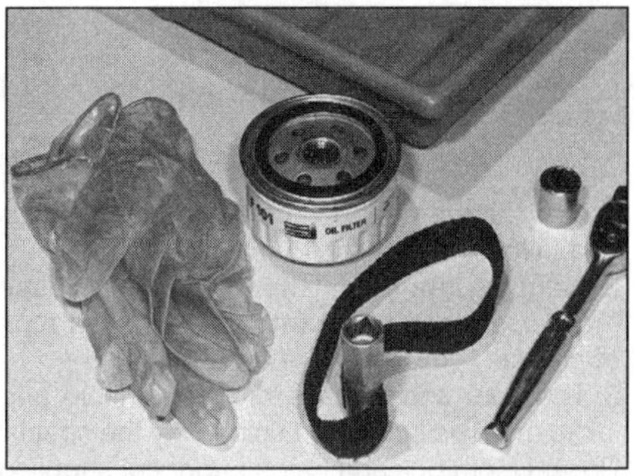

9.2 Requirements for engine oil and filter renewal

from possible skin irritants and other harmful contaminants in used engine oils, it is advisable to wear gloves when carrying out this work.

3 The engine oil drain plug is located on the front of the sump and can be reached easily, without having to raise the vehicle. Remove the oil filler cap and use a spanner, or preferably a suitable socket and bar, to slacken the drain plug about half a turn **(see illustration)**. Position the draining container under the drain plug, then remove the plug completely. If possible, try to keep the plug pressed into the sump while unscrewing it by hand the last couple of turns.

HAYNES HiNT ***Remove the engine oil drain plug quickly so the stream of oil runs into the container, not up your sleeve!***

4 Allow some time for the old oil to drain, noting that it may be necessary to reposition the container as the flow of oil slows to a trickle. Work can be speeded-up by removing the oil filter, as described below, while the oil is draining.

5 After all the oil has drained, wipe off the drain plug with a clean rag and renew its sealing washer. Clean the area around the drain plug opening and refit the plug. Tighten the plug securely, preferably to the specified torque using a torque wrench.

6 Move the container into position under the oil filter, which is located next to the drain plug on the front of the engine.

7 Using an oil filter removal tool, slacken the filter initially then unscrew it by hand the rest of the way **(see illustration)**. Empty the oil in the old filter into the container and allow any residual oil to drain out of the engine.

8 Use a clean rag to remove all oil, dirt and sludge from the filter sealing area on the engine. Check the old filter to make sure that the rubber sealing ring has not stuck to the engine. If it has, carefully remove it.

9 Apply a light coating of clean engine oil to the new filter's sealing ring and screw the filter into position on the engine until it seats, then tighten it through a further half-turn only.

Caution: Tighten the engine oil filter firmly by hand only - do not use any tools.

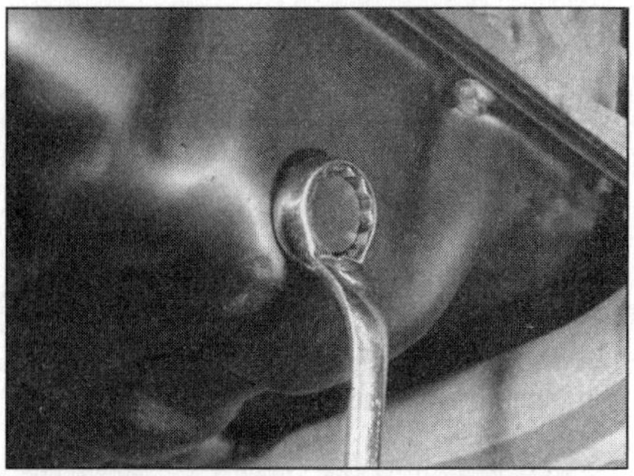

9.3 Unscrewing engine oil drain plug

10 Remove the old oil and all tools from under the vehicle.

11 Refill the engine with fresh oil, using the correct grade and type of oil. Pour in half the specified quantity of oil first, then wait a few minutes for the oil to fall to the sump. Continue adding oil a small quantity at a time until the level is up to the lower mark on the dipstick *(see Weekly Checks)*. Adding a further 1.0 litre will bring the level up to the upper mark on the dipstick.

12 Start the engine and run it for a few minutes while checking for leaks around the oil filter seal and the sump drain plug.

Note: *There may be a delay of a few seconds before the oil pressure warning light goes out when the engine is first started after oil renewal.*

13 Switch off the engine and wait a few minutes for the oil to settle in the sump once more. With the new oil circulated and the filter now completely full, recheck the level on the dipstick and add more oil as necessary.

14 Dispose of the used engine oil safely.

10 Clutch check

Check that the clutch pedal moves smoothly and easily through its full travel and that the clutch itself functions correctly, with no trace of slip or drag. If excessive effort is required to operate the clutch, check first that the cable is correctly routed and undamaged, then remove the pedal to ensure that its pivot

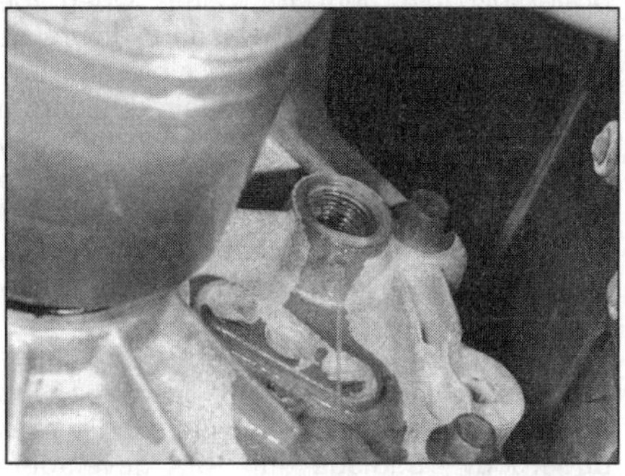

11.3 Oil level is correct when oil has just stopped trickling from filler/level plug hole

9.7 Using an oil filter removal tool to slacken filter

is properly greased before suspecting a fault in the cable itself. If the cable is worn or damaged, or if its self-adjusting mechanism is no longer effective, then it must be renewed.

No adjustment is possible of the cable or of the clutch release. If any fault develops in the clutch, the transmission must be removed so that the clutch can be overhauled.

11 Transmission oil level check

Manual gearbox

1 The oil level must be checked with the vehicle standing on its wheels on level ground. Also, the level must be checked before the vehicle is driven, or at least 5 minutes after the engine has been switched off. If the oil is checked immediately after driving, some of the oil will remain distributed around the gearbox components, resulting in an inaccurate level reading.

HAYNES HiNT ***Gearbox oil can foam when hot and give a false level reading. Allow the gearbox to cool before checking the oil level.***

2 Wipe clean the area around the (hex-head) filler/level plug, which is located at the rear of the gearbox, next to the left-hand driveshaft inner constant velocity joint, then unscrew the plug and clean it. Discard the sealing washer. To avoid rounding-off the corners of the plug hexagon, use only good quality, close-fitting, single-hexagon or surface drive spanners or sockets.

3 The oil level should reach the lower edge of the filler/level hole. A certain amount of oil will have gathered behind the filler/level plug and will trickle out when it is removed; this does not necessarily indicate that the level is correct. To ensure that a true level is established, wait until the initial trickle has stopped, then add oil as necessary until a trickle of new oil can be seen emerging. The level will be correct when the flow ceases. Use only good quality oil of the specified type **(see illustration)**.

1

4 Note that refilling the gearbox is an extremely awkward operation. Above all, allow plenty of time for the oil level to settle properly before checking it. If a large amount had to be added to the gearbox and a large amount flows out on checking the level, refit the filler/level plug and take the vehicle on a short journey so that the new oil is distributed fully around the gearbox components, then recheck the level when it has settled again.

5 If the gearbox has been overfilled so that oil flows out as soon as the filler/level plug is removed, check that the vehicle is completely level (front-to-rear and side-to-side) and allow the surplus to drain off into a container.

6 When the level is correct, fit a new sealing washer and refit the filler/level plug, tightening it to the specified torque wrench setting. Clean away any spilt oil.

Automatic transmission

7 The fluid level must be checked with the vehicle standing on its wheels on level ground.

8 With the dipstick fitted, run the engine until the transmission reaches normal operating temperature.

9 With the engine running at idle speed and the handbrake applied, operate the selector lever through the full range of positions three times and then select "P".

10 With the engine still running, withdraw the dipstick and wipe it with a clean rag.

11 Reinsert the dipstick fully and then withdraw it, this time checking that the fluid level is between the MINIMUM and MAXIMUM marks on the dipstick **(see illustration)**.

12 Stop the engine and if necessary, top-up the transmission fluid to the MAXIMUM mark whilst referring to Chapter 7.

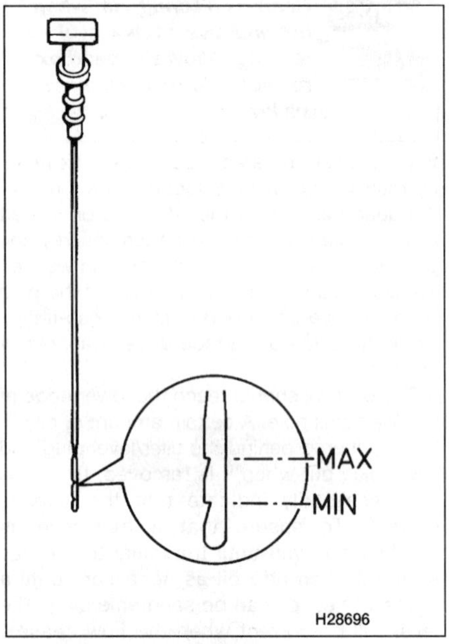

11.11 Automatic transmission dipstick marks

12 Roadwheel nut check

To check that the roadwheel nuts are securely fastened, remove the roadwheel trim (where fitted), then slacken each nut in turn through one-quarter of a turn and tighten it to the specified torque wrench setting. Refit the trim, where applicable.

13 Exterior paintwork, body panel and underbody sealer check

HAYNES HiNT *Steam-cleaning is available at many garages for the purpose of removing any accumulation of oily grime from beneath a vehicle.*

Exterior paintwork and body panels

1 Once the vehicle has been washed and all tar spots and other surface blemishes have been cleaned off, check carefully all paintwork, looking closely for chips or scratches. Check with particular care vulnerable areas such as the front (bonnet and spoiler) and around the wheel arches. Any damage to the paintwork must be rectified as soon as possible to comply with the terms of the manufacturer's cosmetic and anti-corrosion warranties. Check with a Rover dealer for details.

2 If a chip or light scratch is found that is recent and still free from rust, it can be touched-up using the appropriate touch-up pencil. Any more serious damage, or rusted stone chips, can be repaired as described in Chapter 11, but if damage or corrosion is so severe that a panel must be renewed, seek professional advice as soon as possible.

3 Always check that the door and ventilator opening drain holes and pipes are completely clear so that water can be drained out.

Underbody sealer

4 The wax-based underbody protective coating should be inspected annually, preferably just prior to winter, when the underbody should be washed down as thoroughly but gently as possible and any damage to the coating repaired using a proprietary undershield. If any of the body panels are disturbed for repair or renewed, do not forget to replace the coating and to inject wax into door panels, sills, box sections etc, to maintain the level of protection provided by the manufacturer.

5 Check carefully that the wheel arch liners and underwing shields are in place and securely fastened and that there is no sign of underbody damage or of developing corrosion. If any is found, seek immediate professional advice.

14 Lock, hinge and latch mechanism lubrication

1 Lubricate the hinges of the bonnet, doors and tailgate with a light machine oil.

2 Lightly lubricate the bonnet release mechanism and cable with the specified type of grease.

3 The door and tailgate latches, strikers and locks must be lubricated using only the special Rover Door Lock and Latch Lubricant supplied in 25 gram sachets under Part Number VWN 10075. Inject 1 gram into each lock and wipe off any surplus, then apply a thin film to the latches and strikers. Do not lubricate the steering lock mechanism with oil or any other lubricant which might foul the ignition switch contacts. If the lock is stiff, try to introduce a graphite-based powder into the mechanism.

4 If a sunroof is fitted, lubricate very sparingly the seal lip with Rover's Non-Staining Grease available under Part Number BAU 5812.

15 Fuel system components and throttle linkage check

Fuel system components

1 The fuel system is most easily checked with the vehicle raised and suitably supported on axle stands (see "*Jacking and Vehicle Support*") so the components underneath are readily visible and accessible.

2 If the smell of petrol is noticed whilst driving or after the vehicle has been parked in the sun, the system should be thoroughly inspected immediately.

3 Remove the petrol tank filler cap and check for damage, corrosion and an unbroken sealing imprint on the gasket. Renew the cap if necessary.

4 Inspect the petrol tank and filler neck for punctures, cracks and other damage. The connection between the filler neck and tank is especially critical. Sometimes a rubber filler neck or connecting hose will leak due to loose retaining clamps or deteriorated rubber.

5 Carefully check all rubber hoses and metal fuel lines leading away from the petrol tank. Check for loose connections, deteriorated hoses, crimped lines and other damage. Pay particular attention to the vent pipes and hoses which often loop up around the filler neck and can become blocked or crimped. Follow the lines to the front of the vehicle carefully inspecting them all the way. Renew damaged sections as necessary.

6 From within the engine compartment, check the security of all fuel hose attachments and inspect the fuel hoses and vacuum hoses for kinks, chafing and deterioration. Where an evaporative emission control system is fitted, check its hoses and the security of the purge control valve wiring as well as checking the physical condition of the charcoal canister.

Throttle linkage

7 Check the operation of the throttle linkage through its full range and lubricate the linkage components with a few drops of light oil.

16 Exhaust system check

1 With the exhaust system cold, check the complete system from the engine to the end of the tailpipe. Ideally the inspection should be carried out with the vehicle raised and supported on axle stands (see "*Jacking and Vehicle Support*") to permit unrestricted access.

2 Check the exhaust pipes and connections for evidence of leaks, severe corrosion and damage. Make sure that all brackets and mountings are in good condition and tight. Leakage at any of the joints or in other parts of the system will usually show up as a black sooty stain in the vicinity of the leak. Proprietary exhaust repair systems can be used for effective repairs to exhaust pipes and silencer boxes, including ends and bends.

3 Rattles and other noises can often be traced to the exhaust system, especially the brackets and mountings. Try to move the pipes and silencers. If the components can come into contact with the body or suspension parts, secure the system with new mountings or if possible, separate the joints and twist the pipes as necessary to provide additional clearance.

17 Driveshaft gaiter and CV joint check

With the vehicle raised and securely supported on axle stands (see "*Jacking and Vehicle Support*"), turn the steering onto full lock then slowly rotate the roadwheel. Inspect the condition of the outer constant velocity (CV) joint rubber gaiters while squeezing the gaiters to open out the folds **(see illustration)**. Check for signs of cracking, splits or deterioration of the rubber which may allow the grease to escape and lead to the entry of water and grit into the joint. Also check the security and condition of the retaining clips. Repeat these checks on the inner CV joints. If any damage or deterioration is found, the gaiters should be renewed.

At the same time, check the general condition of the CV joints themselves by first holding the driveshaft and attempting to rotate the roadwheel. Repeat this check by holding the inner joint and attempting to rotate the driveshaft. Any appreciable movement indicates wear in the joints, in the driveshaft splines, or a loose driveshaft nut.

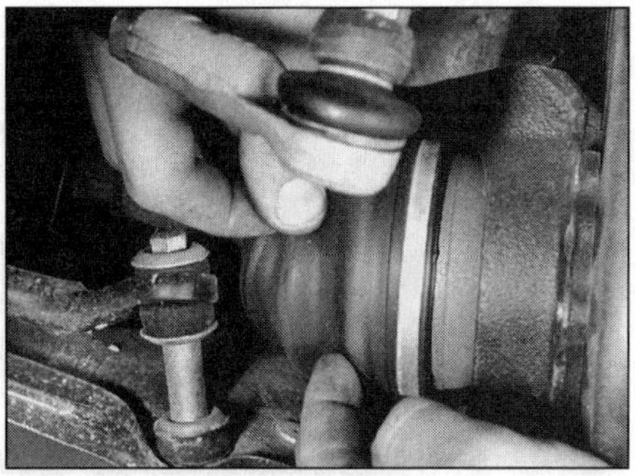

17.1 Checking driveshaft outer CV joint rubber gaiter

18 Front brake pad, caliper and disc check

1 Jack up the front of the vehicle and support it securely on axle stands (see "*Jacking and Vehicle Support*"), then remove the roadwheel.

2 For a quick check, the thickness of friction material remaining on each brake pad can be measured through the slot in the caliper body **(see illustration)**. If any pad's friction material is worn to the specified thickness or less, all four pads must be renewed.

3 For a more comprehensive check, the brake pads should be removed and cleaned. This will facilitate inspection of the caliper.

4 Refer to Chapter 9 and inspect the condition and thickness of each brake disc.

19 Rear brake shoe, wheel cylinder and drum check

Brake shoe, wheel cylinder and drum check

1 Jack up the rear of the vehicle and support it securely on axle stands (see "*Jacking and Vehicle Support*").

2 For a quick check, the thickness of friction material remaining on one of the brake shoes can be measured through the slot in the brake backplate that is exposed by prising out its sealing grommet **(see illustration)**. If a rod of

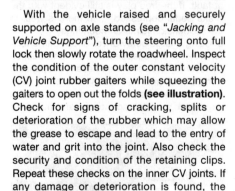

19.2 Brake shoe material can be checked by removing grommet in brake backplate

18.2 Front brake pad friction material can be checked through slot in caliper body

the same diameter as the specified minimum thickness is placed against the shoe friction material, the amount of wear can quickly be assessed. If any shoe's friction material is worn to the specified thickness or less, all four shoes must be renewed.

3 For a comprehensive check, the brake drums should be removed and cleaned. This will permit the wheel cylinders to be checked and the condition of the brake drum itself to be fully examined, see Chapter 9. Upon reassembly, check the shoe adjustment.

Brake shoe adjustment

4 Jack up the rear of the vehicle and support it securely on axle stands (see "*Jacking and Vehicle Support*").

5 Check that the handbrake is fully released and that the roadwheel rotates freely, with no sound of the brake shoes rubbing on the drum.

6 Locate the square-headed brake adjuster on the inboard face of the rear brake backplate, at the top. If it is stuck with corrosion, apply a good quantity of penetrating fluid and allow time for it to work before attempting adjustment. Using a brake-adjusting spanner, rotate the adjuster clockwise (looking at it outwards from the vehicle's centre-line) until the roadwheel locks **(see illustration)**. Do not apply excessive force to the adjuster, but note that it has four tight spots per revolution. Ensure that the roadwheel is locked when the adjuster is backed off from the last (tightest) of these tight spots.

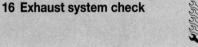

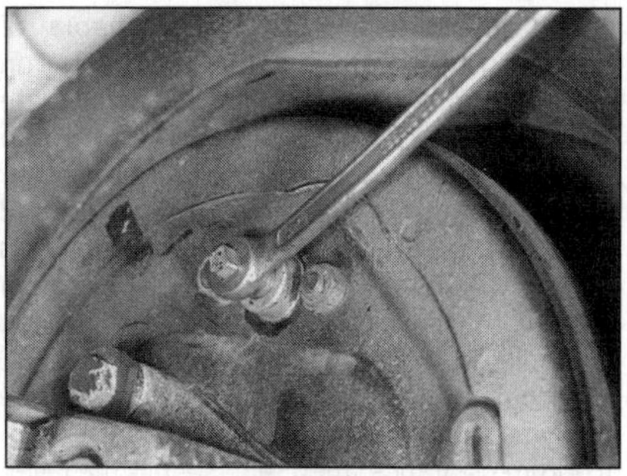

19.6 Using a brake-adjusting spanner to adjust rear brake shoes

7 Now rotate the adjuster anti-clockwise until the roadwheel is just free to rotate with no sound of rubbing. Again, ensure that the final setting is between the tight spots.

8 Apply a smear of grease to the exposed adjuster threads to prevent corrosion, then repeat the operation on the opposite side of the vehicle. Finally, check the handbrake adjustment.

20 Braking system hose, pipe and master cylinder check

1 Check that the brake pedal pivot is properly greased and that the pedal moves smoothly and easily through its full travel. When the engine is switched off, the pedal should have a small amount of free play, then firm resistance. If the pedal feels spongy or if it has a long travel, the system should be checked further, as described in Chapter 9.

2 The brake hydraulic system comprises a number of metal hydraulic pipes which run from the master cylinder around the engine compartment to the front brakes and pressure regulating valves and along the underbody to the rear brakes. Flexible hoses are fitted at front and rear to cater for steering and suspension movement.

3 When checking the system, first look for signs of leakage at the pipe or hose unions, then examine the flexible hoses for signs of cracking, chafing or deterioration of the rubber. Bend them sharply between the fingers (but do not actually bend them double or the casing may be damaged) and check that this does not reveal previously hidden cracks, cuts or splits **(see illustration)**. Check that all pipes and hoses are securely fastened in their clips.

4 Carefully work along the length of the metal hydraulic pipes looking for dents, kinks, damage of any sort or corrosion. Corrosion should be polished off. If the depth of pitting is significant the pipe must be renewed.

20.3 Checking a braking system flexible hose

21 Handbrake adjustment and lubrication

1 The handbrake should be capable of holding the parked car stationary, even on steep slopes, when applied with moderate force. The mechanism should be firm and positive in feel with no trace of stiffness or sponginess from the cables, and should release immediately the handbrake lever is released. If the mechanism is faulty in any of these respects it must be checked immediately.

2 To check the setting, apply the handbrake firmly several times to establish correct shoe-to-drum clearance, then release fully the lever. Applying normal, moderate pressure, pull the handbrake lever to the fully-applied position and count the number of notches required to do so. If the number of notches is more or less than that specified, adjustment is required.

3 To adjust the handbrake, first jack up the rear of the vehicle and support it securely on axle stands (see "*Jacking and Vehicle Support*").

4 Remove the split pin and clevis pin from the left-hand rear brake handbrake lever; do not touch the right-hand brake.

5 Rotate the brake adjusters clockwise until the roadwheels lock, then pump the brake pedal several times to ensure that the shoes are forced firmly into contact with the drums. Check that both rear roadwheels are locked, then rotate both adjusters anti-clockwise through two flats.

6 Working inside the passenger compartment, carefully peel back the carpet between the front seat rear mounting bar and the handbrake lever. Hold the adjuster nut whilst slackening the adjuster locknut **(see illustration)**.

7 Ensuring that the threaded adjuster itself does not rotate, turn the adjuster nut until the holes line up in the end of the left-hand handbrake cable and the rear brake handbrake lever, then refit the clevis pin and secure it with a new split pin, spreading its ends securely. Tighten the adjuster locknut without disturbing the setting.

8 With the handbrake fully released, check that the roadwheels are free to rotate and that they first bind and then lock at the specified number of notches as the lever is pulled on.

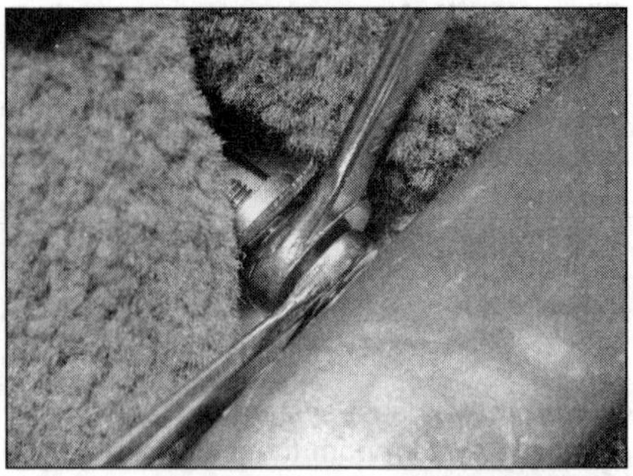

21.6 Adjusting the handbrake

9 If all is well, pull the handbrake to the fully-applied position and then release it. If the left-hand side rear brake still binds, rotate the adjuster anti-clockwise through no more than two flats until the roadwheel rotates freely; do not adjust the right-hand brake.

10 When adjustment is correct, lower the vehicle to the ground.

22 Front suspension check and upper arm pivot bearing lubrication

Suspension check

1 Raise the front of the vehicle and securely support it on axle stands (see "*Jacking and Vehicle Support*").

2 Grasp the roadwheel at the 12 o'clock and 6 o'clock positions and try to rock it **(see illustration)**. Very slight free play may be felt, but if the movement is appreciable further investigation is necessary to determine the source. Continue rocking the wheel while an assistant depresses the brake pedal. If the movement is now eliminated or significantly reduced, it is likely that the hub bearings are at fault. If the free play is still evident with the brake pedal depressed, then there is wear in the suspension joints or mountings.

3 Using a large screwdriver or flat bar, check for wear in the suspension mounting bushes by levering between the relevant suspension component and its attachment point **(see illustration)**. Some movement is to be expected as the mountings are made of

22.2 Rocking the roadwheel to check steering/suspension wear

22.3 Using a lever to check for wear in anti-roll bar mountings

rubber but excessive wear should be obvious. Also check the condition of any visible rubber bushes, looking for splits, cracks or contamination of the rubber.

4 Check the Hydragas system components, looking for signs of fluid leaks from the units and connecting pipes as well as for signs of corrosion or other damage. If any is found, it should be repaired as soon as possible. The manufacturer does not specify a regular check of the ride heights, but these should be checked with reasonable frequency to ensure that the steering and suspension are functioning properly; refer to the relevant Sections of Chapter 10.

5 Where additional dampers are fitted, check for any signs of fluid leakage around the damper body or from the piston rod. Should any fluid be noticed the damper is defective internally and should be renewed. **Note:** *Dampers should always be renewed in pairs on the same axle.*

6 The efficiency of the damper may be checked by bouncing the car at each corner. Generally speaking, the body should return to its normal position and stop after being depressed. If it rises and returns on a rebound, the damper is probably suspect. Examine also the damper upper and lower mountings for any signs of wear.

Suspension upper arm pivot bearing lubrication

7 Rover Metros are unusual for modern cars in that they are still fitted with grease nipples. This is so that highly-stressed bearings can be lubricated regularly using a grease gun instead of having to dismantle them, clean them and re-pack them with grease on reassembly.

8 It is essential that the suspension pivots are greased regularly in accordance with the maintenance schedule or their bearings will wear out very quickly indeed, causing poor handling, a poor ride and instability, poor braking and greatly increased tyre wear, as well as the considerable expense of time and money in effecting repairs. Worn suspension pivot bearings are also a well-known MOT failure point for Metros, so the slight effort spent in greasing the pivots regularly will be well repaid in terms of long bearing life.

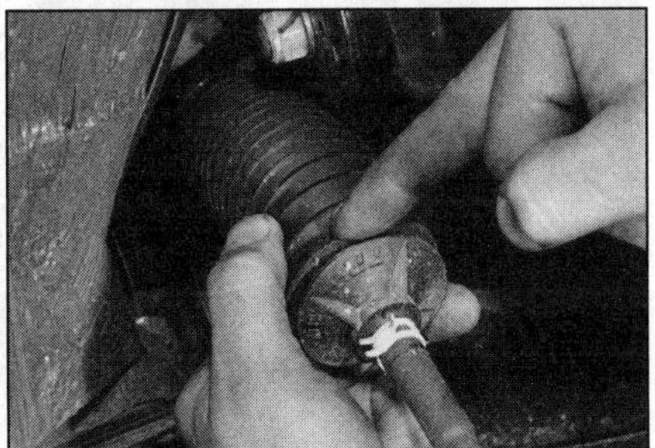

23.2 Checking one of the steering gear rubber gaiters

9 If you do not already possess one, obtain a grease gun which will fit the grease nipples (one with a long, flexible spout would be best) and follow its manufacturer's instructions to fill it with the specified type of grease.

10 When the grease gun is filled, force a little grease out of the nozzle to eject any dirt and check that any air bubbles are removed using the bleed screw. Wipe clean the nozzle.

11 If you don't mind getting dirty, the grease nipple can be reached by turning the steering to the appropriate full lock and working behind the roadwheel. If more than one task is to be carried out however, it is best to jack up the vehicle and to remove the roadwheel. If the roadwheel is not to be removed, take the weight of the vehicle off the pivot by jacking it up until the roadwheel is just clear of the ground and supporting the vehicle on an axle stand.

12 A grease nipple is screwed into the front end of each front suspension upper arm pivot **(see illustration)**. Wipe the nipple clean and press the gun's nozzle firmly and squarely over it. Operate the gun until clean grease can be seen exuding from both ends of the pivot, then remove the gun, wipe clean the nipple and wipe off the excess grease from the pivot. It is essential that as much as possible of the old grease within the pivot is pushed out and replaced by clean grease; if your grease gun has a small capacity, you may have to refill it more than once before the pivot is full.

13 If, on operating the gun, grease just escapes from between the nozzle and the nipple, first reseat the nozzle and try again. If grease still escapes it is probable that the nipple is clogged. This can happen if the suspension has not been greased for some time as the grease can harden in the nipple. To clear the nipple, unscrew it and force grease through it with the gun. If the nipple is still clogged, it must be renewed. although it is always worth trying the effect of immersing it first in boiling water to melt the grease.

14 When the pivot is properly greased, repeat the operation on the other side of the vehicle.

23 Steering gear, rubber gaiter and track rod balljoint check

1 Raise the front of the vehicle and securely support it on axle stands (see "*Jacking and Vehicle Support*").

2 Visually inspect the balljoint dust covers and the steering gear rubber gaiters for splits, chafing or deterioration **(see illustration)**. Any wear of these components will cause loss of lubricant together with dirt and water entry, resulting in rapid deterioration of the balljoints or steering gear.

3 Grasp the roadwheel at the 9 o'clock and 3 o'clock positions and try to rock it. Any movement felt may be caused by wear in the hub bearings, or in the track rod balljoints. If a

22.12 Greasing the front suspension upper arm pivot bearings

balljoint is worn the visual movement will be obvious. If the inner joint is suspect, it can be felt by placing a hand over the steering gear rubber gaiter and gripping the track rod. If the wheel is now rocked, movement will be felt at the inner joint if wear has taken place.

4 With the vehicle standing on its wheels, have an assistant turn the steering wheel back and forth about an eighth of a turn each way. There should be very little, if any, lost movement between the steering wheel and the roadwheels. If this is not the case, closely observe the joints and mountings previously described, but in addition check for wear of the steering column universal joint and the steering gear itself.

24 Rear suspension check and trailing arm pivot bearing lubrication

Suspension check

1 Raise the rear of the vehicle and support it securely on axle stands (see "*Jacking and Vehicle Support*").

2 Working as described above for the front suspension, check the rear hub bearings and the trailing arm pivot bearings for wear, check the security of all component mountings and use a lever to check the condition of the subframe (front) and other mountings **(see illustrations)**.

3 Using a large screwdriver or flat bar, check for wear in the suspension mounting bushes by levering between the relevant suspension

24.2a Using a lever to check for wear in rear suspension trailing arm pivot bearings

24.2b Using a lever to check for wear in rear suspension subframe (front) mountings

component and its attachment point. Some movement is to be expected as the mountings are made of rubber, but excessive wear should be obvious. Also check the condition of any visible rubber bushes, looking for splits, cracks or contamination of the rubber.

4 Check the Hydragas system components, looking for signs of fluid leaks from the units and connecting pipes as well as for signs of corrosion or other damage. If any is found, it should be repaired as soon as possible. The manufacturer does not specify a regular check of the ride heights, but these should be checked with reasonable frequency to ensure that the steering and suspension are functioning properly; refer to the relevant Sections of Chapter 10.

5 Where additional dampers are fitted, check for any signs of fluid leakage around the damper body or from the piston rod. Should any fluid be noticed the damper is defective internally and should be renewed. **Note:** *Dampers should always be renewed in pairs on the same axle.*

6 The efficiency of the damper may be checked by bouncing the car at each corner. Generally speaking, the body should return to its normal position and stop after being depressed. If it rises and returns on a rebound, the damper is probably suspect. Examine also the damper upper and lower mountings for any signs of wear.

Suspension trailing arm pivot bearing lubrication

7 All the general comments made previously about greasing the front suspension upper arm pivot bearings apply equally to the rear suspension trailing arm pivot bearings. However, it is even more important that the trailing arm pivot bearings are regularly greased as the pivots are directly exposed to the road dirt, water and salt thrown up by the rear wheels; this makes the bearings much more vulnerable and even more prone to wearing out if not regularly greased.

8 The actual greasing procedure is exactly the same as that described previously. Read through that procedure before starting work.

9 A grease nipple is screwed into the outboard end of each rear suspension trailing arm pivot **(see illustration)**. Although access is easy, do not forget first to take the weight of the vehicle off the pivot by jacking it up until the roadwheel is just clear of the ground. There is no need to use axle stands if you are not intending to work under the vehicle but take care whilst it is supported only on the jack.

10 When clean grease can be seen exuding from both ends of the pivot, remove the gun and wipe clean the nipple, then wipe off as much excess grease as possible from the pivot and repeat the operation on the other side of the vehicle.

25 Cooling system hose and connection check

1 The engine should be cold for the following cooling system checks.

2 Remove the expansion tank filler cap and clean it thoroughly inside and out with a rag. Also clean the filler neck on the expansion tank. The presence of rust or corrosion in the filler neck indicates that the coolant should be changed. The coolant inside the expansion tank should be relatively clean and transparent. If it is rust-coloured, drain and flush the system and refill with a fresh coolant mixture.

3 Carefully check the radiator hoses and heater hoses along their entire length. Renew any hose which is cracked, swollen or deteriorated. Cracks will show up better if the hose is squeezed. Pay close attention to the hose clips that secure the hoses to the cooling system components. Hose clips can pinch and puncture hoses, resulting in cooling system leaks. If wire type hose clips are used, it may be a good idea to replace them with screw-type clips.

4 Inspect all the cooling system components (hoses, joint faces etc) for leaks. A leak in the cooling system will usually show up as white or rust-coloured deposits on the area adjoining the leak. Where any problems of this nature are found on system components, renew the component or gasket with reference to Chapter 3.

5 Clean the front of the radiator with a soft brush to remove all insects, leaves, etc. imbedded in the radiator fins. Be extremely careful not to damage the radiator fins or cut your fingers on them.

24.9 Greasing the rear suspension trailing arm pivot bearings

26 Radiator electric cooling fan check

Run the engine until normal operating temperature is reached, then allow it to idle. If the fan does not cut in within a few minutes then refer to Chapter 3 for details of further testing.

27 Carburettor piston damper replenishment

1 Unscrew the four screws securing the air cleaner assembly to its mounting bracket and release the quarter-turn fastener securing the inlet duct to the cylinder head support bracket. Carefully lift the air cleaner assembly and disconnect the thermac switch vacuum pipes. Note that these are colour-coded (yellow to the temperature control valve, red to the inlet manifold) to ensure correct reconnection. Place the assembly to one side, clear of the carburettor.

2 Unscrew the piston damper from the top of the carburettor suction chamber and top-up the damper chamber to the top of the damper cylinder with the specified type and viscosity of engine oil **(see illustrations)** . Note that since the advent of modern low-viscosity multigrade engine oils there is no need to use a special carburettor oil in SU carburettors.

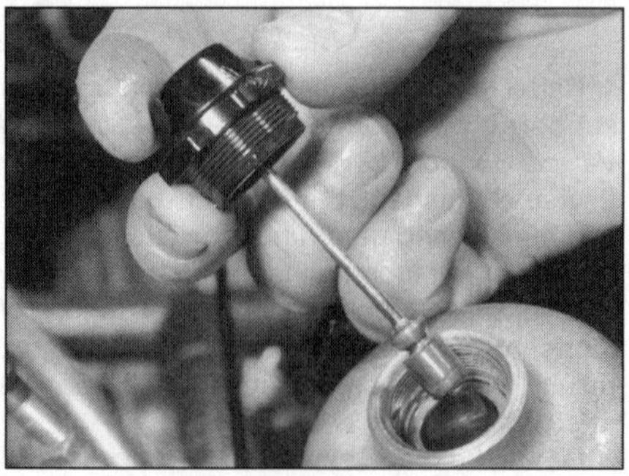

27.2a Unscrew piston damper from carburettor suction chamber . . .

27.2b . . . to top up carburettor damper chamber with engine oil - note identification tag (arrowed)

3 Raise and lower the carburettor piston, ensuring that it moves smoothly and without sticking, then refit and tighten (very carefully, but securely) the piston damper.
4 Refit the air cleaner assembly, ensuring that the vacuum pipes are correctly reconnected.

28 Idle speed and mixture check

Carburettor engines

1 Before beginning any form of carburettor adjustment, always check first the following:
a) Check that the ignition timing is accurate.
b) Check that the spark plugs are in good condition and correctly gapped.
c) Check that the throttle and choke cables are correctly adjusted.
d) Check that the carburettor idle bypass system is functioning correctly.
e) Check that the piston damper is topped-up.
f) Check that the crankcase breather hose(s), the float chamber vent hose and the full load air bleed hose are clear.
g) Check that the air cleaner filter element is clean and that the exhaust system is in good condition.
h) If the engine is running very roughly, check the compression pressures and bear in mind the possibility that one of the hydraulic tappets might be faulty, producing an incorrect valve clearance.

2 Take the car on a journey of sufficient length to warm it up to normal operating temperature. **Note:** *Adjustment should be completed within two minutes of return, without stopping the engine. If this cannot be achieved, or if the radiator electric cooling fan operates, wait for the cooling fan to stop and clear any excess fuel from the inlet manifold by racing the engine two or three times to between 2000 and 3000 rpm, then allow it to idle again.*
3 Ensure that all electrical loads are switched off. If the car is not equipped with a tachometer, connect one following its manufacturer's instructions. Note the idle speed, comparing it with that specified.

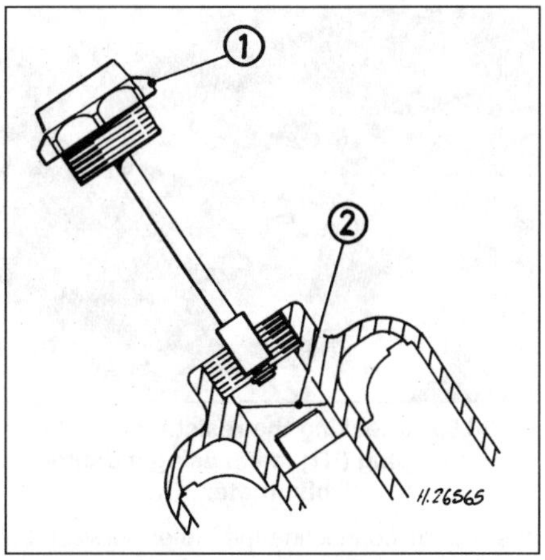

27.2c Topping up carburettor piston damper
1 Piston damper 2 Oil level

4 The idle speed adjusting knob is under the air cleaner assembly, on the rear right-hand corner of the carburettor. Screw it in or out as necessary to obtain the specified speed **(see illustration)**.
5 The idle mixture is set at the factory and should require no further adjustment. If, due to a change in engine characteristics (carbon build-up, bore wear etc.) or after a major carburettor overhaul, the mixture becomes incorrect, it can be reset. Note however, that an exhaust gas analyser (CO meter) will be required to check the mixture and to set it with the necessary standard of accuracy. If this is not available, the car must be taken to a Rover dealer for the work to be carried out.
6 If an exhaust gas analyser is available, follow its manufacturer's instructions to check the CO level. If adjustment is required, it is made by turning the idle air bypass screw, which is set in a deep recess on the carburettor left-hand side, beneath the breather hose **(see illustration)**. Using a Torx-type screwdriver, size TX10, turn the screw in very small increments until the level is correct; screwing it in (clockwise) richens the idle mixture and increases the CO level.
7 When adjustments are complete, disconnect any test equipment and refit any components removed for access.

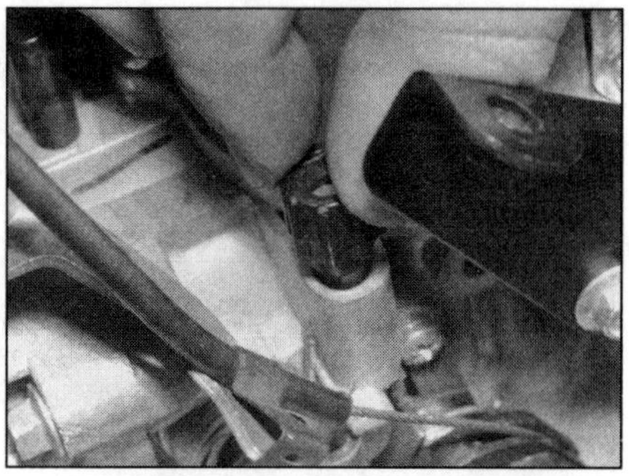

28.4 Turn idle speed adjusting knob to alter engine idle speed

Fuel-injected engines

8 While experienced home mechanics with a considerable amount of skill and equipment (including a good-quality tachometer and a good-quality, carefully-calibrated exhaust gas analyser) may be able to check the exhaust CO level and the idle speed, if these are found to be in need of adjustment the car must be taken to a suitably-equipped Rover dealer. Adjustments can be made only by re-programming the fuel-injection/ignition system ECU using Rover diagnostic equipment connected to the system by the diagnostic connector **(see illustration)**. For most owners the best solution will be to carry out those maintenance operations that they feel able to undertake, with the car then being taken to a Rover dealer for expert attention to the remaining items.

1

29 Lambda sensor check

This task (outlined in Chapter 4) can only be carried out using Rover diagnostic equipment. Do not neglect to have this check made at the specified intervals, especially as the vehicle mileage increases, as it is the only means of checking (in conjunction with a CO level check) whether the catalytic converter's closed-loop control system is working properly or not. Lambda sensors are delicate components working under arduous conditions and do not last for ever. If the sensor is no longer effective, it must be renewed **(see illustration)**.

28.6 Adjusting idle mixture - shown with air cleaner removed for clarity

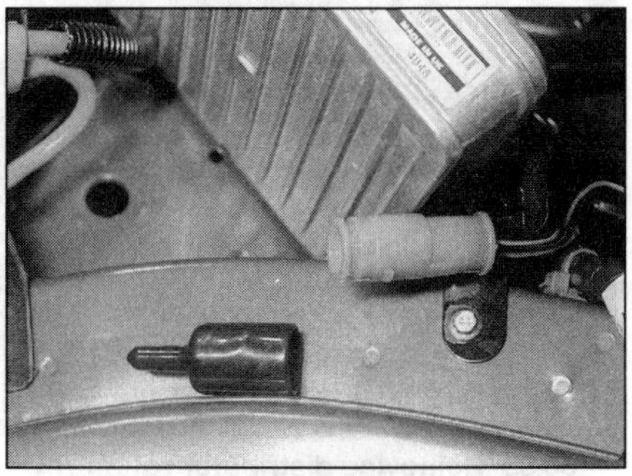

28.8 Fuel-injection/ignition system diagnostic connector (cover removed)

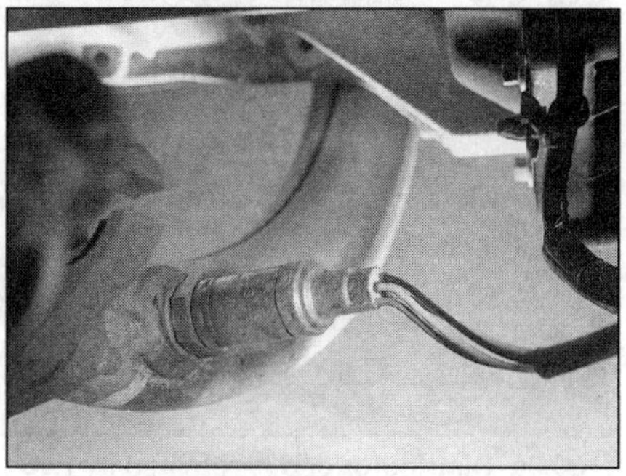

29.1 Lambda sensor location

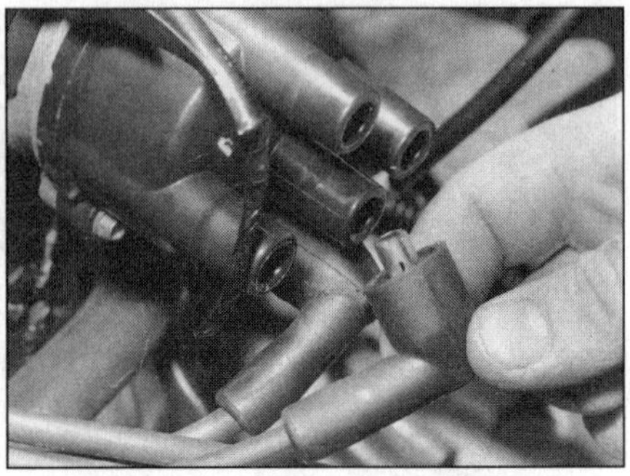

30.5a Disconnecting a spark plug (HT) lead from the distributor cap

30.5b Checking the resistance of the spark plug (HT) leads using a digital ohmmeter

30 Distributor cap and HT lead check

1 The spark plug (HT) leads should be checked whenever new plugs are fitted.
2 Ensure that the leads are numbered before removing them, to avoid confusion when refitting. Pull the leads from the plugs by gripping the end fitting, not the lead, otherwise the lead connection may be fractured.
3 Check inside the end fitting for signs of corrosion, which will look like a white crusty powder. Push the end fitting back onto the spark plug ensuring that it is a tight fit on the plug. If not, remove the lead again and use pliers to carefully crimp the metal connector inside the end fitting until it fits securely on the end of the spark plug.
4 Using a clean rag, wipe the entire length of the lead to remove any built-up dirt and grease. Once the lead is clean, check for burns, cracks and other damage. Do not bend the lead excessively or pull the lead lengthwise - the conductor inside might break.
5 Disconnect the other end of the lead from the distributor cap. Again, pull only on the end fitting. Check for corrosion and a tight fit in the same manner as the spark plug end. If an ohmmeter is available, check the resistance of the lead by connecting the meter between the spark plug end of the lead and the segment inside the distributor cap. Refit the lead securely on completion **(see illustrations)**.
6 Check the remaining leads one at a time, in the same way.
7 If new HT leads are required, purchase a set for your specific vehicle.
8 Remove the distributor cap, wipe it clean and carefully inspect it inside and out for signs of cracks, carbon tracks (tracking) and worn, burned or loose contacts. Check that the cap's carbon brush is unworn, free to move against spring pressure and making good contact with the rotor arm. Similarly inspect the rotor arm, noting that the arm has an in-built resistor. Renew these components if any defects are found. It is common practice to renew the cap and rotor arm whenever new HT leads are fitted. When fitting a new cap, remove the leads from the old cap one at a time and fit them to the new cap in the exact same location. Do not simultaneously remove all the leads from the old cap or firing order confusion may occur. Note that the cap screw locations are offset so that the cap may be refitted only one way. Tighten the screws to their specified torque wrench settings **(see illustrations)**.
9 Even with the ignition system in first class condition, some engines may still occasionally experience poor starting attributable to damp ignition components. To disperse moisture, a proprietary wet start spray can be very effective. A damp start spray should be used for providing a sealing coat to exclude moisture from the ignition system, and in extreme difficulty, a cold start spray will help to start a car when only a very poor spark occurs.

31 Alternator drivebelt check

Inspection

1 The alternator drivebelt is located in the front right-hand corner of the engine compartment, next to the engine oil filter. Due to the belt's function and construction it is subject to wear and will cause poor battery charging, or may even break, if not checked and adjusted at regular intervals.
2 Access to the drivebelt and related components is possible from under the vehicle, but is much improved if the front of the vehicle is raised and supported on axle stands (see "*Jacking and Vehicle Support*") so that the steering can be turned to full right lock and the right-hand underwing shield removed.
3 Check the drivebelt for cracks, splitting, fraying or damage, rotating the crankshaft so that the entire length of the belt is examined. Check also for signs of glazing (shiny patches) and for separation of the belt plies. Renew the belt if worn or damaged.

Adjustment

4 The drivebelt tension is checked by measuring the amount of deflection that takes place when a pressure of 10 kgf is applied (using a spring balance, or similar) midway between the pulleys on the belt's top run **(see illustration)**. If the deflection measured is any more or less than that specified, the drivebelt must be adjusted as follows.
5 Slacken the two pivot bolts securing the top of the alternator to its mounting bracket on the front of the engine, then slacken the

30.8a Distributor cap is retained by two (offset) screws

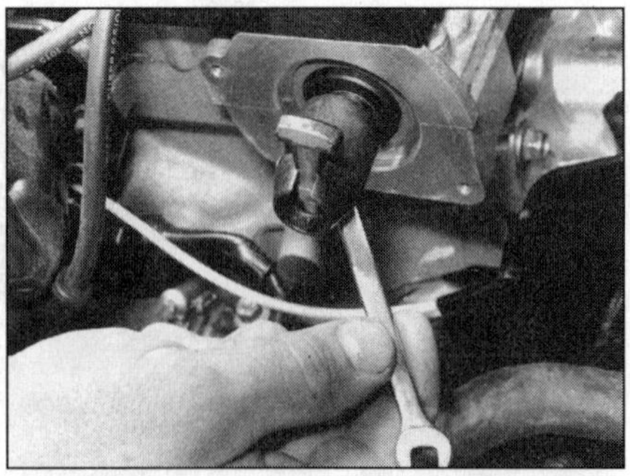

30.8b Removing distributor rotor arm screw - fuel-injected engines

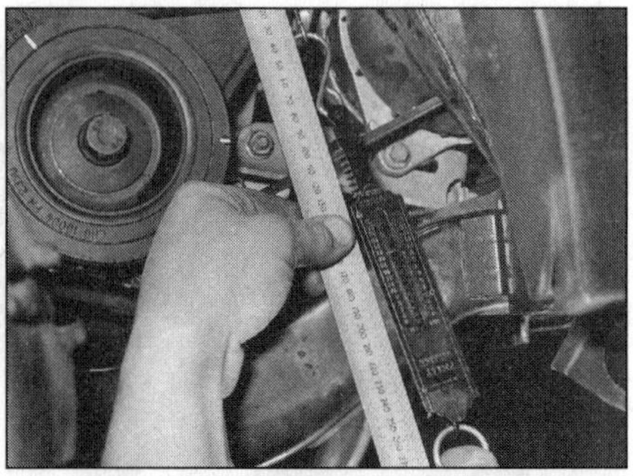

31.4 To check alternator drivebelt tension, measure amount of belt deflection when specified force is applied

adjuster clamp bolt and screw the adjuster bolt in or out as necessary to obtain the correct tension **(see illustration)**.

6 When the correct tension is achieved, tighten the clamp and pivot bolts to their specified torque wrench settings and rotate the crankshaft several times to settle the drivebelt. Recheck the setting, repeating the adjustment if necessary.

Renewal

7 To renew a belt, unscrew the adjuster bolt to fully slacken the drivebelt tension (see above), until the belt can be slipped off the pulleys and withdrawn.

8 Clean the belt pulleys carefully, removing all traces of oil or grease and checking that the grooves are clear, then fit the new belt to the pulleys and tighten the adjuster bolt until the tension is approximately correct, then check and adjust the tension as described above.

9 Refit any components removed and lower the vehicle to the ground.

HAYNES HiNT ***Always recheck the tension of a new drivebelt after the engine has been run for ten minutes.***

31.5 Alternator clamp bolt (A) and adjuster bolt (B)

24 000 Mile/40 000 km or 2 Years

32 Cooling system draining, flushing and refilling

Warning: Wait until the engine is cold before starting the following procedure. Do not allow antifreeze to come in contact with your skin or painted surfaces of the vehicle. Rinse off spills immediately with plenty of water. Never leave antifreeze lying around in an open container or in a puddle in the driveway or on the garage floor. Children and pets are attracted by its sweet smell. Antifreeze is fatal if ingested.

Draining

1 To drain the system, remove the expansion tank filler cap, then move the heater air temperature control to the maximum heat position.

2 Place a large drain tray under the front of the vehicle and disconnect the radiator bottom hose from the radiator. Direct as much of the escaping coolant as possible into the tray **(see illustration)**.

Flushing

3 With time, the cooling system may gradually lose its efficiency due to the radiator core having become choked with rust, scale deposits from the water and other sediment. To minimise this, as well as using only good quality antifreeze and clean soft water, the system should be flushed as follows whenever the coolant is renewed.

4 With the coolant drained, refit the bottom hose and refill the system with fresh water. Refit the expansion tank filler cap, start the engine and warm it up to normal operating temperature, then stop it and (after allowing it to cool down completely) drain the system again. Repeat as necessary until only clean water can be seen to emerge, then refill finally with the specified coolant mixture.

5 If the specified coolant mixture has been used and has been renewed at the specified intervals, the above procedure will be sufficient to keep clean the system for a considerable length of time. If, however, the system has been neglected, a more thorough operation will be required, as follows:

6 First drain the coolant, then disconnect the radiator top hose at the coolant outlet elbow. Insert a garden hose into the top hose and allow water to circulate through the radiator until it runs clean from the bottom outlet.

7 To flush the engine, insert the garden hose into the outlet elbow and allow water to circulate until it runs clear from the bottom hose union. If, after a reasonable period, the water still does not run clear, the radiator should be flushed with a good proprietary cleaning system.

8 In severe cases of contamination, reverse-flushing of the radiator may be necessary. To do this, remove the radiator, invert it and insert a garden hose into the bottom outlet. Continue flushing until clear water runs from the top hose outlet. A similar procedure can be used to flush the heater matrix.

9 The use of chemical cleaners should be necessary only as a last resort. The regular renewal of the coolant will prevent excessive contamination of the system.

Refilling

10 With the cooling system drained and flushed, refit the bottom hose and ensure that all other disturbed hose unions are correctly secured.

11 Prepare a sufficient quantity of the specified coolant mixture, allowing for a surplus so as to have a reserve supply for topping-up.

12 Unscrew the bleed plug from the heater feed hose and the bleed screw from the coolant rail underneath the distributor to allow the escape of air trapped during refilling, thus preventing the formation of air-locks **(see illustrations)**.

13 Fill the system slowly through the expansion tank. When coolant can be seen emerging from the bleed screw in a steady stream, tighten the screw. Continue filling until the same happens at the bleed plug. Tighten the plug securely and top the expansion tank up to the correct level, then refit the filler cap.

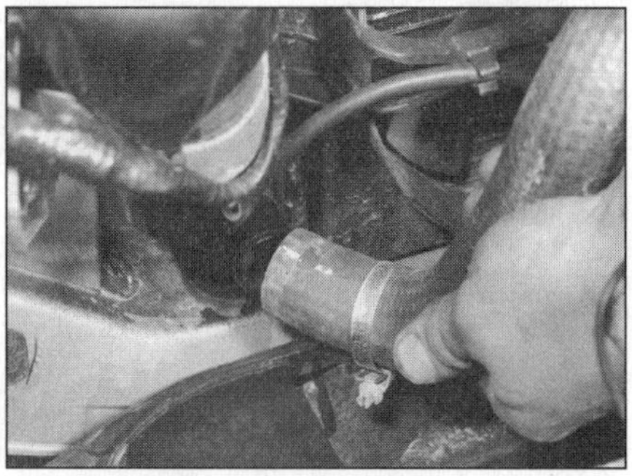

32.2 Cooling system must be drained by disconnecting radiator bottom hose

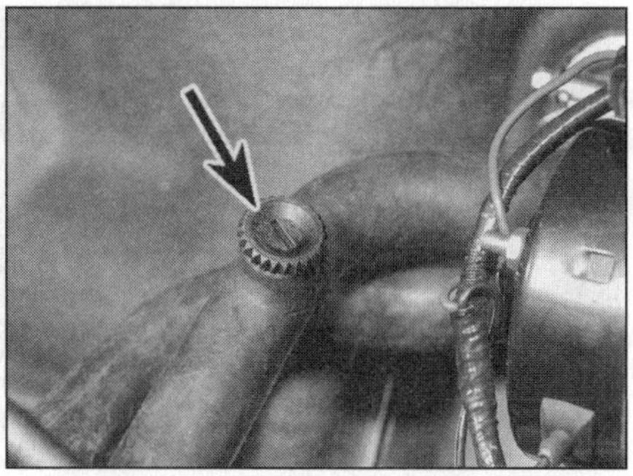

32.12a Cooling system has a bleed plug (arrowed) on heater feed hose . . .

32.12b . . . and a bleed screw (arrowed) on the coolant rail

1

14 Start the engine and run it at no more than idle speed until it has warmed up to normal operating temperature and the radiator electric cooling fan has cut in. Watch the temperature gauge to check for signs of overheating.

15 Stop the engine and allow it to cool down completely, then remove the expansion tank filler cap and top-up the tank to the correct level. Refit the filler cap and wash off all the spilt coolant from the engine compartment and bodywork.

16 After refilling, always check carefully all components of the system (but especially any unions disturbed during draining and flushing) for signs of coolant leaks. Fresh antifreeze has a searching action which will rapidly expose any weak points in the system. A label should be attached to the radiator or expansion tank stating the type and concentration of antifreeze used and the date installed. Any subsequent topping-up should be made with the same type and concentration of antifreeze.

Note: *If, after draining and refilling the system, symptoms of overheating are found which did not occur previously, then the fault is almost certainly due to trapped air at some point in the system causing an air-lock and restricting the flow of coolant. Usually the air is trapped because the system was refilled too quickly. In some cases air-locks can be released by tapping or squeezing the various hoses. If the problem persists, stop the engine and allow it to cool down completely before unscrewing the bleed plug or screw to bleed out the trapped air.*

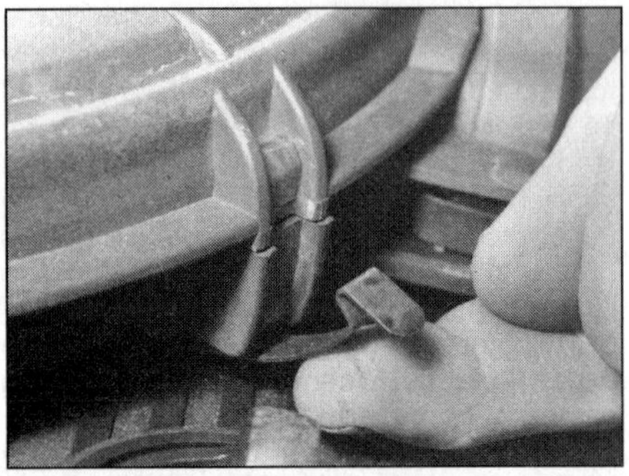

34.1a Release air cleaner assembly cover retaining clips . . .

Antifreeze mixture

17 Always use an ethylene glycol-based antifreeze which is suitable for use in mixed-metal cooling systems. The type of antifreeze and levels of protection afforded are indicated in the Specifications and in *Weekly Checks*. To give the recommended 50% concentration, 2.25 litres of antifreeze must be mixed with 2.25 litres of clean, soft water. This should provide enough to refill the complete system, but it is best to make up a larger amount so that a supply is available for subsequent topping-up.

Caution: Do not use engine antifreeze in the screen washer system, as it will damage the vehicle's paintwork.

33 Braking system hydraulic fluid renewal

1 The procedure is similar to that for the bleeding of the hydraulic system as described in Chapter 9, except that the brake fluid reservoir should be emptied by siphoning, using a clean poultry baster or similar before starting, and allowance should be made for the old fluid to be expelled when bleeding a section of the circuit.

2 Working as described in Chapter 9, open the first bleed nipple in the sequence and pump the brake pedal gently until nearly all the old fluid has been emptied from the master cylinder reservoir. Top-up to the MAX level with new fluid and continue pumping until only the new fluid remains in the reservoir and new fluid can be seen emerging from the bleed nipple. Tighten the nipple and top the reservoir level up to the MAX level line.

3 Old hydraulic fluid is invariably much darker in colour than the new, making it easy to distinguish the two.

4 Work through all the remaining nipples in the sequence until new fluid can be seen at all of them. Be careful to keep the master cylinder reservoir topped up to above the MIN level at all times or air may enter the system and greatly increase the length of the task.

5 When the operation is complete, check that all nipples are securely tightened and that their dust caps are refitted. Wash off all traces of spilt fluid and recheck the master cylinder reservoir fluid level.

6 Check the operation of the brakes before taking the car on the road.

34 Air cleaner filter element renewal

1 Release the clips securing the air cleaner assembly cover, then unscrew the retaining screws (except MPi) and carefully unclip the cover from the assembly **(see illustrations)**. If the assembly is dislodged, lift it carefully and check that none of the vacuum pipes, hoses or wiring (as applicable) connected to its underside have been damaged or disconnected.

2 Lift out the air cleaner filter element and discard it. Wipe clean the inside of the assembly and the cover, then check that there is no foreign matter visible either in the air cleaner inlet duct or in the inlet tract.

3 Place the new element in the air cleaner assembly, ensure that it is correctly seated and clip the cover back onto the assembly. Refit the retaining screws and the clips to secure the cover.

35 Fuel filter renewal

Warning: Always depressurise the fuel system of fuel-injected vehicles before commencing work.

1 Access may be much improved if the air cleaner assembly is removed. Place wads of rag around the fuel filter to catch any spilled fuel.

2 Depressurise the fuel system by slackening the pressure release bolt (fitted in the filter outlet pipe) with a spanner counter-holding the pipe boss **(see illustration)**. When the pressure is released, retighten the bolt to its specified torque wrench setting, again using a spanner to counter-hold the pipe boss, to prevent damage to the pipe or filter.

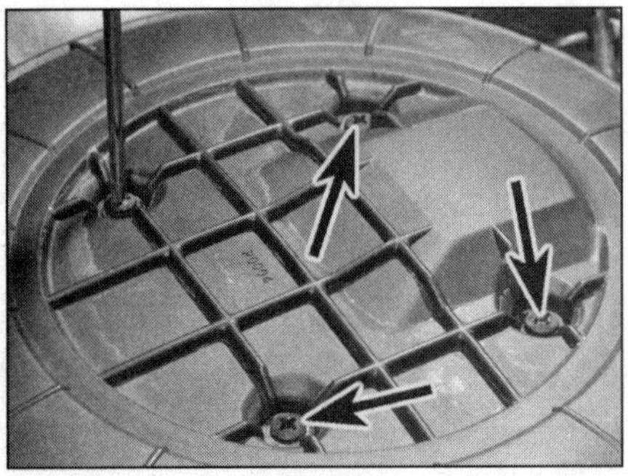

34.1b . . . and remove screws, then unclip cover . . .

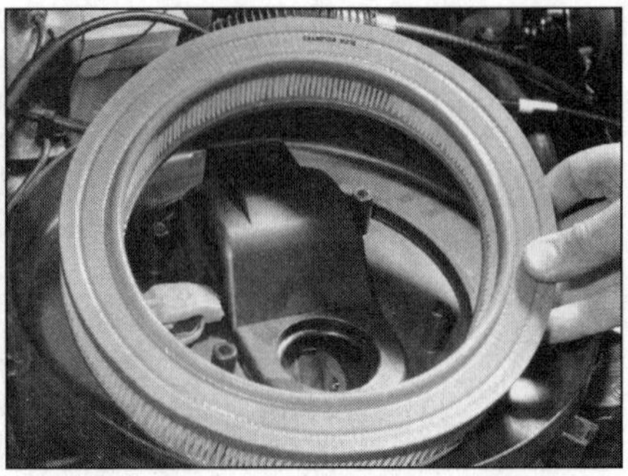

34.1c . . . to expose filter element (carburettor-type shown - Spi similar)

34.1d Mpi-type air filter element and cover

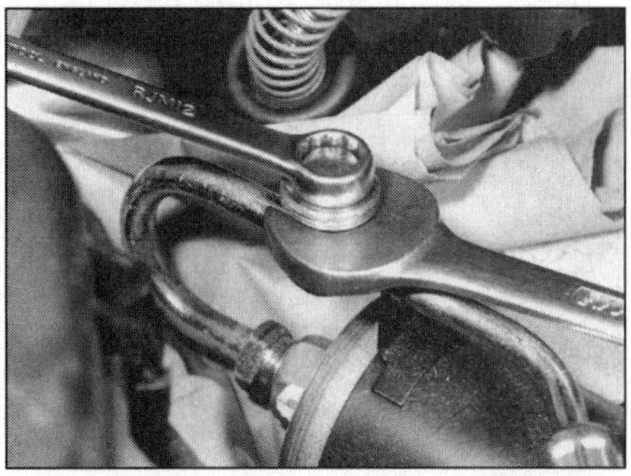

35.2 Slackening fuel pressure release bolt to depressurise fuel system (bolt location differs with model type)

3 Using two spanners to prevent damage to any of the fuel system pipes or components, disconnect the fuel filter inlet and outlet unions and remove the clamp screw to release the filter from its mounting **(see illustration)**.

4 Fit the new filter with the arrows indicating fuel flow pointing to the right of the vehicle **(see illustration)**. Tighten the clamp screw, connect the fuel pipes to the filter and tighten their unions securely, to the specified torque wrench settings if possible. Start the engine and check carefully for any signs of fuel leaks from any of the disturbed components.

5 Dispose safely of the old filter, it will be highly inflammable and may explode if thrown on a fire.

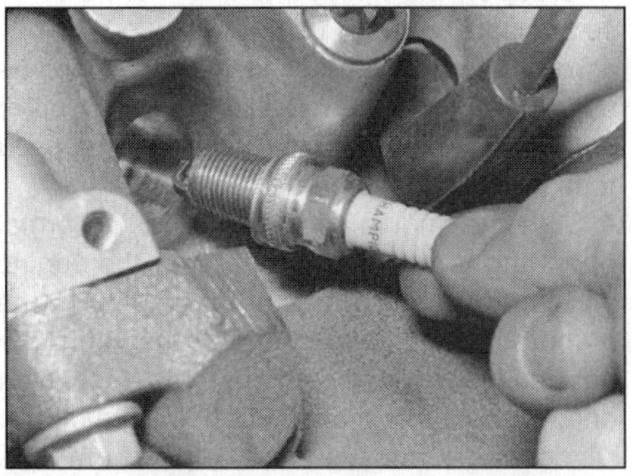

37.2a Spark plugs are easily accessible on K8 engines

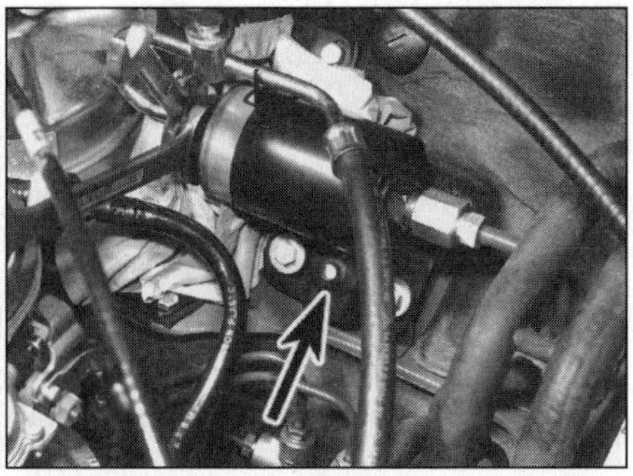

35.3 Use two spanners when slackening fuel filter unions - note filter clamp screw (arrowed)

36 Crankcase breather hose check

Check the security and condition of the crankcase breather hose(s) from the cylinder head cover. Ensure that all cable-ties or securing clips attached to the hose are in place and in good condition. Clips which are broken or missing can lead to chafing of the hose which could cause more serious problems in the future.

37 Spark plug renewal

1 The correct functioning of the spark plugs is vital for the correct running and efficiency of the engine. It is essential that the plugs fitted are of the type specified for the engine. If this type is used and the engine is in good condition, the spark plugs should not need attention between scheduled replacement intervals. Spark plug cleaning is rarely necessary and should not be attempted unless specialised equipment is available as damage can easily be caused to the firing ends.

2 To remove the plugs, first open the bonnet. On K8 engines the plugs are easily reached along the front of the engine **(see illustration)**. On K16 engines, disconnect the vacuum pipe

35.4 Fitting a new fuel filter - ensure arrow marks (arrowed) point to the right of the car

from the air temperature control valve, then undo the single screw securing the inlet duct to its support bracket and unfasten the rubber strap. Release the two clips securing the air inlet duct to the air cleaner assembly and place the duct to one side, taking care not to lose the hot air inlet connector hose. Undo the retaining screws and remove the spark plug cover **(see illustrations)**.

3 If the marks on the original-equipment HT leads cannot be seen, mark the leads one to four to correspond to the cylinder the lead serves (number one cylinder is at the timing belt end of the engine). Pull the leads from the plugs by gripping the end fitting, not the lead, otherwise the lead connection may be fractured.

> **HAYNES HiNT** ***Number each HT lead using sticky tape or paint before removal so as to avoid confusion when refitting.***

4 It is advisable to remove the dirt from the spark plug recesses using a clean brush, vacuum cleaner or compressed air before removing the plugs, to prevent dirt dropping into the cylinders.

5 Unscrew the plugs using a spark plug spanner, suitable box spanner or a deep socket and extension bar. Keep the socket aligned with the spark plug, otherwise if it is forcibly moved to one side, the ceramic insulator may be broken off. As each plug is removed, examine it as follows.

37.2b On K16 engines remove air cleaner intake duct and spark plug cover . . .

37.2c . . . unclip spark plug (HT) leads from clip plate - note identifying numbers . . .

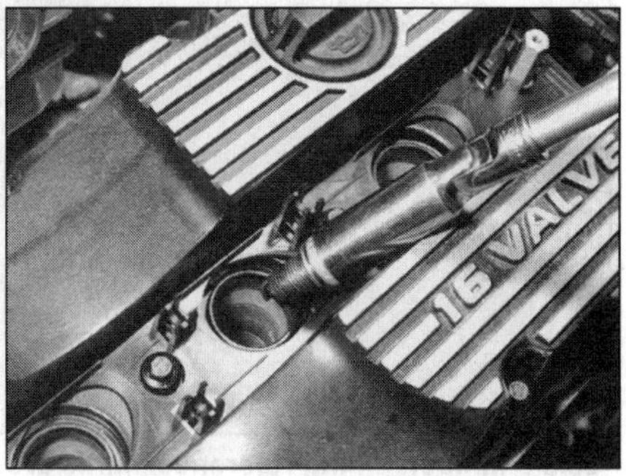

37.2d . . . and remove spark plugs

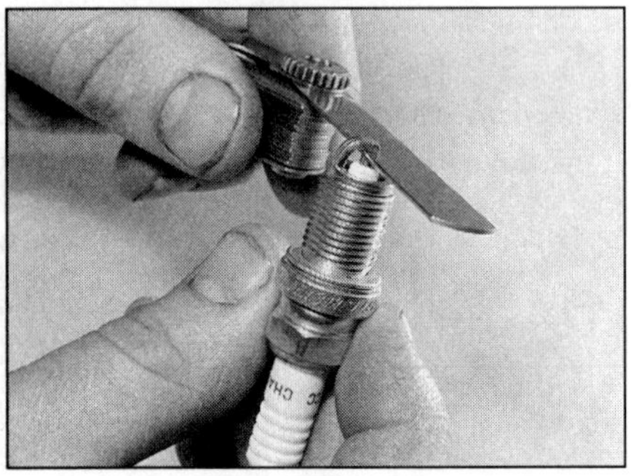

37.10a Measuring the spark plug electrode gap using a feeler blade

6 Examination of the spark plugs will give a good indication of the condition of the engine. If the insulator nose of the spark plug is clean and white, with no deposits, this is indicative of a weak mixture or too hot a plug (a hot plug transfers heat away from the electrode slowly, a cold plug transfers heat away quickly).

7 If the tip and insulator nose are covered with hard black-looking deposits, then this is indicative that the mixture is too rich. Should the plug be black and oily, then it is likely that the engine is fairly worn, as well as the mixture being too rich.

8 If the insulator nose is covered with light tan to greyish brown deposits, then the mixture is correct and it is likely that the engine is in good condition.

9 The spark plug electrode gap is of considerable importance as, if it is too large or too small, the size of the spark and its efficiency will be seriously impaired. The gap should be set to the specified value.

10 To set it, measure the gap with a feeler blade and then bend open, or closed, the outer plug electrode until the correct gap is achieved **(see illustrations)**. The centre electrode should never be bent, as this may crack the insulator and cause plug failure.

11 Special spark plug electrode gap adjusting tools are available from most motor accessory shops **(see illustration)**.

12 Before fitting the spark plugs, check that the threaded connector sleeves are tight and that the plug exterior surfaces and threads are clean.

37.10b Measuring the spark plug electrode gap using a wire gauge

13 Screw in the spark plugs by hand where possible, then tighten them to the specified torque. Take extra care to enter the plug threads correctly as the cylinder head is of aluminium alloy.

14 Reconnect the spark plug (HT) leads in their correct order and refit all components removed for access.

38 Ignition timing check

Warning: Voltages produced by an electronic ignition system are considerably higher than those produced by conventional ignition systems. Extreme care must be taken when working on the system with the ignition switched on. Persons with surgically-implanted cardiac pacemaker devices should keep well clear of the ignition circuits, components and test equipment.

Carburettor engines

1 Access to the alternator drive pulley and the ignition timing marks is only possible with the front of the vehicle raised and supported on axle stands so that the steering can be turned to full right lock (or the roadwheel removed) and the right-hand underwing shield can be removed.

37.11 Adjusting the spark plug electrode gap using a special tool

2 Before the ignition timing can be checked, the timing marks must be clarified. When looking at a brand-new pulley, the only obvious timing mark is the straight line (emphasised by the factory with white paint) cut radially in the pulley's outer (right-hand) face. This is, however, an engine assembly mark only which when aligned with the single, separate mark (at the 12 o'clock position) on the timing belt lower cover sets the crankshaft to 90° BTDC. The ignition timing mark is a tiny notch cut in the rim of the pulley's inner (left-hand) rim at approximately 100° anticlockwise from the engine assembly mark; it is virtually invisible and care is required to identify it.

3 Rotate the pulley so that the engine assembly mark points vertically downwards, whereupon the ignition timing mark can be seen clearly enough to scribe a line squarely across the pulley rims. A hacksaw can then be used to enlarge the mark in the pulley outer (right-hand) rim and white paint can be used to highlight it **(see illustrations)**.

4 Start the engine and warm it up to normal operating temperature, then stop the engine and connect a timing light, according to the manufacturer's instructions. If the vehicle is not equipped with a tachometer then connect one, following its manufacturer's instructions. Disconnect the vacuum pipe from the distributor and plug it temporarily.

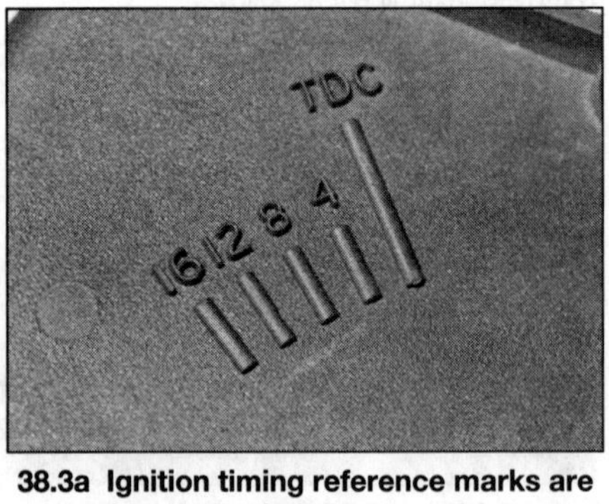

38.3a Ignition timing reference marks are on timing belt lower cover

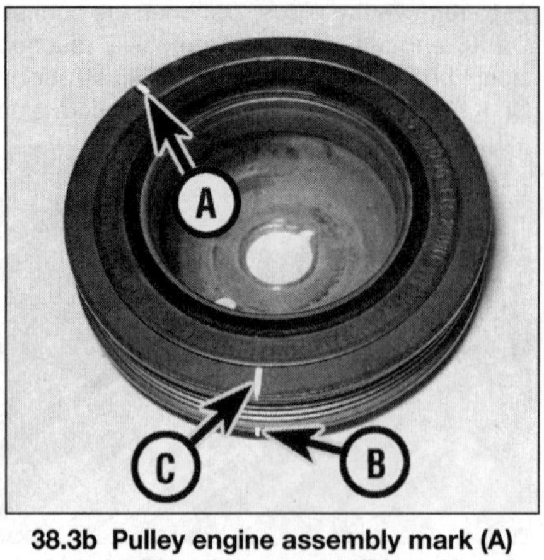

38.3b Pulley engine assembly mark (A) factory ignition timing mark (B) and home-made ignition timing mark (C)

38.3c Ignition timing marks on pulley (arrowed) must be clarified as described before timing can be checked

5 Start the engine and have an assistant increase engine speed to the specified amount, then aim the timing light at the timing marks. The highlighted mark should stand out clearly. Check that the pulley mark aligns with the correct cover reference mark, or within the specified tolerance. The carburettor number (where necessary) is given on the metal identification tag attached to one of the suction chamber screws.

6 If adjustment is required, slacken the distributor mounting bolts until the distributor body is just able to rotate, then turn the body clockwise (viewed from the vehicle's left-hand side) to advance the ignition timing, or anticlockwise to retard it. Tighten the bolts to their specified torque wrench setting when the correct position is found, then recheck the ignition timing to ensure that it has not altered.

7 Increase engine speed and check that the pulley mark advances to beyond the beginning of the cover reference marks, returning to close to the TDC mark when the engine is allowed to idle. This shows that the centrifugal advance mechanism is functioning, but a detailed check must be left to a Rover dealer who has the necessary equipment.

8 Unplug and reconnect the vacuum pipe. The ignition timing should advance as the pipe is reconnected, retarding again when it is disconnected. If the ignition timing does not alter, check that the pipe is clear of blockages or kinks and that it is not leaking. Suck on the carburettor end of the pipe. If there is no effect on the ignition timing, then the vacuum capsule is faulty and must be renewed unless the vehicle is fitted with a catalytic converter, in which case the thermostatically-operated vacuum switch may be at fault. This can be eliminated by connecting a vacuum pipe directly from the carburettor to the distributor. If the vacuum advance is then restored to normal, the switch is faulty and must be renewed. Again, more detailed tests must be left to a Rover dealer.

9 When the ignition timing is correct, stop the engine and disconnect the timing light and tachometer, then reconnect the vacuum pipe. Refit the underwing shield and the roadwheel.

Fuel-injected engines

10 While home mechanics with a timing light and a good-quality tachometer may be able to check the ignition timing (the procedure being as described in paragraphs 1 to 5 above, except that the check should be made at idle speed and there is no vacuum pipe to disconnect), if it is found to be in need of adjustment the car must be taken to a suitably-equipped Rover dealer. Adjustments can be made only by re-programming the fuel-injection/ignition system ECU using Rover diagnostic equipment connected to the system by the diagnostic connector. Note also that the timing and idle speed are under ECU control and may, therefore, vary significantly from the specified nominal values. Without full equipment, any check is therefore nothing more than a rough guide.

48 000 Mile/80 000 km or 4 Years

39 Timing belt check

1 Working as described in Chapter 2, remove the timing belt upper right-hand (outer) cover.

2 Apply the handbrake and ensure that the transmission is in neutral, then jack up the front right-hand side of the vehicle and support it on an axle stand.

3 Remove the roadwheel and the underwing shield to expose the alternator drive pulley, so that the crankshaft can be rotated using a spanner applied to the alternator drive pulley bolt.

4 Rotating the crankshaft so that the full length of the timing belt is checked, examine the belt carefully for any signs of uneven wear, splitting or oil contamination and renew it if there is the slightest doubt about its condition.

5 Note that Rover state that there is no need to adjust the belt tension once it has been installed. If, however, the belt is thought to be incorrectly tensioned, especially if it has been disturbed for other servicing/repair work, the tensioner can be reset following the procedure outlined in Chapter 2.

6 Refit all removed components and lower the vehicle to the ground once the check is complete.

1

60 000 Mile/100 000 km or 5 Years

40 Master cylinder, front brake caliper and rear brake wheel cylinder overhaul

Refer to the appropriate Sections of Chapter 9.

96 000 Mile/160 000 km or 8 Years

41 Timing belt renewal

The timing belt must be renewed as a matter of course at the specified interval, following the procedure given in Chapter 2. If the belt is not renewed as directed, it may break while the engine is running, which will result in serious and expensive engine damage.

Chapter 2 Part A:
Engine in-car repair procedures

Contents

Degrees of difficulty

Easy, suitable for novice with little experience	**Fairly easy,** suitable for beginner with some experience	**Fairly difficult,** suitable for competent DIY mechanic	**Difficult,** suitable for experienced DIY mechanic	**Very difficult,** suitable for expert DIY or professional

Specifications

General

Type	Four-cylinder in-line, four-stroke, liquid-cooled
Designation:	
1.1 and 1.4 8-valve SOHC	K8
1.4 16-valve DOHC	K16
Bore	75.00 mm
Stroke:	
1.1 - K8	63.25 mm
1.4 - K8, K16	79.00 mm
Capacity:	
1.1 - K8	1118 cc
1.4 - K8, K16	1397 cc
Firing order	1-3-4-2 (No 1 cylinder at timing belt end)
Direction of crankshaft rotation	Clockwise (seen from right-hand side of car)
Compression ratio:	
K8	9.75 : 1
K16	9.50 : 1
Minimum compression pressure	10.3 bar
Maximum compression pressure difference between cylinders	1.4 bar
Maximum power (EEC):	
1.1 - K8	60 ps (44 kW) @ 6000 rpm
1.1 - K8 (with catalytic converter)	60 ps (44 kW) @ 5900 rpm
1.4 - K8	76 ps (56 kW) @ 5700 rpm
1.4 - K8 (with catalytic converter)	75 ps (55 kW) @ 5500 rpm
1.4 - K16	95 ps (70 kW) @ 6250 rpm
1.4 - K16 (with catalytic converter)	90 ps (55 kW) @ 6250 rpm
Maximum torque (EEC):	
1.1 - K8	90 Nm (66 lbf ft) @ 3500 rpm
1.4 - K8	117 Nm (86 lbf ft) @ 3500 rpm
1.4 - K16	124 Nm (91 lbf ft) @ 4000 rpm
1.4 - K16 (with catalytic converter)	120 Nm (89 lbf ft) @ 4000 rpm

Cylinder block/crankcase

Note: *Service liners are Grade B*

Material	Aluminium alloy
Cylinder liner bore diameter:	
Wet liner:	
Grade A (Red)	74.975 to 74.985 mm
Grade B (Blue)	74.986 to 74.995 mm
Service limit	75.045 mm
Damp liner:	
Grade A (Red)	74.970 to 74.985 mm
Grade B (Blue)	74.986 to 75.000 mm

Crankshaft

Number of main bearings	5
Main bearing journal diameter	47.979 to 48.000 mm
Main bearing journal size grades:	
Grade 1	47.993 to 48.000 mm
Grade 2	47.986 to 47.993 mm
Grade 3	47.979 to 47.986 mm
Crankpin journal diameter	43.007 to 42.986 mm
Crankpin journal size grades:	
Grade A	43.000 to 43.007 mm
Grade B	42.993 to 43.000 mm
Grade C	42.986 to 42.993 mm
Main bearing and crankpin journal maximum ovality	0.010 mm
Main bearing and big-end bearing running clearance	0.02 to 0.05 mm
Crankshaft endfloat:	
Standard	0.10 to 0.30 mm
Service limit	0.40 mm
Thrustwasher thickness	2.61 to 2.65 mm

Pistons and piston rings - wet liner engines

Note: *Service pistons are Grade B*

Piston diameter - K8:	
Grade A	74.940 to 74.955 mm
Grade B	74.956 to 74.970 mm
Piston diameter - K16 SPI:	
Grade A	74.945 to 74.960 mm
Grade B	74.960 to 74.975 mm
Piston diameter - K16 MPI:	
Grade A	74.940 to 74.955 mm
Grade B	74.956 to 74.970 mm
Piston-to-bore clearance:	
K8 and K16 MPI	0.015 to 0.045 mm
K16 SPI	0.010 to 0.040 mm
Piston ring end gaps (fitted 20 mm from top of bore):	
Top compression ring:	
K8	0.25 to 0.45 mm
K16 SPI	0.30 to 0.50 mm
K16 MPI	0.25 to 0.35 mm
Second compression ring:	
K8	0.25 to 0.50 mm
K16 SPI and MPI	0.30 to 0.50 mm
Oil control ring:	
K8 and K16 MPI	0.25 to 1.00 mm
K16 SPI	0.25 to 0.50 mm
Piston new ring-to-groove clearance:	
Top compression ring:	
K8	0.04 to 0.09 mm
K16 SPI	0.04 to 0.075 mm
K16 MPI	0.04 to 0.085 mm
Second compression ring:	
K8 and K16 MPI	0.04 to 0.08 mm
K16 SPI	0.03 to 0.065 mm
Oil control ring:	
K8 and K16 MPI	0.02 to 0.06 mm
K16 SPI	0.02 to 0.055 mm

Pistons and piston rings - damp liner engines

Piston diameter:	
Grade A	74.940 to 74.955 mm
Grade B	74.956 to 74.970 mm
Piston-to-bore clearance	0.015 to 0.045 mm
Piston ring end gaps (fitted 20 mm from top of bore):	
Top compression ring	0.17 to 0.37 mm
Second compression ring	0.37 to 0.57 mm
Oil control ring	0.15 to 0.40 mm
Piston new ring-to-groove clearance:	
Top compression ring	0.04 to 0.08 mm
Second compression ring	0.03 to 0.062 mm
Oil control ring	0.044 to 0.055 mm

Gudgeon pins

Diameter	18 mm
Fit in connecting rod	Interference

Connecting rods

Length between centres	131.5 mm

Cylinder head

Material	Aluminium alloy
Height	118.95 to 119.05 mm
Reface limit	0.20 mm
Maximum acceptable gasket face distortion	0.05 mm
Valve seat angle	45°
Valve seat width	1.5 mm
Seat cutter correction angle:	
Upper	30°
Lower	60°

Camshaft(s)

Drive	Toothed belt
Number of bearings	6
Bearing journal running clearance:	
Standard	0.060 to 0.094 mm
Service limit	0.150 mm
Camshaft endfloat:	
Standard	0.060 to 0.190 mm
Service limit	0.300 mm
Valve lift:	
1.1 K8	7.9 mm
1.4 K8	9.0 mm
1.4 K16	8.2 mm

Hydraulic tappets

Outside diameter	32.959 to 32.975 mm

Valves

Seat angle	45°
Head diameter:	
Inlet - K8	34 mm
Inlet - K16	28 mm
Exhaust - K8	31 mm
Exhaust - K16	24 mm
Stem diameter:	
Inlet - K8	6.960 to 6.975 mm
Inlet - K16	5.952 to 5.967 mm
Exhaust - K8	6.952 to 6.967 mm
Exhaust - K16	5.947 to 5.962 mm
Guide inside diameter:	
K8	7.000 to 7.025 mm
K16	6.000 to 6.025 mm
Stem-to-guide clearance:	
Inlet - K8	0.025 to 0.065 mm
Inlet - K16	0.033 to 0.063 mm
Inlet - service limit	0.07 mm
Exhaust - K8	0.033 to 0.073 mm
Exhaust - K16	0.038 to 0.078 mm
Exhaust - service limit	0.11 mm

Valves (continued)

Valve timing - 1.1 K8:	
Inlet opens	3° BTDC
Inlet closes	37° ABDC
Exhaust opens	35° BBDC
Exhaust closes	5° ATDC
Valve timing - 1.4 K8:	
Inlet opens	13° BTDC
Inlet closes	47° ABDC
Exhaust opens	53° BBDC
Exhaust closes	7° ATDC
Valve timing - 1.4 K16:	
Inlet opens	15° BTDC
Inlet closes	45° ABDC
Exhaust opens	55° BBDC
Exhaust closes	5° ATDC
Valve spring free length:	
K8	46.2 mm
K16	50.0 mm
Valve guide fitted height:	
K8	10.3 mm
K16	6.0 mm
Valve stem fitted height:	
K8	38.95 to 40.81 mm
Service limit	41.06 mm
K16	38.93 to 39.84 mm
Service limit	40.10 mm

Lubrication system

System pressure at idle speed	1.0 bar
Oil pump type	Trochoidal, eccentric-rotor
Oil pump clearances:	
Rotor endfloat	0.02 to 0.06 mm
Outer rotor-to-body clearance	0.28 to 0.36 mm
Rotor lobe clearance	0.05 to 0.13 mm
Pressure relief valve operating pressure	4.1 bar
Oil pressure warning lamp lights at	Below 0.3 to 0.5 bar

Torque wrench settings

	Nm	lbf ft
Spark plugs	25	18
Spark plug (HT) lead clip screws - K8	9	7
Spark plug cover screws - K16	10	8
Air cleaner support bracket bolts	10	8
Air intake duct support bracket-to-cylinder head screws - K16	4	3
Camshaft cover bolts	10	8
Camshaft bearing cap to cylinder head bolts	10	8
Camshaft carrier to cylinder head bolts	10	8
Blanking plate to camshaft carrier bolts	10	8
Camshaft cover to carrier bolts - K16	25	18
Cylinder head bolts:		
1st stage	20	15
2nd stage	Tighten through 180°	
3rd stage	Tighten through a further 180°	
Timing belt cover screws:		
Upper front	5	4
Lower	10	8
Rear	5	4
Timing belt tensioner pulley bolt	45	33
Timing belt tensioner pulley backplate screw	10	8
Camshaft toothed pulley bolt	35	26
Alternator drive pulley bolt	160	118
Fuel pump blanking plate nuts - K8	25	18
Oil pump-to-cylinder block/crankcase bolt and screws	9	7
Alternator mounting bracket-to-cylinder block/crankcase bolts	45	33
Dipstick tube-to-cylinder block/crankcase bolts	9	7
Flywheel bolts	85	63
Transmission-to-engine bolts	85	63
Crankshaft pulley bolt	205	152

Torque wrench settings (continued)

Torque wrench settings (continued)	Nm	lbf ft
Flywheel cover plate screws	9	7
Flywheel rear cover plate bolt and nut	38	28
Big-end bearing cap bolts:		
1st stage	20	15
2nd stage	Tighten through 45°	
Main bearing ladder-to-cylinder block/crankcase bolts	15	11
Oil rail-to-main bearing ladder bolts	5	4
Oil pump pick-up/strainer pipe screws	10	8
Sump bolts:		
Pressed steel sump - M6 bolts	10	8
Pressed steel sump - M8 bolts	25	18
Alloy sump	25	18
Engine oil drain plug	42	31
Engine/transmission right-hand mounting:		
Bracket-to-cylinder block/crankcase bolts	45	33
Mounting-to-bracket nuts	100	74
Mounting-to-body through-bolt and nut	85	63
Engine/transmission left-hand mounting:		
Support member-to-subframe bolts	45	33
Mounting-to-support member bolts	45	33
Mounting-to-bracket bolts	45	33
Bracket-to-transmission bolts	80	59
Engine/transmission rear mounting:		
Mounting bracket-to-transmission 12 mm bolt(s)	85	63
Mounting bracket-to-transmission 10 mm bolt(s)	45	33
Mounting bracket-to-tie-rod through-bolt	85	63
Tie-rod-to-body bolt and nut	45	33

1 General information and precautions

This Part of the Chapter describes those repair procedures that can reasonably be carried out on the engine whilst it remains in the vehicle. If the engine has been removed from the vehicle and is being dismantled as described in Part B of this Chapter, any preliminary dismantling procedures can be ignored.

Note that whilst it may be possible physically to overhaul items such as the piston/connecting rod assemblies with the engine in the vehicle, such tasks are not usually carried out as separate operations and usually require the execution of several additional procedures (not to mention the cleaning of components and of oilways). For this reason all such tasks are classed as major overhaul procedures and are described in Part B of this Chapter.

Engine description

The engine is of four-cylinder, in-line type, mounted transversely at the front of the vehicle with the clutch and transmission on its left-hand end. Variations in capacity are achieved by altering the stroke dimensions.

Apart from the sump, the timing belt covers and the cylinder head cover, the engine is constructed from three major castings - the cylinder head, the cylinder block/crankcase and the crankshaft main bearing ladder. There is also an oil rail underneath the main bearing ladder and either camshaft carrier/bearing caps or a camshaft carrier (depending on engine type). All these castings are of aluminium alloy, the three major ones being clamped together by ten long through-bolts which perform the dual role of cylinder head bolts and crankshaft main bearing fasteners. Since these bolts pass through the cylinder block/crankcase and the main bearing ladder, the oil rail is secured also to the main bearing ladder (by two nuts) and the main bearing ladder is secured also to the cylinder block/crankcase (by ten smaller bolts) so that the cylinder head can be removed without disturbing the rest of the engine. The passages provided for the bolts in the major castings are used as breather passages or as returns for the oil to the sump.

The crankshaft runs in five main bearings. Thrustwashers are fitted to the centre main bearing (upper half) to control crankshaft endfloat.

The connecting rods rotate on horizontally-split bearing shells at their big-ends. The pistons are attached to the connecting rods by gudgeon pins which are an interference fit in the connecting rod small-end eyes. The aluminium alloy pistons are fitted with three piston rings, comprising two compression rings and an oil control ring.

The cylinder bores are formed by replaceable wet or damp liners (depending on engine type). These are located from their top ends. On wet liners, two sealing O-rings are fitted at the base of each liner to prevent the escape of coolant into the sump. On damp liners, the seal is provided by a continuous bead of sealant.

The inlet and exhaust valves are each closed by coil springs and operate in guides pressed into the cylinder head. The valve seat inserts are pressed into the cylinder head and can be renewed separately if worn.

On the K8 engine, the camshaft is driven by a toothed timing belt and operates the eight valves via self-adjusting hydraulic tappets, thus eliminating the need for routine checking and adjustment of the valve clearances. The camshaft rotates in six bearings that are line-bored direct in the cylinder head and in the bearing caps or camshaft carrier (depending on engine type). This means that the bearing caps are not available separately from the cylinder head and must not be interchanged with others from another engine. Apart from the fact that it has two camshafts, one inlet and one exhaust, each controlling eight valves and both retained by a single camshaft carrier, the same applies to the K16 engine.

On the K8 engine, the distributor and (on carburettor engines only) the mechanical fuel pump are driven from the camshaft left-hand end. On the K16 engine the distributor is driven from the inlet camshaft left-hand end.

On both engine types, the water pump is driven by the timing belt.

Lubrication is by means of an eccentric-rotor trochoidal pump mounted on the crankshaft right-hand end. It draws oil through a strainer located in the sump and then forces it through an externally-mounted full-flow cartridge-type filter into galleries in the oil rail and cylinder block/crankcase, from where it is distributed to the crankshaft (main bearings) and camshaft(s). The big-end bearings are supplied with oil via internal drillings in the crankshaft, while the camshaft bearings and the hydraulic tappets receive a pressurised supply. The camshaft lobes and valves are lubricated by splash, as are all other engine components.

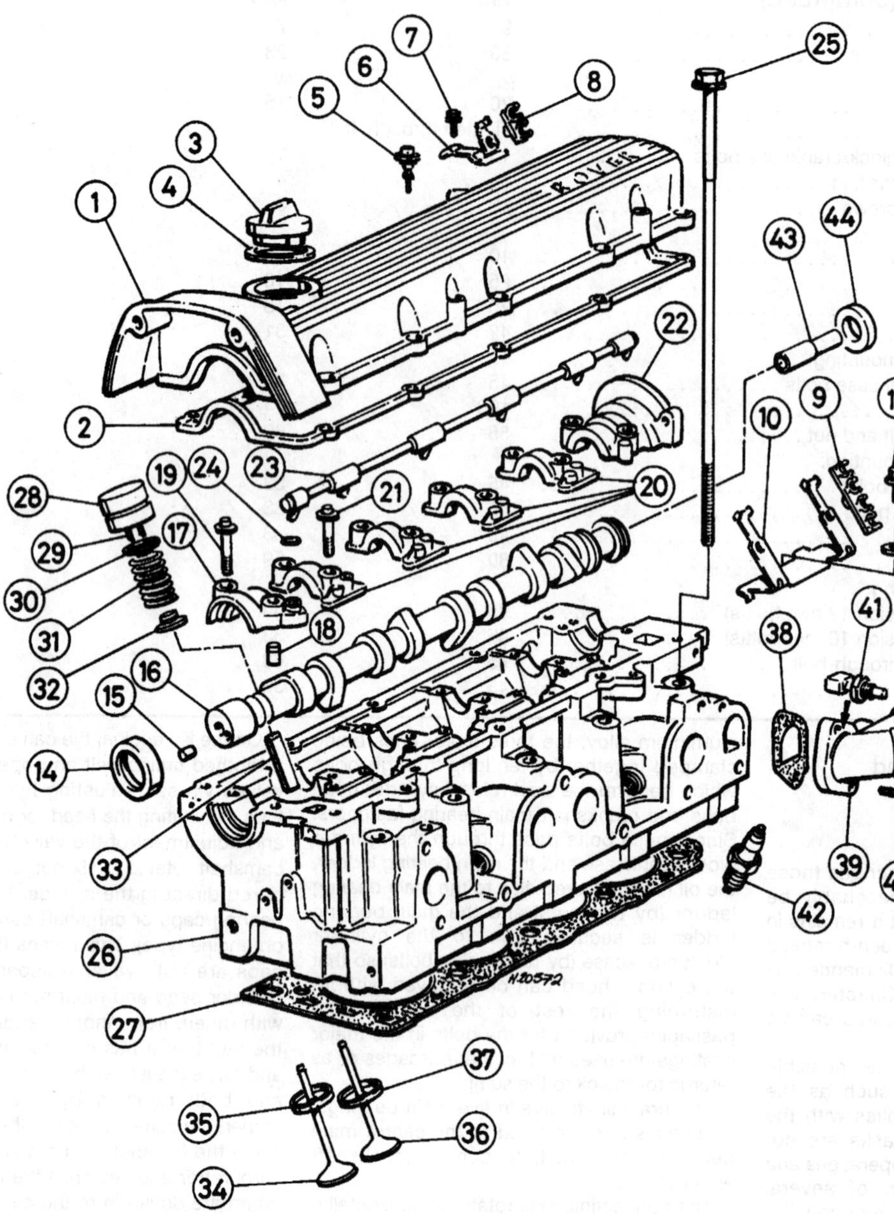

1.0a Top end components - K8 engine (wet liner type)

1 Cylinder head cover
2 Seal
3 Engine oil filler cap
4 Seal
5 Bolt
6 Spark plug (HT) lead clip
7 Screw
8 Plastic insert
9 Plastic insert
10 Spark plug (HT) lead clip
11 Air intake duct support bracket
12 Fastener insert
13 Screw
14 Oil seal
15 Roll pin
16 Camshaft
17 Camshaft right-hand bearing cap*
18 Dowel
19 Bolt
20 Camshaft intermediate bearing cap*
21 Bolt
22 Camshaft left-hand bearing cap*
23 Oil feed tube
24 O-ring
25 Cylinder head bolt
26 Cylinder head
27 Cylinder head gasket
28 Hydraulic tappet
29 Split collets
30 Spring retainer
31 Valve spring
32 Valve stem seal/spring bottom seat
33 Valve guide
34 Inlet valve
35 Valve seat insert
36 Exhaust valve
37 Valve seat insert
38 Gasket
39 Coolant outlet elbow
40 Screw
41 Coolant temperature gauge sender unit
42 Spark plug
43 Rotor arm drive spindle - fuel-injected engines
44 Oil seal - fuel-injected engines

***Note:** Camshaft bearing caps shown for reference only - not available separately from cylinder head*

1.0b Top end components - K8 engine (damp liner type)

1 *Engine oil filler cap*
2 *Filler cap seal*
3 *HT lead clip mounting bracket*
4 *Spark plug (HT) lead clip*
5 *Bolt*
6 *Camshaft cover*
7 *Gasket*
8 *Camshaft cover bolt*
9 *Cylinder head bolt*
10 *HT lead clip mounting bracket*
11 *Spark plug (HT) lead clip*
12 *Bolt*
13 *Mounting bracket (duct)*
14 *Camshaft carrier*
15 *Camshaft carrier bolt - long*
16 *Camshaft carrier bolt - short*
17 *Camshaft carrier dowel*
18 *Camshaft*
19 *Camshaft gear roll pin*
20 *Camshaft front oil seal*
21 *Hydraulic tappet*
22 *Split collets*
23 *Spring retainer*
24 *Valve spring*
25 *Valve stem seal/spring bottom seat*
26 *Valve guide*
27 *Exhaust valve*
28 *Exhaust valve seat insert*
29 *Inlet valve*
30 *Inlet valve seat insert*
31 *Cylinder head*
32 *Coolant temperature sensor*
33 *Coolant outlet elbow*
34 *Bolt*
35 *Gasket*
36 *Spark plug*
37 *Cylinder head gasket*
38 *Fuel pump blanking plate (if fitted)*
39 *Gasket*
40 *Blanking plate nuts*

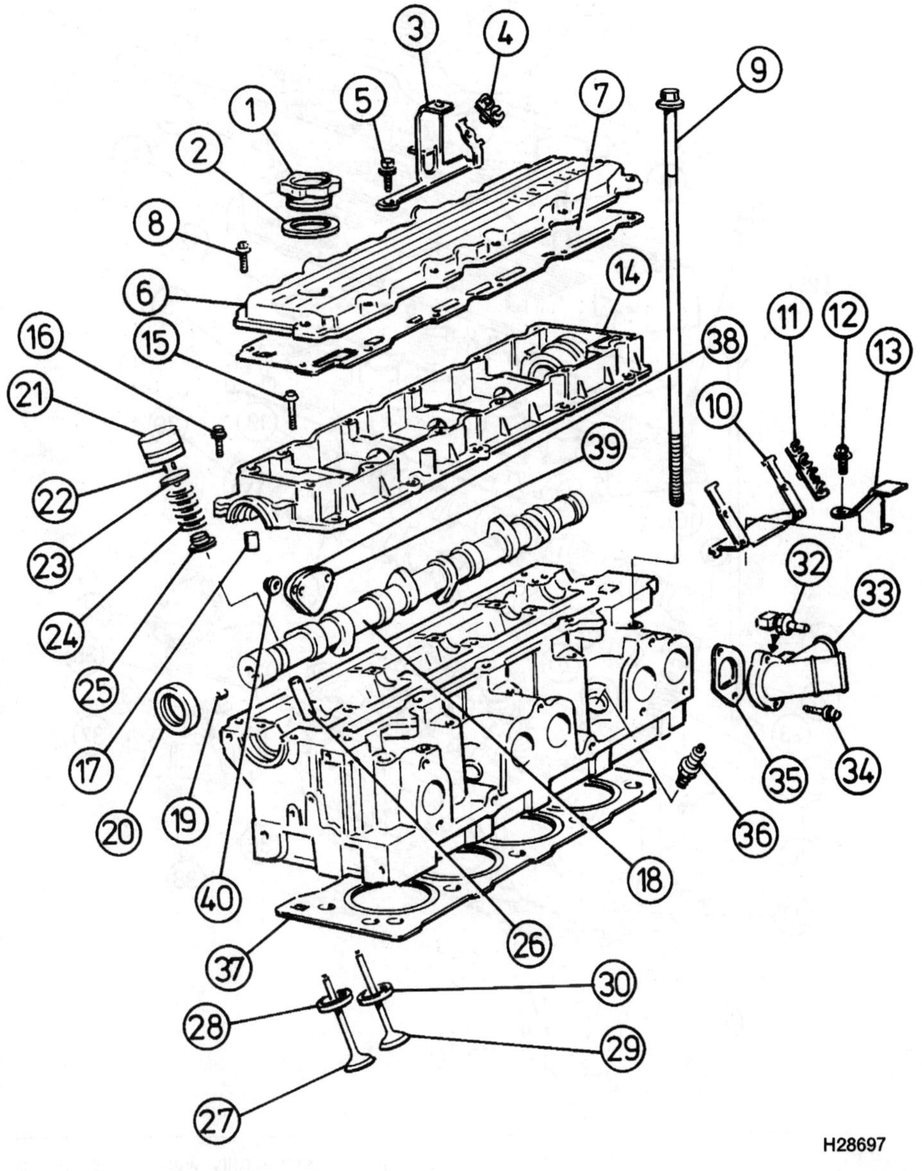

Precautions

Note that a side-effect of the above described engine design is that the crankshaft cannot be rotated once the cylinder head and block through-bolts have been slackened. During any servicing or overhaul work the crankshaft always must be rotated to the desired position before the bolts are disturbed.

Repair operations possible with the engine in the car

The following work can be carried out with the engine in the car **(see illustrations)**:

a) Compression pressure - testing.
b) Cylinder head cover - removal and refitting.
c) Alternator drive pulley - removal and refitting.
d) Timing belt covers - removal and refitting.
e) Timing belt - removal, refitting and adjustment.
f) Timing belt tensioner and toothed pulleys - removal and refitting.
g) Camshaft oil seal(s) - renewal.
h) Camshaft(s) and hydraulic tappets - removal, inspection and refitting.
i) Cylinder head - removal and refitting.
j) Cylinder head and pistons - decarbonising.
k) Sump - removal and refitting.
l) Oil pump - removal, overhaul and refitting.
m Crankshaft oil seals - renewal.
n) Engine/transmission mountings - inspection and renewal.
o) Flywheel - removal, inspection and refitting.

2 Engine oil and filter - renewal

Details of checking the oil level and renewing both the oil and filter are contained in *Weekly Checks* and in Chapter 1, Sections 8 and 9.

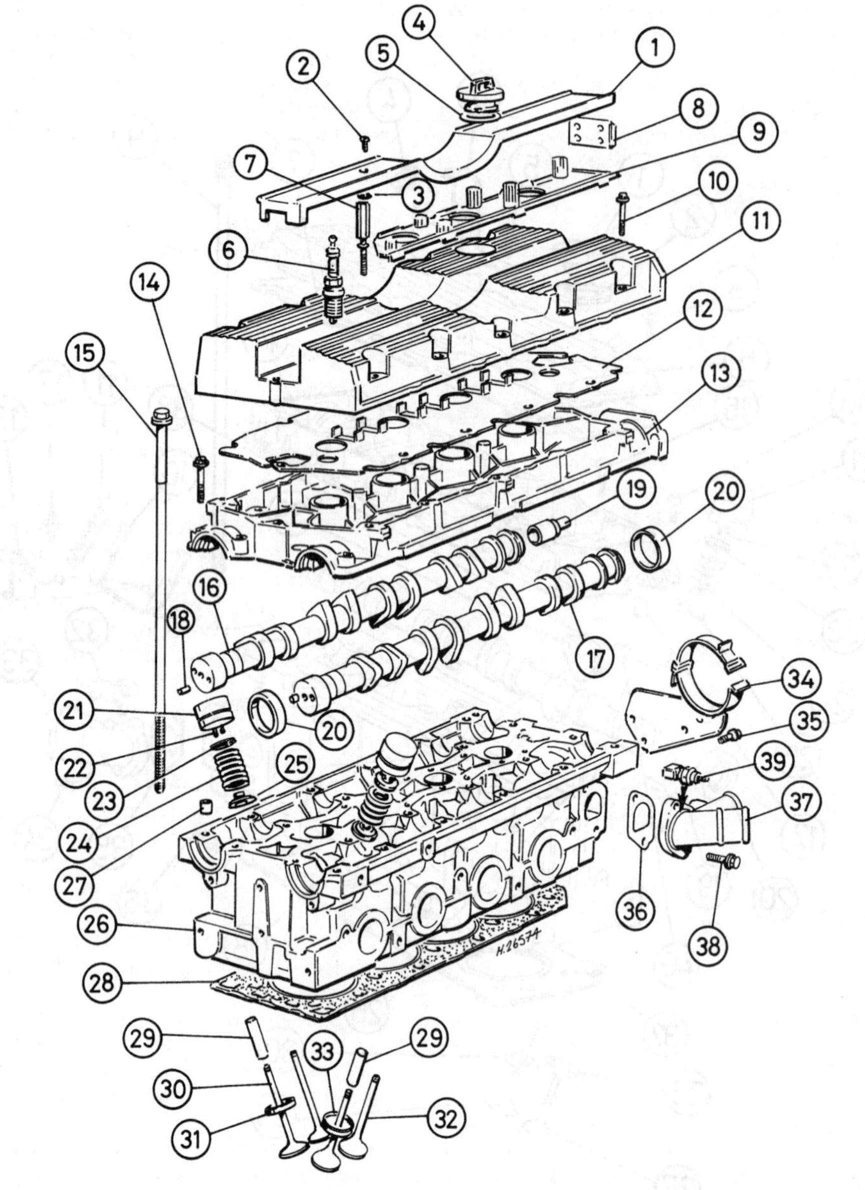

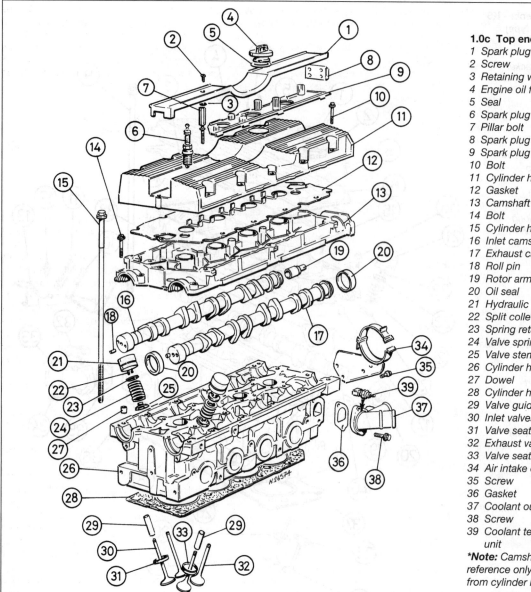

1.0c Top end components - K16 engine
1 Spark plug cover
2 Screw
3 Retaining washer
4 Engine oil filler cap
5 Seal
6 Spark plug
7 Pillar bolt
8 Spark plug (HT) lead grommet
9 Spark plug (HT) lead clip plate
10 Bolt
11 Cylinder head cover
12 Gasket
*13 Camshaft carrier**
14 Bolt
15 Cylinder head bolt
16 Inlet camshaft
17 Exhaust camshaft
18 Roll pin
19 Rotor arm drive spindle
20 Oil seal
21 Hydraulic tappet
22 Split collets
23 Spring retainer
24 Valve spring
25 Valve stem seal/spring bottom seat
26 Cylinder head
27 Dowel
28 Cylinder head gasket
29 Valve guide
30 Inlet valves
31 Valve seat insert
32 Exhaust valves
33 Valve seat insert
34 Air intake duct support bracket
35 Screw
36 Gasket
37 Coolant outlet elbow
38 Screw
39 Coolant temperature gauge sender unit
****Note:** Camshaft carrier shown for reference only - not available separately from cylinder head*

3 Engine - general examination

Refer to Chapter 1, Section 6.

4 Compression test - description and interpretation

1 When engine performance is down, or if misfiring occurs which cannot be attributed to the ignition or fuel systems, a compression test can provide diagnostic clues as to the engine's condition. If the test is performed regularly it can give warning of trouble before any other symptoms become apparent.

2 The engine must be fully warmed up to normal operating temperature, the battery must be fully charged and the spark plugs must be removed. The aid of an assistant will be required.

3 Disable the ignition system by disconnecting the ignition HT coil lead from the distributor cap and earthing it on the cylinder block. Use a jumper lead or similar wire to make a good connection.

4 Fit a compression tester to the number 1 cylinder spark plug hole. The type of tester which screws into the plug thread is to be preferred **(see illustration)**.

5 Have the assistant hold the throttle wide open and crank the engine on the starter motor. After one or two revolutions the compression pressure should build up to a maximum figure and then stabilise. Record the highest reading obtained.

6 Repeat the test on the remaining cylinders, recording the pressure in each.

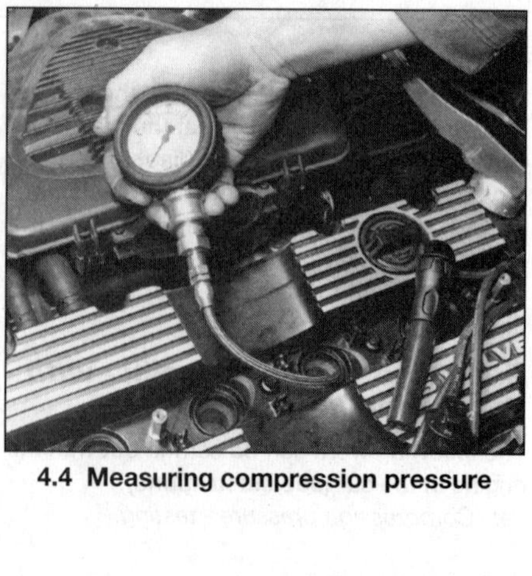

4.4 Measuring compression pressure

7 All cylinders should produce very similar pressures. Any difference greater than that specified indicates the existence of a fault. Note that the compression should build up quickly in a healthy engine; low compression on the first stroke, followed by gradually increasing pressure on successive strokes, indicates worn piston rings. A low compression reading on the first stroke, which does not build up during successive strokes, indicates leaking valves or a blown head gasket (a cracked head could also be the cause). Deposits on the undersides of the valve heads can also cause low compression.

8 If the pressure in any cylinder is reduced to the specified minimum or less, carry out the following test to isolate the cause. Introduce a teaspoonful of clean oil into that cylinder through its spark plug hole and repeat the test.

9 If the addition of oil temporarily improves the compression pressure, this indicates that bore or piston wear is responsible for the pressure loss. No improvement suggests that leaking or burnt valves, or a blown head gasket may be to blame.

10 A low reading from two adjacent cylinders is almost certainly due to the head gasket having blown between them; the presence of coolant in the engine oil will confirm this.

11 If one cylinder is about 20 percent lower than the others and the engine has a slightly rough idle, a worn camshaft lobe could be the cause.

12 If the compression reading is unusually high, the combustion chambers are probably coated with carbon deposits. If this is the case, the cylinder head should be removed and decarbonised.

13 On completion of the test, refit the spark plugs and reconnect the ignition system.

5 Top Dead Centre (TDC) for number one piston - locating

General

Note: *The alternator drive pulley, crankshaft toothed pulley and camshaft toothed pulley(s) are provided by the factory with clear marks which align only at 90° BTDC. This positions the pistons half-way up the bores so that there is no risk of damage as the engine is reassembled. These marks do not indicate TDC. Use only the ignition timing marks, as described in this Section, to find TDC*

1 Top dead centre (TDC) is the highest point in its travel up-and-down the cylinder bore that each piston reaches as the crankshaft rotates. Whilst each piston reaches TDC both at the top of the compression stroke and again at the top of the exhaust stroke, for the purpose of timing the engine, TDC refers to the piston position (usually number 1) at the top of its compression stroke.

2 Whilst all engine reassembly procedures use the factory timing marks (90° BTDC), it is useful for several other servicing procedures to be able to position the engine at TDC.

3 Number 1 piston and cylinder is at the right-hand (timing belt) end of the engine. Note that the crankshaft rotates clockwise when viewed from the right-hand side of the car.

Locating TDC

4 Remove all the spark plugs.

5 Trace number 1 spark plug (HT) lead from the plug back to the distributor cap and use chalk or similar to mark the distributor body or engine casting nearest to the cap's number 1 terminal. Remove the distributor cap.

6 Disconnect both battery leads (unless the starter motor is to be used to turn the engine).

7 Apply the handbrake and ensure that the transmission is in neutral, then jack up the front right-hand side of the car and support it on axle stands (see "*Jacking and Vehicle Support*").

8 Remove the roadwheel and the underwing shield to expose the alternator drive pulley and ignition timing marks.

9 It is best to rotate the crankshaft using a spanner applied to the alternator drive pulley bolt. It is, however, possible to use the starter motor (switched on either by an assistant using the ignition key or by using a remote starter switch) to bring the engine close to TDC, then finish with a spanner. If the starter is used, be sure to disconnect the battery leads immediately it is no longer required.

10 Rotate the crankshaft clockwise until the notch on the alternator drive pulley's inboard (left-hand) rim is aligned with the TDC mark on the timing belt lower cover.

11 Numbers 1 and 4 cylinders are now at TDC, one of them on the compression stroke. If the distributor rotor arm is pointing at (the previously-marked) number 1 terminal, then number 1 cylinder is correctly positioned. If the rotor arm is pointing at number 4 terminal, rotate the crankshaft one full turn (360°) clockwise until the arm points at the marked terminal. Number 1 cylinder will then be at TDC on the compression stroke.

12 Once number 1 cylinder has been positioned at TDC on the compression stroke, TDC for any of the other cylinders can then be located by rotating the crankshaft clockwise 180° at a time and following the firing order (see Specifications).

13 An alternative method of locating TDC is to remove the cylinder head cover and to rotate the crankshaft clockwise until the inlet valve(s) for the cylinder concerned has opened and just closed again. Insert a length of wooden dowel (approximately 150 mm long) or similar into the spark plug hole until it rests on the piston crown and slowly further rotate the crankshaft (taking care not to allow the dowel to be trapped in the cylinder) until the dowel stops rising. The piston is now at the top of its compression stroke and the dowel can be removed.

14 There is a dead area around TDC (as the piston stops rising, pauses and then begins to descend) which makes it difficult to locate the exact TDC position by this method. If absolute accuracy is required, establish carefully the exact mid-point of the dead area or refer to the ignition timing marks.

6 Cylinder head cover - removal and refitting

Removal

K8 engines - wet liner type

1 Disconnect the battery negative lead.

2 Remove the screws securing the air cleaner assembly and release the quarter-turn fastener(s) securing the inlet duct to its cylinder head bracket(s), then disconnect the vacuum pipes from the air cleaner assembly and the air temperature control valve. On fuel-injected engines, the fuel trap vacuum hoses need only be disconnected if extra clearance is required. Withdraw the assembly, taking care not to lose the hot air inlet connector hose and place the assembly to one side, clear of the cylinder head.

3 Disconnect the breather hose(s) from the cover **(see illustration)**.

4 Where they prevent access to the cover's retaining bolts or might hinder its removal, unfasten the spark plug (HT) lead clip(s) and air inlet duct support bracket(s) from the cylinder head or from the cover, and remove them or move them clear of the working area.

5 Remove the two top (hex-head) retaining screws securing the timing belt upper right-hand/outer cover to the cylinder head cover, then slacken the remaining screws and bolts as necessary until the timing belt cover can be prised clear of the cylinder head cover without damaging it.

6 Working progressively and in the reverse of the tightening sequence, unscrew the cylinder head cover retaining bolts.

7 Remove the cover, peel off the rubber seal and check it for cuts, other damage or distortion. Renew the seal if necessary.

6.3 Disconnecting breather hose(s) from cylinder head cover - K8 engine

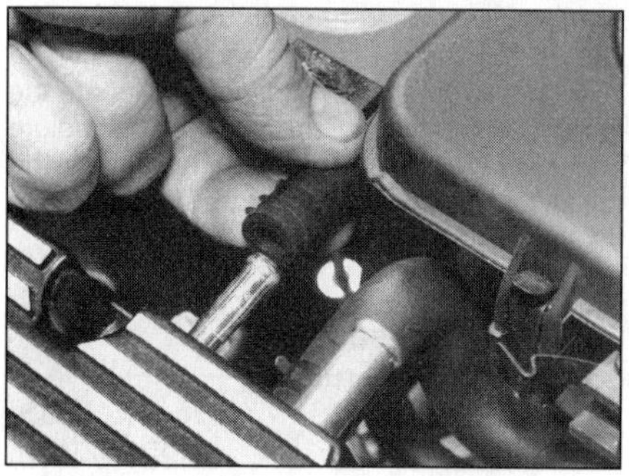

6.11 Disconnecting breather hoses from cylinder head cover - K16 engine

K16 engines

8 Disconnect the battery negative lead.

9 Release the two clips securing the air inlet duct to the air cleaner assembly and unscrew the bolt securing the duct to its support bracket. Unfasten the rubber strap and disconnect the vacuum pipe from the air temperature control valve.

10 Withdraw the assembly, taking care not to lose the hot air inlet connector hose and place the assembly to one side, clear of the cylinder head.

11 Disconnect the breather hoses from the cover **(see illustration)**.

12 Remove the spark plug cover, disconnect the spark plug (HT) leads from the plugs and withdraw them from the cylinder head with the clip plate and the grommet.

13 Working progressively and in the reverse of the tightening sequence, unscrew the cylinder head cover retaining bolts and withdraw the air inlet duct support bracket.

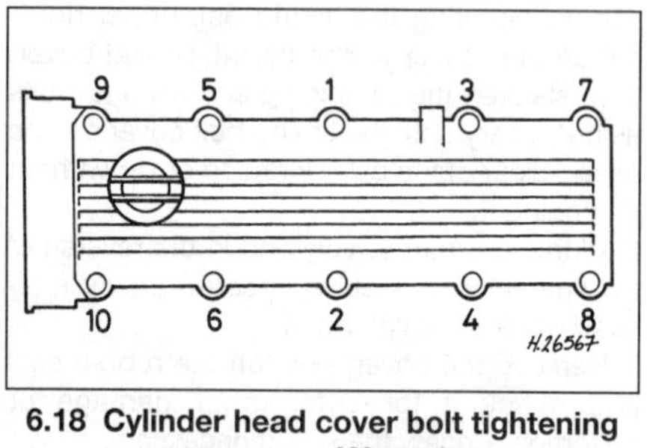

6.18 Cylinder head cover bolt tightening sequence - K8 engine

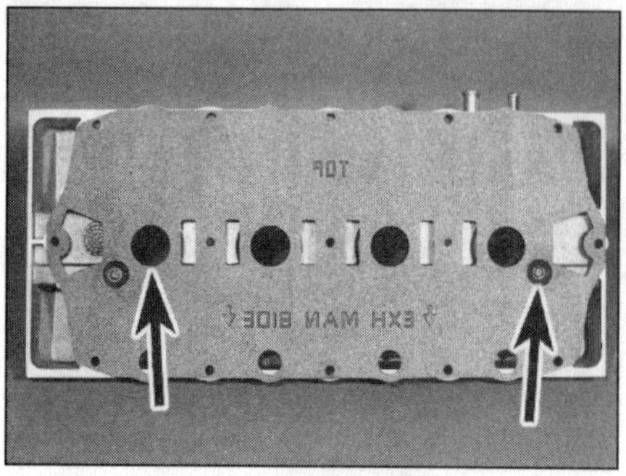

6.24a Fit gasket to cylinder head cover dowels (arrowed) so that . . .

6.16a Ensure cylinder head cover seal is seated correctly in cover groove . . .

14 Withdraw the cover. Take care not to damage the gasket and check that its sealing path is undamaged and attached to the gasket all around the gasket's periphery. If the sealing path is undamaged the gasket is re-usable and should remain in place on the cover until reassembly, unless its removal is necessary for other servicing work.

Refitting

K8 engines - wet liner type

15 On reassembly, carefully clean the cylinder head mating surfaces and the cover seal's groove and remove all traces of oil.

16 Seat the seal in its groove in the cover and refit the bolts, pushing each through the seal, then apply a smear of silicone-RTV sealant to the seal at the points indicated **(see illustrations)**.

17 Refit the cover and start all bolts finger-tight, ensuring that the seal remains seated in its groove.

18 Working in the sequence shown **(see illustration)**, tighten the cylinder head cover bolts to the specified torque wrench setting. Check that the seal has not been displaced.

19 Refit the timing belt upper right-hand/outer cover to the cylinder head cover, then tighten the retaining screws and bolts to the specified torque wrench setting.

20 Refit the removed spark plug (HT) lead clip(s) and air inlet duct support bracket(s), tightening all fasteners to the appropriate torque wrench settings and correctly routing the spark plug (HT) leads.

6.24b . . . stamped markings would appear as shown if gasket were placed on camshaft carrier

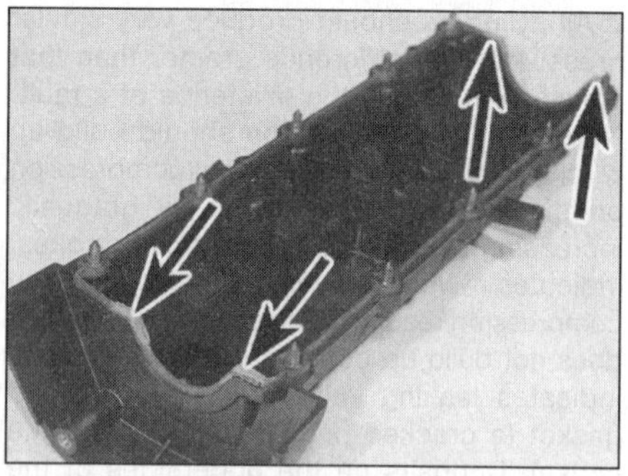

6.16b . . . refit bolts and apply sealant at locations arrowed - K8 engine

21 Connect the breather hose to the cover, then refit the air cleaner assembly, ensuring that all vacuum hoses and pipes are correctly routed and secured. Do not forget to refit the hot air inlet connector hose.

22 Connect the battery negative lead.

K16 engines

23 On reassembly, clean carefully the mating surfaces, removing all traces of oil.

24 If a new gasket is to be fitted, press it onto the cover locating dowels so that if it were laid on the camshaft carrier its stamped markings would be legible. The "TOP" mark should be nearest the inlet manifold and the "EXH MAN SIDE" mark should have its arrows pointing to the exhaust manifold **(see illustrations)**.

25 Refit the cover and start the bolts finger-tight, ensuring that the gasket is not damaged or displaced. Fit the air inlet duct support bracket at the front, in line with number 2 cylinder spark plug.

26 Working in the sequence shown, tighten the cover retaining bolts and pillar bolts to the specified torque wrench setting **(see illustration)**.

27 Reconnect the spark plug (HT) leads to the spark plugs, routing them using the clip plate and grommet, then refit the spark plug cover and reconnect the breather hoses to the cover unions.

28 Ensuring that the hot air inlet connector hose is in place, refit the air inlet duct to the

6.26 Cylinder head cover bolt tightening sequence - K16 engine

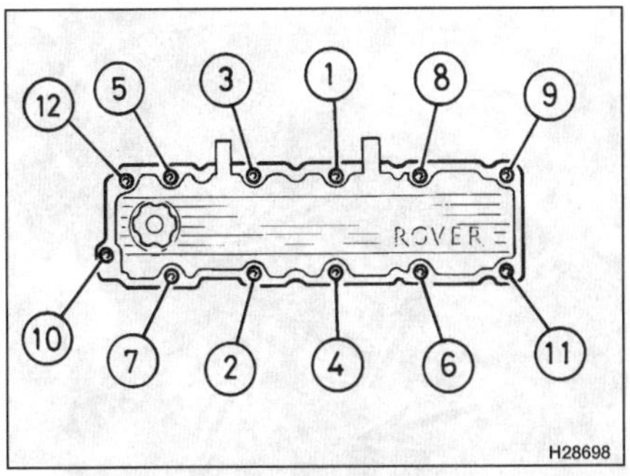

7.8 Camshaft cover bolt tightening sequence

air cleaner assembly, securing it with its clips and rubber strap. Connect the vacuum pipe to the air temperature control valve and tighten the bolt securing the duct to its support bracket to its specified torque wrench setting.

29 Connect the battery negative lead.

7 Camshaft cover (K8 engines - damp liner type) - removal and refitting

Removal

1 Disconnect the battery negative lead.

2 Refer to Chapter 4 and remove the air cleaner assembly to provide clearance to the camshaft cover.

3 Detach the HT leads from the spark plugs and remove the HT lead mounting brackets from the cover. Move the leads clear of the working area.

4 Working progressively and in the reverse sequence for tightening, unscrew the camshaft cover retaining bolts.

5 Remove the cover and discard the gasket.

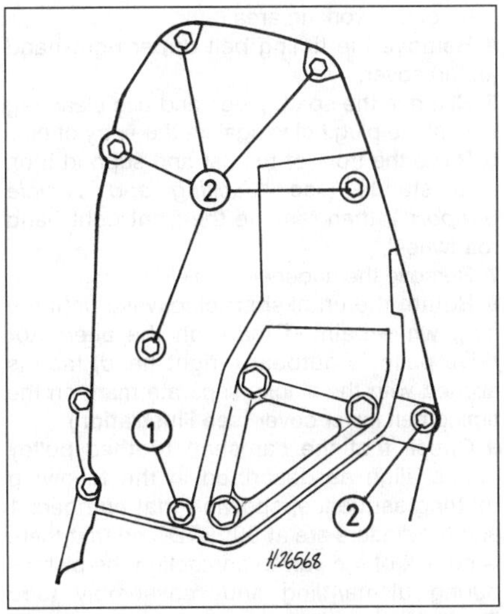

10.2a Location of K8 engine timing belt upper right-hand (outer) cover fasteners

1 Slacken screw - cover should be slotted
2 Remove fasteners

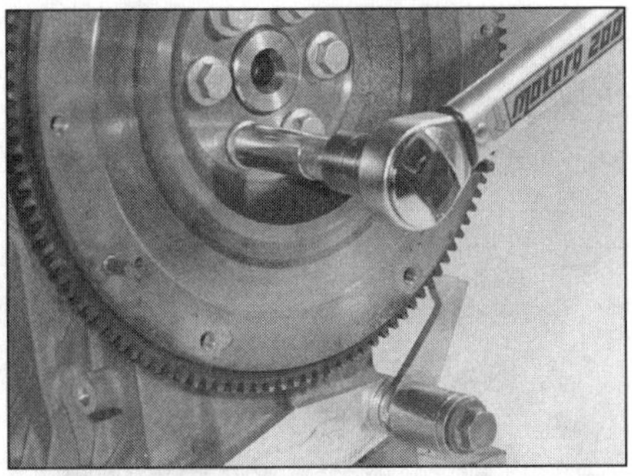

8.5 Use fabricated tool as shown to lock flywheel while slackening or tightening flywheel bolts

Refitting

6 Before refitting, carefully clean and dry the cover and camshaft carrier mating surfaces.

7 Position a new gasket on the cover, ensuring that the spigots on the cover locate in the corresponding gasket holes.

8 Refit the cover to the camshaft carrier, checking that the gasket has not been displaced. Refit the retaining bolts and tighten them to the specified torque loading in the sequence shown **(see illustration)**.

9 Refit the HT lead mounting brackets, tightening all fasteners and correctly routing the HT leads to the spark plugs.

10 Refit the air cleaner assembly, ensuring that all disturbed hoses and pipes are correctly routed and secured.

11 Reconnect the battery negative lead.

8 Alternator drive pulley - removal and refitting

Removal

1 Raise the front right-hand side of the car and support it on an axle stand. Although roadwheel removal is not strictly necessary, access is greatly improved if this is done; otherwise, turn the steering to full right lock.

2 Remove the underwing shield.

3 If necessary, rotate the crankshaft until the timing marks align.

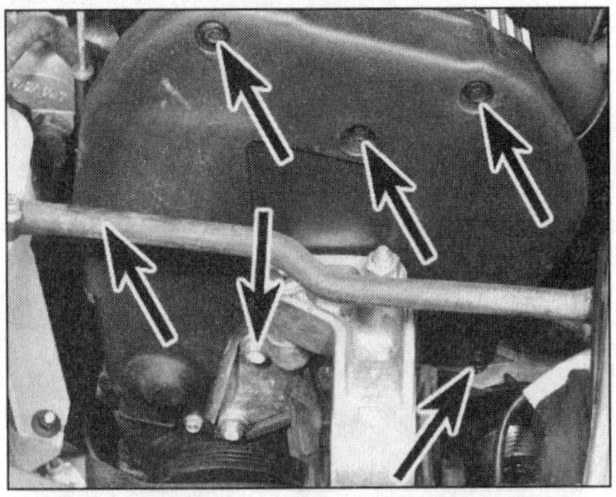

10.2b Location of K16 engine timing belt upper right-hand/outer cover fasteners (arrowed) - engine raised for clarity

8.7 Notch in alternator drive pulley centre fits over crankshaft toothed pulley locating lug (arrowed)

4 Slacken the alternator clamp and pivot bolts, move the alternator as far as possible towards the engine and disengage the drivebelt from the drive pulley.

5 To prevent crankshaft rotation while the pulley bolt is unscrewed, select top gear and have an assistant apply the brakes hard. If the engine has been removed from the car, lock the flywheel using the arrangement shown **(see illustration)**.

6 Unscrew the pulley bolt, noting the special washer behind it, then remove the pulley.

Refitting

7 On refitting, ensure that the notch in the pulley's centre fits over the locating lug on the crankshaft toothed pulley **(see illustration)**.

8 Lock the crankshaft by the method used on removal and tighten the bolt to the specified torque wrench setting.

9 Refit the alternator drivebelt and adjust it.

10 Refit, if removed, the underwing shield and roadwheel.

9 Timing belt - examination

Refer to Chapter 1, Section 39.

10 Timing belt covers - removal and refitting

Removal

Upper right-hand (outer) cover

1 Slacken the (hex-head) screw at the cover's bottom corner, immediately behind the engine/transmission right-hand mounting bracket.

2 Unscrew the remaining cover retaining (hex-head) screws or bolts and withdraw the cover, noting the rubber seal fitted to its mounting bracket edge. Note that if the cover is not slotted at the bottom corner screw's location, the screw will have to be removed fully. If this is the case, the cover can be slotted to ease future removal and refitting **(see illustrations)**.

10.4 Removing timing belt lower cover

10.9c . . . noting that lowermost bolt is accessible only from wheel arch

Lower cover

3 Remove the alternator drive pulley.

4 Remove the cover retaining screws, including the one which also secures the upper cover's bottom front corner and remove the cover, noting the rubber seal fitted to its mounting bracket edge **(see illustration)**.

Upper left-hand (inner) cover

5 Remove the timing belt.

6 Remove the camshaft toothed pulley(s) and the timing belt tensioner.

7 Unscrew the bolt securing the cover to the water pump.

8 On K16 engines, unbolt the engine/transmission right-hand mounting bracket from the cylinder block/crankcase.

10.10 Ensure timing belt upper right-hand (outer) cover engages correctly with cylinder head cover - K8 engine

10.9a Location of K8 engine timing belt upper left-hand (inner) cover fasteners (arrowed)

10.9d Removing K16 engine timing belt upper left-hand (inner) cover

9 Remove the remaining cover retaining bolts **(see illustrations)** and withdraw the cover.

Refitting

Upper right-hand (outer) cover

10 Refitting is the reverse of the removal procedure. Ensure that the seal fits correctly between the cover and the mounting bracket and that the cover edges mate correctly with those of the inner cover and (K8 engines only) cylinder head cover **(see illustration)**.

11 Tighten the cover fasteners to the specified torque wrench setting.

Lower cover

12 Refitting is the reverse of the removal procedure. Ensure that the seal fits correctly between the cover and the mounting bracket and tighten the cover fasteners to the specified torque wrench setting.

13 Refit the alternator drive pulley.

Upper left-hand (inner) cover

14 Refitting is the reverse of the removal procedure. Tighten all disturbed fasteners to their specified torque wrench settings.

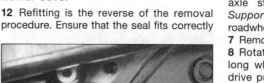

11.8 Alternator drive pulley mark aligned with timing belt lower cover mark at 90° BTDC

10.9b Location of K16 engine timing belt upper left-hand (inner) cover fasteners (arrowed) . . .

11 Timing belt - removal, refitting and adjustment

Removal

1 Disconnect the battery negative lead.

2 Remove its three retaining screws and move the washer system reservoir clear of the working area. Disconnect the pump wiring connector plug(s) if the extra reach is required.

3 Unclip the expansion tank coolant hose from the bonnet lock platform and secure it clear of the working area.

4 Remove the timing belt upper right-hand (outer) cover.

5 Remove the spark plugs and use clean rag to seal the plug holes against the entry of dirt.

6 Raise the front of the car and support it on axle stands (see *"Jacking and Vehicle Support"*), then remove the front right-hand roadwheel.

7 Remove the underwing shield.

8 Rotate the crankshaft clockwise until the long white-painted mark on the alternator drive pulley's outboard (right-hand) face is aligned with the single, separate mark on the timing belt lower cover **(see illustration)**.

9 Check that the camshaft toothed pulley marks align as described in the following refitting sequence, showing that numbers 1 and 4 cylinders are at 90° BTDC so that there is no risk of the valves contacting the pistons during dismantling and reassembly **(see illustration)**.

10 On K16 engines, lock together the camshaft toothed pulleys so that they cannot move under valve spring pressure when the timing belt is removed.

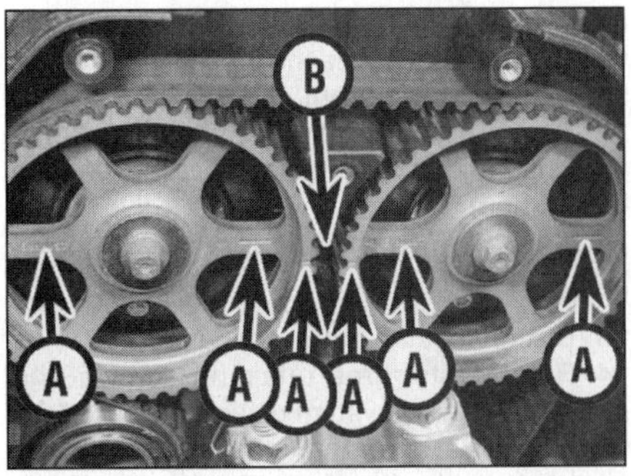

11.9 Camshaft toothed pulley marks (A) aligned with timing belt upper left-hand (inner) cover mark (B) - K16 engine

11 Remove the alternator drive pulley.

12 Remove the timing belt lower cover.

13 Support the weight of the engine/ transmission using a trolley jack, with a wooden spacer to prevent damage to the sump, then unscrew the engine/transmission right-hand mounting through-bolt and nut and the mounting-to-bracket nuts. Remove the mounting, noting the two rubber washers. On K8 engines only, unscrew also the retaining bolts and remove the bracket from the cylinder block/crankcase **(see illustration)**.

14 Slacken through half a turn, the timing belt tensioner pulley Allen screw and the tensioner backplate (hex-head) screw, push the pulley assembly down to the (belt) fully-slack position to release tension from the belt, then re-tighten the backplate screw **(see illustration)**.

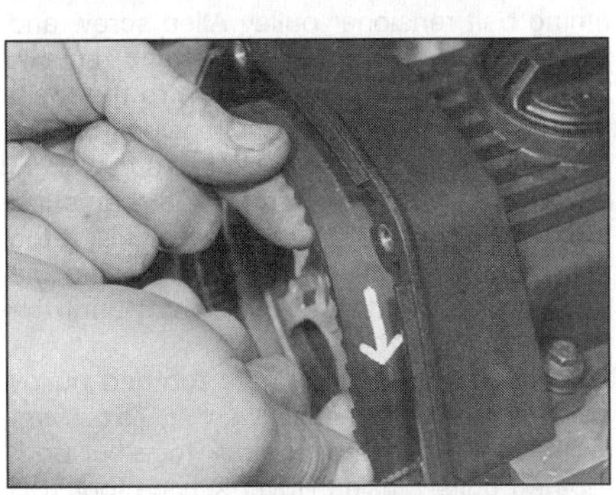

11.15 If timing belt is to be re-used, mark direction of rotation as shown before removing

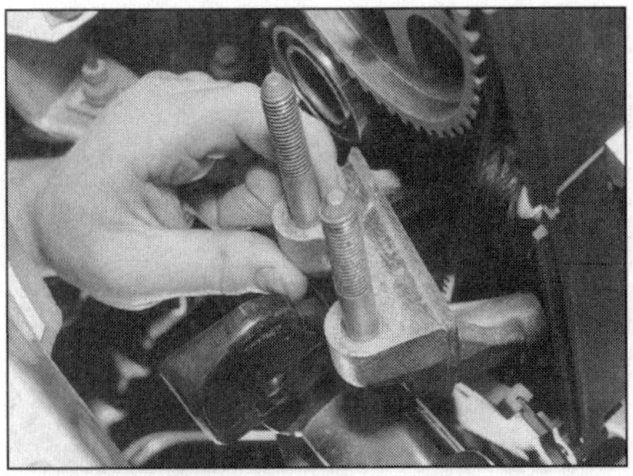

11.13 Removing engine/transmission right-hand mounting bracket - K8 engine

15 If the timing belt is to be re-used, use white paint or similar to mark its direction of rotation **(see illustration)**, then remove it from the toothed pulleys. Do not rotate the crankshaft until the timing belt has been refitted.

16 Check the timing belt carefully for any signs of uneven wear, splitting or oil contamination and renew it if there is the slightest doubt about its condition. If the engine is undergoing an overhaul and has covered more than 48 000 miles (80 000 km) since the original belt was fitted, renew the belt as a matter of course, regardless of its apparent condition. If signs of oil contamination are found, trace the source of the oil leak and rectify it, then wash down the engine timing belt area and all related components to remove all traces of oil.

Refitting

17 On reassembly, thoroughly clean the toothed pulleys and check that they are aligned as follows:

a) ***Camshaft pulley - K8 engine*** *- the "EX" line and the mark stamped in the pulley's rim must be at the front (looking at the pulley from the right-hand side of the car) and aligned exactly with the cylinder head top surface* ***(see illustration).***

b) ***Camshaft pulleys - K16 engine*** *- both "EXHAUST" arrow marks must point to the rear (looking at the pulleys from the right-hand side of the car) with the "IN" lines and the pulley rim marks aligned exactly with the line on the timing belt upper left-hand/inner cover (representing the cylinder head top surface). Refer to illustration 11.9.*

c) ***Crankshaft pulley*** *- the two dots must be on each side of the raised rib on the oil pump body* ***(see illustration).***

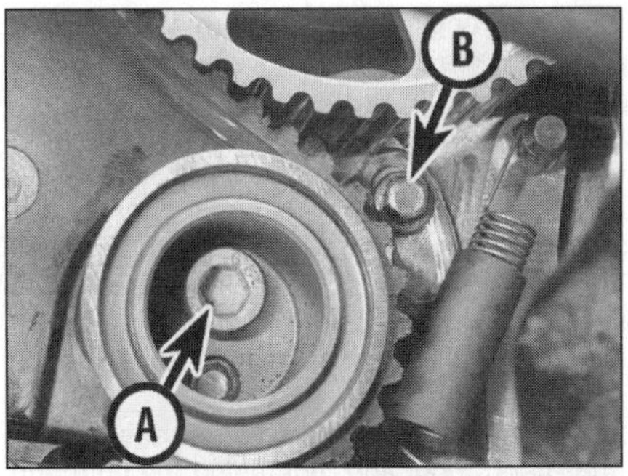

11.14 Timing belt tensioner pulley Allen screw (A) and tensioner backplate screw (B)

Note: *It is most important that these marks are aligned exactly as this sets the valve timing, but note that in this position numbers 1 and 4 cylinders are at 90° BTDC so that there is no risk of the valves contacting the pistons during dismantling and reassembly.*

18 Fit the timing belt over the crankshaft and camshaft toothed pulleys, ensuring that the belt front run (and, on K16 engines, the top run) is taut. That is, all slack is at the tensioner pulley, then over the water pump pulley and tensioner pulley. Do not twist the belt sharply during refitting, ensure that the belt teeth are correctly seated centrally in the pulleys and that the timing marks remain in alignment. If a used belt is being refitted, ensure that the arrow mark made on removal points in the same direction of rotation as before **(see illustration)**.

19 Slacken the tensioner backplate screw and check that the tensioner pulley moves to tension the belt. If the tensioner assembly is not free to move under spring tension, rectify the fault or the timing belt will not be correctly tensioned.

20 On K16 engines, remove the camshaft toothed pulley locking tool.

21 On K8 engines, refit the engine/ transmission right-hand mounting bracket, tightening its bolts to the specified torque wrench setting.

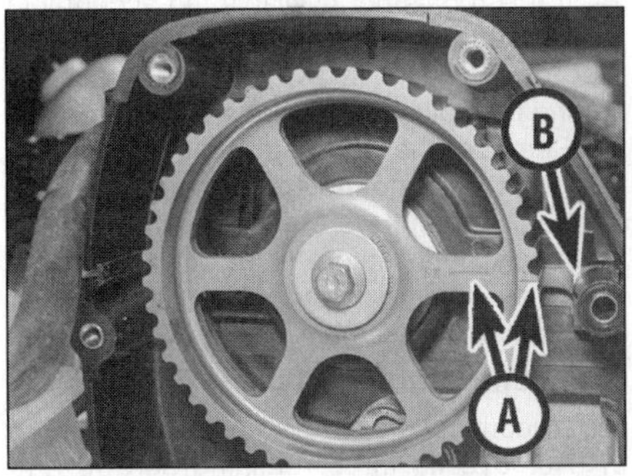

11.17a Camshaft toothed pulley marks (A) aligned with cylinder head top surface (B) - K8 engine

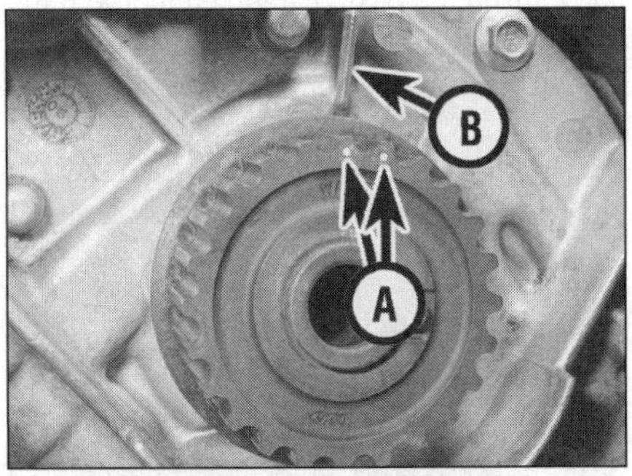

11.17b Crankshaft toothed pulley dots (A) aligned on each side of oil pump raised rib (B)

11.18 Refitting the timing belt - K16 engine

22 On all engines, refit the timing belt lower cover and the alternator drive pulley.
23 Rotate the crankshaft two full turns clockwise to settle and tension the belt. Check that the timing marks are still aligned exactly.
24 The timing belt will now be tensioned correctly. Tighten the tensioner backplate screw, then the tensioner pulley Allen screw (where given) to their specified torque wrench settings.
25 Reassemble the engine/transmission right-hand mounting, tightening the nuts and bolts to their specified torque wrench settings and ensuring that the rubber washers are correctly located.
26 Refit the underwing shield and the roadwheel, then lower the car to the ground.
27 Refit the timing belt upper right-hand (outer) cover, re-route and secure the coolant hose. Refit the spark plugs and the washer system reservoir. Re-connect the battery negative lead.

Adjustment

28 As the timing belt is a “fit-and-forget” type, the manufacturer states that tensioning need be carried out only after a new belt has been fitted (although tensioning is obviously required if the existing belt has been disturbed for other servicing/overhaul work). No re-tensioning is recommended once a belt has been fitted and therefore this operation is not included in the manufacturer’s maintenance schedule.
29 If the timing belt is thought to be incorrectly tensioned, adjust the tension as described in the appropriate preceding paragraphs.
30 If the timing belt has been disturbed, adjust its tension following the same procedure, omitting as appropriate the irrelevant preliminary dismantling/reassembly steps.

12 Timing belt tensioner and toothed pulleys - removal, inspection and refitting

Note: *This Section describes as individual operations the removal and refitting of the components concerned. If more than one component is to be removed at the same time, start by removing the timing belt, then remove the actual component as described below, ignoring the preliminary dismantling steps*

Removal

Camshaft toothed pulley - K8 engine

1 Disconnect the battery negative lead.
2 Remove its three retaining screws and move the washer system reservoir clear of the working area. Disconnect the pump wiring connector plug(s) if the extra reach is required.

12.11 Use fabricated tool shown to hold pulley while bolt is loosened

3 Unclip the expansion tank coolant hose from the bonnet lock platform and secure it clear of the working area.
4 Remove the timing belt upper right-hand (outer) cover.
5 Remove the spark plugs and use clean rag to seal the plug holes against the entry of dirt.
6 Raise the front right-hand side of the car and support it on an axle stand, turn the steering to full right lock and remove the underwing shield.
7 Rotate the crankshaft clockwise until the long white-painted mark on the alternator drive pulley’s outboard (right-hand) face is aligned with the single, separate mark on the timing belt lower cover.
8 Check that the camshaft toothed pulley marks align as described in Section 10.
9 Slacken through half a turn each the timing belt tensioner pulley Allen screw and the tensioner backplate (hex-head) screw, push the pulley assembly down to the (belt) fully-slack position to release tension from the belt, then re-tighten the backplate screw.
10 Remove the belt from the camshaft toothed pulley, taking care not to twist it too sharply. Use the fingers only to handle the belt. Do not rotate the crankshaft until the timing belt is refitted.
11 Unscrew the toothed pulley bolt and remove it, with its washer. To prevent the camshaft from rotating, use Rover service tool 18G 1521. If this is not available, an acceptable substitute can be fabricated from two lengths of steel strip (one long, the other short) and three nuts and bolts; one nut and bolt forming the pivot of a forked tool with the remaining two nuts and bolts at the tips of the forks to engage with the pulley spokes as shown **(see illustration)**.

12.12 Removing camshaft toothed pulley - K8 engine. Note roll pin (arrowed)

12 Remove the toothed pulley from the camshaft end, noting the locating roll pin **(see illustration)**.

Camshaft toothed pulleys - K16 engine

13 Disconnect the battery negative lead.
14 Remove its three retaining screws and move the washer system reservoir clear of the working area. Disconnect the pump wiring connector plug(s) if the extra reach is required.
15 Unclip the expansion tank coolant hose from the bonnet lock platform and secure it clear of the working area.
16 Remove the timing belt upper right-hand (outer) cover.
17 Remove the spark plugs and use clean rag to seal the plug holes against the entry of dirt.
18 Raise the front right-hand side of the car and support it on an axle stand, turn the steering to full right lock and remove the underwing shield.
19 Rotate the crankshaft clockwise until the long white-painted mark on the alternator drive pulley’s outboard (right-hand) face is aligned with the single, separate mark on the timing belt lower cover.
20 Check that the camshaft toothed pulley marks align as described in Section 10.
21 Slacken through half a turn each, the timing belt tensioner pulley Allen screw and the tensioner backplate (hex-head) screw, push the pulley assembly down to the (belt) fully-slack position to release tension from the belt, then re-tighten the backplate screw.
22 Remove the belt from the camshaft toothed pulleys, taking care not to twist it too sharply. Use the fingers only to handle the belt. Do not rotate the crankshaft until the timing belt is refitted.
23 Unscrew the appropriate toothed pulley bolt and remove it, with its washer. To prevent a camshaft from rotating, lock together both toothed pulleys using Rover service tool 18G 1570. This is a metal piece shaped on both sides to fit the pulley teeth and is inserted between the pulleys.
24 If this tool is not available, an acceptable substitute can be cut from a length of steel tube or similar to fit as closely as possible around the pulley spokes **(see illustrations)**.
25 Remove the toothed pulley from the camshaft end, noting the locating roll pin. Although the pulleys are identical it is good practice to mark them (inlet or exhaust) so that they can be returned to their original locations on reassembly.

Crankshaft toothed pulley

26 Disconnect the battery negative lead.
27 Remove its three retaining screws and move the washer system reservoir clear of the working area. Disconnect the pump wiring connector plug(s) if the extra reach is required.

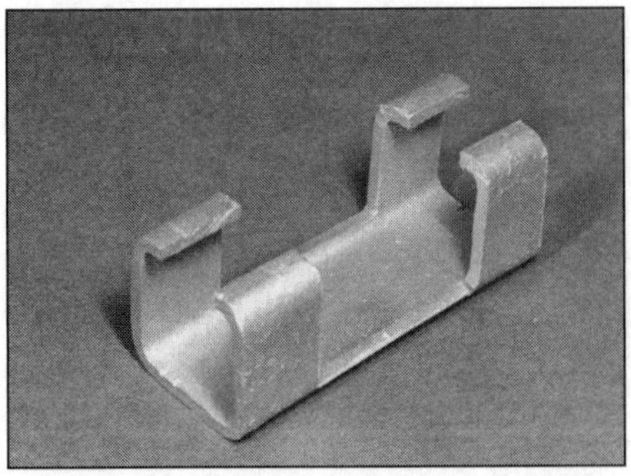

12.24a K16 engine camshaft locking tool cut from steel tube . . .

28 Unclip the expansion tank coolant hose from the bonnet lock platform and secure it clear of the working area.
29 Remove the timing belt upper right-hand (outer) cover.
30 Remove the spark plugs and use clean rag to seal the plug holes.
31 Raise the front right-hand side of the car and support it on an axle stand, then remove the front right-hand roadwheel and the underwing shield.
32 Rotate the crankshaft clockwise until the long white-painted mark on the alternator drive pulley's outboard (right-hand) face is aligned with the single, separate mark on the timing belt lower cover.
33 Check that the camshaft toothed pulley marks align as described in Section 10.
34 On K16 engines, use the tool described above to lock together the camshaft toothed pulleys so that they cannot move under valve spring pressure when the timing belt is removed.
35 Remove the alternator drive pulley.
36 Remove the timing belt lower cover.
37 Slacken through half a turn each the timing belt tensioner pulley Allen screw and the tensioner backplate (hex-head) screw, push the pulley assembly down to the (belt) fully-slack position to release tension from the belt, then re-tighten the backplate screw.
38 Work the belt clear of the crankshaft toothed pulley, taking care not to twist it too sharply. Use the fingers only to handle the belt. Do not rotate the crankshaft until the timing belt is refitted.
39 Remove the pulley.

Tensioner assembly

40 Disconnect the battery negative lead.
41 Remove its three retaining screws and move the washer system reservoir clear of the working area. Disconnect the pump wiring connector plug(s) if the extra reach is required.
42 Unclip the expansion tank coolant hose from the bonnet lock platform and secure it clear of the working area.
43 Remove the timing belt upper right-hand (outer) cover.
44 Remove the spark plugs and use clean rag to cover the plug holes.

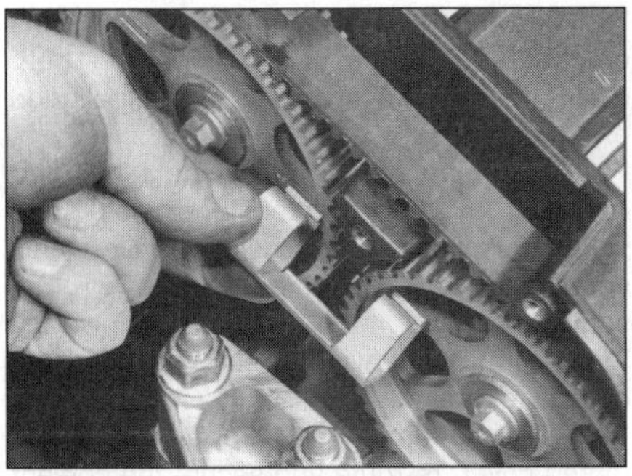

12.24b . . . to fit toothed pulley spokes as closely as possible, as shown

45 Raise the front right-hand side of the car and support it on an axle stand, turn the steering to full right lock and remove the underwing shield.
46 Rotate the crankshaft clockwise until the long white-painted mark on the alternator drive pulley's outboard (right-hand) face is aligned with the single, separate mark on the timing belt lower cover.
47 Check that the camshaft toothed pulley marks align as described in Section 10.
48 On K16 engines, use the tool described above to lock together the camshaft toothed pulleys so that they cannot move under valve spring pressure when the timing belt is slackened.
49 Unhook the tensioner spring from its pillar bolt, then unscrew the tensioner pulley Allen screw and the tensioner backplate (hex-head) screw **(see illustration)**. Withdraw the tensioner assembly. Do not rotate the crankshaft until the timing belt is re-tensioned.

Inspection

50 Clean thoroughly the camshaft/crankshaft pulleys and renew any that show signs of wear, damage or cracks.
51 Clean the tensioner assembly but do not use any strong solvent which may enter the pulley bearing. Check that the pulley rotates freely on the backplate, with no sign of stiffness or of free play. Renew the assembly if there is any doubt about its condition or if there are any obvious signs of wear or damage. The same applies to the tensioner

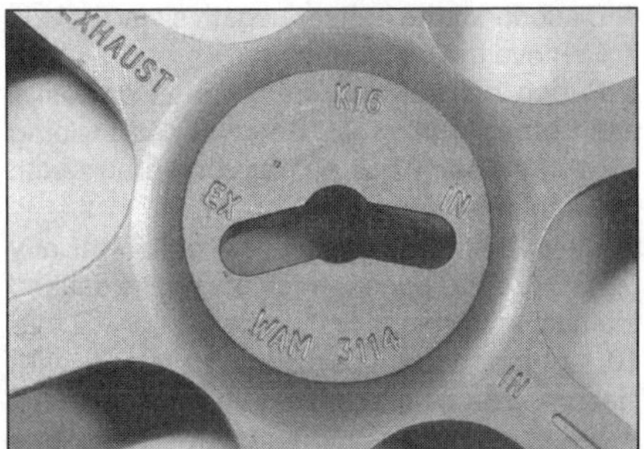

12.59 K16 engine camshaft toothed pulleys have two keyways - engage EX keyway with exhaust camshaft roll pin and IN keyway with inlet camshaft roll pin

12.49 Timing belt tensioner assembly - note spring hooked on pillar bolt (arrowed)

spring, which should be checked with great care as its condition is critical for the correct tensioning of the timing belt.

Refitting

Camshaft toothed pulley - K8 engine

52 On reassembly, refit the pulley so that the timing marks face outwards (to the right) and ensure that the pulley keyway engages with the camshaft roll pin.
53 Refit the pulley bolt and washer, hold the pulley with the tool used on dismantling and tighten the pulley bolt to the specified torque wrench setting. Check that the pulley timing marks align correctly.
54 Refit the timing belt, taking care not to twist it too sharply, then slacken the tensioner backplate screw and check that the tensioner pulley moves to tension the belt. If the tensioner assembly is not free to move under spring tension, rectify the fault or the timing belt will not be correctly tensioned.
55 Rotate the crankshaft two full turns clockwise to settle and tension the belt. Check that the timing marks are still aligned exactly.
56 The timing belt will now be tensioned correctly. Tighten the tensioner backplate screw, followed by the tensioner pulley Allen screw to their specified torque wrench settings (where given).
57 Refit the underwing shield then lower the car to the ground.
58 Refit the timing belt upper right-hand (outer) cover, re-route and secure the coolant hose, refit the spark plugs and the washer system reservoir. Re-connect the battery negative lead.

Camshaft toothed pulleys - K16 engine

59 On reassembly, refit each pulley so that the timing marks face outwards (to the right) and ensure that the appropriate pulley keyway engages with the camshaft roll pin (ie, if refitting the inlet camshaft toothed pulley, engage its "IN" keyway with the roll pin and so on) **(see illustration)**.
60 Refit the pulley bolt and washer, lock the pulleys with the tool used on dismantling and tighten the pulley bolt to the specified torque wrench setting. Check that the pulley timing marks align correctly then remove the locking tool.

2A

61 Refit the timing belt, taking care not to twist it too sharply, then slacken the tensioner backplate screw and check that the tensioner pulley moves to tension the belt. If the tensioner assembly is not free to move under spring tension, rectify the fault or the timing belt will not be correctly tensioned.
62 Rotate the crankshaft two full turns clockwise to settle and tension the belt. Check that the timing marks are still aligned exactly.
63 The timing belt will now be tensioned correctly. Tighten the tensioner backplate screw, followed by the tensioner pulley Allen screw to their specified torque wrench settings (where given).
64 Refit the underwing shield then lower the car to the ground.
65 Refit the timing belt upper right-hand (outer) cover, re-route and secure the coolant hose, refit the spark plugs and the washer system reservoir. Re-connect the battery negative lead.

Crankshaft toothed pulley

66 On reassembly, refit the pulley to the crankshaft so that the pulley locates correctly on the crankshaft's flattened section. The pulley's flange must be inboard so that the two timing marks can be seen from the right-hand side of the car. Check that the pulley timing marks align correctly.
67 Refit the timing belt, taking care not to twist it too sharply, then slacken the tensioner backplate screw and check that the tensioner pulley moves to tension the belt. If the tensioner assembly is not free to move under spring tension, rectify the fault or the timing belt will not be correctly tensioned.
68 On K16 engines, remove the camshaft toothed pulley locking tool.
69 On all engines, refit the timing belt lower cover and the alternator drive pulley.
70 Rotate the crankshaft two full turns clockwise to settle and tension the belt. Check that the timing marks are still aligned exactly.
71 The timing belt will now be tensioned correctly. Tighten the tensioner backplate screw, followed by the tensioner pulley Allen screw to their specified torque wrench settings (where given).
72 Refit the underwing shield then lower the car to the ground.
73 Refit the timing belt upper right-hand (outer) cover, re-route and secure the coolant hose, refit the spark plugs and the washer system reservoir. Re-connect the battery negative lead.

Tensioner assembly

74 On reassembly, loosely refit the tensioner assembly, hook the spring to its pillar bolt and tighten the pulley Allen screw and the backplate screw lightly. Check that the tensioner is free to move under spring tension and that the pulley bears correctly against the belt.
75 On K16 engines, remove the camshaft toothed pulley locking tool.
76 Rotate the crankshaft two full turns clockwise to settle and tension the belt. Check that the timing marks are still aligned exactly.
77 The timing belt will now be tensioned correctly. Tighten the tensioner backplate screw, followed by the tensioner pulley Allen screw, to their specified torque wrench settings.
78 Refit the underwing shield then lower the car to the ground.
79 Refit the timing belt upper right-hand (outer) cover, re-route and secure the coolant hose, refit the spark plugs and the washer system reservoir. Re-connect the battery negative lead.

13 Camshaft oil seal(s) - renewal

Note: *If an oil seal is renewed with the timing belt still in place, check that the belt is free from oil contamination. Renew the belt as a matter of course if signs of oil contamination are found. Cover the belt to protect it from contamination by oil while work is in progress and ensure that all traces of oil are removed from the area before the belt is refitted*

Right-hand seal - K8 engines

1 Remove the camshaft toothed pulley.
2 Punch or drill two small holes opposite each other in the oil seal. Screw a self-tapping screw into each and pull on the screws with pliers to extract the seal.
3 Clean the seal housing and polish off any burrs or raised edges which may have caused the seal to fail in the first place.
4 Lubricate the lips of the new seal with clean engine oil and drive it into position until it seats on its locating shoulder, using a suitable socket or tube. Take care not to damage the seal lips during fitting. Note that the seal lips should face inboard, to the left.
5 Refit the camshaft toothed pulley.

Left-hand seal - K8 fuel-injected engine only

6 Disconnect the battery negative lead.
7 Remove the distributor.
8 Punch or drill two small holes opposite each other in the seal. Screw a self-tapping screw into each and pull on the screws with pliers to extract the seal.
9 Clean the seal housing and polish off any burrs or raised edges which may have caused the seal to fail in the first place.
10 Lubricate the lips of the new seal with clean engine oil and drive it into position until it seats on its locating shoulder, using a suitable deep socket or tube. Take care not to damage the seal lips during fitting. Note that the seal lips should face inboard, to the right.
11 Refit the distributor.
12 Connect the battery negative lead.

13.16 Fitting a new camshaft right-hand oil seal - K16 engine

Right-hand seals - K16 engines

13 Remove the appropriate camshaft toothed pulley.
14 Punch or drill two small holes opposite each other in the seal. Screw a self-tapping screw into each and pull on the screws with pliers to extract the seal.
15 Clean the seal housing and polish off any burrs or raised edges which may have caused the seal to fail in the first place.
16 Lubricate the lips of the new seal with clean engine oil and drive it into position until it seats on its locating shoulder, using a suitable socket or tube **(see illustration)**. Take care not to damage the seal lips during fitting. Note that the seal lips should face inboard, to the left.
17 Refit the camshaft toothed pulley.

Left-hand seals - K16 engines

18 Disconnect the battery negative lead.
19 To reach the inlet camshaft seal, remove the distributor.
20 To reach the exhaust camshaft seal, unfasten the rubber strap securing the air inlet duct to its support bracket, disconnect the vacuum pipe from the air temperature control valve and unclip the pipe from the support bracket, then undo the bracket's retaining (hex-head) screws and remove the bracket from the cylinder head **(see illustration)**.
21 Punch or drill two small holes opposite each other in the seal. Screw a self-tapping screw into each and pull on the screws with pliers to extract the seal.

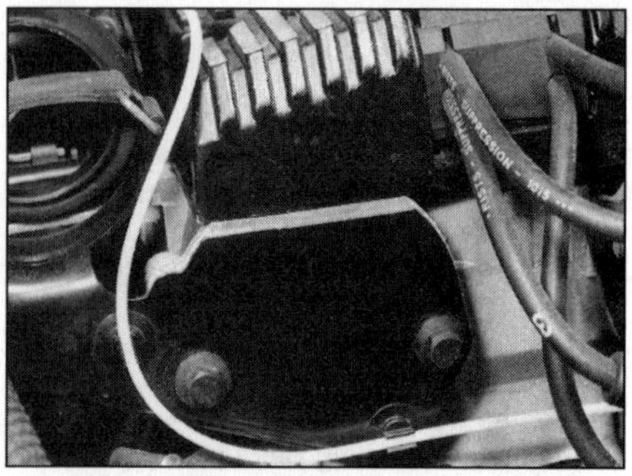

13.20 Remove air intake duct support bracket to reach exhaust camshaft left-hand oil seal - K16 engine

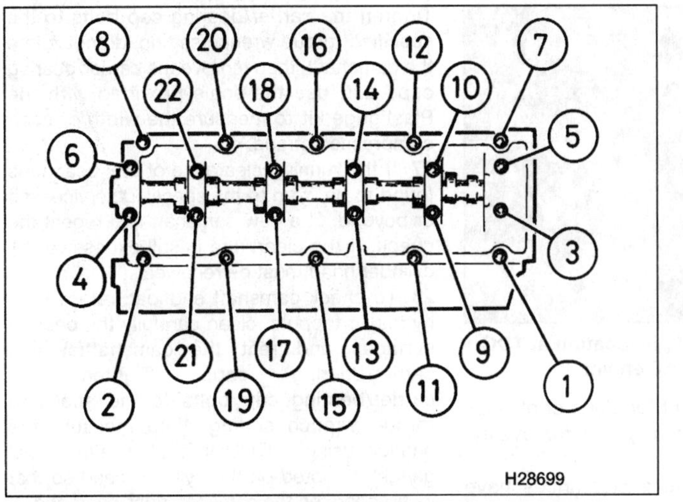

14.12 Camshaft carrier bolt loosening sequence - K8 engine

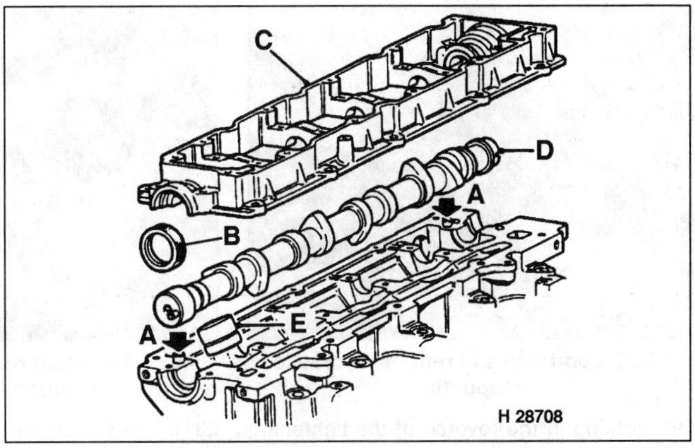

14.13 Camshaft carrier removal - K8 engine

A Locating dowels
B Oil seal
C Camshaft carrier
D Camshaft
E Hydraulic tappet

22 Clean the seal housing and polish off any burrs or raised edges which may have caused the seal to fail in the first place.

23 Lubricate the lips of the new seal with clean engine oil and drive it into position until it seats on its locating shoulder, using a suitable deep socket or tube. Take care not to damage the seal lips during fitting. Note that the seal lips should face inboard, to the right.

24 On the inlet camshaft, refit the distributor.

25 On the exhaust camshaft, refit the air inlet duct support bracket, tightening its screws to their specified torque wrench setting, then reconnect and secure the air temperature control valve vacuum pipe and refit the rubber strap to secure the air inlet duct.

26 Connect the battery negative lead.

14 Camshaft(s) and hydraulic tappets - removal, inspection and refitting

Removal

K8 engine - wet liner type

1 Remove the cylinder head cover.

2 Remove the distributor.

3 Either remove the timing belt from the camshaft toothed pulley so that the camshaft can be withdrawn complete with the pulley and oil seal, or remove the toothed pulley. The second course of action is preferable as the oil seal should be renewed whenever it is disturbed.

4 Carefully prise up the oil feed tube from the camshaft bearing caps and discard the sealing O-rings, which should be renewed whenever they are disturbed.

5 The camshaft right and left-hand end bearing caps are noticeably different and cannot be confused. The intermediate bearing caps (which are all similar) are marked by the manufacturer with a number (1, 2, 3, or 4) stamped in the boss next to the oil feed hole. Before unbolting any of the caps, make written notes to ensure that each can be easily identified and refitted in its original location.

6 Working in the reverse of the tightening sequence, slacken the camshaft bearing cap bolts progressively, and by one turn at a time. Work only as described to release the pressure of the valve springs on the bearing caps gradually and evenly.

7 Withdraw the bearing caps, noting the presence of the locating dowels on the end caps, then remove the camshaft and withdraw the oil seal(s).

8 Obtain eight small, clean plastic containers and number them 1 to 8. Using a rubber sucker, withdraw each hydraulic tappet in turn, invert it to prevent oil loss and place it in its respective container, which should then be filled with clean engine oil. Do not interchange the hydraulic tappets or the rate of wear will be much increased and do not allow them to lose oil or they will take a long time to refill with oil on restarting the engine, resulting in incorrect valve clearances.

K8 engine - damp liner type

9 Remove the camshaft cover.

10 Remove the distributor.

11 Either remove the timing belt from the camshaft toothed pulley so that the camshaft can be withdrawn complete with the pulley and oil seal, or remove the toothed pulley. The second course of action is preferable as the oil seal should be renewed whenever it is disturbed.

12 Working in the sequence shown **(see illustration)**, slacken the camshaft carrier retaining bolts progressively, and by one turn at a time to release the pressure of the valve springs on the bearing caps gradually and evenly.

13 Lift the camshaft carrier off its locating dowels, then remove the camshaft and withdraw the oil seal **(see illustration)**.

14 Obtain eight small, clean plastic containers and number them 1 to 8. Using a rubber sucker, withdraw each hydraulic tappet in turn, invert it to prevent oil loss and place it in its respective container, which should then be filled with clean engine oil. Do not interchange the hydraulic tappets or the rate of wear will be much increased and do not allow them to lose oil or they will take a long time to refill with oil on restarting the engine, resulting in incorrect valve clearances.

K16 engine

15 Remove the timing belt upper left-hand (inner) cover. If it is wished not to remove the timing belt, it is possible to remove both toothed pulleys and to unscrew the inner cover's upper retaining bolts so that the cover can be pulled away from the cylinder head just far enough for adequate working clearance. Take care not to distort or damage the cover or the timing belt **(see illustration)**.

16 Remove the cylinder head cover.

17 Remove the distributor.

18 Unclip the air temperature control valve vacuum pipe from the air inlet duct support bracket, then unbolt the bracket from the cylinder head.

14.15 Securing partly-removed timing belt upper left-hand (inner) cover clear of cylinder head

2A

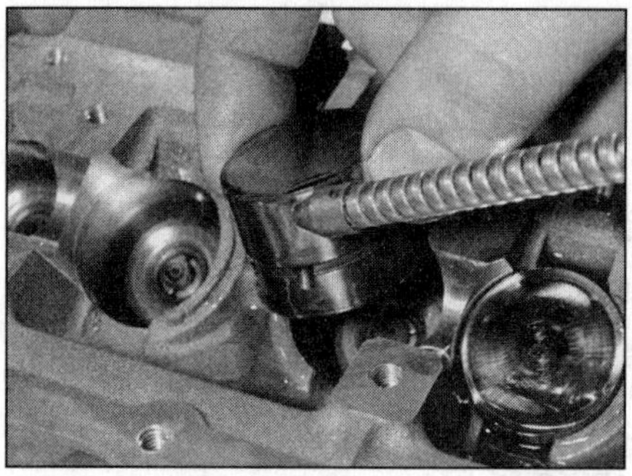

14.32 Lubricate and refit the hydraulic tappets

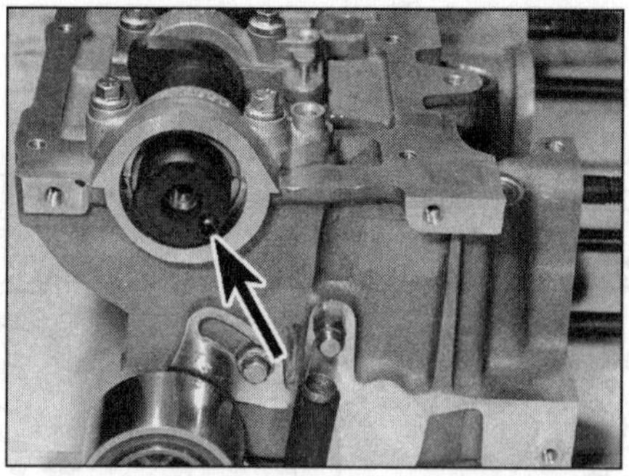

14.33 Camshaft roll pin location at TDC position - K8 engine

19 Working in the reverse of the tightening sequence, slacken the camshaft carrier bolts progressively and by one turn at a time. Work only as described to release the pressure of the valve springs on the carrier gradually and evenly.

20 Withdraw the camshaft carrier, noting the presence of the locating dowels, then remove the camshafts and withdraw their oil seals. The inlet camshaft can be identified by the distributor rotor arm drive spindle (or its location); therefore there is no need to mark the camshafts.

21 Obtain sixteen small, clean plastic containers and number them 1 to 16. Using a rubber sucker, withdraw each hydraulic tappet in turn, invert it to prevent oil loss and place it in its respective container, which should then be filled with clean engine oil. Do not interchange the hydraulic tappets or the rate of wear will be much increased and do not allow them to lose oil or they will take a long time to refill with oil on restarting the engine, resulting in incorrect valve clearances.

Inspection

22 Remove the camshaft(s) and tappets for inspection as described in the relevant sub-Section above.

23 Inspect each tappet for signs of obvious wear (scoring, pitting etc) and for ovality. Renew as necessary.

24 If the engine's valve clearances have sounded noisy, particularly if the noise persists after initial start-up from cold, there is reason to suspect a faulty hydraulic tappet. Only a good mechanic experienced in these engines can tell whether the noise level is typical, or if renewal is warranted of one or more of the tappets. If faulty tappets are diagnosed and the engine's service history is unknown, it is always worth trying the effect of renewing the engine oil and filter, using only good quality engine oil of the recommended viscosity and specification, before going to the expense of renewing any of the tappets. If any tappet operation is faulty, it must be renewed.

25 With the camshaft(s) removed, examine the camshaft bearing journals and the cylinder head bearing surfaces for signs of obvious wear or pitting. If any such signs are evident, renew the component concerned.

26 To check the bearing journal running clearance, remove the hydraulic tappets, clean carefully the bearing surfaces and refit the camshaft(s) and carrier/bearing caps with a strand of Plastigage across each journal. Tighten the carrier/bearing cap bolts to the specified torque wrench setting (do not rotate the camshaft), then remove the carrier/bearing caps and use the scale provided with the Plastigage kit to measure the width of each compressed strand.

27 If the running clearance of any bearing is found to be worn to the specified service limit or beyond, fit a new camshaft and repeat the check. If the clearance is still excessive the cylinder head must be renewed.

28 To check camshaft endfloat, remove the hydraulic tappets, clean carefully the bearing surfaces and refit the camshaft(s) and carrier/bearing caps. Tighten the carrier/bearing cap bolts to the specified torque wrench setting, then measure the endfloat using a DTI (Dial Test Indicator, or dial gauge) mounted on the cylinder head so that its tip bears on the camshaft right-hand end.

29 Tap the camshaft fully towards the gauge, zero the gauge, then tap the camshaft fully away from the gauge and note the gauge reading. If the endfloat measured is found to be worn to the specified service limit or beyond, fit a new camshaft and repeat the check. If the clearance is still excessive, the cylinder head must be renewed.

30 The camshaft itself should show no signs of marks, pitting or scoring on the lobe surfaces. If such marks are evident, renew the camshaft.

31 If a camshaft is renewed, extract the roll pin from the old one and fit the pin to the new camshaft with its split towards the camshaft's centre.

Refitting

K8 engine - wet liner type

32 On reassembly, liberally oil the cylinder head hydraulic tappet bores and the tappets. Note that if new tappets are being fitted, they must be charged with clean engine oil before installation. Carefully refit the tappets to the cylinder head, ensuring that each tappet is refitted to its original bore and is the correct way up **(see illustration)**. Some care will be required to enter the tappets squarely into their bores.

33 Liberally oil the camshaft bearings and lobes then refit the camshaft, rotating it so that number 1 cylinder lobes are pointing away from their valves and the roll pin in the camshaft's right-hand end is in the 4 o'clock position **(see illustration)**.

34 Ensure that the locating dowels are pressed firmly into their recesses, check that the mating surfaces are completely clean, unmarked and free from oil, then apply a thin bead of the special Rover sealant to the mating surfaces of the bearing caps at the points shown. Refer to illustration 14.35. Refit the bearing caps, using the notes made on removal to ensure that each is installed correctly and in its original location.

35 Working in the sequence shown **(see illustration)**, tighten slowly and by one turn at a time the camshaft bearing cap bolts until the

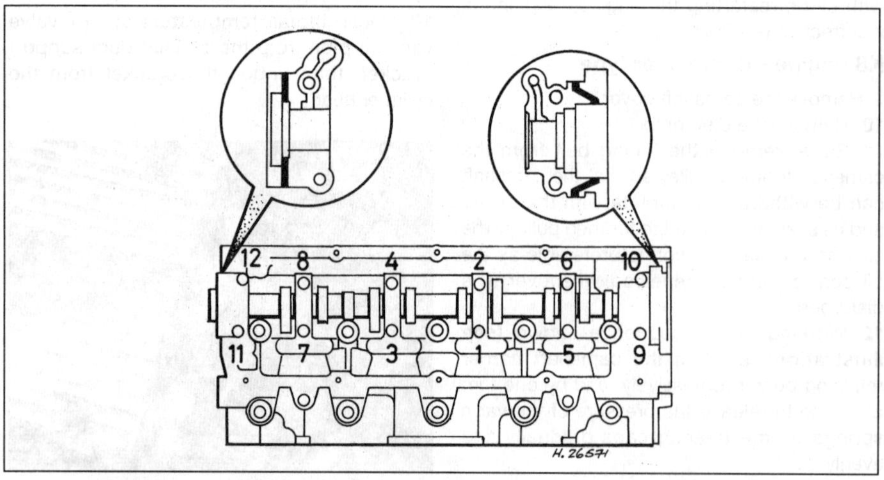

14.35 Camshaft bearing cap bolt tightening sequence - K8 engine
***Note:** Apply thin bead of the special Rover sealant to end bearing cap mating surfaces along paths shown by heavy black lines*

14.37 Fitting a new camshaft oil seal - K8 engine

caps touch the cylinder head evenly, then go round again, in the same sequence, tightening the bolts to the specified torque wrench setting. Work only as described to impose the pressure of the valve springs gradually and evenly on the bearing caps.

36 Wipe off all surplus sealant so that none is left to find its way into any oilways. Follow the sealant manufacturer's instructions as to the time needed for curing. Usually, at least an hour must be allowed between application of the sealant and the starting of the engine.

37 Fit new oil seal(s) **(see illustration)**.

38 Squirt clean engine oil into each camshaft bearing cap oil hole. Fitting new sealing O-rings to each of its stubs, refit the oil feed tube to the bearing caps, pressing it firmly into place **(see illustrations)**.

39 Refit the toothed pulley, if removed. Rotate the pulley until its timing marks align with the cylinder head top surface, then refit the timing belt.

40 Refit the distributor.

41 Refit the cylinder head cover.

K8 engine - damp liner type

42 On reassembly, liberally oil the cylinder head hydraulic tappet bores and the tappets. Note that if new tappets are being fitted, they must be charged with clean engine oil before installation. Carefully refit the tappets to the cylinder head, ensuring that each tappet is

14.38a Fill oil holes with clean oil - note cap identifying number (arrowed)

refitted to its original bore and is the correct way up. Some care will be required to enter the tappets squarely into their bores.

43 Liberally oil the camshaft bearings and lobes then refit the camshaft, rotating it so that number 1 cylinder lobes are pointing away from their valves and the roll pin in the camshaft's right-hand end is in the 4 o'clock position.

44 Ensure that the two locating dowels are pressed firmly into the camshaft carrier. Check that the mating surfaces of the carrier and head are completely clean, unmarked and free from oil, then apply a continuous bead of the recommended sealant to the paths on the mating surface of the carrier as shown **(see illustration)**. Spread the sealant to an even film using a brush or roller, taking care not to allow any to enter the lubrication grooves.

45 Refit the carrier to the cylinder head, pushing it firmly into position. Fit the carrier retaining bolts, finger-tight.

46 Lightly tighten the four bolts indicated **(see illustration)** and then working in the sequence shown, tighten the retaining bolts to the specified torque wrench setting so as to impose pressure of the valve springs gradually and evenly onto the bearing caps.

47 Carefully wipe off all surplus sealant so that none is left to find its way into any oilways. Follow the sealant manufacturer's instructions as to the time needed for curing.

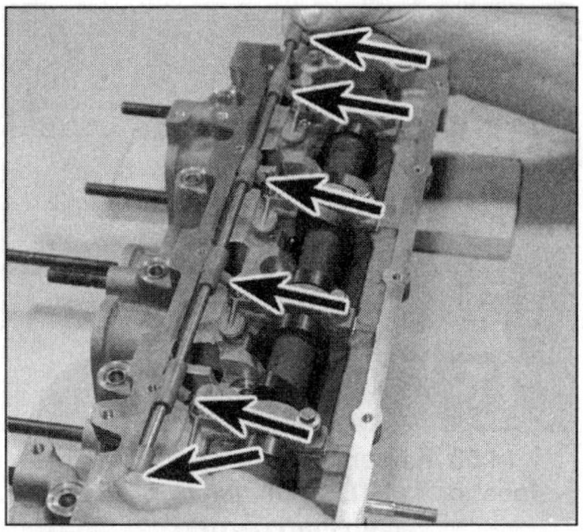

14.38b Renew O-rings (arrowed) before refitting oil feed tube

Usually, at least an hour must be allowed between application of the sealant and the starting of the engine.

48 Fit a new camshaft oil seal.

49 Refit the toothed pulley, if removed. Rotate the pulley until its timing marks align with the cylinder head top surface, then refit the timing belt.

50 Refit the distributor.

51 Refit the camshaft cover.

K16 engine

52 On reassembly, liberally oil the cylinder head hydraulic tappet bores and the tappets. Note that if new tappets are being fitted, they must be charged with clean engine oil before installation. Carefully refit the tappets to the cylinder head, ensuring that each tappet is refitted to its original bore and is the correct way up. Some care will be required to enter the tappets squarely into their bores.

53 Liberally oil the camshaft bearings and lobes. Ensuring that each camshaft is in its original location, refit the camshafts, rotating each so that the number 1 cylinder lobes are pointing away from their valves. The roll pin in the inlet camshaft's right-hand end must be in the 4 o'clock position, whilst that in the exhaust camshaft must be in the 8 o'clock position **(see illustration)**.

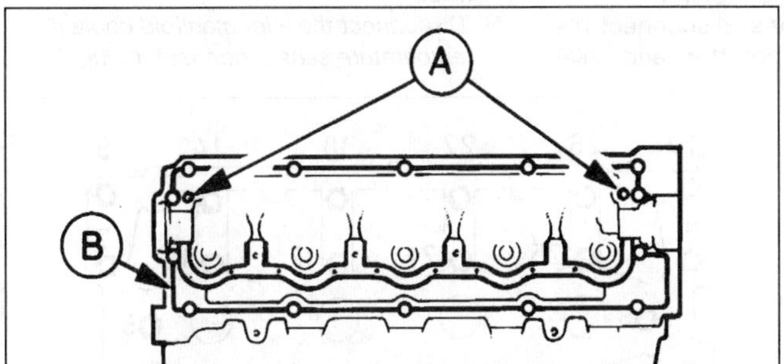

14.44 Application of sealant to camshaft carrier

A Locating dowels
B Continuous bead of sealant

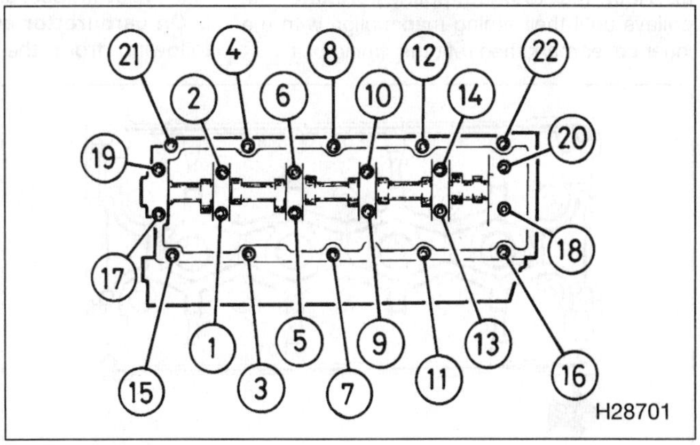

14.46 Camshaft carrier bolt tightening sequence

Note: *Lightly tighten bolts numbered 1, 2, 13 and 14 before tightening all bolts to specified torque loading*

14.53 K16 engine camshaft roll pin locations at TDC position (for refitting camshaft carrier)

54 Ensure that the locating dowels are pressed firmly into their recesses, check that the mating surfaces are completely clean, unmarked and free from oil, then apply a thin bead of the special Rover sealant sealant to the mating surfaces of the carrier as shown **(see illustration)**. Refit the carrier.

55 Working in the sequence shown **(see illustration)**, tighten slowly and by one turn at a time the camshaft carrier bolts until the carrier touches the cylinder head evenly, then go round again, in the same sequence, tightening the bolts to the specified torque wrench setting. Work only as described to impose the pressure of the valve springs gradually and evenly on the carrier.

56 Wipe off all surplus sealant so that none is left to find its way into any oilways. Follow the sealant manufacturer's instructions as to the time needed for curing. Usually, at least an hour must be allowed between application of the sealant and the starting of the engine.

57 Fit new oil seals.

58 Refit the cylinder head cover.

59 Refit the distributor.

60 Refit the air inlet duct support bracket, tightening its screws to their specified torque wrench setting, then reconnect and secure the air temperature control valve vacuum pipe and refit the rubber strap to secure the air inlet duct.

61 Refit the timing belt upper left-hand (inner) cover.

62 Refit the toothed pulleys. Rotate the pulleys until their timing marks align with the inner cover mark then refit the timing belt.

15 Cylinder head - removal and refitting

Caution: Before commencing any servicing or overhaul work on the engine, the crankshaft must always be rotated to the desired position before the cylinder head bolts are disturbed.

Note: *Due to the design of the engine, it will become very difficult, almost impossible, to turn the crankshaft once the cylinder head bolts have been slackened. The manufacturer accordingly states that the crankshaft will be "tight" and should not be rotated more than absolutely necessary once the head has been removed. If the crankshaft cannot be rotated then it must be removed for overhaul work to proceed. With this in mind, during any servicing or overhaul work the crankshaft must always be rotated to the desired position before the bolts are disturbed.*

Removal

1 Disconnect the battery negative lead.

2 Drain the cooling system.

3 Remove the camshaft toothed pulley(s).

4 Unscrew the bolts securing the timing belt upper left-hand (inner) cover to the cylinder head so that the cover can be pulled away from the cylinder head just far enough for adequate working clearance. Take care not to distort or damage the cover or the timing belt.

5 Remove the cylinder head or camshaft cover, as appropriate.

6 Disconnect the exhaust system front pipe from the manifold and where fitted, disconnect or release the lambda sensor wiring so that it is not strained by the weight of the exhaust.

7 Note that the following text assumes that the cylinder head will be removed with both inlet and exhaust manifolds attached. This is easier, but makes it a bulky and heavy assembly to handle. If it is wished first to remove the manifolds, proceed as described in the relevant Sections of Chapter 4.

8 **On carburettor engines,** disconnect the following from the carburettor and inlet manifold as described in the relevant sections of Chapter 4:

a) *Fuel pump feed hose (plug both openings to prevent loss of fuel and the entry of dirt into the system).*
b) *Carburettor idle bypass solenoid wires.*
c) *Throttle cable.*
d) *Choke cable.*
e) *Vacuum servo unit vacuum hose.*
f) *Inlet manifold PTC heater wire.*
g) *Inlet manifold heater temperature switch wiring.*

9 **On single-point fuel-injected engines,** carry out the following operations as described in the relevant sections of Chapter 4:

a) *K8 engines - disconnect the fuel trap vacuum hoses from the air cleaner assembly (if not already disconnected).*
b) *K16 engines - remove the air cleaner assembly.*
c) *Disconnect (where fitted) the charcoal canister purge control valve hose from the throttle body.*
d) *Depressurise the fuel system and disconnect the fuel feed and return hoses from the throttle body pipes - plug both openings of each pipe to prevent loss of fuel and the entry of dirt into the system.*
e) *Disconnect the throttle cable.*
f) *Disconnect the three connector plugs from the throttle body.*
g) *Disconnect the vacuum servo unit vacuum hose from the inlet manifold; discard the sealing washers.*
h) *Disconnect the inlet manifold PTC heater wire.*
i) *Disconnect the inlet manifold coolant temperature sensor connector plug.*

10 **On multi-point fuel-injected engines,** carry out the following operations as described in the relevant sections of Chapter 4:

a) *Remove the throttle housing assembly.*
b) *Depressurise the fuel system and remove the fuel rail assembly.*
c) *Disconnect the vacuum servo unit vacuum hose from the inlet manifold.*
d) *Disconnect the inlet manifold PTC heater wire.*
e) *Disconnect the inlet manifold coolant temperature sensor connector plug.*

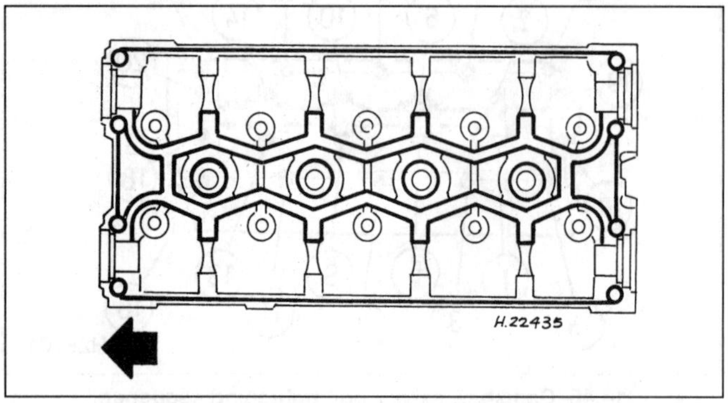

14.54 Apply thin bead of sealant to camshaft carrier mating surface along paths shown by heavy black lines - K16 engine

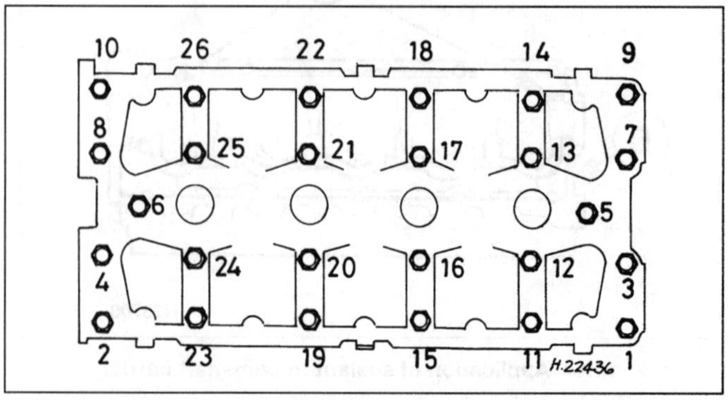

14.55 Camshaft carrier bolt tightening sequence - K16 engine

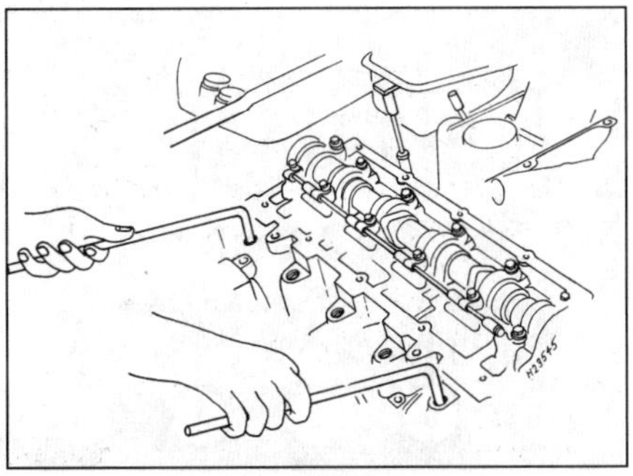

15.16 Using two cranked bars to break cylinder head-to-cylinder block/crankcase joint by rocking

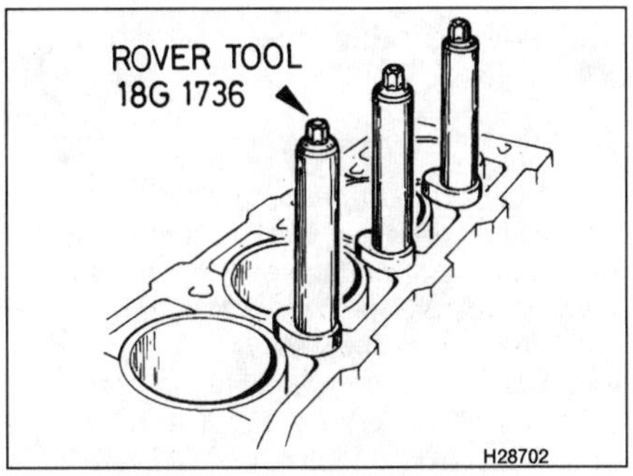

15.18 Use of cylinder liner clamps

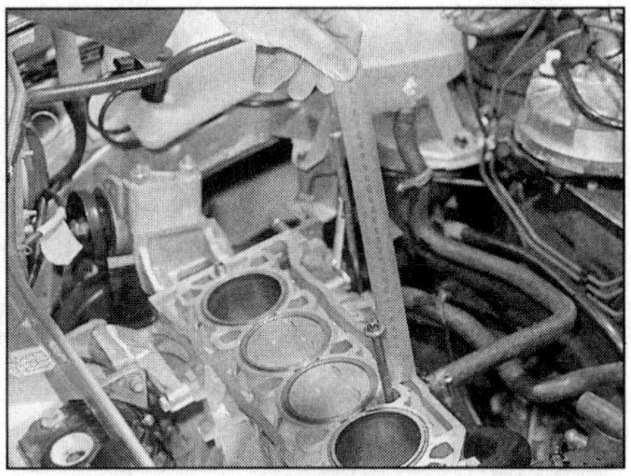

15.20 Checking condition of cylinder head bolt threads - cylinder head removed

11 Working as described in the relevant Sections of Chapter 3, disconnect the connector plug from the coolant temperature sensor screwed into the coolant outlet elbow, then disconnect the coolant hoses from the (three) inlet manifold unions and from the coolant outlet elbow.

12 Unclip the engine wiring harness from the inlet manifold or its support stays, slacken the bolts securing the stays to the manifold, then unbolt the support stays and the carburettor metal overflow pipes from the cylinder block/crankcase.

13 Remove the distributor cap and place it, with the spark plug HT leads, clear of the working area.

14 Working in the reverse of the appropriate sequence shown for tightening, slacken progressively and by one turn at a time the ten cylinder head bolts. A female Torx-type socket (No. 12 size) will be required. Remove each bolt in turn and store it in its correct fitted order by pushing it through a clearly-marked cardboard template.

15 The joint between the cylinder head and gasket and the cylinder block/crankcase must now be broken without disturbing the cylinder liners. Although these liners are better located and sealed than some types, there is still a risk of coolant and foreign matter leaking into the sump if the cylinder head is lifted carelessly. If care is not taken and the liners are moved, there is a possibility of the their seals being disturbed, causing leakage after refitting the head.

16 To break the joint, obtain two L-shaped metal bars which fit into the cylinder head bolt holes and gently rock the cylinder head free towards the front of the car **(see illustration)**. Do not try to swivel the head on the cylinder block/crankcase as it is located by dowels as well as by the tops of the liners.

17 When the joint is broken lift the cylinder head away. Use assistance if possible as it is a heavy assembly, especially if it is complete with the manifolds. Remove the gasket and discard it, noting the two dowels.

18 Note that further to the warnings given in the note at the beginning of this Section, **do not** attempt to rotate the crankshaft with the cylinder head removed, otherwise the liners may be displaced. Operations that require the rotation of the crankshaft (eg. cleaning the piston crowns) can be carried out after fitting cylinder liner clamps. The maker's liner clamps are secured by the cylinder head bolts as shown **(see illustration)**; equivalents can be improvised using large washers and tubular spacers.

19 If the cylinder head is to be dismantled, remove the camshaft(s) then refer to the relevant Sections of Part B of this Chapter.

Refitting

20 Check the condition of the cylinder head bolts and particularly their threads whenever they are removed. Keeping all the bolts in their correct fitted order, wash them and wipe dry, then check each for any sign of visible wear or damage, renewing any bolt if necessary. Lightly oil the threads of each bolt, carefully enter it into its original hole and screw it in, by hand only until finger-tight. Measure the distance from the cylinder block/crankcase gasket surface to under the bolt's head **(see illustration)**.

21 If the distance measured is under 97 mm, the bolt may be re-used. If the distance measured is more than 97 mm, the bolt must be renewed. Considering the task these bolts perform and the pressures they must withstand, owners should consider renewing all the bolts as a matched set if more than one of the originals fail inspection or are close to the limit set.

22 The mating faces of the cylinder head and cylinder block/crankcase must be perfectly clean before refitting the head. Use a hard plastic or wood scraper to remove all traces of gasket and carbon. Also clean the piston crowns. Take particular care as the soft aluminium alloy is damaged easily. Also, make sure that the carbon is not allowed to enter the oil and water passages - this is particularly important for the lubrication system, as carbon could block the oil supply to any of the engine's components. Using adhesive tape and paper, seal the water, oil and bolt holes in the cylinder block/crankcase. To prevent carbon entering the gap between the pistons and bores, smear a little grease in the gap. After cleaning each piston, use a small brush to remove all traces of grease and carbon from the gap, then wipe away the remainder with a clean rag. Clean all the pistons in the same way.

23 Check the mating surfaces of the cylinder block/crankcase and the cylinder head for nicks, deep scratches and other damage. If slight, they may be removed carefully with a file, but if excessive, machining may be the only alternative to renewal.

24 If warpage is suspected of the cylinder head gasket surface, use a straight-edge to check it for distortion. Refer to Part B of this Chapter if necessary.

25 Wipe clean the mating surfaces of the cylinder head and cylinder block/crankcase. Check that the two locating dowels are in position at each end of the cylinder block/crankcase surface.

26 Position a new gasket on the cylinder block/crankcase surface so that the "TOP" mark is uppermost and the "FRONT" arrow points to the timing belt end **(see illustrations)**.

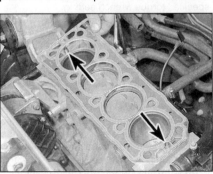

15.26a Fit new cylinder head gasket on two locating dowels (arrowed) . . .

15.26b . . . so that TOP mark is upwards and FRONT arrow points to timing belt end

15.27 Refitting the cylinder head

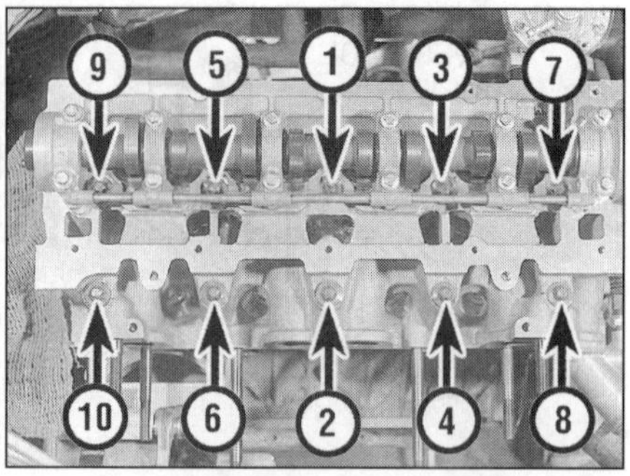

15.29a Cylinder head bolt tightening sequence - K8 engine

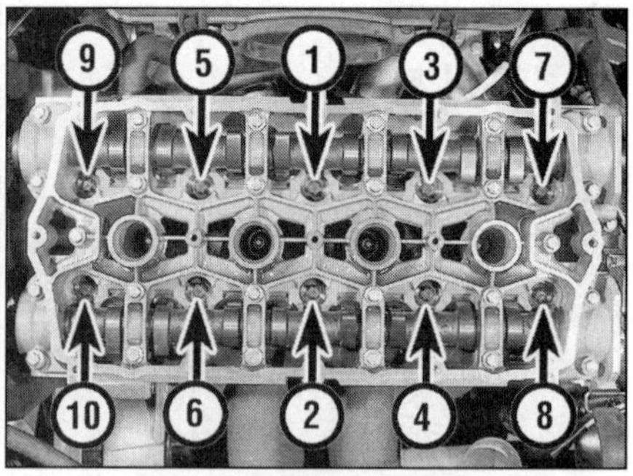

15.29b Cylinder head bolt tightening sequence - K16 engine

27 Refit the cylinder head, locating it on the dowels **(see illustration)**.

28 Keeping all the cylinder head bolts in their correct fitted order, wash them and wipe dry, then lightly oil under the head and on the threads of each bolt, carefully enter it into its original hole and screw it in, by hand only until finger-tight.

29 Working progressively and in the appropriate sequence shown, use first a torque wrench, then an ordinary socket extension bar to tighten the cylinder head bolts in the stages given in the Specifications Section of this Chapter. To tighten the bolts through the angles specified, simply use a felt-tip pen or similar to mark the position on the cylinder head of each bolt head's radial mark. The second stage then tightens each bolt through half a turn so that the marks face away from each other and the third stage tightens them through another half-turn so that all the bolt-head marks will then align again with their cylinder head counterparts. If any bolt is overtightened past its mark, slacken it through 90°, then re-tighten until the marks align **(see illustrations)**.

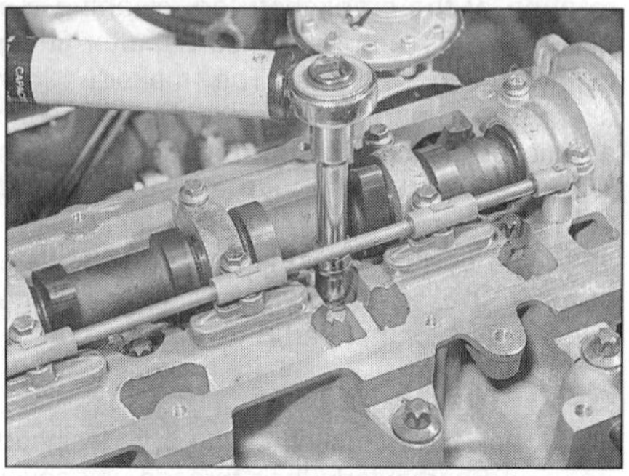

15.29c Tightening cylinder head bolts - first stage . . .

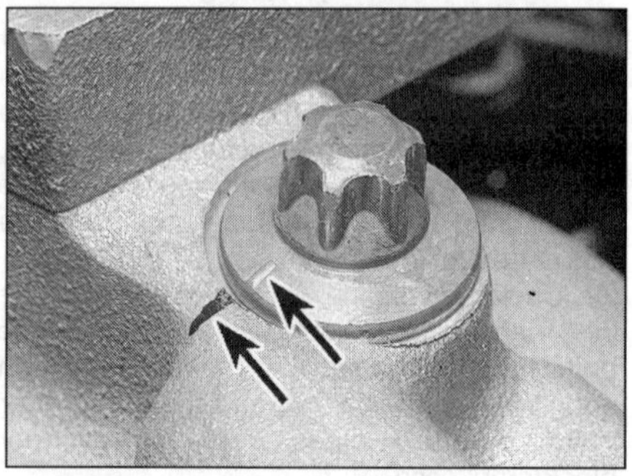

15.29d . . . second and third stages use alignment of bolt head radial marks with cylinder head to establish angles (arrowed)

30 Refit and tighten the inlet manifold support stay bolts, then secure the engine wiring harness using the clips provided.

31 Connect all coolant hoses and refill the cooling system, then reconnect the coolant temperature sensor wiring.

32 Working as described in the relevant Sections of Chapter 4, connect or refit all disturbed wiring, hoses and control cable(s) to the inlet manifold and fuel system components, refit the air cleaner assembly (where appropriate), then adjust the cable(s).

33 Reconnect the exhaust system front pipe to the manifold and (if applicable) reconnect the lambda sensor wiring.

34 Refit the cylinder head cover.

35 Refit the timing belt upper left-hand (inner) cover and the toothed pulley(s).

36 Refit the spark plugs and distributor cap.

37 Connect the battery negative lead.

16 Sump - removal and refitting

Removal

1 Disconnect the battery negative lead.

2 Drain the engine oil, then clean and refit the engine oil drain plug, tightening it to the specified torque wrench setting.

3 Although this is not necessary as part of the dismantling procedure, owners are advised to remove and discard the oil filter so that it can be renewed with the oil.

4 Raise the front of the car and support it on axle stands (see *"Jacking and Vehicle Support"*).

5 Disconnect the exhaust system front pipe from the manifold and where fitted, disconnect or release the lambda sensor wiring so that it is not strained by the weight of the exhaust.

6 Unscrew its three (hex-head) retaining screws and remove the flywheel lower cover plate **(see illustration)**.

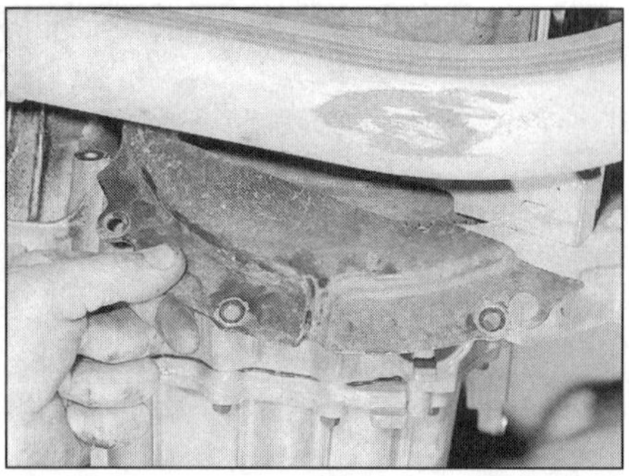

16.6 Remove flywheel lower cover plate to reach sump screws

7 Progressively slacken, then remove the sump (hex-head) retaining bolts. If the sump is the pressed steel type, then the bolts must be renewed.

8 Break the joint by striking the sump with the palm of the hand or a soft-headed mallet, then lower the sump and withdraw it **(see illustration)**.

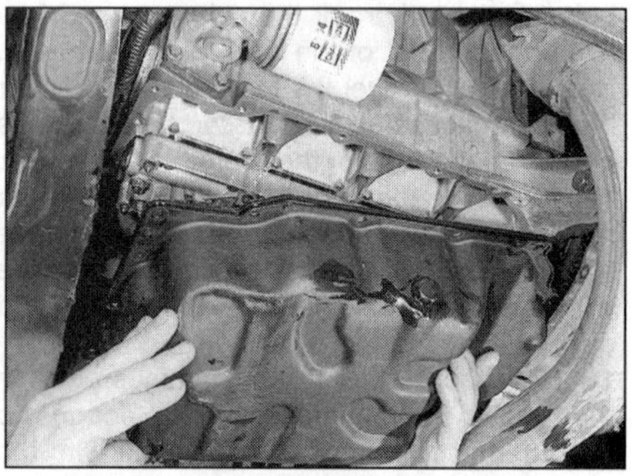

16.8 Removing the sump (pressed steel type)

9 With the sump removed, take the opportunity to unbolt the oil pump pick-up/strainer pipe and clean it - see the relevant Sections of Part B of this Chapter.

Refitting

10 If the oil pump pick-up/strainer pipe has been removed, fit a new O-ring to its end and refit the pipe, tightening its retaining (hex-head) screws to the specified torque wrench setting.

16.12 Sump gasket pegs must engage with sump mating surface holes (pressed steel type)

11 Clean the mating surfaces of the cylinder block/crankcase and sump, then use a clean rag to wipe out the sump and the engine's interior.

Pressed steel sump

12 If the sump gasket is damaged or shows signs of deterioration it must be renewed, otherwise it can be reused. Fit the gasket to the sump mating surface so that its 7 locating pegs fit into the sump holes **(see illustration)**.

13 Offer up the sump to the cylinder block/crankcase and insert the new bolts, tightening them hand-tight at first. Note that early engines will have M6 type bolts fitted, whereas later engines will have M8 type bolts. If in doubt as to the correct type of bolt, consult your Rover dealer. Where an anti-beaming bracket support is fitted, fit and hand-tighten its three retaining bolts.

14 Working in the sequence shown **(see illustration)**, tighten the sump retaining bolts to the specified torque wrench setting.

Alloy sump

15 Apply a continuous 2.0 mm wide by 0.25 mm thick bead of Hylogrip 2000 sealant to the sump mating surface, passing inside the bolt holes, then spread the sealant to an even film using a brush or roller.

16 Make two alignment pins using lengths of M8 studding or by cutting the heads off two M8 bolts. Fit the pins in the positions shown **(see illustration)** before carefully placing the sump over them and pressing it firmly into position.

17 Fit two bolts into the positions shown and tighten them to 4 Nm.

18 Insert the remaining bolts, tightening them hand-tight. Note that the rearmost holes in the sump must contain the M8 x 20 bolts.

19 Remove the alignment pins and fit the remaining two bolts.

20 Using a straight-edge, check that the machined face of the sump flange is level with the rear face of the cylinder block. Carry out this check in three positions, tapping the sump gently to reposition it if necessary.

21 Working in the sequence shown **(see illustration)**, tighten the sump retaining bolts to the specified torque wrench setting.

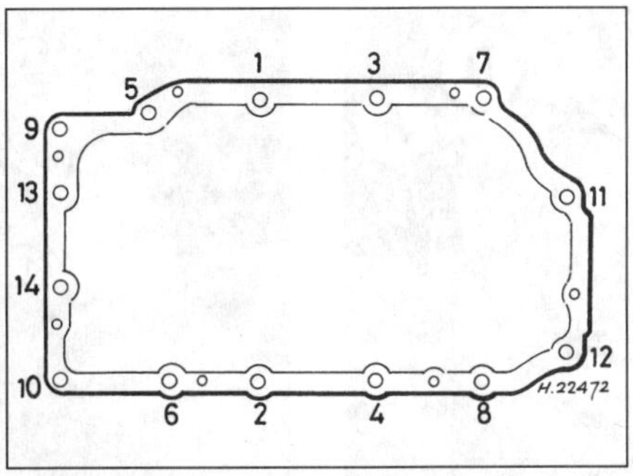

16.14 Sump screw tightening sequence (pressed steel type)

Both types

22 Refit the flywheel lower cover plate and tighten its screws to the specified torque wrench setting.

23 Reconnect the exhaust system front pipe to the manifold and (if applicable) reconnect the lambda sensor wiring.

24 Fit a new oil filter (if applicable) and refill the engine with oil.

25 Connect the battery negative lead.

17 Oil pump - removal and refitting

Note: *The oil pressure relief valve can be dismantled, if required, without removing the oil pump from the car.*

Removal

1 Remove the crankshaft toothed pulley and secure the timing belt clear of the working area so that it cannot be contaminated with oil.

2 Drain the engine oil.

3 Although this is not necessary as part of the dismantling procedure, owners are advised to remove and discard the oil filter so that it can be renewed with the oil.

4 Unscrew the alternator adjuster link retaining nut and unbolt the engine wiring harness guide retaining screws, then move the link and guide clear of the oil pump **(see illustration)**.

5 Unscrew the oil pump retaining bolt and screws and withdraw the oil pump. Recover and discard the gasket. The crankshaft right-hand oil seal should be renewed whenever it is disturbed. If desired, the pump can be dismantled and inspected.

6 Whenever the oil pump is overhauled or renewed, the pump pick-up/ strainer pipe should be cleaned.

Refitting

7 Thoroughly clean the mating faces of the oil pump and cylinder block/crankcase. Use a thin smear of grease to stick the new gasket in place.

2A

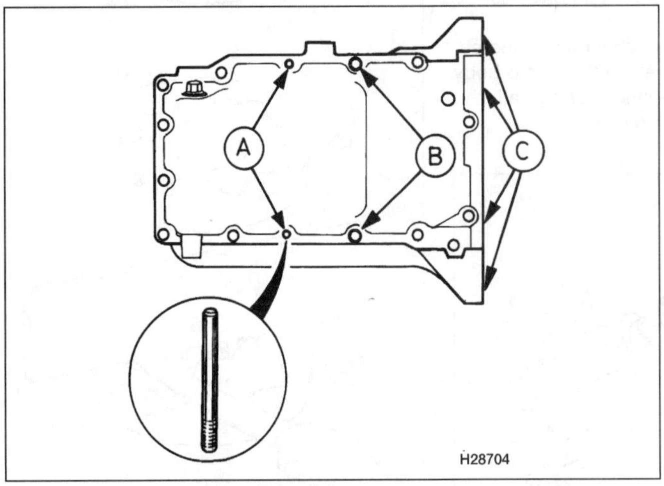

16.16 Fitting an alloy sump

A Alignment pin location
B Initial 2 bolt fitting - torque loading to 4 Nm
C Sump flange to cylinder block rear face alignment

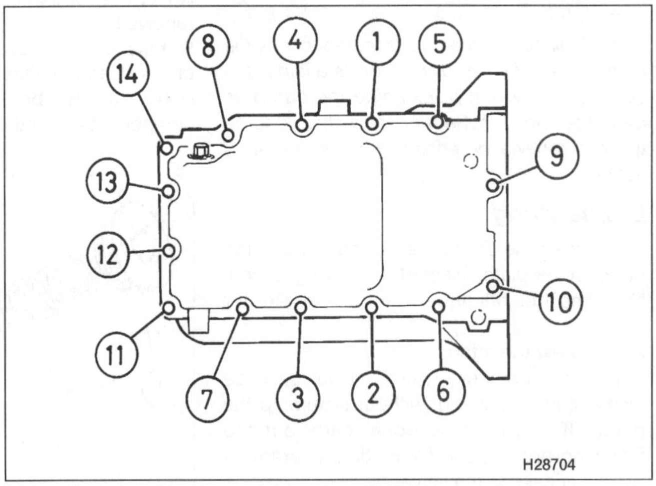

16.21 Sump bolt tightening sequence (alloy type)

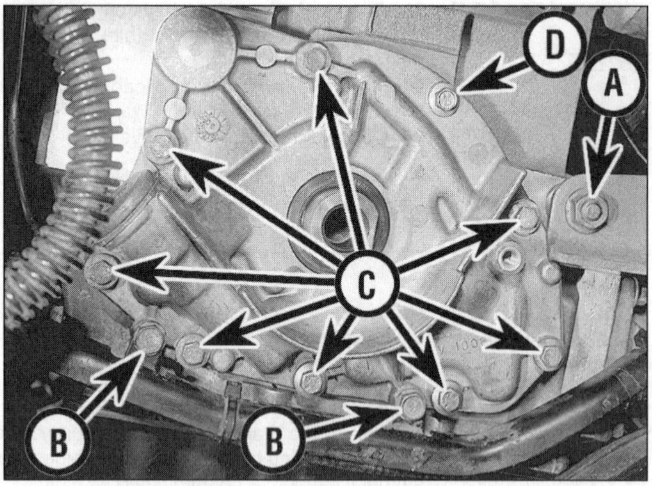

17.4 Alternator link nut (A) wiring guide screws (B) oil pump screws (C) and oil pump bolt (D)

18.4a Unscrewing oil pressure relief valve threaded plug in vehicle

8 Note that whether the original pump is refitted or a new pump is installed, it is essential that the pump is primed before installation by injecting oil into it and turning it by hand.

9 Refit the pump, ensuring that its inner gear engages fully on the crankshaft flats, then push the pump into place.

10 Refit the retaining bolt and screws, tightening them to the specified torque wrench setting.

11 Refit the alternator adjuster link and the engine wiring harness guide, then tighten securely the retaining nut and screws.

12 Fit a new crankshaft right-hand oil seal.

13 Wash off any traces of oil, then refit the crankshaft toothed pulley and the timing belt.

18 Oil pump - dismantling, inspection and reassembly

Note: *If oil pump wear is suspected, check the cost and availability of new parts against the cost of a new pump. Examine the pump as described in this Section and then decide whether renewal or repair is the best course of action.*

Dismantling

1 Unscrew the Torx screws and remove the pump cover plate. Discard the sealing O-ring. Note the identification marks on the outer rotor.

2 Withdraw the rotors.

3 The oil pressure relief valve can be dismantled, if required, without disturbing the pump. If this is to be done, carry out the following preliminary dismantling operations to gain access to the valve.

a) Raise the front right-hand side of the car and support it on an axle stand, then remove the roadwheel.

b) Remove the underwing shield.

4 To dismantle the valve, unscrew the threaded plug and recover the valve spring and plunger, noting their fitted positions **(see illustrations)**. Discard the plug sealing washer.

Inspection

5 Inspect the rotors for obvious signs of wear or damage and renew if necessary. If the pump body or cover plate are scored or damaged, the complete oil pump assembly must be renewed.

6 Using feeler blades of the appropriate thickness, measure the clearance between the outer rotor and the pump body ("A") and between the tips of the inner and outer rotor lobes ("B") **(see illustration)**.

7 Using feeler blades and a straight-edge placed across the top of the pump body and the rotors("C" in illustration 18.6) , measure the rotor endfloat.

8 If any measurement is outside the specified limits, the complete pump assembly must be renewed.

9 If the pressure relief valve plunger is scored, or if it does not slide freely in the pump body bore, it must be renewed, using all the components from the repair kit.

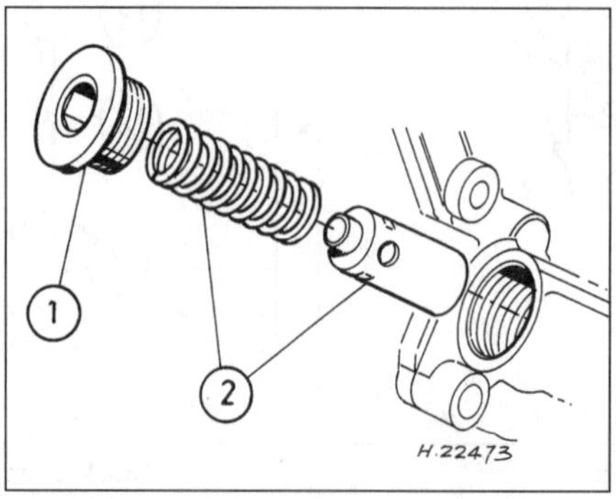

18.4b Oil pressure relief valve components
1 Threaded plug
2 Valve spring and plunger

Reassembly

10 Lubricate the rotors with clean engine oil and refit them to the pump body, ensuring that the outer rotor's identification mark faces outwards **(see illustration)**.

11 Fitting a new O-ring, refit the cover plate. Apply thread-locking compound to their threads and refit the cover plate Torx screws, tightening them securely.

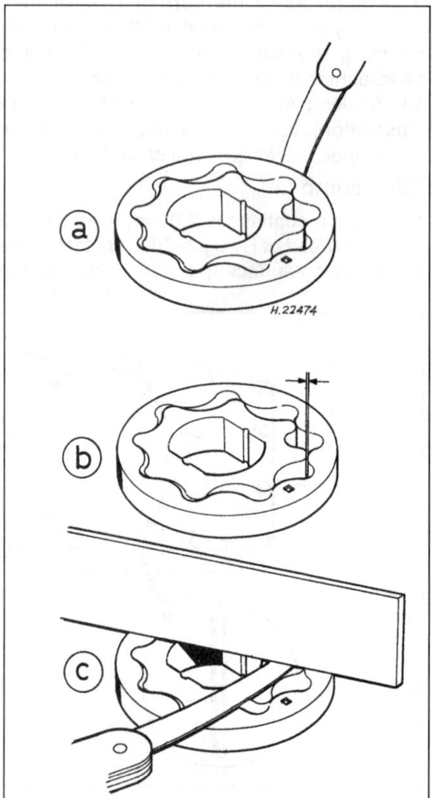

18.6 Checking oil pump rotors for wear - see text for details

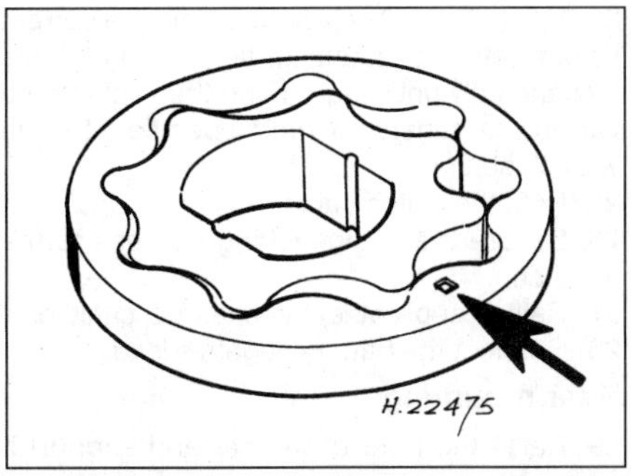

18.10 Oil pump outer rotor outside face identifying mark (arrowed)

12 Check that the pump rotates freely, then prime it by injecting oil into its passages and rotating it. If a long time elapses before the pump is refitted to the engine, prime it again before installation.
13 When reassembling the oil pressure relief valve, ensure that the plunger is refitted the correct way up. Fit a new sealing washer and tighten the threaded plug securely.

19 Crankshaft oil seals - renewal

Right-hand oil seal

1 Remove the crankshaft toothed pulley and secure the timing belt clear of the working area so that it cannot be contaminated with oil.
2 Punch or drill two small holes opposite each other in the seal. Screw a self-tapping screw into each and pull on the screws with pliers to extract the seal.
3 Clean the seal housing and polish off any burrs or raised edges which may have caused the seal to fail in the first place.
4 Lubricate the lips of the new seal with clean engine oil and drive it into position until it seats on its locating shoulder, using a suitable socket or tube. Take care not to damage the seal lips during fitting. Use either grease or a thin layer of insulating tape to protect the seal lips from the edges of the crankshaft flats, but be careful to remove all traces of tape and to lubricate the seal lips if the second method is used. Note that the seal lips should face inboard, to the left.
5 Wash off any traces of oil, then refit the crankshaft toothed pulley and timing belt.

Left-hand oil seal

6 Remove the flywheel.
7 Taking care not to mark either the crankshaft or any part of the cylinder block/crankcase, lever the seal evenly out of its housing.
8 Clean the seal housing and polish off any burrs or raised edges which may have caused the seal to fail in the first place.
9 Lubricate with grease the lips of the new seal and the crankshaft shoulder, then offer up the seal to the cylinder block/crankcase.
10 Feeding the seal's lips over the crankshaft shoulder by hand only, press the seal evenly into its housing and use a soft-faced mallet to tap it gently into place until its outer flange seats evenly on the housing lip.
11 Wash off any traces of oil, then refit the flywheel.

20 Flywheel - removal, inspection and refitting

Removal

1 Remove the transmission.
2 Remove the clutch.
3 Prevent the flywheel from turning by locking the ring gear teeth, or by bolting a strap between the flywheel and the cylinder block/crankcase.
4 Unscrew the bolts and discard them; they must be renewed whenever they are disturbed.
5 Withdraw the flywheel. Do not drop it, it is very heavy.

Inspection

6 If the flywheel's clutch mating surface is deeply scored, cracked or otherwise damaged, the flywheel must be renewed, unless it is possible to have it surface ground. Seek the advice of a Rover dealer or engine reconditioning specialist.
7 If the ring gear is badly worn or has missing teeth it must be renewed, but this job is best left to a Rover dealer or engine reconditioning specialist. The temperature to which the new ring gear must be heated for installation (350°C, shown by an even light blue colour) is critical and, if not done accurately, the hardness of the teeth will be destroyed.
8 If the reluctor ring is damaged, it must be renewed.

Refitting

9 Clean the mating surfaces of the flywheel and crankshaft. Clean any remaining adhesive from the threads of the crankshaft threaded holes by making two saw cuts at opposite points along the (carefully-cleaned) threads of one of the original flywheel bolts and screwing it into each hole in turn. Do not use a tap to clean the threads in this way.
10 Position the flywheel over the crankshaft's locating dowel, press it into place and fit six new bolts.
11 Lock the flywheel by the method used on dismantling and tighten the bolts to the specified torque wrench setting.
12 Refit the clutch then remove the locking tool.
13 Refit the transmission.

21 Engine/transmission mountings - inspection and renewal

Inspection

1 If improved access is required, raise the front of the car and support it securely on axle stands (see "*Jacking and Vehicle Support*").
2 Check the mounting rubber to see if it is cracked, hardened or separated from the metal at any point. Renew the mounting if any such damage or deterioration is evident.
3 Check that all the mounting's fasteners are securely tightened; using a torque wrench to check if possible.
4 Using a large screwdriver or a pry bar, check for wear in the mounting by carefully levering against it to check for free play. Where this is not possible, enlist the aid of an assistant to move the engine/transmission back and forth or from side to side while you watch the mounting. While some free play is to be expected even from new components, excessive wear should be obvious. If excessive free play is found, check first that the fasteners are correctly secured, then renew any worn components as described below.

Renewal

Right-hand mounting

5 Disconnect the battery negative lead.
6 Remove its three retaining screws and move the washer system reservoir clear of the working area. Disconnect the pump wiring connector plug(s) if the extra reach is required.
7 Unclip the expansion tank coolant hose from the bonnet lock platform and secure it clear of the working area.
8 Support the weight of the engine/transmission using a trolley jack (with a wooden spacer to prevent damage to the sump) then unscrew the mounting through-bolt and nut and the mounting-to-bracket nuts. Remove the mounting, noting the two rubber washers **(see illustrations)**.

21.8a Use trolley jack with wooden spacer to adjust height of engine/transmission unit while mountings are renewed

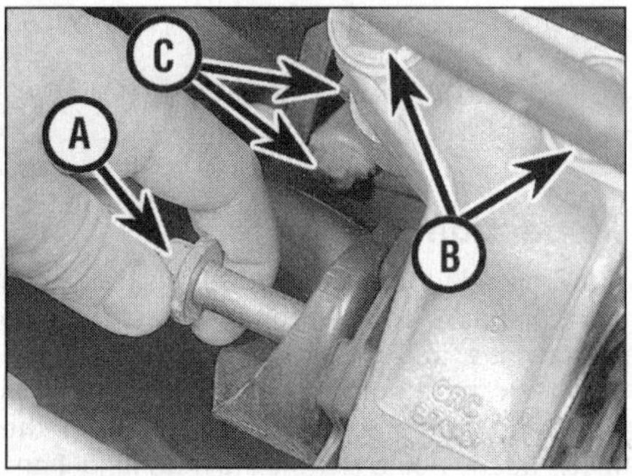

21.8b Right-hand mounting through-bolt (A) mounting-to-bracket nuts (B) and bracket-to-cylinder block/crankcase bolts (two arrowed - C)

9 Where necessary, unscrew also the retaining bolts and remove the bracket from the cylinder block/crankcase.

10 Check carefully for signs of wear or damage all components and renew them where necessary.

11 On reassembly, refit the bracket to the cylinder block/crankcase and tighten its bolts to the specified torque wrench setting.

12 Locate the rubber washers on the mounting, one on each side of its centre boss, then refit it to the bracket and tighten the retaining nuts finger-tight.

13 Using the trolley jack to obtain the correct height, refit from rear to front the mounting-to-body through-bolt, check that the rubber washers are correctly seated and refit the nut **(see illustration)**.

14 Tighten to their specified torque wrench settings the mounting-to-bracket nuts and the through-bolt retaining nut, then lower and remove the jack.

15 Re-route and secure the coolant hose, refit the washer system reservoir, then connect the battery negative lead.

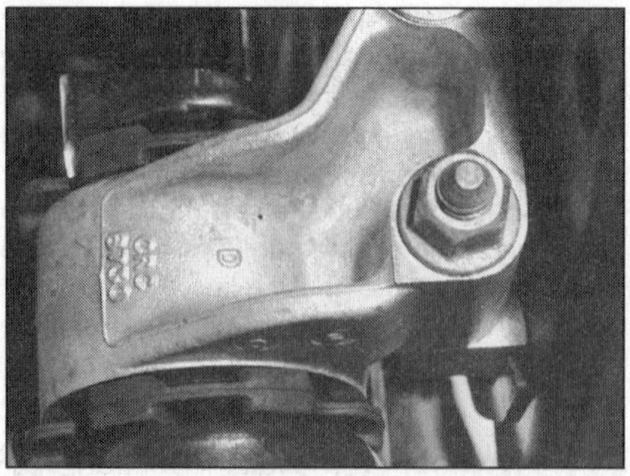

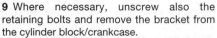

21.13 Check rubber washers are correctly installed before tightening through-bolt nut

Left-hand mounting

16 Disconnect the battery negative lead.

17 Where fitted, remove the charcoal canister.

18 If the mounting's bracket is to be removed, disconnect the clutch cable.

19 Unclip the engine wiring harness from the mounting.

20 Support the weight of the engine/transmission using a trolley jack (with a wooden spacer to prevent damage to the transmission casing) then unbolt the mounting from the bracket on the transmission and also from the support member.

21 If required, unbolt the bracket from the transmission.

22 Although the mounting's rubber is secured by two nuts to a metal outer section, the two parts can be renewed only as a complete assembly. Check all components carefully for signs of wear or damage, and renew them where necessary.

23 On reassembly, refit the bracket to the transmission and tighten its bolts to the specified torque wrench setting.

24 Using the trolley jack to obtain the correct height, refit the mounting, tightening its bolts by hand only until finger-tight, then tighten the various fasteners to their specified torque wrench settings.

25 Refit the clutch cable.

26 Secure the engine wiring harness to the mounting.

27 Refit (if applicable) the charcoal canister.

28 Connect the battery negative lead.

Rear mounting

29 Raise the front of the car and support it securely on axle stands (see "*Jacking and Vehicle Support*").

30 Support the weight of the engine/transmission using a trolley jack (with a wooden spacer to prevent damage to the transmission casing) then unbolt the mounting bracket from the transmission and the tie-rod from the underbody bracket and remove the mounting **(see illustrations)**.

31 Unscrew the through-bolt to separate the tie-rod from the bracket and to release (where fitted) the dynamic absorbers. Check carefully for signs of wear or damage all components and renew them where necessary.

32 Reassembly is the reverse of the removal procedure. If the mounting was removed complete and has not been disturbed, tighten all fasteners to their specified torque wrench settings. If the mounting was dismantled, tighten by hand only all fasteners, lower the car to the ground and rock it to settle the weight of the engine/transmission on the mounting, then use a torque wrench to tighten the fasteners to their specified settings.

21.30a Remove bolts (arrowed) to release . . .

21.30b . . . complete engine/transmission rear mounting

Chapter 2 Part B:
Engine removal and general overhaul procedures

Contents

Degrees of difficulty

Easy, suitable for novice with little experience	**Fairly easy,** suitable for beginner with some experience	**Fairly difficult,** suitable for competent DIY mechanic	**Difficult,** suitable for experienced DIY mechanic	**Very difficult,** suitable for expert DIY or professional

Specifications

Refer to Part A of this Chapter

1 General information

Included in this part of the Chapter are details of removing the engine/transmission unit from the car and general overhaul procedures for the cylinder head, cylinder block/crankcase and all other engine internal components.

The information given ranges from advice concerning preparation for an overhaul and the purchase of replacement parts to detailed step-by-step procedures covering removal, inspection, renovation and refitting of engine internal components.

After Section 5, all instructions are based on the assumption that the engine has been removed from the car. For information concerning in-car engine repair, as well as the removal and refitting of those external components necessary for full overhaul, refer to Part A of this Chapter and to Section 5. Ignore any preliminary dismantling operations described in Part A that are no longer relevant once the engine has been removed from the car.

2 Engine overhaul - general information

It is not always easy to determine when, or if, an engine should be completely overhauled, as a number of factors must be considered.

High mileage is not necessarily an indication that an overhaul is needed, while low mileage does not preclude the need for an overhaul. Frequency of servicing is probably the most important consideration. An engine which has had regular and frequent oil and filter changes, as well as other required maintenance, should give many thousands of miles of reliable service. Conversely, a neglected engine may require an overhaul very early in its life.

Excessive oil consumption is an indication that piston rings, valve seals and/or valve guides are in need of attention. Make sure that oil leaks are not responsible before deciding that the rings and/or guides are worn. Perform a compression test to determine the likely cause of the problem.

Check the oil pressure with a gauge fitted in place of the oil pressure switch and compare it with that specified. If it is extremely low, the main and big-end bearings and/or the oil pump are probably worn out.

Loss of power, rough running, knocking or metallic engine noises, excessive valve gear noise and high fuel consumption may also point to the need for an overhaul, especially if they are all present at the same time. If a complete service does not remedy the situation, major mechanical work is the only solution.

An engine overhaul involves restoring all internal parts to the specification of a new engine **(see illustrations)**. During an overhaul, the cylinder liners, the pistons and the piston rings are renewed. New main and big-end bearings are generally fitted and if necessary, the crankshaft may be renewed to restore the journals. The valves are also serviced as well, since they are usually in less than perfect condition at this point. While the engine is being overhauled, other components, such as the distributor, starter and alternator, can be overhauled as well. The end result should be an as-new engine that will give many trouble-free miles.

Critical cooling system components such as the hoses, thermostat and water pump should be renewed when an engine is overhauled. The radiator should be checked carefully to ensure that it is not clogged or leaking. Also it is a good idea to renew the oil pump whenever the engine is overhauled.

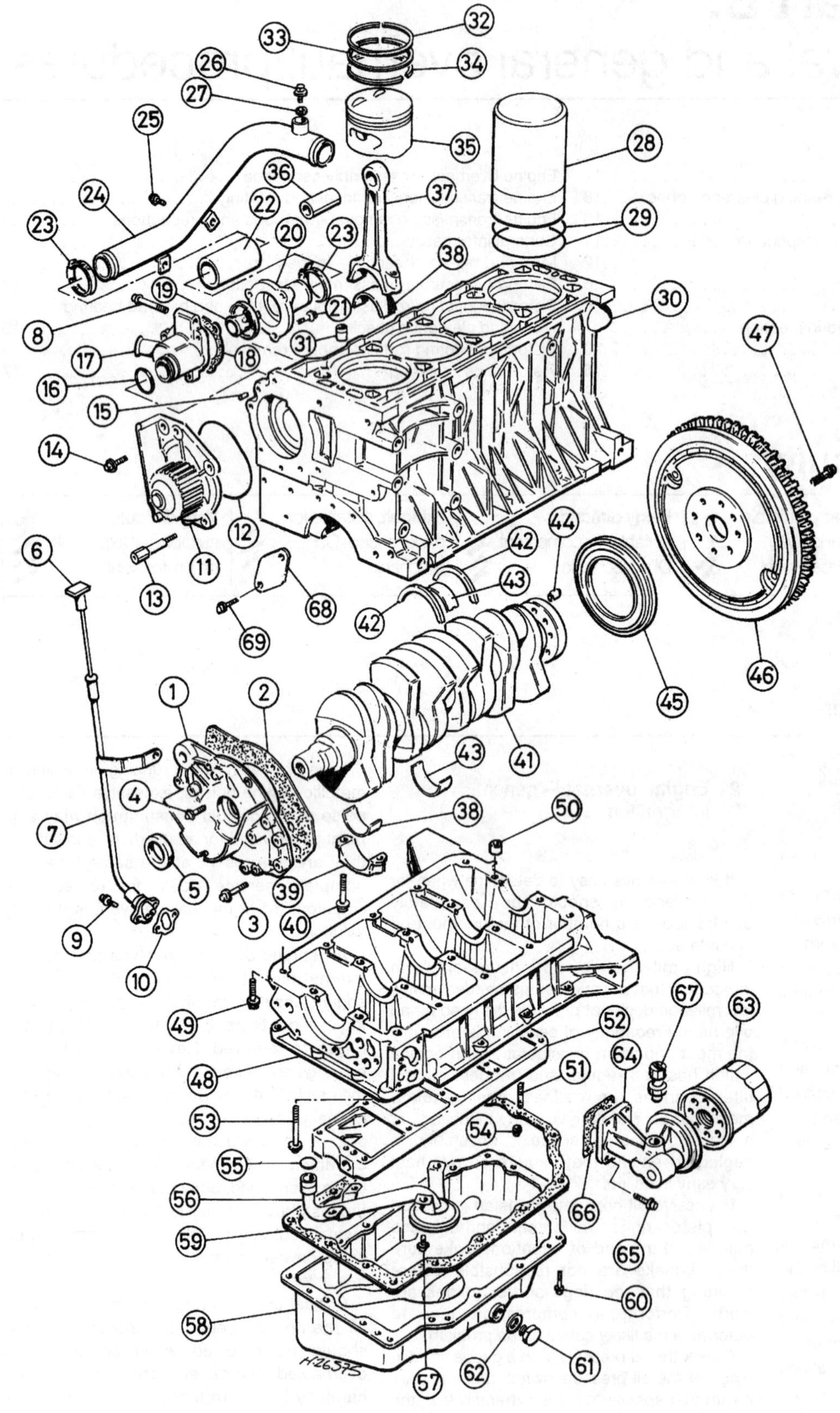

2.6a Engine bottom end components (wet liner engine)

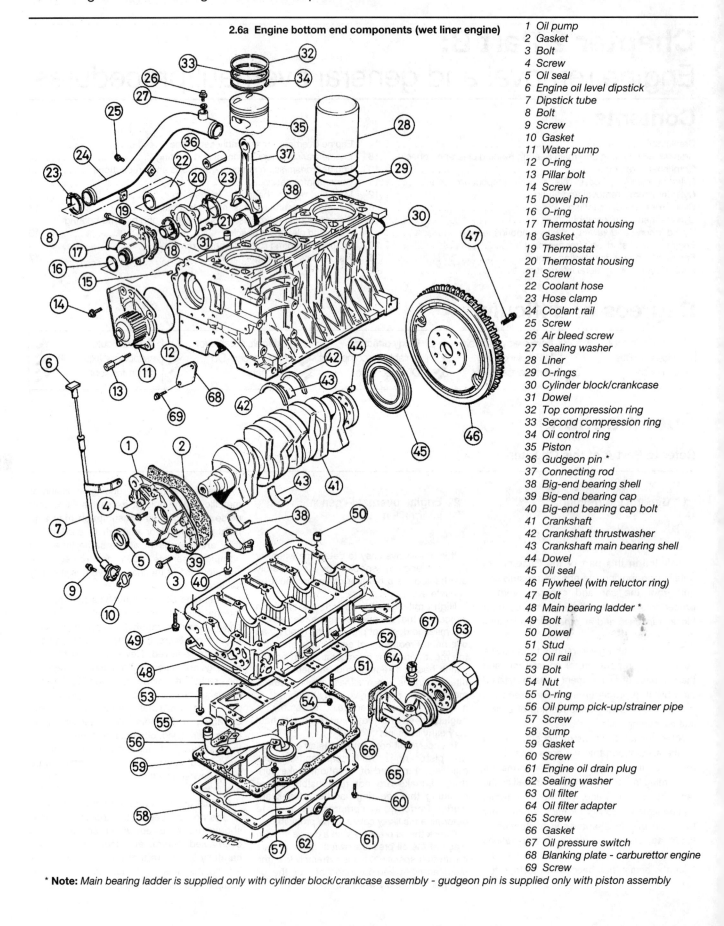

1 Oil pump
2 Gasket
3 Bolt
4 Screw
5 Oil seal
6 Engine oil level dipstick
7 Dipstick tube
8 Bolt
9 Screw
10 Gasket
11 Water pump
12 O-ring
13 Pillar bolt
14 Screw
15 Dowel pin
16 O-ring
17 Thermostat housing
18 Gasket
19 Thermostat
20 Thermostat housing
21 Screw
22 Coolant hose
23 Hose clamp
24 Coolant rail
25 Screw
26 Air bleed screw
27 Sealing washer
28 Liner
29 O-rings
30 Cylinder block/crankcase
31 Dowel
32 Top compression ring
33 Second compression ring
34 Oil control ring
35 Piston
36 Gudgeon pin *
37 Connecting rod
38 Big-end bearing shell
39 Big-end bearing cap
40 Big-end bearing cap bolt
41 Crankshaft
42 Crankshaft thrustwasher
43 Crankshaft main bearing shell
44 Dowel
45 Oil seal
46 Flywheel (with reluctor ring)
47 Bolt
48 Main bearing ladder *
49 Bolt
50 Dowel
51 Stud
52 Oil rail
53 Bolt
54 Nut
55 O-ring
56 Oil pump pick-up/strainer pipe
57 Screw
58 Sump
59 Gasket
60 Screw
61 Engine oil drain plug
62 Sealing washer
63 Oil filter
64 Oil filter adapter
65 Screw
66 Gasket
67 Oil pressure switch
68 Blanking plate - carburettor engine
69 Screw

* **Note:** *Main bearing ladder is supplied only with cylinder block/crankcase assembly - gudgeon pin is supplied only with piston assembly*

1 Oil pump
2 Gasket
3 Screw - M6 X 30
4 Screw - M6 X 20
5 Oil seal
6 Oil level dipstick
7 Dipstick tube
8 Screw
9 Screw
10 Gasket
11 Coolant pump
12 O-ring
13 Pillar bolt
14 Screw
15 Dowel
16 Thermostat housing - plastic
17 O-ring
18 Thermostat seal
19 Thermostat
20 Cover - plastic
21 Screw
22 O-ring
23 Coolant pipe
24 Screw
25 Vent screw - where fitted
26 Sealing washer
27 Cylinder block
28 Liner
29 Dowel
30 Piston/connecting rod assembly
31 Big-end bearing cap
32 Connecting rod bolt
33 Big-end bearing shell
34 Top compression ring
35 Second compression ring
36 Oil control ring
37 Crankshaft
38 Dowel
*39 Main bearing shells **
40 Thrustwashers
41 Oil seal
42 Flywheel assembly
43 Bolt - Patchlok type
44 Main bearing ladder
45 Bolt
46 Bolt
47 Dowel
48 Oil rail
49 Stud
50 Nut
51 Oil filter adapter
52 Gasket
53 Bolt
54 Oil pressure switch
55 Oil filter
56 Sump - pressed steel type
57 Gasket
58 Sump bolt - M6
59 Oil drain plug
60 Sealing washer
61 Sump - alloy type
62 Sump bolt - M8 X 20
63 Sump bolt - M8
64 Oil drain plug
65 Sealing washer
66 Oil pump pick-up/strainer pipe
67 Screw
68 O-ring
69 Blanking plate
70 Screw

2.6b Engine bottom end components (damp liner engine)

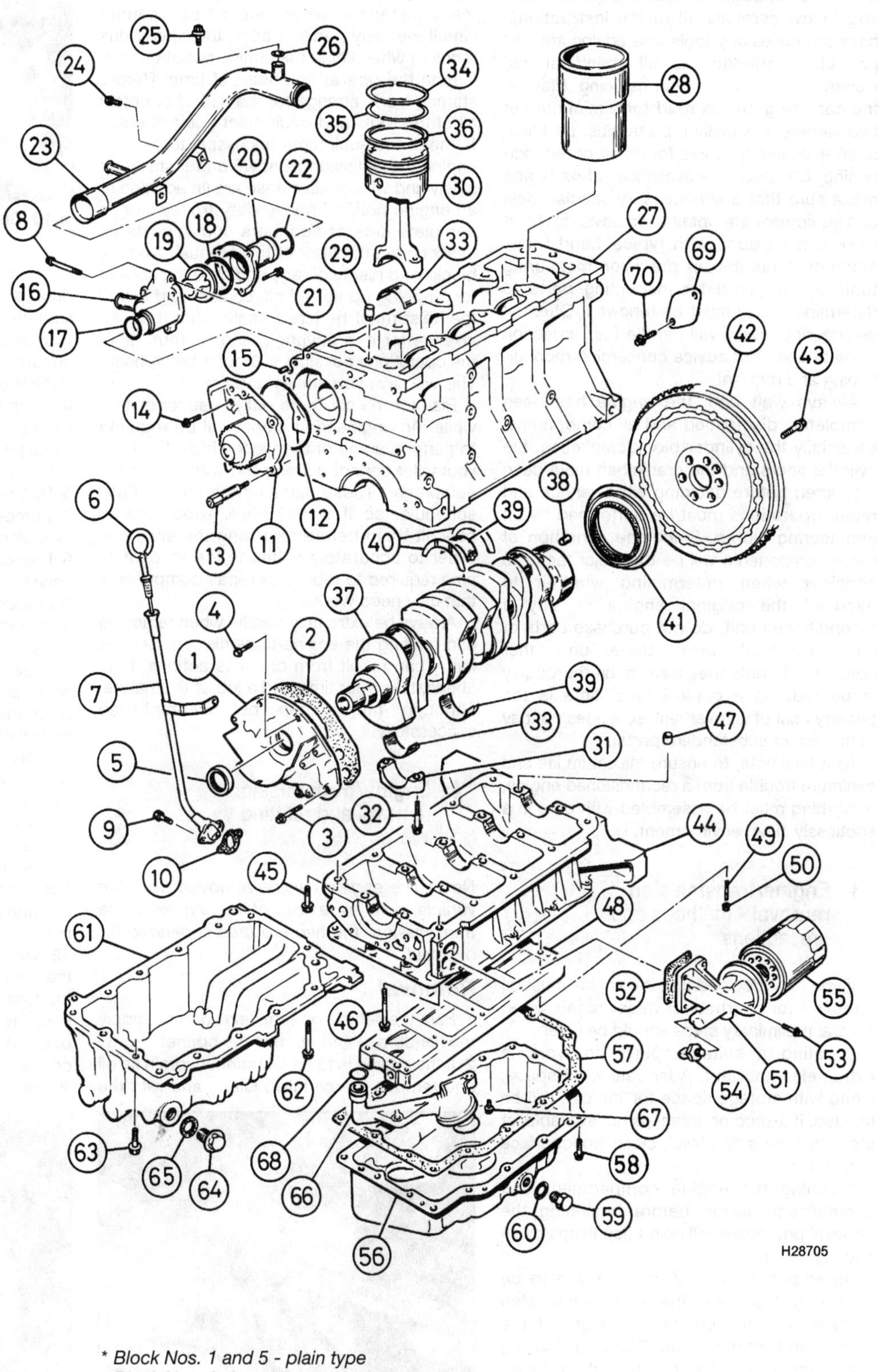

** Block Nos. 1 and 5 - plain type*
Block Nos. 2, 3 and 4 - grooved type
Bearing ladder - plain type

2B

Before beginning the engine overhaul, read through the entire procedure to familiarise yourself with the scope and requirements of the job. Overhauling an engine is not difficult if you follow carefully all of the instructions, have the necessary tools and equipment and pay close attention to all specifications. However, it can be time consuming. Plan on the car being off the road for a minimum of two weeks, especially if parts must be taken to an engineering works for repair or reconditioning. Check on the availability of parts and make sure that any necessary special tools and equipment are obtained in advance. Most work can be done with typical hand tools, although a number of precision measuring tools are required for inspecting parts to determine if they must be renewed. Often an engineering works will handle the inspection of parts and offer advice concerning reconditioning and renewal.

Always wait until the engine has been completely dismantled and all components, especially the cylinder block/crankcase, the cylinder liners and the crankshaft have been inspected before deciding what service and repair operations must be performed by an engineering works. Since the condition of these components will be the major factor to consider when determining whether to overhaul the original engine or buy a reconditioned unit, do not purchase parts or have overhaul work done on other components until they have been thoroughly inspected. As a general rule, time is the primary cost of an overhaul, so it does not pay to fit worn or substandard parts.

As a final note, to ensure maximum life and minimum trouble from a reconditioned engine, everything must be assembled with care in a spotlessly clean environment.

3 Engine/transmission removal - methods and precautions

If you have decided that the engine must be removed for overhaul or major repair work, several preliminary steps should be taken.

Locating a suitable place to work is extremely important. Adequate work space, along with storage space for the car, will be needed. If a shop or garage is not available, at the very least a flat, level, clean work surface is required.

Cleaning the engine compartment and engine/transmission before beginning the removal procedure will help keep things clean and organised.

An engine hoist or A-frame will also be necessary. Make sure the equipment is rated in excess of the combined weight of the engine and transmission (290 lb or 130 kg approximately). Safety is of primary importance, considering the potential hazards involved in lifting the engine/transmission out of the car.

If the engine/transmission is being removed by a novice, a helper should be available. Advice and aid from someone more experienced would also be helpful. There are many instances when one person cannot simultaneously perform all of the operations required when lifting the engine out of the car.

Plan the operation ahead of time. Before starting work, arrange for the hire of or obtain all of the tools and equipment you will need. Some of the equipment necessary to perform engine/transmission removal and installation safely and with relative ease are (in addition to an engine hoist) a heavy duty trolley jack, a complete sets of spanners and sockets as described in the front of this Manual, wooden blocks and plenty of rags and cleaning solvent for mopping up spilled oil, coolant and fuel. If the hoist must be hired, make sure that you arrange for it in advance, and perform all of the operations possible without it beforehand. This will save you money and time.

Plan for the car to be out of use for quite a while. An engineering works will be required to perform some of the work which the do-it-yourselfer cannot accomplish without special equipment. These places often have a busy schedule, so it would be a good idea to consult them before removing the engine in order to accurately estimate the amount of time required to rebuild or repair components that may need work.

Always be extremely careful when removing and refitting the engine/transmission. Serious injury can result from careless actions. Plan ahead, take your time and a job of this nature, although major, can be accomplished successfully.

4 Engine/transmission - removal and refitting

Note: *The engine can be removed from the vehicle only as a complete unit with the transmission; the two are then separated for overhaul.*

Removal

1 Park the vehicle on firm, level ground, apply the handbrake and remove the bonnet.

2 If the engine is to be dismantled, drain its oil and remove the oil filter. Clean and refit the drain plug, tightening it to its specified torque wrench setting.

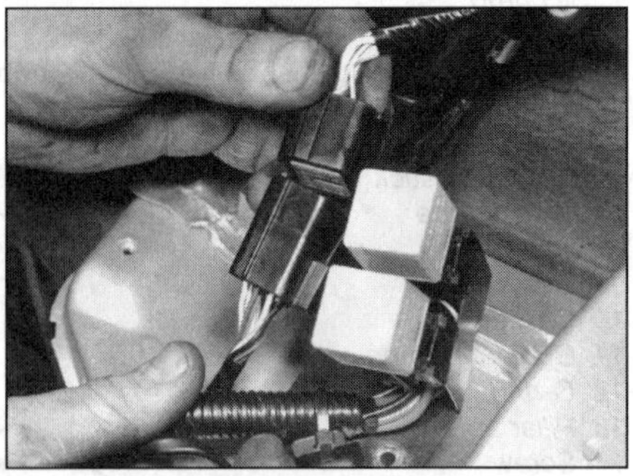

4.10 Disconnecting engine wiring harness from main wiring harness - carburettor models

3 Jack up the front of the car and support it securely on axle stands (see "*Jacking and Vehicle Support*"), then remove the wheels.

4 Drain the transmission oil. Clean and refit the drain plug, tightening it to its specified torque wrench setting.

5 Drain the cooling system.

6 Remove the battery and its tray.

7 Remove the complete air cleaner assembly, including the cold air intake duct.

8 Remove, where fitted, the charcoal canister.

9 Disconnect the ignition HT coil spark plug (HT) lead from the distributor cap.

10 On carburettor engines, unscrew the bolt securing the relay bracket to the inner wing panel and unplug the connector to disconnect the engine wiring harness from the main wiring harness **(see illustration)**.

11 On fuel-injected engines, unplug its wiring connector(s) and disconnect the vacuum hose from the ECU, unplug the two connectors from the relay module and the single connector from the inertia switch, release the lambda sensor relay (where fitted) from its bracket, then unplug the connector to disconnect the engine wiring harness from the main wiring harness.

12 On all models, unscrew the bolt securing the earth lead to the body front panel, remove the fusible link box lid and the 30 amp fusible link, then use a small screwdriver gently to depress the retainer so that the battery lead connector can be removed from the fusible link box **(see illustrations)**.

4.12a Removing bolt securing earth lead to body

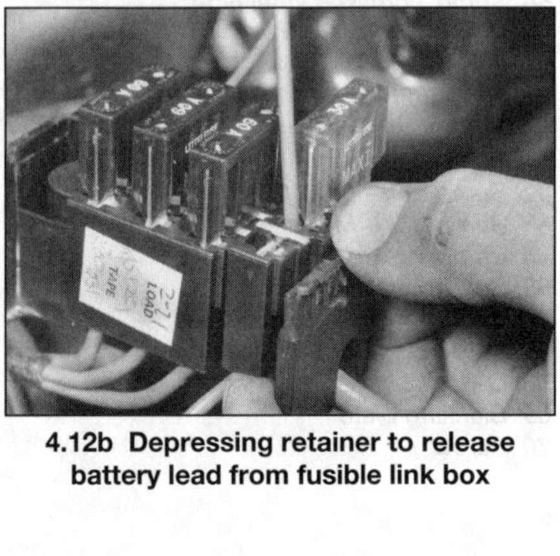

4.12b Depressing retainer to release battery lead from fusible link box

13 Disconnect the remaining wiring from the starter motor and secure all engine/transmission wiring to the unit so that it will not hinder the removal of the engine/transmission from the car.

14 Disconnect the clutch cable and secure it clear of the engine/transmission unit.

15 Disconnect the speedometer drive upper cable from the lower cable, release the upper cable from any securing clips and secure it clear of the engine/transmission unit.

16 Disconnect the washer pump wiring connector plug(s), then remove its three retaining screws and move the washer system reservoir clear of the engine/transmission.

17 Working as described in the relevant Sections of Chapter 3, disconnect the coolant hose from the bottom of the expansion tank, the expansion tank hose from the inlet manifold union, both heater hoses from the heater matrix unions and the radiator top hose from the coolant outlet elbow. Either remove the radiator bottom hose or secure it so that it will not prevent engine/transmission removal.

18 Disconnect the vacuum servo unit vacuum hose from the inlet manifold. Discard the sealing washers.

19 On carburettor engines, disconnect the fuel pump feed hose - plug both openings to prevent loss of fuel and the entry of dirt into the system.

20 On fuel-injected engines, depressurise the fuel system and disconnect the fuel feed and return hoses from the throttle body pipes -

4.26 Bolt lifting brackets to cylinder head using tapped holes provided

plug both openings of each pipe to prevent loss of fuel and the entry of dirt into the system.

21 Disconnect the throttle cable and (on carburettor engines only) the choke cable.

22 Disconnect and release from the engine/transmission unit, the lambda sensor wiring (where fitted), then disconnect the exhaust system front pipe from the manifold.

23 Disconnect the gearchange linkage link rods from the transmission upper and lower selector levers.

24 Either remove the engine/transmission rear mounting or unbolt the mounting bracket from the transmission and slacken the tie-rod-to-body bolt and nut so that the mounting can be swung down clear of the transmission.

25 Dismantle the front suspension and remove both driveshafts.

26 On K8 engines, the cylinder head has a tapped hole provided at the right-hand rear end (above the dipstick tube) and at the left-hand front end (behind the spark plug lead clips). On K16 engine cylinder heads the right-hand end hole is in the same place, but at the left-hand end the air intake duct support bracket mounting points must be used **(see illustration)**. Attach lifting brackets to the engine at these points.

27 Take the weight of the engine/transmission unit using the engine hoist, then unscrew the engine/transmission right-hand mounting through-bolt and nut.

28 Release the engine wiring harness from the clip on the engine/transmission left-hand mounting, unbolt the mounting bracket from the mounting, then unbolt the support member from the front subframe. Remove the support member **(see illustrations)**.

29 Make a final check that all components have been removed or disconnected that will prevent the removal of the engine/transmission unit from the car and ensure that components such as the gearchange linkage link rods are secured so that they cannot be damaged on removal.

30 Lift the engine/transmission unit out of the car, ensuring that nothing is trapped or damaged **(see illustration)**.

31 Lower the engine/transmission unit to the ground and remove the starter motor.

> **HAYNES HiNT** ***After removing the engine, keep it upright until the sump has been removed to prevent sludge from entering the engine internals.***

32 Unbolt the flywheel front, lower and rear cover plates, unscrew the four bolts securing the transmission to the engine and gently prise the transmission off the two locating dowels (at the front and rear of the main bearing ladder). Move the transmission squarely away from the engine, ensuring that the clutch components are not damaged.

33 Remove the clutch. Do not forget to overhaul the clutch components before the engine and transmission are reconnected.

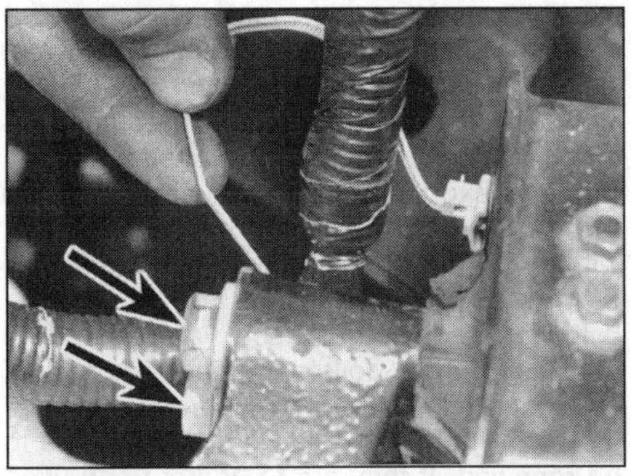

4.28a Release engine wiring harness from mounting clip and unbolt mounting from bracket (arrowed)

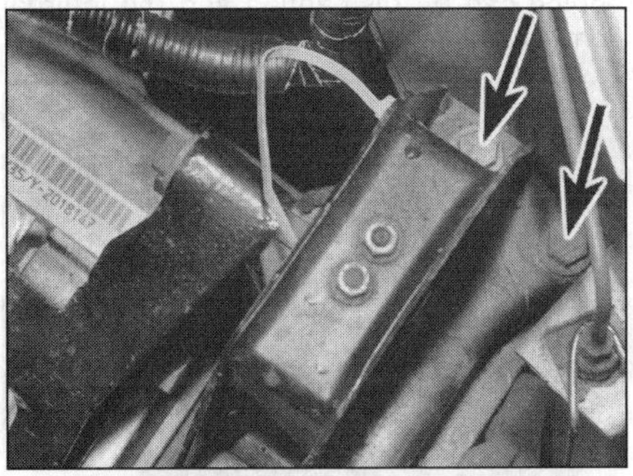

4.28b Unscrew mounting/support member-to-front subframe rear bolts . . .

4.28c . . . and support member-to-front subframe front bolts (arrowed) . . .

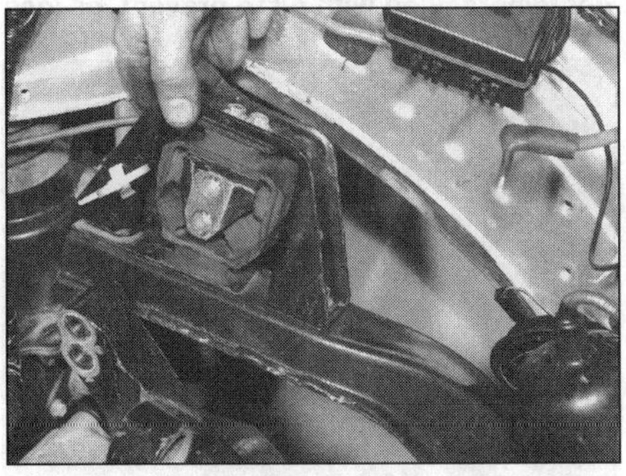

4.28d . . . then remove support member with engine/transmission left-hand mounting

4.30 Lifting out engine/transmission unit

Refitting

34 Refitting is the reverse of removal, following where necessary the instructions given in the other Chapters of this Manual. Note the following additional points:

a) Overhaul and lubricate the clutch components before refitting.
b) When the transmission, starter motor and flywheel cover plates have been refitted, lift the engine/transmission unit and lower it into the engine compartment so that it is slightly tilted (transmission down). Engage both driveshafts then return the unit to the horizontal and refit the engine/transmission mountings.
c) Remove the lifting brackets and refit any components removed to enable them to be fitted.
d) Tighten all fasteners to their specified torque wrench settings.
e) Adjust the control cables.
f) Refill the engine and transmission with oil.
g) Refill the cooling system.

5 Engine overhaul - dismantling sequence

1 It is much easier to dismantle and work on the engine if it is mounted on a portable engine stand. These stands can often be hired from a tool hire shop. Before the engine is mounted on a stand, the flywheel should be removed so that the stand bolts can be tightened into the end of the cylinder block/crankcase (not the main bearing ladder).

2 If a stand is not available, it is possible to dismantle the engine with it blocked up on a sturdy workbench or on the floor. Be extra careful not to tip or drop the engine when working without a stand.

3 If you are going to obtain a reconditioned engine, all external components must be removed first to be transferred to the replacement engine (just as they will if you are doing a complete engine overhaul yourself). These components include the following:

a) Alternator and brackets.
b) Distributor, HT leads and spark plugs.
c) Thermostat and housing, coolant rail, coolant outlet elbow.
d) Dipstick tube.
e) Carburettor/fuel-injection system components.
f) All electrical switches and sensors.
g Inlet and exhaust manifolds.
h) Oil filter.
i) Fuel pump.
j) Engine mountings.
k) Flywheel.

Note: *When removing the external components from the engine, pay close attention to details that may be helpful or important during refitting. Note the fitted position of gaskets, seals, spacers, pins, washers, bolts and other small items.*

4 If you are obtaining a short motor (which comprises the engine cylinder block/crankcase and main bearing ladder, crankshaft, pistons and connecting rods all assembled), then the cylinder head, sump, oil pump, and timing belt will have to be removed also.

5 If you are planning a complete overhaul, the engine can be dismantled and the internal components removed in the following order:

a) Inlet and exhaust manifolds.
b) Timing belt, toothed pulleys, tensioner and timing belt inner cover.
c) Cylinder head.
d) Flywheel.
e) Sump.
f) Oil pump.
g) Piston/connecting rod assemblies.
h) Crankshaft.

6 Before beginning the dismantling and overhaul procedures, make sure that you have the correct tools necessary. See the sections in *"Reference"* at the end of this Manual.

6 Cylinder head - dismantling

Note: *New and reconditioned cylinder heads are available from the manufacturer and from engine overhaul specialists. Due to the fact that some specialist tools are required for the dismantling and inspection procedures, and new components may not be readily available, it may be more practical and economical for the home mechanic to purchase a reconditioned head rather than dismantle, inspect and recondition the original head*

1 Remove the camshaft(s) and hydraulic tappets, being careful to store the tappets in carefully marked containers full of clean engine oil **(see illustrations)**.

2 Remove the cylinder head.

3 Using a valve spring compressor, compress each valve spring in turn until the split collets can be removed. Release the compressor and lift off the spring retainer and spring, then use a pair of pliers to extract the spring bottom seat/stem seal **(see illustrations)**.

4 If, when the valve spring compressor is screwed down, the spring retainer refuses to free and expose the split collets, gently tap the top of the tool directly over the retainer with a light hammer. This will free the retainer.

5 Withdraw the valve.

6 It is essential that each valve is stored together with its collets, retainer and spring, and that all valves are in their correct sequence unless they are so badly worn that they are to be renewed. If they are to be kept and used again, place each valve assembly in a labelled polythene bag or similar small container **(see illustration)**. Note that No 1 valve is nearest to the timing belt end of the engine.

6.1a Use a valve-grinding sucker to extract hydraulic tappets . . .

6.1b . . . and store in clearly-marked containers filled with oil to prevent oil loss

6.3a Using a valve spring compressor to release split collets

6.3b Extracting a valve spring bottom seat/stem seal

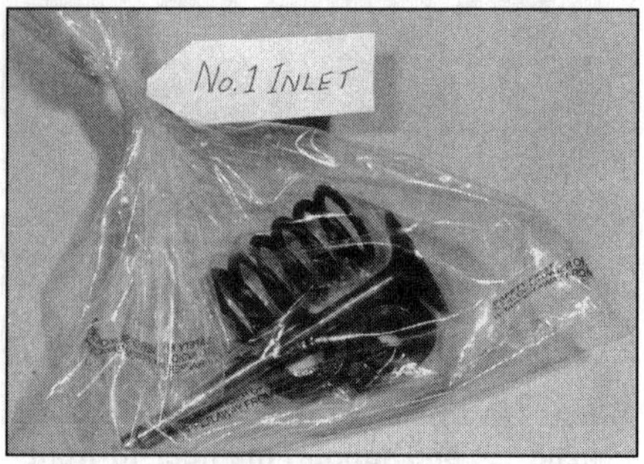

6.6 Use a labelled plastic bag to keep together and identify valve components

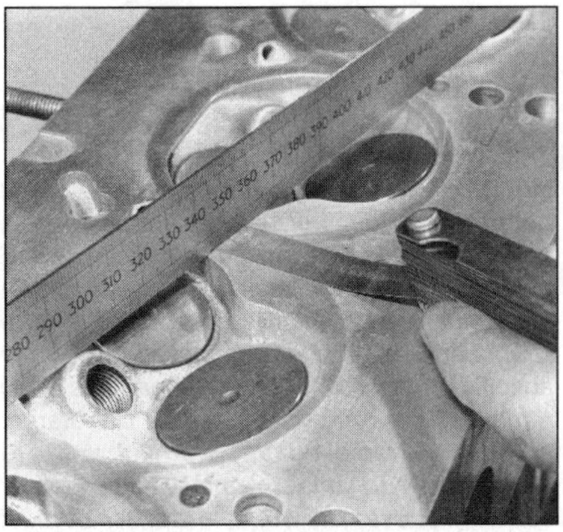

7.6a Checking a cylinder head gasket surface for warpage . . .

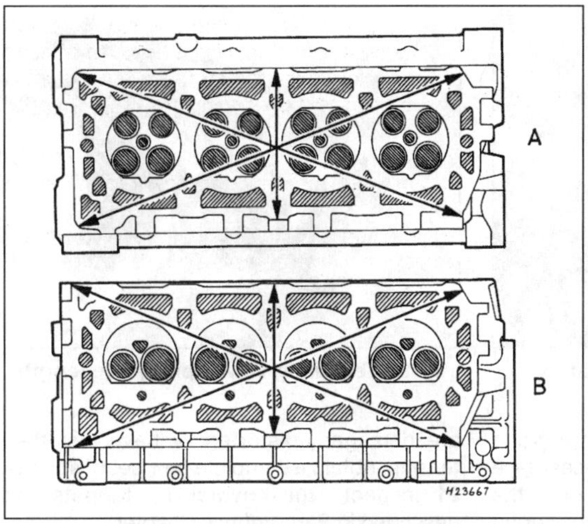

7.6b . . . along the paths shown
A K16 engine B K8 engine

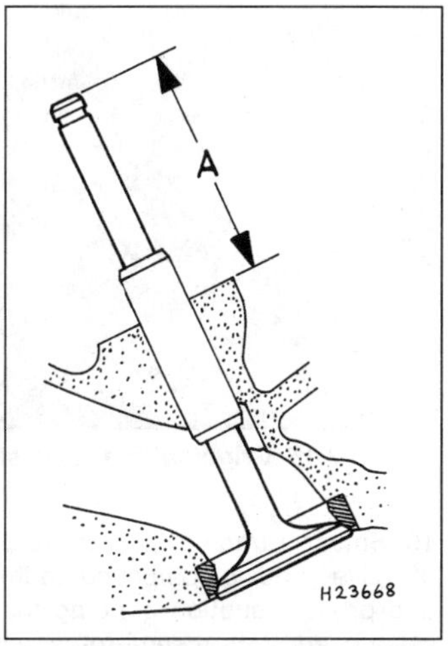

7.7 Check valve seat wear by measuring valve stem installed height (A)

7 Cylinder head and valves - cleaning and inspection

1 Thorough cleaning of the cylinder head and valve components, followed by a detailed inspection, will enable you to decide how much valve service work must be carried out during the engine overhaul. Note that if the engine has been severely overheated, it is best to assume that the cylinder head is warped and to check carefully for signs of this.

Cleaning

2 Scrape away all traces of old gasket material and sealing compound from the cylinder head. Use a hard plastic or wood scraper whilst taking particular care as the soft aluminium alloy is damaged easily. Also, make sure that the carbon is not allowed to enter the oil and water passages.

3 Scrape away the carbon from the combustion chambers and ports, then wash the cylinder head thoroughly with paraffin or a suitable solvent.

4 Scrape off any heavy carbon deposits that may have formed on the valves, then use a power-operated wire brush to remove deposits from the valve heads and stems.

Inspection

Note: *Be sure to perform all the following inspection procedures before concluding that the services of a machine shop or engine overhaul specialist are required. Make a list of all items that require attention:*

Cylinder head

5 Inspect the head very carefully for cracks, evidence of coolant leakage and other damage. If cracks are found, a new cylinder head should be obtained.

6 Use a straight-edge and feeler blade to check that the cylinder head surface is not distorted **(see illustrations)**. If it is, it may be possible to resurface it, provided that the specified reface limit is not exceeded in so doing, or that the cylinder head is not reduced to less than the specified height.

7 Examine the valve seats in each of the combustion chambers. If they are severely pitted, cracked or burned then they will need to be renewed or re-cut by an engine overhaul specialist. If they are only slightly pitted, this can be removed by grinding-in the valve heads and seats with fine valve-grinding compound as described below. To check whether they are excessively worn, refit the valve and measure the installed height of its stem tip above the cylinder head upper surface **(see illustration)**. If the measurement is above the specified limit, repeat the test using a new valve. If the measurement is still excessive, renew the seat insert.

8 If the valve guides are worn (indicated by a side-to-side motion of the valve) new guides must be fitted. Measure the diameter of the existing valve stems and the bore of the guides, then calculate the clearance and compare the result with the specified value. If the clearance is excessive, renew the valves or guides as necessary.

9 The renewal of valve guides is best carried out by an engine overhaul specialist. If the work is to be carried out at home however, use a stepped, double-diameter drift to drive out the worn guide towards the combustion chamber. On fitting the new guide, place it first in a deep-freeze for one hour, then drive it into its cylinder head bore from the camshaft side until it projects the specified amount above the spring bottom seat/stem seal surface.

10 If the valve seats are to be re-cut, this must be done only after the guides have been renewed.

Valves

11 Examine the head of each valve for pitting, burning, cracks and general wear and check the valve stem for scoring and wear ridges. Rotate the valve and check for any obvious indication that it is bent. Look for pits and excessive wear on the tip of each valve stem. Renew any valve that shows any such signs of wear or damage.

12 If the valve appears satisfactory at this stage, measure the valve stem diameter at several points using a micrometer **(see illustration)**. Any significant difference in the readings obtained indicates wear of the valve stem. Should any of these conditions be apparent, the valve(s) must be renewed.

13 If the valves are in satisfactory condition they should be ground (lapped) into their respective seats to ensure a smooth gas-tight seal. If the seat is only lightly pitted, or if it has been re-cut, fine grinding compound only should be used to produce the required finish. Coarse valve-grinding compound should not be used unless a seat is badly burned or deeply pitted. If this is the case, the cylinder head and valves should be inspected by an expert to decide whether seat re-cutting or even the renewal of the valve or seat insert is required.

14 Valve grinding is carried out as follows: Place the cylinder head upside down on a bench.

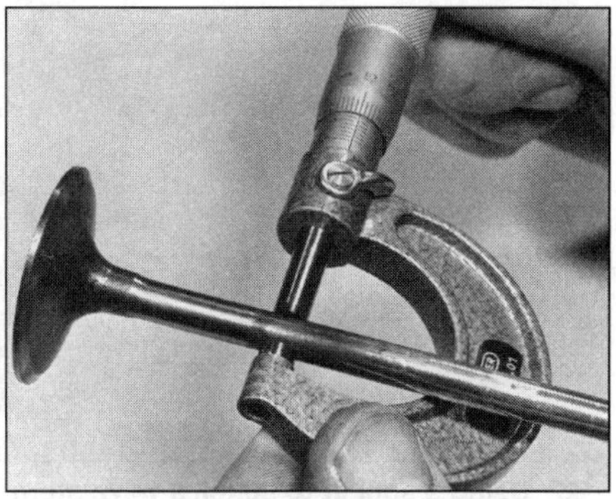

7.12 Measuring valve stem diameter

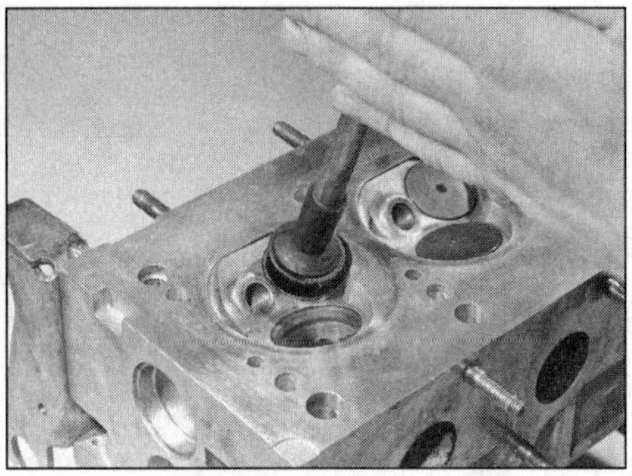

7.15 Grinding-in a valve seat

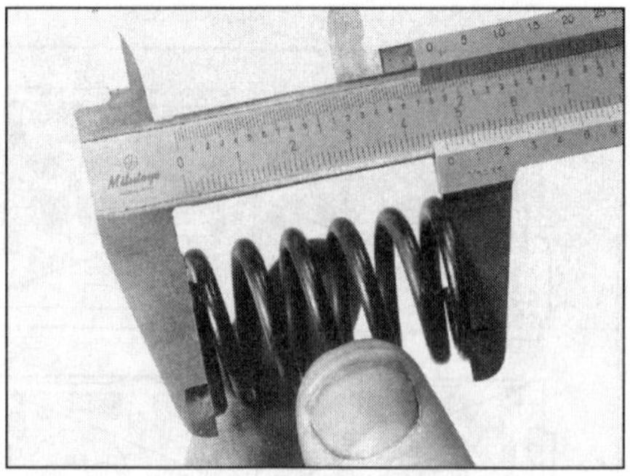

7.19 Measuring valve spring free length

15 Smear a trace of (the appropriate grade of) valve-grinding compound on the seat face and press a suction grinding tool onto the valve head. With a semi-rotary action, grind the valve head to its seat, lifting the valve occasionally to redistribute the grinding compound **(see illustration)**. A light spring placed under the valve head will greatly ease this operation.

16 If coarse grinding compound is being used, work only until a dull, matt even surface is produced on both the valve seat and the valve, then wipe off the used compound and repeat the process with fine compound. When a smooth unbroken ring of light grey matt finish is produced on both the valve and seat, the grinding operation is complete. Do not grind in the valves any further than absolutely necessary, or the seat will be prematurely sunk into the cylinder head.

17 To check that the seat has not been over-ground, measure the valve stem installed height.

18 When all the valves have been ground-in, carefully wash off all traces of grinding compound using paraffin or a suitable solvent before reassembly of the cylinder head.

Valve components

19 Examine the valve springs for signs of damage and discoloration and also measure their free length using vernier calipers **(see illustration)** or by comparing the existing spring with a new component.

20 Stand each spring on a flat surface and check it for squareness. If any of the springs are damaged, distorted or have lost their tension, obtain a complete new set of springs.

21 Inspect the hydraulic tappets as described in Part A of this Chapter.

8 Cylinder head - reassembly

1 Lubricate the stems of the valves and insert them into their original locations. If new valves are being fitted, insert them into the locations to which they have been ground.

2 Working on the first valve, dip the spring bottom seat/stem seal in fresh engine oil then carefully locate it over the valve and onto the guide. Take care not to damage the seal as it is passed over the valve stem. Use a suitable socket or metal tube to press the seal firmly onto the guide **(see illustration)**.

3 Locate the spring on the seat, followed by the spring retainer.

4 Compress the valve spring and locate the split collets in the recess in the valve stem. Use a little grease to hold the collets in place. Release the compressor, then repeat the procedure on the remaining valves.

5 With all the valves installed, place the cylinder head flat on the bench and, using a hammer and interposed block of wood, tap the end of each valve stem to settle the components.

6 Refit the hydraulic tappets and camshaft(s) as described in Part A of this Chapter.

9 Piston/connecting rod assembly - removal

Note: *Due to the design of the engine, it will become very difficult, almost impossible, to turn the crankshaft once the cylinder head bolts have been slackened. The manufacturer accordingly states that the crankshaft will be "tight" and should not be rotated more than absolutely necessary once the head has been removed. If the crankshaft cannot be rotated, it must be removed for overhaul work to proceed. With this in mind, during any servicing or overhaul work the crankshaft must always be rotated to the desired position before the bolts are disturbed*

Removal - without removing crankshaft

1 Remove the timing belt, the camshaft toothed pulley(s) and tensioner, and the timing belt inner cover.

2 Remove the camshaft(s) and hydraulic tappets, being careful to store the hydraulic tappets as described.

3 If the flywheel has been removed, temporarily refit the alternator drive pulley and apply a spanner to its bolt to rotate the crankshaft.

4 Rotate the crankshaft until numbers 2 and 3 cylinder pistons are at the bottom of their stroke.

5 Remove the cylinder head. The crankshaft cannot now be rotated.

6 Unbolt the dipstick tube from the cylinder block/crankcase.

Warning: The tube securing bolts must not be changed for another type. From Engine number 800000 on, the bolts have a flanged head and do not exceed 12 mm length.

7 Remove the sump and unbolt the oil pump pick-up/strainer pipe from the oil rail. Discard its O-ring **(see illustration)**.

8 Unscrew the two retaining nuts and remove the oil rail **(see illustration)**.

8.2 Using a socket to install a valve stem seal

9.7 Removing oil pump pick-up/strainer pipe from oil rail - always renew O-ring (arrowed)

9.8 Oil rail must be removed to reach connecting rod big-end bearings

9.9 Always mark big-end bearing caps before removal (see text) - No.4 cylinder cap shown

9 Using a hammer and centre punch, paint or similar, mark each connecting rod big-end bearing cap with its respective cylinder number on the flat, machined surface provided **(see illustration)**. If the engine has been dismantled before, note carefully any identifying marks made previously. Note that number 1 cylinder is at the timing belt end of the engine.

10 Unscrew and remove the big-end bearing cap bolts and withdraw the cap, complete with bearing shell, from the connecting rod. If only the bearing shells are being attended to, push the connecting rod up and off the crankpin, ensuring that the connecting rod big-ends do not mark the cylinder bore walls, then remove the upper bearing shell. Keep the cap, bolts and (if they are to be refitted) the bearing shells together in their correct sequence.

11 With numbers 2 and 3 cylinder big-ends disconnected, repeat the procedure (exercising great care to prevent damage to any of the components) to remove numbers 1 and 4 cylinder bearing caps.

12 Push each piston/connecting rod assembly up and remove it from the top of the bore. Remove the ridge of carbon from the top of each cylinder bore and ensure that the connecting rod big-ends do not mark the cylinder bore walls. Immediately refit its bearing cap, shells and bolts to each piston/connecting rod assembly so that they are all kept together as a matched set.

13 Note that the number stamped by you on each bearing cap should match the cylinder number stamped on the front (alternator bracket side) of each connecting rod; if any connecting rod number does not match its correct cylinder, mark or label it immediately so that each piston/connecting rod assembly can be refitted to its original bore. Keep each assembly together with its cap, bolts and bearing shells at all times.

Removal - alternative methods

14 If the engine is being completely dismantled and the cylinder head has been removed, either unbolt the main bearing ladder so that the crankshaft can be rotated with care, or remove the crankshaft completely and then remove the connecting rods and pistons.

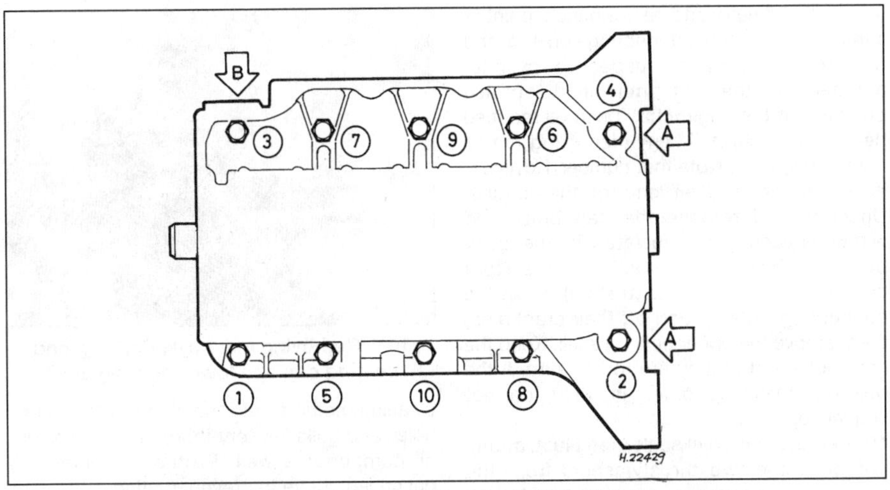

10.8a Crankshaft main bearing ladder bolt slackening sequence
A Bolts hidden in ladder flanges *B Location of single longer bolt*

Cylinder head bolts - inspection

15 Check the condition of the cylinder head bolts and particularly their threads whenever they are removed. If the cylinder head only is removed, check as described in Part A of this Chapter, but if the cylinder head and the oil rail are removed, check as follows:

16 Keeping all the bolts in their correct fitted order, wash them and wipe dry, then check each for any sign of visible wear or damage, renewing any bolt if necessary. Lightly oil the threads of each bolt, carefully enter it into its original hole and screw it in, by hand only until finger-tight. If the full length of thread is engaged, the bolt may be re-used. If the full length of thread is not engaged, measure the distance from the oil rail gasket surface to under the bolt head.

17 If the distance measured is under 378 mm, the bolt may be re-used. If the distance measured is more than 378 mm, the bolt must be renewed. Considering the task these bolts perform and the pressures they must withstand, owners should consider renewing all the bolts as a matched set if more than one of the originals fail inspection or are close to the limit set.

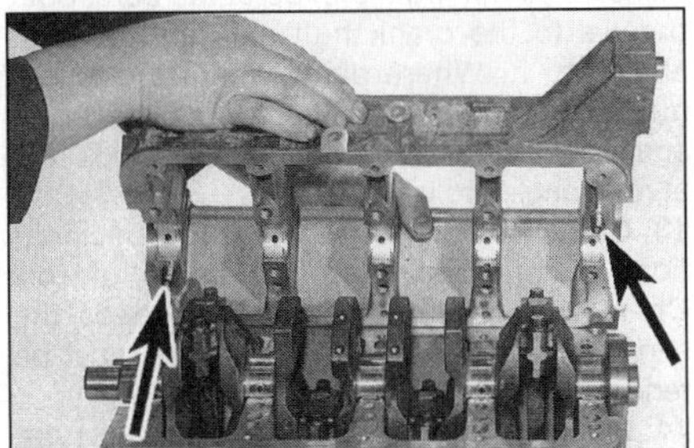

10.8b Removing main bearing ladder - note two locating dowels (arrowed)

18 Note that if any of the cylinder head bolt threads in the oil rail are found to be damaged, the oil rail must be renewed. Thread inserts (eg. Helicoils) are not an acceptable repair in this instance.

10 Crankshaft - removal

Note: *The following procedure assumes that the crankshaft alone is being removed. If the crankshaft endfloat is to be checked, this must be done when the crankshaft is free to move. If a dial gauge is to be used, check after paragraph 1 below, but if feeler gauges are to be used, check after paragraph 9.*

1 Remove the timing belt, the toothed pulley(s) and tensioner, and the timing belt inner cover.

2 Unbolt the dipstick tube from the cylinder block/crankcase.

Warning: The tube securing bolts must not be changed for another type. From Engine number 800000 on, the bolts have a flanged head and do not exceed 12 mm length.

3 Remove the cylinder head. The crankshaft cannot now be rotated.

4 Remove the oil pump.

5 Remove the crankshaft left-hand oil seal.

6 Remove the sump and unbolt the oil pump pick-up/strainer pipe from the oil rail. Discard its O-ring.

7 Unscrew the two retaining nuts and remove the oil rail.

8 Working progressively and in the sequence shown **(see illustration)**, unscrew by a turn at a time the main bearing ladder retaining bolts, then withdraw the ladder **(see illustration)**. Note the two locating dowels and the main bearing shells, which should be removed from the ladder and stored in their correct fitted order.

9 Using a hammer and centre punch, paint or similar, mark each connecting rod big-end bearing cap with its respective cylinder number on the flat, machined surface provided. If the engine has been dismantled before, note carefully any identifying marks made previously. Note that number 1 cylinder is at the timing belt end of the engine. Unscrew and remove the cap bolts and withdraw each cap, complete with the lower bearing shell, from each of the four connecting rods **(see illustration)**. Push the connecting rods up and off their crankpins, then remove the upper bearing shell. Keep the cap, bolts and (if they are to be refitted) the bearing shells together in their correct sequence.

10 Remove the crankshaft **(see illustration)**. Withdraw the two thrustwashers from the number 3 main bearing upper location. Noting the position of the grooved shells, remove the upper main bearing shells, which must be kept with their correct respective partners from the main bearing ladder so that all shells can be identified and (if necessary) refitted in their original locations.

11 Check the condition of the cylinder head bolts.

10.9 Removing (no.1 cylinder) big-end bearing cap and lower bearing shell

10.10 Removing the crankshaft

11 Cylinder block/crankcase - cleaning and inspection

Warning: Wear eye protection when using compressed air or water-dispersant lubricant to clean oil holes and galleries.

Cleaning

1 For complete cleaning, remove the cylinder liners, all external components and electrical switches/sensors.

2 Scrape all traces of gasket from the cylinder block/crankcase, bearing ladder and oil rail, taking care not to damage the gasket/sealing surfaces.

3 Remove all oil gallery plugs (where fitted). The plugs are usually very tight and they may have to be drilled out and the holes re-tapped. Use new plugs when the engine is reassembled.

4 If any of the castings are extremely dirty, all should be steam cleaned.

5 After the castings are returned, clean all oil holes and oil galleries one more time. Flush all internal passages with warm water until the water runs clear, then dry thoroughly and apply a light film of oil to all liner surfaces to prevent rusting. If you have access to compressed air, use it to speed up the drying process and to blow out all the oil holes and galleries.

6 If the castings are not very dirty, you can do an adequate cleaning job with hot, soapy water and a stiff brush. Take plenty of time and do a thorough job. Regardless of the cleaning method used, be sure to clean all oil holes and galleries very thoroughly and to dry all components well. Protect the liners as described above to prevent rusting.

7 All threaded holes must be clean to ensure accurate torque readings during reassembly. Run the proper size tap into each of the holes to remove rust, corrosion, thread sealant or sludge and to restore damaged threads. If possible, use compressed air to clear the holes of debris produced by this operation; a good alternative is to inject aerosol-applied water-dispersant lubricant into each hole, using the long spout usually supplied. Now is a good time to check the condition of the cylinder head bolts.

8 Apply suitable sealant to the new oil gallery plugs and insert them into the holes in the block. Tighten them securely.

9 If the engine is not going to be reassembled right away, cover it with a large plastic bag to keep it clean. Protect the liners as described above to prevent rusting.

Inspection

10 Visually check the castings for cracks and corrosion. Look for stripped threads in the threaded holes. If there has been any history of internal water leakage, it may be worthwhile having an engine overhaul specialist check the cylinder block/crankcase with special equipment. If defects are found have them repaired, if possible, or renew the assembly.

11 Check the bore of each cylinder liner for scuffing and scoring.

12 Measure the diameter of each cylinder liner bore. Where wet liners are fitted, measure 60 mm from the top of the bore, both parallel to the crankshaft axis and at right angles to it. Where damp liners are fitted, measure 65 mm from the top of the bore, again both parallel to the crankshaft axis and at right angles to it.

13 Compare the results with the Specifications at the beginning of Part A of this Chapter. If any measurement exceeds the service limit specified then the liner must be renewed.

14 Measure the piston diameter at right angles to the gudgeon pin axis, 16 mm up from the bottom of the skirt. Compare the results with the Specifications at the beginning of Part A of this Chapter.

15 To measure the piston-to-bore clearance, either measure the bore and piston skirt as described above and subtract the skirt diameter from the bore measurement, or insert each piston into its original bore, select a feeler blade and slip it into the bore along with the piston. The piston must be aligned exactly in its normal attitude and the feeler blade must be between the piston and bore on one of the thrust faces, 20 mm up from the bottom of the bore.

16 If the clearance is excessive a new piston will be required. If the piston binds at the lower end of the bore and is loose towards the top, the bore is tapered. If tight spots are encountered as the piston/feeler blade is rotated in the bore, the bore is out-of-round.

17 Repeat this procedure for the remaining pistons and cylinder liners.

18 If the cylinder liner walls are badly scuffed or scored, or if they are excessively worn, out-of-round or tapered, obtain and fit new cylinder liners. New pistons will also be required.

19 If the bores are in reasonably good condition and not worn to the specified limits and if the piston-to-bore clearances can be maintained properly, then it may only be necessary to renew the piston rings.

20 If this is the case, the bores should be honed to allow the new rings to bed in correctly and provide the best possible seal. The conventional type of hone has spring-loaded stones and is used with a power drill. You will also need some paraffin or honing oil and rags. The hone should be moved up and down the bore to produce a crosshatch pattern and plenty of honing oil should be used. Ideally the crosshatch lines should intersect at approximately a 60° angle. Do not take off more material than is necessary to produce the required finish. If new pistons are being fitted, the piston manufacturers may specify a finish with a different angle, so their instructions should be followed. Do not withdraw the hone from the bore while it is still being turned, but stop it first. After honing a bore, wipe out all traces of the honing oil. If equipment of this type is not available, or if you are not sure whether you are competent to undertake the task yourself, an engine overhaul specialist will carry out the work at moderate cost.

12.2 Always renew liner O-rings whenever liners are removed and oil before refitting

12 Cylinder liners - removal and fitting

Wet liner type

Removal

1 Invert the cylinder block/crankcase and support it on blocks of wood, then use a hard wood drift to tap out each liner from the crankshaft side. When all the liners are released, tip the cylinder block/crankcase on its side and remove each liner from the cylinder head side. Discard the two sealing O-rings from the base of each. If the liners are to be re-used, mark each one by sticking masking tape on its right-hand (timing belt) face and writing the cylinder number on the tape.

Fitting

2 Thoroughly clean the liner mating surfaces in the cylinder block/crankcase and use fine abrasive paper to polish away any burrs or sharp edges which might damage the liner O-rings. Clean the liners and wipe dry, then fit new sealing O-rings to the two grooves at the base of each liner and apply a thin film of oil to the O-rings and to the liner surface on each side of the O-rings **(see illustration)**.

3 If the original liners are being refitted, use the marks made on removal to ensure that each is refitted the same way round into its original bore. Insert each liner into the cylinder

12.3 Ensuring O-rings are not displaced, tap liner as shown onto locating shoulder

block/crankcase taking great care not to displace or damage the O-rings and press it home as far as possible by hand. Using a hammer and a block of wood, tap each liner lightly but fully onto its locating shoulder **(see illustration)**. Wipe clean, then lightly oil all exposed liner surfaces to prevent rusting.

Damp liner type

Removal

4 With the liner clamps removed, position the cylinder block on its side.

5 If the liners are to be re-used, mark each one in relation to the block by using a felt-tipped pen.

6 Applying hand pressure only, push each liner from its location towards the cylinder head side of the block.

7 Clean all old sealant from the cylinder block and from the liners if they are to be reused.

Fitting

8 Thoroughly clean and dry the mating surfaces of the liners and cylinder block.

9 Apply a continuous 2.0 mm thick bead of Hylomar sealant around the shoulder of each liner **(see illustration)**.

10 Positioning each liner so that it is square to the cylinder block, push it fully into position so that its shoulder seats against the block. Do not drop the liner into the block and ensure that any previous alignment marks made on reused liners are correctly positioned before seating the liner.

11 Refit the liner clamps and lightly oil all exposed liner surfaces to prevent rusting.

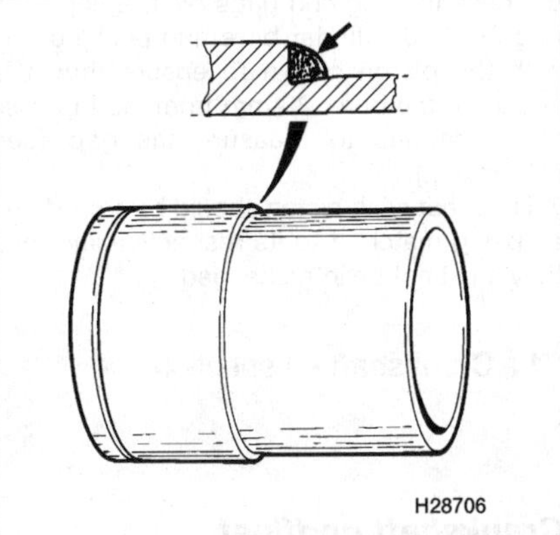

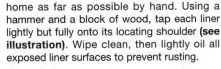

12.9 Apply a continuous 2.0 mm thick bead of sealant around the shoulder of each liner (arrowed)

13 Piston/connecting rod assembly - inspection

1 Examine the pistons for ovality, scoring and scratches, and for wear of the piston ring grooves. Use a micrometer to measure the pistons **(see illustration)**.

2 If the pistons or connecting rods are to be renewed, it is necessary to have this work carried out by a Rover dealer or suitable engine overhaul specialist who will have the necessary tooling to remove and install the gudgeon pins.

3 If new rings are to be fitted to the original pistons, expand the old rings over the top of the pistons. The use of two or three old feeler blades will be helpful in preventing the rings dropping into empty grooves **(see illustration)**.

4 When the original piston rings have been removed, ensure that the ring grooves in the piston are free of carbon by cleaning them using an old ring. Break the ring in half to do this.

5 Check the ring-to-groove clearance by inserting each ring from the outside together with a feeler blade between the ring's top surface and the piston land **(see illustration)**.

2B

13.1 Measuring piston diameter

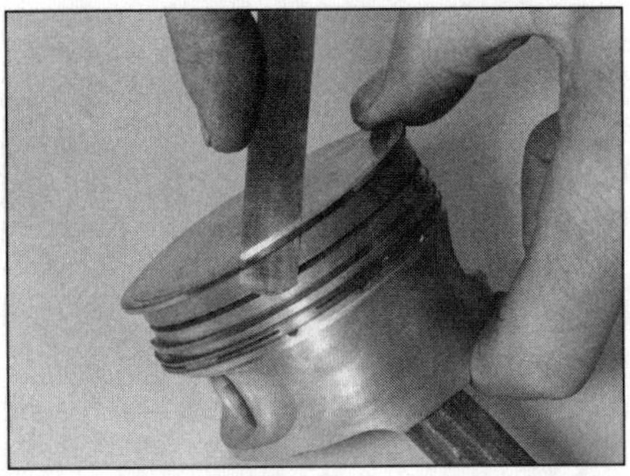

13.3 Removing piston rings using feeler blades

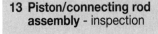

13.5 Measuring piston ring-to-groove clearance

6 Check the ring end gaps by inserting each ring into the cylinder bore and pushing it in with the piston crown to ensure that it is square in the bore, 20 mm from the top. Use feeler gauges to measure the gap **(see illustration).**

7 Note that each piston should be considered as being matched to its respective liner and they must not be interchanged.

14 Crankshaft - inspection

Crankshaft endfloat

1 If the crankshaft endfloat is to be checked, this must be done when the crankshaft is still installed in the cylinder block/crankcase but is free to move.

2 Check the endfloat using a dial gauge in contact with the end of the crankshaft **(see illustration)**. Push the crankshaft fully one way and then zero the gauge. Push the crankshaft fully the other way and check the endfloat. The result can be compared with the specified amount and will give an indication as to whether new thrustwashers are required.

3 If a dial gauge is not available, feeler gauges can be used. First push the crankshaft fully towards the flywheel end of the engine, then use feeler gauges to measure the gap between the web of number 3 crankpin and the thrustwasher.

14.2 Checking crankshaft endfloat using a dial gauge

14.6 Using a penny to check the condition of a crankshaft journal

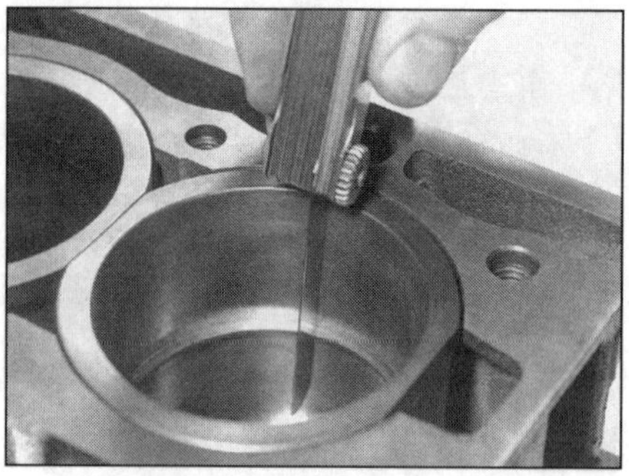

13.6 Measuring piston ring end gap

Crankshaft inspection

4 Clean the crankshaft and dry it with compressed air, if available.

Warning: Wear eye protection when using compressed air! Be sure to clean the oil holes with a pipe cleaner or similar probe.

5 Check the main and crankpin (big-end) bearing journals for uneven wear, scoring, pitting and cracking.

6 Rub a penny across each journal several times **(see illustration).** If a journal picks up copper from the penny, it is too rough.

7 Remove any burrs from the crankshaft oil holes with a stone, file or scraper.

8 Using a micrometer, measure the diameter of the main bearing and crankpin (big-end) journals and compare the results with the Specifications at the beginning of Part A of this Chapter **(see illustration).** Check carefully that each journal diameter is within the tolerances of the size grade corresponding to the code number on the crankshaft right-hand web (main bearing) or indicated by the code letter on the left-hand web (crankpin/big-end bearing). If any diameter measured is incorrect for the grade indicated, re-check the measurement carefully. If the journal is fit for further service, the correct grade code should be substituted when selecting new bearing shells.

9 By measuring the diameter at a number of points around each journal's circumference, you will be able to determine whether or not the journal is out-of-round. Take the measurement at each end of the journal (near the webs) to determine if the journal is tapered.

14.8 Measuring the diameter of a crankshaft journal

10 If the crankshaft journals are damaged, tapered, out-of-round or worn beyond the specified limits, the crankshaft must be renewed unless an engine overhaul specialist can be found who will regrind it and supply the necessary undersize bearing shells.

11 Check the oil seal journals at each end of the crankshaft for wear and damage. If either seal has worn an excessive groove in its journal, consult an engine overhaul specialist who will be able to advise whether a repair is possible or whether a new crankshaft is necessary.

15 Main and big-end bearings - inspection

1 Even though the main and big-end bearings should be renewed during the engine overhaul, the old bearings should be retained for close examination, as they may reveal valuable information about the condition of the engine. The bearing shells are graded by thickness, the grade of each shell being indicated by the colour code marked on it.

2 Bearing failure occurs because of lack of lubrication, the presence of dirt or other foreign particles, overloading the engine and corrosion. Regardless of the cause of bearing failure, it must be corrected before the engine is reassembled to prevent it from happening again.

3 When examining the bearing shells **(see illustration)**, remove them from the cylinder block/crankcase, the main bearing ladder, the connecting rods and the connecting rod big-end bearing caps and lay them out on a clean surface in the same general position as their location in the engine. This will enable you to

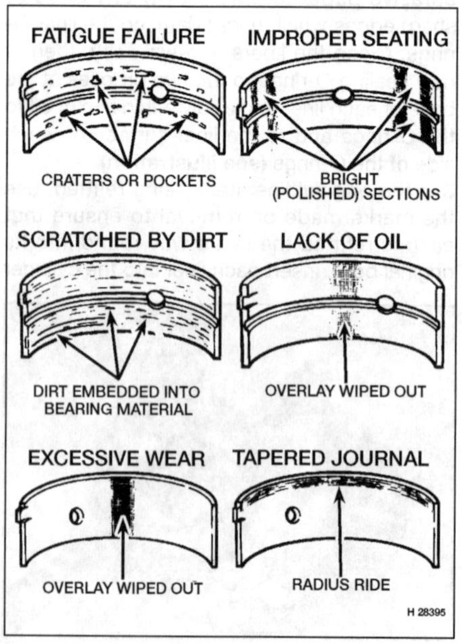

15.3 Typical bearing shell failures

match any bearing problems with the corresponding crankshaft journal. Do not touch any shell's bearing surface with your fingers while checking it, or the delicate surface may be scratched.

4 Dirt and other foreign particles get into the engine in a variety of ways. It may be left in the engine during assembly, or it may pass through filters or the crankcase ventilation system. It may get into the oil and from there into the bearings. Metal chips from machining operations and normal engine wear are often present. Abrasives are sometimes left in engine components after reconditioning, especially when parts are not thoroughly cleaned using the proper cleaning methods. Whatever the source, these foreign objects often end up embedded in the soft bearing material and are easily recognised. Large particles will not embed in the bearing and will score or gouge the bearing and journal. The best prevention for this cause of bearing failure is to clean all parts thoroughly and keep everything spotlessly clean during engine assembly. Frequent and regular engine oil and filter changes are also recommended.

5 Lack of lubrication (or lubrication breakdown) has a number of interrelated causes. Excessive heat (which thins the oil), overloading (which squeezes the oil from the bearing face) and oil leakage (from excessive bearing clearances, worn oil pump or high engine speeds) all contribute to lubrication breakdown. Blocked oil passages, which usually are the result of misaligned oil holes in a bearing shell, will also oil starve a bearing and destroy it. When lack of lubrication is the cause of bearing failure, the bearing material is wiped or extruded from the steel backing of the bearing. Temperatures may increase to the point where the steel backing turns blue from overheating.

6 Driving habits can have a definite effect on bearing life. Full throttle, low speed operation (labouring the engine) puts very high loads on bearings, which tends to squeeze out the oil film. These loads cause the bearings to flex, which produces fine cracks in the bearing face (fatigue failure). Eventually the bearing material will loosen in pieces and tear away from the steel backing. Short-distance driving leads to corrosion of bearings because insufficient engine heat is produced to drive off the condensed water and corrosive gases. These products collect in the engine oil, forming acid and sludge. As the oil is carried to the engine bearings, the acid attacks and corrodes the bearing material.

7 Incorrect bearing installation during engine assembly will lead to bearing failure as well. Tight fitting bearings leave insufficient bearing running clearance and will result in oil starvation. Dirt or foreign particles trapped behind a bearing shell result in high spots on the bearing which lead to failure. Do not touch any shell's bearing surface with your fingers during reassembly; there is a risk of scratching the delicate surface or of depositing particles of dirt on it.

16 Engine overhaul - reassembly sequence

1 Before reassembly begins, ensure that all new parts have been obtained and that all necessary tools are available. Read through the entire procedure to familiarise yourself with the work involved, and to ensure that all items necessary for reassembly of the engine are at hand. In addition to all normal tools and materials, a thread-locking compound will be needed. A tube of liquid sealant will also be required for the joint faces that are fitted without gaskets. It is recommended that Rover's own product is used, which is specially formulated for this purpose.

2 In order to save time and avoid problems, engine reassembly can be carried out in the following order.

a) Crankshaft.
b) Piston/connecting rod assemblies.
c) Oil pump.
d) Sump.
e) Flywheel.
f) Cylinder head.
g) Timing belt inner cover, tensioner and toothed pulleys, and timing belt.
h) Engine external components.

3 At this stage, all engine components should be absolutely clean and dry, with all faults repaired and should be laid out (or in individual containers) on a completely clean work surface.

> **HAYNES HiNT** *Lightly lubricate all engine bearing faces during reassembly.*

17 Piston rings - refitting

1 Before installing new piston rings, check the end gaps. It is assumed that the ring-to-groove clearance has been checked and found to be correct.

2 When measuring new rings, lay out each piston set with a piston/connecting rod assembly and keep them together as a matched set from now on.

3 If the end gap of a new ring is found to be too large or too small, double-check to ensure that you have the correct rings before proceeding. Note that the piston rings fitted to an engine equipped with wet cylinder liners will differ to those fitted to an engine equipped with damp liners. If the end gap is still too small, it must be opened up by careful filing of the ring ends using a fine file. If it is too large, this is not as serious unless the specified service limit is exceeded, in which case very careful checking is required of the dimensions of all components as well as of the new parts.

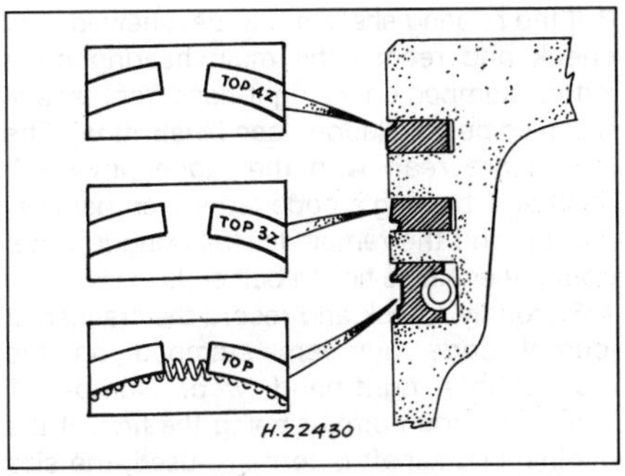

17.5 Piston ring fitting details and top surface markings

4 Once all rings have been checked, they can be installed. Ensure that each ring is refitted only to its matched piston and bore.

5 Install the new rings by fitting them over the top of the piston, starting with the oil control ring spring. Note that all the rings must be fitted with the word TOP uppermost **(see illustration)**.

6 With all the rings in position, space the ring gaps as shown **(see illustration)**, noting that the "FRONT" marking shown is usually in fact an arrow mark on the piston crown and indicates the timing belt end of the engine.

18 Crankshaft - refitting and main bearing running clearance check

2B

Selection of bearing shells

1 The main bearing running clearance is controlled in production by selecting one of three grades of bearing shell. The grades are indicated by a colour-coding marked on the edge of each shell which governs the shell's thickness, as follows:

a) Green - Thin.
b) Blue - Intermediate.
c) Red - Thick.

2 If shells of differing grades are to be fitted to the same journal, the thicker shell must always be fitted to the main bearing ladder location. Bear this carefully in mind when ordering replacement shells for numbers 2, 3 and 4 bearings.

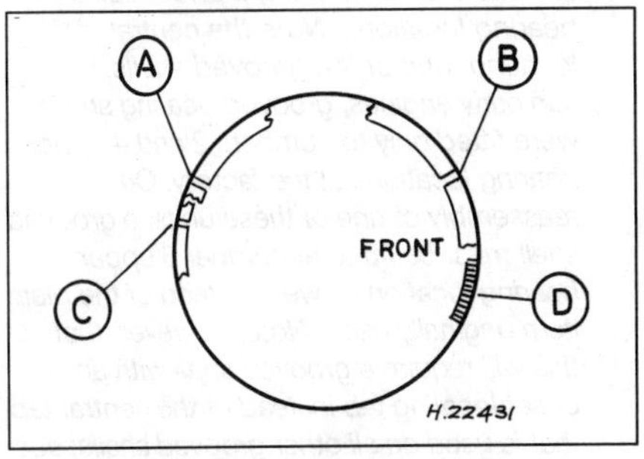

17.6 Piston ring end gap locations
A Top compression ring
B Second compression ring
C Oil control ring
D Oil control ring spring

3 If the bearing shells are to be renewed, first check and record the main bearing code letters stamped on the right-hand front face of the main bearing ladder **(see illustration)**. The letters are read with the ladder inverted, number 1 bearing's code letter then being at the top and the remainder following in order from the engine's timing belt end.

4 Secondly, check and record the crankshaft journal code numbers stamped on the crankshaft's right-hand web. Number 1 journal's code number being the first. If the original crankshaft is to be re-used, the size grade can be checked by direct measurement.

5 Note that if the crankshaft is found to be excessively worn, it must be renewed and the code numbers of the new component must be used instead to select a new set of bearing shells.

6 Matching the codes noted to the following table, select a new set of bearing shells.

Ladder code letter	Crankshaft code number	Shells
A	1	Blue, Blue
A	2	Red, Blue
A	3	Red, Red
B	1	Blue, Green
B	2	Blue, Blue
B	3	Red, Blue
C	1	Green, Green
C	2	Blue, Green
C	3	Blue, Blue

Main bearing running clearance check

7 Clean the backs of the bearing shells and the bearing locations in both the cylinder block/crankcase and the main bearing ladder.

8 Press the bearing shells into their locations, ensuring that the tab on each shell engages in the notch in the cylinder block/crankcase or main bearing ladder location and taking care not to touch any shell's bearing surface with your fingers.

9 Press the bearing shells with the oil grooves into the upper locations (in the cylinder block/crankcase). Note the following points **(see illustration)**:

a) On all engines, grooved bearing shells are fitted to numbers 2, 3 and 4 upper bearing locations. Note the central locating tabs of the grooved shells.

b) On early engines, grooved bearing shells were fitted only to numbers 2 and 4 upper bearing locations at the factory. On reassembly of one of these units, a grooved shell must be fitted at number 3 upper bearing location as well, instead of the plain item originally used. Note, however, that this will require a grooved shell with an offset locating tab instead of the central tab that is used on all other grooved shells; see your Rover dealer for details.

c) If bearing shells of differing grades are to be fitted to the same journal, the thicker shell must always be fitted to the main bearing ladder location.

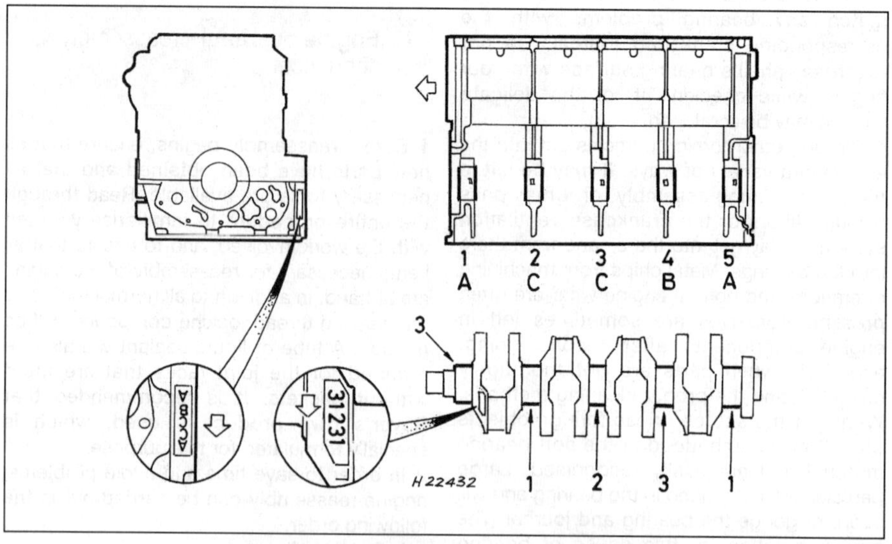

18.3 Crankshaft main bearing size code locations

d) On all engines, if the original main bearing shells are being re-used these must be refitted to their original locations in the cylinder block/crankcase and main bearing ladder.

10 The main bearing running clearance should be checked if there is any doubt about the amount of crankshaft wear that has taken place, if the crankshaft has been reground and is to be refitted with non-genuine undersized bearing shells, or if non-genuine bearing shells are to be fitted. If the original crankshaft or a genuine Rover replacement part is to be installed, the shell selection procedure given above will produce the correct clearances and a further check will not be necessary. If the clearance is to be checked, it can be done in either of two ways:

11 One method (which will be difficult to achieve without a range of internal micrometers or internal/external expanding calipers) is to refit the main bearing ladder to the cylinder block/crankcase, with bearing shells in place. With the ladder retaining bolts tightened to the specified torque, refit the oil rail and the cylinder head, tightening the cylinder head bolts in the approved sequence, then measure the internal diameter of each assembled pair of bearing shells. If the diameter of each corresponding crankshaft journal is measured and then subtracted from the bearing internal diameter, the result will be the main bearing running clearance.

12 The second (and more accurate) method is to use an American product known as Plastigage. This consists of a fine thread of perfectly round plastic which is compressed between the bearing shell and the journal. When the shell is removed, the plastic is deformed and can be measured with a special card gauge supplied with the kit. The running clearance is determined from this gauge. Plastigage is sometimes difficult to obtain but enquiries at one of the larger specialist quality motor factors should produce the name of a stockist in your area. The procedure for using Plastigage is as follows:

13 With the main bearing upper shells in place, carefully lay the crankshaft in position. Do not use any lubricant. The crankshaft journals and bearing shells must be perfectly clean and dry.

14 Cut several lengths of the appropriate size Plastigage (but slightly shorter than the width of the main bearings) and place one length on each crankshaft journal axis **(see illustration)**.

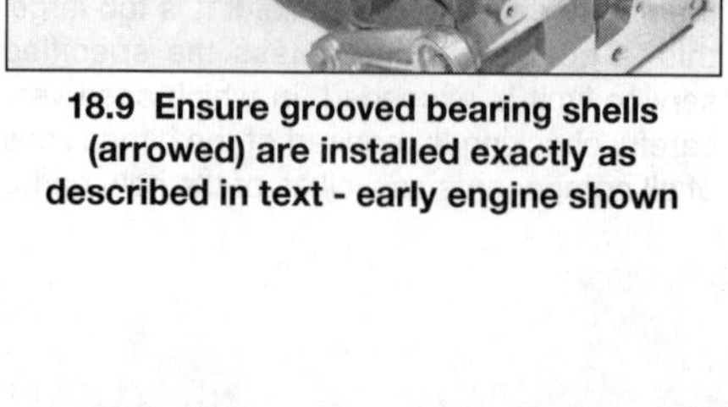
18.9 Ensure grooved bearing shells (arrowed) are installed exactly as described in text - early engine shown

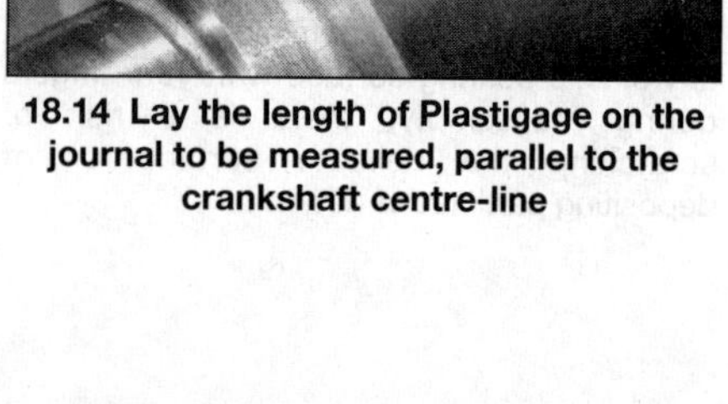
18.14 Lay the length of Plastigage on the journal to be measured, parallel to the crankshaft centre-line

18.18 Using the scale on the envelope provided to check (at its widest point) the width of the crushed Plastigage and measure the bearing running clearance

15 With the main bearing lower shells in position, refit the main bearing ladder (see below) and the oil rail, tightening their fasteners to the specified torque wrench settings. Take care not to disturb the Plastigage.

16 Refit the cylinder head (using the original gasket, to save over-compressing the new one), tightening its bolts in the approved sequence. Do not rotate the crankshaft at any time during this operation.

17 Remove the cylinder head, the oil rail and the main bearing ladder. Do not disturb the Plastigage or rotate the crankshaft.

18 Compare the width of the crushed Plastigage on each journal to the scale printed on the Plastigage envelope to obtain the main bearing running clearance **(see illustration)**.

19 If the clearance is not as specified, the bearing shells may be the wrong grade (or excessively worn if the original shells are being re-used). Before deciding that different grade shells are needed, make sure that no dirt or oil was trapped between the bearing shells and the ladder or cylinder block/crankcase when the clearance was measured. If the Plastigage was wider at one end than at the other, the journal may be tapered.

18.24a If piston/connecting rod assemblies are refitted before the main bearing ladder is installed . . .

20 Carefully scrape away all traces of the Plastigage material from the crankshaft and bearing shells using a fingernail or other object which is unlikely to score the shells.

Final crankshaft refitting

21 Carefully lift the crankshaft out of the cylinder block once more.

22 Using a little grease, stick the thrustwashers to each side of the number 3 main bearing upper location. Ensure that the oilway grooves on each thrustwasher face outwards.

23 Place the bearing shells in their locations as described above. If new shells are being fitted, ensure that all traces of the protective grease are cleaned off using paraffin. Wipe dry the shells and connecting rods with a lint-free cloth. Liberally lubricate each bearing shell in the cylinder block/crankcase, then lower the crankshaft into position so that numbers 2 and 3 cylinder crankpins are at TDC.

24 Refit the piston/connecting rod assemblies. The crankshaft should now be at the (number 1 and 4 cylinders) TDC position **(see illustrations)**.

25 Thoroughly degrease the mating surfaces of the cylinder block/crankcase and the main bearing ladder. Apply continuous thin beads of sealant to the cylinder block/crankcase mating surface as shown **(see illustration)**,

18.24b . . . care is required to hold the crankshaft steady while the connecting rod big-end cap bolts are tightened . . .

18.24c . . . but crankshaft can be rotated to required position

then spread them to an even film with a small brush. **Note:** *If the Rover sealant is being used, assembly must be completed as soon as possible after the sealant has been applied (maximum of 20 minutes). If another sealant is being used, follow its manufacturer's instructions.*

26 Lubricate the bearing shells, then refit the main bearing ladder, ensuring that the shells are not displaced and that the locating dowels engage correctly. Working progressively, by a turn at a time and in the sequence shown **(see illustration)**, tighten the ladder bolts to the specified torque wrench setting; the crankshaft cannot now be rotated.

2B

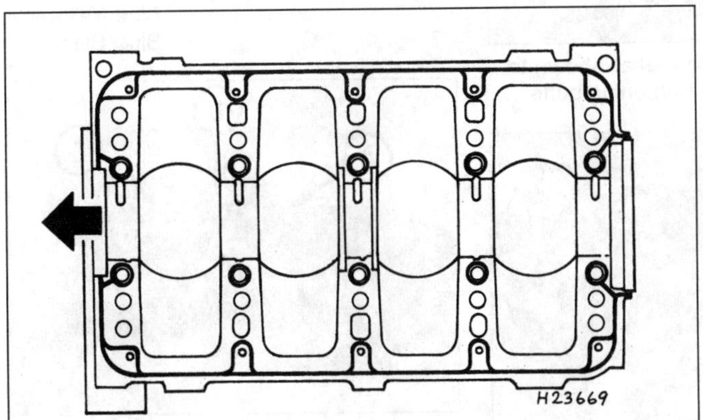

18.25 Apply thin bead of sealant to cylinder block/crankcase mating surface along paths shown by heavy black lines, then spread to an even film

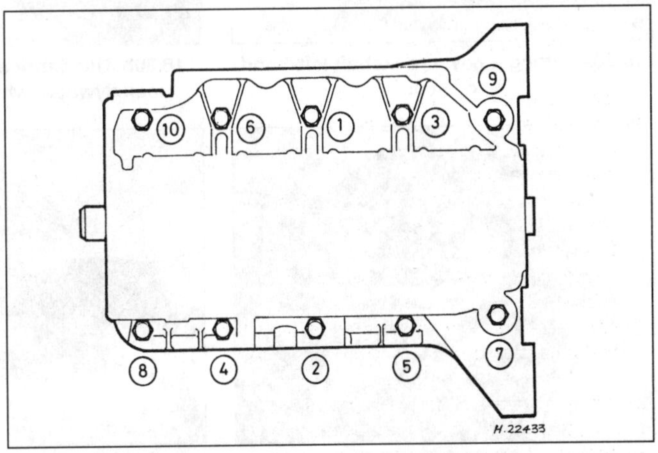

18.26 Crankshaft main bearing ladder bolt tightening sequence

27 Thoroughly degrease the mating surfaces of the oil rail and the main bearing ladder. Apply continuous beads of sealant to the oil rail mating surface as shown **(see illustration)**, then spread them to an even film with a small brush.

28 Refit the oil rail, tightening its nuts to the specified torque wrench setting.

29 Using a new sealing O-ring, refit the oil pump pick-up/strainer pipe to the oil rail, then refit the sump. Tighten all nuts and bolts to their specified torque wrench settings.

30 Fit a new crankshaft left-hand oil seal, then refit the flywheel, using new bolts **(see illustrations)**.

31 Refit the oil pump then install a new crankshaft right-hand oil seal **(see illustrations)**.

32 Refit the cylinder head. Rotate the crankshaft to the 90° BTDC position so that the crankshaft toothed pulley timing marks align correctly.

33 Refit the dipstick tube to the cylinder block/crankcase, tightening its bolts to the specified torque wrench setting.

34 Refit the timing belt inner cover, the toothed pulley(s) and tensioner, and the belt itself.

35 Using a torque wrench, check that the amount of force required to rotate the crankshaft does not exceed 31 Nm. If the effort required is greater than this, the engine must be dismantled again to trace and rectify the cause. This value takes into account the increased friction of a new engine and is much higher than the actual pressure required to rotate a run-in engine, so do not make allowances for tight components. If excessive pressure is required to rotate the crankshaft, the engine has not been rebuilt to the required standard and must be dismantled again.

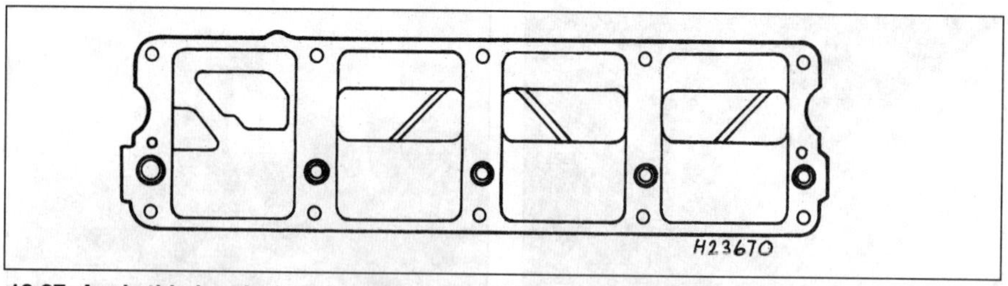

18.27 Apply thin bead of sealant to oil rail mating surface as shown by heavy black lines, then spread to an even film

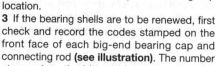

19 Piston/connecting rod assembly - refitting and big-end bearing running clearance check

Selection of bearing shells

1 The big-end bearing running clearance is controlled in production by selecting one of three grades of bearing shell. The grades are indicated by a colour-coding marked on the edge of each shell which governs the shell's thickness, as follows:

a) Yellow - Thin.
b) Blue - Intermediate.
c) Red - Thick.

2 If shells of differing grades are to be fitted to the same journal, the thicker shell must always be fitted to the big-end bearing cap location.

3 If the bearing shells are to be renewed, first check and record the codes stamped on the front face of each big-end bearing cap and connecting rod **(see illustration)**. The number stamped on the big-end bearing cap is the bearing size code, the number stamped on the connecting rod is the piston/rod assembly's cylinder number and the letter stamped on the connecting rod is its weight code.

4 Secondly, check and record the crankpin/big-end journal code letters stamped on the crankshaft's left-hand web **(see illustration)**. Number 1 journal's code letter being the first. If the original crankshaft is to be re-used, the code letter can be checked by direct measurement.

5 Note that if the crankshaft is found to be excessively worn it must be renewed and the code letters of the new component must be used instead to select a new set of bearing shells.

6 Matching the codes noted to the following table, select a new set of bearing shells.

Cap code number	Crankshaft code letter	Shells
5	A	Blue, Blue
5	B	Red, Blue
5	C	Red, Red
6	A	Blue, Yellow
6	B	Blue, Blue
6	C	Red, Blue
7	A	Yellow, Yellow
7	B	Blue, Yellow
7	C	Blue, Blue

18.30a Fitting a new crankshaft left-hand oil seal

18.30b Use fabricated tool as shown to lock flywheel while tightening bolts

18.31a Use grease to stick new gasket in place when refitting oil pump

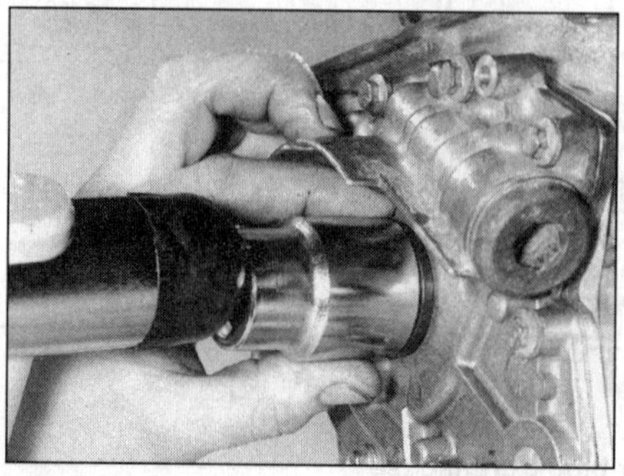

18.31b Fitting a new crankshaft right-hand oil seal

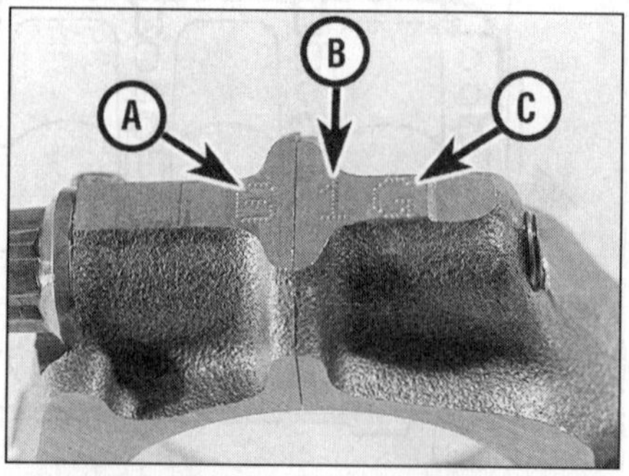

19.3 Big-end bearing size code number (A - on cap) piston/connecting rod assembly cylinder number (B) and connecting rod weight code letter (C)

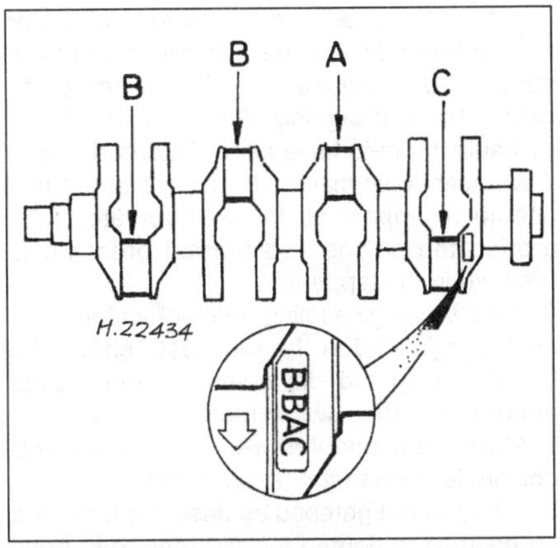

19.4 Crankpin (big-end) journal size code location

Big-end bearing running clearance check

7 If the clearance is to be checked, it can be done in either of two ways:

8 One method is to refit the big-end bearing cap to the connecting rod, with bearing shells in place. With the cap retaining bolts tightened to the specified torque, use an internal micrometer or vernier caliper to measure the internal diameter of each assembled pair of bearing shells. If the diameter of each corresponding crankshaft journal is measured and then subtracted from the bearing internal diameter, the result will be the big-end bearing running clearance.

9 The second method is to use Plastigage. Place a strand of Plastigage on each (cleaned) crankpin journal and refit the (clean) piston/connecting rod assemblies, shells and big-end bearing caps, tightening the bolts to the specified torque wrench settings. Take care not to disturb the Plastigage. Dismantle the assemblies without rotating the crankshaft and use the scale printed on the Plastigage envelope to obtain the big-end bearing running clearance. On completion of the measurement, carefully scrape off all traces of Plastigage from the journal and shells using a fingernail or other object which will not score the components.

Final piston/connecting rod assembly refitting

10 Note that the following procedure assumes that the cylinder liners have been refitted to the cylinder block/crankcase and that the crankshaft and main bearing ladder are in place. It is of course possible to refit the piston/connecting rod assemblies to the cylinder bores, to refit the crankshaft and to reassemble the piston/connecting rods on the crankshaft before refitting the main bearing ladder.

11 Clean the backs of the bearing shells and the bearing recesses in both the connecting rod and the big-end bearing cap. If new shells are being fitted, ensure that all traces of the protective grease are cleaned off using

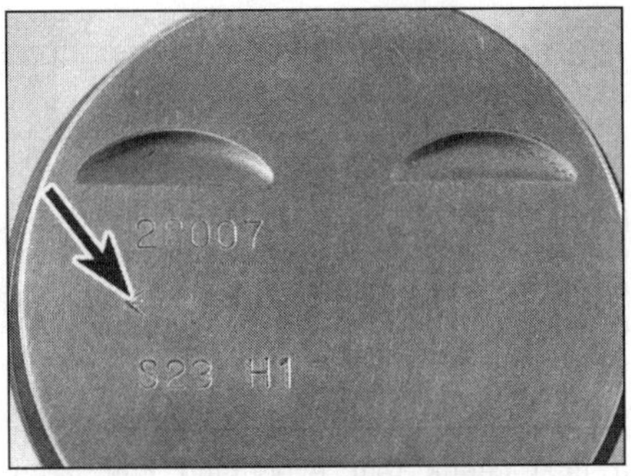

19.15a Arrow (or FRONT marking) on piston crown must point to timing belt end of engine (arrowed)

paraffin. Wipe dry the shells and connecting rods with a lint-free cloth.

12 Press the bearing shells into their locations, ensuring that the tab on each shell engages in the notch in the connecting rod or big-end bearing cap and taking care not to touch any shell's bearing surface with your fingers. Note the following points:

a) *If bearing shells of differing grades are to be fitted to the same journal, the thicker shell must always be fitted to the big-end bearing cap location.*
b) *On all engines, if the original big-end bearing shells are being re-used these must be refitted to their original locations in the connecting rod and big-end bearing cap.*

13 Lubricate the cylinder bores, the pistons and piston rings then lay out each piston/connecting rod assembly in its respective position.

14 Starting with assembly number 1, make sure that the piston rings are still spaced correctly, then clamp them using a piston ring compressor.

15 Insert the piston/connecting rod assembly into the top of liner number 1, ensuring that the arrow (or "FRONT" marking) on the piston crown faces the timing belt end of the engine. Note that the stamped marks on the connecting rod and big-end bearing cap should face the front (alternator bracket side) of the engine. Using a block of wood or hammer handle against the piston crown, tap

19.15b Using a piston ring compressor to clamp piston rings while piston/connecting rod assembly is refitted to cylinder bore

the assembly into the liner until the piston crown is flush with the top of the liner **(see illustrations)**.

16 Ensure that the bearing shell is still correctly installed. Taking care not to mark the liner bores, liberally lubricate the crankpin and both bearing shells, then pull the piston/connecting rod assembly down its bore and onto the crankpin. Noting that the faces with the stamped marks must match (which means that the bearing shell locating tabs abut each other), refit the big-end bearing cap, tightening its bolts finger-tight at first.

17 Use a torque wrench to tighten the bolts evenly to the (first stage) torque wrench setting specified, then use an angular torque gauge to tighten the bolts evenly through the (second stage) angle specified **(see illustrations)**.

18 Repeat the procedure for the remaining three piston/connecting rod assemblies.

19 Thoroughly degrease the mating surfaces of the oil rail and the main bearing ladder. Apply continuous thin beads of sealant to the oil rail mating surface, referring to illustration 18.27, then spread them to an even film with a small brush.

20 Refit the oil rail, tightening its nuts to the specified torque wrench setting.

21 Using a new O-ring, refit the oil pump pick-up/strainer pipe to the oil rail, then refit the sump. Tighten all nuts and bolts to their specified torque wrench settings.

19.17a Tighten connecting rod big-end bearing cap bolts to specified torque wrench setting (first stage) . . .

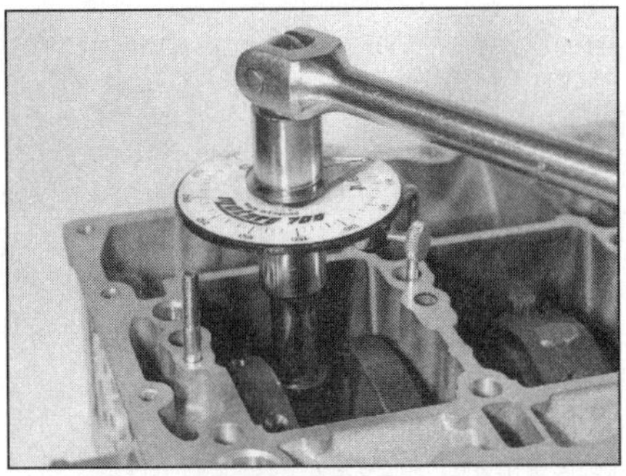

19.17b . . . then use angular torque gauge to tighten bolts through angle specified (second stage)

22 Refit the cylinder head. Rotate the crankshaft to the 90° BTDC position so that the crankshaft toothed pulley timing marks align correctly.

23 Refit the dipstick tube to the cylinder block/crankcase, tightening its bolts to the specified torque wrench setting.

24 Refit the hydraulic tappets and camshaft(s).

25 Refit the timing belt inner cover, the toothed pulley(s) and tensioner, and the belt itself.

26 Using a torque wrench, check that the amount of force required to rotate the crankshaft does not exceed 31 Nm. If the effort required is greater than this, the engine must be dismantled again to trace and rectify the cause. This value takes into account the increased friction of a new engine and is much higher than the actual pressure required to rotate a run-in engine, so do not make allowances for tight components. If excessive pressure is required to rotate the crankshaft, the engine has not been rebuilt to the required standard and must be dismantled again.

20 Engine - initial start-up after overhaul

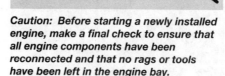

Caution: Before starting a newly installed engine, make a final check to ensure that all engine components have been reconnected and that no rags or tools have been left in the engine bay.

1 With the engine refitted in the car, double-check the engine oil and coolant levels. Make a final check that everything has been reconnected and that there are no tools or rags left in the engine compartment.

2 With the spark plugs removed and the ignition system disabled by earthing the ignition HT coil distributor spark plug (HT) lead with a jumper lead, turn the engine over on the starter until the oil pressure warning lamp goes out.

3 Refit the spark plugs and connect all the spark plug (HT) leads.

4 Start the engine, noting that this may take a little longer than usual due to the fuel system components being empty.

5 With the engine idling, check for fuel, water and oil leaks. Do not be alarmed if there are some odd smells and smoke from parts getting hot and burning off oil deposits. If the hydraulic tappets have been disturbed, some valve gear noise may be heard at first but this should disappear as the oil circulates fully around the engine and normal pressure is restored in the tappets.

6 Keep the engine idling until hot water is felt circulating through the top hose, check the ignition timing and idle speed and mixture (as appropriate), then switch it off.

7 After a few minutes, recheck the oil and coolant levels and top up as necessary.

8 If they were tightened as described, there is no need to re-tighten the cylinder head bolts once the engine has first run after reassembly.

9 If new pistons, rings or crankshaft bearings have been fitted, the engine must be run-in for the first 500 miles (800 km). Do not operate the engine at full throttle or allow it to labour in any gear during this period. It is recommended that the oil and filter be changed at the end of this period.

Chapter 3
Cooling, heating and ventilation systems

Contents

Degrees of difficulty

Easy, suitable for novice with little experience	**Fairly easy,** suitable for beginner with some experience	**Fairly difficult,** suitable for competent DIY mechanic	**Difficult,** suitable for experienced DIY mechanic	**Very difficult,** suitable for expert DIY or professional

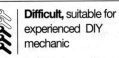

3

Specifications

System

Type	Pressurised, pump-assisted, thermo-syphon with front-mounted radiator and thermostatically-controlled electric cooling fan.

Thermostat

Type	Wax
Start to open temperature	76 to 80°C
Fully open temperature	82 or 88°C (actual value stamped in unit end)
Full lift height	9.0 mm

Expansion tank

Cap pressure	0.9 to 1.0 bar

Cooling fan

Operating temperature	88 to 92°C

Torque wrench settings

Torque wrench settings	Nm	lbf ft
Coolant temperature gauge sender unit	15	11
Inlet manifold pre-heater temperature switch (carburettor engines)	15	11
Coolant temperature sensor (fuel-injected engines)	15	11
Thermostat housing cover bolts:		
Alloy housing	10	8
Plastic housing	8	6
Thermostat housing/dipstick tube-to-cylinder block/crankcase bolt	10	8
Coolant rail-to-cylinder block/crankcase bolts	10	8
Coolant pump fasteners:		
Pump-to-timing belt upper left-hand (inner) cover bolt	10	8
Pump-to-cylinder block/crankcase bolts	10	8
Heater air inlet box and blower motor-to-body bolts and nuts	7	5

1 General information and precautions

General information

Cooling system

The cooling system is of the pressurised, pump-assisted thermo-syphon type. It comprises the front-mounted radiator (which is of copper/brass, with moulded plastic side tanks), a translucent expansion tank mounted on the right-hand inner wing, a thermostatically-controlled electric cooling fan mounted on the rear of the radiator, a thermostat and a centrifugal water pump, as well as the connecting hoses. The water pump is driven by the engine timing belt.

Heating and ventilation systems

The heater has a three-speed blower housed in the engine compartment, face level vents in the centre and at each end of the facia and air ducts to the front footwells. Illuminated sliding controls for air temperature and distribution are housed, with the heater blower switch, in the facia instrument panel and operate flap valves to deflect the air flowing through the heater. Cold air enters through the grille at the rear of the bonnet, is boosted when required by the blower's radial fan and flows through the ducts, according to the control setting; stale air is exhausted through tailgate ducts. If warm air is required, the cold air is passed over the copper/brass heater matrix which is heated by the engine coolant.

The blower motor is controlled by a switch mounted in the instrument panel. The blower fan and its motor are mounted in the engine compartment, in the heater air inlet/blower motor assembly. The motor is regulated to any one of three speeds by switching in elements of a resistor unit which is mounted on the heater air inlet/blower motor assembly. The circuit is supplied with current via a fuse and ignition relay.

Precautions

Do not attempt to remove the expansion tank filler cap or to disturb any part of the cooling system whilst it or the engine is hot, as there is a very great risk of scalding. If the expansion tank filler cap must be removed before the engine and radiator have fully cooled down (even though this is not recommended) the pressure in the cooling system must first be released. Cover the cap with a thick layer of cloth, to avoid scalding, and slowly unscrew the filler cap until a hissing sound can be heard. When the hissing has stopped, showing that pressure is released, slowly unscrew the filler cap until it can be removed; if more hissing sounds are heard, wait until they have stopped before unscrewing the cap completely. At all times keep well away from the filler opening.

Do not allow antifreeze to come in contact with your skin or painted surfaces of the vehicle. Rinse off spills immediately with plenty of water. Never leave antifreeze lying around, it is fatal if ingested.

If the engine is hot, the electric cooling fan may start rotating even if the engine is not running, so be careful to keep hands, hair and loose clothing well clear when working in the engine compartment.

2 Cooling system - draining, flushing and refilling

Refer to Chapter 1, Section 32.

3 Cooling system - general inspection

Refer to Chapter 1 for details of system inspection, antifreeze mixture and checking the system coolant level.

4 Cooling system hoses - renewal

Caution: Never work on the cooling system when it is hot. Release any pressure from the system by loosening the expansion tank cap, having first covered it with a cloth to avoid any possibility of scalding.

1 If inspection of the system reveals a faulty hose, it must be renewed as follows:

2 First drain the cooling system. If the coolant is not due for renewal, it may be re-used if collected in a clean container.

3 To disconnect any hose, use a screwdriver to slacken the clips then move them along the hose clear of the outlet. Carefully work the hose off its outlets. **Do not** attempt to disconnect any part of the system when still hot.

4 Note that the radiator hose outlets are fragile; do not use excessive force when attempting to remove the hoses. If a hose proves stubborn try to release it by rotating it on its outlets before attempting to work it off. If all else fails, cut the hose with a sharp knife then slit it so that it can be peeled off in two pieces. While expensive, this is preferable to buying a new radiator.

5 When refitting a hose, first slide the clips onto the hose then work the hose onto its outlets **(see illustration)**. If the hose is stiff, use soap as a lubricant or soften it by first soaking it in boiling water, but take care to prevent scalding.

6 Work each hose end fully onto its outlet, check that the hose is settled correctly and is properly routed, then slide each clip along the hose until it is behind the outlet flared end before tightening it securely.

7 Refill the system with coolant.

8 Check carefully for leaks as soon as possible after disturbing any part of the cooling system.

4.5 Connecting the radiator top hose to the coolant outlet elbow

5 Radiator and expansion tank - removal, inspection and refitting

Removal

Radiator

1 Drain the cooling system.

2 Remove the electric cooling fan assembly.

3 Disconnect the remaining coolant hoses from the radiator as required. If necessary, the radiator top hose and expansion tank hose can be disconnected so that the coolant cross-pipe is removed with the radiator and subsequently disconnected.

4 Disconnect the electric cooling fan thermostatic switch wires.

5 Withdraw the radiator, taking care not to damage its matrix on the exhaust manifold **(see illustration)**. Detach the cross-pipe (where appropriate).

Expansion tank

6 The expansion tank can be removed, as soon as the system has been drained by unscrewing its mounting nuts and disconnecting its hoses.

Expansion tank filler cap

7 Unscrew the filler cap from the top of the expansion tank.

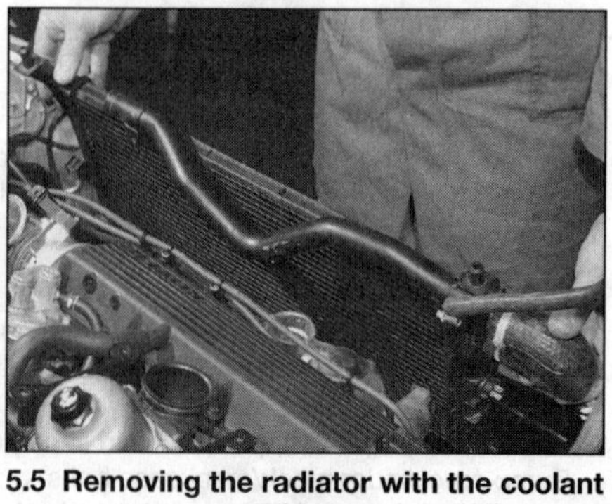

5.5 Removing the radiator with the coolant cross-pipe

Inspection

Radiator

8 If the radiator was removed because of clogging, then try reverse flushing or, in severe cases, use a radiator cleanser strictly in accordance with the manufacturer's instructions; ensure that the cleanser is suitable for use in a copper/brass radiator.
9 Use a soft brush and an air line or garden hose to clear the radiator matrix of leaves, insects etc.
10 Minor leaks from the radiator can be cured using a proprietary product. Major leaks or extensive damage should be repaired by a specialist, or the radiator should be renewed or exchanged for a reconditioned unit.
11 If the radiator is to be repaired or exchanged, detach the thermostatic switch and any remaining coolant hoses.
12 Check the condition of the mountings and renew them if necessary.

Expansion tank

13 Empty any remaining coolant from the tank and flush it with fresh water to clean it. If the tank is leaking it must be renewed, but it is worth first attempting a repair using a proprietary sealant or suitable adhesive.

Expansion tank filler cap

14 The cap should be cleaned and checked whenever it is removed. Check that its sealing surfaces and threads are clean and undamaged and that they mate correctly with those of the expansion tank.
15 The cap's performance can be checked only using a cap pressure-tester (cooling system tester) with a suitable adapter. On applying pressure, the cap's pressure relief valve should hold until the specified pressure is reached, at which point the valve should open.
16 If there is any doubt about the cap's performance, it must be renewed; ensure that the replacement is of exactly the correct type and rating.

Refitting

Radiator

17 Refitting is the reverse of the removal procedure, noting the following points.

a) Ensure that the radiator is seated correctly and without strain on its mountings.
b) Position the hose clips carefully so that they do not foul any other component.
c) Refill the cooling system.

Expansion tank

18 Refitting is the reverse of the removal procedure, noting the following points.

a) Ensure that the hoses, especially that between the tank and the radiator, are correctly routed with no kinks or sharp bends and are secured by the clips provided.
b) Refill the cooling system.

6.1 The thermostat can be removed without disturbing its housing if the inlet manifold is removed first

Expansion tank filler cap

19 Refitting is a reversal of removal.

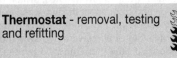

6 Thermostat - removal, testing and refitting

Removal

1 Note that access to the thermostat is very limited, depending on the tools available. It may be easier to raise the front of the car and to work from underneath - ensure that the car is securely supported on axle stands (see "*Jacking and Vehicle Support*"). In most cases however, access is better if the air cleaner and carburettor/throttle body (as appropriate) are removed first and is best if the complete inlet manifold is removed. If the inlet manifold is removed, the thermostat housing cover can be unbolted to remove the thermostat without disturbing the housing itself **(see illustration)**.
2 On models equipped with Multi Point Injection incorporating an alloy inlet manifold, if the manifold is to be removed, loosen the bolt securing the manifold stay to the cylinder block. Detach the stay from the manifold and pivot the stay to one side.
3 Whichever method is used, first drain the cooling system.
4 Where fitted, either remove the thermostatically-operated vacuum switch or disconnect the vacuum pipes from the switch so that it can be removed with the thermostat housing.

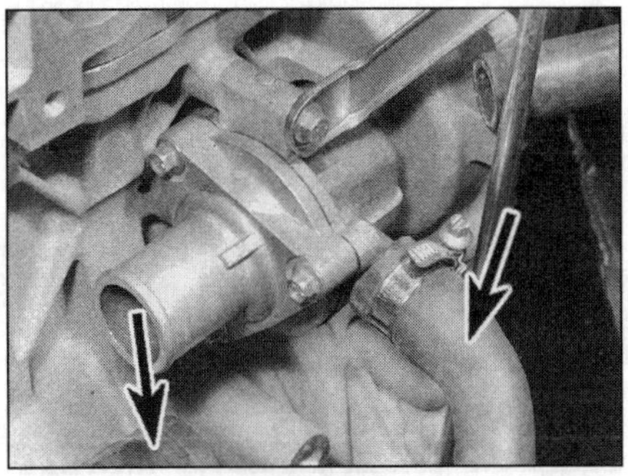

6.5 Thermostat removal - inlet manifold removed for clarity - disconnecting coolant hoses (arrowed) . . .

5 Unbolt the coolant rail from the rear of the cylinder block/crankcase, then slacken their clips and disconnect the coolant rail hose and heater/inlet manifold return hose from the thermostat housing **(see illustration)**.
6 Undo the thermostat housing/dipstick tube-to-cylinder block/crankcase bolt **(see illustration)**.
7 Remove the thermostat housing from the cylinder block/crankcase **(see illustration)**.
8 Remove the sealing O-ring; this must be renewed whenever it is disturbed. Unbolt the housing cover and discard the gasket, then withdraw the thermostat.

Testing

9 If the thermostat remains in the open position at room temperature it is faulty and must be renewed as a matter of course.
10 To test it fully, suspend the (closed) thermostat on a length of string in a container of cold water, with a thermometer beside it; ensure that neither touches the side of the container.
11 Heat the water and check the temperature at which the thermostat begins to open. Compare this value with that specified. Continue to heat the water until the thermostat is fully open; the temperature at which this should happen is stamped in the unit's end **(see illustration)**. Remove the thermostat and measure the height of the fully opened valve, then allow the thermostat to cool down and check that it closes fully.

6.6 . . . unscrew bolt securing dipstick tube and thermostat housing to cylinder block/crankcase . . .

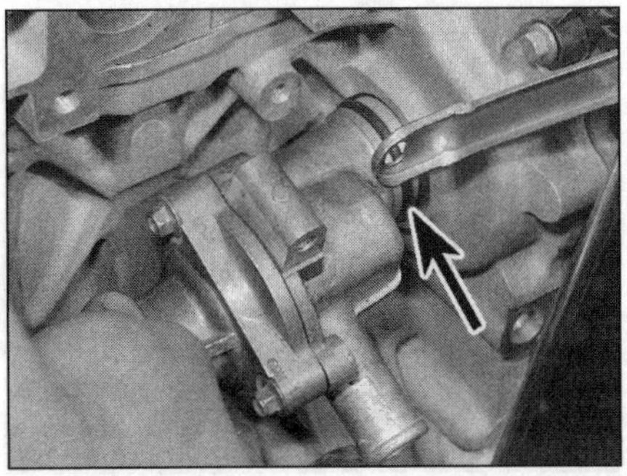

6.7 . . . and withdraw complete thermostat housing - always renew O-ring (arrowed)

3

6.11 Note temperature specification stamped in thermostat end

12 If the thermostat does not open and close as described, if it sticks in either position, or if it does not open at the specified temperature, it must be renewed.

Refitting

13 Refitting is the reverse of the removal procedure, noting the following points **(see illustration)**:

- *a) Clean the thermostat housing, housing cover and cylinder block/crankcase mating surfaces thoroughly.*
- *b) Always fit a new cover gasket and sealing O-ring. Smear the O-ring with grease to aid refitting.*
- *c) Tighten all bolts to their specified torque wrench settings.*
- *d) Ensure that the coolant hose clips are positioned so that they do not foul any other component, then tighten them securely.*
- *e) Refit any components removed for improved access.*
- *f) Refill the cooling system.*

7 Electric cooling fan - testing, removal and refitting

Testing

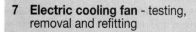

1 The cooling fan motor is supplied with current via the ignition switch and fuse, the circuit being completed by the radiator-mounted thermostatic switch.

6.13 Thermostat housing refitted and coolant hoses correctly secured

2 If the fan does not appear to work, run the engine until normal operating temperature is reached, then allow it to idle. If the fan does not cut in within a few minutes, switch off the ignition and disconnect the two wires from the thermostatic switch. Bridge these two wires with a length of spare wire and switch on the ignition. If the fan now operates, the thermostatic switch is probably faulty and must be tested further.

3 If the fan still fails to operate, check that full battery voltage is available at the switch's light green wire terminal. If not, check the feed for a blown fuse or other fault. If the feed is good, check that there is continuity between the fan motor's black wire terminal and a good earth point on the body; if not, then the earth connection is faulty and must be remade.

4 If the switch and wiring are in good condition, the fault must be in the motor itself. This can be checked by disconnecting it from the wiring loom and connecting a 12 volt supply directly to it. If the motor does not work it must be renewed; see the note at the end of the removal sequence below.

Removal

Carburettor and single-point injection models

5 Disconnect the battery negative lead.

6 Disconnect the vacuum pipe from the inlet air temperature control valve, release the two clips securing the air inlet duct to the air

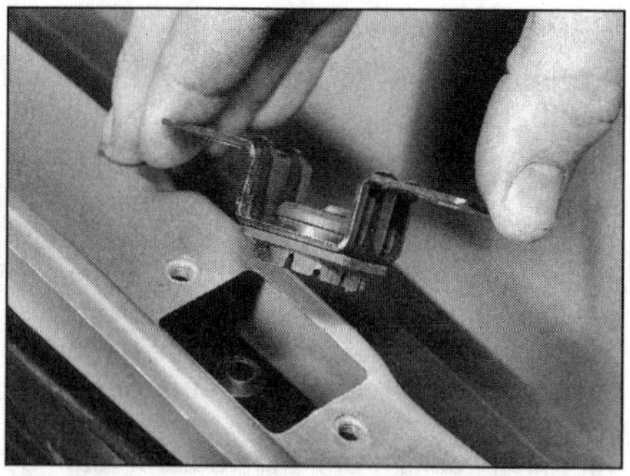

7.9 Unscrew bolts to release radiator top mountings from bonnet lock platform and check condition of mounting rubbers - renew if necessary

cleaner assembly and (as appropriate) unscrew the bolt or release the quarter-turn fastener(s) securing the duct to its support bracket(s).

7 Where fitted, unfasten the rubber strap and unbolt the support bracket from the cylinder head; unclip the vacuum pipe and withdraw the bracket.

8 Remove the two screws securing the cold air inlet duct to the body front panel, then withdraw the complete inlet duct assembly, taking care not to lose the hot air inlet connector hose.

9 Unbolt the radiator top mountings from the bonnet lock platform and remove both mounting brackets **(see illustration)**.

10 Remove the two (hex-head) screws securing the coolant cross-pipe to the radiator, release the cross-pipe and secure it as far away from the working area as possible, over the cylinder head and exhaust manifold. **Note:** *The cooling fan and cowl assembly are very difficult to remove past the cross-pipe.* If the extra room is needed, drain the cooling system and disconnect the radiator top hose from the cross-pipe **(see illustrations)**.

11 Unscrew the remaining (hex-head) screw securing the cooling fan and cowl assembly to the radiator **(see illustration)**.

12 Disconnect the fan motor wires and release the wiring from the cowl clip **(see illustration)**.

7.10a Pull radiator backwards at top edge to undo cross-pipe screw at right-hand end (arrowed) . . .

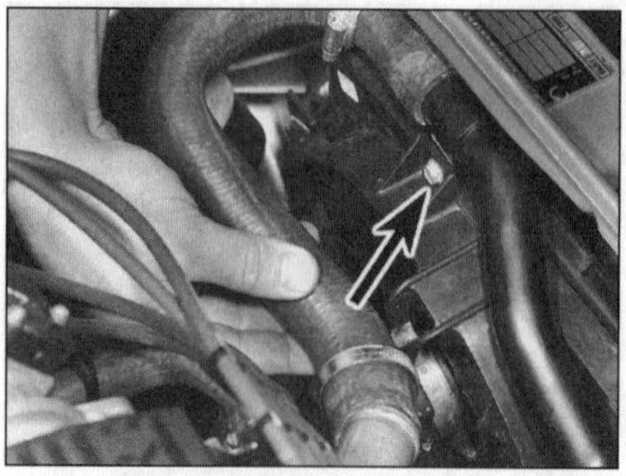

7.10b . . . it may be necessary to disconnect radiator top hose from cross-pipe - note remaining cross-pipe screw (arrowed)

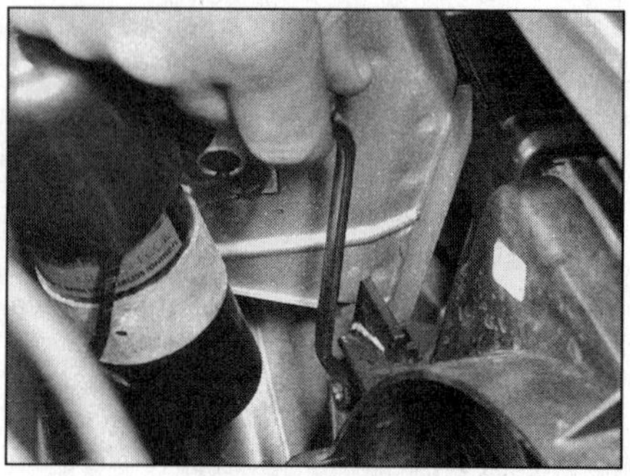

7.11 Unscrewing remaining screw securing electric cooling fan and cowl assembly

13 Release the radiator from its lower mountings; it is seated on two pegs on its bottom edge which locate in rubber bushes in the body front panel.

14 Slide the cooling fan and cowl assembly towards the centre of the radiator, rotate it to release it from the radiator and withdraw it **(see illustration)**. Take care not to damage the radiator matrix.

15 Note that if only the fan, its motor or the cowl is to be renewed, check with a Rover dealer before attempting to strip the assembly. If the separate items are not available, the assembly must be renewed complete and there is no point in trying to dismantle it. If they are available separately, the fan motor is secured by pop rivets to the cowl; these must be drilled out to release the motor and new rivets must be inserted on reassembly. The fan is secured by a clip to the motor shaft **(see illustrations)**.

Multi-point injection models

16 Disconnect the battery negative lead.

17 Remove the air cleaner assembly.

18 Unbolt the radiator top mountings from the bonnet lock platform and remove both mounting brackets.

19 Unscrew the single bolt securing the fan cowl to the radiator.

20 Disconnect the fan motor multiplug and release the wiring from the cowl clip.

21 Release the radiator from its two lower mountings. It is seated on two pegs on its bottom edge which locate in rubber bushes in the body front panel.

22 Remove the nut and bolt securing the coolant pipe to the radiator. Detach the pipe and move it to one side.

23 Slide the cooling fan and cowl assembly towards the centre of the radiator, rotate it to release it from the radiator and withdraw it. Take care not to damage the radiator matrix.

24 Note that if only the fan, its motor or the cowl is to be renewed, check with a Rover dealer before attempting to strip the assembly. If the separate items are not available, the assembly must be renewed complete and there is no point in trying to dismantle it. If they are available separately, the fan motor is secured by pop rivets to the cowl; these must be drilled out to release the motor and new rivets must be inserted on reassembly. The fan is secured by a clip to the motor shaft.

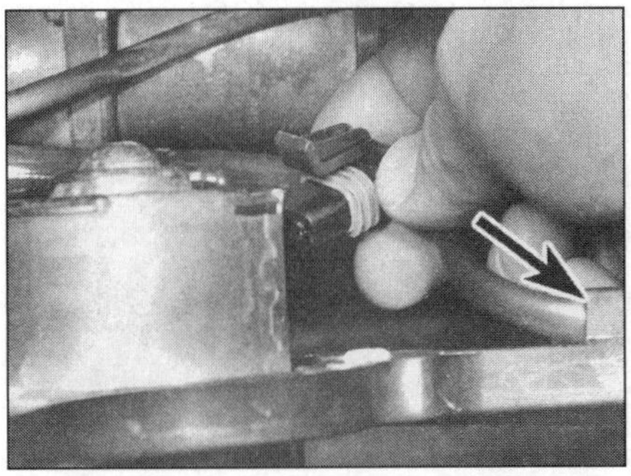

7.12 Disconnecting radiator electric cooling fan wiring - note cowl wiring clip (arrowed)

Refitting

25 Refitting is the reverse of the removal procedure; if the coolant was drained, refill the system.

8 Cooling system electrical switches - testing, removal and refitting

Testing

Electric cooling fan thermostatic switch

1 If the switch is to be tested thoroughly, it must be removed.

2 To test the switch, use two spare wires to connect to it either a multimeter (set to the resistance function) or a battery and bulb test circuit. Suspend the switch in a pan of water which is being heated. Measure the temperature of the water with a thermometer. Do not let either the switch or the thermometer touch the pan itself.

3 The switch contacts should close to the "On" position (ie, continuity should exist) when the water reaches the temperature specified. Stop heating the water and allow it to cool down; the switch contacts should open at the same temperature or just below.

4 If the switch's performance is significantly different from that specified, or if it does not work at all, it must be renewed.

7.14 Withdrawing electric cooling fan and cowl assembly - note cross-pipe had to be disconnected in this case

Coolant temperature gauge sender unit

5 The coolant temperature gauge mounted in the instrument panel is fed with a stabilised 10 volt supply from the instrument panel feed (via the ignition switch and fuse), its earth being controlled by the sender unit.

6 The sender unit is screwed into the coolant outlet elbow mounted on the left-hand end of the cylinder head, underneath the distributor **(see illustration)**. It contains a thermistor, which is an element whose electrical resistance decreases at a predetermined rate as its temperature rises. Thus when the coolant is cold, the sender's resistance is high, current flow through the gauge is reduced and the gauge needle points to the "C" (cold) end of the scale. If the unit is faulty it must be renewed.

7 If the gauge develops a fault, check first the other instruments; if they do not work at all, check the instrument panel feed. If the readings are erratic, there may be a fault in the voltage stabiliser which will necessitate the renewal of the gauge unit or printed circuit. If the fault is in the temperature gauge alone, check it as follows.

8 If the gauge needle remains at the "C" end of the scale, disconnect the sender unit wire and earth it to the cylinder head. If the needle then deflects when the ignition is switched on, the sender unit is proven faulty and must be renewed. If the needle still does not move, remove the instrument panel and check the continuity of the wire between the gauge and

7.15a Drilling out rivets securing fan to cowl . . .

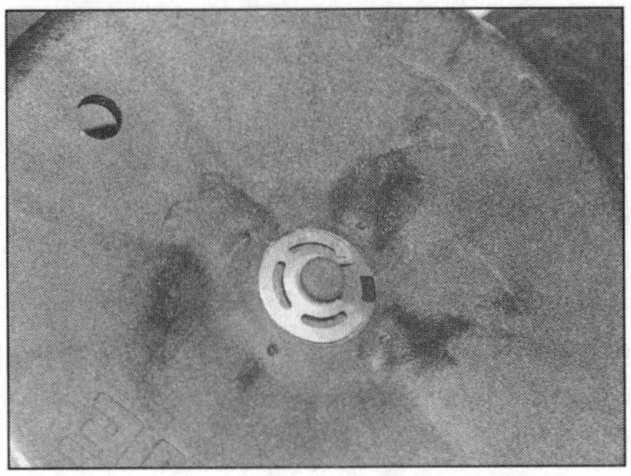

7.15b . . . cooling fan is clipped to motor shaft

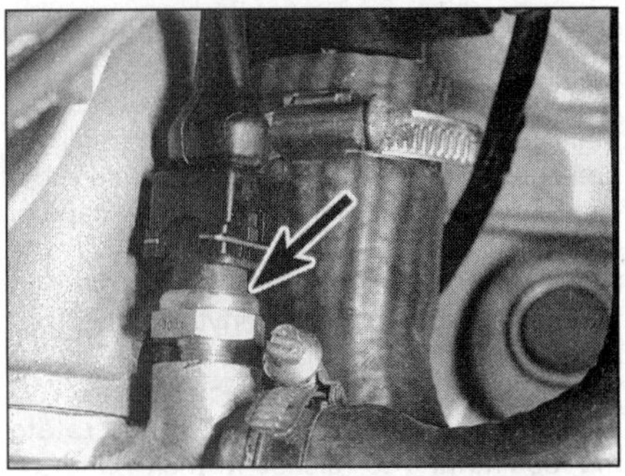

8.6 Coolant temperature gauge sender unit (arrowed)

the sender unit and the feed to the gauge unit. If continuity is shown, and the fault still exists, then the gauge is faulty and the gauge unit must be renewed.

9 If the gauge needle remains at the "H" end of the scale, disconnect the sender unit wire. If the needle then returns to the "C" end of the scale when the ignition is switched on, the sender unit is proven faulty and must be renewed. If the needle still does not move, check the remainder of the circuit as described above.

Inlet manifold pre-heater temperature switch - carburettor engines

10 The switch screwed into the underside of the inlet manifold controls the inlet manifold heater circuit. Refer to Chapter 4 for details **(see illustration)**.

11 The switch contacts should be closed to the "On" position (ie, continuity should exist) only at temperatures below 50°C. Test the switch as described for the electric cooling fan thermostatic switch.

Thermostatically-operated vacuum switch

12 Refer to Chapter 5.

Coolant temperature sensor - fuel-injected engines

13 The sensor, screwed into the underside of the inlet manifold (Spi models) or into the top coolant hose adapter (Mpi models) is a thermistor which is supplied with approximately 5 volts by the engine management system ECU. The ECU also controls the sensor's earth path and, by measuring the amount of current in the sensor circuit, determines the engine's temperature. This information is used, in conjunction with other inputs, to control idle speed, injector opening time duration and ignition timing.

14 If the sensor circuit should fail to provide adequate information, the ECU's back-up facility assumes a value corresponding to 60°C. The sensor itself can be tested only by having a Rover dealer check the complete system using the correct diagnostic equipment. Do not attempt to test the circuit using any other equipment, or the ECU will be damaged.

Removal

Electric cooling fan thermostatic switch

15 When the engine and radiator are cold, either drain the cooling system down to the level of the switch or unscrew the expansion tank filler cap to release any remaining pressure and have ready a suitable plug that can be used temporarily to stop the escape of coolant while the switch is removed. If the latter method is used, take care not to damage the radiator and do not use anything which will leave foreign matter inside the radiator.

16 Disconnect the battery negative lead.

17 Disconnect the switch wires and rotate the locking ring to release it, then withdraw the switch from the radiator and prise out the sealing ring **(see illustration)**.

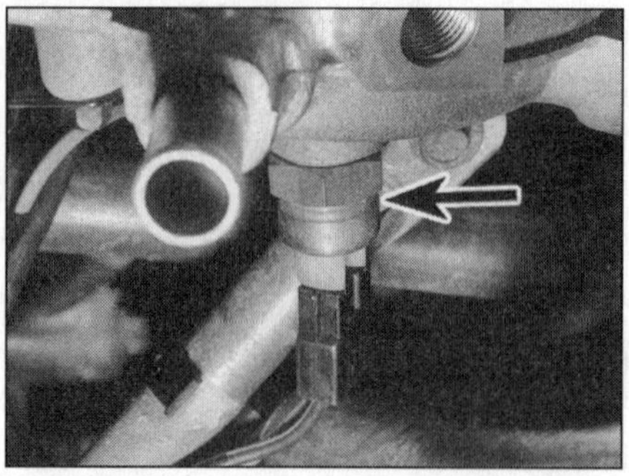

8.10 Inlet manifold pre-heater temperature switch - carburettor engines (arrowed)

Coolant temperature gauge sender unit

18 When the engine and radiator are cold, either drain the cooling system down to the level of the sender unit or unscrew the expansion tank filler cap to release any remaining pressure and have ready a suitable plug that can be used temporarily to stop the escape of coolant while the unit is removed. If the latter method is used, take care not to damage the threads and do not use anything which will leave foreign matter inside the cooling system.

19 Disconnect the battery negative lead.

20 Disconnect the unit's wiring and unscrew the unit from the coolant outlet elbow.

Inlet manifold pre-heater temperature switch - carburettor engines

21 Removal is as described for the coolant temperature gauge sender unit.

Thermostatically-operated vacuum switch

22 Refer to Chapter 5.

Coolant temperature sensor - fuel-injected engines

23 Removal is as described for the coolant temperature gauge sender unit.

Refitting

Electric cooling fan thermostatic switch

24 On refitting, renew the sealing ring if it is worn or compressed and clean carefully the radiator seat before pressing in the sealing ring and switch. Refit the locking ring and rotate it to tighten securely. Reconnect the switch and battery, then refill the cooling system or check the coolant level, as necessary.

Coolant temperature gauge sender unit

25 On refitting, apply a suitable sealant to the unit threads and tighten it to its specified torque wrench setting. Reconnect the unit and battery, then refill the cooling system or check the coolant level, as necessary.

Inlet manifold pre-heater temperature switch - carburettor engines

26 Refitting is a reversal of removal. Note that the switch is fitted with a sealing washer that must be renewed whenever the switch is removed. Tighten the switch to the specified torque wrench setting.

Thermostatically-operated vacuum switch

27 Refer to Chapter 5.

Coolant temperature sensor - fuel-injected engines

28 Refitting is a reversal of removal. Note the specified torque wrench setting for the sensor.

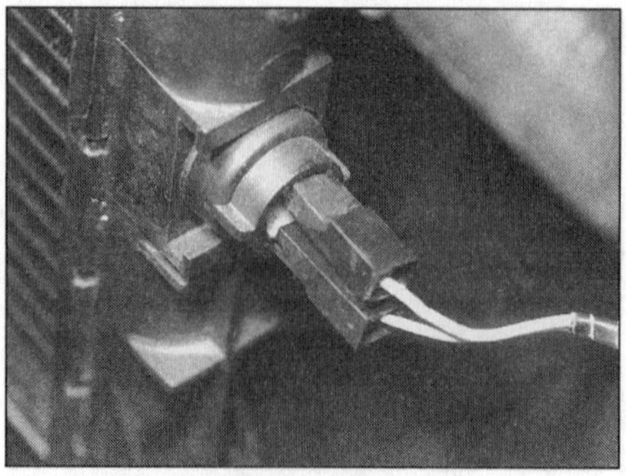

8.17 Radiator electric cooling fan thermostatic switch

9 Coolant pump - removal and refitting

Removal

1 Pump failure is usually indicated by coolant leaking from the gland behind the pump's bearing, or by rough and noisy operation, usually accompanied by excessive pump spindle play. If the pump shows any of these symptoms it must be renewed as follows.

2 Drain the cooling system.

3 Remove the timing belt.

4 Noting the locations of the two pillar bolts, unscrew the five bolts securing the water pump to the cylinder block/crankcase, then unscrew the single bolt securing the pump to the timing belt upper left-hand (inner) cover.

5 Withdraw the water pump and discard its sealing O-ring which should never be re-used **(see illustration)**. Carefully clean the cylinder block/crankcase mating surface and the pump socket.

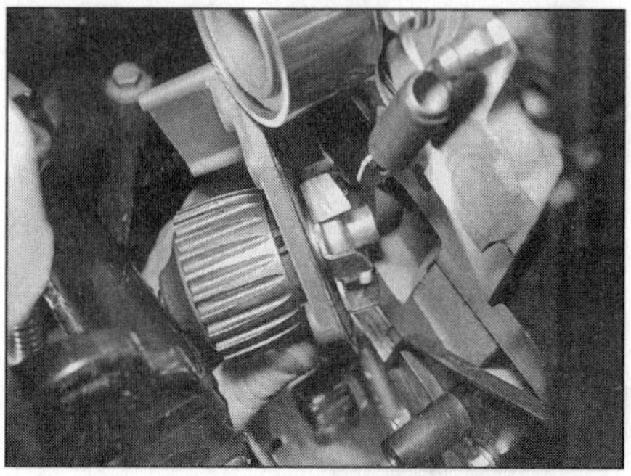

9.5 Removing the water pump

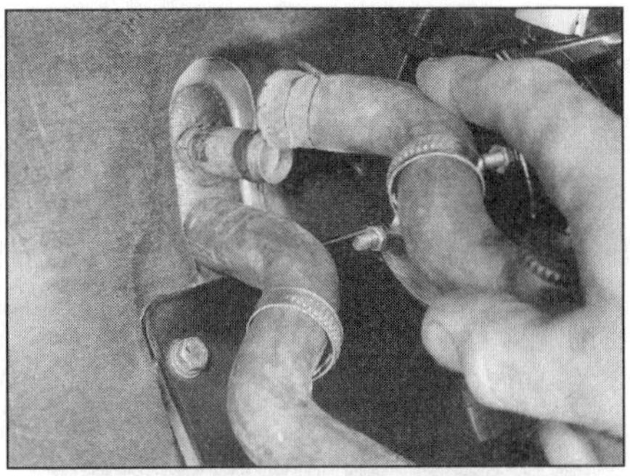

10.2 Slacken hose clips to disconnect heater feed and return hoses from bulkhead unions

Refitting

6 On refitting, install the pump using a new sealing O-ring and tighten the bolts to their specified torque wrench settings. The remainder of the refitting procedure is the reverse of removal.

10 Heater components - removal and refitting

Removal

Heater unit

1 Drain the cooling system.
2 Slacken the hose clips and disconnect the heater feed and return hoses from the heater matrix outlets on the bulkhead **(see illustration)**.
3 Remove the facia.

10.14 Heater blower motor wiring connector plug (arrowed)

10.15 Heater air inlet box and blower motor assembly mountings visible from engine compartment (arrowed) . . .

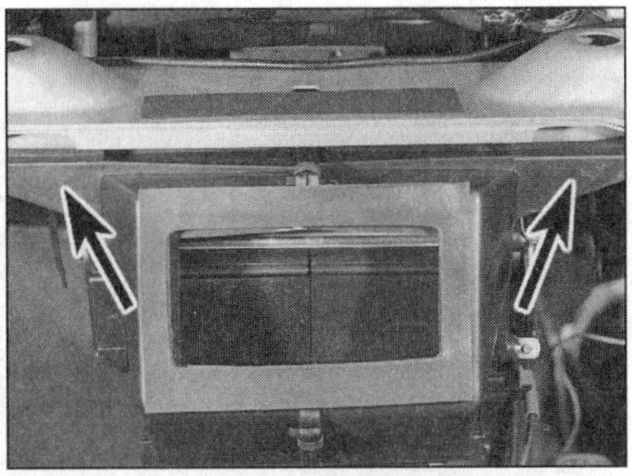

10.5a Unscrew heater securing bolts (arrowed) . . .

4 Remove the side window demister ducts, the facia rail support stays, the face-level air duct and the windscreen demister ducts.
5 Unscrew the two bolts securing the heater to the body crossmember, then prise the heater off the clip securing it to the bulkhead and remove it, along with the control panel. Use old towels or rag to soak up any remaining coolant that is released from the matrix. Note that the heater is a tight fit on the clip and will require considerable effort to remove it; take care not to damage the heater or any other component **(see illustrations)**.
6 The heater control cables can now be disconnected, if required, and the matrix removed (see below).

Heater matrix

7 Remove the heater unit.
8 Withdraw the foam seal from the matrix pipes, remove the two screws and withdraw the pipe clamp.
9 Remove the four screws securing the heater end plate and withdraw the end plate, followed by the matrix **(see illustration)**.
10 If the matrix is leaking, it is best to obtain a new or reconditioned unit as home repairs are seldom successful. If it is blocked it can be cleared sometimes by reverse flushing using a garden hose, using a proprietary radiator cleaning product if absolutely necessary.

Heater air inlet box and blower motor

11 Disconnect the battery negative terminal.
12 On cars with fuel-injected engines, remove the ECU mounting bracket-to-body screws and move aside the ECU.
13 If the extra working space is needed, remove also (if fitted) the charcoal canister.

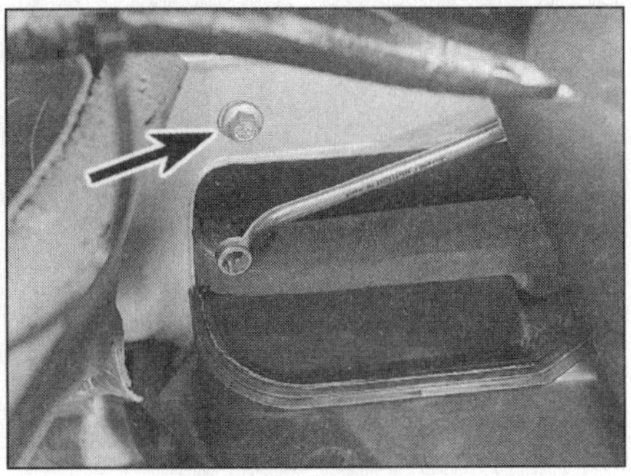

10.17 . . . and through glovebox opening in facia (arrowed)

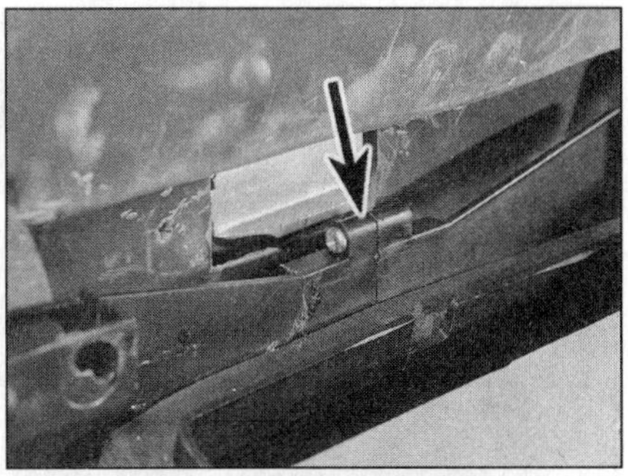

10.5b . . . and release heater from bulkhead clip with care

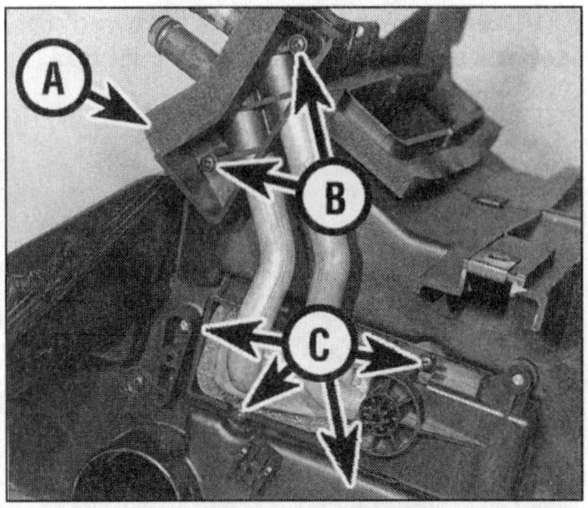

10.9 Heater matrix pipe seal (A) pipe clamp screws (B) end plate screws (C) (arrowed)

14 Disconnect the blower motor wiring by unplugging the connector on the top of the unit **(see illustration)**. Release the clutch cable from its clip.
15 Unscrew the four bolts and three nuts securing the assembly's mounting plate to the bulkhead; be careful that all are unscrewed, as some are difficult to see **(see illustration)**.
16 Working inside the car, remove the glovebox.
17 Unscrew the remaining two bolts and one nut securing the assembly to the bulkhead. Again, check carefully that all fasteners are unscrewed, as they are difficult to see **(see illustration)**.
18 Remove the heater air inlet box and blower motor as an assembly, with its mounting plate **(see illustration)**. If it resists removal, do not use force but check instead that all fasteners have been removed.

10.18 Remove heater air inlet box and motor as an assembly with the mounting

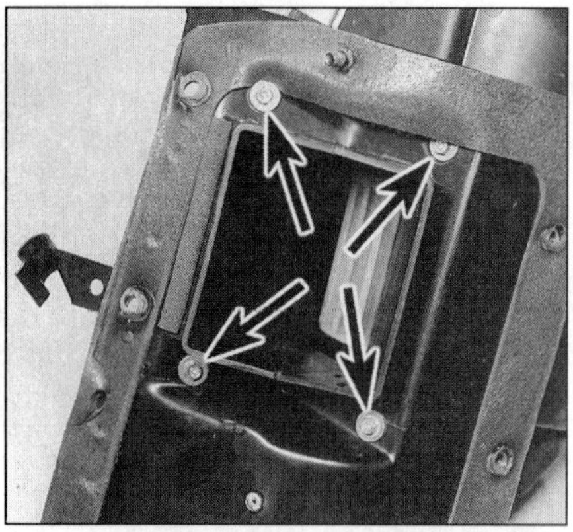

10.19a Remove four bolts (arrowed) to separate mounting plate from inlet box . . .

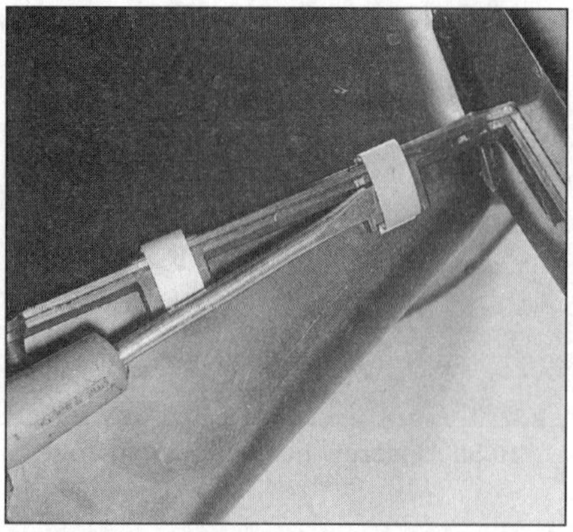

10.19b . . . remove drain tube, release clips . . .

10.19c . . . and remove screws (arrowed) . . .

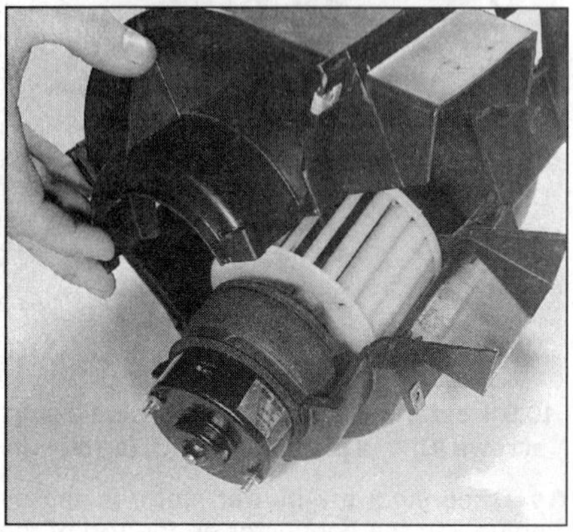

10.19d . . . to separate inlet box halves

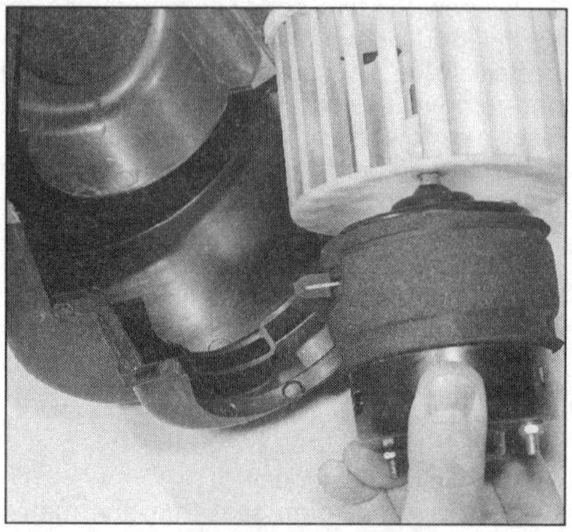

10.19e Remove blower motor, noting locating tongue . . .

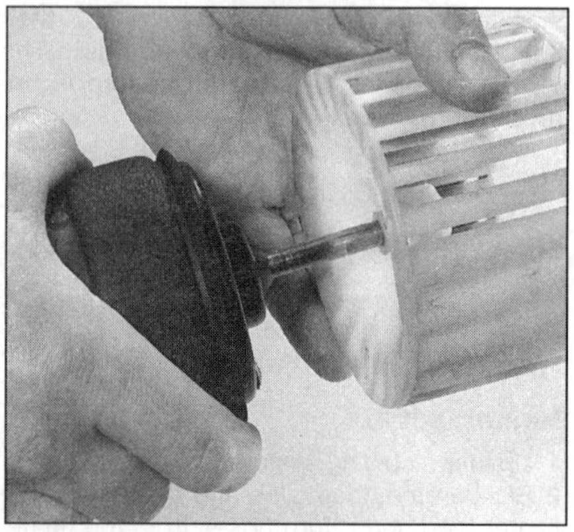

10.19f . . . and withdraw fan from motor shaft

19 Note that if only the blower fan, its motor or the air inlet box is to be renewed, check with a Rover dealer before attempting to strip the assembly. If the separate items are not available, the assembly must be renewed complete and there is no point in trying to dismantle it. If they are available separately, the assembly can be dismantled by disconnecting the motor wires, unbolting the air inlet box from the mounting plate and removing the box-to-bonnet seal (three clips) and drain tube. The two halves of the inlet box are secured by eight clips and by three screws around the motor. The fan is pressed on to the motor shaft **(see illustrations)**. On reassembly, clean off the old adhesive from the mating surfaces of the inlet box halves and apply a bead of suitable adhesive such as Bostik Sealer P.34 44S.

Heater blower motor resistor

Note: *If the resistor is thought to be faulty, check first with a Rover dealer as to whether it is available separately or not; it may only be available as part of the complete heater air inlet box/blower motor/mounting plate assembly*

20 Remove the heater air inlet box and blower motor assembly.

21 Disconnect the wiring from the blower motor.

22 Drill out the two pop rivets securing the resistor and cowl to the assembly's mounting plate **(see illustration)**.

Heater blower switch

23 Refer to Chapter 12.

Refitting

Heater unit

24 Refitting is the reverse of the removal procedure, noting the following points.

a) *Ensure that the foam rubber seals are refitted correctly so that all bulkhead apertures are closed off and that the sound deadening material is correctly replaced.*
b) *Ensure that the heater ducts are connected so that there can be no gaps or air leaks.*
c) *Ensure that the heater hoses are correctly reconnected; the feed hose (with the bleed plug) is connected to the heater matrix upper union.*
d) *Refill the cooling system.*

10.22 Heater blower motor resistor unit and cowl

Heater matrix

25 Refitting is the reverse of the removal procedure.

Heater air inlet box and blower motor

26 Refitting is the reverse of the removal procedure, noting the following points.

a) *Clean the mating surfaces of the bulkhead and of the assembly's mounting plate thoroughly.*
b) *Ensure that the foam rubber seal is refitted correctly so that the bulkhead aperture is closed off; if necessary slacken the heater return hose clip so that the seal can be properly located.*
c) *Ensure that the assembly mates correctly with the duct's seal, then tighten all fasteners to the specified torque wrench setting.*

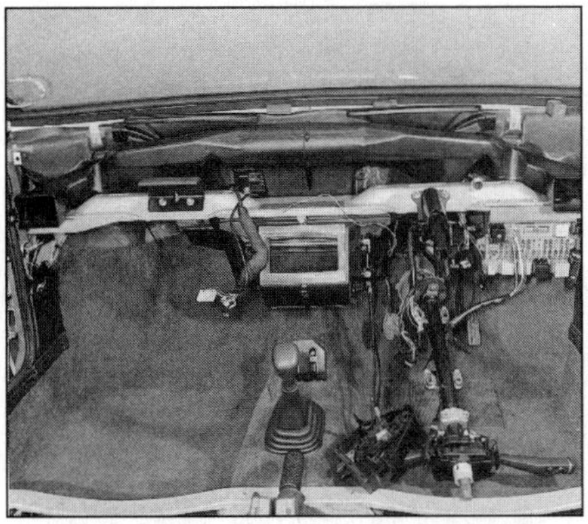

11.1 Remove the facia to reach heater components

d) If coolant was lost on disturbing the heater hose, top-up the system.

Heater blower motor resistor

27 Refitting is the reverse of the removal procedure.

Heater blower switch

28 Refer to Chapter 12.

11 Heater ducts and vents - removal and refitting

Removal

Ducts

1 Remove the facia **(see illustration)**.
2 Withdraw the side window demister ducts **(see illustration)**.
3 Unbolt the facia rail support stays **(see illustration)**.
4 Unclip the face-level air duct. It has a clip at each end and two in the centre.
5 Unscrew the two plastic nuts to release each of the windscreen demister ducts **(see illustration)**.

Vents

6 The adjustable face-level vents can be removed by prising them gently out of the facia until their clips are released. Take care not to mark the facia **(see illustration)**.
7 The side window demister vents are secured by sealing flanges from behind the facia and so cannot be removed until the facia has been withdrawn.

Refitting

Ducts

8 Refitting is the reverse of the removal procedure. Ensure that the ducts mate correctly with each other and with their respective vents, so that there are no air leaks.

Vents

9 Refitting is a reversal of removal. Fit new self-adhesive sealing strips on reassembly.

11.2 Withdrawing a side window demister duct

11.5 Windscreen demister duct mounting nuts (arrowed)

12 Heater controls - removal, refitting and adjustment

Removal

1 Remove the facia.
2 Remove the three screws securing the control panel to the facia, release the panel and disconnect the illuminating bulb wires **(see illustration)**.
3 Note that the control cables and their fittings on the heater unit are colour-coded; the temperature control being brown, while the distribution control is black.

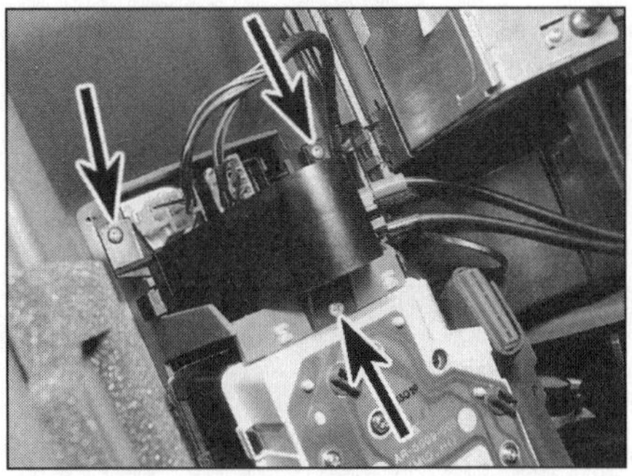

12.2 Heater control panel retaining screws (arrowed) on rear of facia

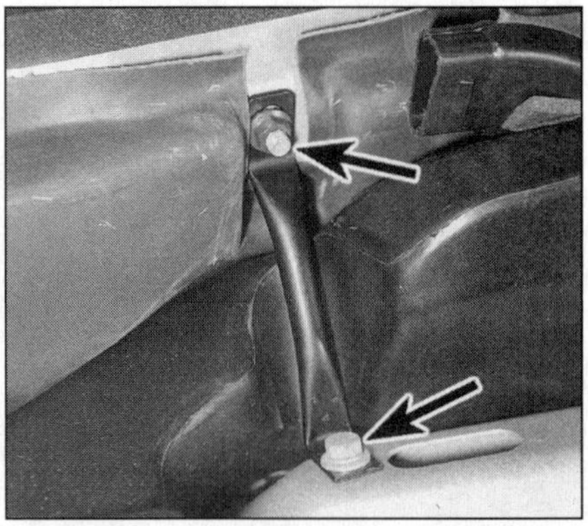

11.3 Facia rail support stay mountings (arrowed)

11.6 Removing a face-level vent - take care not to mark the facia

4 Release the clip securing each cable outer to the heater unit and unclip each cable inner wire from its respective control lever. Withdraw the control panel **(see illustration)**. **Note:** *The heater control cables are not available separately, do not attempt to disconnect them from the control panel levers.*

Refitting

5 Refitting is the reverse of the removal procedure.

Adjustment

6 No adjustment is possible; if the heater does not work properly, either the control panel or the assembly must be renewed to cure the fault.

12.4 Control cable clips on heater unit (arrowed)

Chapter 4 Part A:
Fuel and exhaust systems - carburettor models

Contents

Degrees of difficulty

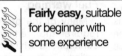

Easy, suitable for novice with little experience	**Fairly easy,** suitable for beginner with some experience	**Fairly difficult,** suitable for competent DIY mechanic	**Difficult,** suitable for experienced DIY mechanic	**Very difficult,** suitable for expert DIY or professional

Specifications

Fuel pump

Type	Mechanical, driven by eccentric on camshaft	

Carburettor

Type	Hobourn-SU constant-depression/variable choke	
Designation:		
1.1 models	KIF 38	
1.4 models	KIF 44	
	1.1 models	**1.4 models**
Carburettor number:		
Without catalytic converter	MAC 10003 or 10043	MAC 10004
With catalytic converter	MAC 10010	MAC 10011
Throttle bore diameter	38 mm	44 mm
Piston spring colour code	Red	Red
Damper	LZX 2337	LZX 2337
Jet size	LZX 2211 (0.090 in)	LZX 2237 (0.100 in)
Needle:		
Without catalytic converter	AEH (MAC 10003) or AEK (MAC 10043)	BGZ
With catalytic converter	AEJ	BGZ
Needle valve seat	LZX 1756	LZX 1756
Fast idle speed - at choke control first detent	1200 rpm	1200 rpm
Idle speed	850 ± 50 rpm	850 ± 50 rpm
CO level at idle speed - engine at normal operating temperature:		
Without catalytic converter	2.0 to 3.0%	2.0 to 3.0%
With catalytic converter - at gas sampling pipe	1.0 to 3.0%	1.0 to 3.0%
Choke type	Manual	Manual

Recommended fuel

Minimum octane rating:	
Without catalytic converter	95 RON unleaded (ie unleaded Premium) or 97 RON leaded (ie 4-star)
With catalytic converter	95 RON unleaded (ie unleaded Premium) **only**

Torque wrench settings

	Nm	lbf ft
Fuel system		
Fuel tank mounting bolts	12	9
Two-way valve-to-fuel tank filler neck nut	5	3.5
Fuel tank filler neck-to-body fasteners:		
Screws - three-door	5	3.5
Nuts - five-door	9	6.5
Fuel pump-to-cylinder head mounting nuts	10	7.5
Inlet manifold mounting nuts and bolts	25	18.5
Inlet manifold support stays-to-cylinder block/crankcase bolts	25	18.5
Upper-to-lower inlet manifold Torx screws	10	7.5
Air cleaner assembly support bracket-to-carburettor screws	5	3.5
Throttle pedal mounting nuts	25	18.5
Coolant temperature sensor	15	11
Carburettor vent and air bleed pipe mounting bolts	9	6.5
Exhaust system		
Exhaust manifold mounting nuts	45	33
Exhaust system front pipe-to-manifold nuts:		
Without catalytic converter (spring-loaded mounting)	see text	see text
With catalytic converter	50	37
All exhaust system flange securing nuts	45	33
Exhaust system intermediate pipe-to-tailpipe clamp nut	18	13
Lambda sensor	45	33

1 General information and precautions

General information

The fuel system comprises a fuel tank mounted under the rear of the car, a mechanical fuel pump and a carburettor. The fuel pump is operated by an eccentric on the camshaft and is mounted on the rear of the cylinder head. The air cleaner contains a disposable paper filter element and incorporates a flap valve air temperature control system which allows cold air from the outside of the car and warm air from the exhaust manifold to enter the air cleaner in the correct proportions.

The carburettor is the Hobourn SU-manufactured KIF type, a development by Rover of the previous HIF instrument. To reduce emissions and to improve driveability when the engine is cold, the inlet manifold is heated by the cooling system coolant and by an electric pre-heater system. Mixture enrichment for cold starting is by a manually-operated choke control.

The carburettor features an electrically-controlled idle bypass system that is separate from the main fuel/air mixture circuit provided by the piston, jet and metering needle, a manual choke, an overrun valve and a full load enrichment device.

The manual choke uses the constant manifold depression to draw fuel and air into a fixed orifice; a helical groove in the spindle keyed to the choke cam is arranged so that extra fuel/air mixture can pass from the orifice only when the choke cam is rotated slightly from the at-rest position; the amount of extra fuel delivered increases to a maximum point when the choke cam is rotated through 60°.

The full load enrichment device also uses manifold depression. At light engine loads, with the throttle partially closed (idling, cruising or decelerating) a high depression is generated in the manifold, downstream of the throttle disc. A passage connects the space behind a diaphragm to this point so that the diaphragm is sucked off its seat against spring pressure; the air passing through the air bleed hose can then enter through two passages which means that the depression across the fuel pick-up is too low for fuel to be drawn from the float chamber into the system.

At high engine loads, with the throttle fully open (accelerating, full-throttle running) manifold depression drops to the point where the diaphragm is seated by its spring and the air can enter only through a small jet; this increases air speed and raises the depression over the fuel pick-up to the point where additional fuel is drawn up from the float chamber, mixed with the air bleed and passed into the carburettor venturi downstream of the piston.

Some models are fitted with a spring-loaded poppet valve in the throttle disc, so that when the throttle is closed at high engine speeds the high manifold depression sucks the valve open, admitting enough air to burn completely the small amount of fuel that is sucked through the jet under these conditions, thus reducing exhaust emissions.

The (service replacement) exhaust system consists of three sections; the front pipe and front silencer box, the intermediate pipe and middle silencer box, and the tailpipe and main silencer box. The system fitted in production differs in that the intermediate pipe and tailpipe are in one piece. The system is suspended throughout its entire length by rubber mountings. If a catalytic converter is fitted, it is situated between the front pipe and the (much shorter) intermediate pipe.

Precautions

Fuel warning

Many of the procedures in this Chapter require the removal of fuel lines and connections which may result in some fuel spillage. Before carrying out any operation on the fuel system refer to the precautions given in Safety first! at the beginning of this Manual and follow them implicitly. Petrol is a highly dangerous and volatile liquid and the precautions necessary when handling it cannot be overstressed.

Unleaded petrol - usage

The information given in this Chapter is correct at the time of writing and applies only to petrols currently available in the UK. If updated information is thought to be required, check with a Rover dealer. If travelling abroad consult one of the motoring organisations (or a similar authority) for advice on the petrols available and their suitability for your vehicle

The fuel recommended by Rover for Metro and 100 series models is shown in the Specifications of this Chapter, followed by the equivalent petrol currently on sale in the UK. RON and MON are different testing standards; RON (or RM) stands for Research Octane Number, while MON (or MM) stands for Motor Octane Number.

All Rover Metro models are designed to run on 95 (RON) octane petrol. Super/Super Plus (unleaded) petrols can be used without modification, if nothing else is available; 4-star (leaded) petrol can only be used if the car is not fitted with a catalytic converter.

Note: *The only cars which MUST use unleaded petrol at all times are those with catalytic converters.*

Catalytic converters

Before attempting work on these items, carefully read the precautions listed in Part D of this Chapter.

3.2 Note colour-coding of thermac switch vacuum pipes before disconnecting

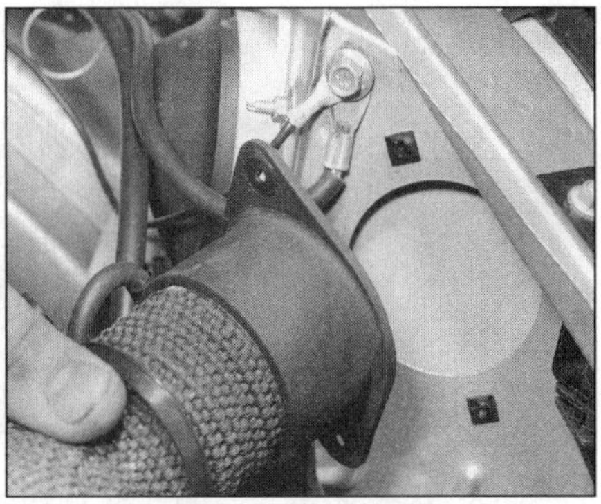

3.5a Cold air intake duct is secured by two screws to body front panel

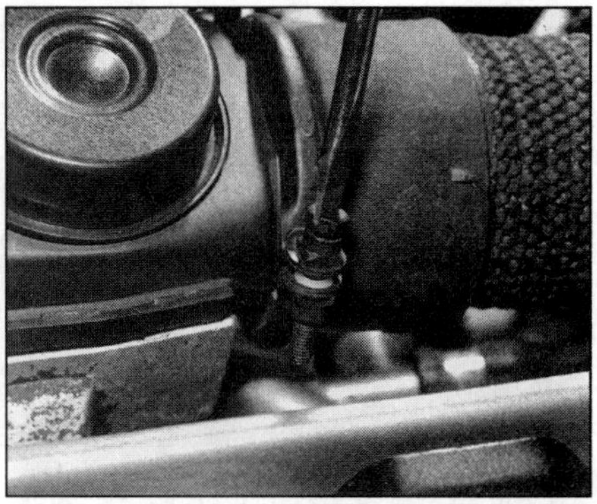

3.5b Slacken clamp to disconnect cold air intake duct from air cleaner intake duct

2 Air cleaner element - renewal

Refer to Chapter 1, Section 34.

3 Air cleaner assembly - removal and refitting

Removal

1 Release the two clips securing the air inlet duct to the assembly, then undo the four screws securing the assembly to its mounting bracket.

2 Release the assembly from the inlet duct and withdraw it until the thermac switch vacuum pipes can be disconnected; note that these are colour-coded (yellow to the temperature control valve, red to the inlet manifold) to ensure correct reconnection **(see illustration)**.

3 Withdraw the assembly. Check the condition of the O-ring around the carburettor inlet and renew it if worn or damaged.

4 To remove the inlet duct, refer to the following Section.

5 To remove the cold air inlet duct remove the two retaining screws and disconnect the duct from the body front panel, release the clip securing the ignition HT lead, then slacken the clamp to separate the cold air duct from the inlet duct **(see illustrations)**.

Refitting

6 Refitting is the reverse of the removal procedure; ensure that the vacuum pipes are correctly reconnected and are not trapped as the assembly is refitted, then check that the assembly sits properly on the carburettor inlet before tightening the screws securely.

4 Air cleaner air temperature control system - inspection and component renewal

Inspection

1 The system is controlled by a thermac switch mounted in the air cleaner assembly; when the engine is started from cold, the switch is closed to allow inlet manifold depression to act on the air temperature control valve in the inlet duct. This raises a vacuum servo in the valve assembly and draws a flap valve across the cold air inlet, thus allowing only (warmed) air from the exhaust manifold to enter the air cleaner.

2 As the temperature rises of the exhaust-warmed air in the air cleaner, a bi-metallic strip in the thermac switch deforms and opens the switch to shut off the depression in the air temperature control valve assembly; the flap is lowered gradually across the hot air inlet until, when the engine is fully warmed up to normal operating temperature, only cold air from the front of the car is entering the air cleaner.

3 To check the system, allow the engine to cool down completely, then disconnect the cold air inlet duct from the air cleaner inlet duct; the flap valve should be securely seated across the hot air inlet. Start the engine; the flap should immediately rise to close off the cold air inlet and should then lower steadily as the engine warms up until it is eventually seated across the hot air inlet again.

4 To check the thermac switch, disconnect the vacuum pipe from the control valve when the engine is running **(see illustration)**. With the engine cold, full inlet manifold depression should be felt sucking at the pipe end; none at all when the engine is fully warmed up.

5 To check the air temperature control valve, disconnect the cold air inlet duct from the air cleaner inlet duct; the flap valve should be securely seated across the hot air inlet. Disconnect the vacuum pipe and suck hard at the control valve stub; the flap should rise to shut off the cold air inlet.

6 If either the thermac switch or temperature control valve are faulty, then they must be renewed as followed:

Thermac switch - renewal

7 Remove the air cleaner assembly.

8 Remove the air cleaner filter element.

9 Bend up the tags on the switch clip and remove the clip, then withdraw the switch and its seal **(see illustration)**.

10 Refitting is the reverse of the removal procedure; ensure that the switch mating surfaces are clean and that the switch and seal are correctly located before fastening the clip.

Air temperature control valve - renewal

11 Disconnect the vacuum pipe from the air temperature control valve, then disconnect the cold air inlet duct from the air cleaner inlet duct.

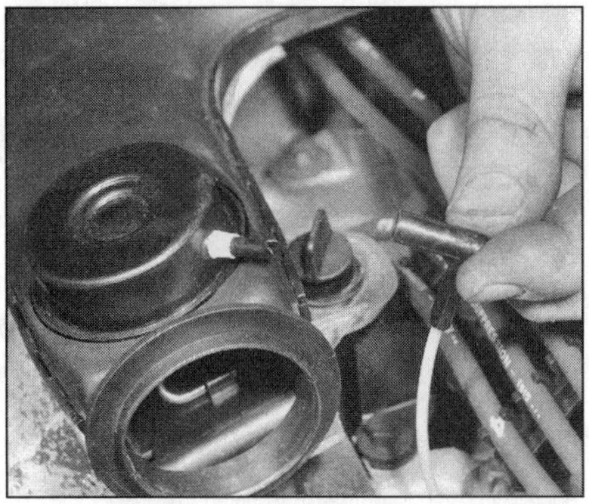

4.4 Disconnect vacuum pipe from control valve to check operation of system components

4.9 Thermac switch is clipped into air cleaner assembly

4A

4.12 Do not lose hot air inlet connector hose when removing air cleaner intake duct

6.3 Plug fuel hoses when disconnecting - pump inlet hose disconnected, outlet hose arrowed

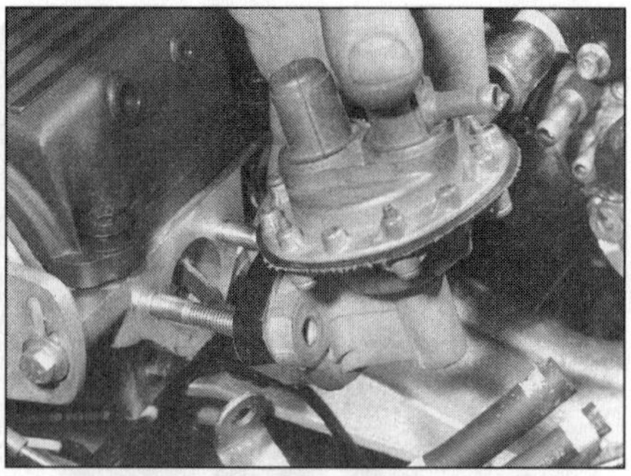

6.5 Removing fuel pump and insulating block

12 Release the two clips securing the air inlet duct to the air cleaner assembly and withdraw the duct, taking care not to lose the hot air inlet connector hose **(see illustration)**.

13 The air temperature control valve can be renewed only with the complete inlet duct assembly.

14 Refitting is the reverse of the removal procedure.

5 Fuel system - inspection

Refer to Chapter 1, Section 15.

6 Fuel pump - testing, removal and refitting

Testing

1 To test the fuel pump on the engine, temporarily disconnect the outlet pipe which leads to the carburettor, and hold a wad of rag over the pump outlet while an assistant spins the engine on the starter. *Keep the hands away from the electric cooling fan.* Regular spurts of fuel should be ejected as the engine turns.

2 The pump can also be tested by removing it. With the pump outlet pipe disconnected but the inlet pipe still connected, hold the wad of rag by the outlet. Operate the pump lever by hand, moving it in and out; if the pump is in a satisfactory condition a strong jet of fuel should be ejected.

Removal

3 Identify the pump inlet and outlet hoses then disconnect and plug them **(see illustration)**. Place wads of rag to catch any spilled fuel and cover the hose unions to prevent the entry of dirt and the escape of fuel.

4 Unscrew the nuts securing the pump to the cylinder head and remove the washers.

5 Withdraw the fuel pump from the engine and remove the insulating block **(see illustration)**.

Refitting

6 Refitting is the reverse of the removal procedure; clean the mating surfaces and renew the insulating block if its sealing surfaces are marked or damaged. Tighten the pump mounting nuts to the specified torque wrench setting.

7 Fuel gauge sender unit - removal, refitting and testing

Removal

1 Jack up the rear of the car and support it on axle stands (see "*Jacking and Vehicle Support*").

2 Disconnect the battery negative lead.

3 Drain the fuel tank and slacken the tank rear mounting bolts, then remove the tank front mounting bolts and lower the tank until the sender unit (in the tank's front left-hand corner) can be reached.

4 Disconnect the sender unit wiring and hose **(see illustration)**.

5 Release the sender unit's locking ring by turning it anti-clockwise; Rover recommend the use of Service Tool Number 18G 1001, but for those without access to such equipment a pair of slip-jointed pliers will serve as an adequate substitute.

6 Withdraw the sender unit, noting the sealing ring; this must be renewed if worn or damaged.

Refitting

7 Refitting is the reverse of the removal procedure.

Testing

8 The fuel gauge mounted in the instrument panel is fed with a stabilised 10 volt supply from the instrument panel feed (via the ignition switch and fuse 3), its earth being controlled by the sender unit.

9 If the gauge develops a fault, check first the other instruments; if they do not work at all, check the instrument panel feed. If the readings are erratic, there may be a fault in the voltage stabiliser which will necessitate the renewal of the gauge unit or printed circuit. If the fault is in the fuel gauge alone, check it as follows.

10 If the gauge needle remains at the "E" end of the scale, disconnect the sender unit wire and earth it; if the needle then deflects when the ignition is switched on, the sender unit is proven faulty and must be renewed. If the needle still does not move, remove the instrument panel and check the continuity of the green/black wire between the gauge and the sender unit and the feed to the gauge unit. If continuity is shown, and the fault still exists, then the gauge is faulty and the gauge unit must be renewed.

11 If the gauge needle remains at the "F" end of the scale, disconnect the sender unit wire; if the needle then returns to the "E" end of the scale when the ignition is switched on check the sender unit as described below, then check that the green/black wire is sound. If the needle still does not move, check the remainder of the circuit as described above.

12 To test the sender unit, remove it from the tank and connect a multimeter (set to its resistance function) between the wire terminals and measure the resistance with the float in various positions; when the float is lowered to the empty position a reading of approximately 270 ohms should be obtained, decreasing steadily through 65 ohms at the half-full point, to a reading of 15.5 ohms when the float is raised to the full position. If the unit is faulty it must be renewed.

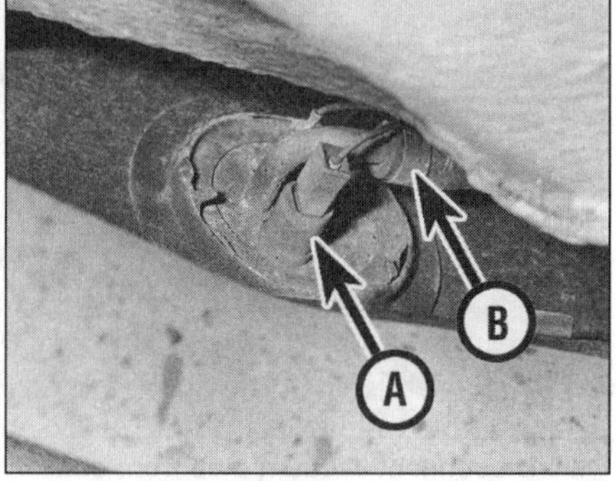

7.4 Location of fuel gauge sender unit and hose clamp (arrowed)

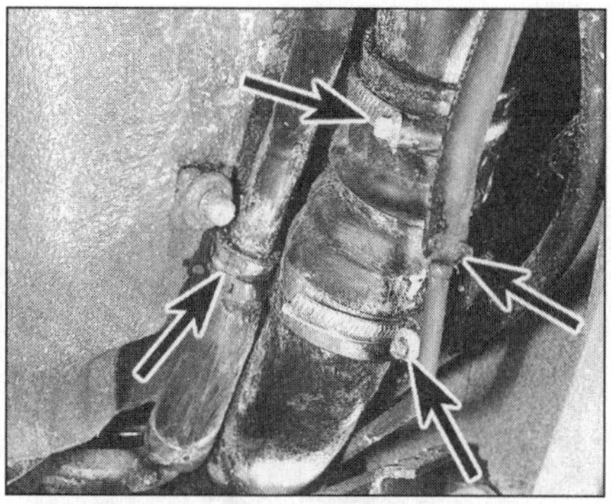
8.5 Slacken or release clips (arrowed) to disconnect hoses from tank

9.5 Fuel tank filler neck is secured by two nuts (one shown) on five-door models

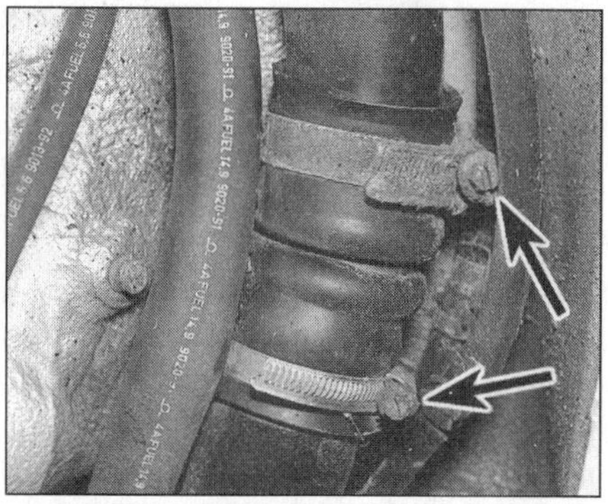
9.6 Slacken filler hose clips (arrowed) to release filler neck

8 Fuel tank - removal and refitting

Removal

1 A fuel tank drain plug is not provided; it is therefore preferable to carry out the removal operation when the tank is nearly empty. Before proceeding, disconnect the battery negative lead and syphon or hand pump the remaining fuel from the tank.

2 Chock the front wheels, then jack up the rear of the car and support its body on axle stands. Remove the right-hand roadwheel.

3 Remove the exhaust tailpipe. If the production-fit system is still fitted, unhook its rubber mountings and move the system aside without straining it, but be careful to support its weight as much as possible. If the tailpipe does become a hindrance, it must be removed, even if this means cutting a perfectly good component.

4 Use a trolley jack to support the weight of the rear suspension subframe, then remove the subframe right-hand (front) mounting and lower the subframe as far as possible without straining the brake flexible hose.

5 Slacken its retaining clip and disconnect the filler hose from the tank, then release their clips and disconnect the various fuel feed, breather and vent hoses from the tank **(see illustration)**. Plug all hoses and cover their unions to prevent the entry of dirt and the escape of fuel.

6 Disconnect the wiring from the fuel gauge sender unit.

7 Release the handbrake cable from its retaining clips and move it above the tank.

8 Unbolt the tank from the body and withdraw it from the car.

9 If the tank is contaminated with sediment or water, remove the sender unit and swill the tank out with clean fuel. If the tank is damaged or leaks, it should be repaired by a specialist or alternatively renewed. *Do not under any circumstances attempt to solder or weld a fuel tank.*

Refitting

10 Refitting is the reverse of the removal procedure; tighten all nuts and bolts to their specified torque wrench settings and ensure that all hoses are correctly routed and securely fastened so that there can be no risk of fuel leakage.

9 Fuel tank filler components - removal and refitting

Removal

1 A fuel tank drain plug is not provided; it is therefore preferable to carry out the removal operation when the tank is nearly empty. Before proceeding, disconnect the battery negative lead and syphon or hand pump the remaining fuel from the tank.

2 Chock the front wheels, then jack up the rear of the car and support it on axle stands (see "*Jacking and Vehicle Support*"). Remove the right-hand roadwheel.

3 Remove the fuel filler cap.

4 On three-door models, remove the two screws securing the filler neck to the body.

5 On five-door models, remove the filler neck grommet, then undo the two nuts securing the filler neck to the body **(see illustration)**.

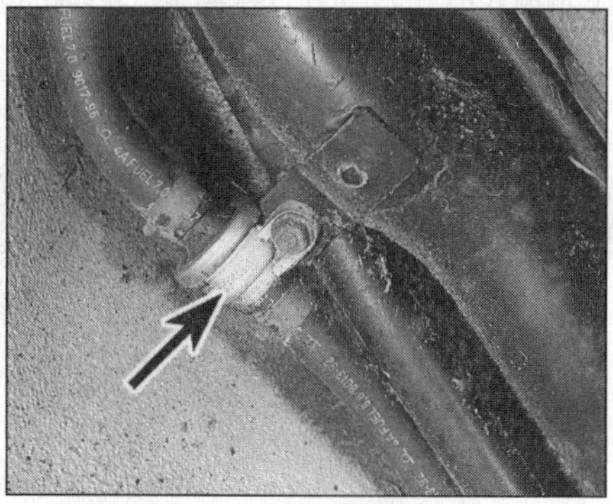
9.7 Fuel tank breather two-way valve and mounting nut (arrowed)

6 On all models, slacken the clips of the filler hose and of the large- and small-diameter vent hoses, then disconnect the hoses and remove the filler neck and hose assembly **(see illustration)**. Plug all hoses and cover their unions to prevent the entry of dirt and the escape of fuel.

7 The hoses can be disconnected, if required, by releasing their clips. Note that the breather two-way valve is secured by a nut **(see illustration)**.

Refitting

8 Refitting is the reverse of the removal procedure; tighten all nuts and bolts to their specified torque wrench settings and ensure that all hoses are correctly routed and securely fastened so that there can be no risk of fuel leakage.

10 Throttle cable - removal, refitting and adjustment

Removal

1 Working inside the car, release the clip securing the cable inner wire to the pedal **(see illustration)**.

2 Working inside the engine compartment, slacken the cable adjuster nut and locknut,

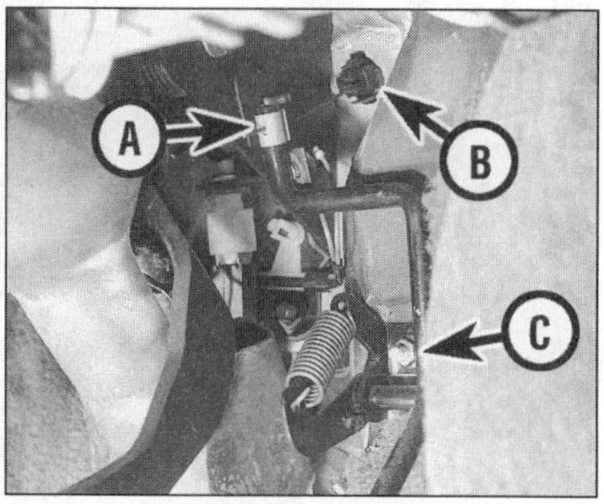

10.1 Throttle cable inner wire securing clip (A) cable fastener (B) and throttle pedal mounting nut (C)

release the cable from the adjuster bracket and disengage the cable end nipple from the carburettor pulley **(see illustration)**.

3 Release the cable fastener from the bulkhead and withdraw the cable into the engine compartment.

Refitting

4 Refitting is the reverse of the removal procedure; adjust the cable as follows.

Adjustment

5 With the pedal fully released, check that there is maximum clearance at the lost motion gap **(see illustration)** and no slack in the cable. Have an assistant fully depress the pedal and check that the throttle opens fully, then check that it returns to the at-rest position when released.

6 To adjust the cable, slacken the adjuster locknut (underneath the adjuster bracket) and pull the cable upwards until the lost motion gap clearance is felt to have been taken up, all cable free play has been taken up and the throttle spindle is just starting to move.

7 From this position, unscrew the adjuster nut until a gap of 5 mm is present between the underside of the nut and the top of the adjuster bracket; tighten the locknut without disturbing this setting.

8 Recheck the adjustment.

11 Throttle pedal - removal and refitting

Note: *Refer to Chapter 12 for details of throttle pedal switch removal and refitting*

Removal

1 Disconnect the throttle cable inner wire from the pedal.

2 Unhook the return spring and undo the nuts securing the pedal assembly to the bulkhead; withdraw the pedal.

Refitting

3 Refitting is the reverse of the removal procedure; tighten to the specified torque wrench setting the pedal nuts, then adjust the throttle cable.

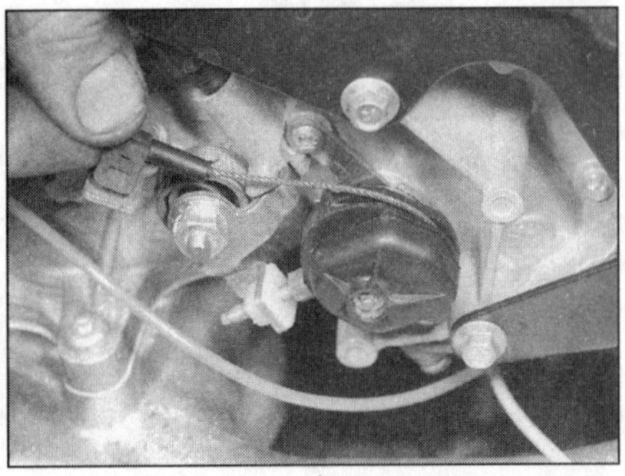

12.2 Release clip to disconnect choke cable from carburettor - note fast idle adjusting screw

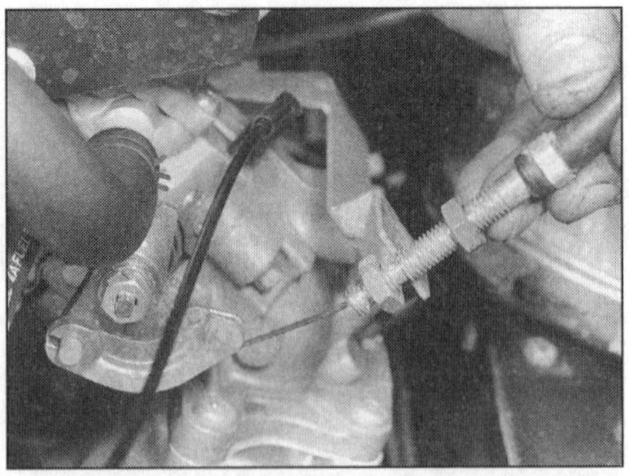

10.2 Disconnecting throttle cable from carburettor

12 Choke cable - removal, refitting and adjustment

Note: *Refer to Chapter 12 for details of choke switch removal and refitting*

Removal

1 Remove the air cleaner assembly.

2 Release the clip securing the cable outer to the carburettor, then disconnect the cable inner from the carburettor pulley **(see illustration)**.

3 Prise the cable sealing grommet out of the bulkhead aperture and slide the grommet off the cable **(see illustration)**. Tie a length of string to the end of the cable.

4 Working inside the car, remove the ashtray and disconnect the switch wire from the choke cable, then prise out the clip securing the cable to the facia and withdraw the cable, removing the switch if required. Untie the drawstring as soon as it appears.

Refitting and adjustment

5 Refitting is the reverse of the removal procedure; use the drawstring to pull the new cable through the facia and bulkhead into the engine compartment.

6 Adjust the cable so that when the choke control is pulled fully out the choke cam has no further travel. When the control is pushed fully in the choke cam should return to the fully-off position so that there is clearance between the cam and the fast idle adjusting

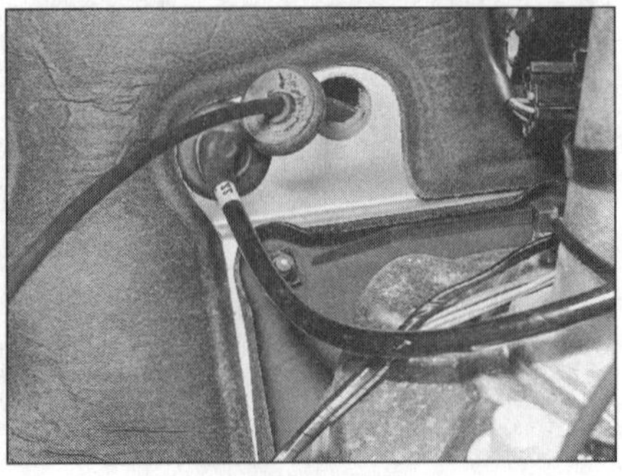

12.3 Remove cable sealing grommet from bulkhead to remove choke cable

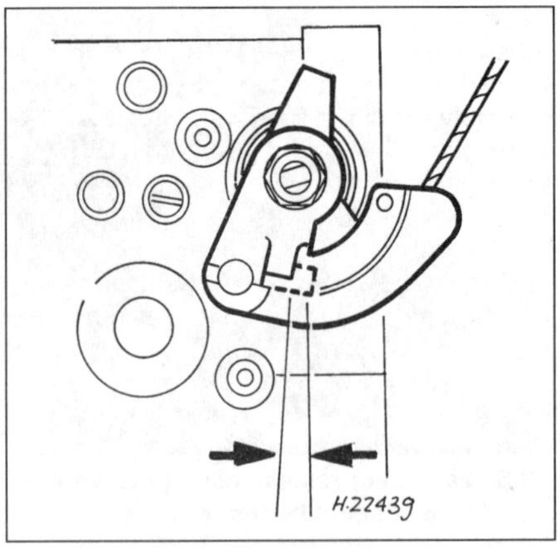

10.5 Throttle lost motion gap (arrowed)

screw; provided that the choke returns fully, no cable free play should be evident.

7 The cable is adjusted by releasing the carburettor clip and repositioning the cable outer as necessary.

13 Carburettor - removal and refitting

Removal

1 Remove the air cleaner assembly.

2 Disconnect the throttle cable.

3 Disconnect the choke cable.

4 Disconnect the breather hose and the vacuum pipes; if required they can (where possible) be removed with the carburettor. Disconnect the idle bypass solenoid wiring, making notes of the connections so that they can be correctly reconnected, then disconnect the float chamber vent hose and the full load air bleed hose **(see illustration)**.

5 Release its clip and disconnect the fuel pump outlet hose from the carburettor. Place wads of rag around the union to catch any spilled fuel, plug the hose as soon as it is disconnected and cover the hose union to prevent the entry of dirt and the escape of fuel.

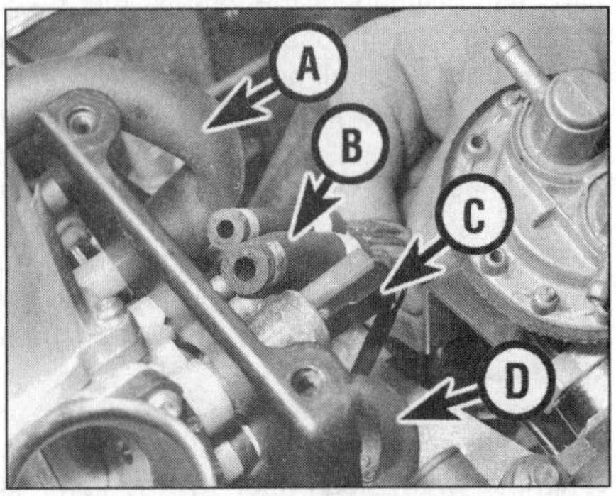

13.4 Breather hose (A) float chamber vent and full load air bleed hoses (B) idle bypass solenoid wiring (C) and fuel pump outlet hose (D)

6 Unscrew the four Torx screws securing the upper inlet manifold to the lower inlet manifold, then remove the carburettor assembly. Plug the inlet port with a wad of clean cloth, then check that the manifold mating surfaces are clean and flat and renew the gasket if necessary **(see illustrations)**.

7 If required, the air cleaner assembly support brackets, the air cleaner adapter and the upper inlet manifold can be unbolted from the carburettor body. Again, check that the mating surfaces are clean and flat, renew the sealing O-rings as a matter of course and renew the gasket if it is damaged.

Refitting

8 Refitting is the reverse of the removal procedure; tighten all screws and bolts to their specified torque wrench settings (where given). Check, and adjust if necessary, the cable adjustments and the idle speed and mixture.

14 Carburettor - diagnosis, overhaul and adjustments

Diagnosis

1 The SU carburettor does not usually suffer from jet blockages and wear is usually only found between the needle and jet, although it is worth checking the fit of the piston in the suction chamber whenever the carburettor is dismantled. If the idle speed is too high and cannot be reduced by normal adjustment, it is worth checking the throttle disc overrun valve spring (if fitted); if this has weakened, the throttle disc must be renewed.

2 If a carburettor fault is suspected, always check first that the ignition timing is accurate and the spark plugs are in good condition and correctly gapped, that the throttle and choke cables are correctly adjusted, that the carburettor piston damper is topped-up, that the float chamber vent hose and (especially if the mixture is very rich) the full load air bleed hose are clear and that the air cleaner filter element is clean. If the engine is running very roughly, check the compression pressures (Chapter 2) and bear in mind the possibility that one of the hydraulic tappets might be faulty, producing an incorrect valve clearance.

3 If careful checking of all of the above produces no improvement, the carburettor must be removed for cleaning and overhaul.

Overhaul

4 A complete strip-down of a carburettor is unlikely to cure a fault which is not immediately obvious without introducing new problems. If persistent carburation problems are encountered, it is recommended that the advice of a Rover dealer or carburettor specialist is sought. Most dealers will be able to provide carburettor re-jetting and servicing facilities and if necessary, it should be possible to purchase a reconditioned carburettor of the relevant type.

13.6a Unscrew upper-to-lower inlet manifold Torx screws . . .

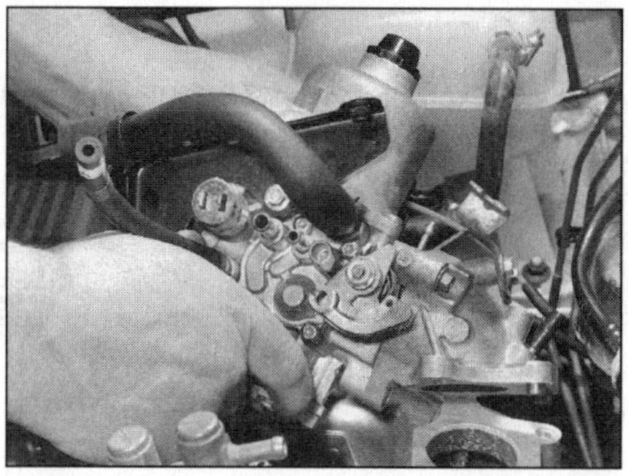

13.6b . . . to remove carburettor assembly

5 If it is decided to go ahead and service a carburettor, check the cost and availability of spare parts before commencement. Obtain a carburettor repair kit, which will contain the necessary gaskets, diaphragms and other renewable items.

6 When working on carburettors, scrupulous cleanliness must be observed and care must be taken not to introduce any foreign matter into components. Carburettors are delicate instruments and care should be taken not to disturb any components unnecessarily.

7 Referring to the relevant exploded view of the carburettor **(see illustration),** remove each component part whilst making a note of its fitted position. Make alignment marks on linkages etc.

8 Reassemble the carburettor in the reverse order to dismantling, using new gaskets, O-rings etc. Be careful not to kink any diaphragms.

Adjustments

Idle speed and mixture

9 Refer to Chapter 1, Section 28.

Fast idle speed

10 Check the throttle and choke cable adjustments.

11 Warm the engine up to normal operating temperature and check that the idle speed and mixture are correctly set. If the car is not equipped with a tachometer, connect a tachometer to the engine following its manufacturer's instructions.

12 Pull out the choke control to the first detent position and check that the engine speed increases to the specified amount.

13 If adjustment is required, screw in or out the fast idle adjusting screw until the engine speed is correct.

Fuel level

14 The carburettor fuel level is adjusted by bending the float arm to alter the float height, usually measured with the carburettor inverted. However, since the necessary information is not provided by the manufacturer, the car should be taken to a Rover dealer or SU carburettor specialist if the fuel level is thought to be incorrect.

Jet adjustment

Note: *Accurate jet adjustment is not easy for the inexperienced and can only be carried out using an exhaust gas analyser. If the jet adjustment is thought to be incorrect or is to be checked, owners without the required equipment and the skill to use it are advised to have the work carried out by a Rover dealer or SU carburettor specialist*

15 Warm the engine up to normal operating temperature and check that the ignition timing, idle speed and mixture are correctly set and that the carburettor piston damper is topped-up. Connect a tachometer to the engine following its manufacturer's instructions.

16 Remove the tamperproof cap from the jet adjusting screw recess at the front left-hand corner of the carburettor body.

17 Counting the exact number of turns required to do so, screw the idle air bypass screw anti-clockwise until it seats lightly, then start the engine, switch on the headlamps, heated rear window and heater blower motor (first speed only) and adjust the idle speed to 700 to 750 rpm.

18 Connect the exhaust gas analyser following its manufacturer's instructions.

19 Turning the jet adjusting screw either way (clockwise to richen the mixture) by half a turn at a time and waiting for the analyser reading to respond and stabilise before making a further alteration, set the mixture to a base CO level of 5.5% ± 0.5%. When the analyser reading is steady at the correct level, switch off all electrical loads.

20 Screw the idle air bypass screw clockwise by the number of turns previously noted to return it to its original setting, then set the true idle mixture to the specified value.

21 Stop the engine when the adjustment is correct, disconnect the test equipment and fit a new tamperproof cap to the jet adjusting screw recess.

Idle bypass system

22 As well as the carburettor idle air bypass passage and screw, the system incorporates the solenoid and the throttle pedal switch and is supplied with current via fusible link number 1, the ignition switch and fuse number 1.

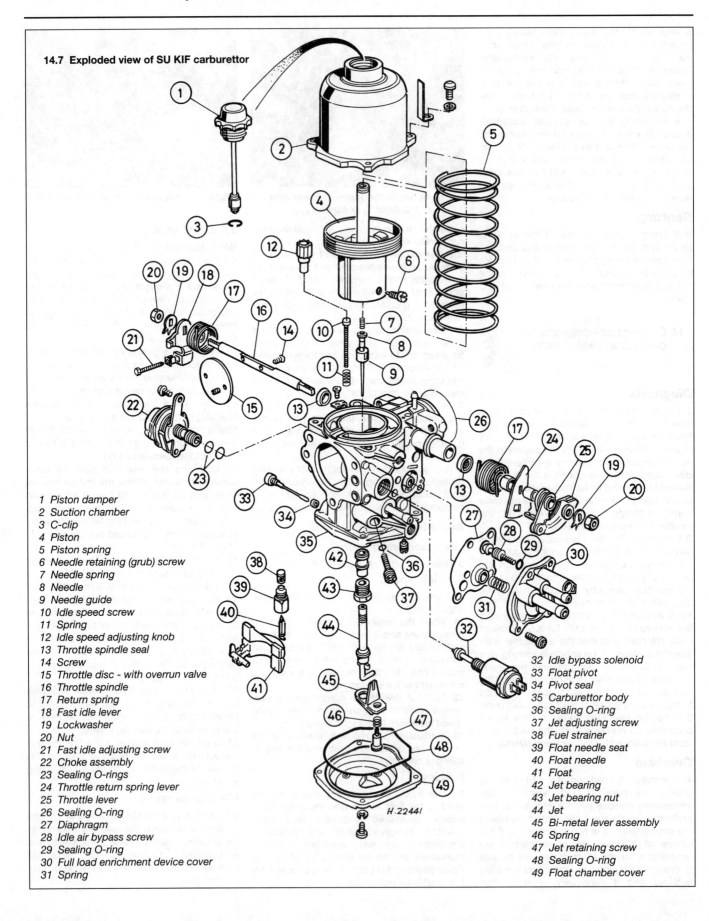

14.7 Exploded view of SU KIF carburettor

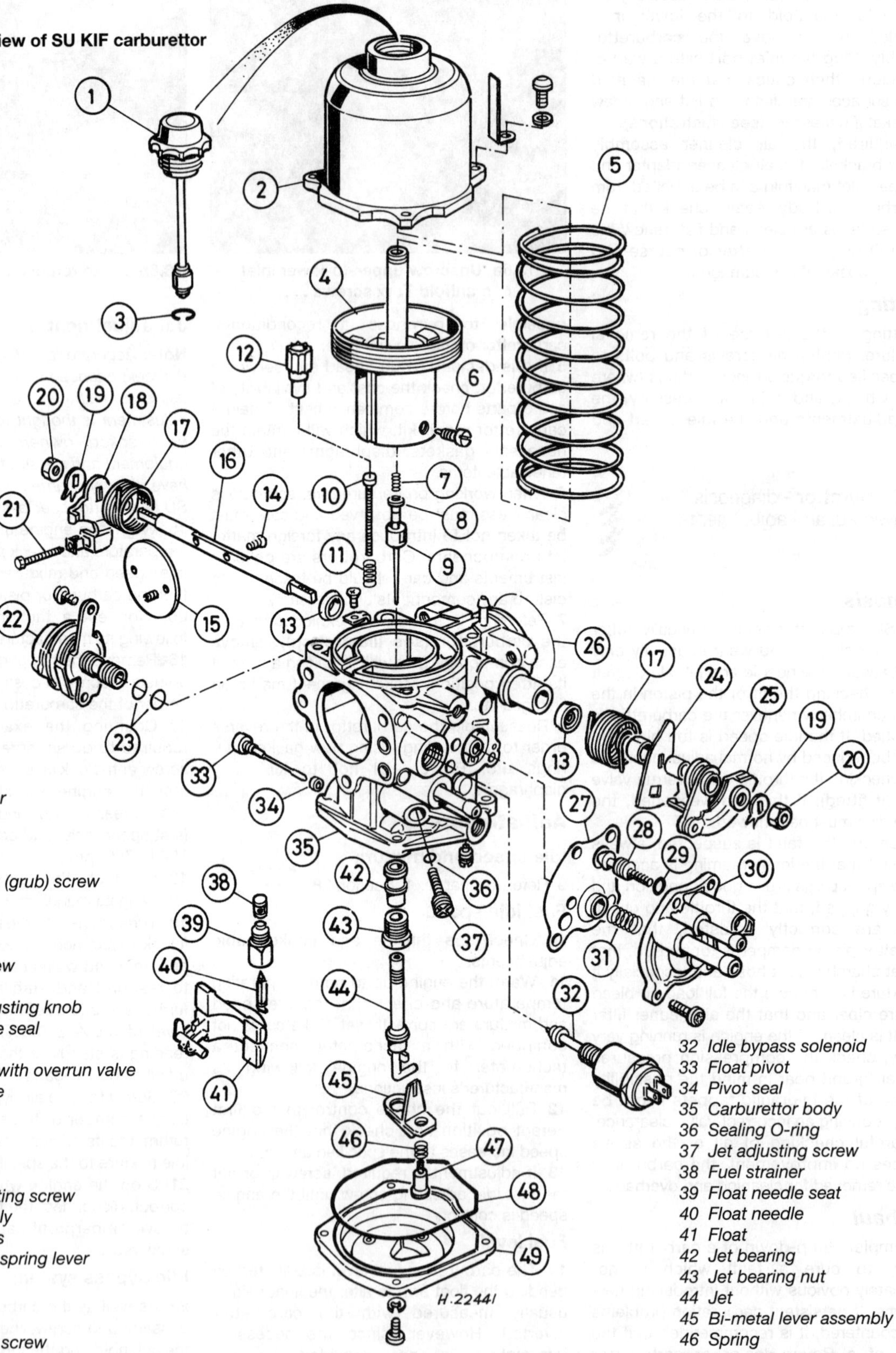

1 Piston damper
2 Suction chamber
3 C-clip
4 Piston
5 Piston spring
6 Needle retaining (grub) screw
7 Needle spring
8 Needle
9 Needle guide
10 Idle speed screw
11 Spring
12 Idle speed adjusting knob
13 Throttle spindle seal
14 Screw
15 Throttle disc - with overrun valve
16 Throttle spindle
17 Return spring
18 Fast idle lever
19 Lockwasher
20 Nut
21 Fast idle adjusting screw
22 Choke assembly
23 Sealing O-rings
24 Throttle return spring lever
25 Throttle lever
26 Sealing O-ring
27 Diaphragm
28 Idle air bypass screw
29 Sealing O-ring
30 Full load enrichment device cover
31 Spring
32 Idle bypass solenoid
33 Float pivot
34 Pivot seal
35 Carburettor body
36 Sealing O-ring
37 Jet adjusting screw
38 Fuel strainer
39 Float needle seat
40 Float needle
41 Float
42 Jet bearing
43 Jet bearing nut
44 Jet
45 Bi-metal lever assembly
46 Spring
47 Jet retaining screw
48 Sealing O-ring
49 Float chamber cover

14.26 Note connections before disconnecting idle bypass solenoid wiring

23 When the throttle is closed and the ignition is switched on the solenoid is energised, its plunger being retracted to open the bypass passage, this allows air to bypass the carburettor piston and thus makes the idle mixture independent of the needle metering. Screwing in (clockwise) the idle air bypass screw reduces the amount of air bypassing the piston and richens the idle mixture.

24 As soon as the throttle pedal is depressed, the throttle pedal switch opens, the solenoid is de-energised and the bypass passage is shut off.

25 To check the system, listen closely by the carburettor while an assistant switches on the ignition and depresses and releases the throttle pedal several times; the solenoid should be heard to be clicking in and out.

26 If no clicking can be heard, remove the air cleaner assembly and use a meter or similar to check the solenoid earth and feed; use a meter to check that the throttle pedal switch contacts open and close as described. If the solenoid or switch is faulty it must be renewed. Note that fuse number 1 also controls the ignition system; if it blows repeatedly, the solenoid may be at fault **(see illustration)**.

27 Refer to Chapter 12 for details of throttle pedal switch removal and refitting.

15 Inlet manifold pre-heater - operation, removal and refitting

Operation

1 The system incorporates the manifold PTC (Positive Temperature Coefficient) heater, the relay and the manifold temperature switch; the relay energising coil is supplied with current via fusible link number 1, the ignition switch and fuse number 1.

2 When the ignition is switched on and the engine (coolant) is cold, the relay-energising current earths through the manifold temperature switch, closing the relay contacts and allowing current to flow from the battery via fusible link number 4 to the heater. This ensures that the inlet manifold is warm enough, even before the effect of the coolant

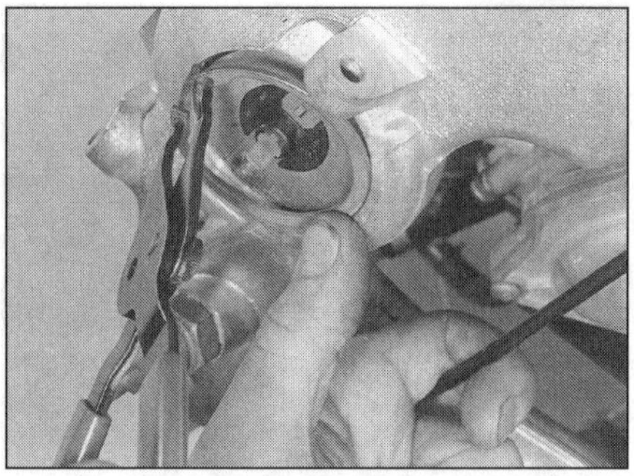

15.6a Remove inlet manifold and extract circlip . . .

heating becomes apparent, to prevent fuel droplets condensing in the manifold, thus improving driveability and reducing exhaust emissions when the engine is cold.

3 As soon as the engine warms up to temperatures above 50°C, the switch contacts close and the circuit is shut off.

4 If the engine suddenly develops flat spots when cold, the system may be faulty.

Manifold PTC heater - removal and refitting

Removal

5 Remove the inlet manifold.

6 Extract the circlip securing the heater to the manifold, then withdraw the heater and prise out and discard the rubber sealing ring **(see illustrations)**.

Refitting

7 Refitting is the reverse of the removal procedure; fit a new sealing ring as a matter of course and ensure that the heater locating projection is correctly engaged in the manifold recess.

Inlet manifold pre-heater temperature switch - testing, removal and refitting

8 Refer to Chapter 3 for details of switch testing, removal and refitting **(see illustration)**.

Manifold heater relay

9 Refer to Chapter 12 for details.

15.8 Location of inlet manifold pre-heater temperature switch

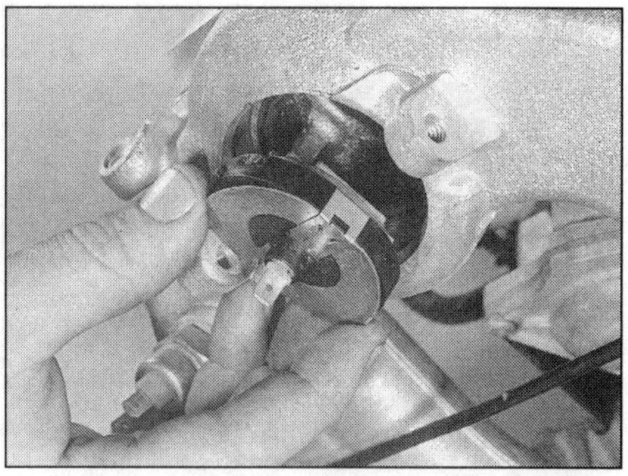

15.6b . . . to remove manifold PTC heater

16 Inlet manifold - removal and refitting

Removal

Note: *The following procedure describes the removal of the manifold with the carburettor. Access to some of the components concerned is, however, much better if the carburettor is first removed separately. If this is done, the following procedure should be amended as required*

1 Disconnect the battery negative lead.

2 Remove the air cleaner assembly.

3 Either drain the cooling system completely, or clamp the coolant hoses connected to the inlet manifold to minimise coolant loss and be prepared to catch the coolant that will be released from the manifold and cylinder head.

4 Disconnect all coolant hoses from the manifold **(see illustration)**.

5 Trace the float chamber vent hose and the full load air bleed hose from the carburettor down to their metal pipes and unscrew the nut and bolts securing the pipes to the cylinder block/crankcase.

6 Disconnect the breather hose from the cylinder head cover.

7 Disconnect the idle bypass solenoid wiring, making notes of the connections so that they can be correctly reconnected, then disconnect the manifold pre-heater switch and heater wiring.

16.4 Disconnect hoses (arrowed) when removing inlet manifold

16.11 Inlet manifold support stay upper end bolt (arrowed)

8 Release its clip and disconnect the fuel pump outlet hose from the carburettor. Place wads of rag around the union to catch any spilled fuel, plug the hose as soon as it is disconnected and cover the hose union to prevent the entry of dirt and the escape of fuel.

9 Disconnect the vacuum pipe from the distributor; secure the pipes so that they cannot be damaged during removal and refitting.

10 Disconnect the brake vacuum servo unit vacuum hose from the manifold and discard the sealing washers.

11 The manifold support stays are bolted to the manifold at their upper ends and to the cylinder block/crankcase at their lower ends; slacken the bolts at one end and unbolt the other as convenient **(see illustration)**.

12 Unscrew the nuts and bolts securing the manifold to the cylinder head and withdraw it **(see illustration)**. Remove and discard the gasket.

13 Clean the manifold and cylinder head mating surfaces and check that they are flat and unmarked.

Refitting

14 Refitting is the reverse of the removal procedure, noting the following points:

a) *Always fit a new manifold gasket **(see illustration)**.*

b) *Working in the sequence shown **(see illustration)**, tighten the manifold retaining nuts and bolts evenly, to the specified torque wrench setting.*

16.12 Removing the inlet manifold complete with carburettor

c) *Refill the cooling system or check the coolant level as required, then wash off any spilt coolant.*

d) *Renew the vacuum servo unit vacuum hose banjo union sealing washers.*

e) *Tighten all other disturbed nuts and bolts to their specified torque wrench settings (where given).*

17 Exhaust manifold - removal and refitting

Removal

1 Disconnect the battery negative lead.

2 Jack up the front of the car and support it securely on axle stands (see "*Jacking and Vehicle Support*").

3 Unbolt the radiator top mountings to permit movement.

4 Disconnect the exhaust front pipe from the manifold.

5 Remove the cold air inlet duct and the air cleaner inlet duct.

6 Unscrew the nuts securing the manifold to the cylinder head and withdraw it; remove and discard the gasket.

7 Clean the manifold and cylinder head mating surfaces and check that they are flat and unmarked. Check all threads and the exhaust front pipe mating surface; clean off any corrosion and repair or renew any damaged component.

16.14a Always fit a new manifold gasket

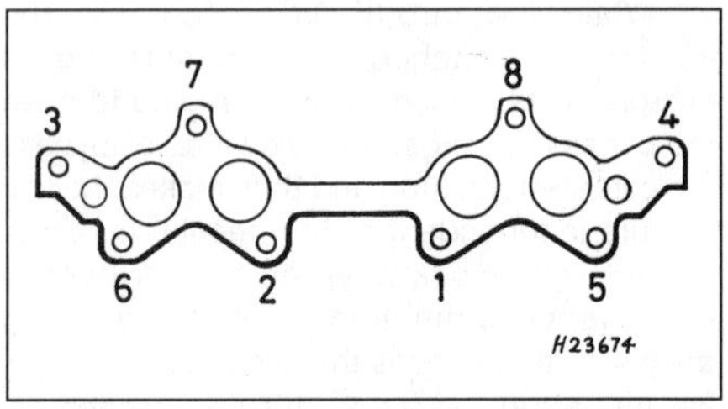

16.14b Inlet manifold fastener tightening sequence

Refitting

8 Refitting is the reverse of the removal procedure, noting the following points:

a) *Always fit a new manifold gasket **(see illustration)**.*

b) *Working in the sequence shown **(see illustration)**, tighten the manifold retaining nuts evenly to the specified torque wrench setting.*

c) *Tighten all other disturbed nuts and bolts to their specified torque wrench settings (where given).*

18 Exhaust system - inspection and component renewal

Note: *If a catalytic converter is fitted, remember that it is FRAGILE - do not use hammers, mallets etc to strike any part of the system and take care not to drop it or strike it against anything else while handling it*

Inspection

Refer to Chapter 1, Section 16.

System assembly

1 The exhaust system components are assembled as shown **(see illustrations)**. The (service replacement) exhaust system is in three sections; the front pipe (attached to the exhaust manifold by a spring-tensioned flange on models without catalytic converters, by a flanged joint on models with catalytic converters) and front silencer box, the intermediate pipe and middle silencer box (attached to the front pipe by a flanged joint) and the tailpipe and main silencer box

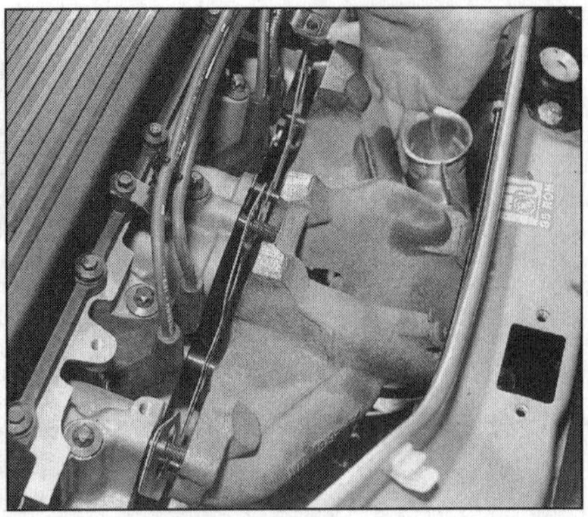

17.8a Refitting exhaust manifold - always renew gasket

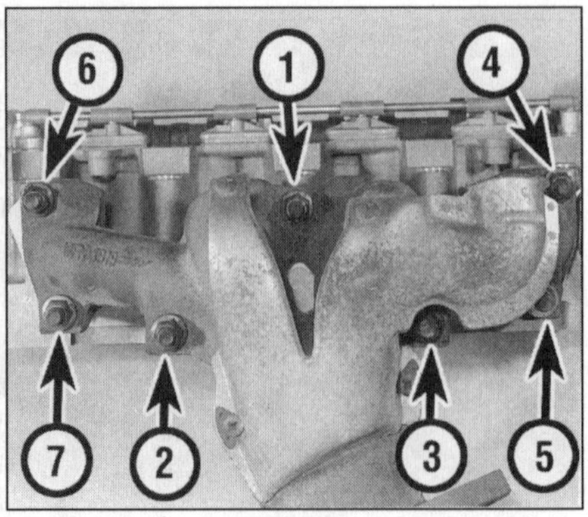

17.8b Exhaust manifold nut tightening sequence

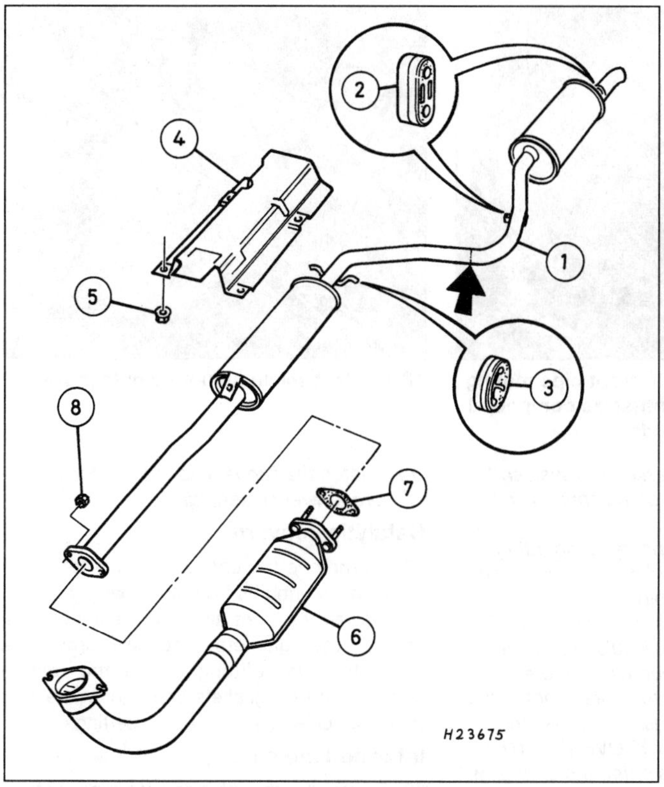

18.1a Typical exhaust system components without catalytic converter

1 *Intermediate pipe and tailpipe - production fit*
2 *Rubber mounting*
3 *Rubber mounting*
4 *Heat shield*
5 *Nut*
6 *Front pipe*
7 *Gasket*
8 *Nut*

***Note:** Arrow indicates cutting point for removal of production-fit intermediate pipe and tailpipe*

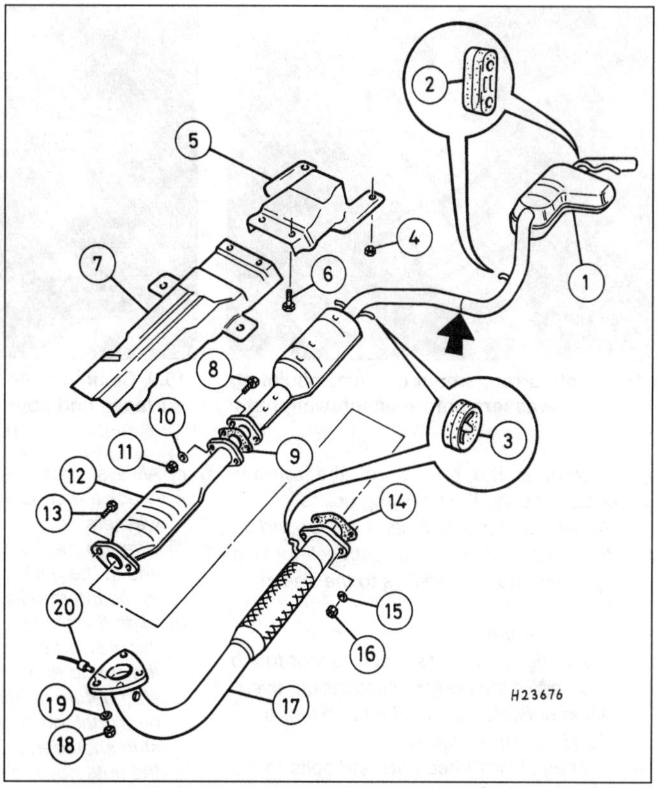

18.1b Typical exhaust system components with catalytic converter

1 *Intermediate pipe and tailpipe - production fit*
2 *Rubber mounting*
3 *Rubber mounting*
4 *Nut*
5 *Rear heat shield*
6 *Bolt*
7 *Front heat shield*
8 *Bolt*
9 *Gasket*
10 *Washer*
11 *Nut*
12 *Catalytic converter*
13 *Bolt*
14 *Gasket*
15 *Washer*
16 *Nut*
17 *Front pipe*
18 *Nut*
19 *Washer*
20 *Gas-sampling pipe*

***Note:** Arrow indicates cutting point for removal of production-fit intermediate pipe and tailpipe.*

(attached to the intermediate pipe by a clamped sleeve joint). If a catalytic converter is fitted, it is situated between the front pipe and the (much shorter) intermediate pipe, with a flanged joint at each end; the front pipe then has a gas-sampling pipe (fitted to permit mixture checks using an exhaust gas analyser) and a flexible section. **Note:** *The exhaust system fitted in production differs in that the intermediate pipe and tailpipe are in one piece; the pipe must be cut to separate the two when either is to be renewed.*

2 The system is suspended throughout its entire length by rubber mountings.

3 If the car still has the exhaust system fitted in production by the factory, the tailpipe and intermediate pipe must be cut at the point marked by two dimples in the pipe; the two can then be removed individually **(see illustration)**. On fitting new components, the service replacement tailpipe has a sleeved joint which fits over the intermediate pipe and is secured by a clamp; if the intermediate pipe is to be renewed first, an adapter sleeve (which will require securing clamps) is available from Rover dealers. Apart from this complication, all sections can be removed individually if required, in no particular sequence.

4 To remove the system or part of the system, first jack up the front or rear of the car and support it on axle stands (see "*Jacking and Vehicle Support*"). Alternatively position the car over an inspection pit or on car ramps.

System renewal

5 Disconnect the front pipe from the exhaust manifold and cut or disconnect (as appropriate) the intermediate pipe from the tailpipe. Unhook the rubber mountings and withdraw the tailpipe from above the rear suspension subframe, then remove the front part of the system.

6 Renew all gaskets and seals as a matter of course; check, and renew if necessary, all fasteners, the clamp (if appropriate) and the rubber mountings.

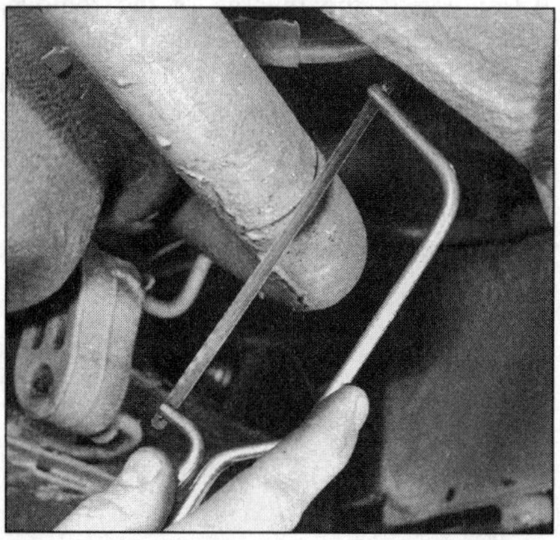

18.3 Cutting production-fit intermediate pipe and tailpipe to remove

4A

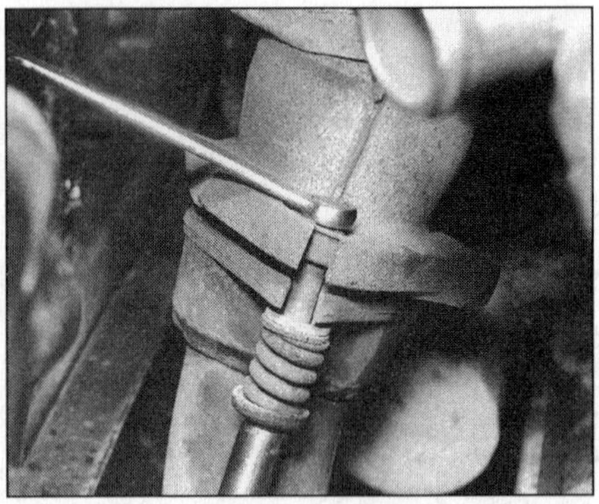

18.8 Note arrangement of plain, insulating and cup washers before unscrewing nuts

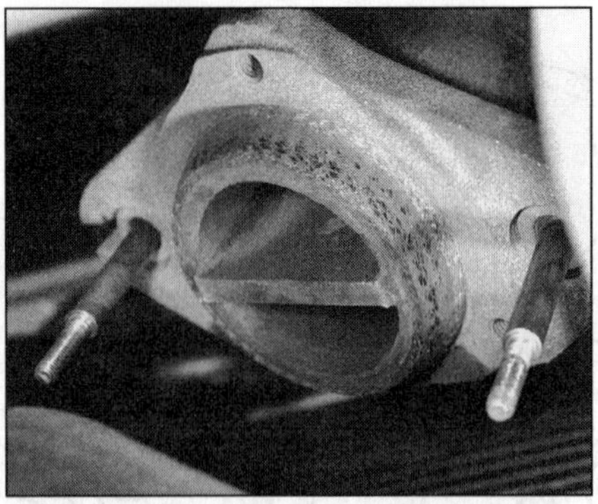

18.9 Clean manifold-to-front pipe mating surfaces and apply anti-seize compound to studs

18.15 Heat shield mounting nuts (arrowed)

7 Refitting is the reverse of the removal procedure, noting the following points.

a) *Apply a smear of anti-seize compound to the threads of all nuts (except self-locking nuts) and bolts as well as to the sleeve joint.*
b) *Assemble the system loosely on its mountings and check that it cannot touch any part of the body or suspension, even when deflected within the full extent of the rubber mountings.*
c) *Tighten all disturbed nuts and bolts to their specified torque wrench settings.*
d) *Start the engine and check the system for leaks, especially once it is fully warmed up; check-tighten all fasteners after the system has cooled.*

Component renewal

Front pipe

8 To remove the front pipe on cars without catalytic converters, unscrew and remove the two nuts, then remove the cup washers, the springs and the plain washers securing the pipe to the manifold **(see illustration)**. Unscrew the nuts and prise the intermediate pipe away from the front pipe, then withdraw the front pipe; collect the seal from its upper end and the gasket from its lower end.

9 Refitting is the reverse of the removal procedure, noting the following points:

a) *Clean the mating surfaces of the front pipe and of the manifold and intermediate pipe* ***(see illustration).***
b) *Apply a smear of anti-seize compound to the bolts and to the threads of the studs and nuts (except self-locking nuts).*
c) *Always renew the gasket and seal, and check the condition of the springs and washers.*
d) *Offer up the front pipe to its mountings and fit the gasket and nuts to connect it to the intermediate pipe.*
e) *Align the pipe on the manifold then refit the plain washer, the insulating washer, the spring and the cup washer to each stud before refitting the nuts. Tighten the nuts until the cup washer touches the stud shoulder. DO NOT OVERTIGHTEN the nuts beyond this point; the springs will provide the seal required.*
f) *Tighten the front-to-intermediate pipe flange nuts to the specified torque wrench setting.*

10 To remove the front pipe on cars with catalytic converters, unscrew the three nuts securing the pipe to the manifold and the two nuts securing the front pipe to the catalytic converter; prise the converter away from the front pipe, unhook the rubber mounting and withdraw the front pipe. Collect the seal from its upper end and the gasket from its lower end.

11 Refitting is the reverse of the removal procedure, noting the following points.

a) *Clean the mating surfaces of the front pipe and of the manifold and the catalytic converter.*
b) *Apply a smear of anti-seize compound to the threads of the studs and nuts (except self-locking nuts).*
c) *Always renew the gasket and seal and check carefully the condition of the rubber mounting.*
d) *Offer up the front pipe and hook it onto the rubber mounting, then fit the seal, gasket and nuts to connect it to the manifold and catalytic converter.*
e) *Tighten the flange nuts to their specified torque wrench settings.*

Catalytic converter

12 To remove the catalytic converter, undo the nuts securing its front and rear ends, then prise away the front and intermediate pipes; collect the gaskets and withdraw the converter. On refitting, clean the mating surfaces, fit new gaskets and tighten the nuts to the specified torque wrench settings.

Intermediate pipe

13 To remove the intermediate pipe first cut or disconnect the tailpipe (as appropriate). Unscrew the nuts and prise away the front pipe/catalytic converter; collect the gasket. Unhook the rubber mountings and remove the intermediate pipe. On refitting, clean the mating surfaces, fit new gaskets, renew the rubber mountings if necessary and tighten the nuts to the specified torque wrench setting.

Tailpipe

14 To remove the tailpipe, either cut it or slacken the clamp nut and separate the tailpipe from the intermediate pipe. Unhook the rubber mountings and remove the tailpipe. Refitting is the reverse of the removal procedure; tighten the clamp nut to its specified torque wrench setting and renew the rubber mountings if necessary.

Heat shields

15 The various heat shields can be unfastened from the body and manoeuvred clear of the exhaust system; it may be necessary to unhook one or more of the system's rubber mountings if the extra space is required **(see illustration)**.

Chapter 4 Part B:
Fuel and exhaust systems - single-point fuel injection models

Contents

Degrees of difficulty

Easy, suitable for novice with little experience	**Fairly easy,** suitable for beginner with some experience	**Fairly difficult,** suitable for competent DIY mechanic	**Difficult,** suitable for experienced DIY mechanic	**Very difficult,** suitable for expert DIY or professional

Specifications

System

Type	Rover/Motorola Modular Engine Management System, using ECU-controlled single-point injection (MEMS-SPi) and speed/density method of airflow measurement

MEMS-SPi system data

Fuel pump type	Electric, immersed in fuel tank
Fuel pump pressure:	
Maximum - at 16 volts	2.7 bar
Regulated constant pressure:	
1.4 K16-engined models with closed-loop catalytic converter	1.1 ± 0.1 bar
All other models	1.0 to 1.1 bar
Injector/pressure regulator assembly:	
1.1 models	JZX 3300
1.4 K8-engined models	JZX 3296
1.4 K16-engined models	JZX 3028
Throttle potentiometer voltage:	
Throttle closed	0 to 1 volt
Throttle open	4 to 5 volt
Idle speed - nominal value given for reference purposes only:	
1.4 K16-engined models with closed-loop catalytic converter	875 ± 50 rpm
All other models	850 ± 50 rpm
CO level at idle speed - engine at normal operating temperature:	
Without catalytic converter - at tailpipe	0.5 to 2.0%
With open-loop catalytic converter - at gas sampling pipe	0.5 to 2.0%
With closed-loop catalytic converter - at tailpipe	0.75% maximum - not adjustable

Recommended fuel

Minimum octane rating:	
Without catalytic converter	95 RON unleaded (ie unleaded Premium) or 97 RON leaded (ie 4-star)
With catalytic converter	95 RON unleaded (ie unleaded Premium) **only**

Torque wrench settings

	Nm	lbf ft
Fuel system		
Fuel tank mounting bolts	12	9
Two-way valve-to-fuel tank filler neck nut	5	3.5
Fuel tank filler neck-to-body fasteners:		
Screws - three-door	5	3.5
Nuts - five-door	9	6.5
Electric fuel pump-to-fuel tank mounting nuts	9	6.5
Inlet manifold mounting nuts and bolts	25	18.5
Inlet manifold support stays-to-cylinder block/crankcase bolts	25	18.5
Air inlet duct-to-cylinder head support bracket screw - K16 engine	8	6
Coolant temperature sensor to cylinder block	15	11
Fuel system pressure release bolt - at fuel filter	12	9
Fuel filter inlet union	40	29.5
Fuel filter outlet union	35	26
Throttle pedal mounting nuts	25	18.5
Inlet air temperature sensor	7	5
Fuel pipe union nuts - at injector housing	24	17.5
Injector housing fuel pipe union adapters	24	17.5
Injector housing-to-throttle body screws	5	3.5
Throttle body-to-inlet manifold nuts	18	13
Throttle potentiometer mounting screws	2	1.5
Exhaust system		
Exhaust manifold mounting nuts	45	33
Exhaust system front pipe-to-manifold nuts:		
Without catalytic converter (spring-loaded mounting)	see text	see text
With catalytic converter	50	37
All exhaust system flange securing nuts	45	33
Exhaust system intermediate pipe-to-tailpipe clamp nut	18	13
Lambda sensor	45	33

1 General information and precautions

General information

The fuel system comprises a fuel tank mounted under the rear of the car with an integral electric fuel pump, a fuel filter, fuel feed and return lines and the throttle body assembly (which incorporates the single fuel injector and the fuel pressure regulator), as well as the Electronic Control Unit (ECU) and the various sensors, electrical components and related wiring. The ECU fully controls both the ignition system and the fuel injection system, integrating the two in a complete engine management system.

The Rover/Motorola Modular Engine Management System uses the ECU-controlled single-point injection (MEMS-SPi) and the speed/density method of airflow measurement. The whole system is best explained if considered as three sub-systems; the fuel delivery, the air metering and the electrical control:

The fuel delivery system incorporates the fuel tank, which has an electric fuel pump immersed in a swirl pot inside it to prevent aeration of the fuel. When the ignition is switched on, the pump is supplied with current through one of the relays incorporated in the relay module. Under the control of the ECU, the pump feeds petrol via a non-return valve (to prevent fuel draining out of the system components and back to the tank when the pump is not working) to the fuel filter and from the filter to the injector. Fuel pressure is controlled by the pressure regulator, which lifts to allow excess fuel to return to the tank swirl pot, where a venturi causes the returning fuel to draw cool fuel from the tank into the swirl pot. In the event of sudden deceleration (ie, an accident) the inertia switch cuts off the power to the pump so that the risk of fire is minimised from fuel spraying out of broken fuel lines under pressure.

The air metering system includes the inlet air temperature control system and the air cleaner, but its main components are in the throttle body assembly. This incorporates the injector, which sprays fuel onto the back of the throttle disc, the throttle potentiometer, which is linked to the throttle disc spindle and sends the ECU information on the rate of throttle opening by transmitting a varying voltage, and the stepper motor, which is controlled by the ECU and operates the throttle disc spindle lever via a cam and pushrod to provide idle speed control. **Note:** *There is no provision for the adjustment or alteration of the idle speed except by reprogramming the ECU using Rover diagnostic equipment; if checking the idle speed, remember that it will vary constantly under ECU control.*

The electrical control system comprises the ECU, with all the sensors that provide it with information and the actuators by which it controls the whole system's operation. The ECUs manifold absolute pressure sensor is connected, by hoses and a fuel (vapour) trap mounted in the air cleaner assembly, to the inlet manifold. Variations in manifold pressure are converted into graduated electrical signals which are used by the ECU to determine the load on the engine. The inlet air temperature sensor is self-explanatory, the crankshaft sensor gives it the engine speed and crankshaft position, the coolant temperature sensor gives it the engine temperature, the throttle pedal switch tells it when the throttle is closed. In addition, the ECU senses battery voltage (adjusting the injector pulse width to suit and using the stepper motor to increase the idle speed and, therefore, the alternator output if it is too low), incorporates short-circuit protection and diagnostic capabilities and can both receive and transmit information via the diagnostic connector, thus permitting engine diagnosis and tuning by Rover diagnostic equipment. If either the coolant temperature sensor, the inlet air temperature sensor or the manifold absolute pressure sensor circuits should fail to provide adequate information, the ECU has a back-up facility which assumes a value corresponding to a coolant temperature of 60°C, an inlet air temperature of 35°C and an engine load based on the engine speed and throttle position; these are used to implement a back-up air/fuel mixture ratio.

All these signals are compared by the ECU, using digital techniques, with set values pre-programmed (mapped) into its memory; based on this information, the ECU selects the response appropriate to those values and controls the ignition HT coil (varying the ignition timing as required), the fuel injector (varying its pulse width - the length of time the injector is held open - to provide a richer or weaker mixture, as appropriate), the stepper motor (controlling the idle and fast idle speeds), the fuel pump relay (controlling the fuel delivery), the manifold heater relay (controlling the inlet manifold pre-heater system) and the main relay, the purge control valve (where fitted) and the lambda sensor and relay (where fitted) accordingly. The mixture, idle speed and ignition timing are constantly varied by the ECU to provide the best settings for cranking, starting and engine warm-up (with either a hot or cold engine), idle, cruising and acceleration. A rev-limiter circuit is built into the ECU which switches off the injector earth (ie, the fuel supply) if engine speed exceeds 6860 rpm, switching it back on at 6820 rpm. The injector earth is also switched off on the overrun (coolant temperature above 80°C, throttle pedal switch contacts closed, engine speed above 1500 rpm) to improve fuel economy and reduce exhaust emissions.

The ECU idle control is an adaptive system; it learns the engine load and wear characteristics over a period of time and adjusts the idle speed to suit. If the ECU is renewed, or one from another car is fitted, it will take a short period of normal driving for the new ECU to learn the engine's characteristics and restore full idle control.

The air cleaner contains a disposable paper filter element and incorporates a flap valve air temperature control system which allows cold air from the outside of the car and warm air from the exhaust manifold to enter the air cleaner in the correct proportions.

To reduce emissions and to improve driveability when the engine is cold, the inlet manifold is heated by the cooling system coolant and by an electric pre-heater system. Mixture enrichment for cold starting is a pre-programmed function of the system.

The exhaust system is as described in Part A of this Chapter.

Precautions

Fuel warning

Many of the procedures in this Chapter require the removal of fuel lines and connections which may result in some fuel spillage. Before carrying out any operation on the fuel system refer to the precautions given in Safety first! at the beginning of this Manual and follow them implicitly. Petrol is a highly dangerous and volatile liquid and the precautions necessary when handling it cannot be overstressed.

Fuel injection system warning

Residual pressure will remain in the fuel lines long after the vehicle was last used, therefore extra care must be taken when disconnecting a fuel line hose. Loosen any fuel hose slowly to avoid a sudden release of pressure which may cause fuel spray. As an added precaution place a rag over each union as it is disconnected to catch any fuel which is forcibly expelled.

Unleaded petrol - usage

The information given in this Chapter is correct at the time of writing and applies only to petrols currently available in the UK. If updated information is thought to be required, check with a Rover dealer. If travelling abroad consult one of the motoring organisations (or a similar authority) for advice on the petrols available and their suitability for your vehicle

The fuel recommended by Rover for Metro and 100 series models is given in the Specifications Section of this Chapter, followed by the equivalent petrol currently on sale in the UK. RON and MON are different testing standards; RON stands for Research Octane Number (also written as RM), while MON stands for Motor Octane Number (also written as MM).

All Rover Metro models are designed to run on 95 (RON) octane petrol. Super/Super Plus (unleaded) petrols can be used without modification, if nothing else is available; 4-star (leaded) petrol can **only** be used if the car is **not** fitted with a catalytic converter.

Note: *The only cars which MUST use unleaded petrol at all times are those with catalytic converters.*

Catalytic converters

Before attempting work on these items, carefully read the precautions listed in Part D of this Chapter.

2 Air cleaner element - renewal

Refer to Chapter 1, Section 34.

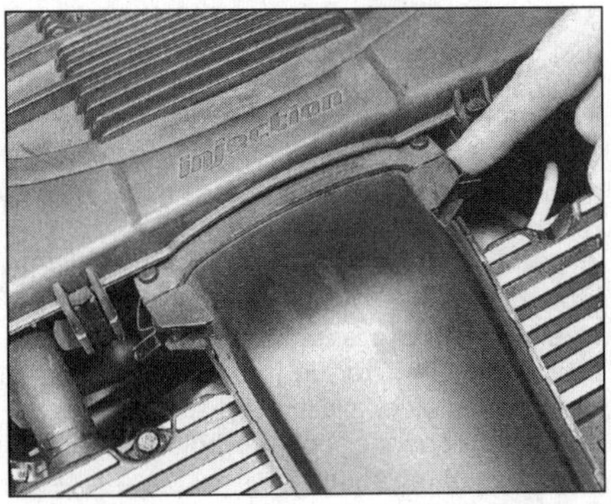

3.1 Releasing clips to separate inlet duct from air cleaner assembly

3 Air cleaner assembly - removal and refitting

Removal

1 Release the two clips securing the air inlet duct to the assembly, then undo the three screws securing the assembly to the throttle body **(see illustration)**.

2 Release the assembly from the inlet duct and withdraw it, collecting the throttle body seal and the inlet duct sealing O-ring (where fitted), then disconnect the following **(see illustration)**.

a) Disconnect the thermac switch vacuum pipes; note that these are colour-coded (yellow to the temperature control valve, red to the inlet manifold) to ensure correct reconnection.

b) Disconnect the ECU manifold absolute pressure sensor fuel trap vacuum hoses; note that these are colour-coded (green to the ECU, white to the inlet manifold) to ensure correct reconnection.

c) Release its wire clip and disconnect the inlet air temperature sensor wiring.

3 Check the condition of the throttle body seal and the inlet duct sealing O-ring (where fitted); renew either if worn or damaged.

4 To remove the inlet duct, refer to the following Section.

5 To remove the cold air inlet duct, remove the two retaining screws and disconnect the duct from the body front panel. Release the clip securing the ignition HT lead, then slacken the clamp and unfasten the rubber strap (where fitted) to separate the cold air duct from the inlet duct.

Refitting

6 Refitting is the reverse of the removal procedure; ensure that the vacuum pipes and hoses are correctly reconnected and are not trapped as the assembly is refitted, then check that the assembly sits properly on the throttle body before tightening the screws securely.

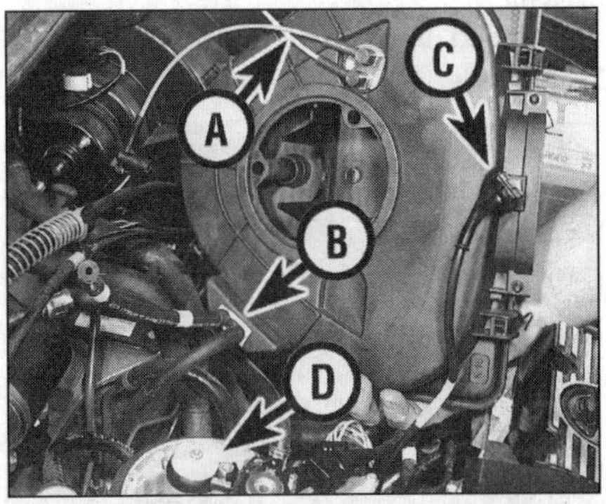

3.2 Thermac switch vacuum pipes (A) fuel trap vacuum hoses (B) intake air temperature sensor wiring (C) throttle body seal (D)

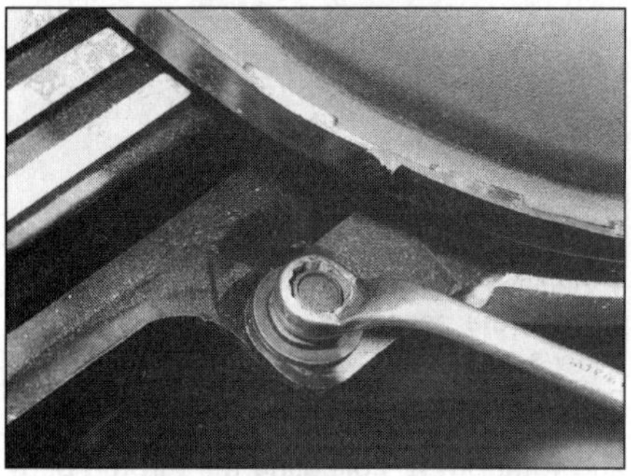

4.5a Unfastening screw securing inlet duct to support bracket

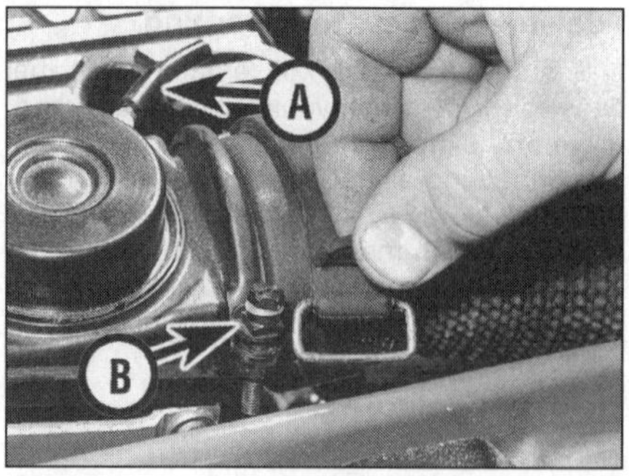

4.5b Unfastening cold air inlet duct rubber strap - note vacuum pipe (A) and clamp screw (B)

4 Air cleaner air temperature control system - inspection and component renewal

Inspection

1 Refer to Section 4 in Part A of this Chapter.

Thermac switch - renewal

2 Refer to Section 4 in Part A of this Chapter, removing the air cleaner assembly as described in the previous Section.

Air temperature control valve - renewal

3 Disconnect the vacuum pipe from the air temperature control valve, then slacken the clamp and disconnect the cold air inlet duct from the air cleaner inlet duct.
4 On K8-engined models, release the two quarter-turn fasteners securing the inlet duct to its support bracket.
5 On K16-engined models, undo the single screw securing the inlet duct to its support bracket, then unfasten the rubber strap **(see illustrations)**.
6 Release the two clips securing the air inlet duct to the air cleaner assembly and withdraw the duct, taking care not to lose the hot air inlet connector hose.
7 The air temperature control valve can be renewed only with the complete inlet duct assembly.
8 Refitting is the reverse of the removal procedure.

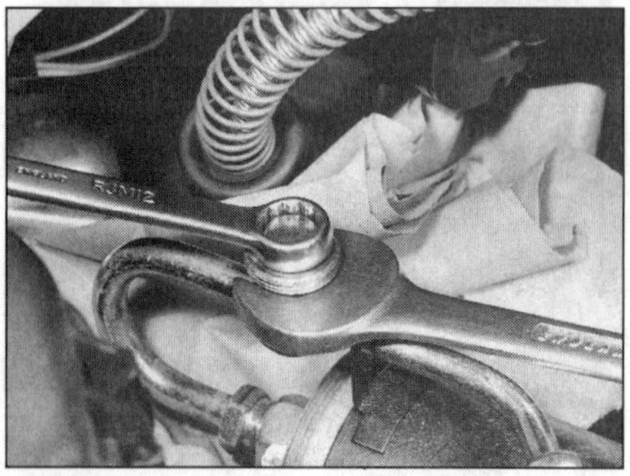

6.4 Slackening pressure release bolt to depressurise fuel system

5 Fuel system - inspection

Refer to Chapter 1, Section 15.

6 Fuel system - depressurisation

Warning: The following procedures will merely relieve the pressure in the fuel system - remember that fuel will still be present in the system components and take precautions accordingly before disconnecting any of them

1 The fuel system referred to in this Section is defined as the tank-mounted fuel pump, the fuel filter, the fuel injector and the pressure regulator in the injector housing, and the metal pipes and flexible hoses of the fuel lines between these components. All these contain fuel which will be under pressure while the engine is running and/or while the ignition is switched on.
2 The pressure will remain for some time after the ignition has been switched off and must be relieved before any of these components is disturbed for servicing work.
3 The first method is simply to remove the fuel pump fuse (number 17) and to start the engine; allow the engine to idle until it dies. Turn the engine over once or twice on the starter to ensure that all pressure is released, then switch off the ignition; do not forget to refit the fuse when work is complete.
4 The second method is to place wads of rag around the area to catch the spilled fuel and to slacken the pressure release bolt fitted above the fuel filter, in the filter outlet pipe. Remove the black plastic cap and slacken the bolt with a spanner counter-holding the pipe boss **(see illustration)**.
5 When all pressure is released, tighten the bolt to its specified torque wrench setting; again, use a spanner to counter-hold the pipe boss, to prevent damage to the pipe or filter.

7 Fuel system - pressure check

1 The following procedure is based on the use of the Rover pressure gauge and adapter (Service Tool Numbers 18G 1500 and 18G 1500/3).
2 Depressurise the fuel system.
3 Unscrew the pressure release bolt and screw in the adapter, then connect the pressure gauge.
4 Turn the engine over on the starter motor; the pressure should reach the specified value. Stop cranking the engine and watch the gauge. The pressure drop in the first minute should not exceed 0.7 bar.
5 If the pressure first recorded was too high, renew the pressure regulator; this means renewing the complete injector housing assembly.
6 If the pressure first recorded was too low or if it falls too quickly, check the system carefully for leaks. If no leaks are found check the pump by substituting a new one and recheck the pressure. If the pressure does not improve the fault is in the pressure regulator and the complete injector housing assembly must be renewed; if this is the case it is worth dismantling the regulator to check that the fault is not due to its being jammed open with dirt, or similar.

8 Fuel pump - removal and refitting

Removal

1 Remove the fuel tank.
2 Release the clips and disconnect the fuel feed (yellow band) and return (unmarked) hoses from the pump unions.
3 Release the pump wiring from any clamps or ties securing it.
4 Unscrew the mounting nuts and withdraw the pump from the tank, then remove the pump seal.

Refitting

5 Refitting is the reverse of the removal procedure, noting the following points.

a) *Renew the pump seal if there is any doubt about its condition.*
b) *Tighten the pump mounting nuts to the specified torque wrench setting.*
c) *Ensure that the hoses are connected to the correct unions* ***(see illustration)*** *and that their clips are securely fastened.*

9 Fuel gauge sender unit - removal and refitting

Refer to Section 7 in Part A of this Chapter.

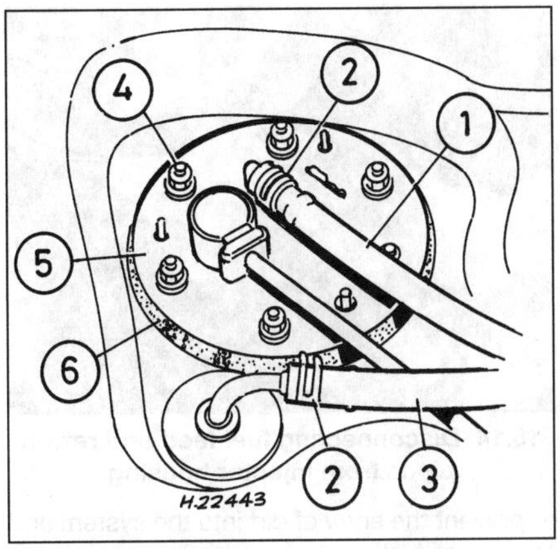

8.5 Fuel pump mountings

1 *Fuel feed hose (yellow band)*
2 *Clip*
3 *Fuel return hose (unmarked)*
4 *Nut*
5 *Fuel pump*
6 *Pump seal*

10 Fuel tank - removal and refitting

Proceed as described in Section 8 in Part A of this Chapter but depressurise the fuel system before disconnecting any of the fuel lines.

Note that the fuel feed hose is identified by a yellow band and that there is also an (unmarked) fuel return hose to be disconnected. Unclip the pump wiring connector from the tank bracket and unplug it to disconnect the pump wiring.

11 Fuel tank filler components - removal and refitting

Refer to Section 9 in Part A of this Chapter.

12 Fuel filter - renewal

Refer to Chapter 1, Section 35.

13 Throttle cable - removal, refitting and adjustment

Removal

1 Working inside the car, release the clip securing the cable inner wire to the pedal.
2 Working inside the engine compartment, remove the air cleaner assembly.
3 Slacken the cable adjuster nut and locknut, release the cable from the adjuster bracket and disengage the cable end nipple from the throttle cam **(see illustration)**.

13.3 Disconnecting throttle cable from throttle cam pulley

4 Release the cable fastener from the bulkhead and withdraw the cable into the engine compartment.

Refitting

5 Refitting is the reverse of the removal procedure; adjust the cable as follows.

a) *With the cable connected to the throttle cam and (loosely) engaged on the adjuster bracket, switch on the ignition and position the stepper motor by MOVING THE CAM ONLY to open and fully close the throttle.*
b) *Tighten the adjuster nut (underneath the adjuster bracket) until the clearance is equal on each side of the throttle lever at the lost motion link **(see illustration)**.*
c) *Tighten the locknut securely and recheck the setting.*
d) *Switch off the ignition and refit the air cleaner assembly.*

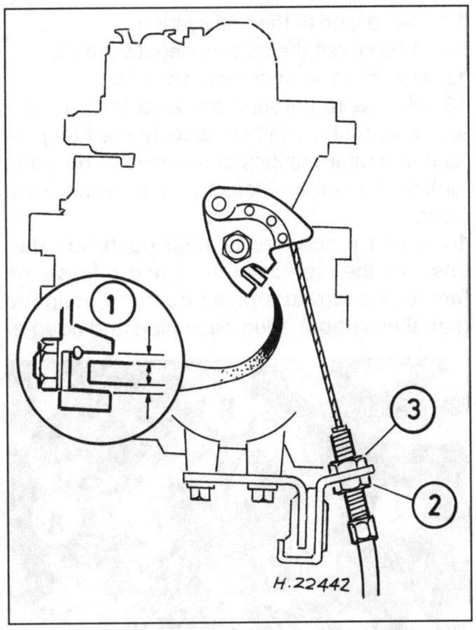

13.5 Throttle cable adjustment

1 *Throttle lever-to-lost motion link clearance - should be equal on each side*
2 *Adjuster nut*
3 *Adjuster locknut*

Adjustment

6 With the pedal fully released, check that there is equal clearance on each side of the throttle lever at the lost motion link, see illustration 13.5, and no slack in the cable. Have an assistant fully depress the pedal and check that the throttle opens fully, then check that it returns to the at-rest position when released.
7 To adjust the cable, switch on the ignition and position the stepper motor by moving the cam only to open and fully close the throttle. Note that it is essential for accurate positioning of the stepper motor that the throttle pedal switch contacts remain closed, so that the ECU recognises the throttle movement as a command and indexes the stepper motor to 25 steps.
8 Slacken the adjuster locknut (above the adjuster bracket) and adjuster nut, then tighten the adjuster nut until the clearance is equal on each side of the throttle lever at the lost motion link; tighten the locknut without disturbing this setting. Recheck the adjustment and switch off the ignition.

14 Throttle pedal - removal and refitting

Refer to Section 11 in Part A of this Chapter.

15 Fuel-injection system - adjustment, testing, component removal and refitting

4B

Adjustment

Idle speed and mixture

Refer to Chapter 1, Section 28.

Testing

1 Apart from the following tests, there is nothing that can be done by the owner to test individual fuel system components:

a) *The basic electrical tests outlined in Chapter 12.*
b) *The ignition system checks given in Chapter 5.*
c) *The tests for the coolant temperature sensor given in Chapter 3.*
d) *The test for the throttle pedal switch given in Section 14 in Part A of this Chapter.*
e) *The test for the fuel cut-off inertia switch given in Chapter 12.*

2 Remember that the ECU's back-up facility will keep the engine running, albeit at reduced efficiency, if certain sensor circuits should fail. Unfortunately, the effect of this will be that whilst a system fault will be evident to the driver, it will be masked in such a way as to make fault diagnosis very difficult; the only solution is to have the complete system checked using Rover diagnostic equipment.

15.9a Remove screw to release injector connector . . .

15.9b . . . then withdraw injector

15.14 Disconnecting fuel feed and return pipes from injector housing

3 If a fault arises, check first that it is not due to poor maintenance; ie, check that the air cleaner filter element is clean, the spark plugs are in good condition and correctly gapped, that the engine breather hoses are clear and undamaged and that the throttle cable is correctly adjusted. If the engine is running very roughly check the compression pressures, bearing in mind the possibility that one of the hydraulic tappets might be faulty, producing an incorrect valve clearance.

4 If the fault is thought to be due to a dirty injector, it is worth trying one of the proprietary injector-cleaning treatments before renewing, perhaps unnecessarily, the injector.

5 If the fault persists, check the ignition system components as far as is possible.

6 If the fault is still not eliminated, work methodically through the system, checking all fuses, fusible links, wiring connectors and wiring, looking for any signs of poor connections, damp, dirt or other faults.

7 Once the system components have been checked for signs of obvious faults such as dirty or poorly-fastened connections, damp, or "tracking" and have been tested as far as is possible take the car to a suitably-equipped Rover dealer for the full engine management system to be tested on the correct equipment.

8 Do not attempt to test any component, particularly the ECU, with anything other than the correct test equipment, which will be available only at a good Rover dealer. If any of the wires are to be checked which lead to a component such as the ECU, always first unplug the relevant connector from the system components so that there is no risk of their being damaged by the application of incorrect voltages from test equipment.

Component removal and refitting

Fuel injector

9 As a Rover replacement part, the injector is available only as part of the injector housing; it is removed and refitted as described below. Note, however that it is a Bosch-manufactured component and can be obtained separately through Bosch agents; to remove it from the housing, proceed as described in paragraphs 10 to 12 and 15 below, then remove the retaining screw to release its connector. The injector can then be lifted out of the housing **(see illustrations)**. Refitting is the reverse of the removal procedure; ensure that the connector makes good contact with the injector pins.

Injector housing

10 Depressurise the fuel system.

11 Disconnect the battery negative lead.

12 Remove the air cleaner assembly.

13 Place a rag around the area to catch the spilled fuel and examine closely the fuel pipe feed and return unions at the injector housing, looking for signs of leakage, then wipe them clean.

14 Using a spanner to hold each adapter, unscrew the pipe union nuts and release the fuel feed and return pipes from the adapters **(see illustration)**. Plug each pipe and adapter to prevent the entry of dirt into the system and the loss of fuel.

15 Release its wire clip and disconnect the injector wiring connector plug **(see illustration)**.

16 Remove the injector housing-to-throttle body screws and withdraw the housing, collecting the gasket **(see illustrations)**.

17 If leakage is detected from the feed and return pipes or their union nuts, check the sealing surfaces of the nuts and adapters, renewing as necessary the adapter or the pipe assembly. If leakage is detected from the adapters, unscrew each through one turn with a spanner, then through two turns by hand; if either is tight, the housing must be renewed. If the threads are sound, fit new sealing washers to the adapters and refit them, tightening them to their specified torque wrench setting.

18 Refitting is the reverse of the removal procedure, noting the following points.

a) *Clean the mating surfaces of the injector housing and the throttle body and renew the gasket if there is any doubt about its condition.*

b) *Apply thread-locking compound (Rover recommend Loctite Screwlock or Nutlock) to the threads of the injector housing screws and tighten them to their specified torque wrench setting.*

c) *Unplug the fuel pipes and adapters, clean the unions and refit the pipes, tightening them finger-tight only at first, then tighten them to their specified torque wrench setting WITHOUT using a holding spanner on the adapters. To tighten a nut to a*

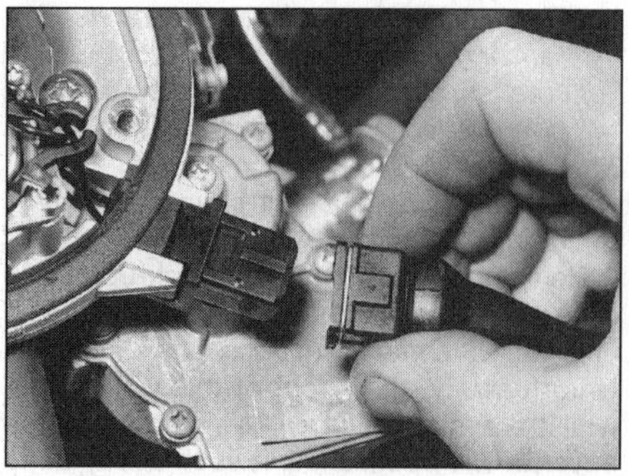

15.15 Disconnecting injector wiring

15.16a Injector housing-to-throttle body screws (A) injector connector screw (B) pressure regulator screws (C)

15.16b Note gasket when removing injector housing from throttle body

15.21 Disconnecting stepper motor wiring

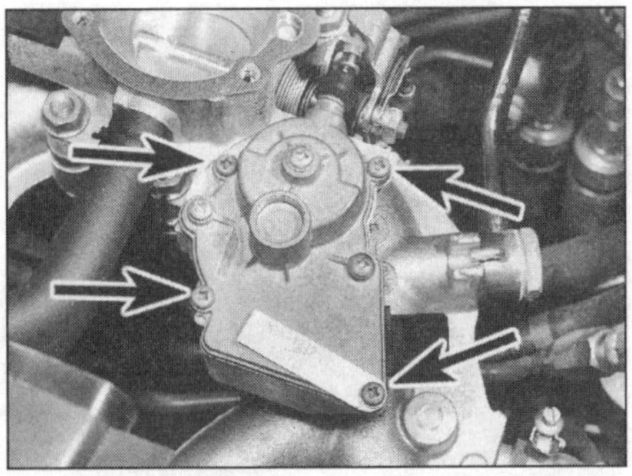

15.22a Location of stepper motor screws

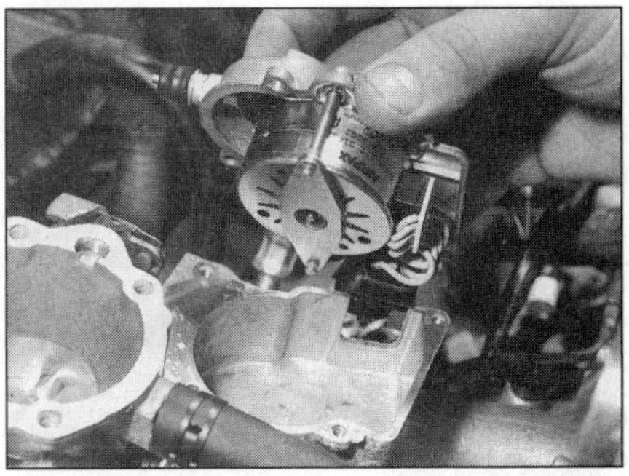

15.22b Removing stepper motor assembly

torque value using an open-ended spanner, hook a spring balance to the spanner's outer end and apply the desired force by pulling the spring balance. Since a torque setting of 17.5 lbf ft is a turning force of 17.5 lb applied at a distance of 1 ft from the nut's centre, it is easy to calculate that a force of 17.5 x 2 (ie 35 lb) must be applied if the spanner is only 6 inches long; if the spanner is longer, the applied force can be reduced proportionately.

Fuel pressure regulator

19 The pressure regulator is available only as part of the injector housing; it is removed and refitted as described above.

Stepper motor

20 Remove the injector housing; see above.

21 Release its clip and disconnect the stepper motor wiring connector plug **(see illustration)**.

22 Remove the stepper motor screws and withdraw the stepper motor assembly **(see illustrations)**. Do not attempt to dismantle the assembly.

23 Refitting is the reverse of the removal procedure. Adjust the throttle cable to ensure that the stepper motor is correctly indexed.

Throttle potentiometer

24 Although not strictly necessary, access is greatly improved if the air cleaner assembly is first removed.

25 Disconnect the battery negative lead.

26 Release its wire clip and disconnect the potentiometer wiring connector plug **(see illustration)**.

27 Remove the two screws and withdraw the potentiometer, noting how its tongue engages with the throttle disc spindle lever **(see illustration)**. Withdraw the spacer if required.

28 Refitting is the reverse of the removal procedure, noting the following points.

a) *Carefully clean the mating surfaces of the throttle body, the spacer and the potentiometer, then refit the spacer.*
b) *Refit the potentiometer so that its tongue engages FORWARD of (ie `inside') the throttle disc spindle lever, then rotate the throttle cam to check the action of the lever and tongue.*

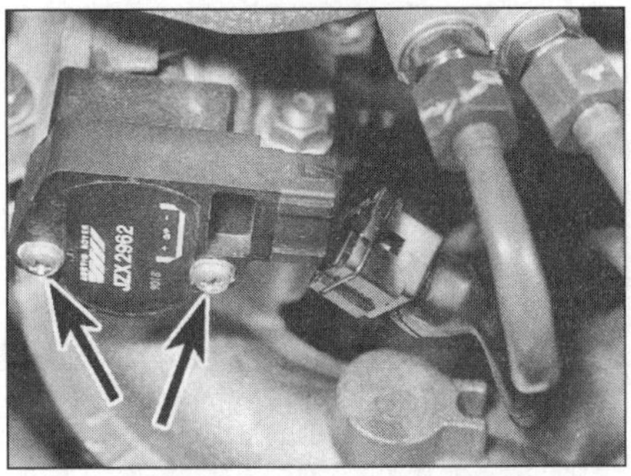

15.26 Disconnecting throttle potentiometer wiring - note mounting screws (arrowed)

c) *Tighten the potentiometer screws to their specified torque wrench setting and rotate the cam to recheck the potentiometer action before reconnecting the wiring.*

Throttle body

Note: *This refers to the throttle body assembly, complete with the injector housing and stepper motor; it is also possible to remove these separately, as described above, before removing the throttle body itself*

29 Depressurise the fuel system.

30 Disconnect the battery negative lead.

31 Remove the air cleaner assembly.

32 Disconnect the fuel feed and return pipes from the injector housing; see paragraphs 13, 14 and 17 above.

33 Releasing their clips, unplug the connectors to disconnect the injector, stepper motor and throttle potentiometer wiring.

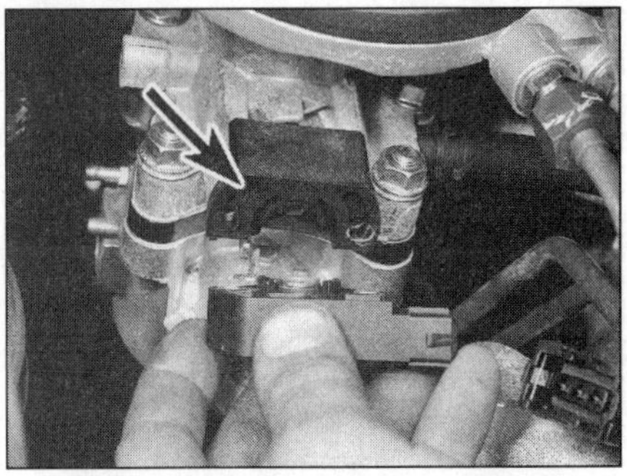

15.27 Ensure potentiometer tongue engages correctly with throttle lever - note spacer (arrowed)

34 Disconnect the throttle cable.

35 Release their clips and disconnect the breather hoses **(see illustration)**.

36 Unscrew the retaining nuts and remove the complete throttle body assembly from the inlet manifold **(see illustration)**.

37 Refitting is the reverse of the removal procedure, noting the following points:

a) *Carefully clean the mating surfaces of the throttle body and the inlet manifold.*
b) *Renew the gasket spacer if there is any doubt about its condition **(see illustration)**.*
c) *Tighten the throttle body-to-inlet manifold nuts to their specified torque wrench setting.*
d) *Adjust the throttle cable.*
e) *Reconnect the fuel feed and return pipes as described in paragraph 18 c) above.*

15.35 Disconnecting breather hoses from throttle body

15.36 Removing throttle body assembly from inlet manifold

15.37 Renew throttle body gasket spacer if worn or damaged

15.39 Disconnecting ECU wiring

15.41 ECU mounting bracket retaining screws (arrowed)

15.44 Manifold absolute pressure sensor is mounted in air cleaner assembly

15.50 Remove air cleaner inlet duct to reach intake air temperature sensor

15.52 Location of coolant temperature sensor (arrowed)

Fuel-injection/ignition system ECU

38 Disconnect the battery negative lead.

39 Unplug the connectors from the ECU and from the relay module **(see illustration)**.

40 Release the engine wiring harness connector plug from the ECU mounting bracket, then undo the three screws securing the bracket to the body. Withdraw the assembly until the manifold absolute pressure sensor vacuum hose can be disconnected from the ECU.

41 Undo the three screws securing the ECU to its mounting bracket, then withdraw it **(see illustration)**.

42 Refitting is the reverse of the removal procedure; if a new or different ECU has been fitted, it may take a short while for full idle control to be restored.

Manifold absolute pressure sensor

43 This is part of the ECU and is removed and refitted as described above.

44 The sensor's vacuum hose runs from the inlet manifold to the ECU via a fuel (vapour) trap mounted in the air cleaner assembly **(see illustration)**.

45 To remove the fuel trap, remove the air cleaner assembly cover, release their clips and disconnect the hoses, then remove the single retaining screw and withdraw the trap.

46 On refitting, note that the hoses are colour-coded (green to the ECU, white to the inlet manifold) to ensure correct reconnection.

Inlet air temperature sensor

47 Disconnect the battery negative lead.

48 Remove the air cleaner assembly inlet duct.

49 Release its wire clip and disconnect the sensor wiring.

50 Unscrew the sensor and remove it **(see illustration)**.

51 Refitting is the reverse of the removal procedure; tighten the sensor to its specified torque wrench setting.

Coolant temperature sensor

52 Refer to Chapter 3 **(see illustration)**.

Relay module

53 Refer to Chapter 12. Note that the module contains the main relay, the starter relay, the fuel pump relay and the manifold pre-heater relay and cannot be dismantled. If any of these relays is faulty, the complete unit must be renewed.

Accelerator pedal switch

54 Refer to Chapter 12.

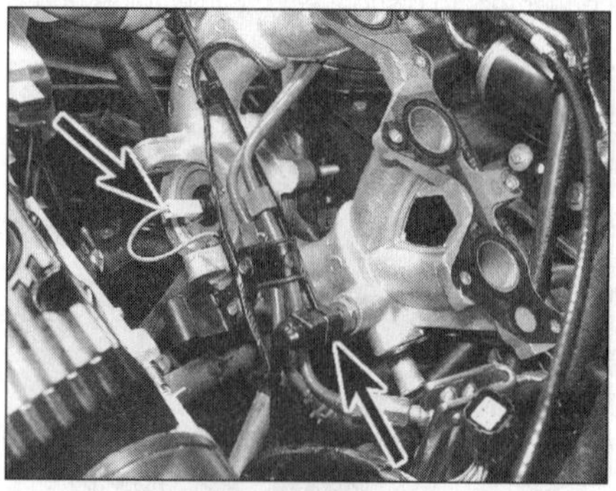

16.1 Inlet manifold partially removed to show manifold PTC heater and coolant temperature sensor (arrowed)

Fuel cut-off inertia switch

55 Refer to Chapter 12.

16 Inlet manifold pre-heater - removal and refitting

The system is as described in Section 15 in Part A of this Chapter, noting the following points **(see illustration)**.

a) The manifold pre-heater relay is one of those in the relay module; it is energised under ECU control.

b) There is no separate pre-heater temperature switch - the ECU uses the coolant temperature sensor.

c) Inlet manifold removal and refitting is as described in the following Section.

17 Inlet manifold - removal and refitting

Removal

Note: *The following procedure describes the removal of the manifold with the throttle body assembly. Access to some of the components concerned is, however, much better if the throttle body is first removed separately; if this is done, the following procedure should be amended as required.*

1 Depressurise the fuel system.

2 Disconnect the battery negative lead.

3 Remove the air cleaner assembly.

17.5 Disconnect coolant hoses (arrowed) from inlet manifold

4 Either drain the cooling system completely or clamp the coolant hoses connected to the inlet manifold to minimise coolant loss and be prepared to catch the coolant that will be released from the manifold and cylinder head.
5 Disconnect all coolant hoses from the manifold **(see illustration)**.
6 Release their clips and disconnect the breather hoses from the cylinder head cover.
7 Disconnect the brake vacuum servo unit vacuum hose from the manifold and discard the sealing washers.
8 Releasing their clips, unplug the connectors to disconnect the injector, stepper motor and throttle potentiometer wiring.
9 Disconnect the coolant temperature sensor and manifold pre-heater wiring.
10 Disconnect the throttle cable.
11 Working as described in Section 15, disconnect the fuel feed and return pipes from the injector housing.
12 Disconnect the vacuum pipes and hoses as necessary. Secure them so that they cannot be damaged during removal and refitting.

17.16a Always renew gasket when refitting manifold

13 The manifold support stays are bolted to the manifold at their upper ends and to the cylinder block/crankcase at their lower ends; slacken the bolts at one end and unbolt the other, as convenient.
14 Unscrew the nuts and bolts securing the manifold to the cylinder head and withdraw it. Remove and discard the gasket.
15 Clean the manifold and cylinder head mating surfaces and check that they are flat and unmarked.

Refitting

16 Refitting is the reverse of the removal procedure, noting the following points:

a) *Always fit a new manifold gasket **(see illustration)**.*
b) *Working in the appropriate sequence for the engine type **(see illustration)**, tighten the manifold retaining nuts and bolts evenly, to the specified torque wrench setting.*
c) *Adjust the throttle cable.*
d) *Reconnect the fuel feed and return pipes as described in Section 15.*
e) *Refill the cooling system or check the coolant level as required, then wash off any spilt coolant.*
f) *Renew the vacuum servo unit vacuum hose banjo union sealing washers.*
g) *Tighten all disturbed fasteners to their specified torque wrench settings (where given).*

18 Exhaust manifold - removal and refitting

Proceed as described in Section 17 in Part A of this Chapter but on refitting, tighten the manifold nuts in the appropriate sequence for the engine type **(see illustration)**.

19 Exhaust system - inspection and component renewal

Proceed as described in Section 18 in Part A of this Chapter. Note that on models with closed-loop catalytic converters, the lambda sensor must be removed or its wiring must be disconnected whenever the exhaust system front pipe is disconnected from the manifold or removed.

4B

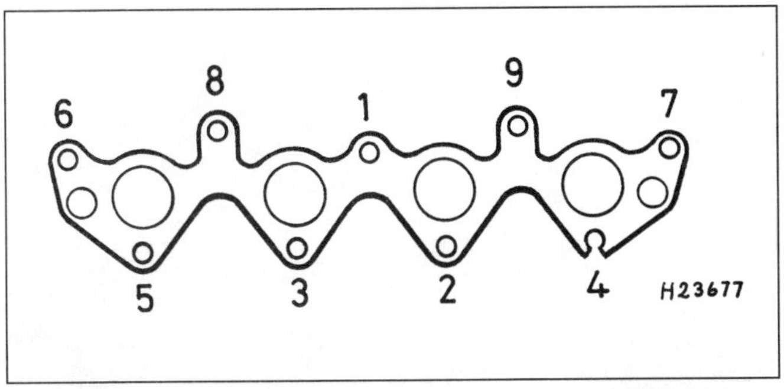

17.16b Inlet manifold fastener tightening sequence - K16 engines

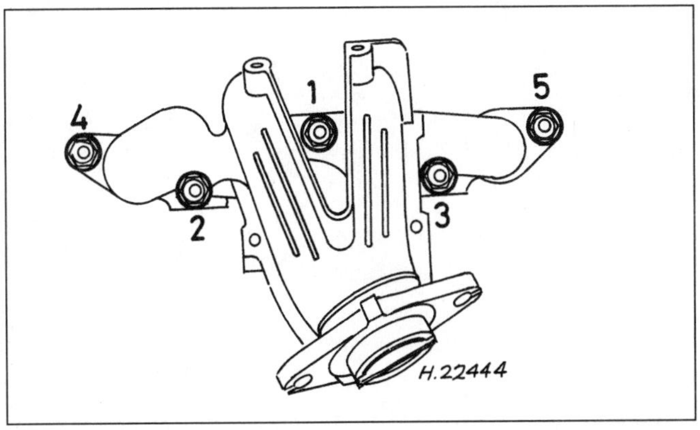

18.1 Exhaust manifold nut tightening sequence - K16 engines

Chapter 4 Part C:
Fuel and exhaust systems - multi-point fuel injection models

Contents

Degrees of difficulty

Easy, suitable for novice with little experience	**Fairly easy,** suitable for beginner with some experience	**Fairly difficult,** suitable for competent DIY mechanic	**Difficult,** suitable for experienced DIY mechanic	**Very difficult,** suitable for expert DIY or professional

Specifications

System

Type	Rover/Motorola Modular Engine Management System, using ECU-controlled multi-point injection (MEMS-MPi) and speed/density method of airflow measurement

MEMS-MPi system data

Fuel pump type	Electric, immersed in fuel tank
Maximum fuel pump pressure at 16 volts	3.0 bar
Regulated injection pressure	3.0 ± 0.2 bar
MEMS - ECU assembly	MKC 10027
Throttle body assembly	MHB 10057
Throttle potentiometer voltage:	
Throttle closed	0 to 1 volt
Throttle open	4 to 5 volt
Idle speed - controlled by ECU	850 ± 50 rpm
CO level at idle speed - engine at normal operating temperature	0.75 % maximum - not adjustable

Recommended fuel

Minimum octane rating	95 RON unleaded (ie unleaded Premium) **only**

Torque wrench settings

	Nm	lbf ft
Fuel system		
Fuel tank mounting bolts	12	9
Two-way valve-to-fuel tank filler neck nut	5	3.5
Fuel tank filler neck-to-body fasteners:		
Screws - three-door	5	3.5
Nuts - five-door	9	6.5
Electric fuel pump-to-fuel tank mounting nuts	9	6.5
Throttle housing to alloy manifold chamber nuts	7	5
Support stay to inlet manifold bolt	25	18.5
Fuel system pressure release bolt - at fuel filter	12	9
Fuel pressure regulator to fuel rail bolts - alloy manifold	9	7
Fuel rail to inlet manifold bolts - alloy manifold	9	7
Fuel feed hose union to fuel rail bolts - alloy manifold	7	5
Fuel rail bolts - plastic manifold	10	7.5
Fuel feed hose bolts - plastic manifold	10	7.5
Throttle housing bolts - plastic manifold	4	3
Throttle potentiometer mounting screws - plastic manifold	1.5	1
Stepper motor securing screws - plastic manifold	1.5	1
Coolant temperature sensor to adapter pipe	15	11
Inlet air temperature sensor to inlet manifold	7	5
Oxygen sensor	45	33
Throttle pedal mounting nuts	25	18.5
Inlet manifold mounting nuts and bolts	25	18.5
Exhaust system		
Exhaust manifold mounting nuts	45	33
Exhaust system front pipe-to-manifold nuts:		
With catalytic converter	50	37
All exhaust system flange securing nuts	45	33
Exhaust system intermediate pipe-to-tailpipe clamp nut	18	13
Lambda sensor	45	33

1 General information and precautions

General information

The fuel system comprises a fuel tank which is mounted under the rear of the car with an electric fuel pump immersed in it, a fuel filter, fuel feed and return lines which service four fuel injectors interlinked by a rail, as well as the Electronic Control Unit (ECU) and the various sensors, electrical components and related wiring which make up the system as a whole. Inlet manifolds of either alloy or plastic construction are fitted.

The air cleaner contains a disposable paper filter element and incorporates a flap valve air temperature control system which allows cold air from the outside of the car and warm air from the exhaust manifold to enter the air cleaner in the correct proportions.

To reduce emissions and to improve driveability when the engine is cold, the inlet manifold is heated by the cooling system coolant. Mixture enrichment for cold starting is a pre-programmed function of the system.

The ECU fully controls both the ignition system and the fuel injection system, integrating the two in a complete engine management system (MEMS-MPi). Refer to Chapter 5 for information on the ignition side of the system and to Chapter 12 for details of electrical components such as the ignition switch, throttle pedal switch, fuel cut-off inertia switch and the relays.

The exhaust system is as described in Section 1 of Chapter 4A.

Precautions

Refer to the precautions shown in Section 1 in Chapter 4B

2 Air cleaner element - renewal

Refer to Chapter 1, Section 34.

3 Air cleaner assembly - removal and refitting

Removal

1 Remove the battery.

2 Disconnect the HT lead from the distributor cap and from its retaining clip on the air inlet hose **(see illustration)**.

3 Detach the speedometer cable from the air inlet hose by releasing its securing clip (where fitted).

4 Detach the air inlet hose from the air cleaner after loosening its securing clip.

5 Remove the two battery tray to air cleaner securing bolts.

6 Pull the air cleaner assembly free of its lower mounting rubber and remove the assembly from the vehicle.

7 Remove the HT lead retaining clip from the air inlet hose.

Refitting

8 Refitting is the reverse of the removal procedure; ensuring that the inlet hose is securely reconnected.

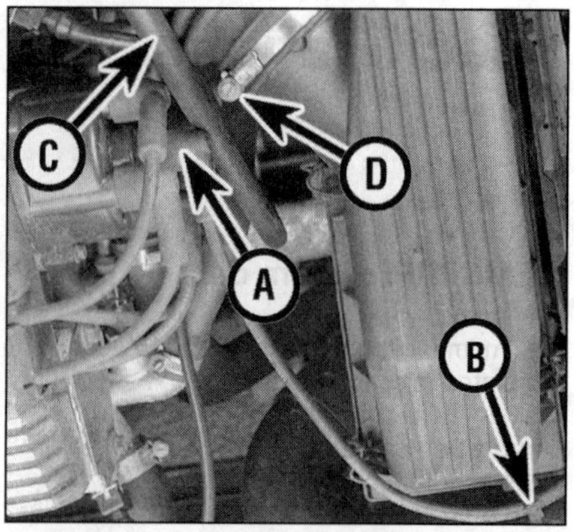

3.2 Removing the air cleaner assembly

A HT lead distributor cap connection
B HT lead retaining clip
C Speedometer cable
D Air inlet hose securing clip

4 Fuel system - inspection

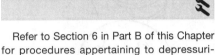

Refer to Chapter 1, Section 15.

5 Fuel system - depressurisation

Refer to Section 6 in Part B of this Chapter for procedures appertaining to depressurisation of a fuel system.

6 Fuel system - pressure check

1 The testing of the fuel system will involve the use of specialist Rover tools. Consult your Rover dealer as to the availability of these tools and refer to Section 7 in Part B of this Chapter and to the figures given in the Specifications Section before proceeding.

7 Fuel pump - removal and refitting

Refer to Section 8 in Part B of this Chapter.

8 Fuel gauge sender unit - removal and refitting

Refer to Section 7 in Part A of this Chapter.

9 Fuel tank - removal and refitting

Proceed as described in Section 8 in Part A of this Chapter but depressurise the fuel system before disconnecting any of the fuel lines.

Note that the fuel feed hose is identified by a yellow band and that there is also an (unmarked) fuel return hose to be disconnected. Unclip the pump wiring connector from the tank bracket and unplug it to disconnect the pump wiring.

10 Fuel tank filler components - removal and refitting

Refer to Section 9 in Part A of this Chapter.

11 Fuel filter - renewal

Refer to Chapter 1, Section 35.

12 Throttle cable - removal, refitting and adjustment

Removal

Alloy and plastic inlet manifolds

1 Release the cable from its retaining clip on the manifold chamber.

2 Detach the cable end from its abutment bracket and disengage the cable end nipple from the throttle cam **(see illustration)**.

3 Release the cable outer from the bulkhead by turning its retaining clip.

Plastic inlet manifold only

4 Release the cable to expansion tank hose retaining clip.

5 Release the cable to heater hose retaining clip (LHD models only).

Alloy and plastic inlet manifolds

6 Remove the cable inner to throttle pedal securing clip and detach the cable from the pedal.

7 Withdraw the cable from the vehicle.

Refitting

8 Refitting is the reverse of the removal procedure; adjust the cable as follows:

Adjustment

Note: *Before proceeding with adjustment, ensure that the cable is correctly routed. Do not attempt to adjust the cable by means of the throttle stop screw.*

Alloy inlet manifold only

9 Ensure that the throttle potentiometer and stepper motor are synchronised.

10 Turn the ignition on and wait for 10 seconds before turning the ignition off to ensure that the stepper motor is in the setting position.

Alloy and plastic inlet manifolds

11 Detach the cable adjuster nut from its abutment bracket and reposition the cable outer in the bracket.

12 Turn the cable adjuster nut until it just makes contact with the top of the abutment bracket.

Alloy inlet manifold only

13 Hold the cam in the "throttle closed" position and ensure that the screw is in contact with the stepper motor pin. Turn the cable adjuster nut until all slack is removed from the cable inner. Any linkage gap must be removed without opening of the throttle **(see illustration)**.

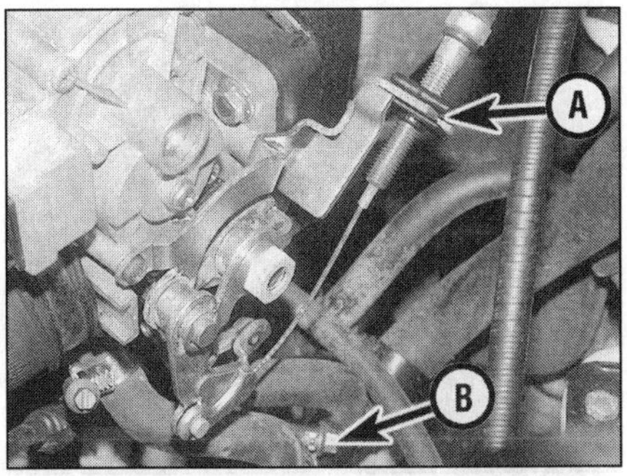

12.2 Throttle cable attachment points
A Abutment bracket B Throttle cam

Plastic inlet manifold only

14 Hold the throttle cam in contact with the throttle stop screw and turn the cable adjuster nut until all slack is removed from the cable inner.

This must be achieved without opening of the throttle.

Alloy and plastic inlet manifolds

15 Check that there is no free play in the cable outer and refit the cable adjuster nut into its abutment bracket.

16 Operate the throttle pedal, checking that the throttle opens to its stop.

13 Throttle pedal - removal and refitting

Refer to Section 11 in Part A of this Chapter.

14 Fuel-injection system - adjustment, testing, component removal and refitting

4C

Adjustment

Idle speed and mixture

Refer to Chapter 1, Section 28.

Testing

1 Apart from the following tests, there is nothing that can be done by the owner to test individual fuel system components:

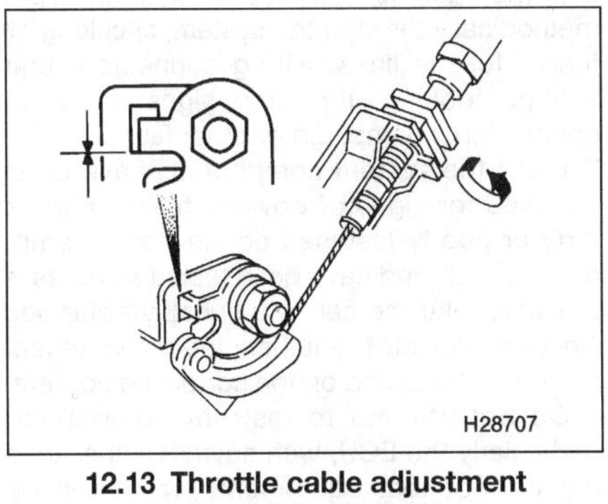

12.13 Throttle cable adjustment (alloy inlet manifold)

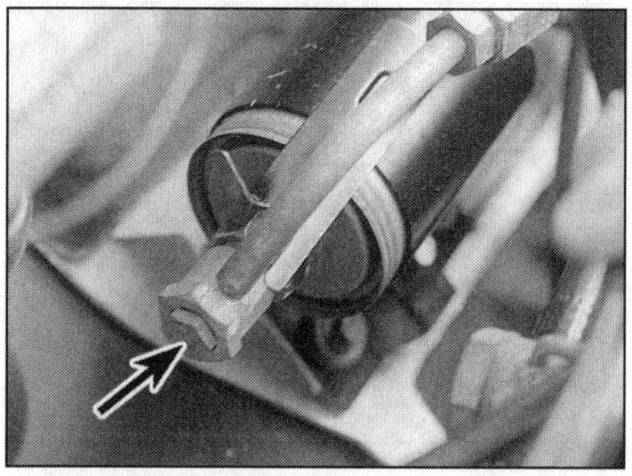

14.9 **Fuel system pressure release bolt (arrowed)**

a) The basic electrical tests outlined in Chapter 12.
b) The ignition system checks given in Chapter 5.
c) The tests for the coolant temperature sensor given in Chapter 3.
d) The test for the throttle pedal switch given in Section 14 in Part A of this Chapter.
e) The test for the fuel cut-off inertia switch given in Chapter 12.

2 Remember that the ECU's back-up facility will keep the engine running, albeit at reduced efficiency, if certain sensor circuits should fail. Unfortunately, the effect of this will be that whilst a system fault will be evident to the driver, it will be masked in such a way as to make fault diagnosis very difficult; the only solution is to have the complete system checked using Rover diagnostic equipment.

3 If a fault arises, check first that it is not due to poor maintenance; ie, check that the air cleaner filter element is clean, the spark plugs are in good condition and correctly gapped, that the engine breather hoses are clear and undamaged and that the throttle cable is correctly adjusted. If the engine is running very roughly check the compression pressures, bearing in mind the possibility that one of the hydraulic tappets might be faulty, producing an incorrect valve clearance.

4 If the fault is thought to be due to a dirty injector, it is worth trying one of the proprietary injector-cleaning treatments before renewing, perhaps unnecessarily, the injector.

5 If the fault persists, check the ignition system components as far as is possible.

6 If the fault is still not eliminated, work methodically through the system, checking all fuses, fusible links, wiring connectors and wiring, looking for any signs of poor connections, damp, dirt or other faults.

7 Once the system components have been checked for signs of obvious faults such as dirty or poorly-fastened connections, damp, or "tracking" and have been tested as far as is possible take the car to a suitably-equipped Rover dealer for the full engine management system to be tested on the correct equipment.

8 Do not attempt to test any component, particularly the ECU, with anything other than the correct test equipment, which will be available only at a good Rover dealer. If any of the wires are to be checked which lead to a component such as the ECU, always first unplug the relevant connector from the system components so that there is no risk of their being damaged by the application of incorrect voltages from test equipment.

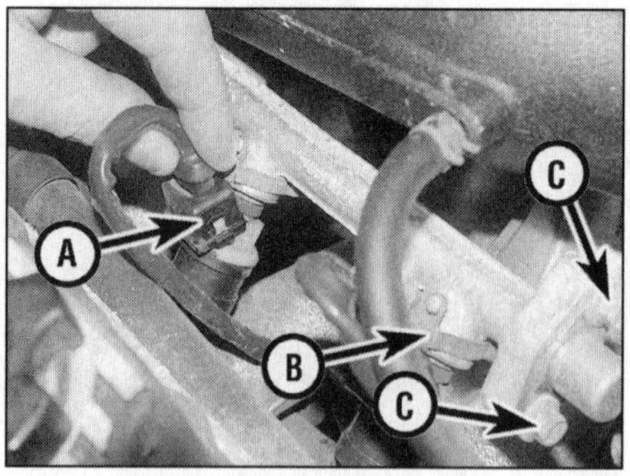

14.11 Fuel rail components

A Injector multiplug
B Injector securing clip
C Fuel feed hose union securing bolts

Component removal and refitting

Fuel rail

Alloy inlet manifold

9 Wrap a length of absorbent cloth around the system pressure release bolt and slowly loosen the bolt to release system pressure **(see illustration)**. On completion, retighten the bolt to the specified torque loading.

10 Detach the inlet manifold from the cylinder head and discard the gasket.

11 Disconnect the four injector multiplugs and remove the spring clips which secure the injectors to the fuel rail **(see illustration)**.

12 Remove the two bolts securing the fuel feed hose union to the fuel rail and release the union from the rail, detaching the O-ring.

13 Remove the two bolts which secure the fuel pressure regulator to the fuel rail, remove the regulator and detach the O-ring and spacer **(see illustration)**.

14 Remove the two bolts securing the fuel rail to the inlet manifold, release the rail from the injectors and detach the O-ring from each injector. If unions are to be left disconnected for any length of time, then plug them with clean cloth to prevent the ingress of dirt or moisture into the system.

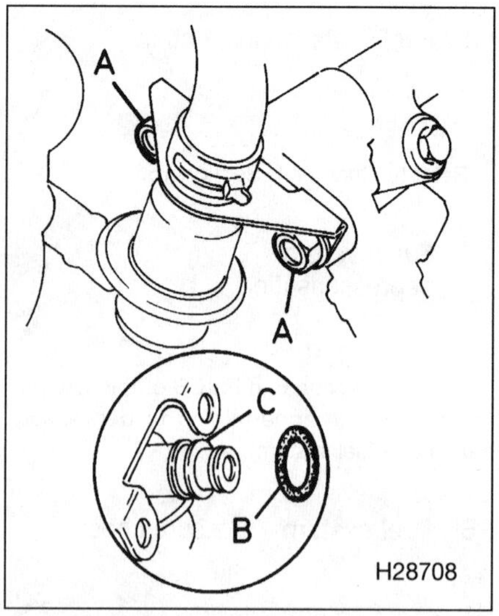

14.13 Fuel pressure regulator components

A Securing bolts B O-ring C Spacer

15 Refitting is the reverse of the removal procedure, noting the following points.

a) Thoroughly clean all component parts, paying particular attention to the mating surfaces.
b) Fit new O-rings, lubricating them with clean fuel.
c) Where applicable, tighten all securing bolts to the specified torque wrench settings.
d) Fit a new inlet manifold gasket.

Plastic inlet manifold

16 Disconnect the battery earth lead.

17 Wrap a length of absorbent cloth around the fuel filter union and slowly loosen the union to release system pressure. On completion, retighten the union.

18 Loosen the throttle housing breather hose to camshaft cover retaining clip and detach the hose **(see illustration)**.

19 Disconnect the multiplug from the stepper motor.

20 Disconnect the inlet manifold breather hose from the camshaft cover.

21 Disconnect the vacuum pipe from the fuel pressure regulator.

22 Loosen the retaining clip and disconnect the fuel return hose from the fuel rail.

23 Remove the two bolts which secure the fuel feed pipe to the fuel rail and release the pipe from the rail, detaching the O-ring.

24 Disconnect each injector multiplug and securing clip.

25 Remove the two bolts securing the fuel rail to the inlet manifold and detach the rail from the manifold, together with the fuel pressure regulator.

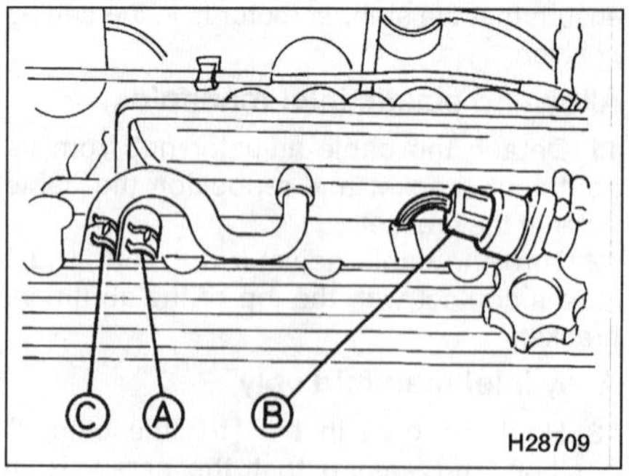

14.18 Fuel rail removal (plastic inlet manifold)

A Throttle housing breather hose
B Stepper motor multiplug
C Inlet manifold breather hose

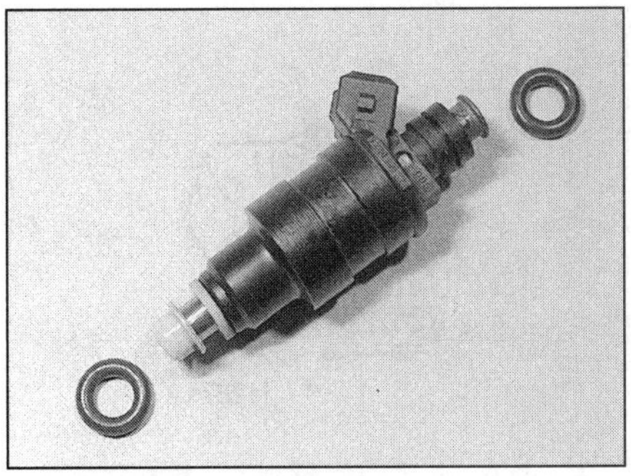

14.29 Fuel injector with seals removed

26 Note that the rail and regulator are serviced as an assembly and should not be separated. If unions are to be left disconnected for any length of time, then plug them with clean cloth to prevent the ingress of dirt or moisture into the system.
27 Refitting is the reverse of the removal procedure, noting the following points.

a) Thoroughly clean all component parts, paying particular attention to the mating surfaces.
b) Fit new O-rings, lubricating them with silicone grease.
c) Where applicable, tighten all securing bolts to the specified torque wrench settings.

Fuel injectors

Alloy inlet manifold

28 Refer to the appropriate sub Section and remove the fuel rail from the inlet manifold.
29 Pull each injector from its location in the inlet manifold and discard its O-rings **(see illustration)**.
30 Before fitting an injector, thoroughly clean its mating surface with the manifold. Fit a new O-ring and lubricate it with clean fuel before carefully pushing the injector into position.
31 Refer to the appropriate sub Section and refit the fuel rail to the inlet manifold.

Plastic inlet manifold

32 Refer to the appropriate sub Section and remove the fuel rail from the inlet manifold.
33 Pull each injector from its location in the inlet manifold and discard its O-ring.
34 Before fitting an injector, thoroughly clean its mating surface with the manifold. Fit a new O-ring and lubricate it with silicone grease before carefully pushing the injector into the manifold.
35 Refer to the appropriate sub Section and refit the fuel rail to the inlet manifold.

Throttle housing

Alloy inlet manifold

36 Position a container beneath the throttle housing to catch any coolant released during the removal procedure.
37 Loosen the inlet hose to throttle housing retaining clip and detach the hose from the housing **(see illustration)**.
38 Detach the stepper motor and throttle potentiometer multiplugs and release the speedometer cable from its retaining bracket on the throttle housing.
39 Pull the throttle cable from its abutment bracket and release the cable inner from the throttle cam.
40 Loosen the two coolant hose retaining clips and pull each hose from the throttle housing, allowing coolant to drain into the container **(see illustration)**.
41 Remove the four nuts securing the throttle housing to the manifold chamber, detaching the speedometer cable retaining bracket in the process, and detach the housing from the chamber.
42 Loosen the three breather hose retaining clips and detach the hoses from the housing.
43 Remove the throttle housing with its gasket.
44 Refitting is the reverse of the removal procedure, noting the following points.

a) Thoroughly clean all component parts, paying particular attention to the mating surfaces.
b) Fit a new throttle housing gasket.
c) Where applicable, tighten all securing bolts to the specified torque wrench settings.
d) Replenish the cooling system on completion.
e) Check throttle cable adjustment.

Plastic inlet manifold

45 Disconnect the battery earth lead.
46 Disconnect the hose from between the throttle housing and air cleaner assembly by releasing its retaining clips and pulling it from position.
47 Loosen the stepper motor hose to throttle housing retaining clip and detach the hose from the housing.
48 Disconnect the multiplug from the throttle potentiometer.
49 Disconnect the breather hose from the throttle housing after loosening its retaining clip.
50 Pull the throttle cable from its abutment bracket and release the cable inner from the throttle cam.

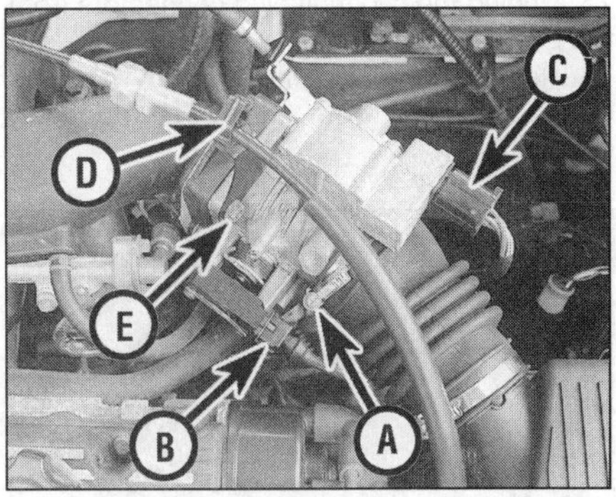

14.37 Throttle housing removal

A Inlet hose retaining clip
B Throttle potentiometer multiplug
C Stepper motor multiplug
D Speedometer cable retaining bracket
E Housing securing bolts

51 Remove the four bolts securing the throttle housing to the inlet manifold, moving the speedometer cable and retaining bracket to one side in the process.
52 Detach the throttle housing from the manifold and discard the sealing ring.
53 Refitting is the reverse of the removal procedure, noting the following points.

a) Thoroughly clean all component parts, paying particular attention to the mating surfaces.
b) Fit a new throttle housing sealing ring, lubricating it with silicone grease.
c) Where applicable, tighten all securing bolts to the specified torque wrench settings.
d) Check throttle cable adjustment.

Fuel pressure regulator

Alloy inlet manifold

54 Wrap a length of absorbent cloth around the system pressure release bolt and slowly loosen the bolt to release system pressure. On completion, retighten the bolt to the specified torque loading.
55 Pull the top coolant rail hose from the expansion tank after loosening its retaining clip. Do this when the system is cool and catch any spilt coolant.
56 Remove the three nuts securing the expansion tank to the vehicle body and move the tank to one side.
57 Remove the engine oil level dipstick.
58 Detach the vacuum hose and the fuel return hose from the fuel pressure regulator.
59 Remove the two bolts securing the fuel pressure regulator to the fuel rail and detach the regulator, removing the O-ring and spacer.
60 Refitting is the reverse of the removal procedure, noting the following points.

a) Thoroughly clean all component parts, paying particular attention to the mating surfaces.
b) Fit a new O-ring to the regulator, lubricating it with clean fuel.
c) Tighten the regulator securing bolts to the specified torque wrench setting.
d) Check the cooling system level on completion.

Plastic inlet manifold

61 The fuel pressure regulator is available only as part of the fuel rail and should not be separated from the same.

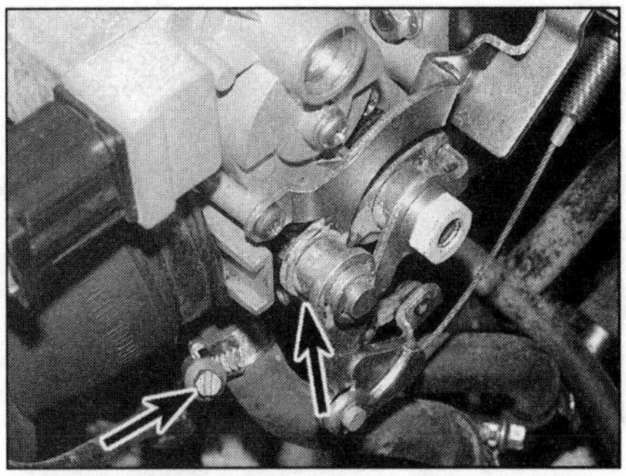

14.40 Throttle housing coolant hose retaining clips (arrowed)

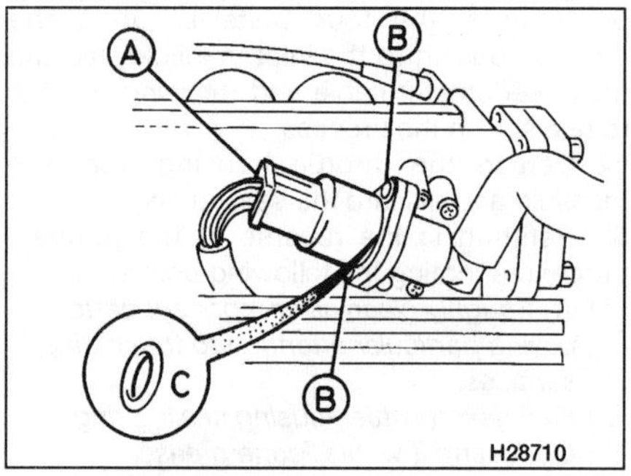

14.63 Stepper motor removal (plastic inlet manifold)
A Multiplug B Securing screws C O-ring

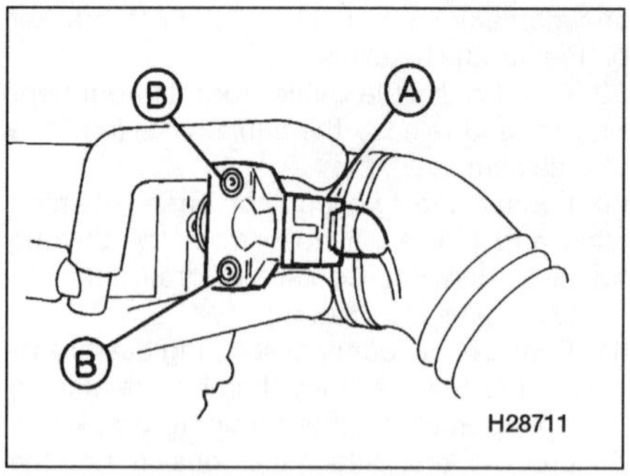

14.70 Potentiometer removal (plastic inlet manifold)
A Multiplug B Securing screws

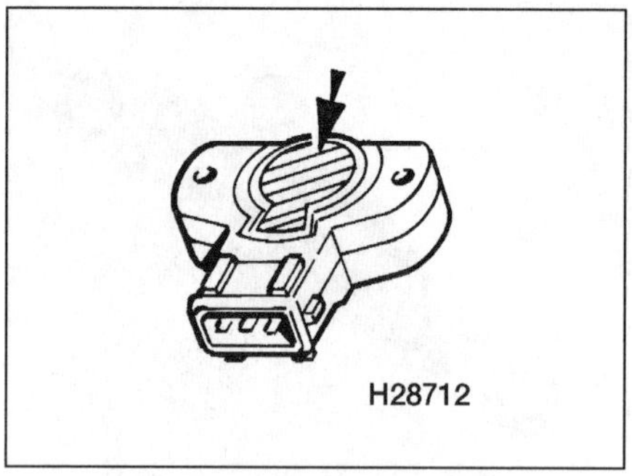

14.73 Apply finger pressure only to the shaded area of the potentiometer (arrowed)

Stepper motor

Alloy inlet manifold

62 The stepper motor fitted to this type of manifold is an integral part of the throttle housing and as a consequence, cannot be removed.

Plastic inlet manifold

63 Disconnect the multiplug from the stepper motor **(see illustration)**..

64 Remove the two Torx screws which secure the motor to the inlet manifold and remove the motor, discarding its O-ring.

65 Refitting is the reverse of the removal procedure, noting the following points.

a) Thoroughly clean the mating surfaces.
b) Fit a new O-ring to the motor, lubricating it with silicone grease.
c) Tighten the motor securing bolts to the specified torque wrench setting.

Throttle potentiometer

Alloy inlet manifold

66 Disconnect the battery earth lead.

67 Disconnect the multiplug from the potentiometer.

68 Remove the two securing screws and detach the potentiometer from the throttle housing.

69 Refitting is the reverse of the removal procedure, noting the following points.

a) Thoroughly clean the mating surfaces.
b) Ensure correct engagement of the potentiometer before fitting the securing screws.

Plastic inlet manifold

70 Disconnect the potentiometer multiplug **(see illustration)**.

71 Remove and discard the two securing screws and wavewashers and remove the clamping plate.

72 Pull the potentiometer off the throttle spindle being careful not to apply leverage or twist the potentiometer.

73 Refitting is the reverse of the removal procedure, noting the following points.

a) Carefully clean the mating surfaces of the throttle housing and potentiometer.
b) Refit the potentiometer so that the flat on the spindle is aligned with the mating portion of the potentiometer.
*c) When pressing the potentiometer onto the spindle, apply finger pressure only to the shaded area shown **(see illustration)**.*
d) Rotate the potentiometer anti-clockwise only to align the fixing holes.
e) Tighten the potentiometer screws to their specified torque wrench setting.
f) Operate the throttle cam 2 or 3 times and ensure that full travel exists between the throttle open and closed positions.

Fuel-injection/ignition system ECU

74 Disconnect the battery negative lead.

75 Unplug the two multiplug connectors from the ECU and from the relay module.

76 Release the engine wiring harness connector plug from the ECU mounting bracket.

77 Release the charcoal canister from the mounting bracket to gain access to the ECU mounting bolts, then undo the three bolts securing the mounting bracket to the body. Withdraw the assembly until the vacuum hose can be disconnected from the ECU.

78 Undo the three screws securing the ECU to its mounting bracket, then withdraw it.

79 Refitting is the reverse of the removal procedure; if a new or different ECU has been fitted, it may take a short while for full idle control to be restored.

Inlet air temperature sensor

80 Disconnect the battery earth lead.

81 Disconnect the sensor multiplug and unscrew the sensor from the inlet manifold **(see illustration)**.

82 Refitting is the reverse of the removal procedure; tighten the sensor to its specified torque wrench setting.

Coolant temperature sensor

83 Refer to Chapter 3 **(see illustration)**.

Throttle pedal switch

84 Refer to Chapter 12.

Charcoal canister

85 Refer to Part D of this Chapter.

Purge control valve

86 Refer to Part D of this Chapter.

Fuel vapour trap

87 Detach the charcoal canister from its mounting bracket.

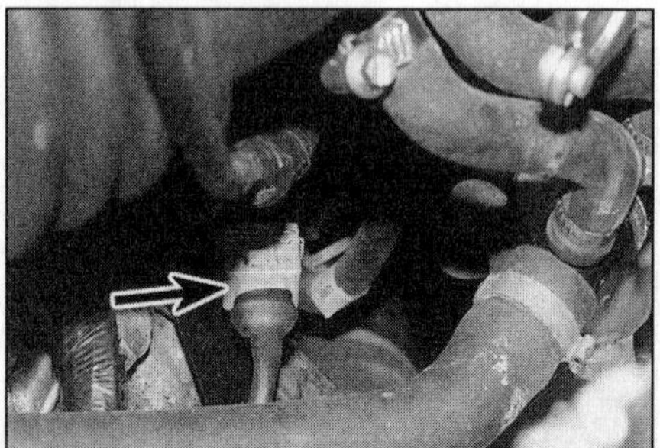

14.81 Inlet air temperature sensor (arrowed)

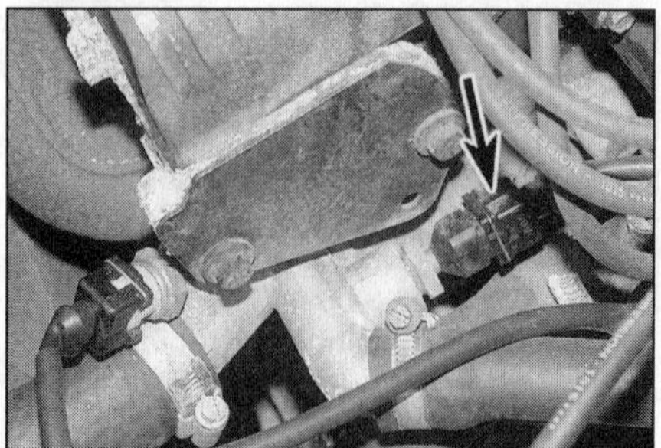

14.83 Coolant temperature sensor (arrowed)

14.89 Fuel vapour trap (arrowed)

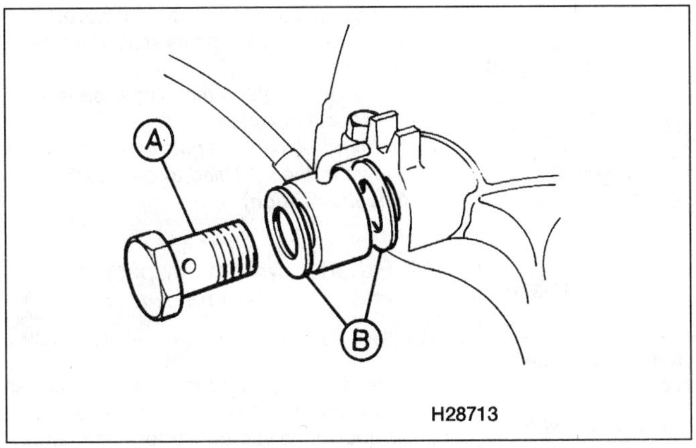

15.6 Alloy inlet manifold brake servo line connector bolt (A) and sealing washers (B)

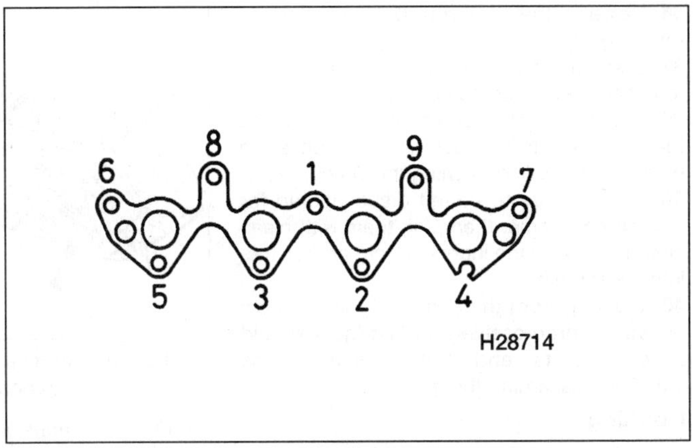

15.20 Alloy inlet manifold tightening sequence

88 Remove the three screws securing the ECU mounting bracket to the body and release the bracket to gain access to the fuel vapour trap.

89 Release the two hoses from the vapour trap, marking them to ensure correct refitting, and remove the trap from its mounting bracket **(see illustration)**.

90 Refitting is the reverse of the removal procedure.

Oxygen sensor

91 Refer to Part D of this Chapter.

15 Inlet manifold - removal and refitting

Alloy inlet manifold

Removal

1 Disconnect the battery earth lead.

2 Wrap a length of absorbent cloth around the system pressure release bolt and slowly loosen the bolt to release system pressure. On completion, retighten the bolt to the specified torque loading.

3 Refer to Chapter 1 and drain the cooling system.

4 Pull the throttle cable from its abutment bracket and release the cable inner from the throttle cam.

5 Release the two coolant hoses from the throttle housing by loosening their retaining clips and pulling them from position.

6 Unscrew the brake servo line connector bolt from the manifold **(see illustration)**, discarding both sealing washers.

7 Detach the throttle potentiometer multiplug and place the electrical lead to one side.

8 Remove the manifold chamber and discard its gasket.

9 Release the three breather hoses from the throttle housing and position the manifold chamber and throttle housing assembly to one side.

10 Remove the breather hose bracket securing bolt from the inlet manifold.

11 Remove the engine oil dipstick.

12 Disconnect the four injector multiplugs and remove the spring clips which secure the injectors to the fuel rail.

13 Remove the two bolts securing the fuel feed hose union to the fuel rail and release the union from the rail, detaching the O-ring.

14 Detach the inlet air temperature sensor multiplug and place the electrical lead to one side.

15 Remove the two bolts which secure the fuel pressure regulator to the fuel rail, remove the regulator and detach the O-ring and spacer.

16 Remove the two bolts securing the fuel rail to the inlet manifold, release the rail from the injectors and detach the O-ring from each injector. If unions are to be left disconnected for any length of time, then plug them with clean cloth to prevent the ingress of dirt or moisture into the system.

17 Release the coolant hose from the inlet manifold.

18 Remove the bolt securing the support stay to the manifold and remove the two bolts securing the engine wiring harness brackets to the manifold.

19 Remove the manifold securing bolts and nuts, in the reverse order shown for tightening, and remove the manifold, discarding the gasket.

Refitting

20 Refitting is the reverse of the removal procedure, noting the following points.

a) Thoroughly clean all component parts, paying particular attention to the mating surfaces.

b) Always fit a new manifold gasket.

c) Working in the sequence shown ***(see illustration)****, tighten the manifold retaining nuts and bolts evenly to the specified torque wrench setting.*

d) Tighten all disturbed fasteners to their specified torque wrench settings (where given).

e) Fit new O-rings, lubricating them with clean fuel.

f) Renew the brake servo connector sealing washers.

g) Adjust the throttle cable.

h) Refill the cooling system and check the coolant level, then wash off any spilt coolant.

Plastic inlet manifold

Removal

21 Disconnect the battery earth lead.

22 Wrap a length of absorbent cloth around the system pressure release bolt and slowly loosen the bolt to release system pressure. On completion, retighten the bolt to the specified torque loading.

23 Refer to Chapter 1 and drain the cooling system.

24 Disconnect the hose from the air cleaner assembly by releasing its retaining clip and pulling it from position.

25 Release the retaining clip and detach the purge hose from the manifold.

26 Disconnect the breather hose from the throttle housing after loosening its retaining clip.

27 Disconnect the multiplug from the throttle potentiometer.

28 Loosen the stepper motor hose to abutment retaining clip and detach the hose, moving it to one side.

29 Remove the four bolts securing the throttle housing to the inlet manifold, moving the speedometer cable and retaining bracket to one side in the process.

30 Detach the throttle housing from the manifold and discard the sealing ring.

31 Disconnect the multiplug from the stepper motor.

32 Release the breather hose from the inlet manifold and depress the plastic collar of the brake servo hose quick-fit connector to release it from the manifold.

33 Disconnect the ECU vacuum pipe from the manifold.

34 Loosen the retaining clip and disconnect the fuel return hose from the fuel rail.

35 Disconnect the coolant system expansion tank hose from the manifold.

36 Release the fuel return hose from its retaining clips.

37 Disconnect the injector harness and air temperature sensor multiplugs.

38 Remove the two bolts which secure the fuel feed pipe to the fuel rail and release the pipe from the rail, detaching the O-ring.

39 If unions are to be left disconnected for any length of time, then plug them with clean cloth to prevent the ingress of dirt or moisture into the system.

40 Working from the centre of the manifold outwards, progressively loosen the manifold securing nuts and bolts. Remove the manifold, discarding the gasket.

Refitting

41 Refitting is the reverse of the removal procedure, noting the following points.

a) Thoroughly clean all component parts, paying particular attention to the mating surfaces.

b) Ensure that a metal insert is located in each manifold stud or bolt hole.

c) Always fit a new manifold gasket ***(see illustration).***

d) Working in the sequence shown ***(see illustration),*** *tighten the manifold retaining nuts and bolts evenly to the specified torque wrench setting.*

e) Tighten all disturbed fasteners to their specified torque wrench settings (where given).

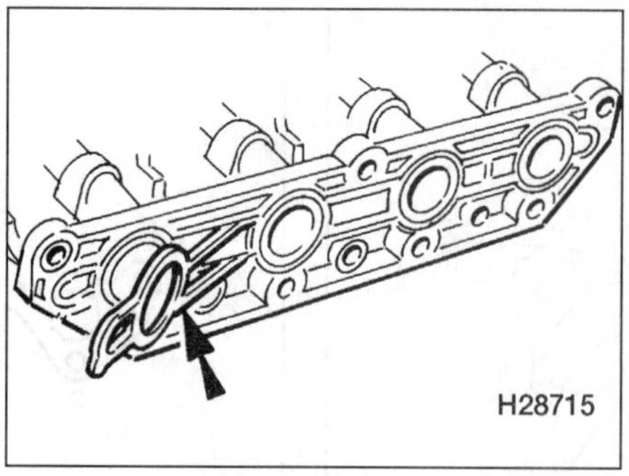

15.41a Plastic inlet manifold gasket location (arrowed)

f) Fit new O-rings, lubricating them with silicone grease.

g) Refill the cooling system and check the coolant level, then wash off any spilt coolant.

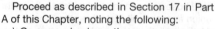

16 Exhaust manifold - removal and refitting

Proceed as described in Section 17 in Part A of this Chapter, noting the following:

a) On removal, release the oxygen sensor multiplug from the gearbox bracket and disconnect the plug from the engine wiring harness.

b) The oxygen sensor must be removed from the manifold and its sealing washer renewed.

c) On refitting, tighten the oxygen sensor to the specified torque loading.

d) Tighten the manifold nuts in the sequence shown to the specified torque loading ***(see illustration).***

17 Exhaust system - inspection and component renewal

Proceed as described in Section 18 in Part A of this Chapter. Note that on models with closed-loop catalytic converters, the lambda sensor must be removed or its wiring must be disconnected whenever the exhaust system front pipe is disconnected from the manifold or removed.

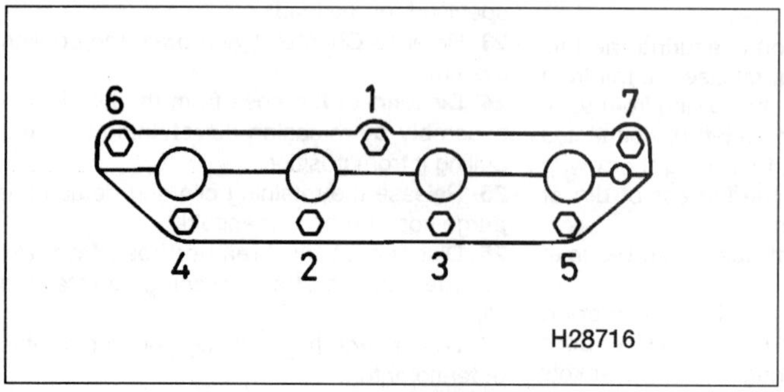

15.41b Plastic inlet manifold tightening sequence

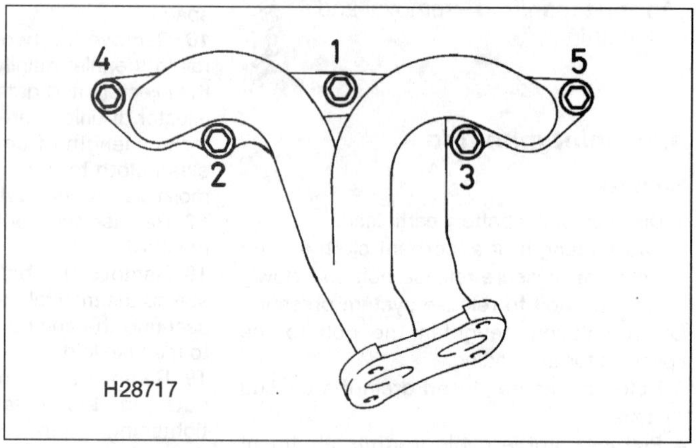

16.1 Exhaust manifold tightening sequence

Chapter 4 Part D: Emission control systems

Contents

Degrees of difficulty

Easy, suitable for novice with little experience	**Fairly easy,** suitable for beginner with some experience	**Fairly difficult,** suitable for competent DIY mechanic	**Difficult,** suitable for experienced DIY mechanic	**Very difficult,** suitable for expert DIY or professional

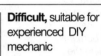

Specifications

Torque wrench settings	**Nm**	**lbf ft**
Oxygen (Lambda) sensor	45	33

1 General information

Apart from their ability to use unleaded petrol and the various features which help to minimise emissions and which are built into the fuel system, Rover Metro and 100 series models have at least, the crankcase emission-control system fitted and may be fitted with one or both of the other two systems described below:

Crankcase emission control

To reduce the emission of unburned hydrocarbons from the crankcase into the atmosphere, the engine is sealed and the blow-by gases and oil vapour are drawn from the crankcase through a wire mesh oil separator in the cylinder head cover, into the inlet tract to be burned by the engine during normal combustion. On carburettor engines, a single breather hose connects the cylinder head cover to the carburettor continuous-depression area. On fuel-injected engines, a small-bore breather hose connects the cylinder head cover to the throttle body downstream of the throttle disc, whilst a larger-bore hose is connected above the throttle disc so that the same effect is obtained at all states of manifold depression.

Under conditions of high manifold depression (idling, deceleration), the gases will be sucked positively out of the crankcase. Under conditions of low manifold depression (acceleration, full-throttle running), the gases are forced out of the crankcase by the (relatively) higher crankcase pressure. If the engine is worn, the raised crankcase pressure (due to increased blow-by) will cause some of the flow to return under all manifold conditions.

Evaporative emission control

To minimise the escape into the atmosphere of unburned hydrocarbons, an evaporative emissions control system is fitted to some models. The fuel tank filler cap is sealed and a charcoal canister is mounted in the engine compartment to collect the petrol vapours generated in the tank when the car is parked. It stores them until they can be cleared from the canister (under the control of the fuel-injection/ignition system ECU via the purge control valve) into the inlet tract to be burned by the engine during normal combustion.

To ensure that the engine runs correctly when it is cold and/or idling and to protect the catalytic converter from the effects of an over-rich mixture, the purge control valve is not opened by the ECU until the engine has warmed up to above 70°C, the engine speed exceeds 1500 rpm and manifold absolute pressure is below 30 kPa; the valve solenoid is then modulated on and off to allow the stored vapour to pass into the inlet.

Exhaust emission control

To minimise the amount of pollutants which escape into the atmosphere, some models are fitted with a catalytic converter in the exhaust system. Either an open-loop control system, which has no feedback from the converter to the fuel system, or a closed-loop control system, in which an oxygen sensor in the exhaust system provides the fuel-injection/ignition system ECU with constant feedback (which enables it to adjust the mixture to provide the best possible conditions for the converter to operate) may be fitted.

If an oxygen sensor (also known as a lambda sensor) is fitted, it has a heating element built-in that is controlled by the ECU through the oxygen sensor relay to quickly bring the sensor's tip to an efficient operating temperature. The sensor's tip is sensitive to oxygen and sends the ECU a varying voltage depending on the amount of oxygen in the exhaust gases; if the intake air/fuel mixture is too rich, the exhaust gases are low in oxygen so the sensor sends a low-voltage signal, the voltage rising as the mixture weakens and the amount of oxygen rises in the exhaust gases. Peak conversion efficiency of all major pollutants occurs if the intake air/fuel mixture is maintained at the chemically-correct ratio for the complete combustion of petrol of 14.7 parts (by weight) of air to 1 part of fuel (the `stoichiometric' ratio). The sensor output voltage alters in a large step at this point, the ECU using the signal change as a reference point and correcting the intake air/fuel mixture accordingly by altering the fuel injector pulse width.

2 Catalytic converters - general information and precautions

The catalytic converter is a reliable and simple device which needs no maintenance in itself, but there are some facts of which an owner should be aware if the converter is to function properly for its full service life.

a) *DO NOT use leaded petrol in a car equipped with a catalytic converter - the lead will poison the catalyst.*
b) *Always keep the ignition and fuel systems well-maintained in accordance with the manufacturer's schedule - particularly, ensure that the air cleaner filter element, the fuel filter (where fitted) and the spark plugs are renewed at the correct interval. If the intake air/fuel mixture is allowed to become too rich due to neglect, the unburned surplus will enter and burn in the catalytic converter, overheating the element.*
c) *If the engine develops a misfire, do not drive the car at all (or at least as little as possible) until the fault is cured - the misfire will allow unburned fuel to enter the converter, which will result in its overheating, as noted above.*
d) *DO NOT push- or tow-start the car - this will soak the catalytic converter in unburned fuel, causing it to overheat when the engine does start - see (b) above.*
e) *DO NOT switch off the ignition at high engine speeds. If the ignition is switched off at anything above idle speed, unburned fuel will enter the (very hot) catalytic converter, with the possible risk of its igniting on the element and damaging the converter.*
f) *DO NOT use fuel or engine oil additives - these may contain substances harmful to the catalytic converter.*
g) *DO NOT continue to use the car if the engine burns oil to the extent of leaving a visible trail of blue smoke - the unburned carbon deposits will clog the converter passages and reduce its efficiency; in severe cases the element will overheat.*
h) *Remember that the catalytic converter operates at very high temperatures and the casing will become hot enough to ignite combustible materials which brush against it. DO NOT, therefore, park the car in dry undergrowth, over long grass or piles of dead leaves.*
i) *Remember that the catalytic converter is FRAGILE. Do not strike it with tools during servicing work. Take care when working on the exhaust system, ensure that the converter is well clear of any jacks or other lifting gear used to raise the car and do not drive the car over rough ground, road humps etc in such a way as to "ground" the exhaust system.*
j) *In some cases, particularly when the car is new and/or is used for stop/start driving, a sulphurous smell (like that of rotten eggs) may be noticed from the exhaust. This is common to many catalytic converter-equipped cars and seems to be due to the small amount of sulphur found in some petrols reacting with hydrogen in the exhaust to produce hydrogen sulphide (H_2S) gas; while this gas is toxic, it is not produced in sufficient amounts to be a problem. Once the car has covered a few thousand miles the problem should disappear - in the meanwhile a change of driving style or of the brand of petrol used may effect a solution.*
k) *The catalytic converter, used on a well-maintained and well-driven car, should last for between 50 000 and 100 000 miles. From this point on, careful checks should be made at all specified service intervals of the CO level to ensure that the converter is still operating efficiently - if the converter is no longer effective it must be renewed.*

3 Emission control system components - testing and renewal

Crankcase emission control

1 Apart from the checks described in Chapter 1, the components of this system require no attention other than to check that the hose(s) are clear and that the wire mesh oil separators are flushed clean with a suitable solvent whenever the cylinder head cover is removed, as described in Chapter 2 **(see illustration)**.

3.1 Always clean oil separators whenever cylinder head cover is removed

Evaporative emission control

Testing

2 If the system is thought to be faulty, disconnect the hoses from the charcoal canister/purge control valve assembly **(see illustration)** and check that they are clear by blowing through them. If the purge control valve or charcoal canister are thought to be faulty, the assembly must be renewed.

Renewal

3 Disconnect the battery negative lead.

4 Release their clips and disconnect the hoses from the valve and canister.

5 Unplug the connector to disconnect the purge control valve wiring.

6 Remove the assembly from its mounting bracket; do not attempt to dismantle it.

7 Refitting is the reverse of the removal procedure; the hose from the (underbody) fuel filler breather pipe is connected to the charcoal canister, while the hose from the inlet is connected to the purge control valve.

Exhaust emission control

Note: *If the CO level reading is too high (or if any other symptom is encountered which causes you to suspect a fault in the exhaust emission control system) always check first that the air cleaner filter element is clean, the spark plugs are in good condition and correctly gapped, that the engine breather and vacuum hoses are clear and undamaged and that the throttle cable is correctly adjusted. If the engine is running very roughly, check the compression pressures and bear in mind the possibility that one of the hydraulic tappets might be faulty, producing an incorrect valve clearance. Check also that all wiring is in good*

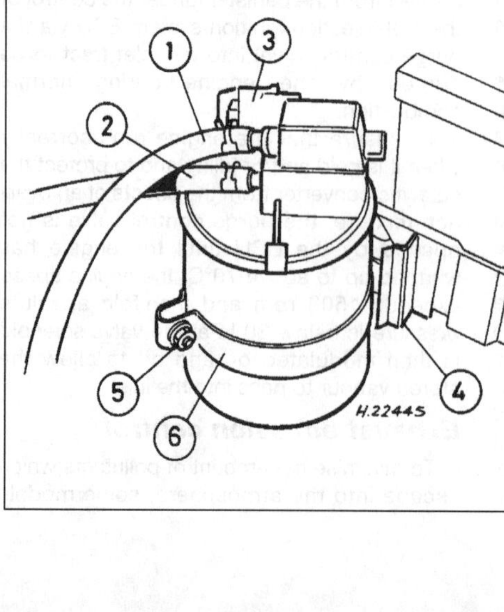

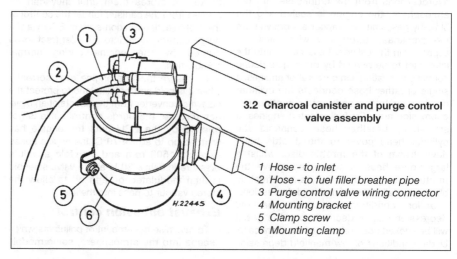

3.2 Charcoal canister and purge control valve assembly

1 *Hose - to inlet*
2 *Hose - to fuel filler breather pipe*
3 *Purge control valve wiring connector*
4 *Mounting bracket*
5 *Clamp screw*
6 *Mounting clamp*

condition, with securely-fastened connectors, that the fuel filter (fuel-injected engines only) has been renewed at the recommended intervals and that the exhaust system is entirely free of air leaks which might upset the operation of the catalytic converter. Only when all these have been checked and found to be in serviceable condition should the converter be suspected

Testing - open-loop system

8 The performance of the catalytic converter can only be checked by using a good-quality, carefully-calibrated exhaust gas analyser.

9 Check that the CO level is as specified at the gas-sampling pipe when the engine is fully warmed up to normal operating temperature; if not, check the fuel and ignition systems until the fault is found and the level is restored to its correct value.

10 Once the CO level is known to be correct upstream of the catalytic converter, take the car on a brisk 4-mile road test and check the CO level at the tailpipe **immediately** on return; it should be significantly lower than the level at the gas-sampling pipe (below 0.5% approximately on fuel-injected engines, slightly higher on carburettor engines).

11 If the tailpipe CO level is little different from that at the gas-sampling pipe, repeat the check ensuring that it is made **immediately** on return from road test or the converter may not be at normal operating temperature and will not have reached its peak conversion efficiency. If the results are the same, the catalytic converter is proven faulty and must be renewed.

Testing - closed-loop system

12 The performance of the catalytic converter can only be checked by using a good-quality, carefully-calibrated exhaust gas analyser.

13 Where a gas-sampling pipe is fitted, the test described above can be carried out. If the CO level at the tailpipe is little different from that at the gas-sampling pipe, the catalytic converter is probably faulty and must be renewed, once the fuel-injection and ignition systems have been checked thoroughly using Rover diagnostic equipment and are known to be free from faults.

14 If a gas-sampling pipe is not fitted and the CO level at the tailpipe is too high, the complete fuel-injection and ignition systems must be checked thoroughly using Rover diagnostic equipment. Once these have been checked and are known to be free from faults, the fault must be in the catalytic converter, which must be renewed.

Catalytic converter - renewal

15 Refer to Section 18 in Part A of this Chapter.

Oxygen sensor - operational check

16 The manufacturer's maintenance schedule calls for regular checks of the oxygen sensor's operation. This can be done only by attaching Rover diagnostic equipment to the sensor wiring and checking that the voltage varies from low to high values when the engine is running; **do not** attempt to `test' any part of the system with anything other than the correct test equipment.

Oxygen sensor - renewal

Note: *The oxygen sensor is delicate and will not work if it is dropped or knocked, if its power supply is disrupted, or if any cleaning materials are used on it*

17 Release the sensor's wiring connector from its bracket on the transmission and unplug it to disconnect the sensor.

18 Raising and supporting the front of the car, if required, to remove the sensor from underneath, unscrew the sensor from the exhaust system front pipe; collect the sealing washer **(see illustration)**.

19 On refitting, clean the sealing washer and renew it if it is damaged or worn, then refit the sensor, tightening it to its specified torque wrench setting. Reconnect the wiring and refit the connector plug.

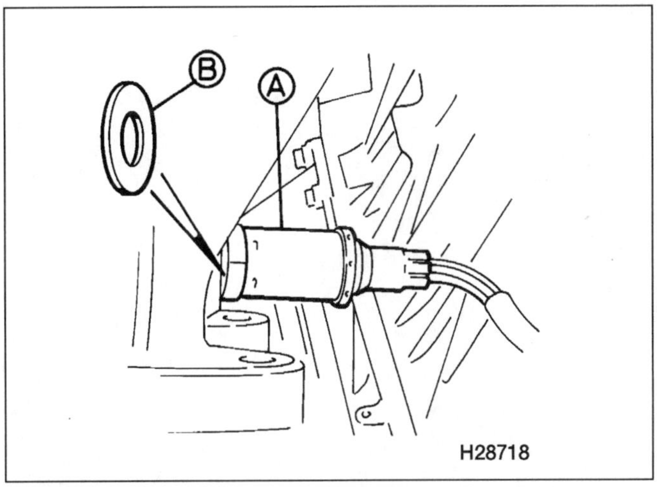

3.18 Oxygen sensor (A) and sealing washer (B)

Chapter 5 Part A:
Ignition system - carburettor models

Contents

Degrees of difficulty

Easy, suitable for novice with little experience	**Fairly easy,** suitable for beginner with some experience	**Fairly difficult,** suitable for competent DIY mechanic	**Difficult,** suitable for experienced DIY mechanic	**Very difficult,** suitable for expert DIY or professional

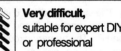

Specifications

General

System type	Lucas constant energy inductive
Firing order	1-3-4-2 (No 1 cylinder at timing belt end)
Direction of crankshaft rotation	Clockwise (viewed from right-hand side of car)

Distributor

Type	Lucas 67 DM4, incorporating centrifugal and vacuum advance mechanisms and externally-mounted amplifier module
Identification:	
1.1 models	NJC 10024
1.4 models	NJC 10026
Direction of rotor arm rotation	Anti-clockwise (viewed from left-hand side of car)
Rotor arm type	GRA 2143
Amplifier module type	CDU 4175/NJQ 10001
Pick-up coil resistance	950 to 1150 ohms
Vacuum capsule identification:	
1.1 models	80-270-7
1.4 models	80-200-8
Vacuum advance commences	107 mbar (80 mm Hg)
Maximum vacuum advance:	
1.1 models	14° @ 360 mbar (270 mm Hg)
1.4 models	16° @ 267 mbar (200 mm Hg)
Deceleration check - vacuum disconnected:	
1.1 models	6° to 10° @ 2000 rpm
1.4 models	4° to 8° @ 2500 rpm

Note: *Degree and speed values to be measured at crankshaft*

Ignition HT coil

Type	AUU 1326 or ADU 8779
Manufacturer	Bosch, Ducellier or Rudi Cajavec
Current consumption - average	0.25 to 0.75 amps @ idle speed
Winding resistances:	
Primary	0.71 to 0.81 ohms @ 20°C
Secondary	5 to 15 K ohms @ 20°C

Ignition timing - @ 1500 rpm (vacuum pipe disconnected)

1.1 models:	
Carburettor numbers MAC 10003 and MAC 10010	8° ± 1° BTDC
Carburettor number MAC 10043	10° ± 1° BTDC
1.4 models	9° ± 1° BTDC

Torque wrench settings

	Nm	lbf ft
Spark plugs	25	19
Distributor cap screws	2	2
Amplifier module-to-distributor body (hex-head) screws	5	4
Distributor mounting bolts	25	19
Reluctor ring-to-flywheel setscrews	3	2
Ignition HT coil mounting screws	7	5

1 General information and precautions

General information

The ignition system is fully-electronic in operation and of the inductive type, incorporating a contact-less distributor (driven off the camshaft left-hand end) and an amplifier module as well as the spark plugs, HT leads, ignition HT coil and associated wiring. The system is divided into two circuits; primary (low tension/LT) and secondary (high tension/HT). The primary circuit comprises the battery, ignition switch, ignition HT coil primary windings, amplifier module and distributor pick-up coil and wiring. The secondary circuit comprises the ignition HT coil secondary windings, the distributor cap and rotor arm, the spark plugs and the HT leads connecting these.

The distributor incorporates features which advance the ignition timing both mechanically and by vacuum operation. Its shaft, driven by the camshaft, incorporates a reluctor which has four shaped poles and is mounted on the centre of a centrifugal advance assembly whose two weights move outwards under centrifugal force as engine speed rises, thus rotating the reluctor on the shaft and advancing or retarding the spark; the amount of movement being controlled by light springs. A pick-up coil generates a weak magnetic field whenever the ignition is switched on; as the engine rotates the reluctor poles pass the coil, disturbing the field each time and sending a signal current to the amplifier module. Whenever this signal exceeds a threshold level determined by engine speed a high-voltage transistor in the amplifier is switched on, thus allowing HT coil current to flow; when this current has reached the required level it is held constant until the transistor is switched off, thus triggering the spark. The pick-up coil is clamped to a stator pack that is able to rotate under the control of the vacuum capsule mounted on the side of the distributor. The capsule comprises a diaphragm, one side of which is connected via a small-bore pipe to the carburettor and the other side to the stator pack. Inlet manifold depression, which varies with engine speed and throttle position, causes the diaphragm to move thus rotating the stator pack and advancing or retarding the spark.

Models fitted with catalytic converters have a thermostatically-operated vacuum switch screwed into the cooling system thermostat housing; the small-bore vacuum pipe being in two lengths that are connected from the carburettor to the switch and from the switch to the distributor. At coolant temperatures below 70°C the switch prevents any vacuum advance from taking place, causing raised exhaust gas temperatures due to the retarded ignition timing, thus bringing the catalytic converter more quickly to its efficient operating temperature. Once coolant temperatures rise above this point, the switch opens and normal vacuum advance is restored.

Precautions

General

It is necessary to take extra care when working on the electrical system to avoid damage to semi-conductor devices (diodes and transistors), and to avoid the risk of personal injury. In addition to the precautions given in the *"Safety first!"* Section at the beginning of this manual, take note of the following points when working on the system.

Always remove rings, watches, etc before working on the electrical system. Even with the battery disconnected, capacitive discharge could occur if a component live terminal is earthed through a metal object. This could cause a shock or nasty burn.

Do not reverse the battery connections. Components such as the alternator or any other having semi-conductor circuitry could be irreparably damaged.

If the engine is being started using jump leads and a slave battery, connect the batteries *positive to positive* and *negative to negative.* This also applies when connecting a battery charger.

Never disconnect the battery terminals, or alternator multi-plug connector, when the engine is running.

The battery leads and alternator multi-plug must be disconnected before carrying out any electric welding on the car.

Never use an ohmmeter of the type incorporating a hand cranked generator for circuit or continuity testing.

Ignition and engine management systems

The HT voltage generated by an electronic ignition system is extremely high, and in certain circumstances could prove fatal. Take care to avoid receiving electric shocks from the HT side of the ignition system. *Persons with surgically-implanted cardiac pacemaker devices should keep well clear of the ignition circuits, components and test equipment.*

Do not handle HT leads, or touch the distributor or coil when the engine is running. If tracing faults in the HT circuit, use well insulated tools to manipulate live leads.

Engine management modules are very sensitive components, and certain precautions must be taken to avoid damage to the module when working on a vehicle equipped with an engine management system as follows.

When carrying out welding operations on the vehicle using electric welding equipment, the battery and alternator should be disconnected.

Although underbonnet-mounted modules will tolerate normal underbonnet conditions, they can be adversely affected by excess heat or moisture. If using welding equipment or pressure washing equipment in the vicinity of the module, take care not to direct heat, or jets of water or steam at the module. If this cannot be avoided, remove the module from the vehicle, and protect its wiring plug with a plastic bag.

Before disconnecting any wiring, or removing components, always ensure that the ignition is switched off.

On models with underbonnet-mounted modules, do not run the engine with the module detached from the body panel, as the body acts as an effective heat sink, and the module may be damaged due to internal overheating.

Do not attempt to improvise fault diagnosis procedures using a test lamp or multimeter, as irreparable damage could be caused to the module.

Ensure that all the wiring is correctly reconnected before connecting the battery or switching on the ignition when working on ignition/engine management system components.

2 Spark plugs - renewal

Refer to Chapter 1, Section 37.

3 HT leads, distributor cap and rotor arm - inspection and renewal

Refer to Chapter 1, Section 30.

4 Ignition timing - checking and adjustment

Refer to Chapter 1, Section 38.

5.2 Disconnecting the distributor wiring - note amplifier module screws (arrowed)

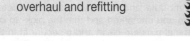

5 Distributor - removal, overhaul and refitting

Removal

1 Disconnect the battery negative terminal.
2 Releasing its wire clip, unplug the wiring connector from the distributor **(see illustration).**
3 Disconnect and plug the vacuum pipe **(see illustration).**
4 Position the engine so that number 1 cylinder is at TDC on the compression stroke.
5 Remove the distributor cap (and rotor arm, if required).
6 Mark the relationship of the distributor body to the cylinder head, using a scriber or similar **(see illustration).**

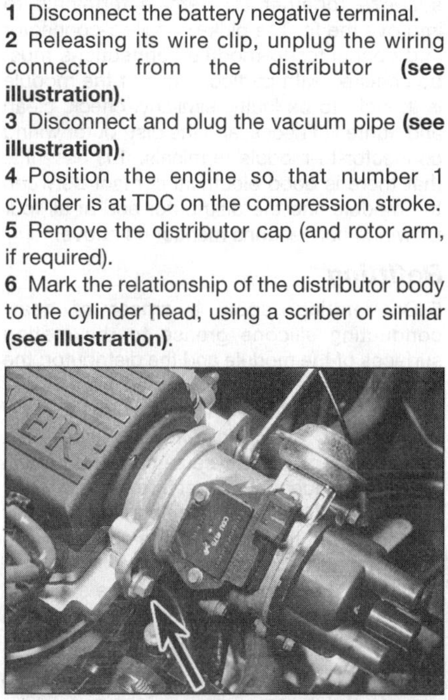

5.7 Unscrewing distributor mounting bolts - remaining bolt arrowed

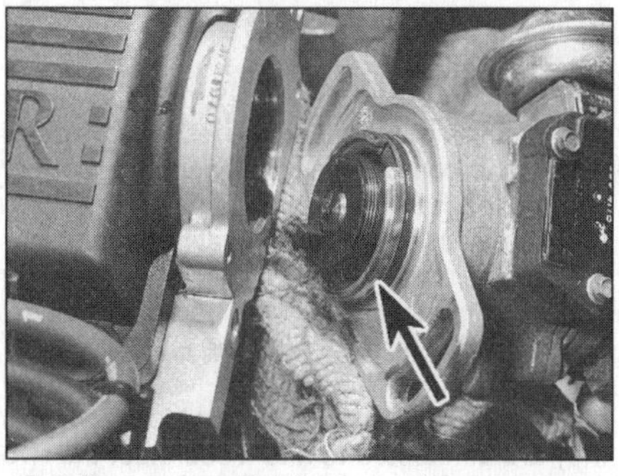

5.8 Removing distributor - always renew O-ring (arrowed)

5.3 Disconnecting vacuum pipe from distributor vacuum capsule

7 Unscrew the distributor mounting bolts and withdraw the distributor **(see illustration).** Do not disturb the crankshaft setting while the distributor is removed, or rotate the distributor shaft (unless the unit is to be overhauled).
8 Remove the distributor body sealing O-ring which must be renewed whenever it is disturbed **(see illustration).**

Overhaul

9 Remove the distributor and withdraw the cap and rotor arm, if not already removed **(see illustration).**
10 Remove the amplifier module, then remove its gasket and withdraw the connector.
11 Remove the screws and separate the upper housing from the lower.
12 Remove the clamp ring and pick-up coil from the upper housing.
13 Remove the circlip (and first thrustwasher, if fitted) from the underside of the upper housing, disengage the stator pack from the vacuum capsule arm and withdraw the stator pack, followed by the (second) thrustwasher.
14 Remove its retaining screw and withdraw the vacuum capsule. Note the numbers stamped on the capsule's mounting bracket; the eight-digit number is the Lucas part number, but the three remaining numbers indicate the capsule's design characteristics -

5.6 Marking relationship of distributor body to cylinder head

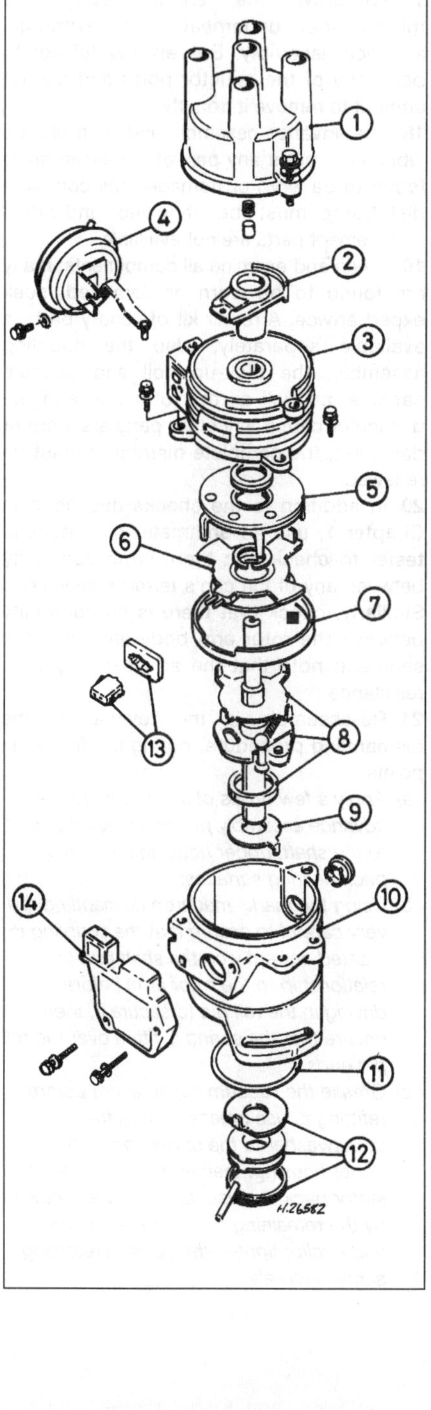

5.9 Exploded view of the Lucas 67 DM4 distributor

1 Distributor cap
2 Rotor arm
3 Upper housing
4 Vacuum capsule
5 Stator pack, including thrust washer(s) and circlip
6 Pick-up coil
7 Clamp ring
8 Distributor shaft, including reluctor and advance assembly
9 Thrust washer
10 Lower housing
11 Sealing O-ring
12 Drive coupling, including thrust washer, spring and roll pin
13 Connector and gasket
14 Amplifier module

the first and second numbers show (in mm Hg) the pressure at which vacuum advance begins and reaches its maximum, while the third shows the capsule's total advance in (distributor) degrees. Check that the capsule is the correct one for the car (see Specifications).

15 Check the distributor shaft endfloat; if it seems excessive, seek expert advice.

16 Remove the spring from the distributor drive coupling, then use a scriber or similar to mark the relationship of the coupling to the shaft; it is essential that the coupling is refitted correctly in relationship to the rotor arm on refitting. Release the distributor shaft by driving out the retaining roll pin and removing the coupling; note the thrustwasher behind it.

17 Withdraw the shaft, noting the thrustwasher underneath the centrifugal advance assembly. Be very careful not to bend any of the reluctor poles and do not attempt to remove it from the shaft.

18 The advance assembly and shaft can be lubricated, but if any part of the assembly is found to be worn or damaged the complete distributor must be renewed; individual replacement parts are not available.

19 Clean and examine all components; if any are found to be worn or damaged, seek expert advice. A repair kit of sundry parts is available separately, also the coupling assembly, the pick-up coil and vacuum capsule, as well as the rotor arm and the distributor cap; if any other parts are worn or damaged, the complete distributor must be renewed.

20 In addition to the checks described in Chapter 1, use an ohmmeter or continuity tester to check that there is no continuity between any of the cap's terminal segments. Similarly, check that there is no continuity between the rotor arm body and its brass segment; note that the arm has a built-in resistance.

21 Re-assembly is the reverse of the dismantling procedure, noting the following points.

a) *Apply a few drops of suitable oil to the advance assembly pivots and springs and to the shaft, upper housing and stator pack bearing surfaces.*
b) *Using the marks made on dismantling, be very careful to ensure that the coupling is located correctly on the shaft end (in relationship to the rotor arm) before driving in the roll pin to secure it, then ensure that the spring is fitted over the roll pin ends.*
c) *Grease the vacuum capsule arm before refitting it, use grease to stick the thrustwasher to the underside of the upper housing, then refit and connect the stator pack and vacuum capsule, followed by the remaining thrustwasher, if fitted, and circlip; tighten the capsule retaining screw securely.*
d) *Refit the pick-up coil to the upper housing and centre its terminals in the aperture before fitting the clamp ring so that its cut-out is over the aperture.*
e) *Refit the upper housing to the lower, tighten the screws lightly and check that the shaft is free to rotate - there must be no sign of the reluctor poles touching the stator pack arms, as either can easily be bent - before tightening the screws securely.*
f) *Refit the connector and its gasket.*
g) *Refit the amplifier module and the rotor arm.*
h) *Fit a new sealing O-ring to the distributor body.*

Refitting

Normal procedure

22 First check that number 1 cylinder is at TDC, then rotate the rotor arm to align with the distributor cap's number 1 terminal. Fit a new sealing O-ring to the distributor body and lubricate it with a smear of engine oil.

23 Aligning the marks made on removal, refit the distributor. If necessary, rotate the rotor arm very slightly to help the distributor drive dogs locate in the camshaft slots; they are offset and so will fit only one way. Refit the mounting bolts, tightening them to the specified torque wrench setting.

24 Refit the distributor cap, ensuring it is correctly located, then reconnect the HT leads.

25 Reconnect the vacuum pipe and distributor wiring.

26 Check, and adjust if necessary, the ignition timing.

Full procedure

27 If a new distributor is to be fitted (or no marks were made on removal), the following procedure will produce a basic setting which will enable the engine to start and run while the ignition timing is accurately set.

28 Remove the cylinder head cover and position the engine so that number 1 cylinder is at TDC on the compression stroke, then rotate the crankshaft slightly anti-clockwise until the flywheel mark aligns with the appropriate scale mark (see Specifications), so that the engine is in the firing position.

29 Rotate the distributor rotor arm to align with the distributor cap's number 1 terminal.

30 Refit the distributor, positioning its body so that the mounting bolts are in the middle of their respective slots. Refit the cylinder head cover and connect the HT leads to the cap and spark plugs, ensuring that the leads are correctly routed and secured in their guides and that the firing order is followed.

31 Check, and adjust if necessary, the ignition timing.

6 Ignition amplifier module - removal and refitting

> **Warning:** ***Do not attempt to open or repair the module; if it is faulty, it must be renewed***

Removal

1 Disconnect the battery negative terminal.

2 Releasing its wire clip, unplug the wiring connector from the distributor.

3 Remove the two screws and withdraw the module, taking care not to damage the terminal pins.

4 Check carefully that the mating surfaces of the module and distributor are completely clean and unmarked and that the pick-up coil terminal pins are clean and a secure fit in the module; if in doubt, it is permissible to remove the connector and its gasket and to gently squeeze together the female terminals to improve the fit. The pick-up coil-to-connector and connector-to-module connections must be checked with particular care if the module is thought to be faulty; similarly, check, clean and tighten (if necessary) the distributor wiring connector-to-module terminals. It is essential that there is good electrical contact between the module and the distributor and at all four LT wiring connections mentioned above.

Refitting

5 On refitting, apply a smear of heat-conducting silicone grease to the mating surfaces of the module and the distributor; the correct grease can be obtained from Rover dealers under Part Number BAU 5812, but if this is not available either a heat-sink compound, or an anti-seize compound, will serve as an adequate substitute.

6 Check that the terminal pins are not bent or damaged and that they engage correctly with the module's connections.

7 Tighten the module screws to the specified torque wrench setting, then reconnect the distributor wiring and battery.

7 Ignition HT coil - removal, testing and refitting

Removal

1 The coil is mounted on the left-hand side of the engine compartment, between the battery and the left-hand headlamp unit.

2 Disconnect the battery negative terminal.

3 Remove the two retaining screws securing the cold air inlet duct to the body front panel and move the hose clear of the HT coil.

4 Peel back the rubber cover, then disconnect the HT lead. Note which terminals they are connected to and disconnect the two pairs of LT wires from the coil **(see illustration).**

7.4 Peel back the cover to expose the HT coil connections

5 Slacken the two coil mounting screws, noting the location of the suppressor, and withdraw the coil; slacken its clamp screw, if required, to release it from its bracket.

Testing

6 Testing of the coil consists of using a multimeter set to its resistance function, or a low-wattage test lamp, to check the primary (LT "+ " to "-" terminals) and secondary (LT "+" to HT lead terminals) windings for continuity. If the meter is used the resistance of either winding can be checked and compared with the specified value. Note that since the readings obtained will vary slightly with temperature, the coil should be tested (where possible) after the engine has been running for at least 15 minutes so that the coil is at its normal operating temperature.

7 Using an ohmmeter or continuity tester, check that there is no continuity between the HT lead terminal and the coil body.

8 If the coil is faulty it must be renewed.

Refitting

9 Refitting is the reverse of the removal procedure.

8 Crankshaft sensor and reluctor ring - removal, inspection and refitting

Removal

Crankshaft sensor

1 Disconnect the battery negative lead.

2 Disconnect the sensor wiring at its connector plug on the flywheel rear cover plate, then undo the retaining screw to release the wiring lead **(see illustration)**.

3 Remove the two retaining screws and withdraw the sensor from the cylinder block/crankcase.

Reluctor ring

Note: *While a reluctor ring is fitted to the flywheel of carburettor engines, it has no function on these models but should be checked whenever the flywheel is removed to ensure that its mountings are securely fastened*

4 Remove the gearbox, clutch and flywheel.

5 Remove the setscrews securing the reluctor ring to the flywheel and withdraw it **(see illustration)**.

Inspection

Crankshaft sensor

6 Check the sensor for obvious signs of wear or damage and renew it if any are found. As no data is available to enable the sensor to be tested, if it is thought to be faulty it can be checked only by the substitution of a new component.

Reluctor ring

7 Check the ring for any signs of wear or damage and renew it if any are found.

Refitting

Crankshaft sensor

8 Refitting is the reverse of the removal procedure; tighten the screws to their specified torque wrench setting.

Reluctor ring

9 Refitting is the reverse of the removal procedure; tighten the screws to their specified torque wrench setting.

9 Thermostatically-operated vacuum switch - removal and refitting

Removal

1 Either drain the cooling system, or be prepared for some loss of coolant as the switch is unscrewed.

2 Access to the thermostat housing is possible with the inlet manifold and carburettor in place, but is made much easier if these are first removed.

3 Disconnect and plug the vacuum pipes.

4 Unscrew the switch and withdraw it, then plug the opening to prevent the entry of dirt; if the cooling system has not been drained, work quickly to minimise coolant loss.

Refitting

5 Refitting is the reverse of the removal procedure, noting the following points.

a) *Wipe clean the threads of the switch and of the thermostat housing.*
b) *If a sealing washer is fitted, renew it whenever it is disturbed to prevent leaks; if no sealing washer is fitted, apply a smear of sealant to the switch threads.*
c) *Tighten the switch securely and reconnect the vacuum pipes.*
d) *Refit any components removed to improve access.*
e) *Refill or top-up the cooling system.*

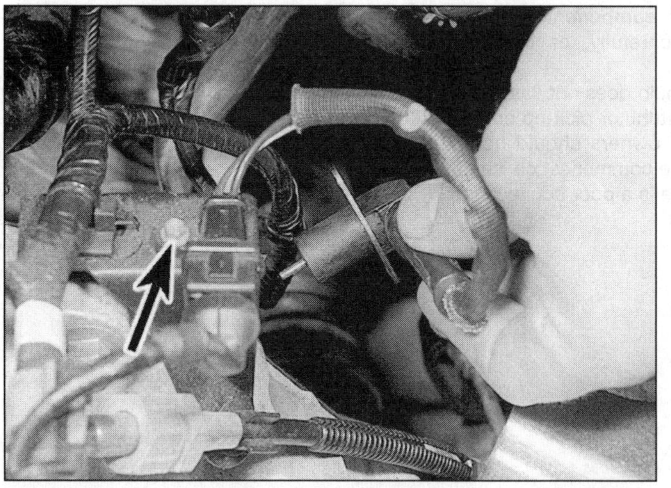

8.2 Removing crankshaft sensor - wiring lead screw arrowed

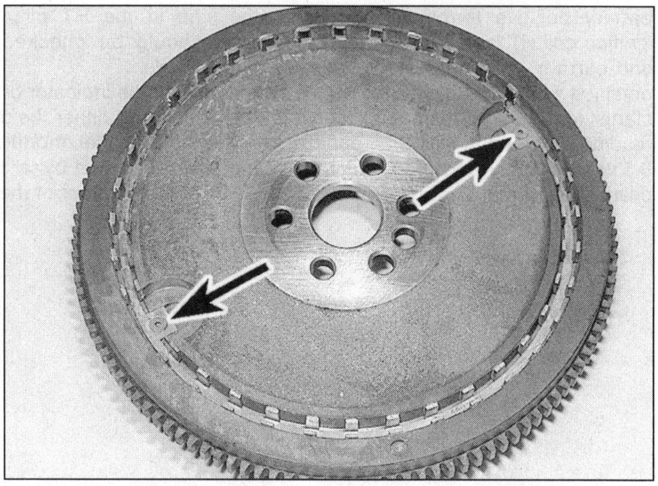

8.5 Reluctor ring-to-flywheel setscrews (arrowed)

10 Electronic control unit (ECU) - removal and refitting

Refer to Chapter 4, Part A or B.

11 Ignition system - testing

Note: *Refer to the warning given in Section 1 of this Chapter before starting work. Always switch off the ignition before disconnecting or connecting any component and when using a multi-meter to check resistances. Any voltmeter or multi-meter used to test ignition system components must have an impedance of 10 M ohms or greater*

General

1 The components of electronic ignition systems are normally very reliable; most faults are far more likely to be due to loose or dirty connections or to "tracking" of HT voltage due to dirt, dampness or damaged insulation than to the failure of any of the system's components. **Always** check all wiring thoroughly before condemning an electrical component and work methodically to eliminate all other possibilities before deciding that a particular component is faulty.

2 The old practice of checking for a spark by holding the live end of an HT lead a short distance away from the engine is not recommended; not only is there a high risk of a powerful electric shock, but the HT coil or amplifier module will be damaged. Similarly, **never** try to "diagnose" misfires by pulling off one HT lead at a time.

Engine will not start

3 If the engine either will not turn over at all, or only turns very slowly, check the battery and starter motor. Connect a voltmeter across the battery terminals (meter positive probe to battery positive terminal), disconnect the ignition coil HT lead from the distributor cap and earth it, then note the voltage reading obtained while turning over the engine on the starter for (no more than) ten seconds. If the reading obtained is less than approximately 9.5 volts, check the battery, starter motor and charging system.

4 If the engine turns over at normal speed but will not start, check the HT circuit by connecting a timing light (following the manufacturer's instructions) and turning the engine over on the starter motor; if the light flashes, voltage is reaching the spark plugs, so these should be checked first. If the light does not flash, check the HT leads themselves followed by the distributor cap, carbon brush and rotor arm but note also the tests given in Section 5, paragraph 20 of this Chapter).

5 If there is a spark, check the fuel system for faults.

6 If there is still no spark, check the voltage at the ignition HT coil "+" terminal (white wires); it should be the same as the battery voltage (ie, at least 11.7 volts). If the voltage at the coil is more than 1 volt less than that at the battery, check the feed back through the fusebox and ignition switch to the battery and its earth until the fault is found.

7 If the feed to the HT coil is sound, check the coil's primary winding (and also the secondary winding, while the opportunity exists) as described in Section 7, paragraph 6. Renew the coil if faulty but be careful to check carefully the condition of the LT connections themselves before doing so, to ensure that the fault is not due to dirty or poorly-fastened connectors.

8 If the HT coil is in good condition, the fault is probably within the amplifier module or distributor pick-up coil. So that the operation of these two can be checked quickly, Rover dealers have a Neon indicator, which when connected across the HT coil's LT terminals, flashes every time the amplifier triggers an HT pulse in the coil if the ignition is switched on and the engine is turned over on the starter. Owners can substitute a low-wattage bulb; if the bulb flickers or flashes when the engine is turned over, the amplifier and distributor are sound.

9 If the amplifier and distributor are sound, and the entire LT circuit is in good condition, the fault, if it lies in the ignition system, must be in the HT circuit components. These should be checked carefully, as outlined above.

10 If the indicator or bulb does not flash, the fault is in either the distributor pick-up coil or the amplifier module; owners should note, however, that by far the commonest cause of failure of either of these is a poor connection, either between the amplifier module and the distributor body or in the LT circuit wiring connections themselves. If a voltmeter or multi-meter is available, check the feed to the amplifier (the voltage reading obtained should be the same as that measured at the HT coil LT "+" terminal), then check that there is no measurable resistance between the amplifier module fixing screws and engine earth and that there is no continuity between either module terminal and earth. If any doubt exists as to the condition of the connections, remove the module, clean and check carefully the module earth and the connections and, if necessary, improve their fit. If these checks fail to correct the fault, measure the resistance of the pick-up coil, comparing it with the specified value; renew the coil if the reading obtained differs significantly from that given. If the fault still exists, the only solution is to try the effect of renewing the amplifier module.

Engine misfires

11 An irregular misfire suggests either a loose connection or intermittent fault on the primary circuit, or an HT fault on the coil side of the rotor arm.

12 With the ignition switched off, check carefully through the system ensuring that all connections are clean and securely fastened. If the equipment is available, check the LT circuit as described in paragraphs 6 to 10 above.

13 Check that the HT coil, the distributor cap and the HT leads are clean and dry. Check the leads themselves and the spark plugs (by substitution, if necessary), then check the distributor cap, carbon brush and rotor arm.

14 Regular misfiring is almost certainly due to a fault in the distributor cap, HT leads or spark plugs. Use a timing light (paragraph 4 above) to check whether HT voltage is present at all leads.

15 If HT voltage is not present on any particular lead, the fault will be in that lead or in the distributor cap. If HT is present on all leads, the fault will be in the spark plugs; check and renew them if there is any doubt about their condition.

16 If no HT is present, check the HT coil; its secondary windings may be breaking down under load.

Chapter 5 Part B:
Ignition system - fuel injection models

Contents

Degrees of difficulty

Easy, suitable for novice with little experience	**Fairly easy,** suitable for beginner with some experience	**Fairly difficult,** suitable for competent DIY mechanic	**Difficult,** suitable for experienced DIY mechanic	**Very difficult,** suitable for expert DIY or professional

Specifications

General

System type	Rover/Motorola Modular Engine Management System (MEMS), fully electronic, controlled by ECU
Firing order	1-3-4-2 (No 1 cylinder at timing belt end)
Direction of crankshaft rotation	Clockwise (viewed from right-hand side of car)

Distributor

Type	Spark distribution only (ignition timing entirely controlled by ECU)
Direction of rotor arm rotation	Anti-clockwise (viewed from left-hand side of car)
Distributor cap:	
Early 1.4 K16-engined models	AUU 1186
All other models	NJD 10005
Rotor arm	AUU 1641 (resistive type)

Electronic Control Unit (ECU)

1.1 K8-engined models	MN3 10015
1.4 K8-engined models	MNE 10016
1.4 K16-engined models - without catalytic converter:	
Up to VIN 662512	AUU 1518 or MNE 10039
VIN 662513 on	MNE 10050
1.4 K16-engined models - with open-loop catalytic converter	MNE 10009 or MNE 10041
1.4 K16-engined models - with closed-loop catalytic converter	MNE 10022 or MNE 10062

Ignition timing - @ idle speed (ECU-controlled)

1.1 K8-engined models	15° BTDC
1.4 K8-engined models	10° BTDC
1.4 K16-engined models - by ECU number:	
AUU 1518, MNE 10039	13° ± 2° BTDC
MNE 10009, MNE 10041, MNE 10050	14° ± 2° BTDC
MNE 10062	14° ± 5° BTDC
MNE 10022	Not available

Note: *Nominal value given for checking purposes only - not adjustable and may vary under ECU control*

Crankshaft sensor

Type	ADU 7340

Ignition HT coil

Type:	
Early 1.4 K16-engined models	NEC 10002 or NEC 10003
All other models	AUU 1326 or ADU 8779
Manufacturer	Bosch, Ducellier or Rudi Cajavec
Current consumption - average	0.25 to 0.75 amps @ idle speed
Winding resistances:	
Primary	0.71 to 0.81 ohms @ 20°C
Secondary	5 to 15 K ohms @ 20°C

Torque wrench settings

	Nm	lbf ft
Spark plugs	25	19
Distributor cap screws	2	2
Distributor rotor arm (hex-head) screw	10	8
Reluctor ring-to-flywheel setscrews	3	2
Ignition HT coil mounting screws	7	5
Crankshaft sensor mounting screws	6	4.5
Crankshaft sensor lead-to-flywheel cover plate screw	6	4.5

1 General information and precautions

General information

The ignition system is fully electronic in operation, incorporating the Electronic Control Unit (ECU) mounted on the engine compartment bulkhead, a distributor (driven off the inlet camshaft left-hand end) and a crankshaft sensor mounted in the left-hand rear end of the engine's cylinder block/crankcase to register with the reluctor ring fixed to the flywheel, as well as the spark plugs, HT leads, ignition HT coil and associated wiring. The system is divided into two circuits; primary (low tension - LT) and secondary (high tension - HT). The primary circuit consists of the battery, ignition switch, ignition HT coil primary windings, ECU and wiring. The secondary circuit consists of the ignition HT coil secondary windings, the distributor cap and rotor arm, the spark plugs and the HT leads connecting these **(see illustration)**.

The ECU controls both the ignition system and the fuel injection system, integrating the two in a complete engine management system.

As far as the ignition system is concerned, the ECU receives information in the form of electrical impulses or signals from the crankshaft sensor (which gives it the engine speed and crankshaft position), from the coolant temperature sensor (which gives it the engine temperature), from the throttle pedal switch (which tells it when the throttle is closed) and from the manifold absolute pressure sensor (which gives it the load on the engine). All these signals are compared by the ECU, using digital techniques, with set values pre-programmed (mapped) into its memory; based on this information, the ECU selects the ignition timing appropriate to those values and controls the ignition HT coil accordingly.

Note that this means that the distributor is just that, a distributor of the HT pulse to the appropriate spark plug; it has no effect whatsoever on the ignition timing. Also, the system is so sensitive that, at idle speed, the ignition timing may be constantly changing and this should be remembered if trying to check the ignition timing.

Precautions

General

It is necessary to take extra care when working on the electrical system to avoid damage to semi-conductor devices (diodes and transistors), and to avoid the risk of personal injury. In addition to the precautions given in the *"Safety first!"* Section at the beginning of this manual, take note of the following points when working on the system.

Always remove rings, watches, etc before working on the electrical system. Even with the battery disconnected, capacitive discharge could occur if a component live terminal is earthed through a metal object. This could cause a shock or nasty burn.

Do not reverse the battery connections. Components such as the alternator or any other having semi-conductor circuitry could be irreparably damaged.

If the engine is being started using jump leads and a slave battery, connect the batteries *positive to positive* and *negative to negative.* This also applies when connecting a battery charger.

Never disconnect the battery terminals, or alternator multi-plug connector, when the engine is running.

The battery leads and alternator multi-plug must be disconnected before carrying out any electric welding on the car.

Never use an ohmmeter of the type incorporating a hand cranked generator for circuit or continuity testing.

Ignition and engine management systems

The HT voltage generated by an electronic ignition system is extremely high, and in certain circumstances could prove fatal. Take care to avoid receiving electric shocks from the HT side of the ignition system. *Persons with surgically-implanted cardiac pacemaker devices should keep well clear of the ignition circuits, components and test equipment.*

Do not handle HT leads, or touch the distributor or coil when the engine is running. If tracing faults in the HT circuit, use well insulated tools to manipulate live leads.

Engine management modules are very sensitive components, and certain precautions must be taken to avoid damage to the module when working on a vehicle equipped with an engine management system as follows.

When carrying out welding operations on the vehicle using electric welding equipment, the battery and alternator should be disconnected.

Although underbonnet-mounted modules will tolerate normal underbonnet conditions, they can be adversely affected by excess heat or moisture. If using welding equipment or pressure washing equipment in the vicinity of the module, take care not to direct heat, or jets of water or steam at the module. If this cannot be avoided, remove the module from the vehicle, and protect its wiring plug with a plastic bag.

Before disconnecting any wiring, or removing components, always ensure that the ignition is switched off.

On models with underbonnet-mounted modules, do not run the engine with the module detached from the body panel, as the body acts as an effective heat sink, and the module may be damaged due to internal overheating.

Do not attempt to improvise fault diagnosis procedures using a test lamp or multimeter, as irreparable damage could be caused to the module.

After working on ignition/engine management system components, ensure that all wiring is correctly reconnected before reconnecting the battery or switching on the ignition.

1.1 Modular Engine Management System components

1 Oxygen sensor
2 Inertia switch
3 Fuel pump
4 Throttle potentiometer
5 Fuel pressure regulator
6 Injector
7 Stepper motor
8 Inlet air temperature sensor
9 Manifold PTC sensor
10 Coolant temperature sensor
11 Distributor cap
12 Crankshaft sensor
13 Diagnostic sensor
14 ECU
15 Relay module
16 Ignition coil
17 Oxygen sensor relay
18 Purge valve
19 Charcoal canister
20 Lambda sensor

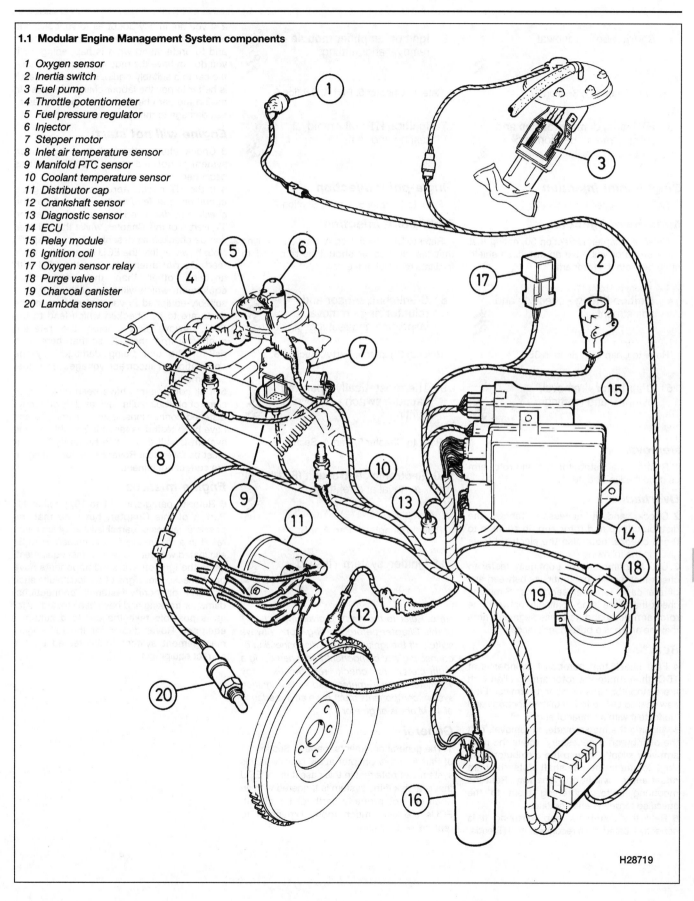

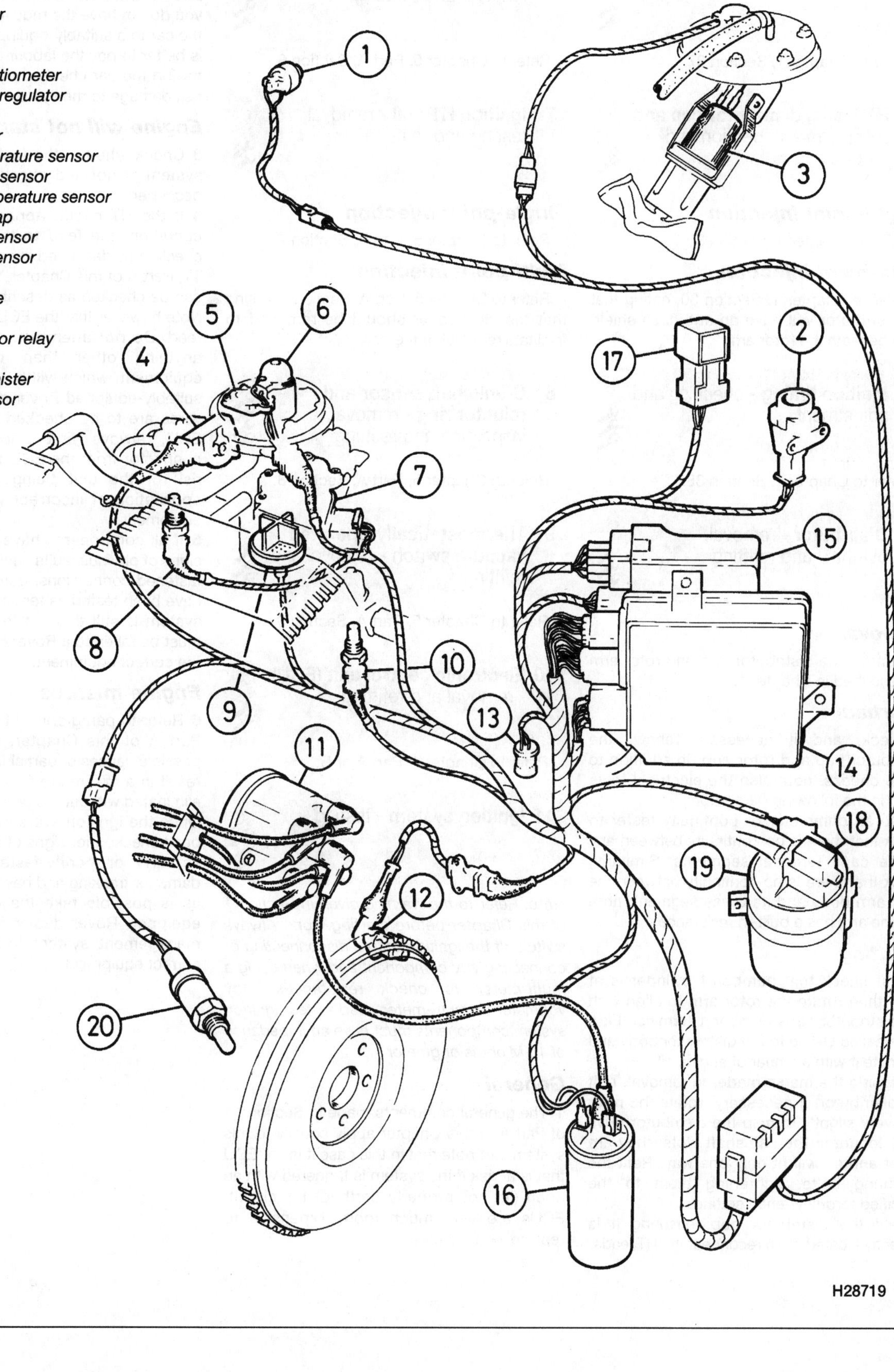

H28719

2 Spark plugs - renewal

Refer to Chapter 1, Section 37.

3 HT leads, distributor cap and rotor arm - inspection and renewal

Single-point injection

Refer to Chapter 1, Section 30.

Multi-point injection

Refer to Chapter 1, Section 30, noting that the distributor will have an anti-flash shield fitted beneath the rotor arm.

4 Ignition timing - checking and adjustment

Refer to Chapter 1, Section 38.

5 Distributor - removal, overhaul and refitting

Removal

1 Remove the distributor cap and rotor arm as described in Chapter 1.

Overhaul

2 Check, and if necessary renew, the distributor cap and rotor arm. In addition to those checks, note also the electrical tests given in the following paragraph:

3 Use an ohmmeter or continuity tester to check that there is no continuity between any of the caps terminal segments. Similarly, check that there is no continuity between the rotor arm body and its brass segment; note that the arm has a built-in resistance.

Refitting

4 First check that number 1 cylinder is at TDC, then rotate the rotor arm to align with the distributor caps number 1 terminal. Fit a new sealing O-ring to the distributor body and lubricate it with a smear of engine oil.

5 Aligning the marks made on removal, refit the distributor. If necessary, rotate the rotor arm very slightly to help the distributor drive dogs locate in the camshaft slots; they are offset and so will fit only one way. Refit the mounting bolts, tightening them to the specified torque wrench setting.

6 Refit the distributor cap, ensuring it is correctly located, then reconnect the HT leads.

6 Ignition amplifier module - removal and refitting

Refer to Chapter 5, Part A, Section 6.

7 Ignition HT coil - removal, testing and refitting

Single-point injection

Refer to Chapter 5, Part A, Section 7.

Multi-point injection

Refer to Chapter 5, Part A, Section 7, noting that the air cleaner should be removed to facilitate removal of the coil.

8 Crankshaft sensor and reluctor ring - removal, inspection and refitting

Refer to Chapter 5, Part A, Section 8.

9 Thermostatically-operated vacuum switch - removal and refitting

Refer to Chapter 5, Part A, Section 9.

10 Electronic control unit (ECU) - removal and refitting

Refer to Chapter 4, Part A or B.

11 Ignition system - testing

Note: *Refer to the warning given in Section 1 of this Chapter before starting work. Always switch off the ignition before disconnecting or connecting any component and when using a multi-meter to check resistances. Any voltmeter or multi-meter used to test ignition system components must have an impedance of 10 M ohms or greater*

General

1 The general comments made in Section 11 of Part A of this Chapter apply equally to this system, but note that in this case it is the ECU that is at risk if the system is triggered with an open (ie, not properly earthed) HT circuit. ECUs are very much more expensive to replace, so take care!

2 If you are in any doubt as to your skill and ability to test the ignition system components and to understand what is happening, or if you do not have the required equipment, take the car to a suitably-equipped Rover dealer; it is better to pay the labour charges involved in having the car checked by an expert than to risk damage to the system or to yourself.

Engine will not start

3 Check whether the fault is in the ignition system or not and check the HT circuit as described.

4 If the HT circuit appears to be in good condition, the feed to the HT coil can be checked as described in paragraph 6, Section 11, Part A of this Chapter, whilst the coil itself can be checked as described in paragraph 7. Note however that the ECU controls the coil's feed. **Do not** attempt to test the ECU with anything other than the correct test equipment, which will be available only at a suitably-equipped Rover dealer. If any of the wires are to be checked which lead to the ECU, always first unplug the relevant connector from the ECU so that there is no risk of the unit being damaged by the application of incorrect voltages from test equipment.

5 If all components have been checked for signs of obvious faults such as dirty or poorly-fastened connections, damp, or tracking and have been tested as far as is possible but the system is still thought to be faulty, the car must be taken to a Rover dealer for testing on the correct equipment.

Engine misfires

6 Refer to paragraphs 11 to 16, Section 11, Part A of this Chapter, but note that the possible causes of partial failures which might result in a misfire are far too numerous to be eliminated without the correct test equipment. Once the ignition system components have been checked for signs of obvious faults such as dirty or poorly-fastened connections, damp, or tracking and have been tested as far as is possible take the car to a suitably-equipped Rover dealer for the full engine management system to be tested on the correct equipment.

Chapter 5 Part C:
Starting and charging systems

Contents

Degrees of difficulty

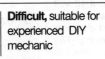

Easy, suitable for novice with little experience	**Fairly easy,** suitable for beginner with some experience	**Fairly difficult,** suitable for competent DIY mechanic	**Difficult,** suitable for experienced DIY mechanic	**Very difficult,** suitable for expert DIY or professional

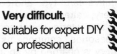

Specifications

System

Type	12 volt, negative earth

Battery

Type	Maintenance-free (sealed for life) lead-acid	
Code (Lucas):		
K8-engined models:		
Standard equipment	007	
Cold climates	063	
K16-engined models:		
Standard equipment	063	
Cold climates	063S	
Police versions	063S	
Performance:	**Cold cranking**	**Reserve capacity**
007	280 amps	50 minutes
063	360 amps	60 minutes
063S	405 amps	70 minutes

Alternator

Type	Lucas/Magneti Marelli A127
Output - @ 14 volts and 6000 rpm:	
GTi 16v	65 amps
All other models	55 amps
Regulated voltage	14 volts maximum
Voltage regulator	Lucas 21TR
Brush minimum protrusion	5 mm approx. (see text)
Brush spring pressure - brush end flush with brushbox	1.3 to 2.7 N
Stator winding resistance - @ 20°C:	
A127/55	0.18 ohms ± 5%
A127/65	0.15 ohms ± 5%
Rotor field winding resistance - @ 20°C	3.2 ohms ± 5%
Drivebelt deflection	6 to 8 mm @ 10 kg pressure

Starter motor

Type	Lucas M79
Rating	0.8 kW
Commutator minimum diameter	28.8 mm
Brush minimum length	3.5 mm approx. (see text)
Brush spring tension	12 to 20 N

Torque wrench settings

	Nm	lbf ft
Battery tray and fusible link box mounting bracket bolts	9	6.5
Alternator pivot and clamp bolts:		
10 mm	45	33
8 mm	25	18.5
Alternator pulley nut	25	18.5
Alternator mounting bracket-to-cylinder block/crankcase bolts	45	33
Starter motor-to-transmission bolts	45	33
Starter motor support bracket (where fitted) fasteners:		
Bracket front half-to-motor nuts	25	18.5
Bracket front half-to-rear half bolt	45	33
Bracket rear half-to-transmission bolts	25	18.5

1 General information and precautions

General information

The electrical system is of the 12 volt negative earth type and comprises a 12 volt battery, alternator with integral voltage regulator, starter motor and related electrical accessories, components and wiring. The battery is charged by an alternator which is belt-driven.

The starter motor is of the pre-engaged type incorporating an integral solenoid. On starting, the solenoid moves the drive pinion into engagement with the flywheel ring gear before the starter motor is energised. Once the engine has started, a one-way clutch prevents the motor armature being driven by the engine until the pinion disengages from the flywheel.

Precautions

It is necessary to take extra care when working on the electrical system to avoid damage to semi-conductor devices (diodes and transistors), and to avoid the risk of personal injury. In addition to the precautions given in the *"Safety first!"* Section at the beginning of this manual, take note of the following points when working on the system.

Always remove rings, watches, etc before working on the electrical system. Even with the battery disconnected, capacitive discharge could occur if a component live terminal is earthed through a metal object. This could cause a shock or nasty burn.

Do not reverse the battery connections. Components such as the alternator or any other having semi-conductor circuitry could be irreparably damaged.

If the engine is being started using jump leads and a slave battery, connect the batteries *positive to positive* and *negative to negative.* This also applies when connecting a battery charger.

Never disconnect the battery terminals, or alternator multi-plug connector, when the engine is running.

The battery leads and alternator multi-plug must be disconnected before carrying out any electric welding on the car.

Never use an ohmmeter of the type incorporating a hand cranked generator for circuit or continuity testing.

2 Battery - maintenance

Refer to Chapter 1, Section 7 and *"Weekly Checks"*.

3 Battery - testing and charging

Caution: Specially rapid "boost" charges which are claimed to restore the power of a battery in 1 to 2 hours are not recommended as they can cause serious damage to the battery plates through overheating.
Caution: During battery electrolyte replenishment, never add water to sulphuric acid otherwise it will explode. Always pour the acid slowly onto the water.

Testing

1 In normal use, the battery should not require charging from an external source unless very heavy use is made of electrical equipment over a series of journeys that are too short to allow the charging system to keep pace with demand. Otherwise, a need for regular recharging points to a fault either in the battery or in the charging system.

2 If, however, the car is laid up for long periods (in excess of thirty days at a time) the battery will lose approximately 1% of its charge per week. This figure is for a disconnected battery; if the battery is left connected, circuits such as the clock (where fitted) will drain it at a faster rate. To prevent this happening, always disconnect the battery negative lead whenever the car is to be laid up for a long period. To keep the battery fully charged it should be given regular 'refresher' charges every six weeks or so. This is particularly important on 'maintenance-free' batteries, which will suffer permanent reduction of charge capacity if allowed to become fully discharged.

3 If a discharged battery is suspected the simplest test for most owners is as follows. Leave the battery disconnected for at least two hours, then measure the (open circuit, or no-load) voltage using a sensitive voltmeter connected across the battery terminals. Compare the reading obtained with the following

Voltmeter reading	Charge condition
10.50 volts	*Fully discharged*
12.30 volts	*50% charged*
12.48 volts	*75% charged*
12.66 volts or more	*Fully charged*

4 If frequent topping-up is required and the battery case is not fractured, then the battery is being over-charged. The voltage regulator will have to be checked.

5 If the car covers a very small annual mileage, it is worthwhile checking the specific gravity of the electrolyte every three months to determine the state of charge of the battery. Use a hydrometer to make the check, and compare the results with the following table

	Normal climates	Tropics
Discharged	*1.120*	*1.080*
Half charged	*1.200*	*1.160*
Fully charged	*1.280*	*1.230*

6 If the battery condition is suspect, first check the specific gravity of electrolyte in each cell. A variation of 0.040 or more between any cells indicates loss of electrolyte or deterioration of the internal plates.

7 A further test can be made only by a battery specialist using a battery heavy discharge meter. Alternatively, connect a voltmeter across the battery terminals and operate the starter motor with the ignition coil HT lead disconnected from the distributor and earthed, and with the headlamps, heated rear window and heater blower switched on. If the voltmeter reading remains above approximately 9.5 volts, the battery condition is satisfactory. If the voltmeter reading drops below 9.5 volts and the battery has already been charged, it is proven faulty.

Charging

8 In winter when heavy demand is placed on the battery (starting from cold and using more electrical equipment), it is a good idea occasionally to have the battery fully charged from an external source. The battery's bench charge rate depends on its code (see a Rover dealer or Lucas agent for details); for most owners the best method will be to use a trickle-charger overnight, charging at a rate of 1.5 amps. Rapid 'boost' charges which are claimed to restore the power of the battery in 1 to 2 hours are **not** recommended, as they can cause serious damage to the battery plates through overheating and may cause a sealed battery to explode.

9 Ideally, the battery should be removed from the car before charging and moved to a well-ventilated area. As a minimum precaution, both battery terminal leads must be disconnected (disconnect the negative lead first) before connecting the charger leads.

Warning: The battery will be emitting significant quantities of (highly-inflammable) hydrogen gas during charging and for approximately 15 minutes afterwards; do not allow sparks or naked flames near the battery or it may explode.

10 Continue to charge the battery until all cells are gassing vigorously and no further rise in specific gravity or increase in no-load voltage is noted over a four-hour period. When charging is complete, turn the charger off before disconnecting the leads from the battery.

4 Battery - removal and refitting

Removal

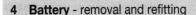

1 First check that all electrical components are switched off to avoid a spark occurring as the negative lead is disconnected. If the radio/cassette unit has a security code, de-activate the code temporarily and re-activate it when the battery is re-connected; refer to the instructions and code supplied with the unit.

2 Slacken the terminal clamp nut, then lift the clamp and negative lead from the terminal. This is the terminal to disconnect before working on any electrical component on the car. If the terminal is tight, carefully ease it off by moving it from side to side.

3 Raise the plastic cover from the positive terminal clamp and slacken the clamp nut, then lift the clamp and lead from the terminal.

4 Unscrew the clamp bolt and remove the clamp from the front of the battery **(see illustration)**.

5 Lift the battery from the tray keeping it upright and taking care not to allow it to contact your clothing.

6 If the battery tray is to be removed, release the two wiring harness clips from the tray and remove the cable-tie from the wiring, then release its two retainers and pull the fusible link box off its mounting bracket. Unscrew the five bolts securing the battery tray and fusible link mounting bracket to the body side member and remove the tray, collecting the bracket **(see illustrations)**.

7 Clean the battery terminal posts, clamps, tray and battery casing. If the bodywork is rusted as a result of battery acid spilling onto it, clean it thoroughly and re-paint.

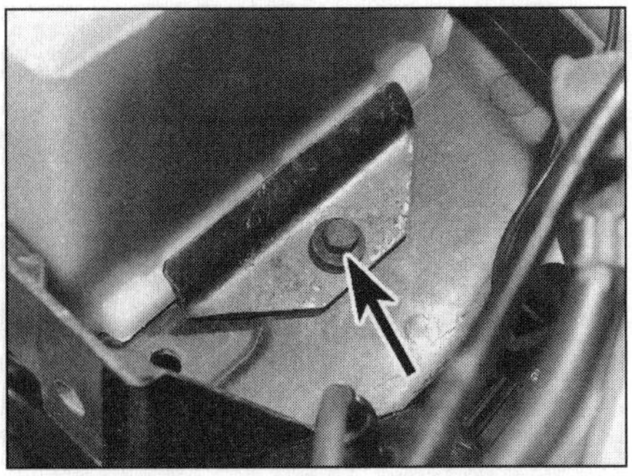

4.4 Battery clamp bolt (arrowed)

8 Whenever the battery is removed, check it for cracks and leakage.

Refitting

9 Refitting is the reverse of the removal procedure. Ensure that the terminal posts and leads are cleaned before re-connection. Smear petroleum jelly on the terminals after reconnecting the leads. Always connect the positive terminal clamp first and the negative terminal clamp last.

5 Charging system - testing

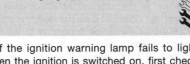

1 If the ignition warning lamp fails to light when the ignition is switched on, first check the alternator wiring connections for security. If satisfactory, check that the warning lamp bulb has not blown and is secure in its holder. If the lamp still fails to light, check the continuity of the warning lamp feed wire from the alternator to the bulbholder. If all is satisfactory, the alternator is at fault and should be renewed or taken to an auto-electrician for testing and repair.

2 If the ignition warning lamp lights when the engine is running, stop the engine and check that the drivebelt is correctly tensioned and that the alternator connections are secure. If all is so far satisfactory, check the alternator brushes and commutator. If the fault persists, the alternator should be renewed or taken to an auto-electrician for testing and repair.

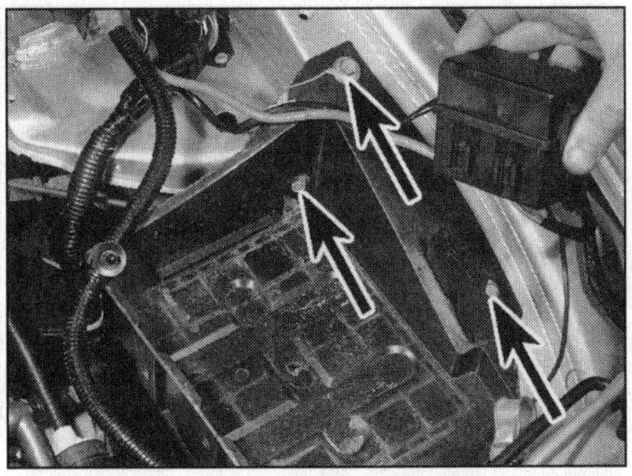

4.6a Battery tray/fusible link box mounting bracket upper (arrowed) . . .

3 If the alternator output is suspect even though the warning lamp functions correctly, the regulated voltage may be checked as follows.

4 Connect a voltmeter across the battery terminals and start the engine.

5 Increase engine speed until the voltmeter reading remains steady; this should be approximately 12 to 13 volts and no more than 14 volts.

6 Switch on as many electrical accessories (eg the headlamps, heated rear window and heater blower) as possible and check that the alternator maintains the regulated voltage at around 13 to 14 volts.

7 If the voltage is not as stated, the fault may be due to worn brushes, weak brush springs, a faulty voltage regulator, a faulty diode, a severed phase winding or a worn or damaged commutator. The brushes and commutator may be checked but if the fault persists, the alternator should be renewed or taken to an auto-electrician for testing and repair.

6 Alternator - drivebelt inspection, adjustment and renewal

Refer to Chapter 1, Section 31.

7 Alternator - removal and refitting

Removal

1 Disconnect the battery negative lead.

2 Remove its three retaining screws and move the washer system reservoir clear of the working area. Disconnect the wiring connector plug(s) if the extra reach is required.

3 If a cover is fitted over the alternator left-hand end, unscrew its three retaining nuts and washers and withdraw it. Release the wire clip and unplug the connector to disconnect the alternator wiring **(see illustration)**.

4 Remove the alternator drivebelt.

5 If not already done, jack up the front of the car and support it securely on axle stands (see "*Jacking and Vehicle Support*") so that the steering can be turned to full right lock and the right-hand underwing shield can be removed.

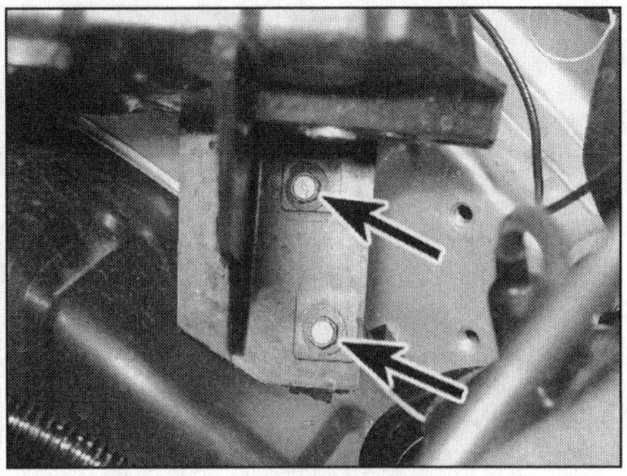

4.6b . . . and lower mounting bolts (arrowed)

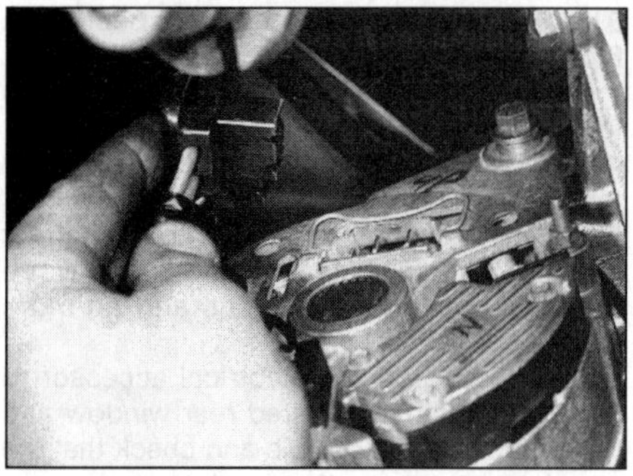

7.3 Disconnecting alternator wiring

6 Remove the oil filter element, having placed a suitable container under the filter adapter to catch the spilt oil. Unless the filter was installed only recently, it should be discarded and a new filter should be installed on reassembly; this of course means that the engine oil should be changed at the same time.

7 Support the weight of the engine/transmission by using a trolley jack, with a wooden spacer interposed to prevent damage to the sump, then unscrew the engine/transmission right-hand mounting through-bolt and nut and jack up the unit by approximately 60 mm.

8 Unscrew the alternator clamp and pivot bolts and manoeuvre the alternator out of the car **(see illustrations)**.

9 The alternator adjuster link and mounting bracket can be unbolted from the cylinder block/crankcase if required.

10 If the alternator is to be renewed, the pulley must be transferred to the new unit. Clamp the pulley firmly in a vice with padded jaws and unscrew the pulley nut, taking care not to damage the pulley. Withdraw the pulley. On reassembly, tighten the pulley nut to its specified torque wrench setting.

Refitting

11 Refitting is the reverse of the removal procedure, noting the following points.

a) Tighten the alternator clamp and pivot bolts loosely, then refit the drivebelt and adjust it before tightening the bolts to their specified torque wrench settings.

b) Connect the alternator wiring and refit the cover (where fitted).

c) Fit the oil filter.

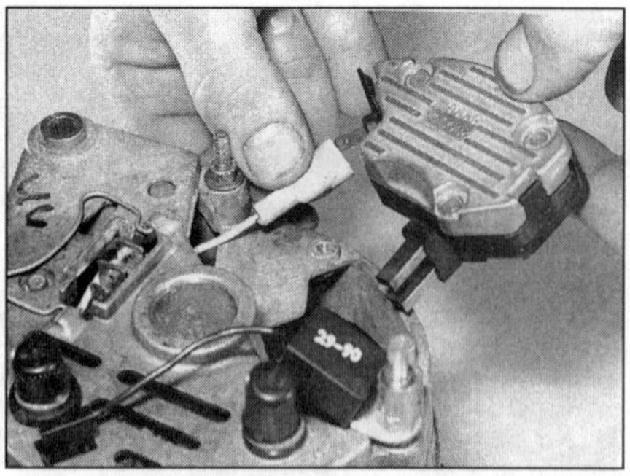

8.2 Disconnecting wire to release voltage regulator/brushbox from alternator

7.8a Removing alternator pivot bolts (one arrowed) . . .

d) Lower the engine/transmission and refit the mounting through-bolt and nut, tightening them to their specified torque wrench settings.

e) Check the engine oil level and top-up if necessary.

8 Alternator - brush and voltage regulator renewal

Note: *The vast majority of actual alternator faults are due to the voltage regulator or to the brushes. If the renewal of either of these assemblies does not cure the fault, the advice of an expert should be sought as to the best approach. For most owners the best course of action will be to renew the alternator as a complete unit. In many cases overhaul will not be viable on economic grounds alone.*

1 Whilst it is physically possible to remove the voltage regulator and brushbox assembly with the alternator in place on the car, owners are advised to remove the alternator so that it can be serviced in clean working conditions.

2 Unscrew the three small screws securing the voltage regulator and brushbox assembly to the alternator. Lift off the regulator/brushbox, disconnect the electrical lead and remove the regulator/brushbox from the alternator **(see illustration)**.

3 In most cases the brushes will have wear limit marks in the form of a groove etched along one face of each brush. When these marks are erased by wear, the brushes are worn out **(see illustration)**. If no marks are

8.3 When brushes are worn to the wear limit marks (arrowed) they must be renewed

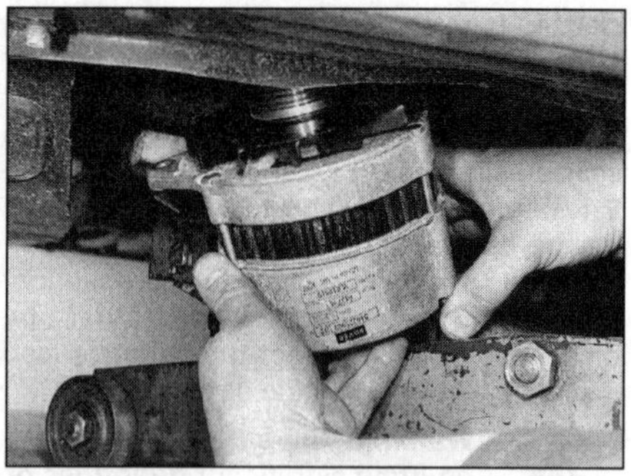

7.8b . . . and removing alternator

provided, measure the protrusion of each brush from the brushbox end to the tip of the brush. No dimension is given by Rover but as a rough guide 5 mm should be regarded as a minimum. If either brush is worn to or below this amount, renew the voltage regulator and brushbox assembly. If the brushes are still serviceable, clean them with a solvent-moistened cloth. Check that the brush spring pressure is equal for both brushes and holds the brushes securely against the slip rings. If in doubt about the condition of the brushes and springs, compare them with new components.

4 Clean the slip rings with a solvent-moistened cloth, then check for signs of scoring, burning or severe pitting. If worn or damaged, the slip rings should be attended to by an auto-electrician.

5 Refitting is the reverse of the removal procedure.

9 Starting system - testing

1 If the starter motor fails to operate when the switch is operated, the causes may be:

a) The battery is faulty.

b) One of the electrical connections between the switch, solenoid, battery and starter motor is failing to pass the necessary current from the battery through the starter to earth.

c) The solenoid is faulty.

d) The starter motor is mechanically or electrically defective.

2 To check the battery, switch on the headlamps. If they dim after a few seconds the battery is discharged. Recharge or renew the battery. If the lamps glow brightly, operate the ignition switch and see what happens to the lamps. If they dim then you know that power is reaching the starter motor, therefore the starter motor must be removed and renewed or overhauled to cure the fault. If the lamps stay bright (and no clicking sound can be heard from the solenoid) there is a fault in the circuit or solenoid, see below. If the starter turns slowly when switched on, but the battery is in good condition, then either the starter must be faulty or there is considerable resistance in the circuit.

3 If the circuit is suspected, disconnect the battery terminals (including the earth connection to the body), the starter/solenoid wiring and the engine/transmission earth lead. Thoroughly clean their connections and refit them, then use a meter or test lamp to check that full battery voltage is available at the solenoid terminal of the battery positive lead and that the earth is sound. Smear petroleum jelly around the battery terminals to prevent corrosion. Corroded connections are the most frequent cause of electric system malfunctions.
4 If the battery and all connections are in good condition, check the circuit first by disconnecting the wire from the solenoid blade terminal. Connect a meter or test lamp between the wire end and the terminal and check that the wire is live when the ignition switch is operated. If it is, then the circuit is sound. If not, proceed to paragraph 7.
5 The solenoid contacts can be checked by putting a voltmeter or test lamp across the main cable connection on the starter side of the solenoid and earth. When the switch is operated, there should be a reading or lighted bulb. If there is no reading or lighted bulb, the solenoid is faulty and should be renewed.
6 If the circuit and solenoid are proved sound, the fault must be in the starter motor. Remove the motor and check the brushes. If the fault does not lie in the brushes, the motor windings must be faulty. In this event the motor must be renewed, unless an auto-electrical specialist can be found who will overhaul the unit at a cost significantly less than that of a new or exchange starter motor.
7 If the circuit is thought to be faulty, check it as follows whilst referring to the wiring diagrams for details.
8 Disconnect the connector plug from the starter relay or relay module and use a meter or test lamp to check that the white/red wire is live when the ignition switch is operated. If it is not live, then the fault is either in the ignition switch or in the wiring between the switch and the relay. If it is live, then check that the earth connection is sound on the black wire. If the relay-energising wiring is good, proceed to the next check.
9 Using a multimeter set to the resistance function or a battery and bulb test circuit, check that there is continuity between the brown/red wire terminals on the relay connector and the solenoid. Renew or repair the wire if a fault is found. Using a meter or test lamp, check that full battery voltage is available at the brown wire terminal. If not, check the feed wires back through the fusible link to the battery. If the wiring is in good condition the fault must lie in the relay itself; check it by substituting a new one. On models with fuel-injection, note that this means renewing the complete relay module.

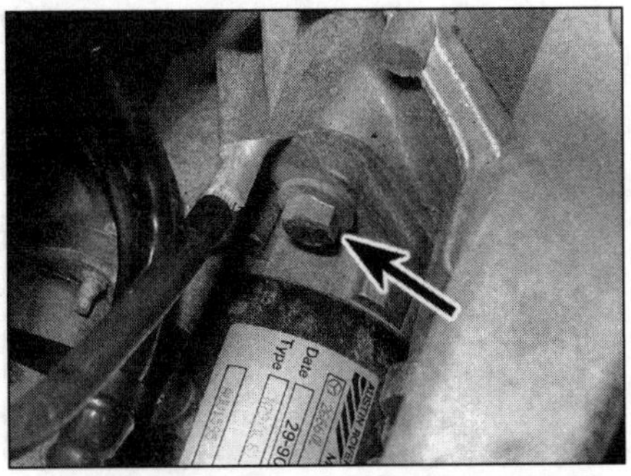

10.3 Starter motor-to-transmission upper bolt (arrowed) also secures engine earth lead

10 Starter motor - removal and refitting

Removal

1 Disconnect the battery negative lead.
2 Disconnect the wiring from the starter motor solenoid. To prevent damage to the solenoid blade terminal, slide up the plastic sleeve and use a small pointed instrument to depress the release tag before pulling the wire off the terminal.
3 Unscrew the starter motor-to-transmission upper bolt, disconnecting the engine/transmission earth lead **(see illustration)**.
4 Jack up the front of the car and support it securely on axle stands (see "*Jacking and Vehicle Support*").
5 Unbolt the starter motor support bracket (where fitted) from the transmission **(see illustration)**.

10.5 Starter motor support bracket-to-transmission bolts (A) and starter motor-to-transmission lower bolts (B)

6 Remove the two remaining starter motor-to-transmission bolts and withdraw the motor **(see illustration)**.
7 If the motor is to be exchanged or renewed, remove the support bracket (where fitted).

Refitting

8 Refitting is the reverse of the removal procedure; tighten all bolts and nuts to their specified torque wrench settings.

11 Starter motor - brush and solenoid renewal

General

1 Whilst it is physically possible to remove the solenoid and brushes with the starter motor in place on the car, owners are advised to remove the motor so that it can be serviced in clean working conditions.

Brushes

Removal

2 Undo the two screws and remove the cover and gasket from the commutator end bracket, then prise out the C-clip and withdraw any thrustwashers fitted **(see illustration)**.
3 Noting the alignment marks between the end bracket or grommet and the yoke, unscrew the two retaining screws and withdraw the end bracket **(see illustrations)**.

5C

10.6 Removing the starter motor

11.2 Remove the commutator end cover - note the gasket and C-clip (arrowed)

11.3a Note alignment marks between yoke and grommet (arrowed) . . .

11.3b . . . and withdraw commutator end bracket

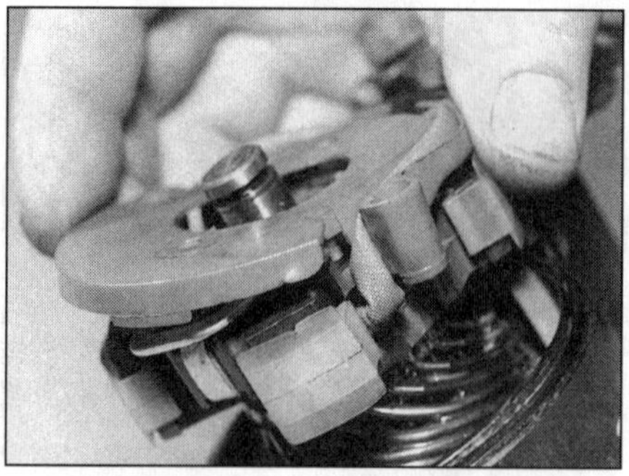

11.4a Removing plastic insulating plate

11.4b Releasing brush springs

11.4c Removing positive brushes and bus bar from brushbox

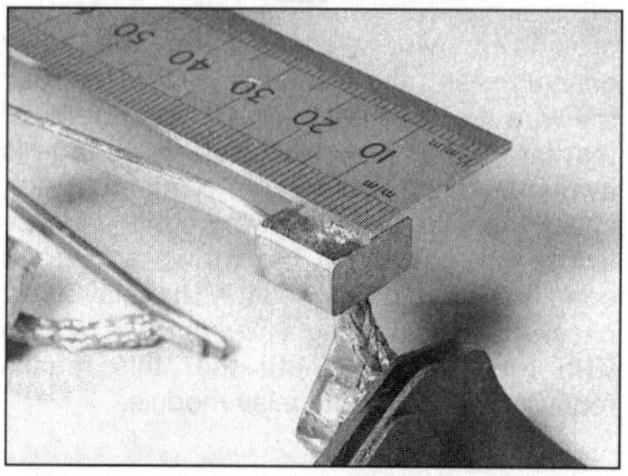

11.5 Measuring length of starter motor brushes

11.10 Unscrew nut to disconnect motor lead from solenoid terminal

4 Release the brush springs and withdraw the negative brushes, then unscrew the nut securing the positive brush lead to the solenoid terminal. Remove the brushbox, withdraw the plastic insulating plate and remove the positive brushes complete with the bus bar **(see illustrations)**.

5 In most cases the brushes will have wear limit marks in the form of a groove etched along one face of each brush; when the brushes are worn down to these marks, they are worn out and must be renewed **(see illustration)**. If no marks are provided, measure the length of each brush. No dimension is given by Rover but as a rough guide 3.5 mm should be regarded as a minimum. If any brush is worn below this amount, renew the brushes as a set. If the brushes are still serviceable, clean them with a solvent-moistened cloth. Check that the brush spring pressure is equal for all brushes and holds the brushes securely against the commutator. If in doubt about the condition of the brushes and springs compare them with new components.

6 Clean the commutator with a solvent-moistened cloth, then check for signs of scoring, burning, excessive wear or severe pitting. If worn or damaged, the commutator should be attended to by an auto-electrician.

Refitting

7 On refitting, place the bus bar on the brushbox, then fit the brushes and insulating plate, insert the negative brushes and fit the clips.

8 Fit the brushbox assembly to the commutator and fit the brush springs. Check that the brushes are free to move in their holders against spring pressure, then refit the commutator end bracket over the springs, engaging it with the grommet, align the marks noted on removal and tighten the retaining screws securely.

9 Refit the thrustwashers and C-clip, the gasket and the cover, tightening the two screws securely. Connect the positive brush lead to the solenoid terminal and tighten the nut securely.

Solenoid

Removal

10 Unscrew the nut, noting the lockwasher(s) and disconnect the motor (positive brush) lead from the solenoid terminal **(see illustration)**.

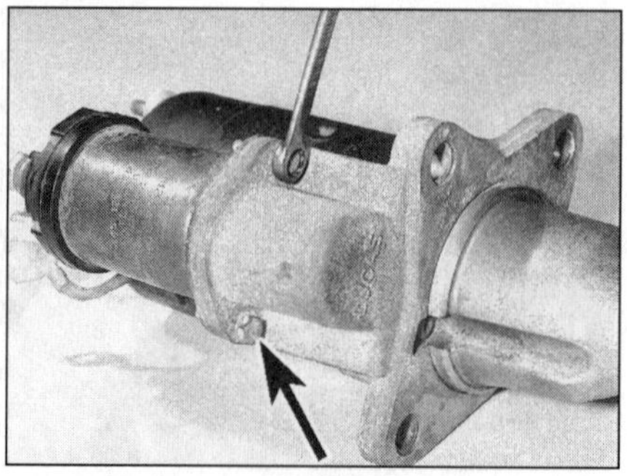

11.11 Unscrewing solenoid retaining bolts (one arrowed)

11 Unscrew the two bolts securing the solenoid to the motor drive end bracket **(see illustration)**.

12 Release the solenoid plunger from the starter engaging lever, then withdraw the solenoid, noting the spring **(see illustration)**.

Refitting

13 Refitting is the reverse of the removal procedure. Clean the solenoid, its plunger and the motor/solenoid mating surfaces carefully and lubricate the plunger/starter engaging lever surfaces with a smear of grease (Rover recommend Shell Alvania).

11.12 Removing solenoid from starter engaging lever

Chapter 6
Clutch

Contents

Degrees of difficulty

Easy, suitable for novice with little experience	**Fairly easy,** suitable for beginner with some experience	**Fairly difficult,** suitable for competent DIY mechanic	**Difficult,** suitable for experienced DIY mechanic	**Very difficult,** suitable for expert DIY or professional

Specifications

Clutch

Type	Single dry plate with diaphragm spring, cable-operated, self-adjusting

Friction plate

Diameter:	
1.1	180 mm
1.4	190 mm
Friction material total thickness - AP plate only:	
1.1 models:	
New plate	8.30 to 8.80 mm
Service limit	6.60 mm
1.4 models:	
New plate	8.00 to 8.40 mm
Service limit	6.30 mm
Rivet depth - distance from friction material surface to rivet heads:	
AP:	
New plate	1.3 mm minimum
Service limit	0.2 mm
Valeo:	
New plate	0.9 mm minimum
Service limit	0.1 mm
Maximum run-out - at outer edge of friction material:	
AP	1.3 mm
Valeo	1.0 mm

Pressure plate

Diaphragm spring finger maximum clearance:	
AP	0.65 mm
Valeo	1.00 mm
Diaphragm spring finger height above flywheel surface:	
1.1 models:	
AP:	
New plate	27.0 to 33.2 mm
Service limit	38.3 mm
Valeo:	
New plate	30.1 to 32.0 mm
Service limit	37.3 mm
1.4 models:	
AP:	
New plate	27.6 to 33.1 mm
Service limit	39.4 mm
Valeo:	
New plate	29.1 to 32.0 mm
Service limit	35.9 mm
Maximum warpage of machined surface:	
AP	0.08 mm
Valeo	0.20 mm

6

Torque wrench settings	Nm	lbf ft
Pressure plate-to-flywheel bolts	18	13
Release bearing guide sleeve-to-bellhousing bolts	5	4

1 General information and precautions

General information

The clutch comprises a friction plate, a pressure plate assembly, a release bearing and the release mechanism. All of these components are contained in the large cast aluminium alloy bellhousing, sandwiched between the engine and the gearbox. The release mechanism is mechanical, being operated by a cable.

The friction plate is fitted between the engine flywheel and the clutch pressure plate and is allowed to slide on the gearbox input shaft splines. It comprises two circular facings of friction material riveted in position to provide the clutch bearing surface, and a spring-cushioned hub to damp out transmission shocks.

The pressure plate assembly is bolted to the engine flywheel and is located by three dowel pins. It comprises the clutch cover, the diaphragm spring and the pressure plate. When the engine is running, drive is transmitted from the crankshaft via the flywheel and clutch cover to the friction plate (these last three components being clamped securely together by the pressure plate and diaphragm spring) and from the friction plate to the gearbox input shaft.

To interrupt the drive the spring pressure must be relaxed. This is achieved by a sealed release bearing fitted concentrically around the gearbox input shaft. When the driver depresses the clutch pedal, the release bearing is pressed against the fingers at the centre of the diaphragm spring. Since the spring is held by rivets between two annular fulcrum rings the pressure at its centre causes it to deform so that it flattens and thus releases the clamping force it exerts, at its periphery, on the pressure plate.

Depressing the clutch pedal pulls the control cable inner wire and this in turn rotates the release fork by acting on the lever at the fork's upper end, above the bellhousing. The fork itself is clipped to the left of the release bearing.

As the friction plate facings wear, the pressure plate moves towards the flywheel which causes the diaphragm spring fingers to push against the release bearing, thus reducing the clearance which must be present in the mechanism. To ensure correct operation, the clutch cable incorporates a spring-loaded self-adjusting mechanism, eliminating the need for periodic adjustments.

Precautions

The clutch friction and pressure plates are manufactured by two suppliers, AP (Automotive Products) and Valeo. Both the friction plate and the pressure plate must come from the same supplier; they are not interchangeable between the two. Apart from the manufacturer's name which may be stamped on either component, AP components can be identified by the part number being applied with white paint, while on Valeo components the part number is applied either with green paint or with black paint with a green spot. All other clutch components are the same, irrespective of supplier.

Dust, created by clutch wear and deposited on the clutch components, may contain asbestos which is a health hazard. DO NOT blow it out with compressed air or inhale any of it. DO NOT use petrol or petroleum-based solvents to clean off the dust. Brake system cleaner or methylated spirit should be used to flush the dust into a suitable receptacle. After the clutch components are wiped clean with rags, dispose of the contaminated rags and cleaner in a sealed, marked container

2 Clutch - operation check

Refer to Chapter 1, Section 10.

3 Clutch cable - removal, inspection and refitting

Removal

1 Working in the engine compartment, compress the cable spring and remove the C-clip, then unhook the cable end fitting from the release fork lever **(see illustrations)**.

2 Release the cable from the bracket bolted to the gearbox and from the bulkhead clip.

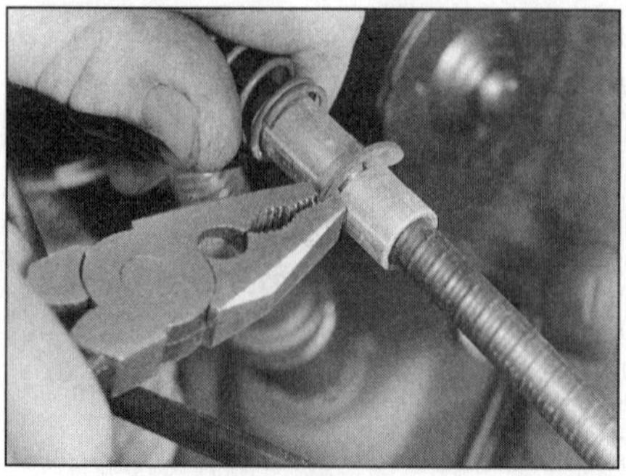

3.1a Compress cable spring and remove C-clip . . .

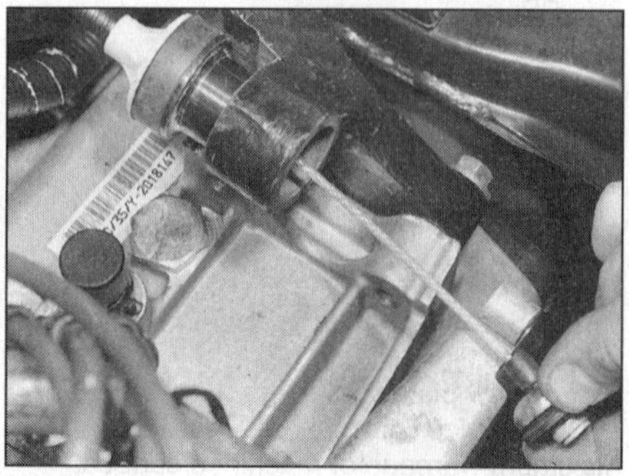

3.1b . . . then unhook cable from release lever and withdraw from bracket

3 Working inside the car, unhook the cable from the pedal **(see illustration).**

4 Return to the engine compartment and withdraw the cable forwards through the bulkhead.

Inspection

5 Examine the cable, looking for worn end fittings or a damaged outer casing and for signs of fraying of the inner wire. Check cable operation. The inner wire should move smoothly and easily through the outer casing, but remember that a cable that appears serviceable when tested off the car may well be much heavier in operation when compressed into its working position. Renew the cable if it shows any signs of excessive wear or of damage.

Refitting

6 Refitting is the reverse of the removal procedure, but apply a thin smear of multi-purpose grease to the cable end fittings. Align the slot in the inner wire's end with the pedal hook and smear petroleum jelly on the cable outer's rubber bush before hooking the cable onto the pedal. Press the bush firmly into the bulkhead so that the steel washer butts firmly against the bulkhead boss.

7 Ensure that the cable is routed correctly, with no sharp bends or kinks, also that it is secured clear of components such as brake pipes, coolant hoses and wiring.

8 When the cable is refitted, depress the pedal several times through its full travel, releasing it fully at each stroke, to enable the self-adjusting mechanism to set itself. Check that the clutch operation is correct.

4 Clutch pedal - removal, inspection and refitting

Removal

1 Disconnect the cable from the pedal.

2 Remove the circlip and withdraw the pedal from its pivot.

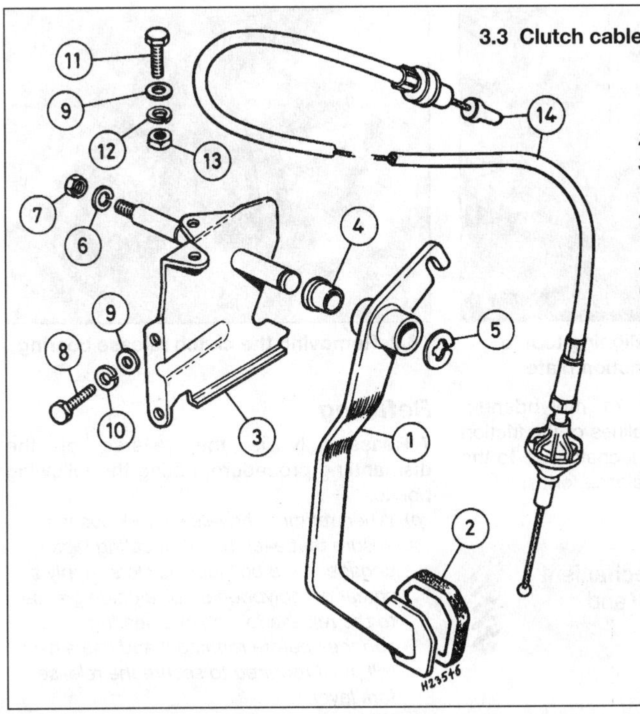

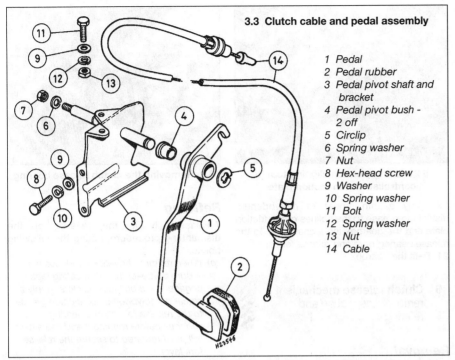

3.3 Clutch cable and pedal assembly

1 Pedal
2 Pedal rubber
3 Pedal pivot shaft and bracket
4 Pedal pivot bush - 2 off
5 Circlip
6 Spring washer
7 Nut
8 Hex-head screw
9 Washer
10 Spring washer
11 Bolt
12 Spring washer
13 Nut
14 Cable

Inspection

3 Carefully clean all components and renew any that are worn or damaged. Check the bearing surfaces of the pivot bushes and shaft with particular care; the bushes can be renewed separately if worn.

Refitting

4 Refitting is the reverse of the removal procedure, but apply a smear of multi-purpose grease to the pedal pivot bearing surfaces.

5 Clutch assembly - removal, inspection and refitting

Removal

1 Unless the complete engine/gearbox unit is to be removed from the car and separated for major overhaul, the clutch can be reached by removing the gearbox.

2 Before disturbing the clutch, use chalk or a felt-tip pen to mark the relationship of the pressure plate assembly to the flywheel.

3 Working in a diagonal sequence, slacken by half a turn at a time the pressure plate bolts until spring pressure is released and the bolts can be unscrewed by hand.

4 Prise the pressure plate assembly off its locating dowels and collect the friction plate, noting which way round the friction plate is fitted **(see illustration)**.

Inspection

Note: *Due to the amount of work necessary to remove and refit clutch components, it is usually considered good practice to renew the clutch friction plate, pressure plate assembly and release bearing as a matched set, even if only one of these is actually worn enough to require renewal.*

5 Remove the clutch assembly.

6 When cleaning clutch components, read first the precautions given in Section 1. Remove dust using a clean, dry cloth whilst working in a well-ventilated atmosphere.

7 Check the friction plate facings for signs of wear, damage or oil contamination. If the friction material is cracked, burnt, scored or damaged, or if it is contaminated with oil or grease (shown by shiny black patches), the friction plate must be renewed.

8 If the depth from the friction material surface to any of the rivets is worn to the service limit specified or less, the friction plate must be renewed.

9 If the friction plate is an AP item, the total thickness of friction material can be measured **(see illustration)** and compared with the Specifications at the beginning of this Chapter. If the plate is excessively worn, or even close to the service limit, it must be renewed.

10 If the friction material is still serviceable, check that the centre boss splines are unworn, that the torsion springs are in good condition and securely fastened and that all the rivets are tightly fastened. If any wear or damage is found, the friction plate must be renewed.

11 If the friction material is fouled with oil, this must be due to an oil leak from the crankshaft left-hand oil seal, from the sump-to-main bearing ladder joint, from the main bearing ladder-to-cylinder block/crankcase joint or from the gearbox input shaft. Renew the seal or repair the joint, as appropriate.

12 Check the pressure plate assembly for obvious signs of wear or damage; shake it to check for loose rivets or worn or damaged fulcrum rings and check that the drive straps securing the pressure plate to the cover do not show signs (such as a deep yellow or blue discoloration) of overheating. If the diaphragm spring is worn or damaged, or if its pressure is in any way suspect, the pressure plate assembly should be renewed.

13 To check the condition of the diaphragm spring, place a circular piece of flat plate across the tips of the spring fingers and use feeler blades to measure the clearance between each finger's tip and the plate. If any finger is distorted so that the clearance between its tip and the plate is at the specified service limit or greater, the pressure plate must be renewed.

14 To check the condition of the complete pressure plate assembly, first check that the friction plate is within tolerances, then refit the clutch assembly to the flywheel. Measure the height of each diaphragm spring finger from the flywheel's machined bearing surface. If any finger's height is at the service limit specified or greater, the pressure plate assembly must be renewed.

15 Examine the machined bearing surfaces of the pressure plate and of the flywheel; they should be clean, completely flat and free from scratches or scoring. If either is discoloured from excessive heat or shows signs of cracks it should be renewed, although minor damage

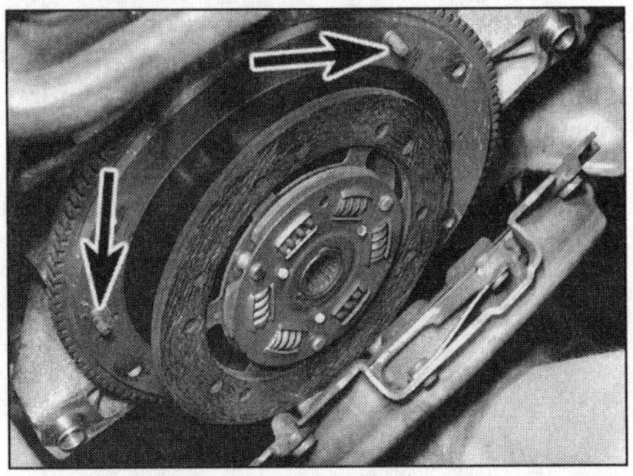

5.4 Note locating dowels (two arrowed) and which way round friction plate is fitted on removing clutch components

5.9 Measuring friction plate total thickness

6

5.18 Check friction plate for markings on refitting - this side must be refitted next to the flywheel

of this nature can sometimes be polished away using emery paper. Use a straight-edge, placed across the pressure plate surface at four different points, and feeler blades to check the pressure plate surface, comparing any warpage found with the specified service limit.

16 Inspect the release bearing.

Refitting

17 On reassembly, ensure that the bearing surfaces of the flywheel and pressure plate are completely clean, smooth and free from oil or grease. Use solvent to remove any protective grease from new components.

18 Fit the friction plate so that the longer part of its central splined boss is towards the flywheel and so that its spring hub assembly faces away from the flywheel; there may also be a marking showing which way round the plate is to be refitted **(see illustration)**.

19 Refit the pressure plate assembly, aligning the marks made on dismantling (if the original pressure plate is re-used) and locating the pressure plate on its three locating dowels. Fit the pressure plate bolts, but tighten them only finger-tight so that the friction plate can still be moved.

20 The friction plate must now be centralised so that when the gearbox is refitted its input shaft will pass through the splines at the centre of the friction plate.

21 Centralisation can be achieved by passing a screwdriver or other long bar through the friction plate and into the hole in the crankshaft. The friction plate can then be moved around until it is centred on the crankshaft hole. Alternatively, a clutch aligning tool **(see illustration)** can be used to eliminate the guesswork; these can be obtained from most accessory shops or can be made up from a length of metal rod or wooden dowel which fits closely inside the crankshaft hole and has insulating tape wound around it to match the diameter of the friction plate splined hole.

22 When the friction plate is centralised, tighten the pressure plate bolts evenly and in a diagonal sequence to the specified torque setting.

5.21 Using a clutch aligning tool to centralise clutch friction plate

23 Apply a thin smear of molybdenum disulphide grease to the splines of the friction plate and the gearbox input shaft, also to the release bearing bore and release fork shaft.

24 Refit the gearbox.

6 Clutch release mechanism - removal, inspection and refitting

Removal

1 Unless the complete engine/gearbox unit is to be removed from the car and separated for major overhaul, the clutch release mechanism can be reached only by removing the gearbox.

2 Disengaging the release bearing from the fork ends, pull the release bearing off its guide sleeve **(see illustration)**.

3 Drive out the roll pin from the top of the release fork using a hammer and a parallel punch, remove the lever and prise up the fork upper bush. Withdraw the release fork and extract the lower bush **(see illustration)**.

Inspection

4 Check the release mechanism, renewing any component which is worn or damaged. Carefully check all bearing surfaces and points of contact.

5 When checking the release bearing itself, note that it is often considered worthwhile to renew it as a matter of course. Check that the contact surface rotates smoothly and easily with no sign of noise or roughness and that the surface itself is smooth and unworn with no signs of cracks, pitting or scoring. If there is any doubt about its condition the bearing must be renewed.

6 Note that when cleaning clutch components, **do not** use solvents on the release bearing; it is packed with grease which may be washed out if care is not taken.

6.2 Removing the clutch release bearing

Refitting

7 Reassembly is the reverse of the dismantling procedure, noting the following points.

a) When refitting the release fork bushes, ensure that each bush's locating tags engage in the bellhousing slots. Apply a smear of molybdenum disulphide grease to the release fork shaft's bearing surfaces before refitting it and use a new roll pin if required to secure the release fork lever.

b) Clean the release bearing bore and guide sleeve, then apply a smear of molybdenum disulphide grease to both bearing surfaces before engaging the bearing on the fork ends and sliding it onto the sleeve.

c) Move the fork up and down to check that it fits correctly against the bearing, then move the release lever to check that the fork and bearing operate properly.

d) Refit the gearbox.

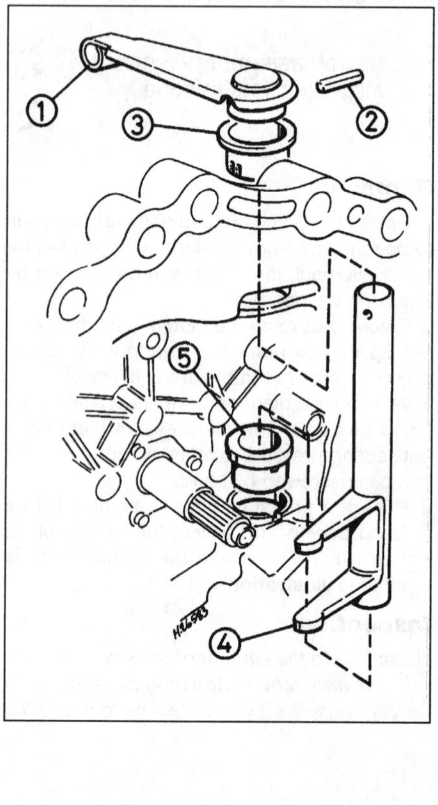

6.3 Release fork and bushes

1 Release lever
2 Roll pin
3 Upper bush
4 Release fork
5 Lower bush

Chapter 7 Part A:
Manual gearbox

Contents

Degrees of difficulty

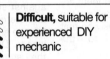

Easy, suitable for novice with little experience	**Fairly easy,** suitable for beginner with some experience	**Fairly difficult,** suitable for competent DIY mechanic	**Difficult,** suitable for experienced DIY mechanic	**Very difficult,** suitable for expert DIY or professional

Specifications

Gearbox

Type	4 or 5 forward speeds and reverse. Synchromesh on all forward speeds
Designation	Rover R65 or R65u

Torque wrench settings

	Nm	lbf ft
General		
Oil filler/level and drain plugs	25	19
Speedometer upper-to-lower cable nut	9	7
Speedometer pinion housing screw	18	13
Gearbox-to-engine bolts	85	63
Flywheel cover plate screws	9	7
Flywheel rear cover plate bolt and nut	38	28
Engine/gearbox left-hand mounting:		
Support member-to-subframe bolts	45	33
Mounting-to-support member bolts	45	33
Mounting-to-bracket bolts	45	33
Bracket-to-gearbox bolts	80	59
Engine/gearbox rear mounting:		
Mounting bracket-to-gearbox 12 mm bolt(s)	85	63
Mounting bracket-to-gearbox 10 mm bolt(s)	45	33
Mounting bracket-to-tie-rod through-bolt	85	63
Tie-rod-to-body bolt and nut	45	33
Overhaul		
Intermediate plate-to-bellhousing:		
Bolts	28	21
Torx screws	60	44
Gearbox casing-to-bellhousing bolts	28	21
Input and output shaft left-hand bearing retainer Torx screws	30	22
Output shaft left-hand end nut	150	111
Left-hand end cover bolts	28	21

1 General information

The vehicle transmission assembly is contained in a cast aluminium alloy casing bolted to the engine's left-hand end and consists of the gearbox and final drive differential, often called a transaxle.

Drive is transmitted from the crankshaft via the clutch to the input shaft, which has a splined extension to accept the clutch friction plate, and rotates in sealed ball-bearings. From the input shaft, drive is transmitted to the output shaft which rotates in a roller bearing at its right-hand end and a sealed ball-bearing at its left-hand end. From the output shaft, the drive is transmitted to the differential crownwheel which rotates with the differential case and planetary gears, thus driving the sun gears and driveshafts. The rotation of the planetary gears on their shaft allows the inner roadwheel to rotate at a slower speed than the outer roadwheel when the car is cornering.

The input and output shafts are arranged side by side, parallel to the crankshaft and driveshafts, so that their gear pinion teeth are in constant mesh. In the neutral position, the output shaft gear pinions rotate freely so that drive cannot be transmitted to the crownwheel.

Gear selection is by a floor-mounted lever acting through a remote control linkage on the selector mechanism. The selector mechanism causes the appropriate selector fork to move its respective synchro-sleeve along the shaft to lock the gear pinion to the synchro-hub. Since the synchro-hubs are splined to the output shaft, this locks the pinion to the shaft so that drive can be transmitted. To ensure that gear changing can be made quickly and quietly a synchro-mesh system is fitted to all forward gears, consisting of baulk rings and spring-loaded fingers as well as the gear pinions and synchro-hubs; the synchro-mesh cones are formed on the mating faces of the baulk rings and gear pinions.

2 Gearbox oil - renewal

Draining

1 This operation is much quicker and more efficient if the car is first taken on a journey of sufficient length to warm the engine/gearbox unit up to normal operating temperature.

2 Park the car on level ground, switch off the ignition and apply the handbrake firmly. For improved access, jack up the front of the car and support it securely on axle stands (see "*Jacking and Vehicle Support*"). Note that the car must be lowered to the ground and level, to ensure accuracy, when refilling and checking the oil level.

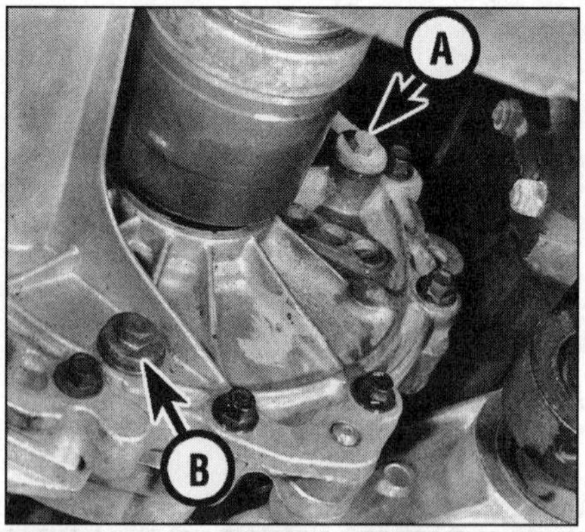

2.3 Gearbox oil filler/level plug (A) and drain plug (B)

3 To avoid rounding-off the corners of the filler/level and drain plug hexagons, use only good quality close-fitting single-hexagon or surface drive spanners or sockets. Unscrew the filler/level plug, then position a container under the drain plug at the rear of the gearbox, below the left-hand driveshaft inner constant velocity joint. Unscrew the plug **(see illustration)**.

4 Allow the oil to drain completely into the container. If the oil is hot, take precautions against scalding. Clean both the filler/level and the drain plugs, being especially careful to wipe any metallic particles off the magnetic inserts. Discard the original sealing washers; they should be renewed whenever they are disturbed.

5 When the oil has finished draining, clean the drain plug threads and those of the gearbox casing, fit a new sealing washer and refit the drain plug, tightening it to the specified torque wrench setting. It the car was raised for the draining operation, now lower it to the ground.

Filling

6 Refilling the gearbox is an extremely awkward operation. Above all, allow plenty of time for the oil level to settle properly before checking it. Note that the car must be parked on flat level ground when checking the oil level.

7 Refill the gearbox with the exact amount of oil. Allow time for the oil to settle.

8 Check the oil level (Chapter 1). If the correct amount was poured into the gearbox and a large amount flows out on checking the level, refit the filler/level plug and take the car on a short journey so that the new oil is distributed fully around the gearbox components, then check the level again.

9 Dispose of the old oil safely.

OIL CARE
FOLLOW THE CODE
OIL BANK LINE
0800 66 33 66

Note: It is antisocial and illegal to dump oil down the drain. To find the location of your local oil recycling bank, call this number free.

3 Gearchange linkage - adjustment

1 If a stiff, sloppy or imprecise gearchange leads you to suspect that a fault exists within the linkage, first dismantle it completely and check it for wear or damage, then reassemble it, applying a smear of the specified grease to all bearing surfaces **(see illustration).**

2 If this does not cure the fault, the car should be examined by an expert, as the fault must lie within the gearbox itself. There is no adjustment as such in the linkage. Note that while the length of the link rods can be altered, this is for initial setting-up only and is not intended to provide a form of compensation for wear.

3 If the link rods have been renewed, or if the length of the originals is incorrect, adjust them as follows.

4 Ensure that the car is parked on level ground, with the ignition switched off, the handbrake firmly applied and neutral selected. Remembering that the selector mechanism is spring-loaded so that the gearchange lever rests naturally between the third and fourth gear positions, have an assistant hold the gearchange lever in its normal position in relation to the front seats.

5 Working in (or under) the engine compartment, slacken the locknut at each end of the rod to be adjusted; if not already done, disconnect the rod(s) from the gearbox selector levers.

6 Check that the selector lever concerned is in its neutral position, with no signs of free play or damage, then hold the rod end socket over the lever ball and prevent the socket from rotating while turning the rod itself to alter its length by screwing it in or out of its end sockets.

7 When the rod's length is correct, check that the same amount of thread is visible at each end before tightening the locknuts securely; be careful not to alter the position of either socket when tightening the locknuts.

8 Connect the link rod(s) to the selector lever(s) and check that all gears can be selected, with the gearchange lever returning properly to its correct at-rest position.

4 Gearchange linkage - removal, overhaul and refitting

Removal

1 Park the car on level ground, switch off the ignition, check that the gearbox is in neutral and apply the handbrake firmly. Jack up the front of the car and support it securely on axle stands (see "*Jacking and Vehicle Support*").

2 Although not strictly necessary, work is a great deal easier if the exhaust front pipe is first removed.

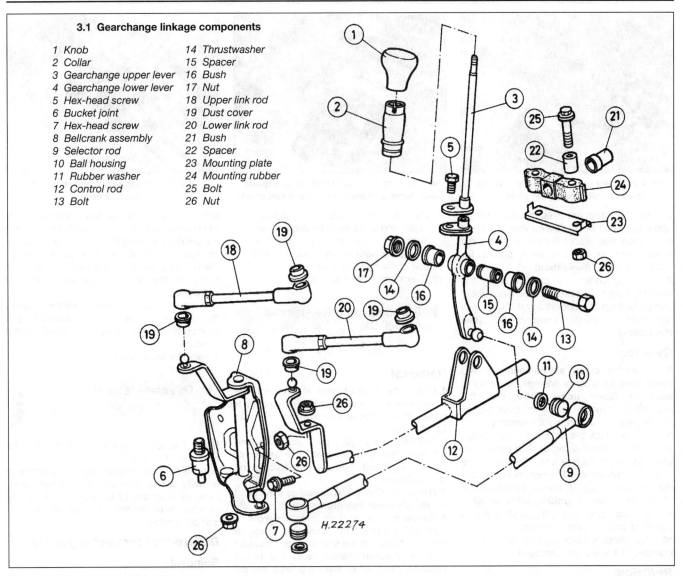

3.1 Gearchange linkage components

1 Knob	*14 Thrustwasher*
2 Collar	*15 Spacer*
3 Gearchange upper lever	*16 Bush*
4 Gearchange lower lever	*17 Nut*
5 Hex-head screw	*18 Upper link rod*
6 Bucket joint	*19 Dust cover*
7 Hex-head screw	*20 Lower link rod*
8 Bellcrank assembly	*21 Bush*
9 Selector rod	*22 Spacer*
10 Ball housing	*23 Mounting plate*
11 Rubber washer	*24 Mounting rubber*
12 Control rod	*25 Bolt*
13 Bolt	*26 Nut*

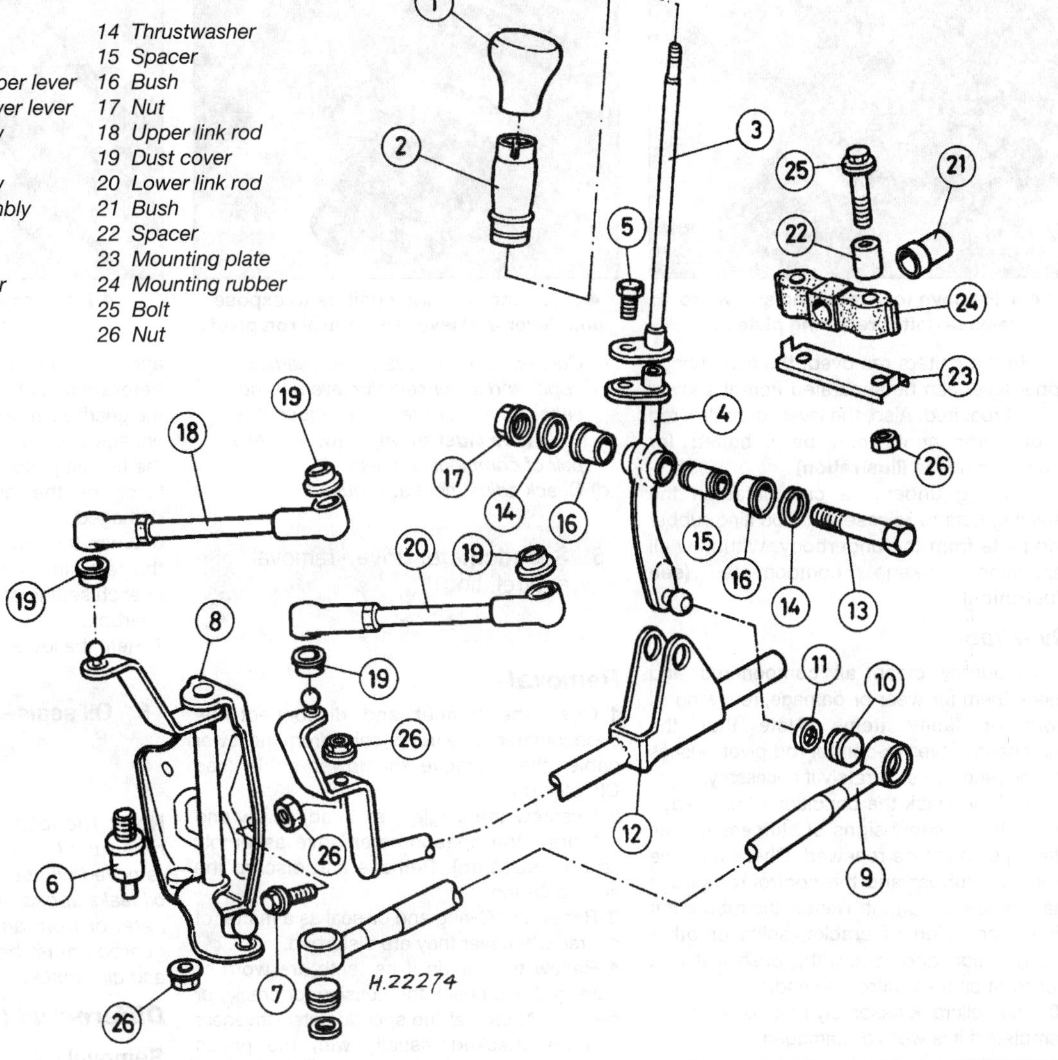

3 Disconnect the link rods from the gearbox upper and lower selector levers using either Rover service tool Number 18G 1592 **(see illustration)** or a fabricated copy of it, or (with care) a pair of needle-nosed pliers.

4 Unscrewing the nuts and/or releasing the balljoints as necessary, disconnect the gearchange control and selector rods from the bellcrank assembly. The assembly can now be unbolted from the suspension front subframe if required **(see illustrations)**.

5 Move inside the car. Although not strictly necessary, work is a great deal easier if the cassette storage holder is removed first. Unscrew the gearchange knob and collar, then remove the four screws and withdraw the gearchange lever outer gaiter, its retaining plate and the inner gaiter **(see illustration)**.

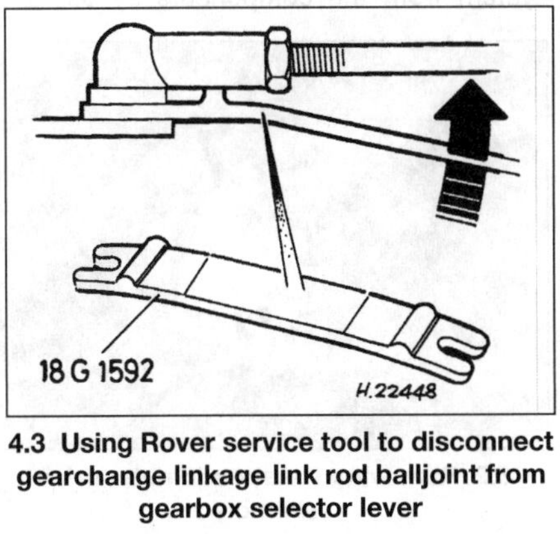

4.3 Using Rover service tool to disconnect gearchange linkage link rod balljoint from gearbox selector lever

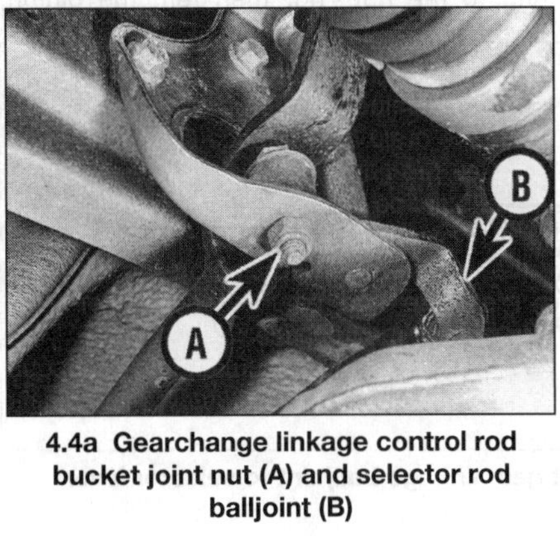

4.4a Gearchange linkage control rod bucket joint nut (A) and selector rod balljoint (B)

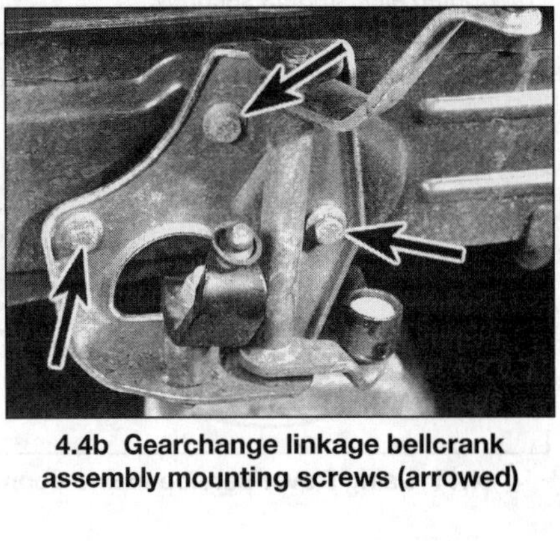

4.4b Gearchange linkage bellcrank assembly mounting screws (arrowed)

4.5 Remove four retaining screws to release gaiter retaining plate . . .

4.6 . . . and withdraw gaiters to expose gear lever and lever-to-control rod pivot

4.7 Gearchange linkage rear end components

6 With the gaiters removed, the gearchange upper lever can be separated from the lower lever, if required. Also, the lever-to-control rod pivot components can be unbolted for examination **(see illustration)**.

7 Returning under the car, unfasten the retaining nuts to release the mounting rubber and plate from the underbody. Withdraw all remaining linkage components **(see illustration)**.

Overhaul

8 Thoroughly clean all components and check them for wear or damage, renewing all worn or faulty items. Note that the gearchange lever-to-control rod pivot bushes can be renewed separately if necessary.

9 Carefully check the condition of all linkage joints. If any show signs of stiffness or free play, they must be renewed. Check also the mounting rubber and the control rods bush that passes through it. Renew the rubber if it shows any sign of cracks, splits or other deterioration and renew the bush if it is a sloppy fit on the control rod end.

10 The bellcrank assembly must be renewed complete if it is worn or damaged.

Refitting

11 Refitting is the reverse of the removal procedure, noting the following points.

a) *Apply a smear of the specified grease to all pivots and bearing surfaces. Pack the gearchange lever-to-control rod pivot with grease.*
b) *Tighten all fasteners securely.*
c) *Connect the link rods to the gearbox upper and lower selector levers using either Rover service tool Number 18G 1594* ***(see illustration)*** *or (with care) a pair of combination pliers.*
d) *Check adjustment as required.*

5 Speedometer drive - removal and refitting

Removal

1 Open the bonnet and disconnect the speedometer drive upper cable from the lower cable, then remove the lower cable (see Chapter 12).

2 Unscrew the single (hex-head) screw and withdraw the speedometer drive assembly **(see illustration)**. Remove and discard the sealing O-ring.

3 Renew the O-ring and oil seal as a matter of course whenever they are disturbed.

4 Renew the pinion if its teeth are worn or damaged and check the housing for cracks or damage. Note that the speedometer drivegear can be checked visually with the pinion assembly removed by shining a torch into the aperture. If any of the gear teeth are damaged, the gearbox must be removed from the car and dismantled so that the gear can be renewed (it is pressed onto the differential case).

Refitting

5 On reassembly, fit the new oil seal and O-ring to the housing, then refit the pinion, applying a smear of grease to all components before installation. Insert the assembly into the gearbox, rotating the pinion until it is felt to engage the teeth of the drivegear, then press the housing into place. **Do not** use excessive force or the drive components may be damaged.

6 When the drive is correctly refitted, tighten the retaining screw to the specified torque wrench setting and connect the cable(s) to the gearbox.

7 Refit the lower cable.

6 Oil seals - renewal

Note: *The following text describes only the renewal of those oil seals which can be removed without dismantling the gearbox. If oil leaks appear from any seal not mentioned here, or from any of the joint surfaces, the gearbox must be removed from the vehicle and dismantled.*

Differential (driveshaft) seals

Removal

1 Jack up the front of the car and support it securely on axle stands (see "*Jacking and Vehicle Support*"), then remove the appropriate roadwheel.

2 Drain the gearbox oil.

3 Remove the underwing shield.

4 Relieve the pressure of the Hydragas system from the components by using a

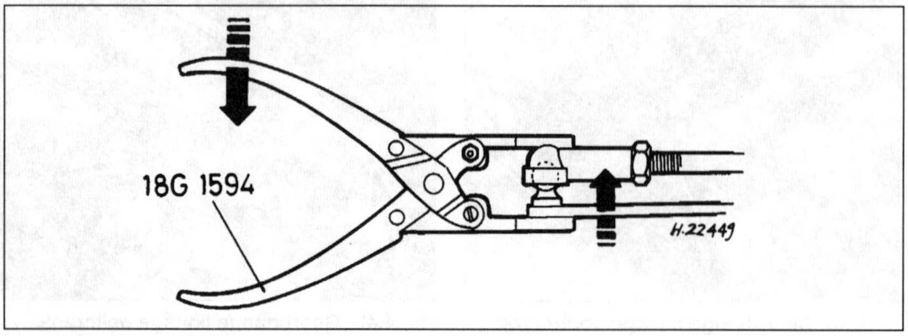

4.11 Using Rover service tool to connect gear linkage balljoint to selector lever

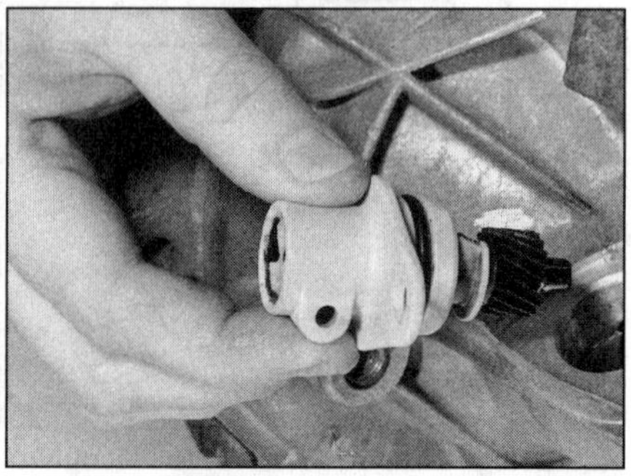

5.2 Removing the speedometer drive assembly

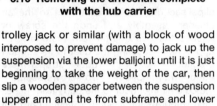

6.10 Removing the driveshaft complete with the hub carrier

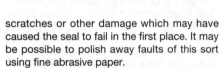

6.11 Prising out a driveshaft oil seal

6.12 Fitting a new driveshaft oil seal

trolley jack or similar (with a block of wood interposed to prevent damage) to jack up the suspension via the lower balljoint until it is just beginning to take the weight of the car, then slip a wooden spacer between the suspension upper arm and the front subframe and lower the jack.

5 Unscrew the brake caliper mounting bolts, remove the caliper from the hub carrier and slip a clean spacer (of the same thickness as the brake disc) between the pads, then secure the caliper clear of the working area without stretching or kinking the brake flexible hose.

6 Disconnect the track rod balljoint from the hub carrier steering arm.

7 Disconnect the suspension upper balljoint from the upper arm and discard the lockwasher.

8 Unscrew the nut and completely remove the pinch-bolt, then disconnect the suspension lower balljoint from the hub carrier.

9 Use a suitable lever to prise out the driveshaft until the circlip compresses into its groove and is released from the differential sun gear.

10 Withdraw the driveshaft assembly complete with the hub carrier **(see illustration)**. Check the circlip at the driveshaft's inboard end; renew it if there is any doubt about its condition. To prevent the risk of the sun gear falling down inside the gearbox, insert a clean metal rod or wooden dowel of the same diameter as the driveshaft into the aperture until the gear is securely supported.

11 Prise out the seal, taking care not to scratch the seal housing **(see illustration)**. If difficulty is experienced, use an internally-expanding claw-type puller to extract the seal.

Refitting

12 Dip the new seal in clean oil, fit it to the gearbox aperture and drive it squarely into place until it seats on its locating shoulder by using a piece of tubing (such as a socket) which bears only on the seal's hard outer edge as a drift **(see illustration)**.

13 Before refitting the driveshaft check its seal rubbing surface for signs of burrs, scratches or other damage which may have caused the seal to fail in the first place. It may be possible to polish away faults of this sort using fine abrasive paper.

14 Thoroughly clean the driveshaft and the aperture in the gearbox to prevent the entry of dirt during reassembly. Apply a thin film of grease to the oil seal lips and to the driveshaft shoulder.

15 Ensure that the circlip fitted to the inboard end of each driveshaft is in good condition and is located securely in its groove. Remove the sun gear support.

16 Taking care not to damage the oil seal lips, insert the driveshaft into the gearbox and engage its splines with those of the sun gear. Press the driveshaft firmly into place until the circlip engages correctly behind (inboard of) the sun gear. If it is necessary to use tools to tap the driveshaft into place, be very careful not to damage the rubber gaiter.

17 Check that the circlip is properly engaged by grasping the inner joint body firmly and trying to pull the driveshaft out of the sun gear.

18 Refit the lower balljoint to the hub carrier, tightening the pinch-bolt and nut to the specified torque wrench setting.

19 Refit the upper balljoint to the suspension upper arm, fit a new lockwasher and tighten the balljoint-to-upper arm nut to the specified torque wrench setting. Secure the nut by bending the washer tab up against one of its flats.

20 Connect the track rod balljoint to the hub carrier steering arm and tighten the balljoint nut to the specified torque wrench setting.

21 Refit the brake caliper, tightening its bolts to the specified torque wrench setting.

22 Jack up the suspension, remove the spacer and lower the suspension again, then refit the underwing shield and the roadwheel.

23 Refill the gearbox with oil and check the level, removing any spilt oil.

Input shaft (clutch) seal

Note: *On later gearboxes, the clutch release bearing guide sleeve and the input shaft oil seal are an assembly and must be renewed as one unit*

Removal

24 Remove the gearbox from the vehicle and remove the clutch release fork.

25 Unbolt the clutch release bearing guide sleeve and remove it, with the oil seal, from the bellhousing. Discard the bolts, they must be renewed whenever disturbed. Clean any locking material from the bellhousing threads using Loctite Chisel and a suitable tap, then degrease thoroughly.

Refitting

26 Before fitting a new seal, check the input shaft's seal rubbing surface for signs of burrs, scratches or other damage which may have caused the seal to fail in the first place. It may be possible to polish away faults of this sort using fine abrasive paper. Ensure that the input shaft is clean and greased to protect the seal lips on refitting.

27 Dip the new seal in clean oil and (where separate) fit it to the guide sleeve, then refit the guide sleeve, tightening the **new** bolts to the specified torque wrench setting.

28 Reassemble and lubricate the clutch release mechanism. Wipe off any surplus oil or grease, then refit the gearbox.

Gear selector lower lever seal

Removal

29 Disconnect the gearchange linkage link rod from the gearbox lower selector lever.

30 Using a hammer and a parallel punch, drive out the roll pin securing the lever to its shaft and remove the lever.

31 Prise out the seal, taking care not to scratch the seal housing.

32 Clean and check both housing and shaft for signs of wear or damage which might have caused the seal to fail in the first place.

Refitting

33 Dip the new seal in clean oil and drive it into the housing, using a piece of tubing (such as a socket) which bears only on the seal's hard outer edge as a drift, until it seats on its locating shoulder.

34 Reassemble the gearchange linkage, check the gearbox oil level and top-up if necessary then wash off any spilt oil.

7 Reversing lamp switch - testing, removal and refitting

Testing

1 The reversing lamp circuit is controlled by a plunger-type switch that is screwed into the gearbox casing **(see illustration).**

2 To test the switch, disconnect its wires and use a multimeter (set to the resistance function) or a battery and bulb test circuit to check that there is continuity between the switch terminals only when reverse gear is selected. If this is not the case and there are no obvious breaks or other damage to the wires, the switch is faulty and must be renewed.

Removal

3 To remove the switch, disconnect its wires and unscrew it.

Refitting

4 On refitting, apply a smear of sealant to the switch threads and tighten it securely, but do not overtighten it. Re-connect its wires and test the circuit.

8 Gearbox - removal and refitting

Note: *To carry out this task an engine hoist or similar will be required to lift out the gearbox and a second, similar, piece of equipment must be available to take the weight of the engine while it is moved sideways and raised or lowered. A strong trolley jack would be useful in the latter case, provided that a wooden spacer is available to spread the load and prevent the risk of damage to the sump*

Removal

All models

1 Park the car on firm, level ground, apply the handbrake and remove the bonnet. Jack up the front of the vehicle, supporting it securely on axle stands (see "*Jacking and Vehicle Support*").

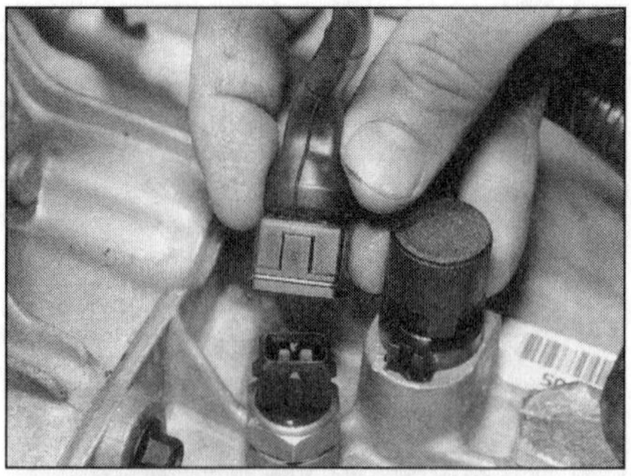

7.1 Disconnecting reversing lamp switch wires

2 Drain the gearbox oil. Clean and refit the drain plug, tightening it to its specified torque wrench setting.

3 Remove the battery and where fitted, the charcoal canister. Remove the battery tray, having first released all electrical leads from the tray retaining clips and released the fusebox from its bracket by depressing its two retaining tags.

Multi-point injected engines

4 Remove the air cleaner assembly. Remove the two nuts which secure the air cleaner support bracket to the wing valance. Remove the bolts securing the support bracket to the battery tray and to the bottom coolant hose clip and then remove the bracket.

Carburettor engines

5 Remove the distributor. Remove its clamp and undo the two screws securing the cold air duct to the body front panel, then withdraw it.

6 Detach the vacuum hose from the air temperature control diaphragm **(see illustration).**

7 Remove the air cleaner inlet hose retaining clip. Remove the screws and washers securing the inlet hose adapter to the vehicle body behind the left-hand headlamp and withdraw the hose assembly.

All fuel-injected engines

8 Disconnect the HT coil lead from the distributor cap.

Single-point injected engines

9 Disconnect the vacuum pipe from the inlet air temperature control valve, release the two

8.6 Detaching the vacuum hose from the air temperature control diaphragm

clips securing the air inlet duct to the air cleaner assembly and undo the screw or release the two quarter-turn fasteners, as appropriate, securing the duct to its support bracket. Unfasten the rubber strap (where fitted) and remove the two screws securing the cold air inlet duct to the body front panel, then withdraw the assembly, taking care not to lose the hot air inlet connector hose.

All models

10 Disconnect the clutch cable and secure it clear of the engine/gearbox unit.

11 Disconnect the reversing lamp switch.

12 Disconnect the speedometer drive upper cable from the lower cable, release the upper cable from any securing clips and secure it clear of the engine/gearbox unit.

13 Disconnect the gearchange linkage link rods from the gearbox upper and lower selector levers.

14 Either remove the engine/gearbox unit rear mounting or unbolt the mounting bracket from the gearbox and slacken the tie-rod-to-body bolt and nut so that the mounting can be swung down clear of the gearbox.

15 Remove the starter motor.

16 Unbolt the flywheel front, lower and rear cover plates, disconnecting the clips (where fitted) securing the engine wiring harness **(see illustrations).**

17 Dismantle the front suspension and remove both driveshafts (see Chapter 8 for full details, but for simplicity follow the abbreviated procedure given in Section 6, paragraphs 1 to 10).

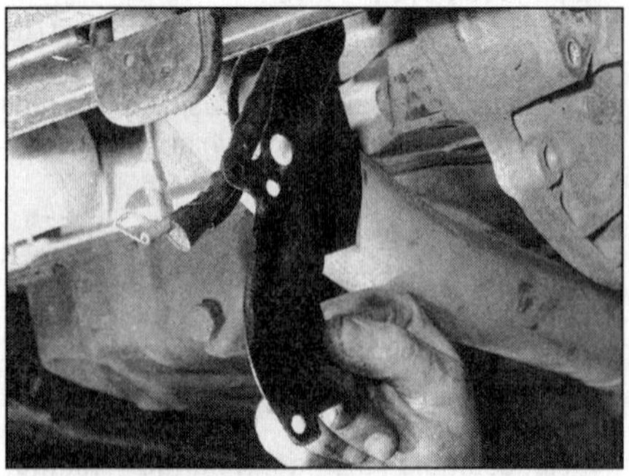

8.16a Removing the flywheel front cover plate

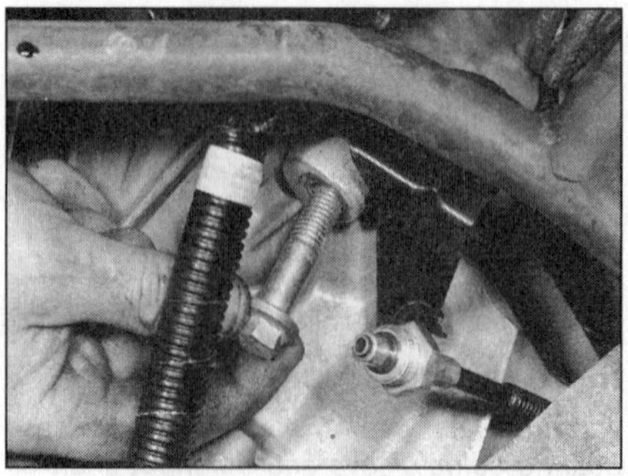

8.16b Remove large bolt and nut as well as mounting screws . . .

8.16c . . . to release flywheel rear cover plate

8.18 Attach lifting equipment using lifting eye provided in casing flange

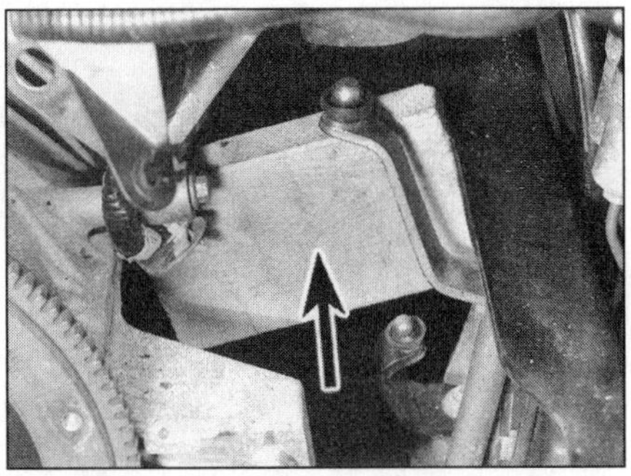

8.20 Lever engine forwards and use wooden block (arrowed) to hold it in place

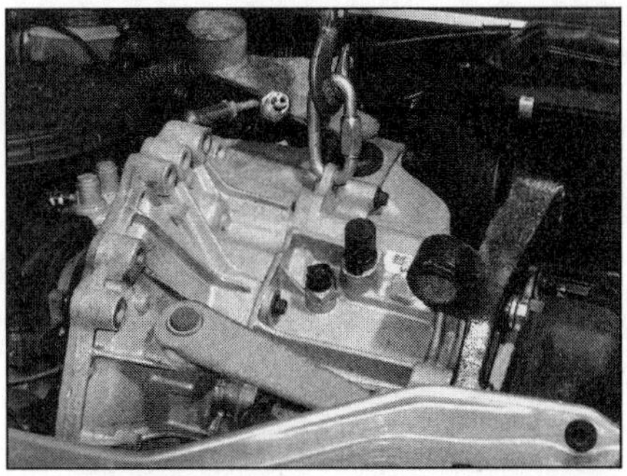

8.23 Lifting the gearbox out of the car

18 Attaching the lifting equipment to the lifting eye formed in the gearbox casing flange **(see illustration)**, take the weight of the gearbox and support the weight of the engine using a trolley jack, with a wooden spacer to prevent damage to the sump.

19 Release the engine wiring harness from the clip on the engine/gearbox unit left-hand mounting, unbolt the mounting bracket from the mounting, then unbolt the support member from the front subframe. Remove the support member.

20 Lever forwards the engine/gearbox unit by approximately 25 mm and insert a wooden block (measuring 150 x 80 mm) lengthways between the front subframe and the rear of the cylinder block/crankcase to hold it forwards **(see illustration)**.

21 Make a final check that all components have been removed or disconnected that will prevent the removal of the gearbox from the car and ensure that components such as the gearchange linkage link rods are secured so that they cannot be damaged on removal.

22 Unscrew the four bolts securing the gearbox to the engine (noting that the top two are shorter) and gently prise the gearbox off the two locating dowels (at the front and rear of the main bearing ladder). Move the gearbox squarely away from the engine, ensuring that the clutch components are not damaged.

23 Lift the gearbox out of the car, ensuring that nothing is trapped or damaged **(see illustration)**.

24 Whenever the gearbox is removed, check the mountings and renew them if necessary. Overhaul the clutch components. If the gearbox is to be overhauled or renewed, unbolt the mounting bracket and remove the clutch release mechanism and speedometer drive assembly.

Refitting

25 Check that the mating surfaces of the engine and gearbox are completely clean and dry, that all clutch components are in good condition and correctly installed and that the locating dowels are clean and lubricated with a smear of anti-seize compound.

26 Apply a thin smear of molybdenum disulphide grease to the splines of the clutch friction plate and the gearbox input shaft, also to the release fork shaft's bearing surfaces, the release bearing bore and the guide sleeve. Push the release bearing as far towards the gearbox as possible, then hold the release fork's lever in that position by locking it with a spanner applied to the nearest gearbox casing-to-bellhousing bolt head.

27 Offer up the gearbox to the engine and engage the input shaft with the clutch friction plate; ensure that the gearbox is absolutely square to the engine.

28 Push the gearbox into full engagement with the engine, ensuring that it seats correctly on the dowels. If the gearbox proves reluctant to mate with the engine, try swivelling it slightly, or have an assistant rotate the crankshaft via the alternator drive pulley bolt, until the input shaft splines engage with those of the friction plate.

29 Once the gearbox is fully engaged, refit the bolts securing it to the engine, remove the wooden block and refit the engine/gearbox unit mountings; tighten all nuts and bolts to their specified torque wrench settings. Unlock the release fork's lever.

30 The remainder of the refitting procedure is the reverse of removal, noting the following points.

a) *Tighten all nuts and bolts to their specified torque wrench settings.*
b) *Ensuring that they are clean and greased, refit the driveshafts.*
c) *For full details of refitting all ancillary components, refer to the relevant Sections of this Chapter or of the other Chapters mentioned during removal.*
d) *On carburettor engines, check the ignition timing.*

9 Gearbox - overhaul

Overhauling a gearbox is a difficult and involved job for the DIY home mechanic. In addition to dismantling and reassembling many small parts, clearances must be precisely measured and, if necessary, changed by selecting shims and spacers. Gearbox internal components are also often difficult to obtain and in many instances extremely expensive. Because of this, if the gearbox develops a fault or becomes noisy, the best course of action is to have the unit overhauled by a specialist or to obtain an exchange reconditioned unit.

Nevertheless, it is not impossible for the more experienced mechanic to overhaul a gearbox provided that the special tools are available and the job is done in a deliberate step-by-step manner so that nothing is overlooked.

The tools necessary for a typical overhaul include internal and external circlip pliers, bearing pullers, a slide-hammer, a set of pin punches, a dial test indicator and possibly an hydraulic press. In addition, a large sturdy workbench and a vice will be required.

All work should be done in conditions of extreme cleanliness. When dismantling, make careful notes of how each component is fitted. This will facilitate accurate and straightforward reassembly.

Before dismantling the gearbox, it will help to have some idea of which component is malfunctioning. Certain problems can be related to specific areas in the gearbox which can in turn make component examination and replacement more straightforward. Refer to the Fault Finding Section of this Manual for more information.

Chapter 7 Part B:
Automatic transmission

Contents

Degrees of difficulty

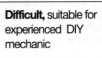

Easy, suitable for novice with little experience	**Fairly easy,** suitable for beginner with some experience	**Fairly difficult,** suitable for competent DIY mechanic	**Difficult,** suitable for experienced DIY mechanic	**Very difficult,** suitable for expert DIY or professional

Specifications

Transmission

Type	Constantly Variable Transmission (CVT)
Designation	VT - 1

Torque wrench settings

	Nm	lbf ft
Fluid cooler union nut	15	11
Fluid pan bolts	10	7
Transmission fluid hose adapters	37	28
Selector lever to cable nut	7	5
Selector shaft nut	15	11
Starter inhibitor/reverse switch	12	9
Dipstick tube retaining bolt	25	18
Primary cover bolts	10	7
Secondary cover bolts	10	7
Flywheel cover plate bolts	8	6
Transmission-to-engine bolts	85	63
Mounting bracket-to-transmission bolts	80	59
Unit mounting bracket-to-engine mounting bolts	45	33
Support member to subframe bolts	45	33
Engine steady bar bracket-to-body bolts	45	33
Engine steady bar bracket-to-transmission bolts	85	63
Fluid drain plug	30	22

1 General information and precautions

General information

The Continuously Variable Transmission (CVT) differs from conventional automatic transmissions in that it has been specifically designed for use with transverse-mounted engines fitted to front wheel drive vehicles and provides an infinite number of gear ratios in a stepless shifting pattern.

The transmission is driven via a torsion damper bolted to the engine flywheel. Power is transmitted to the input shaft, which in turn drives a planet carrier. Depending on forward or reverse gear being selected through one of two multiplate wet clutch assemblies, a primary pulley will rotate and transmit torque to a secondary pulley via a steel belt, thus causing the vehicle to move in the desired direction.

To enable the vehicle to move away in a low gear, the two halves of the primary pulley are parted, thus obliging the belt to run on its smaller diameter and allowing it to run on the larger diameter of the closed secondary pulley. As engine speed increases, hydraulic pressure causes the halves of the primary pulley to close, thereby increasing its effective diameter. As the belt is forced up the increasing diameter of the primary pulley, its increasing tension forces the halves of the secondary pulley to part against spring pressure, thereby increasing the gear ratio. With the primary pulley fully closed and the secondary pulley fully open, the secondary pulley is rotating at 2.5 times that of the primary pulley and this effectively provides an overdrive ratio.

The gear selector control resembles that fitted to conventional automatic transmissions. The control positions are as follows:

P ***(Parking)*** *The transmission is mechanically locked by the engagement of a pawl with the secondary pulley.*

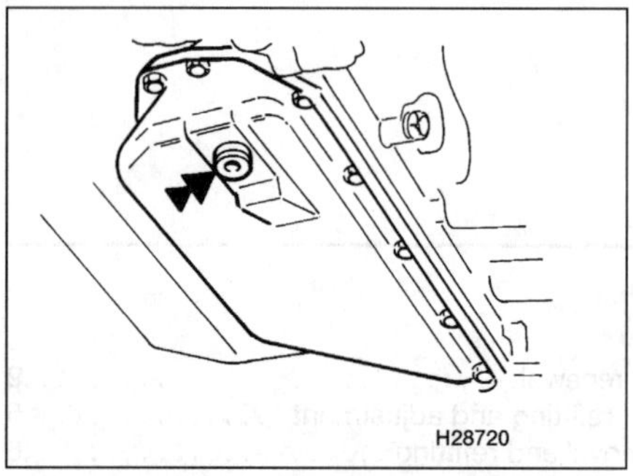

2.4 Transmission fluid drain plug location (arrowed)

***R* (Reverse)** *The reverse clutch is activated and the forward clutch inhibited.*

***N* (Neutral)** *The transmission is in neutral, both forward and reverse clutches being inhibited.*

***D* (Drive)** *Normal driving position, the forward clutch being activated and the reverse clutch inhibited. Transmission ratio is varied automatically to suit prevailing speed and load.*

***L* (Low drive)** *Prevents the transmission moving into high ratios. Provides maximum acceleration and maximum engine braking.*

Due to the complexity of the transmission, any repair or overhaul work must be referred to a Rover dealer or automatic transmission specialist with the necessary equipment for fault diagnosis and repair. The contents of this Chapter are therefore confined to supplying any service information and instructions which can be used by the home mechanic.

Precautions

Observe the following precautions to avoid damage to the automatic transmission:

a) *Do not attempt to start the engine by pushing or towing the car.*

b) *If the car has to be towed for recovery, only tow the car with the front wheels clear of the ground.*

c) *Only engage 'P' when the vehicle is stationary.*

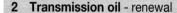

2 Transmission oil - renewal

Draining

1 This operation must be undertaken with the transmission at normal operating temperature. **Note:** *the fluid will be very hot when drained.* Drain the fluid as follows.

2 Park the vehicle on level ground, switch off the ignition and apply the handbrake firmly. Remove the transmission dipstick and jack up the front of the vehicle, supporting it securely on axle stands (see "*Jacking and Vehicle Support*").

3 Position a container of at least 5 litres capacity under the transmission drain plug.

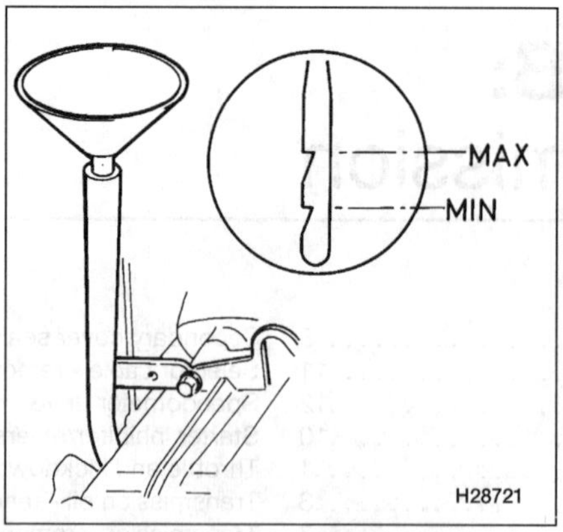

2.8 Transmission dipstick tube and dipstick end markings

4 To avoid rounding-off the corners of the drain plug hexagon, use only a good quality close-fitting spanner or socket. Unscrew the plug **(see illustration)**.

5 Allow the fluid to drain completely into the container, taking precautions against scalding from the hot fluid. Approximately 1 litre of fluid will be retained in the primary and secondary cylinders of the transmission.

6 Clean the plug, being especially careful to wipe any metallic particles off the magnetic insert. Discard the original sealing washer which must be renewed.

7 When the fluid has finished draining, wipe clean the drain plug threads and those of the gearbox casing, fit the new sealing washer and refit the plug, tightening it to the specified torque wrench setting. Lower the vehicle to the ground so that it is level.

Filling

8 Position a funnel securely into the dipstick tube and fill the transmission with the specified type of fluid to the minimum mark on the dipstick, taking care not to overfill and allowing time for the fluid to settle **(see illustration)**.

9 Refit the dipstick and run the engine until the transmission reaches normal operating temperature. Operate the selector lever through the full range of positions three times so that the new fluid is distributed fully around the transmission components. Stop the engine.

10 Recheck the fluid level and if necessary, top it up until the level is maintained between the minimum and maximum marks on the dipstick.

11 Dispose of the used fluid safely; do not pour it down a drain

3 Kickdown cable - removal and refitting

Note: *Rover tool no. 18G 1650 will be required to release the kickdown cable from the transmission casing.*

Removal

1 Park the vehicle on level ground, switch off the ignition and apply the handbrake firmly.

2 Disconnect the battery earth lead and remove the air cleaner assembly

3 Jack up the front of the vehicle, supporting it securely on axle stands (see "*Jacking and Vehicle Support*").

4 Refer to Chapter 5 and remove the starter motor.

5 Refer to the appropriate Section of this Chapter and remove the fluid pan.

6 Go to the throttle end of the cable and loosen the cable adjuster locknuts.

7 Detach the cable inner from the throttle cam and the cable adjuster from its mounting bracket.

8 Locate the valve cam inside the transmission and release the cable inner from it, using a hooked tool fabricated from a length of stiff wire **(see illustration)**.

9 Release the cable outer from the transmission casing, using the recommended tool (Rover tool 18G 1650) **(see illustration)** and withdraw the cable from the vehicle.

Refitting

10 Refitting the kickdown cable is a reversal of the removal procedure, noting the following points:

11 Push the cable outer firmly into the transmission casing to lock it in position and use the hooked tool to locate the cable inner over the valve cam.

12 With the fluid pan and starter motor refitted, lower the vehicle to the ground and refill the transmission with the recommended fluid.

13 Adjust the kickdown and throttle cables as described in the next Section.

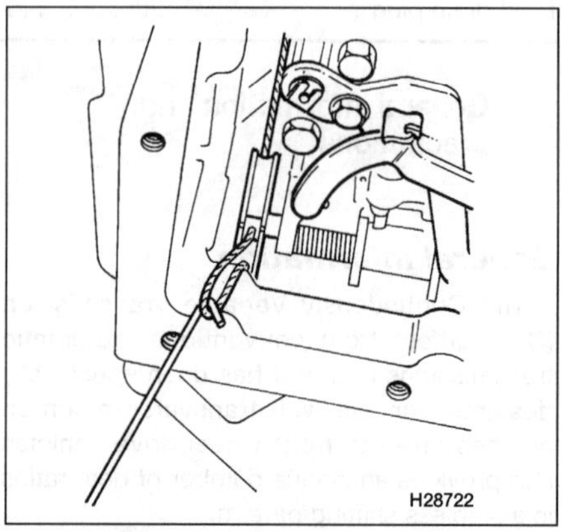

3.8 Use a hooked tool to release the cable from the transmission valve cam

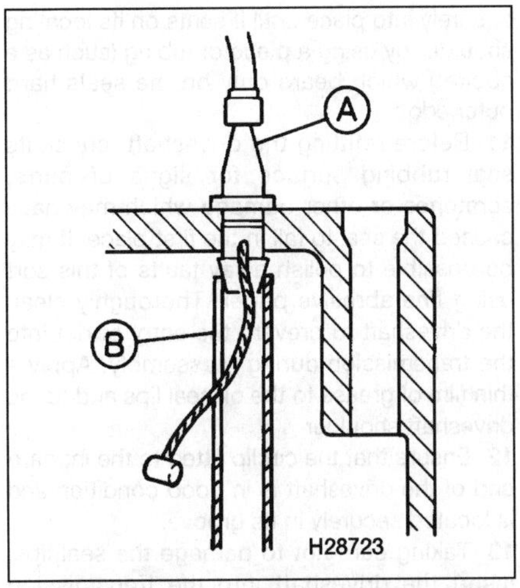

3.9 Releasing the kickdown cable from the transmission casing

A Cable end B Rover tool 18G 1650

4 Throttle and kickdown cables - adjustment

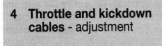

1 Remove the air cleaner assembly.

2 Disconnect the multiplug from the fuel injector unit and turn on the ignition for 5 seconds to ensure that the stepper motor and ECU are referenced. Turn off the ignition.

3 Loosen the throttle cable adjuster locknuts and adjust the cable so that the spigots of the throttle cam are at the position indicated **(see illustration)** and all "lost motion gap" is removed. Lightly retighten the locknuts.

4 Loosen the kickdown cable adjuster locknuts and adjust the cable so that there is a 9.0mm clearance between the cable crimp and adjuster end **(see illustration)**. Lightly retighten the locknuts.

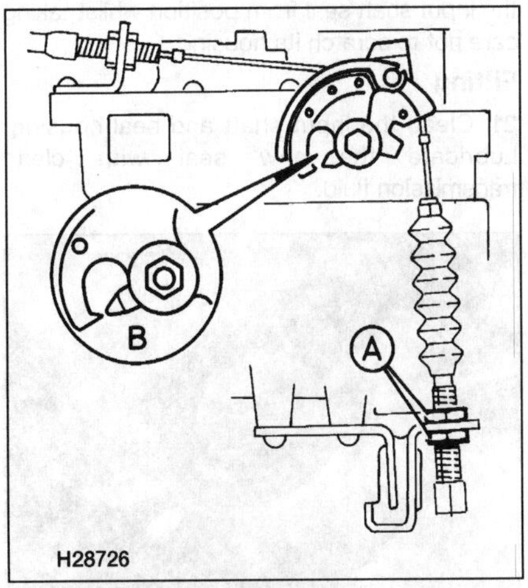

4.6 Throttle cable adjustment

A Cable adjuster locknuts
B Throttle and lost motion lever pointer alignment

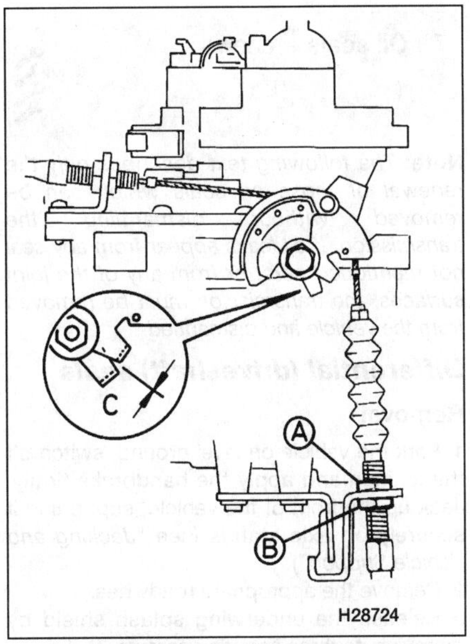

4.3 Throttle cable adjustment

A Cable locknut
B Cable adjuster nut
C Throttle cam spigots

5 Now loosen the throttle cable adjuster locknuts and firmly tighten those of the kickdown cable.

6 Adjust the throttle cable so that the pointers of the throttle lever and lost motion lever are aligned as shown **(see illustration)**. Tighten the cable adjuster locknuts.

7 Reconnect the injector unit multiplug and refit the air cleaner assembly.

5 Selector cable - removal, refitting and adjustment

Removal

1 Park the vehicle on level ground, switch off the ignition and apply the handbrake firmly. Jack up the front of the vehicle, supporting it

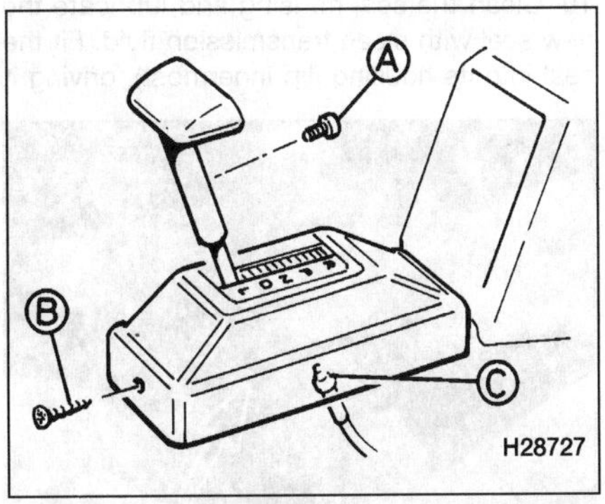

5.2 Selector lever and housing removal

A Lever knob securing screw
B Housing securing screw
C Indicator light

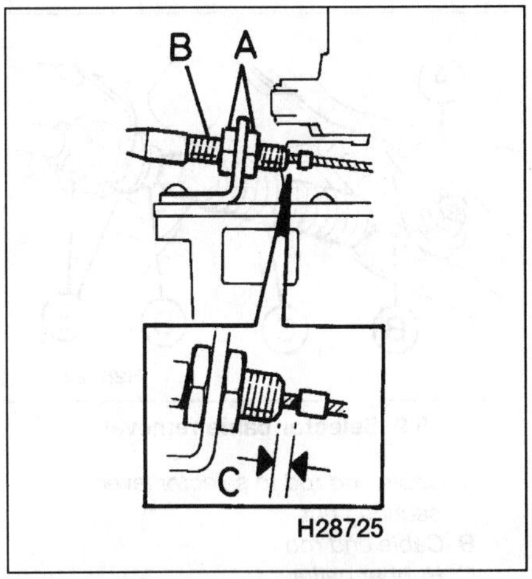

4.4 Kickdown cable adjustment

A Cable adjuster locknuts
B Cable adjuster
C 9.0 mm clearance

securely on axle stands (see "*Jacking and Vehicle Support*").

2 Move the gear selector lever to the "L" position and remove the lever knob securing screw **(see illustration)**. Pull the knob from the lever.

3 Detach the selector lever housing by removing its rear securing screw and then unclipping it from the cassette storage box. Lift the housing carefully and release the indicator light bulb from its housing.

4 Release the cassette storage box by removing its two securing screws.

5 Gain access to the selector cable abutment bracket by lifting the carpet over the cassette storage box retaining bracket.

6 Loosen the selector cable locknut and release the cable from the abutment bracket **(see illustration)**.

7 Release the cable from the selector lever balljoint.

8 Refer to Chapter 4 and remove the heat shield from the catalytic converter.

9 Remove the cable end-rod to selector lever securing nut **(see illustration)** and pull the rod from the lever.

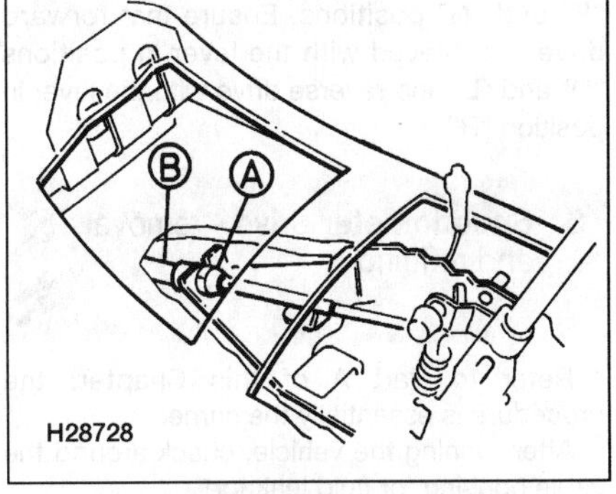

5.6 Selector cable locknut (A) and abutment bracket (B)

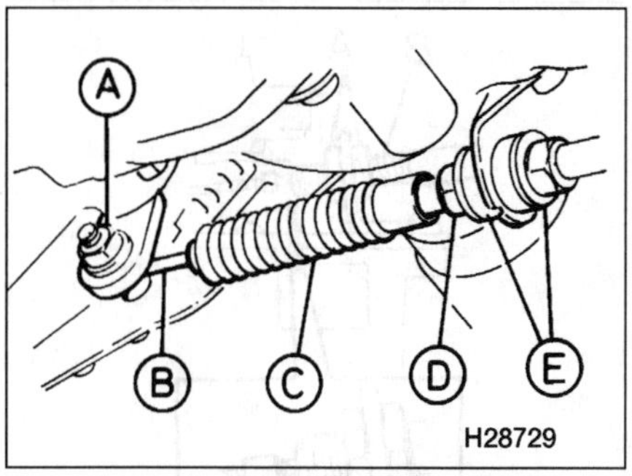

5.9 Selector cable removal

A Cable end rod to selector lever securing nut
B Cable end rod
C Rubber gaiter
D Cable rod locknut
E Anti-vibration rubbers

10 Ease the rubber gaiter back to expose the cable rod locknut and loosen the nut.

11 Separate the anti-vibration rubbers and release the cable from its abutment bracket.

12 Use a screwdriver to prise the cable grommet from the floor of the vehicle and withdraw the cable.

Refitting

13 Refitting the selector cable is a reversal of the removal procedure. When fitted, adjust the cable as follows:

Adjustment

14 With the front of the vehicle jacked up and supported securely on axle stands (see "*Jacking and Vehicle Support*"), move the gear selector lever to the "P" position.

15 Loosen the cable end-rod to selector lever securing nut and move the selector lever to its fully forward position.

16 Check that the "park" mechanism is properly engaged by trying to rotate each front roadwheel in its driving direction.

17 Tighten the cable end-rod to selector lever securing nut to the specified torque loading and lower the vehicle to the ground.

18 Carry out a final check for correct cable adjustment by ensuring that the engine will only start with the gear selector lever in the "P" and "N" positions. Ensure that forward drive is achieved with the lever in positions "D" and "L" and reverse drive with the lever in position "R".

6 **Speedometer drive** - removal and refitting

Refer to Part A of this Chapter; the procedure is essentially the same.

After running the vehicle, check around the cable housing for fluid leakage.

7 **Oil seals** - renewal

Note: *The following text describes only the renewal of those oil seals which can be removed without dismantling the transmission. If oil leaks appear from any seal not mentioned here, or from any of the joint surfaces, the transmission must be removed from the vehicle and dismantled.*

Differential (driveshaft) seals

Removal

1 Park the vehicle on level ground, switch off the ignition and apply the handbrake firmly. Jack up the front of the vehicle, supporting it securely on axle stands (see "*Jacking and Vehicle Support*").

2 Remove the appropriate roadwheel.

3 Release the underwing splash shield by removing its three securing screws.

4 Position a suitable container of at least 5 litres capacity under the appropriate driveshaft to catch fluid spillage.

5 Release the driveshaft from the differential housing by levering them apart.

6 Remove the two brake caliper to hub securing bolts and carefully move the caliper to one side, tying it in position so that no strain is placed on the brake hose.

7 Position a jack beneath the wheel hub and raise the hub to allow a wooden wedge to be fitted between the suspension arm and the subframe. Lower the suspension onto the wedge and remove the jack **(see illustration).**

8 Refer to Chapter 10 and disconnect the track rod balljoint and the upper and lower hub balljoints, allowing the wheelhub and driveshaft assembly to be removed.

9 Clean the transmission casing around the seal location and using a screwdriver, lever the differential seal from position whilst taking care not to scratch its housing **(see illustration).**

Fitting

10 Clean the seal housing and lubricate the new seal with clean transmission fluid. Fit the seal into its housing (lip innermost), driving it squarely into place until it seats on its locating shoulder by using a piece of tubing (such as a socket) which bears only on the seals hard outer edge.

11 Before refitting the driveshaft, check its seal rubbing surface for signs of burrs, scratches or other damage which may have caused the seal to fail in the first place. It may be possible to polish away faults of this sort using fine abrasive paper. Thoroughly clean the driveshaft to prevent the entry of dirt into the transmission during reassembly. Apply a thin film of grease to the oil seal lips and to the driveshaft shoulder.

12 Ensure that the circlip fitted to the inboard end of the driveshaft is in good condition and is located securely in its groove.

13 Taking care not to damage the seal lips, insert the driveshaft into the transmission pressing it firmly into place until the circlip engages. Check that the circlip is properly engaged by grasping the shaft firmly and trying to pull it out of its location.

14 Refer to Chapter 10 and reconnect the lower and upper hub and trackrod balljoints.

15 Refer to Chapter 9 and refit the brake caliper.

16 Jack up the wheel hub, remove the wooden wedge and lower the hub again, then refit the underwing shield.

17 Fit the roadwheel and tighten its securing nuts to the torque loading specified in Chapter 10.

18 Lower the vehicle to the ground and replenish the transmission fluid. After running the vehicle, check around the renewed seal for leakage.

Input shaft seal

Removal

19 Remove the transmission.

20 Clean the transmission casing around the seal location and using a screwdriver, lever the input shaft seal from position whilst taking care not to scratch its housing.

Fitting

21 Clean the input shaft and seal housing. Lubricate the new seal with clean transmission fluid.

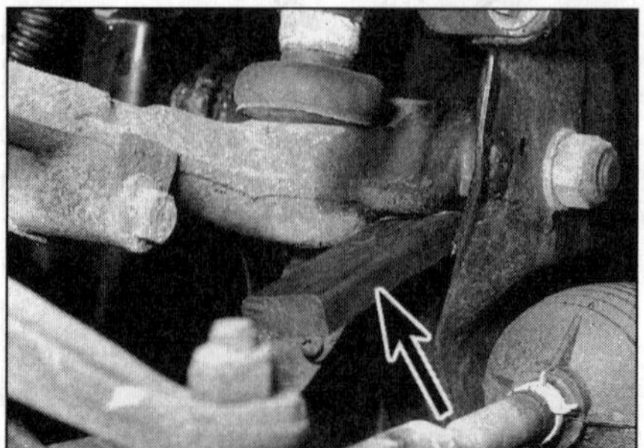

7.7 Wedge a wooden spacer (arrowed) between the suspension arm and subframe

7.9 Levering the differential seal from position

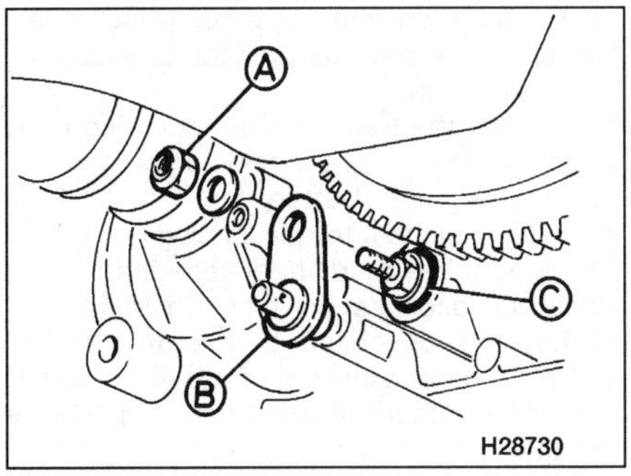

7.28 Removing the selector lever from its shaft

A Lever securing nut
B Selector lever
C Selector shaft seal

22 Fit the seal over the input shaft and into its housing (lip innermost), driving it squarely into place until it seats on its locating shoulder by using a piece of tubing (such as a socket) which bears only on the seals hard outer edge.

23 Refit the transmission.

Selector shaft seal

Removal

24 Park the vehicle on level ground, switch off the ignition and apply the handbrake firmly. Ensure that the gear selector lever is in the "P" position. Jack up the front of the vehicle, supporting it securely on axle stands (see "*Jacking and Vehicle Support*").

25 Refer to Chapter 4 and remove the front pipe of the exhaust system.

26 Remove the cable end-rod to selector lever securing nut and pull the rod from the lever.

27 Remove the three bolts which secure the flywheel lower cover plate to the engine and remove the plate.

28 Unscrew the nut securing the selector lever to the selector shaft. Remove the washer and release the lever to expose the shaft seal **(see illustration)**.

29 Clean the casing around the seal location and using a screwdriver, carefully lever the shaft seal from position whilst taking care not to scratch the casing.

Fitting

30 Clean the selector lever, shaft and seal housing. Lubricate the new seal with clean transmission fluid and slide it over the shaft .

31 Push the seal squarely into place until it seats in its housing by using a piece of tubing (such as a socket).

32 Refitting the remaining components is a reversal of the removal procedure, noting the following points:

33 Where applicable, tighten nuts and bolts to the specified torque loading figures.

34 Ensure that the selector cable is correctly adjusted before lowering the vehicle to the ground and replenishing the transmission fluid. After running the vehicle, check around the renewed seal for leakage.

8 Dipstick tube seal - renewal

1 Thoroughly clean the dipstick tube and the area where it enters the transmission casing.

2 Withdraw the dipstick from its tube. Remove the tube-to-transmission casing securing bolt and withdraw the tube from the casing.

3 Carefully remove the O-ring seal from its location in the transmission casing. *Under no circumstances must foreign matter be allowed to enter the transmission casing.* Discard the O-ring.

4 Clean the end of the dipstick tube and its mating face in the transmission casing. Lubricate each face with clean transmission fluid and fit a new O-ring over the end of the tube.

5 Taking care not to damage the O-ring, refit the dipstick tube into the casing and push it fully home. Fit and tighten the tube securing bolt to the specified torque loading.

6 Clean and refit the dipstick. After running the vehicle, check around the base of the tube for fluid leakage.

9 Secondary cover seals - renewal

Removal

1 Park the vehicle on level ground, switch off the ignition and apply the handbrake firmly. Remove the battery and jack up the front of the vehicle, supporting it securely on axle stands (see "*Jacking and Vehicle Support*").

2 Remove the left-hand front roadwheel.

3 Release the splash shield from the rear of the wheel arch by removing its three securing screws.

4 Detach the charcoal canister from its mounting bracket on the battery tray and ease it to one side.

5 Release the battery positive lead and the main feed wires to the fusebox from their respective clips on the battery tray.

6 Detach the fusebox from its mounting bracket by depressing its two retaining clips and then ease the fusebox and wiring harness to one side.

7 Disconnect the electrical lead from the horn, unscrew the two retaining bolts and remove the horn.

8 Remove the five battery tray retaining bolts, remove the fusebox mounting bracket and then the battery tray.

9 Position a jack beneath the engine to support it, protecting the engine from damage by placing a block of wood between it and the jack.

10 Remove the two bolts securing the transmission mounting bracket to its mounting and loosen the two bolts securing the mounting to its support member **(see illustration)**.

11 Remove the four bolts securing the support member to the subframe and then remove the support member and mounting assembly from the vehicle **(see illustration)**.

12 Raise the engine/transmission to gain access to the lower rear secondary cover securing bolt, then clean the secondary cover and the area of transmission casing surrounding it.

13 Remove the four cover securing bolts and remove the cover **(see illustration)**.

14 Remove and discard the one split-ring and two O-rings from inside the cover.

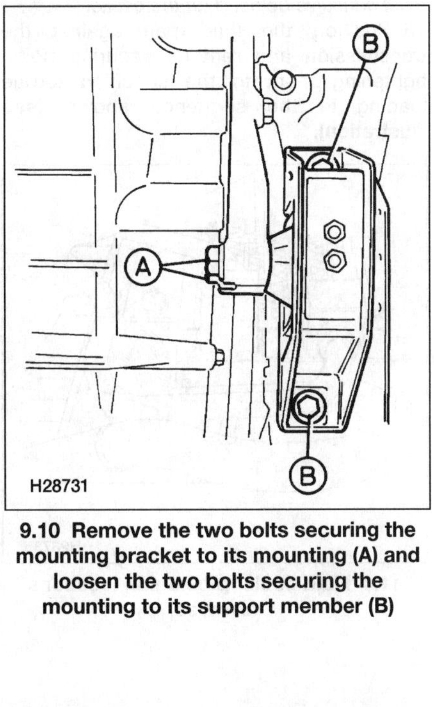

9.10 Remove the two bolts securing the mounting bracket to its mounting (A) and loosen the two bolts securing the mounting to its support member (B)

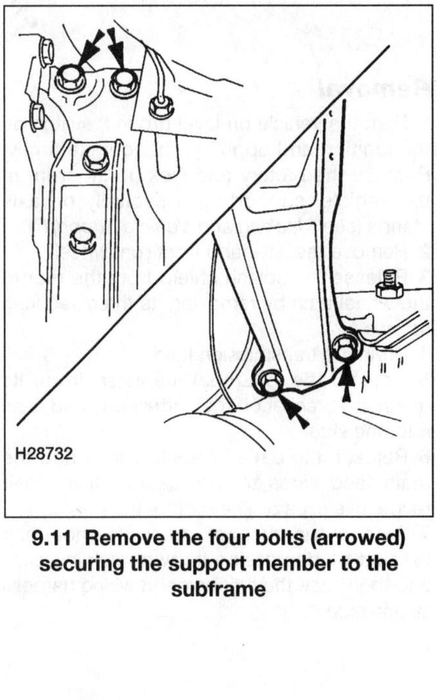

9.11 Remove the four bolts (arrowed) securing the support member to the subframe

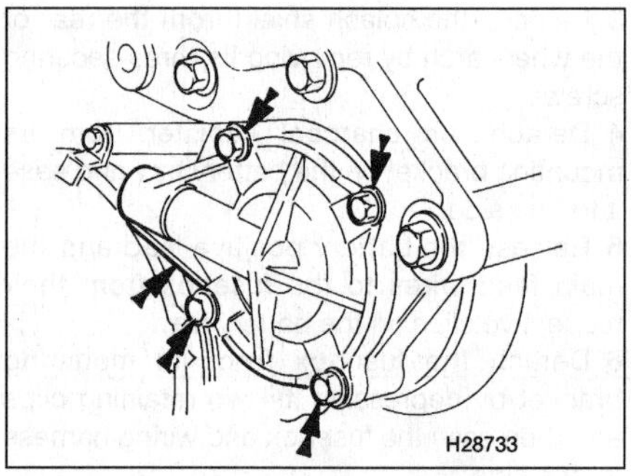

9.13 Remove the four bolts (arrowed) securing the secondary cover

Fitting

15 Thoroughly clean the secondary cover and its mating face on the transmission. Lubricate the new O-rings with clean transmission fluid and fit them to the cover. Fit a new split-ring.

16 Position the cover against the transmission and refit its securing bolts, tightening them to the specified torque loading.

17 Refitting the remaining components is a reversal of the removal procedure, noting the following points:

18 Tighten the transmission mounting and support member bolts to the specified torque loading of 45 Nm.

19 Tighten the battery tray and horn mounting bolts to a torque loading of 9 Nm.

20 Tighten the roadwheel securing nuts to the torque loading specified in Chapter 10.

21 Lower the vehicle to the ground and check the transmission fluid level. After running the vehicle, check around the cover for leakage.

10 Fluid pan gasket - renewal

Removal

1 Park the vehicle on level ground, switch off the ignition and apply the handbrake firmly. Remove the battery and jack up the front of the vehicle, supporting it securely on axle stands (see "*Jacking and Vehicle Support*").

2 Remove the left-hand front roadwheel.

3 Release the splash shield from the rear of the wheel arch by removing its three securing screws.

4 Drain the transmission fluid.

5 Detach the charcoal canister from its mounting bracket on the battery tray and ease it to one side.

6 Release the battery positive lead and the main feed wires to the fusebox from their respective clips on the battery tray.

7 Detach the fusebox from its mounting bracket by depressing its two retaining clips and then ease the fusebox and wiring harness to one side.

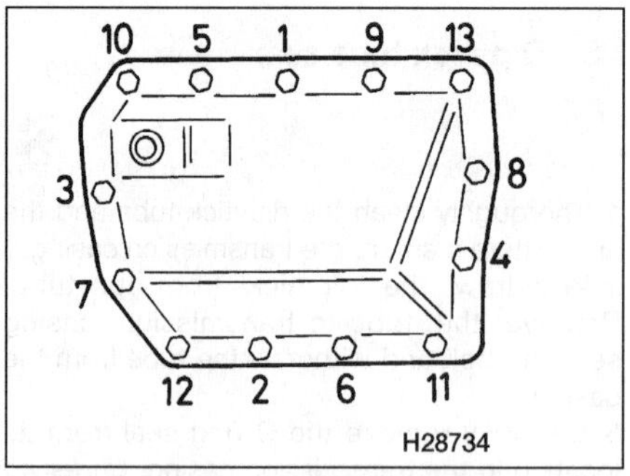

10.15 Tighten the fluid pan securing bolts in the sequence shown

8 Disconnect the electrical lead from the horn, unscrew the two retaining bolts and remove the horn.

9 Remove the five battery tray retaining bolts, remove the fusebox mounting bracket and then the battery tray.

10 Position a jack beneath the flywheel housing to support the engine/transmission, taking care to prevent the housing being damaged by the jack.

11 Remove the two bolts securing the transmission mounting bracket to its mounting and loosen the two bolts securing the mounting to its support member, see illustration 9.10.

12 Raise the engine/transmission to gain access to the fluid pan securing bolts. Working in the reverse of the tightening sequence (see illustration 10.15), loosen and remove the pan retaining bolts.

13 Ease the fluid pan away from the transmission and discard the gasket.

Fitting

14 Thoroughly clean the fluid pan and its mating face on the transmission. Lubricate the new gasket with clean transmission fluid and fit it to the fluid pan. *Under no circumstances must adhesive be used on the gasket.*

15 Position the fluid pan against the transmission and refit its securing bolts, tightening them to the specified torque loading in the sequence shown **(see illustration)**.

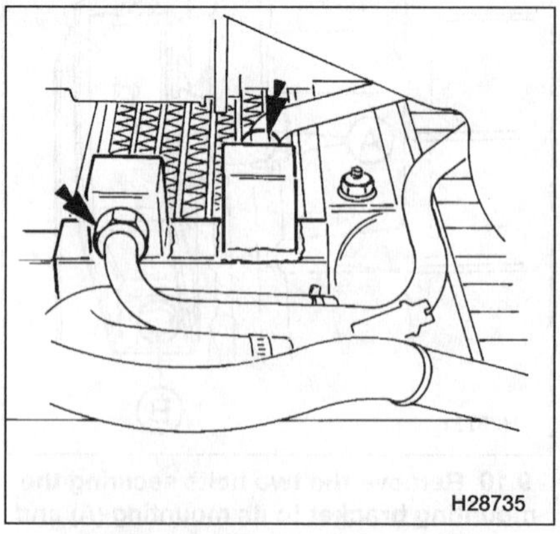

11.4 Fluid cooler pipe union locations (arrowed)

16 Refitting the remaining components is a reversal of the removal procedure, noting the following points:

17 Tighten the transmission mounting bolts to the specified torque loading of 45 Nm.

18 Tighten the battery tray and horn mounting bolts to a torque loading of 9 Nm.

19 Tighten the roadwheel securing nuts to the torque loading specified in Chapter 10.

20 Lower the vehicle to the ground and replenish the transmission fluid. After running the vehicle, check around the fluid pan for leakage.

11 Fluid cooler - removal and refitting

Removal

1 Park the vehicle on level ground, switch off the ignition and apply the handbrake firmly. Disconnect the battery earth lead and jack up the front of the vehicle, supporting it securely on axle stands (see "*Jacking and Vehicle Support*").

2 Remove the alternator.

3 Remove the cooler pipes to radiator securing bolt and bracket.

4 Place a container beneath the fluid cooler to catch any spillage of fluid and unscrew each cooler pipe union. **Note:** *Each fluid cooler boss must be firmly held as the pipe union is unscrewed* **(see illustration).** Move each pipe clear of the cooler unit.

5 Prevent ingress of dirt into the cooling system by plugging the exposed connections.

6 Remove the two bolts from each of the two radiator top mounting brackets and remove the brackets **(see illustration).**

7 Remove the two nuts securing the fluid cooler to the radiator, tilt the top of the radiator forward and remove the two bolts.

8 Lift the radiator with the cooler to release the cooler unit from its lower mounting. Separate the cooler unit from the radiator and remove it from the vehicle.

Refitting

9 Refitting the fluid cooler is a reversal of the removal procedure, noting the following points:

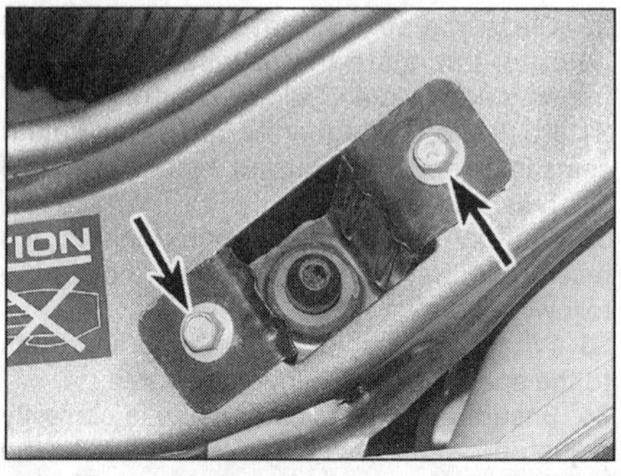

11.6 Remove the two bolts (arrowed) from each of the two radiator top mounting brackets

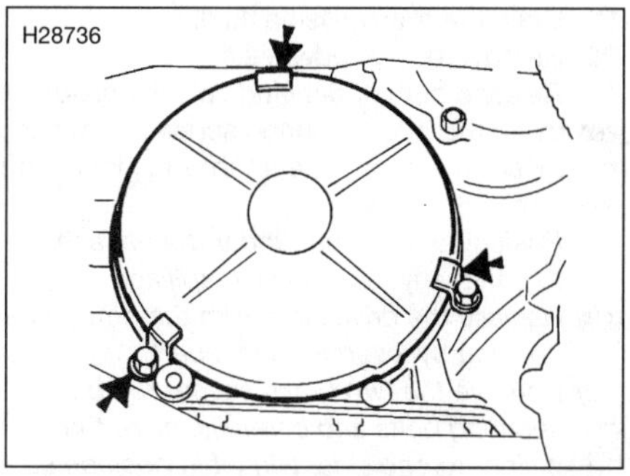

13.5 Primary cover securing screws and brackets (arrowed)

10 Before reconnecting the pipes, ensure that the connections are unplugged and their mating surfaces cleaned.

11 Fit each pipe to the fluid cooler but do not fully tighten until the pipes have been secured to the radiator. Tighten the pipe unions to the specified torque loading.

12 Refit the alternator, then lower the vehicle and reconnect the battery.

13 Replenish the fluid level and after operating the system, check each disturbed connection for leaks.

12 Fluid cooler hoses - removal and refitting

Removal

1 Park the vehicle on level ground, switch off the ignition and apply the handbrake firmly. Disconnect the battery earth lead and jack up the front of the vehicle, supporting it securely on axle stands (see "*Jacking and Vehicle Support*").

2 If removing the return hose, then remove the alternator.

3 Remove the cooler pipes to radiator securing bolt and bracket.

4 Place a container beneath the fluid cooler to catch any spillage of fluid and unscrew each cooler pipe union. **Note:** *Each fluid cooler boss must be firmly held as the pipe union is unscrewed.*

5 Unscrew each hose union from its adapter in the transmission casing and remove each hose assembly from the vehicle.

6 Prevent ingress of dirt into the cooling system by plugging all exposed connections.

Refitting

7 Before refitting either hose assembly, ensure that all connections are unplugged and clean the mating surfaces of each connection.

8 Fit each hose to the transmission casing and tighten to the specified torque loading.

9 Fit each pipe to the fluid cooler but do not fully tighten at this stage.

10 Align the cooler pipes to the radiator, refit the retaining bracket and secure it with the bolt. Now tighten the fluid cooler unions to the specified torque loading.

11 If necessary, refit the alternator, then lower the vehicle and reconnect the battery.

12 Replenish the fluid level and after operating the system, check each disturbed connection for leaks.

13 Primary cover - removal and refitting

Removal

1 Park the vehicle on level ground, switch off the ignition and apply the handbrake firmly. Jack up the front of the vehicle, supporting it securely on axle stands (see "*Jacking and Vehicle Support*").

2 Remove the left-hand front roadwheel.

3 Release the splash shield from the rear of the wheel arch by removing its three securing screws.

4 Clean the primary cover and the area of transmission casing surrounding it.

5 Release the three cover securing brackets and remove the cover **(see illustration).**

Refitting

6 Thoroughly clean the primary cover and its mating face on the transmission. Position the cover against the transmission and refit its securing bolts with brackets, tightening them to the specified torque loading.

7 Refitting the remaining components is a reversal of the removal procedure, noting the following points:

8 Tighten the roadwheel securing nuts to the torque loading specified in Chapter 10.

9 Lower the vehicle to the ground and check the transmission fluid level. After running the vehicle, check around the cover for leakage.

14 Starter inhibitor/reversing lamp switch - removal and refitting

Removal

1 Park the vehicle on level ground, switch off the ignition and apply the handbrake firmly. Jack up the front of the vehicle, supporting it securely on axle stands (see "*Jacking and Vehicle Support*").

2 Disconnect the multi-plug from the switch **(see illustration).**

3 Position a container beneath the switch to catch any fluid spillage and unscrew the switch from the transmission housing. Recover and discard the O-ring.

Refitting

4 Before fitting the switch, clean both the switch and its mating surface on the transmission casing.

5 Lightly lubricate the switch thread with clean transmission fluid and fit a new O-ring.

6 Fit the switch and tighten it to the specified torque loading.

7 Reconnect the multi-plug and check the operation of the switch. The starter motor must only operate in positions "P" and "N", and the reversing lights must only come on in position "R". Adjustment can only be made to the selector cable, the switch itself is not adjustable.

8 Lower the vehicle to the ground and check the transmission fluid level, replenishing it if necessary. After running the vehicle, check around the switch for fluid leakage.

14.2 Removing the starter inhibitor/reversing lamp switch

A Multiplug connection
B O-ring
C Cable securing bracket

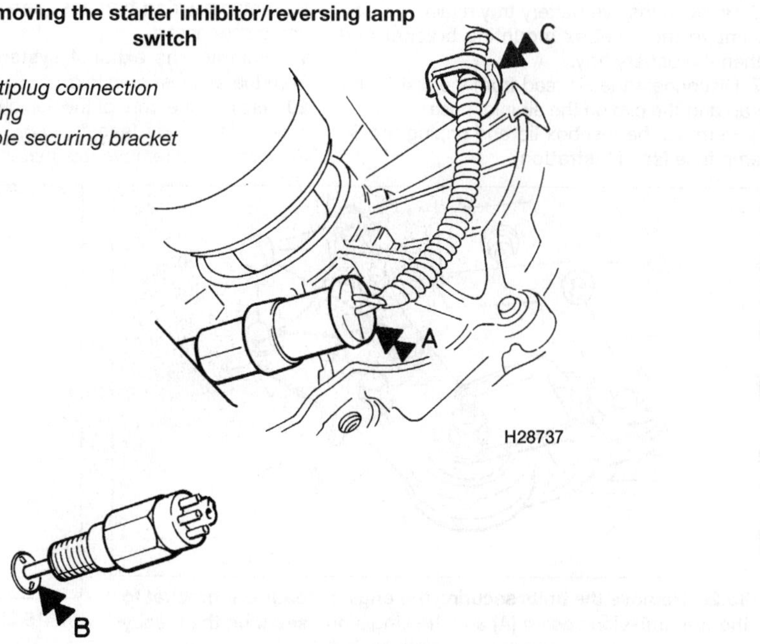

7B

15.8 Remove the fusebox lid to expose the 30 amp fuse (arrowed)

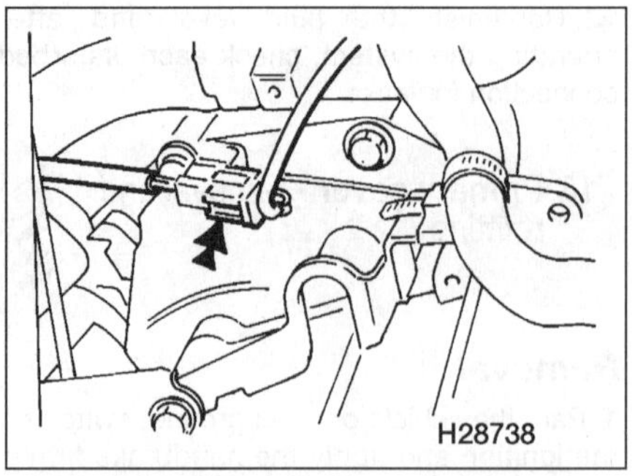

15.18 Disconnect the oxygen sensor multiplug from the engine wiring harness (arrowed)

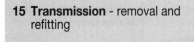

15 Transmission - removal and refitting

Note: *If the transmission is being removed for repair by a specialist, make sure that the specialist does not wish to test the transmission whilst it is still in the vehicle.*

Removal

1 Park the vehicle on level ground, switch off the ignition and apply the handbrake firmly. Remove the bonnet and battery.

2 Detach the charcoal canister from its mounting bracket on the battery tray and ease it to one side.

3 Release the battery positive lead and the main feed wires to the fusebox from their respective clips on the battery tray.

4 Detach the fusebox from its mounting bracket by depressing its two retaining clips and then ease the fusebox and wiring harness to one side.

5 Disconnect the electrical lead from the horn, unscrew the two retaining bolts and remove the horn.

6 Remove the five battery tray retaining bolts, remove the fusebox mounting bracket and then the battery tray.

7 Disconnect the HT lead from the distributor cap and the clip on the air inlet hose.

8 Remove the fusebox lid and unplug the 30 amp fuse **(see illustration).**

9 Detach the battery lead from the fusebox by depressing its retainer then sliding its connector out of the box.

10 Remove the air cleaner assembly.

11 Release the air inlet hose from its adapter behind the left-hand headlamp by removing the two securing screws. Remove the hose.

12 Loosen the two bolts holding the HT coil to the vehicle body, ease the coil free and position it to one side.

13 Release the speedometer cable from its housing on the transmission casing by first pulling out its securing pin and then pulling out the cable. Move the cable to one side.

14 Go to the throttle end of the kickdown cable and loosen the cable adjuster locknuts.

15 Detach the cable inner from the throttle cam and the cable adjuster from its mounting bracket.

16 Place a container beneath the radiator bottom hose, loosen the hose retaining clip and pull the hose off its connector, allowing the coolant to drain.

17 Release the radiator top hose from the cylinder head.

18 Locate the oxygen sensor multiplug on the engine wiring harness **(see illustration)** and disconnect it.

19 Remove the exhaust system front pipe from the exhaust manifold.

20 Jack up the front of the vehicle, supporting it on axle stands (see "*Jacking and Vehicle Support*"), and remove the starter motor.

21 Drain the transmission fluid.

22 Remove both roadwheels.

23 Release both underwing splash shields by removing the three securing screws from each one. Remove each wheelhub and driveshaft assembly as follows:

a) Position a container under the driveshaft to catch any residual fluid spillage.

b) Release the driveshaft from the differential housing by levering them apart.

c) Remove the two brake caliper to hub securing bolts and carefully move the caliper to one side, tying it in position so that no strain is placed on the brake hose.

d) Position a jack beneath the wheel hub and raise the hub to allow a wooden wedge to be fitted between the suspension arm and the subframe. Lower the suspension onto the wedge and remove the jack.

e) Refer to Chapter 10 and disconnect the track rod balljoint and the upper and lower hub balljoints, allowing the wheelhub and driveshaft assembly to be withdrawn.

24 Disconnect the multiplug from the starter inhibitor/reversing lamp switch and release its cable from the transmission casing, (see illustration 14.2).

25 Remove the selector cable end-rod to selector lever securing nut and pull the rod from the lever.

26 Remove the three bolts securing the engine steady bar bracket to the transmission casing and the single bolt securing the steady bar to the vehicle body **(see illustration).** Remove the steady bar and bracket assembly.

27 Unscrew each fluid cooler hose union from its adapter in the transmission casing and position the hoses to one side. Prevent ingress of dirt into the cooling system by plugging all exposed connections.

28 Remove the three bolts which secure the flywheel lower cover plate to the engine and remove the plate.

29 Remove the three bolts which secure the flywheel front cover plate to the engine **(see illustration)** and remove the plate.

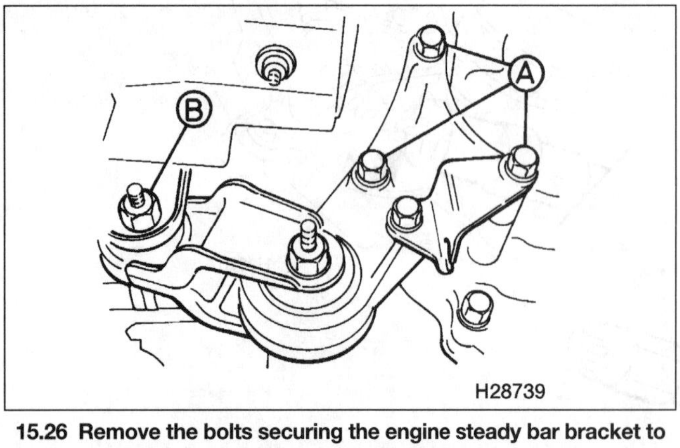

15.26 Remove the bolts securing the engine steady bar bracket to the transmission casing (A) and the single bolt securing the steady bar to the vehicle body (B)

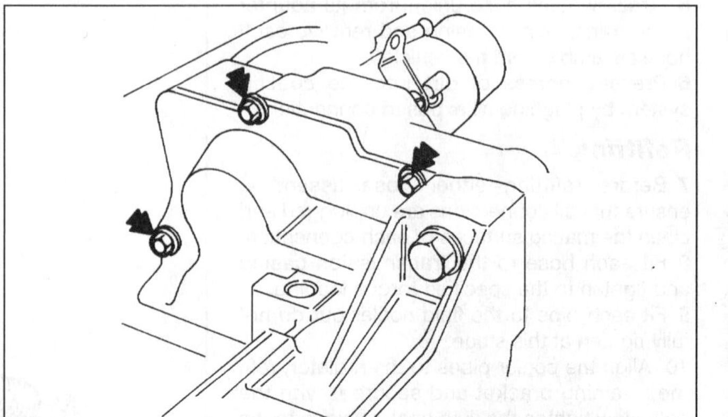

15.29 Remove the flywheel front cover plate securing bolts (arrowed)

30 Locate the crankshaft sensor multiplug on the engine wiring harness **(see illustration)** and disconnect it.
31 Remove the two bolts which secure the flywheel rear cover plate and crankshaft sensor multiplug. Release the wiring harness bracket and remove the cover plate.
32 Release the multiplug from the ECU mounting and disconnect it from the main wiring harness, (Chapter 4). Remove the three bolts securing the ECU mounting bracket to the vehicle body and carefully retain the ECU.
33 Disconnect the multiplug from the inertia switch and release the oxygen sensor relay from its mounting bracket **(see illustration)**.
34 Disconnect the engine wiring harness from the transmission lifting bracket and place the harness and ECU to one side.
35 Bolt a lifting bracket (Rover tool no. 18G 1572/2) to the cylinder head, tightening the bolt to a torque loading of 9 Nm. Connect a hoist to the lifting bracket and take the weight of the engine/transmission.
36 Remove the two bolts securing the transmission mounting bracket to its mounting and loosen the two bolts securing the mounting to its support member, see illustration 9.10.
37 Remove the four bolts securing the support member to the subframe and then remove the support member and mounting assembly from the vehicle, see illustration 9.11.
38 Lift the engine/transmission to provide clearance for separation of the two components.
39 Secure a second lifting chain to the transmission casing eye and tension it to take the weight of the unit.
40 Remove the four bolts securing the engine to the transmission, retaining the oxygen sensor multiplug mounting bracket. Ease the unit away from the engine and clear of the vehicle.
41 Remove the three mounting bracket securing bolts from the transmission casing and detach the mounting.

Refitting

42 With the new transmission on the workbench, fit the mounting bracket and tighten its securing bolts to 80 Nm.
43 Clean the mating faces of the engine and transmission. Clean the two dowels and their holes, then fit the dowels.
44 Lower the transmission into the engine compartment and align it over the dowels, pressing the mating faces together. *Take care to ensure that the input shaft is correctly engaged in the drive plate.*
45 Refit the four bolts securing the engine to the transmission, relocating the oxygen sensor multiplug mounting bracket beneath the appropriate bolt head. Tighten the bolts to the specified torque loading and detach the lifting chain from the transmission..
46 The remainder of the refitting procedure is the reverse of removal, noting the following points:

a) *Tighten all nuts and bolts to their specified torque wrench settings.*
b) *For full details of refitting (and adjusting) all ancillary components, refer to the relevant Sections of this, or other Chapters.*
c) *Top-up the cooling system.*
d) *Fill the transmission with fluid of the specified type to the correct level.*

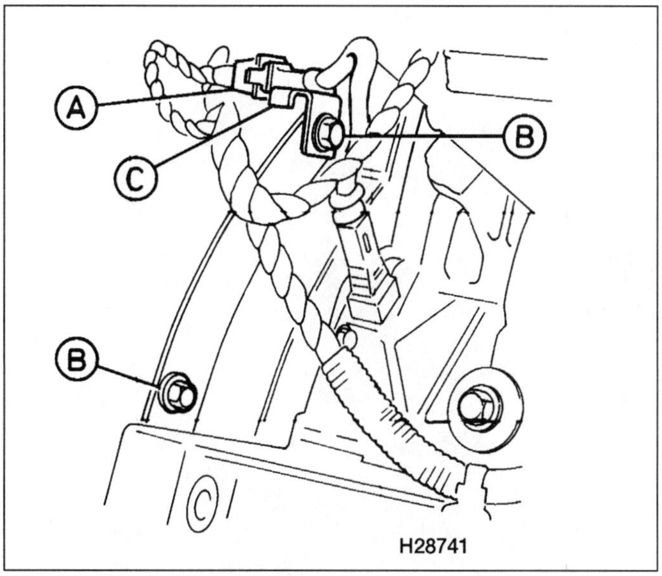

15.30 Removing the crankshaft sensor multiplug and flywheel rear cover plate

A *Crankshaft sensor multiplug*
B *Flywheel rear cover plate securing bolts*
C *Wiring harness bracket*

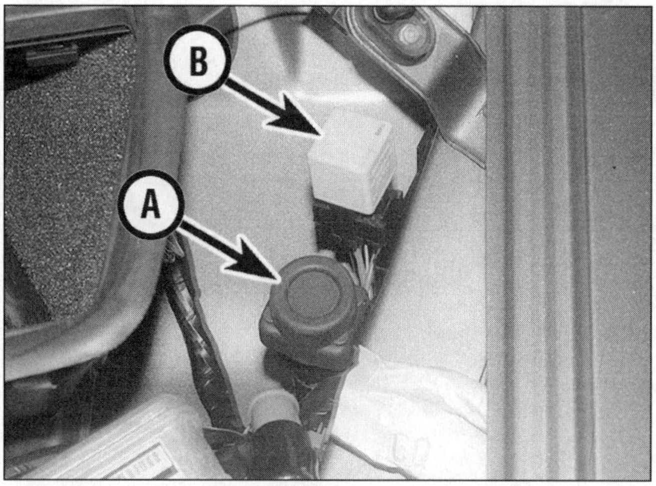

15.33 Disconnect the multiplug from the inertia switch (A) and release the oxygen sensor relay from its mounting bracket (B)

7B

Notes

Chapter 8
Driveshafts

Contents

Degrees of difficulty

Easy, suitable for novice with little experience	**Fairly easy,** suitable for beginner with some experience	**Fairly difficult,** suitable for competent DIY mechanic	**Difficult,** suitable for experienced DIY mechanic	**Very difficult,** suitable for expert DIY or professional

Specifications

Driveshafts

Type	Unequal-length solid steel shafts, splined to inner and outer constant velocity joints, dynamic damper on right-hand shaft

Torque wrench settings

	Nm	lbf ft
Driveshaft nut	210	155

1 General information and precautions

General information

Drive is transmitted from the differential to the front roadwheels by two unequal-length steel driveshaft assemblies. The (longer) right-hand driveshaft is fitted with a dynamic damper to reduce harmonic vibrations and resonance.

Both driveshafts are splined at their outer ends to accept the wheel hubs and are threaded so that each hub can be fastened by a large nut. The inner end of each driveshaft is splined to accept the differential gear and has a groove to accept the circlip which secures the driveshaft to the gear.

Two constant velocity joints are fitted to each driveshaft to ensure that the smooth and efficient transmission of drive at all possible angles as the roadwheels move up and down with the suspension, and as they turn from side to side under steering. Each outer joint is of the Birfield-Rzeppa ball-and-cage type, but the inner joint is of the tripod type and is plunge-accepting, to allow for the differences in driveshaft effective length at the extremes of suspension travel.

Precautions

The only replacement parts listed are the inner constant velocity joint and shaft assemblies, the outer constant velocity joint assemblies and the rubber gaiters. The gaiters are supplied in a kit with the necessary sachets of grease and their clips. If any joint is worn or damaged it cannot be reconditioned but must be renewed. In the case of the inner joints, this means that the complete joint/shaft assembly must be renewed.

2 Driveshafts - general inspection

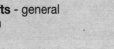

Refer to Chapter 1, Section 17.

3 Driveshafts - overhaul

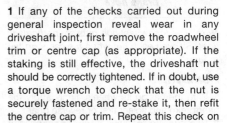

1 If any of the checks carried out during general inspection reveal wear in any driveshaft joint, first remove the roadwheel trim or centre cap (as appropriate). If the staking is still effective, the driveshaft nut should be correctly tightened. If in doubt, use a torque wrench to check that the nut is securely fastened and re-stake it, then refit the centre cap or trim. Repeat this check on the other driveshaft nut.

2 Road test the vehicle and listen for a metallic clicking from the front as the vehicle is driven slowly in a circle on full lock. If a clicking noise is heard, this indicates wear in the outer constant velocity joint. This means that the joint must be renewed as reconditioning is not possible.

3 If the outer joint is worn then it can be renewed separately.

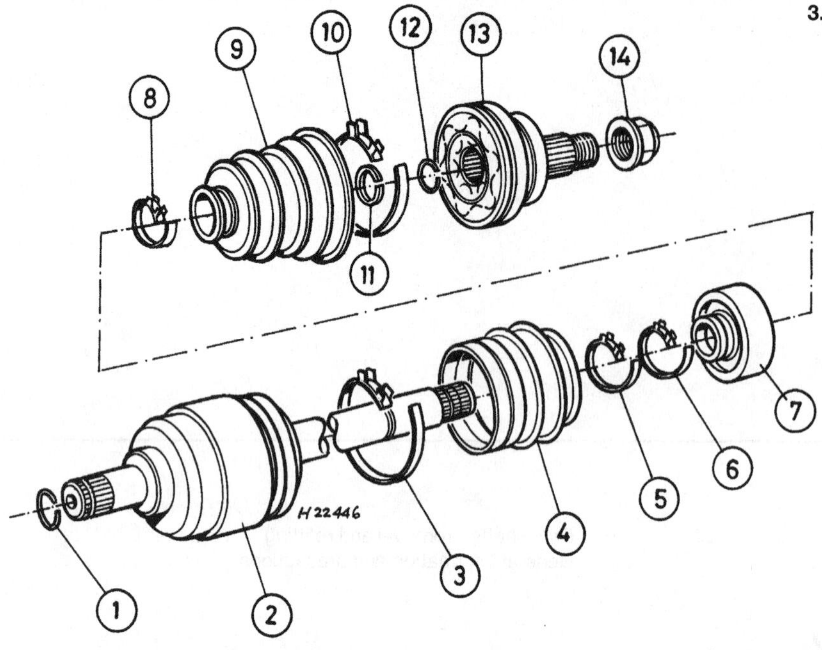

3.5 Exploded view of driveshaft assembly

1 Circlip
2 Inner joint and shaft assembly
3 Large gaiter clip
4 Gaiter
5 Small gaiter clip
6 Damper clip
7 Dynamic damper - right-hand driveshaft only
8 Small gaiter clip
9 Gaiter
10 Large gaiter clip
11 Stopper ring
12 Circlip
13 Outer joint assembly
14 Driveshaft nut

4 If vibration consistent with road speed is felt through the car when accelerating, there is a possibility of wear in the inner constant velocity joints.

5 Remove the driveshafts then dismantle them and check the joints **(see illustration)**. If any wear or free play is found, the inner joints are worn and must be renewed, complete with the shaft assembly.

4 Driveshafts - removal and refitting

HAYNES HiNT ***Always tie an unbolted brake caliper to the suspension strut so as to prevent strain on the flexible brake hose.***

Note: *The roadwheel hub nuts are particularly tight. Slacken each nut when the car is on the ground.*

Removal

1 With the car on its wheels, firmly apply the handbrake and select first or reverse gear.

2 Remove the roadwheel trim or centre cap (as appropriate) **(see illustration)**. Relieve the staking of the driveshaft nut using a hammer and punch or (if necessary) an electric drill, then use a suitable socket, a strong T-bar and a long extension tube to slacken the nut; do not unscrew it yet. If the nut is particularly tight, have an assistant apply the brakes hard.

3 Slacken the roadwheel nuts, then jack up the front of the car and support it securely on axle stands (see "*Jacking and Vehicle Support*"). Remove the roadwheel, then unscrew the driveshaft nut and discard it; it must be renewed as a matter of course whenever disturbed.

4 Drain the transmission oil.

5 Remove the underwing shield.

6 Relieve the pressure of the Hydragas system from the components by using a trolley jack or similar (with a block of wood interposed to prevent damage) to jack up the suspension via the lower balljoint until it is just beginning to take the weight of the car, then slip a wooden spacer between the suspension upper arm and the front subframe and lower the jack.

7 Unscrew the brake caliper mounting bolts, remove the caliper from the hub carrier and slip a clean spacer (of the same thickness as the brake disc) between the pads, then secure the caliper clear of the working area without stretching or kinking the brake flexible hose.

8 Disconnect the track rod balljoint from the hub carrier steering arm.

4.2 On cars with alloy wheels, remove the centre cap to expose driveshaft nut

9 Disconnect the suspension upper balljoint from the upper suspension arm and discard the lockwasher.

10 Sharply tug the hub carrier outwards off the driveshaft splines. It may be necessary to use a soft-faced mallet (having first refitted the driveshaft nut to protect the shaft's threaded end) to tap the driveshaft out of the hub.

11 Use a suitable lever to prise out the driveshaft until the circlip compresses into its groove and is released from the differential gear **(see illustration)**.

12 Withdraw the driveshaft assembly. Check the circlip at the driveshaft's inboard end carefully, renewing it if there is any doubt about its condition. To prevent the risk of the differential gear becoming displaced, insert a clean metal rod or wooden dowel of the same diameter as the driveshaft into the transmission aperture until the gear is securely supported.

Refitting

13 On refitting, proceed as follows.

4.11 Levering driveshaft out of transmission

4.23a Tighten driveshaft nut to specified torque wrench setting . . .

4.23b . . . and stake into driveshaft groove to secure it

14 Thoroughly clean the driveshaft itself and the apertures in the transmission and hub carrier to prevent the entry of dirt during reassembly. Apply a thin film of grease to the oil seal lips and to the driveshaft splines and shoulders. Check that all gaiter clips are securely fastened.
15 Ensure that the circlip fitted to the inboard end of each driveshaft is in good condition and is located securely in its groove. Remove the differential gear support.
16 Taking care not to damage the oil seal lips, insert the driveshaft into the transmission and engage its splines with those of the gear. Press the driveshaft firmly into place until the circlip engages correctly behind (inboard of) the gear. If it is necessary to use tools to tap the driveshaft into place, be very careful not to damage the rubber gaiter.
17 Check that the circlip is properly engaged by grasping the inner joint body firmly and trying to pull the driveshaft out of the differential.
18 Refit the driveshaft to the hub carrier and fit a new driveshaft nut.
19 Refit the upper balljoint to the suspension upper arm, fit a new lockwasher and tighten the balljoint-to-upper suspension arm nut to the specified torque wrench setting, then secure the nut by bending the washer tab up against one of its flats.
20 Connect the track rod balljoint to the hub carrier steering arm and tighten the balljoint nut to the specified torque wrench setting.
21 Refit the brake caliper, tightening its bolts to the specified torque wrench setting.
22 Jack up the suspension, remove the spacer and lower the suspension again, then refit the underwing shield and the roadwheel.
23 Lower the car to the ground and tighten the driveshaft nut and roadwheel nuts to their specified torque settings. Using a hammer and punch, secure the driveshaft nut by staking its collar into the driveshaft groove **(see illustrations)**.
24 Refit the roadwheel trim or centre cap.
25 Refill the transmission with oil.

5 Driveshafts - gaiter renewal

Outer joint

Note: *This operation is a great deal easier if the driveshaft is removed from the vehicle. However, it is possible to dismantle an outer joint without removing the driveshaft from the transmission, provided that care is taken to hold the driveshaft into the transmission whilst the hub carrier and outer joint are removed.*
1 Remove the driveshaft.
2 Cut the gaiter clips and peel back the gaiter from the joint **(see illustration)**.
3 Clamp the driveshaft in a soft-jawed vice.
4 Using a sharply-pointed punch or scribing tool, mark the relationship of the joint body to the driveshaft itself, then use a hammer and a drift (applied to the joint inner race only) to tap the joint off the shaft splines until the circlip compresses into its groove and is released from the inner race **(see illustration)**.
5 Withdraw the joint from the driveshaft and slide off the gaiter. If it is to be re-used, wrap insulating tape around the shaft to protect the gaiter from any sharp edges. Check the gaiter for splits, cracking or other signs of damage and renew it if necessary. Renew both clips.
6 Remove and discard the circlip from the driveshaft end.
7 On refitting, proceed as follows.
8 Wind a thin layer of insulating tape around the shaft to protect the gaiter from the shaft splines and other sharp edges. Fit the small gaiter clip, then slide on the gaiter and check that it is seated correctly before removing the tape.
9 Ensuring that the stopper ring is securely located in its groove, fit a **new** circlip to the groove nearest the driveshaft's end, apply a smear of grease and press the outer joint into place so that the driveshaft end, the circlip and the joint inner race are all aligned. Using a soft-faced mallet and protecting the joint's threaded end by refitting temporarily the driveshaft nut, tap the outer joint onto the driveshaft until the circlip compresses into its groove and passes through the inner race **(see illustration)**.
10 Check that the circlip is correctly engaged by trying to pull the joint off the shaft.
11 Fill the joint with the grease provided in sachets in the gaiter kit, packing any surplus into the gaiter.
12 Position the gaiter on the joint groove, fasten the large gaiter clip and expel all air from the gaiter before fastening the small gaiter clip.

Inner joint

13 Remove the outer joint as described above.
14 On right-hand shafts only, remove the clip and withdraw the dynamic damper; use liquid soap if necessary to aid damper removal and clean off any rust deposits or similar using emery cloth.

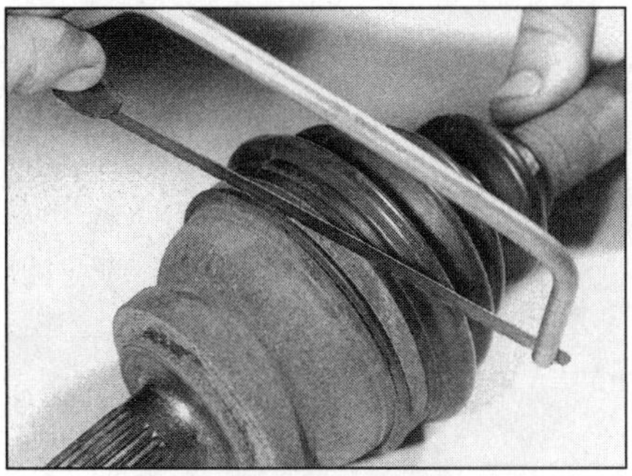

5.2 It may be necessary to cut gaiter clips to release gaiters

5.4 Driving outer constant velocity joint off driveshaft end

5.9 Refitting outer constant velocity joint to driveshaft

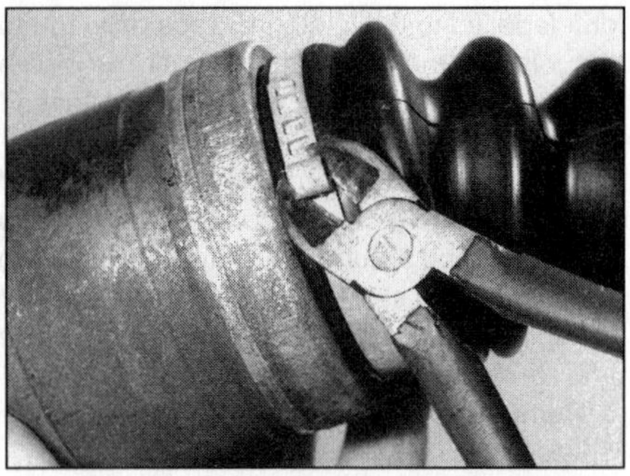

5.15 Cutting inner constant velocity joint gaiter clip to release it

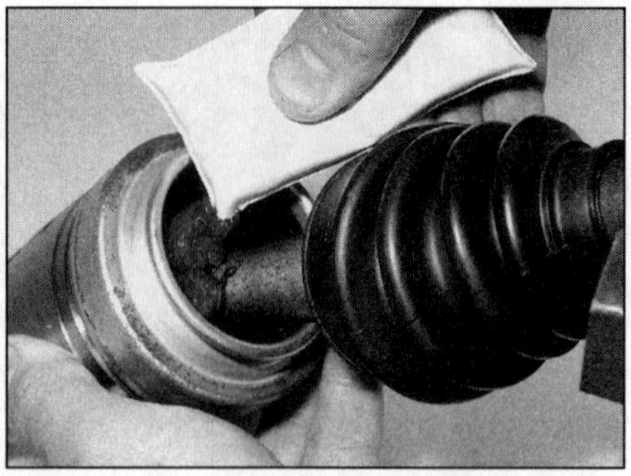

5.17 Using sachets supplied with gaiter kit to fill inner joint with grease

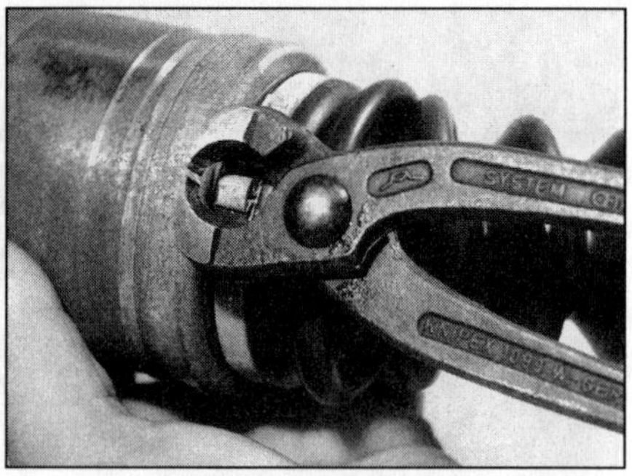

5.18 Using correct tool to tighten gaiter clip - end cutters can be used instead, if care is exercised

15 Cut the clips **(see illustration)** and withdraw the gaiter. If it is to be re-used, wrap insulating tape around the shaft to protect the gaiter from any sharp edges. Check the gaiter for splits, cracking or other signs of damage and renew it if necessary. Renew both clips.

16 Clean the shaft (using emery cloth to polish away any rust or sharp edges which might damage the new gaiter's sealing lip) and joint, renewing any worn or damaged items.

17 On reassembly, pack the joint with the grease provided in sachets in the gaiter kit **(see illustration)** then slide the new gaiter onto the shaft, taking care not to damage the gaiter lip.

18 Position the gaiter on the joint groove, fasten the large gaiter clip and expel all air from the gaiter before fastening the small gaiter clip **(see illustration)**.

19 On left-hand shafts, refit the outer joint. On right-hand shafts, lubricate the shaft and refit the dynamic damper (with a new clip) so that its clip flange is inboard, towards the inner joint. Reassemble the outer joint, then position the damper as shown **(see illustration)** and secure its clip. Clean off any surplus lubricant.

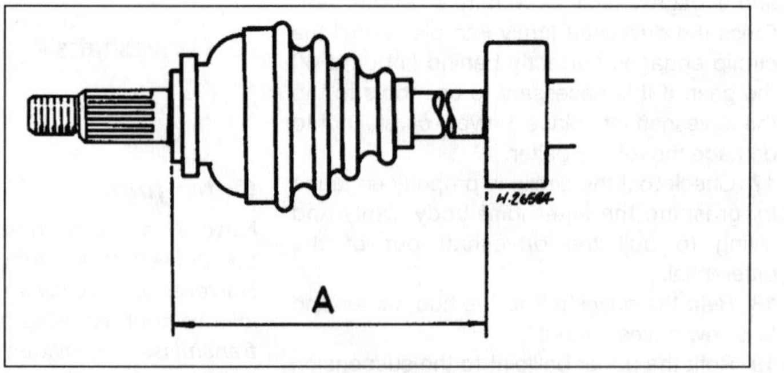

5.19 Position the dynamic damper the specified distance from the outer joint flange, then secure the clip

A = 393.25 to 399.25 mm

Chapter 9
Braking system

Contents

Degrees of difficulty

Easy, suitable for novice with little experience	**Fairly easy,** suitable for beginner with some experience	**Fairly difficult,** suitable for competent DIY mechanic	**Difficult,** suitable for experienced DIY mechanic	**Very difficult,** suitable for expert DIY or professional

Specifications

Brake system

Type	Hydraulically-operated diagonally split dual circuit with pressure regulating valves to rear brakes, vacuum servo-assisted, discs front, drums rear. Handbrake cable-operated on rear drums

Front brakes

Type	Disc, with single-piston sliding caliper
Disc diameter	238 mm
Disc thickness:	
New	12.76 mm
Minimum	10.80 mm
Maximum thickness variation	0.015 mm
Disc maximum run-out	0.150 mm
Brake pad friction material minimum thickness	3.0 mm

Rear brakes

Type	Single leading shoe drum
Drum diameter:	
New	177.90 mm
Maximum	179.00 mm
Drum maximum ovality	0.050 mm
Brake shoe friction material minimum thickness	1.5 mm

Handbrake

Roadwheels bind at:	
Up to VIN 661301	2 to 3 notches
VIN 661301 on	1 notch
Roadwheels lock at:	
Up to VIN 661301	3 to 4 notches
VIN 661301 on	1 to 2 notches

Torque wrench settings

	Nm	lbf ft
Vacuum servo unit mounting nuts	13	10
Master cylinder-to-vacuum servo unit mounting nuts	13	10
Vacuum servo unit vacuum hose banjo union bolt - alloy inlet manifold	50	37
Brake pipe union nuts	15	11
Rear brake pressure regulating valve mounting bolt	25	19
Front brake caliper:		
Bleed nipple	13	10
Brake flexible hose banjo union bolt	35	26
Guide pin bolts	30	22
Caliper-to-hub carrier mounting bolts	85	63
Front brake disc securing screws	7	5
Front brake disc shield mounting bolts	10	8
Rear brake drum securing screw	7	5
Rear brake (wheel cylinder) bleed nipple	7	5
Rear brake backplate-to-suspension trailing arm nuts and bolts	25	19
Handbrake lever assembly-to-body mounting nuts and bolts	25	19

1 General information and precautions

General information

The braking system is hydraulically-operated and incorporates a vacuum servo unit and master cylinder mounted on the right-hand side of the engine compartment bulkhead, with disc brakes at the front wheels and drums at the rear.

The master cylinder is of the tandem type and, with the connecting metal pipes and flexible hoses, provides a diagonally-split dual circuit system. The primary circuit operates the right-hand front and left-hand rear brakes whilst the secondary operates the left-hand front and right-hand rear. Under normal conditions both circuits operate in unison, but in the event of hydraulic failure of one of the circuits full brake pressure will still be available at two of the brakes, thus allowing the car to be stopped in a stable manner, albeit with increased pedal movement.

To prevent the rear wheels locking under heavy braking, a pressure-sensitive regulating valve is fitted into each circuit to control the amount of hydraulic pressure at the rear brakes.

The handbrake operates the rear brakes through a lever assembly bolted to the floor and a cable to the brake backplates.

In addition to the stop-lamps, there is a brake warning lamp in the instrument panel. This is activated by a plunger switch mounted at the base of the handbrake lever, so that the lamp lights whenever the handbrake is applied, and also by a float-type sender unit in the master cylinder reservoir filler cap, so that the lamp lights whenever the fluid level falls to a dangerously low level.

The vacuum servo unit uses inlet manifold depression (generated only while the engine is running) to boost the effort applied by the driver at the brake pedal and transmits this increased effort to the master cylinder pistons. It is direct-acting, with its input rod connected directly to the brake pedal and is of the suspended-vacuum type.

The front brake calipers are of the single-piston sliding type in which the main caliper body slides on a mounting bracket rigidly attached to the hub carrier. Full braking efficiency relies on the ability of the caliper body to slide easily on its mounting bracket, as well as on the condition of the pads and the caliper bore, piston and seals.

The rear brakes consist of the drum, which is of cast iron and is fastened to the hub and roadwheel, as well as the backplate which is mounted on the rear suspension trailing arm to carry the shoes and wheel cylinder.

Precautions

Hydraulic fluid is poisonous; wash off immediately and thoroughly in the case of skin contact and seek immediate medical advice if any fluid is swallowed or gets into the eyes. Certain types of hydraulic fluid are inflammable and may ignite when allowed into contact with hot components; when servicing any hydraulic system it is safest to assume that the fluid is inflammable and to take precautions against the risk of fire as though it is petrol that is being handled. Hydraulic fluid is also an effective paint stripper and will attack plastics; if any is spilt, it should be washed off immediately using copious quantities of fresh water. Finally, it is hygroscopic (it absorbs moisture from the air) old fluid may be contaminated and unfit for further use. When topping-up or renewing the fluid, always use the recommended type and ensure that it comes from a freshly-opened sealed container

When working on the brake components, take care not to disperse brake dust into the air, or to inhale it, since it may contain asbestos which is injurious to health

When servicing any part of the system, work carefully and methodically; also observe scrupulous cleanliness when overhauling any part of the hydraulic system. Always renew components (in axle sets, where applicable) if in doubt about their condition and use only genuine Rover replacement parts, or at least those of known good quality.

2 Brake pedal - removal, inspection and refitting

Warning: Read carefully the precautions listed in Chapter 12, Section 1, appertaining to vehicles equipped with airbags (SRS) before attempting removal of the steering column.

Removal

1 Release the retaining fasteners and remove the fusebox cover.

2 Remove its retaining screw and bolt and withdraw the steering column cover, then unfasten the column from its remaining mountings and lower it as far as possible without stretching the wiring.

3 Remove its split pin and withdraw the pedal-to-vacuum servo unit fork clevis pin, then unhook the pedal return spring from the pedal **(see illustration)**.

4 Undo the nuts and bolt securing the pedal pivot bracket (and the vacuum servo unit) to the bulkhead, then unbolt the pedal pivot bracket from the steering column lower mounting bracket.

5 Unscrew the nut securing the bracket to the pedal pivot shaft and withdraw the bracket far enough to permit the pedal to be removed. Disconnect or release the wiring as necessary.

Inspection

6 Carefully clean all components and renew any that are worn or damaged. Check the return spring and the bearing surfaces of the pivot bushes and shaft with particular care. The bushes can be renewed separately if required.

Refitting

7 Refitting is the reverse of the removal procedure, but apply a thin smear of Molykote 44 lubricant to the pedal-to-vacuum servo unit fork clevis pin and multi-purpose grease to all other pivots and bearing surfaces.

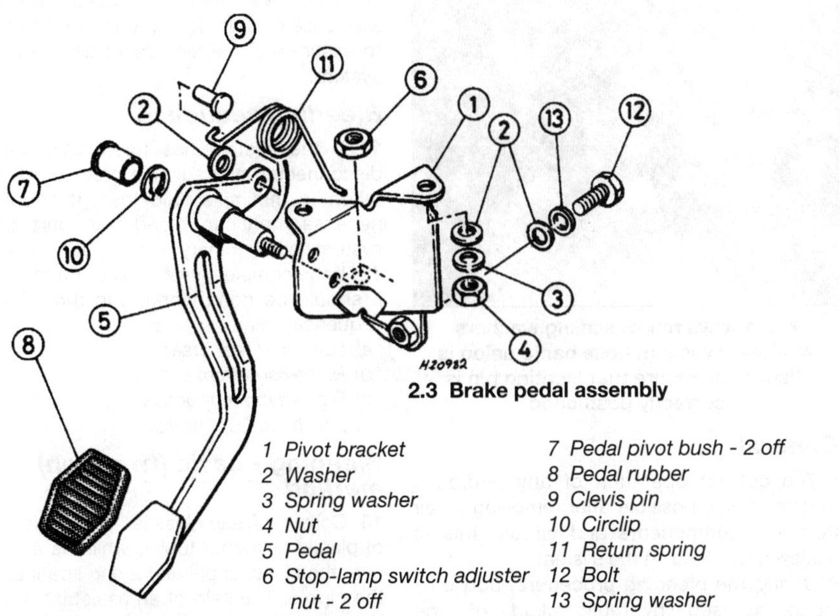

2.3 Brake pedal assembly

1 Pivot bracket
2 Washer
3 Spring washer
4 Nut
5 Pedal
6 Stop-lamp switch adjuster nut - 2 off
7 Pedal pivot bush - 2 off
8 Pedal rubber
9 Clevis pin
10 Circlip
11 Return spring
12 Bolt
13 Spring washer

3 Vacuum servo unit - inspection

1 In normal use, any failure of the vacuum servo unit will be evident to the driver due to the increased pedal effort required to achieve normal braking. To test the unit, park the car on level ground and release the handbrake, then proceed as follows.

2 Switch off the engine and destroy the vacuum in the unit by depressing the brake pedal five to six times. Check that there is no significant change in pedal travel after the first two or three strokes.

3 Apply normal pressure to the brake pedal and maintain it while the engine is started. If the unit is operating correctly the pedal should move down slightly as vacuum is restored in the unit.

4 To check whether the unit is completely airtight, start the engine and run it for one or two minutes, then switch off the ignition. Depress the brake pedal slowly several times using the same, normal, pressure at each stroke. If the unit is airtight the pedal should go down to the normal depressed height on the first one or two strokes, but after that the depressed height should gradually rise as the vacuum is destroyed and the level of assistance decreases.

5 Finally start the engine again, apply normal pressure to the brake pedal and maintain it while the engine is switched off. There should be no change in pedal height for at least thirty seconds.

6 If the vacuum servo unit proves faulty as a result of the above tests it must be renewed, although it is worth checking first that the non-return check valve is not faulty or that the vacuum hose from the inlet manifold is not kinked, blocked or leaking. Whilst a repair kit is available from Rover dealers, no details are available of how to overhaul the unit, so this task must be left to a Rover dealer or similar expert. Always check first the cost of a replacement unit against that of a kit and labour charges to establish whether repairs are economically viable.

4 Vacuum servo unit - removal and refitting

Removal

1 Open the bonnet. If the extra clearance is required, remove the air cleaner assembly.

2 Unscrew the two nuts securing the master cylinder to the vacuum servo unit and very carefully lift the master cylinder upwards clear of the servo unit studs and pushrod, taking great care not to kink or damage the metal brake pipes. If there is any risk of kinking or damaging the pipes, either unclip them from the bulkhead or disconnect them until the master cylinder can be moved clear, or removed, as required **(see illustration)**.

3 Carefully unplug the vacuum hose adapter from the vacuum servo unit.

4 Working inside the vehicle, release the retaining fasteners and remove the fusebox cover.

5 Remove its retaining screw and bolt and withdraw the steering column cover, then unfasten the column from its remaining mountings and lower it as far as possible without stretching the wiring.

6 Remove its split pin and withdraw the brake pedal-to-vacuum servo unit fork clevis pin.

7 Unscrew the four nuts securing the vacuum servo unit (and the brake pedal pivot bracket) to its mounting plate and the bulkhead. Whilst three of the nuts are unscrewed from inside the car, immediately above the brake pedal pivot, the fourth is reached from beneath the front edge of the mounting plate, inside the engine compartment.

8 Withdraw the vacuum servo unit and discard the gasket.

9 If the vacuum servo unit is faulty it must be renewed. Renew the gasket as a matter of course.

Refitting

10 Refitting is the reverse of the removal procedure, noting the following points.

a) Tighten all nuts and bolts securely, to the specified torque wrench settings, where given.

b) Lubricate the pedal-to-servo unit fork clevis pin.

c) If any brake pipes were disconnected, bleed any air from the system and wash off any spilt hydraulic fluid.

d) When refitting the vacuum hose adapter, take note of the comments made in Section 6.

e) Check the operation of the brakes in general and of the vacuum servo unit in particular.

5 Vacuum servo unit non-return check valve - testing

1 When testing the valve, remember that its function is to allow air to flow in one direction only, out of the vacuum servo unit. If it allows air to flow in both directions, or in neither, it is faulty and must be renewed.

2 To test the valve, carefully unplug the vacuum hose adapter from the vacuum servo unit and blow through the hose from the adapter. Air should pass freely through the valve. Now disconnect the hose from the inlet manifold, block the manifold banjo union holes and suck hard on the adapter end. There should be no leakage at all back through the valve.

3 If the valve is faulty it must be renewed, do not try to separate it from its hose.

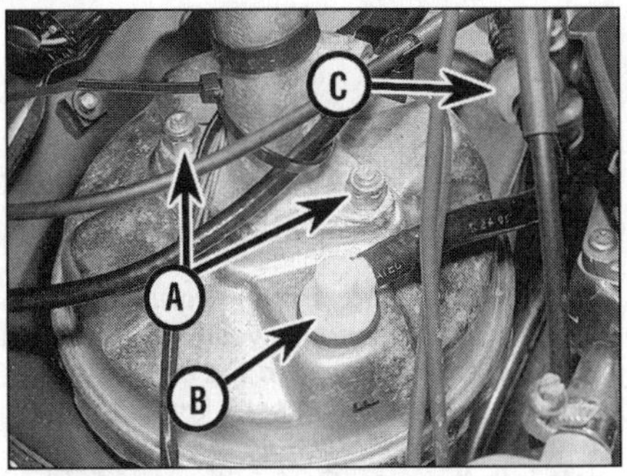

4.2 Master cylinder mounting nuts (A) vacuum hose adapter (B) and non-return check valve (C)

6 Vacuum servo unit non-return check valve - removal and refitting

Note: *The valve is only available as part of the vacuum hose assembly. Do not try to remove it, the adapter, or the banjo union from the hose or air leaks may ensue, necessitating the renewal of the assembly.*

Removal

1 The valve is set in the vacuum hose from the inlet manifold which is plugged into the top of the vacuum servo unit.

2 To remove the valve, carefully unplug the hose adapter from the vacuum servo unit. On models fitted with an alloy inlet manifold, unscrew the banjo union bolt from the manifold and withdraw the hose assembly **(see illustration)**. Discard the sealing washers; they must be renewed whenever disturbed. On models fitted with a plastic inlet manifold, depress the plastic collar to release the quick-fit hose connector from the manifold.

Refitting

3 Refitting is the reverse of the removal procedure, noting the following points:

a) *Use new sealing washers when refitting the alloy inlet manifold banjo union (one on each side of the hose union) and tighten the bolt to its specified torque wrench setting, ensuring that the union's locating pin is correctly engaged between the manifold lugs and that the union does not twist as the bolt is tightened.*

b) *When plugging the hose adapter into the vacuum servo unit, take care not to distort or displace the sealing grommet. Note that if the grommet is displaced into the vacuum servo unit, the unit must be renewed.*

c) *As soon as the engine is restarted check that there are no signs of air leaks.*

7 Hydraulic fluid - level check and renewal

Refer to *Weekly Checks* and Chapter 1, Section 33.

8 Hydraulic system - bleeding

Warning: Brake hydraulic fluid is poisonous; wash off immediately in the case of skin contact and seek immediate medical advice if any fluid is swallowed or gets into the eyes. Certain types of fluid are inflammable and may ignite when allowed into contact with hot components.

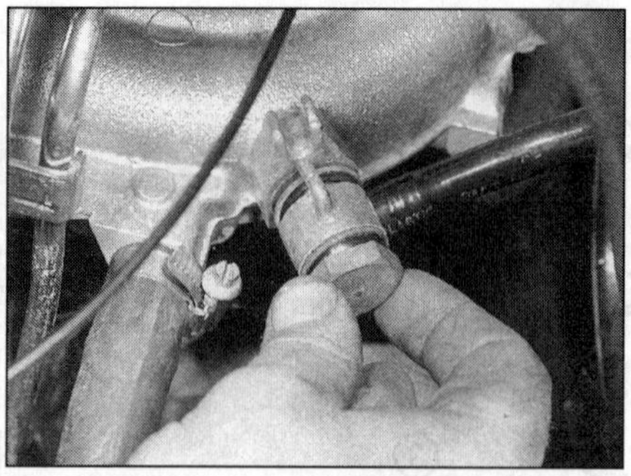

6.2 Always renew sealing washers whenever vacuum hose banjo union is disturbed. Ensure that locating pin is correctly positioned

General

1 The correct operation of any hydraulic system is only possible after removing all air from the components and circuit; this is achieved by bleeding the system.

2 During the bleeding procedure, add only clean, unused hydraulic fluid of the recommended type. Never re-use fluid that has already been bled from the system. Ensure that sufficient fluid is available before starting work.

3 If there is any possibility of incorrect fluid being already in the system, the brake components and circuit must be flushed completely with uncontaminated, correct fluid and new seals should be fitted to the various components.

4 If hydraulic fluid has been lost from the system, or air has entered because of a leak, ensure that the fault is cured before proceeding further.

5 Park the car on level ground, switch off the engine and select first or reverse gear, then chock the wheels and release the handbrake.

6 Check that all pipes and hoses are secure, unions tight and bleed nipples closed. Clean any dirt from around the bleed nipples.

7 Top the master cylinder reservoir up to the MAX level line. Refit the cap loosely and remember to maintain the fluid level at least above the MIN level line throughout the procedure or there is a risk of further air entering the system.

8 There are a number of one-man, do-it-yourself brake bleeding kits currently available from car accessory shops. It is recommended that one of these kits is used whenever possible as they greatly simplify the bleeding operation and also reduce the risk of expelled air and fluid being drawn back into the system. If such a kit is not available the basic (two-man) method must be used which is described in detail below.

9 If a kit is to be used, prepare the car as described previously and follow the kit manufacturer's instructions as the procedure may vary slightly according to the type being used. Generally they are as outlined below in the relevant sub-section.

10 Whichever method is used, the same sequence must be followed (paras 11 and 12) to ensure that the removal of all air from the system.

Bleeding sequence

11 If the system has been only partially disconnected and suitable precautions were taken to minimise fluid loss, it should be necessary only to bleed that part of the system (ie the primary or secondary circuit).

12 If the complete system is to be bled, then it should be done working in the following sequence:

a) *Left-hand rear brake.*

b) *Right-hand front brake.*

c) *Right-hand rear brake.*

d) *Left-hand front brake.*

Bleeding - basic (two-man) method

13 Collect a clean glass jar, a suitable length of plastic or rubber tubing which is a tight fit over the bleed nipple and a ring spanner to fit the nipple. The help of an assistant will also be required.

14 Remove the dust cap from the first nipple in the sequence. Fit the spanner and tube to the nipple, place the other end of the tube in the jar and pour in sufficient fluid to cover the end of the tube.

15 Ensure that the master cylinder reservoir fluid level is maintained at least above the MIN level line throughout the procedure.

16 Have the assistant fully depress the brake pedal several times to build up pressure, then maintain it on the final stroke.

17 Whilst pedal pressure is maintained, unscrew the bleed nipple (approximately one turn) and allow the compressed fluid and air to flow into the jar. The assistant should maintain pedal pressure, following it down to the floor if necessary and should not release it until instructed to do so. When the flow stops, tighten the bleed nipple again, release the pedal slowly and recheck the reservoir fluid level.

18 Repeat the steps given in paragraphs 16 and 17 until the fluid emerging from the bleed nipple is free from air bubbles. If the master cylinder has been drained and refilled and air is being bled from the first nipple in the sequence, allow approximately five seconds between cycles for the master cylinder passages to refill.

19 When no more air bubbles appear, tighten the bleed nipple securely, remove the tube and spanner and refit the dust cap. Do not overtighten the bleed nipple. Note the specified torque wrench settings.

20 Repeat the procedure on the remaining nipples in the sequence until all air is removed from the system and the brake pedal feels firm again.

Bleeding - using a one-way valve kit

21 As their name implies, these kits consist of a length of tubing with a one-way valve fitted to prevent expelled air and fluid being

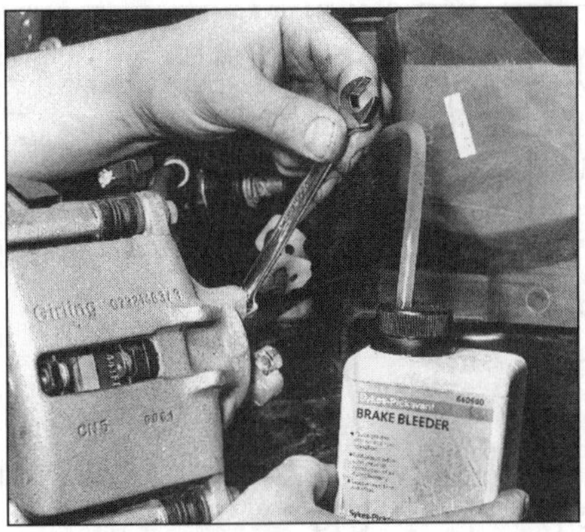

8.21 Bleeding the brake hydraulic system using a typical one-way valve kit

drawn back into the system. Some kits include a translucent container which can be positioned so that the air bubbles can be more easily seen flowing from the end of the tube **(see illustration)**.

22 The kit is connected to the bleed nipple, which is then opened. The user returns to the driver's seat and depresses the brake pedal with a smooth, steady stroke and slowly releases it. This is repeated until the expelled fluid is clear of air bubbles.

23 Note that these kits simplify work so much that it is easy to forget the master cylinder reservoir fluid level. Ensure that this is maintained at least above the MIN level line at all times.

Bleeding - using a pressure bleeding kit

24 These kits are usually operated by the reservoir of pressurised air contained in the spare tyre, although note that it will probably be necessary to reduce the pressure to a lower limit than normal. Refer to the instructions supplied with the kit.

25 By connecting a pressurised fluid-filled container to the master cylinder reservoir, bleeding can be carried out simply by opening each nipple in turn (in the specified sequence) and allowing the fluid to flow out until no more air bubbles can be seen in the expelled fluid.

26 This method has the advantage that the large reservoir of fluid provides an additional safeguard against air being drawn into the system during bleeding.

27 Pressure bleeding is particularly effective when bleeding difficult systems or when bleeding the complete system at the time of routine fluid renewal.

All methods

28 When bleeding is complete and firm pedal feel is restored, wash off any spilt fluid, tighten the bleed nipples securely and refit their dust caps. Do not overtighten the bleed nipples; note their specified torque wrench settings.

29 Check the hydraulic fluid level and top-up if necessary.

30 Discard any hydraulic fluid that has been bled from the system; it will not be fit for re-use.

31 Check the feel of the brake pedal. If it feels at all spongy, air must still be present in the system and further bleeding is required. Failure to bleed satisfactorily after a reasonable repetition of the bleeding procedure may be due to worn master cylinder seals.

9 Hydraulic pipes and hoses - inspection

Refer to Chapter 1, Section 20.

10 Hydraulic pipes and hoses - renewal

1 If any pipe or hose is to be renewed, minimise fluid loss by removing the master cylinder reservoir cap and then tightening it down onto a piece of polythene (taking care not to damage the sender unit) to obtain an airtight seal. Alternatively flexible hoses can be sealed, if required, using a proprietary brake hose clamp **(see illustration)**, whilst metal brake pipe unions can be plugged or capped immediately they are disconnected. Place a wad of rag under any union that is to be disconnected to catch any spilt fluid.

2 If a flexible hose is to be disconnected, unscrew the brake pipe union nut before removing the spring clip which secures the hose to its mounting bracket.

3 To unscrew the union nuts, it is preferable to obtain a brake pipe spanner of the correct size. These are available from most large motor accessory shops. Failing this, a close-fitting open-ended spanner will be required, though if the nuts are tight or corroded their flats may be rounded-off if the spanner slips. In such a case a self-locking wrench is often the only way to unscrew a stubborn union, but it follows that the pipe and the damaged nuts must be renewed on reassembly. Always clean a union and surrounding area before disconnecting it. If disconnecting a component with more than one union, make a careful note of the connections before disturbing any of them.

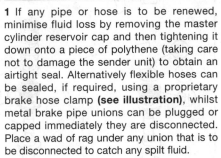

10.1 Using a brake hose clamp will minimise fluid loss when brake flexible hoses are disconnected

4 If a brake pipe is to be renewed, it can be obtained from a Rover dealer, cut to length and with the union nuts and end flares in place. All that is then necessary is to bend it to shape, following the line of the original, before fitting it to the car. Alternatively, most motor accessory shops can make up brake pipes from kits, but this requires very careful measurement of the original to ensure that the replacement is of the correct length. The safest answer is usually to take the original to the shop as a pattern.

5 On refitting, do not overtighten the union nuts. The specified torque wrench settings are not high and it is not necessary to exercise brute force to obtain a sound joint. When refitting flexible hoses, always renew any sealing washers used and note the torque settings specified.

6 Ensure that the pipes and hoses are correctly routed with no kinks and that they are secured in the clips or brackets provided. After fitting, remove the polythene from the reservoir and bleed the hydraulic system. Wash off any spilt fluid and check carefully for fluid leaks.

11 Master cylinder - removal, overhaul and refitting

Removal

1 Remove the master cylinder reservoir cap, having disconnected the sender unit wires, and syphon the hydraulic fluid from the reservoir. *Do not syphon the fluid by mouth as it is poisonous.* Alternatively, open any convenient bleed nipple in the system and gently pump the brake pedal to expel the fluid through a plastic tube connected to the nipple.

2 Release their clips and move the clutch and speedometer drive cables and the wiring clear of the master cylinder.

3 Unscrew the union nuts and disconnect the metal brake pipes. Try to keep fluid spillage to a minimum and wash off any spilt fluid as soon as possible.

4 Unscrew the two nuts securing the master cylinder to the vacuum servo unit and withdraw it. Remove and discard the sealing O-ring.

Overhaul

Note: *Before attempting to overhaul the unit, check the price and availability of individual components and compare this with the price of a new or reconditioned unit, as overhaul may not be viable on economic grounds alone. Also, read through the procedure and check that the special tools and facilities required are available*

5 Remove the master cylinder from the car and clean it thoroughly.

6 Extract the roll pin, then prise the reservoir from the master cylinder body and remove the two seals and their baffle plates from the body ports **(see illustration)**.

7 Press the primary piston in as far as possible and extract the secondary piston stop pin from the reservoir inlet port, then remove the retaining circlip.

8 Noting the order of removal and the direction of fitting of each component, withdraw the piston assemblies with their springs and seals, tapping the body on to a clean wooden surface to dislodge them. If necessary, clamp the master cylinder body in a vice (fitted with soft jaw covers) and use compressed air (applied through the secondary circuit fluid port) to assist the removal of the secondary piston assembly.

9 Undo the retaining screw to separate the spring retainer and spring from the primary piston and remove the circlip to release the spring seat, the piston seal and its washer.

10 Thoroughly clean all components using only methylated spirit, isopropyl alcohol or clean hydraulic fluid as a cleaning medium. Never use mineral-based solvents such as petrol or paraffin which will attack the hydraulic system's rubber components. Dry the components immediately using compressed air or a clean, lint-free cloth.

11 Check all components and renew any that are worn or damaged. Check particularly the cylinder bores and pistons. The complete assembly should be renewed if these are scratched, worn or corroded. If there is any doubt about the condition of the assembly or of any of its components, renew it. Check that the body's inlet and bypass ports are clear.

12 If the assembly is fit for further use, obtain a repair kit. Renew all seals and sealing O-rings disturbed on dismantling as a matter of course; these should never be re-used. Renew also any other items included in the repair kit.

13 On reassembly, soak the pistons and the new seals in clean hydraulic fluid. Smear clean fluid into the cylinder bore.

14 Fit the new seals to their pistons using only the fingers to manipulate them into the grooves.

15 Insert the pistons into the bore using a twisting motion to avoid trapping the seal lips. Ensure that all components are refitted in the correct order and the right way round.

16 Press the secondary piston assembly fully up into the bore using a clean metal rod, then refit the stop pin.

17 Refit the primary piston assembly, then secure it with a new circlip.

18 Refit the baffle plates and press new seals into the body ports, then refit the reservoir and secure it with the roll pin.

19 Refit the master cylinder to the car, using a new sealing O-ring.

Refitting

20 Refitting is the reverse of the removal procedure, noting the following points:

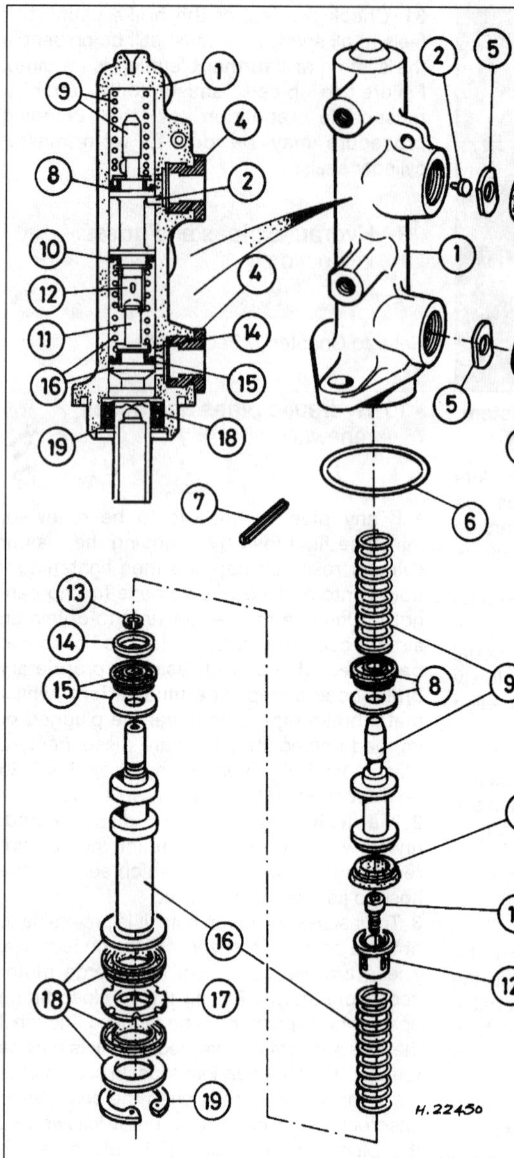

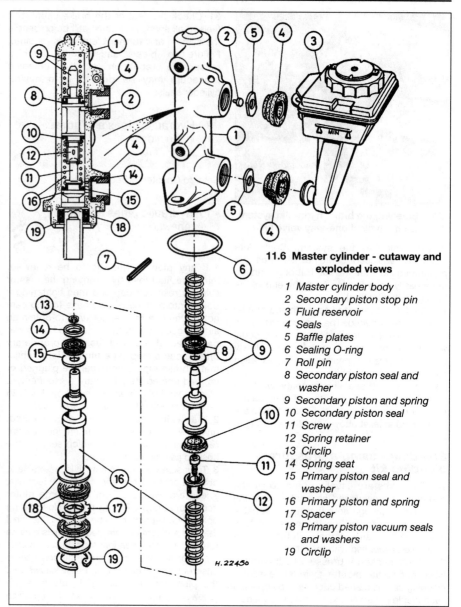

11.6 Master cylinder - cutaway and exploded views

1 Master cylinder body
2 Secondary piston stop pin
3 Fluid reservoir
4 Seals
5 Baffle plates
6 Sealing O-ring
7 Roll pin
8 Secondary piston seal and washer
9 Secondary piston and spring
10 Secondary piston seal
11 Screw
12 Spring retainer
13 Circlip
14 Spring seat
15 Primary piston seal and washer
16 Primary piston and spring
17 Spacer
18 Primary piston vacuum seals and washers
19 Circlip

a) Refit the master cylinder to the vacuum servo unit, aligning the servo's pushrod with the master cylinder primary piston.
b) Fit a new sealing O-ring and tighten the mounting nuts to their specified torque wrench setting.
c) Refill the reservoir with new fluid and bleed the system.
d) If a new master cylinder has been fitted (or the original was fully drained) start the bleeding procedure by disconnecting each metal brake pipe in turn (top first) and gently pumping the brake pedal until only clear hydraulic fluid emerges. Catch the ejected fluid with a rag wrapped around the master cylinder.
e) In very difficult cases, disconnect both pipes, plug their ports with the fingers, then uncover each one in turn as the brake pedal is depressed and plug it again as the pedal is released, so that fluid is forcibly drawn in from the reservoir. Refit and tighten securely all pipe unions as soon as the master cylinder is cleared of air and is pumping correctly, then proceed with the normal bleeding procedure.
f) Ensure that the disturbed cables and wiring are correctly re-routed, check the hydraulic fluid level and top-up if necessary, then reconnect the sender unit wires.

12 Front brake pads - inspection

Refer to Chapter 1, Section 18.

13.4 Unscrew caliper bottom guide pin bolt and swing up caliper body . . .

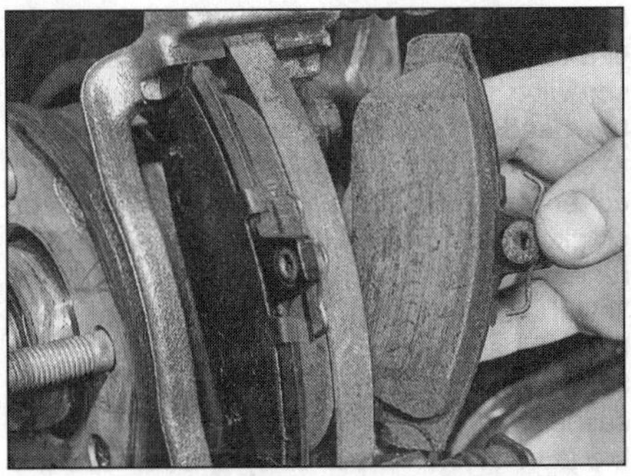

13.5 . . . note location of anti-rattle springs before removing brake pads

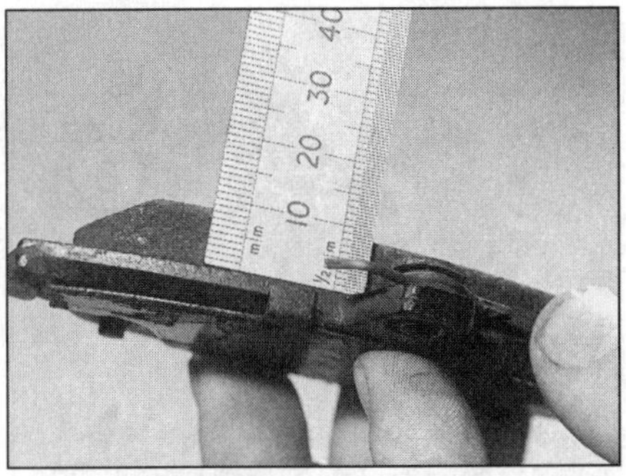

13.6 Measuring thickness of brake pad friction material

13 Front brake pads - renewal

Warning: When working on brake components, take care not to disperse brake dust into the air or to inhale it, since it may contain asbestos which is injurious to health.

Warning: Always support the vehicle on axle stands before removing the roadwheel to service brake assemblies.

1 Jack up the front of the car and support it securely on axle stands (see *"Jacking and Vehicle Support"*), then remove the roadwheel.

2 If the inspection described in Chapter 1 has shown the condition of the brake pads to be doubtful, they must be removed and checked, as follows.

3 Pull the caliper body outwards to compress the piston into the cylinder, then check that the caliper body slides smoothly and easily in the mounting bracket. If not, the guide pins must be cleaned, checked for wear and lubricated before reassembly.

4 Unscrew the caliper bottom guide pin bolt, if necessary using a slim open-ended spanner to counterhold the head of the guide pin itself **(see illustration)**. Pivot the caliper body upwards to expose the brake pads. Do not depress the brake pedal until the caliper is reassembled.

5 Noting the exact location of the anti-rattle springs, withdraw the brake pads **(see illustration)**. Mark them so that they will be refitted in their original locations. Do not be tempted to interchange pads to compensate for uneven wear.

6 First measure the thickness of friction material remaining on each brake pad **(see illustration)**. If either pad is worn at any point to the specified minimum thickness or less, all four pads must be renewed as a set. Also, the pads should be renewed if any are fouled with oil or grease; there is no satisfactory way of degreasing friction material once contaminated.

7 If any of the brake pads are worn unevenly or fouled with oil or grease, trace and rectify the cause before reassembly.

8 If the brake pads are still serviceable, carefully clean them using a clean, fine wire brush or similar, paying particular attention to the sides and back of the metal backing. Clean out the grooves in the friction material (where applicable) and pick out any large embedded particles of dirt or debris. Carefully clean the anti-rattle springs and the pad locations in the caliper body and mounting bracket.

9 If there is any doubt about the ability of the caliper to slide in the mounting bracket, dismantle, clean and lubricate the guide pins **(see illustration)**. Inspect the brake disc.

10 On reassembly, fit the anti-rattle springs to the brake pads and apply a thin smear of high-temperature brake grease (silicone- or PBC/Poly Butyl Cuprysil-based) or anti-seize compound to the sides and back of each pad's metal backing and to those surfaces of the caliper body and mounting bracket which bear on the pads. Do not allow the lubricant to foul the friction material.

11 Refit the brake pads, ensuring that the friction material is against the disc.

12 If new brake pads have been fitted, the caliper piston must be pushed back into the cylinder to make room for them. Either use a G-clamp or similar tool, or use suitable pieces of wood as levers. Provided that the master cylinder reservoir has not been overfilled with hydraulic fluid there should be no spillage, but keep a careful watch on the fluid level while retracting the piston. If the fluid level rises above the MAX level line at any time the surplus should be siphoned off or ejected via a plastic tube connected to the bleed nipple.

13.9 Remove, clean and lubricate guide pins if caliper body is not free to slide on mounting bracket

13 Pivot the caliper body down over the brake pads, refit the bottom guide pin bolt and tighten it to the specified torque wrench setting.

14 Check that the caliper body slides smoothly in the mounting bracket, then depress the brake pedal repeatedly until the pads are pressed into firm contact with the brake disc and normal (non-assisted) pedal pressure is restored. Refit the roadwheel.

15 Repeat the full procedure on the opposite brake caliper, then lower the car to the ground and tighten the roadwheel nuts to the specified torque wrench setting.

16 Check the hydraulic fluid level.

14 Front brake caliper - removal and refitting

Warning: Brake hydraulic fluid may be under considerable pressure in a pipeline, take care not to allow hydraulic fluid to spray into the face or eyes when loosening a connection.

Removal

1 Jack up the front of the car and support it securely on axle stands (see *"Jacking and Vehicle Support"*), then remove the roadwheel.

2 Minimise fluid loss either by removing the master cylinder reservoir cap and then tightening it down onto a piece of polythene to obtain an airtight seal (taking care not to damage the sender unit), or by using a brake hose clamp, a G-clamp or a similar tool to clamp the flexible hose.

3 Clean the area around the union, then unscrew the flexible hose banjo union bolt. Discard the sealing washers, they must be renewed whenever disturbed. If the caliper is not to be dismantled, plug the fluid orifice to prevent the entry of dirt. Similarly, plug or wrap the flexible hose banjo union tightly with polythene.

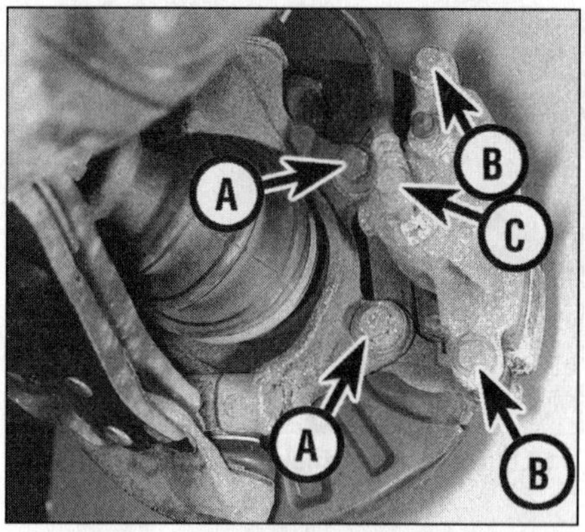

14.4 Caliper mounting bracket-to-hub carrier bolts (A) guide pin bolts (B) and flexible hose banjo union bolt (C)

4 Unscrew the two caliper mounting bracket-to-hub carrier bolts **(see illustration)**.

5 Withdraw the brake caliper assembly and slip a clean wooden spacer (of the same thickness as the brake disc) between the brake pads to retain them.

Refitting

6 Refitting is the reverse of the removal procedure, noting the following points.

a) *Tighten all nuts and bolts to the specified torque wrench settings.*
b) *Renew the flexible hose union sealing washers as a matter of course.*
c) *Ensure that the flexible hose is correctly routed and secured by the clamp provided, without being twisted.*
d) *Bleed any air from the system.*
e) *Check the hydraulic fluid level.*

15 Front brake caliper - overhaul

Caution: Never refit old seals when reassembling brake system components

1 Jack up the front of the car and support it securely on axle stands (see "*Jacking and Vehicle Support*"), then remove the roadwheel.

2 Minimise fluid loss either by removing the master cylinder reservoir cap and then tightening it down onto a piece of polythene to obtain an airtight seal (taking care not to damage the sender unit), or by using a brake hose clamp, a G-clamp or a similar tool to clamp the flexible hose.

3 Clean the area around the union, then unscrew the flexible hose banjo union bolt. Discard the sealing washers; they must be renewed whenever disturbed. Wrap polythene tightly around the flexible hose banjo union to prevent the entry of dirt.

4 Unscrew the caliper guide pin bolts **(see illustration)**, if necessary using a slim open-ended spanner to counterhold the head of each guide pin. Withdraw the caliper body.

5 Remove and check the brake pads.

6 Extract the guide pins, if necessary by screwing their bolts into them and pulling on the head of each bolt using a self-locking wrench or similar. Peel off the rubber dust cover from each guide pin and check it for cracks, splits or other damage; these can be renewed separately if required.

7 Unbolt the caliper mounting bracket from the hub carrier.

8 Prise off the piston dust seal lip from the caliper body. Place a small block of wood in the jaws of the caliper body and remove the piston, including dust seal, by applying a jet of low-pressure compressed air (such as that from a tyre pump) to the fluid entry port.

9 Peel the dust seal off the piston and use a blunt instrument such as a knitting needle to extract the piston (fluid) seal from the caliper cylinder bore.

10 Thoroughly clean all components using only methylated spirit, isopropyl alcohol or clean hydraulic fluid as a cleaning medium. Never use mineral-based solvents such as petrol or paraffin which will attack the hydraulic system's rubber components. Dry the components immediately using compressed air or a clean, lint-free cloth. Use compressed air to blow clear the fluid passages.

11 Check all components and renew any that are worn or damaged. Check particularly the cylinder bore and piston; these should be renewed (note that this means the renewal of the complete body assembly) if they are scratched, worn or corroded in any way. Similarly check the condition of the guide pins and their bores in the mounting bracket. Both guide pins should be undamaged and (when cleaned) a reasonably tight sliding fit in the mounting bracket bores. If there is any doubt about the condition of any components, renew it.

12 If the assembly is fit for further use, obtain the appropriate repair kit. The components are available from Rover dealers in various combinations.

13 Renew all rubber seals, dust covers and caps, and also the sealing washers disturbed on dismantling as a matter of course. These should never be re-used.

14 On reassembly, ensure that all components are absolutely clean and dry.

15 Soak the piston and the new piston (fluid) seal in clean hydraulic fluid. Smear clean fluid on the cylinder bore surface.

16 Fit the new piston (fluid) seal using only the fingers to manipulate it into the cylinder bore groove. Fit the new dust seal to the

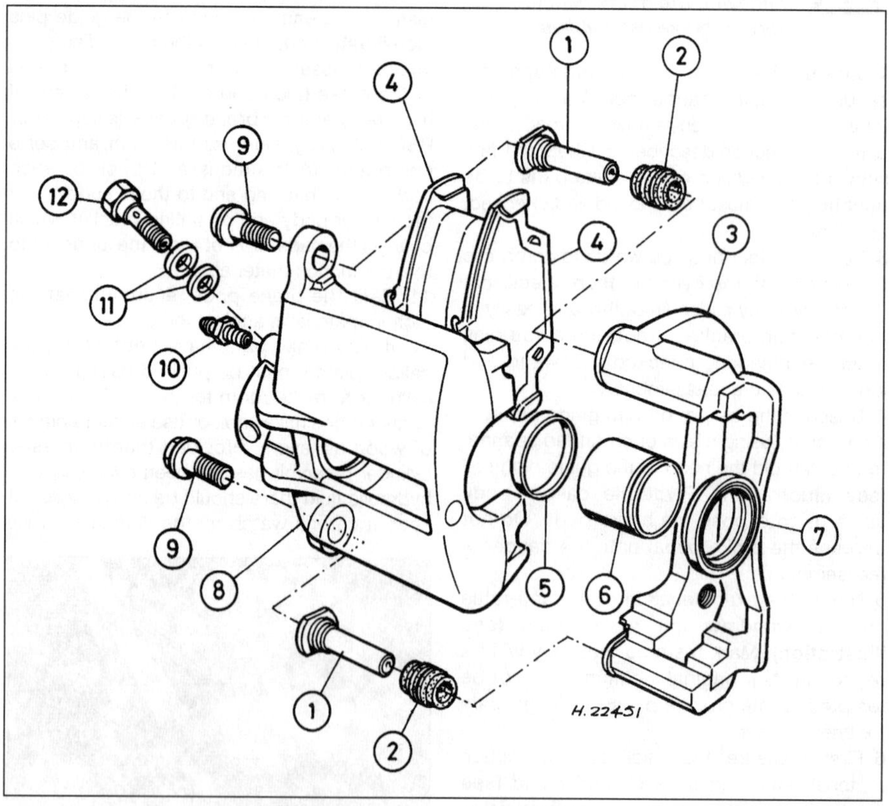

15.4 Exploded view of front brake caliper

1 Guide pins
2 Rubber dust covers
3 Caliper mounting bracket
4 Brake pads
5 Piston (fluid) seal
6 Piston
7 Piston (dust) seal
8 Caliper body
9 Guide pin bolts
10 Bleed nipple
11 Sealing washers
12 Flexible hose banjo bolt

piston and refit it to the cylinder bore using a twisting motion, and ensure that the piston enters squarely into the bore. Press the piston fully into the bore, then secure the dust seal to the caliper body.

17 Refit the caliper mounting bracket to the hub carrier, tightening the two bolts to the specified torque wrench setting.

18 Fit a new rubber dust cover to each guide pin and apply a thin smear of grease to the guide pins before refitting them to their bores. Rover recommend Molykote 111 for this purpose; a sachet is included in all appropriate repair kits. If it is not available, any good quality silicone- or PBC/Poly Butyl Cuprysil-based high-temperature brake grease or anti-seize compound can be used.

19 Refit the brake pads.

20 Fit the caliper body over the mounting bracket and brake pads, refit the guide pin bolts and tighten them to the torque wrench setting specified. Check that the caliper body slides smoothly in the mounting bracket.

21 Ensuring that the flexible hose is correctly routed and secured by the clamp provided without being twisted, refit the hose banjo union to the caliper body so that the union's locating peg is between the two body lugs, fit two new sealing washers (one on each side of the hose union), then refit the banjo union bolt and tighten it to its specified torque wrench setting, ensuring that the union does not twist as the bolt is tightened.

22 Bleed any air from the system, then depress the brake pedal repeatedly until the pads are pressed into firm contact with the brake disc and normal (non-assisted) pedal pressure is restored.

23 Wash off any spilt fluid and check for any fluid leaks while an assistant applies full pressure to the brake pedal. Refit the roadwheel.

24 Repeat the full procedure on the opposite brake caliper, then lower the car to the ground and tighten the roadwheel nuts to the specified torque wrench setting.

25 Check the hydraulic fluid level. Check for any fluid leaks which might subsequently appear.

16 Front brake disc - inspection, removal and refitting

Inspection

Note: *To ensure even and consistent braking, both discs should be renewed at the same time, even if only one is faulty*

1 Jack up the front of the car and support it securely on axle stands (see "*Jacking and Vehicle Support*"), then remove the roadwheel.

2 Slowly rotate the brake disc so that the full area of both sides can be checked. Remove the brake pads if better access is required to the inboard surface. Light scoring is normal in

16.8 Front brake disc securing screws (arrowed)

the area swept by the brake pads, but if heavy scoring is found the disc must be renewed. The only alternative to this is to have the disc surface-ground until it is flat again, but this must not reduce the disc to less than the minimum thickness specified.

3 It is normal to find a lip of rust and brake dust around the disc's perimeter; this can be scraped off if required. If, however, a lip has formed due to excessive wear of the brake pad swept area then the disc's thickness must be measured using a micrometer. Take measurements at four places around the disc at the inside and outside of the pad swept area. If the disc has worn at any point to the specified minimum thickness or less, or if any measurement differs from the others by more than the maximum specified variation, the disc must be renewed.

4 If the disc is thought to be warped, it can be checked for run-out (6 mm in from the disc's outer edge) either using a dial gauge mounted on any convenient fixed point, whilst the disc is slowly rotated, or by using feeler blades to measure (at several points all around the disc) the clearance between the disc and a fixed point such as the caliper mounting bracket. If the measurements obtained are at the specified maximum or beyond, the disc is excessively warped and must be renewed. However, it is worth checking first that the hub bearing is in good condition. Also try the effect of removing the disc and turning it through 180° to reposition it on the hub. If run-out is still excessive the disc must be renewed.

5 Check the disc for cracks, especially around the stud holes, and any other wear or damage. Renew it if any of these are found.

Removal

6 Jack up the front of the car and support it securely on axle stands (see "*Jacking and Vehicle Support*"), then remove the roadwheel.

7 Unscrew the two brake caliper mounting bracket-to-hub carrier bolts, then withdraw the caliper assembly and secure it out of harm's way without stretching or kinking the brake hose. Place a clean spacer (of the same thickness as the brake disc) between the pads to prevent them being dislodged.

8 Use chalk or paint to mark the relationship of the disc to the hub, then undo the disc securing screws **(see illustration)** and withdraw the disc.

Refitting

9 Refitting is the reverse of the removal procedure, noting the following points.

a) Ensure that the mating surfaces of the disc and hub are clean and flat.

b) Align (if applicable) the marks made on removal.

c) If a new disc has been fitted, use a suitable solvent to wipe any preservative coating from the disc before refitting the caliper.

d) Tighten the screws, bolts and roadwheel nuts to their specified torque wrench settings.

17 Front brake disc shield - removal and refitting

Removal

1 Remove the brake disc.

2 Unbolt the brake disc shield from the hub carrier and withdraw it.

Refitting

3 Refitting is the reverse of the removal procedure. Tighten the shield mounting bolts to the specified torque wrench setting.

18 Pressure regulating valve - removal and refitting

1 If one or both rear roadwheels lock repeatedly under heavy braking, first check that this is not due to adverse road conditions or to incorrectly inflated or badly-worn tyres, then check the condition of all four brake assemblies before suspecting a pressure regulating valve fault. Note that the right-hand valve serves only the primary circuit, which includes the left-hand rear brake, whilst the left-hand valve serves the secondary circuit and the right-hand rear brake. If a fault appears, this may help to isolate the cause.

2 If either valve is thought to be faulty it must be renewed. The valves are available only as complete units and must not be dismantled.

Removal

3 The two pressure regulating valves are bolted to the engine compartment bulkhead **(see illustration)**. Remove the air cleaner assembly, if required, to gain better working space.

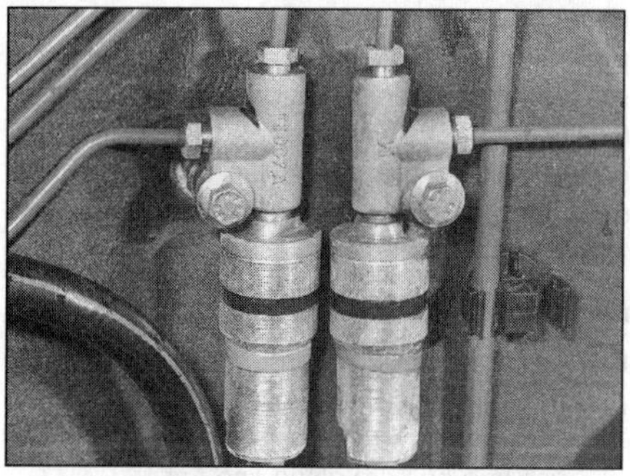

18.3 Rear brake pressure regulating valves on engine compartment bulkhead

4 Minimise fluid loss either by removing the master cylinder reservoir cap and then tightening it down onto a piece of polythene to obtain an airtight seal (taking care not to damage the sender unit), or by capping or plugging each metal brake pipe as it is disconnected from the valve. Also plug the valve orifices, whilst taking great care not to allow dirt into the system.
5 Unbolt the valve from the bulkhead, noting the spacer and withdraw it.

Refitting

6 Refitting is the reverse of the removal procedure, noting the following points.

a) Prevent the valve from rotating while tightening the bolt to its specified torque wrench setting.
b) When the metal brake pipe unions are secured, bleed any air from the system and wash off any spilt fluid.
c) Check the hydraulic fluid level.

20.5a Releasing brake shoe retainer components

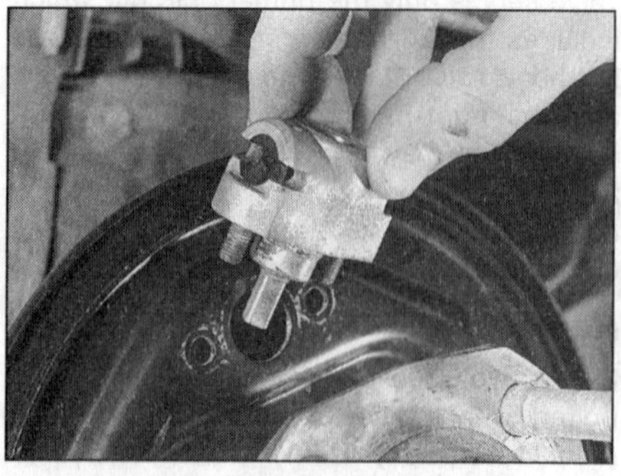

20.7a Rear brake shoe adjuster assembly . . .

19 Rear brake shoes - wear check and adjustment

Refer to Chapter 1, Section 19.

20 Rear brake shoes - renewal

1 Remove and inspect the brake drum.
2 Remove all traces of brake dust from the brake drum, backplate and shoes.
3 Measure the thickness of friction material remaining on each brake shoe at several points. If either shoe is worn at any point to the specified minimum thickness or less, all four shoes must be renewed (replacement shoes from Rover dealers are only available as an axle set). Also, the shoes should be renewed if any are fouled with oil or grease as there is no satisfactory way of degreasing friction material once contaminated.
4 If any of the brake shoes are worn unevenly or fouled with oil or grease, trace and rectify the cause before reassembly.
5 To remove the brake shoes, first remove the shoe retainer springs and pins, using a pair of pliers to press in each retainer washer until it can be rotated through 90° and released. Release the shoes one at a time from the adjuster, then from the wheel cylinder and handbrake lever assembly, unhook the bottom return spring and withdraw the shoes from the backplate **(see illustrations)**. Do not depress the brake pedal until the brakes are reassembled. Wrap a strong elastic band around the wheel cylinder pistons to retain them.
6 Clean the backplate and apply a thin smear of high-temperature brake grease (silicone- or PBC/Poly Butyl Cuprysil-based) or anti-seize compound to all those surfaces of the backplate which bear on the shoes, particularly the adjuster and the wheel cylinder pistons. Do not allow the lubricant to foul the friction material.
7 Check the adjuster for wear or damage; it can be unbolted and renewed separately if necessary **(see illustrations)**.
8 Peel back the rubber protective caps and check the wheel cylinder for fluid leaks or other damage.
9 Check the handbrake lever assembly for wear or damage and renew it if necessary. Apply a smear of lubricant to its bearing surfaces.
10 Fit the shoe assembly to the backplate, being careful not to get grease onto the friction material. Ensure that the shoe ends engage properly with the wheel cylinder piston and adjuster grooves, then hook on the bottom return spring and engage the shoes on the handbrake lever assembly **(see illustration)**.
11 Tap the shoes to centralise them on the backplate, then refit the shoe retainer pins, springs and washers. If new shoes have been fitted, slacken off the adjuster to provide sufficient clearance for them.
12 Refit the brake drum.
13 Repeat the procedure on the opposite brake.

20.5b Removing brake shoes

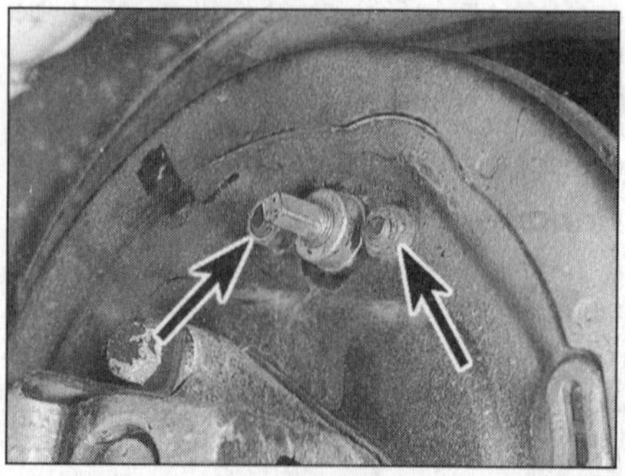

20.7b . . . is secured by two nuts (arrowed)

21 Rear brake drum - removal, inspection and refitting

Removal

1 Jack up the rear of the car and support it securely on axle stands (see "*Jacking and Vehicle Support*"), then remove the roadwheel.
2 Use chalk or paint to mark the relationship of the drum to the hub.

20.10 Brake shoe and handbrake lever assembly correctly refitted

21.3 Removing the rear brake drum securing screw

3 With the handbrake firmly applied to prevent drum rotation, unscrew the drum securing screw **(see illustration)**. Fully release the handbrake and withdraw the drum.

4 If the drum will not pull away, first check that the handbrake is fully released, then slacken off the brake shoe adjustment until the drum can be removed. If the drum still will not move it is probably stuck to the hub flange with corrosion; use a soft-faced mallet to gently tap the drum off the hub. Discard the drum gasket which must be renewed whenever the drum is disturbed.

Inspection

Note: *If either drum requires renewal, both should be renewed at the same time to ensure even and consistent braking*

5 Remove all traces of brake dust from the drum, noting the precautions given in Section 1.

6 Scrub clean the outside of the drum and check it for obvious signs of wear or damage such as cracks around the roadwheel stud holes. Renew the drum if necessary.

7 Examine carefully the inside of the drum. Light scoring of the friction surface is normal, but if heavy scoring is found the drum must be renewed. It is usual to find a lip on the drum's inboard edge which consists of a mixture of rust and brake dust; this should be scraped away to leave a smooth surface which can be polished with fine (120 to 150 grade) emery paper. If, however, the lip is due to the friction surface being recessed by excessive wear, then the drum must be renewed.

8 If the drum is thought to be excessively worn, or oval, its internal diameter must be measured at several points using an internal micrometer. Take measurements in pairs, the second at right angles to the first, and compare the two to check for signs of ovality. Provided that it does not enlarge the drum to beyond the specified maximum diameter, it may be possible to have the drum refinished by skimming or grinding but if this is not possible, the drums on both sides must be renewed.

Refitting

9 Refitting is the reverse of the removal procedure, noting the following points.

a) On fitting a new brake drum, use a suitable solvent to remove any preservative coating that may have been applied to its interior.

b) Use a clean wire brush to remove all traces of dirt, brake dust and corrosion from the mating surfaces of the drum and the hub flange. Always fit a new gasket to the hub flange.

c) Align (if applicable) the marks made on removal.

d) Tighten the drum securing screw and the roadwheel nuts to their specified torque wrench settings.

e) Depress the brake pedal several times until the wheel cylinder(s) and brake shoes have taken up their correct working positions and normal (non-assisted) pedal pressure is restored.

f) Check, and correct if necessary, the brake shoe adjustment.

g) Check, and correct if necessary, the handbrake adjustment. Ensure that the roadwheels rotate easily, with no (or very slight) sound of brake shoe-to-drum contact.

22 Rear wheel cylinder - removal, overhaul and refitting

Removal

1 Remove the brake drum.

2 Remove the brake shoes.

3 Minimise fluid loss by removing the master cylinder reservoir cap and then tightening it down onto a piece of polythene to obtain an airtight seal (taking care not to damage the sender unit), or by using a brake hose clamp, a G-clamp or a similar tool to clamp the flexible hose, or by capping or plugging the metal brake pipe as it is disconnected from the cylinder. Unscrew the bleed nipple. Plug the cylinder orifices, taking great care not to allow dirt into the system.

4 Noting how it is fitted, prise out the circlip securing the cylinder to the backplate. Withdraw the cylinder and its gasket.

Overhaul

Note: *Before attempting to overhaul the unit, check the price and availability of individual components and the price of a new or reconditioned unit, as overhaul may not be viable on economic grounds alone. Also, read through the procedure and check that the special tools and facilities required are available*

5 Remove the wheel cylinder from the car and clean it thoroughly.

6 Mount the wheel cylinder in a soft-jawed vice and remove the rubber protective caps. Extract the piston assemblies.

7 Thoroughly clean all components using only methylated spirit, isopropyl alcohol or clean hydraulic fluid as a cleaning medium. Never use mineral-based solvents such as petrol or paraffin which will attack the hydraulic system's rubber components. Dry the components immediately using compressed air or a clean, lint-free cloth.

8 Check all components and renew any that are worn or damaged. Check particularly the cylinder bore and pistons. The complete assembly must be renewed if these are scratched, worn or corroded. If there is any doubt about the condition of the assembly or of any of its components, renew it. Check that the fluid entry port and bleed nipple passage are clear.

9 If the assembly is fit for further use, obtain a repair kit. Renew the rubber protective caps, dust caps and seals disturbed on dismantling as a matter of course; these should never be re-used. Renew also any other items included in the repair kit.

10 On reassembly, soak the pistons and the new seals in clean hydraulic fluid. Smear clean fluid on the cylinder bore surface.

11 Fit the new seals to their pistons using only the fingers to manipulate them into the grooves. Ensure that all components are refitted in the correct order and the right way round.

12 Insert the pistons into the bore using a twisting motion to avoid trapping the seal lips. Apply a smear of rubber lubricant to each piston before fitting the new rubber protective caps.

13 Refit the wheel cylinder to the car.

Refitting

14 Refitting is the reverse of the removal procedure, noting the following points.

a) Fit the gasket to the cylinder and refit the cylinder, ensuring that the circlip is fitted correctly.

b) Refit the bleed nipple, then connect the metal brake pipe to the cylinder and refit the brake shoes and drum.

c) Bleed any air from the system and check for leaks while an assistant applies full pressure to the brake pedal, then wash off any spilt fluid.

d) Check the brake hydraulic fluid level. Check for any fluid leaks which might subsequently appear.

23 Rear brake backplate - removal and refitting

Removal

1 Remove the rear hub.

2 Remove the brake shoes.

3 Minimise fluid loss by removing the master cylinder reservoir cap and then tightening it down onto a piece of polythene to obtain an airtight seal (taking care not to damage the sender unit), or by using a brake hose clamp, a G-clamp or a similar tool to clamp the flexible hose, or by capping or plugging the

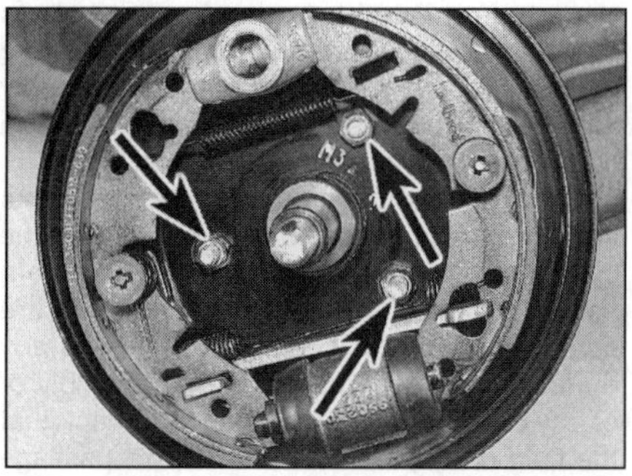

23.5 Brake backplate mounting bolts/nuts (arrowed)

metal brake pipe as it is disconnected from the wheel cylinder. Also plug the cylinder orifices, taking great care not to allow dirt into the hydraulic system.

4 Disconnect the handbrake cable from the lever assembly.

5 Unbolt the backplate from the rear suspension trailing arm and withdraw it, noting the arrangement of the handbrake cable bracket and, where fitted, the anti-roll bar link bracket **(see illustration)**.

Refitting

6 Refitting is the reverse of the removal procedure, but apply a smear of sealant to the backplate/trailing arm mating surfaces. Tighten all nuts and bolts to their specified torque wrench settings. Refer to the relevant Sections of Chapter 10 as well as this Chapter for detailed instructions.

24 Handbrake - inspection and adjustment

Refer to Chapter 1, Section 21.

25 Handbrake lever - removal and refitting

Removal

1 With the car parked on level ground, switch off the ignition, select first or reverse gear and chock the roadwheels so that the car cannot move.

2 Referring to the relevant Sections of Chapter 11, carry out the following **(see illustration)**.

a) Remove the front seats and the front seat rear mounting bar.

b) Unscrew the rear seat mountings; remove the seats if required.

c) Remove all door sill trim panels.

d) Unbolt the front seat belt bottom anchorages and the stalks.

3 Withdraw the two covering plastic mouldings from the floor front crossmember, lift the carpet and peel it forwards, clear of the handbrake lever.

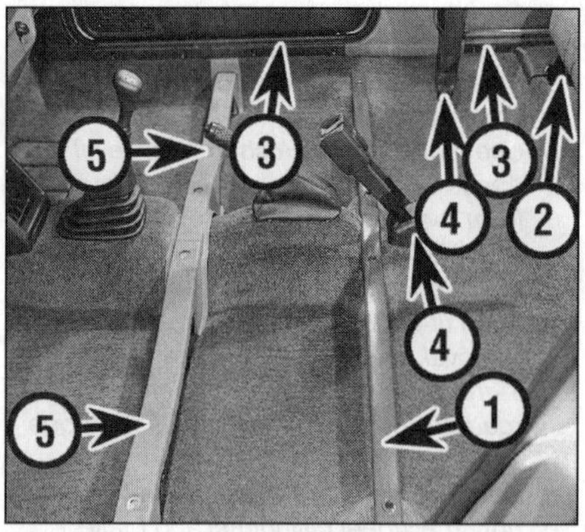

25.2 Remove front seat rear mounting bar (1) rear seat mountings (2) door sill trim panels (3) seat belt anchorages and stalks (4) and front crossmember covers (5) to lift carpet for access to handbrake

4 Either disconnect the handbrake switch wires or remove its retaining screws and withdraw the switch from the lever.

5 Remove its split pin and withdraw the clevis pin securing the cable yoke to the handbrake lever **(see illustration)**.

6 Unbolt the handbrake lever from the floor.

Refitting

7 Refitting is the reverse of the removal procedure. Apply a smear of grease (Rover recommend Molykote 44) to all pivots, the cable yoke fittings and the adjuster threads. Adjust the handbrake.

26 Handbrake cable - removal, inspection and refitting

Removal

1 Gain access to the cable assembly by carrying out the preliminary dismantling described in Section 25.

2 Remove its split pin and withdraw the clevis pin securing the cable yoke to the handbrake lever. Unscrew the cable adjuster nuts and remove the yoke and nuts from the cable **(see illustration)**.

26.2 Lift floor carpet to expose handbrake cable yoke and adjuster

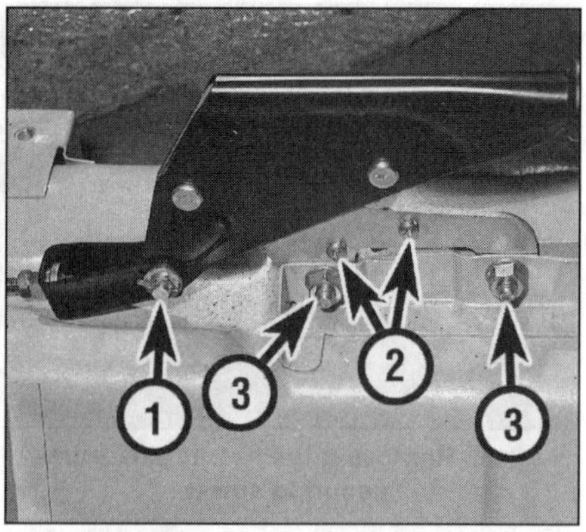

25.5 Handbrake lever-to-cable clevis pin (1) switch mounting screws (2) and lever mounting nuts and bolts (3)

3 Drill out the pop rivet securing the cable cover plate to the floor, then remove the cover and withdraw the seal from the cable.

4 Jack up the rear of the car and support it securely on axle stands (see "*Jacking and Vehicle Support*").

5 Release the cable from the clips securing it to the fuel tank left-hand end.

6 Remove the clip securing the front end of the cable outer to the underbody bracket (immediately above the exhaust intermediate pipe rubber mounting), release the cable from the bracket and pull it down clear of the car.

7 Disconnect the cable from both rear brake handbrake lever assemblies by removing its split pin and withdrawing the clevis pin securing each cable yoke **(see illustration)**.

8 Remove the clip securing each rear end of the cable outer to its respective suspension trailing arm bracket, release each cable seal and the cable-tie securing the cable to the trailing arm, then release the cable from the trailing arm.

9 Remove the clip securing the cable outer to each end of the rear suspension subframe **(see illustration)**, release each cable seal and move the cable into the larger subframe aperture, then remove both cable ends from the subframe.

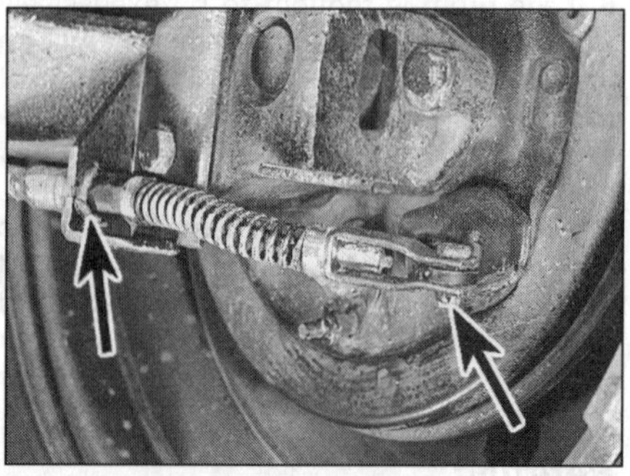

26.7 Handbrake cable-to-lever assembly clevis pin and trailing arm bracket clip (arrowed)

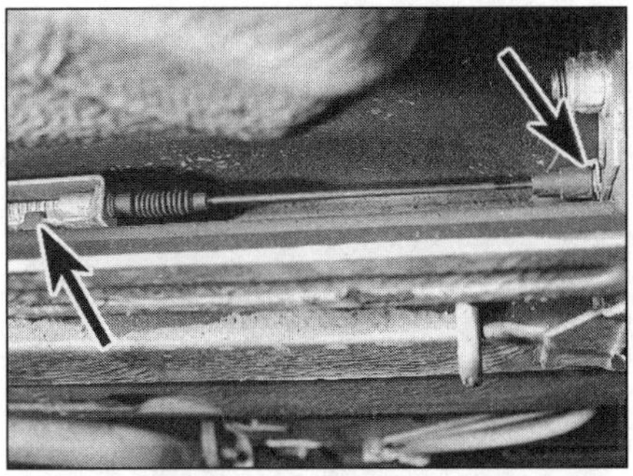

26.9 Handbrake cable and compensator clips (arrowed)

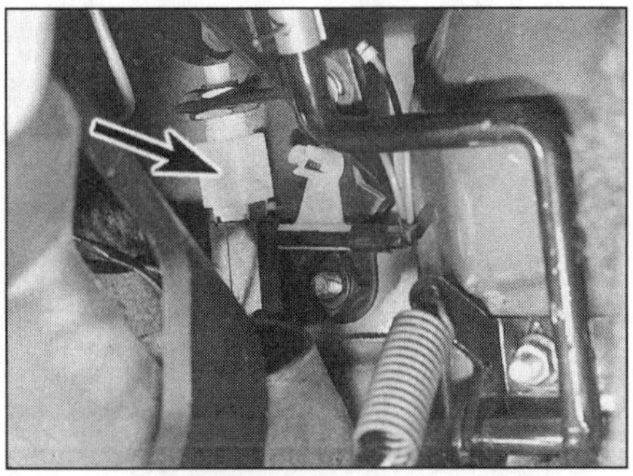

27.4 Location of stop-lamp switch (arrowed)

28.6 Location of handbrake switch (arrowed)

10 Release the compensator assembly from the subframe clip and withdraw the cable assembly from the car, noting carefully how it is routed.

Inspection

11 Check the cable for wear or damage and renew it if necessary.

12 Clean the adjuster threads thoroughly and apply a smear of grease to the yokes. Check and lubricate the compensator and, if required, the rear brake lever assembly.

Refitting

13 Refitting is the reverse of the removal procedure, noting the following points.

a) Lay out the cable under the car so that it is in its correct relative position, then pass the front end over the subframe.

b) Feed each cable rear end through the subframe and route it along the trailing arm, then clip the compensator into place, push each cable outer into the subframe smaller aperture, refit the clips to secure them and position the cable seals.

c) Refit each cable rear end to its trailing arm bracket, refit the clip to secure it and position the cable seal.

d) Lubricate the clevis pins (Rover recommend Molykote 44) before connecting each cable rear end to its respective rear brake lever assembly.

e) Pass the cable's front end into the car, secure the cable outer with the clip and fasten the clips securing the cable to the fuel tank.

f) Check the cable seal and renew it if necessary, then connect the cable to the handbrake lever and pop-rivet the cover plate to the floor.

g) Adjust the handbrake.

h) Use new cable-ties to secure the cables to the trailing arms, then lower the car to the ground.

i) Refit the carpet, the seat belts and the seats.

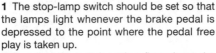

27 Stop-lamp switch - adjustment

1 The stop-lamp switch should be set so that the lamps light whenever the brake pedal is depressed to the point where the pedal free play is taken up.

2 To adjust the switch setting, first release the retaining fasteners and remove the fusebox cover.

3 Remove its retaining screw and bolt and withdraw the steering column cover, then unfasten the column from its remaining mountings and lower it as far as possible without stretching the wiring. Peel back the carpet if better access is required.

4 Slacken the two nuts securing the switch **(see illustration)** and reposition the switch until the lamps light at the correct moment. Either have an assistant check the stop-lamps for you or disconnect the switch wires and use a multimeter set to the resistance scale to check when the switch contacts close, allowing current to flow. Tighten the two nuts securely, then switch on the ignition and check the operation of the stop-lamps.

5 Refit the steering column, its cover and the fusebox cover.

28 Brake system warning lamps - testing and renewal

Stop-lamp

1 The stop-lamp circuit is controlled by a plunger-type switch mounted on the brake pedal bracket.

2 Check and adjust the switch setting.

3 If the switch is thought to be faulty, it can be tested by disconnecting its wires and connecting either a multimeter (set to the resistance function) or a battery and bulb test circuit across the switch terminals. The switch should allow current to flow only when it is extended. If the switch is faulty it must be renewed.

4 To remove the switch, disconnect its wires and unscrew the adjuster locknut to remove it from its bracket.

5 Refitting is the reverse of the removal procedure; adjust the switch setting.

Brake warning lamp

6 The handbrake circuit of the instrument panel brake warning lamp is activated by a plunger switch mounted at the base of the handbrake lever. The lamp lights whenever the handbrake is applied or whenever the brake fluid in the master cylinder falls to a dangerously low level **(see illustration)**.

7 Unless the switch, its mounting screws and connector can be reached by (carefully) lifting the handbrake lever gaiter and peeling back the carpet, the switch can be reached only by lifting the carpet.

8 The switch is not adjustable and is secured by two screws. To remove it, undo the screws and unplug the wiring connector.

9 To test the switch, remove it and use the equipment described in paragraph 3 to check that continuity exists between the switch's terminal and its earth only when the plunger is extended. If the switch is faulty it must be renewed.

10 Refitting is the reverse of the removal procedure.

11 The brake fluid level circuit of the instrument panel brake warning lamp is activated by a float-type sender unit in the master cylinder reservoir filler cap. The lamp lights whenever the fluid level falls to a dangerously low level or the handbrake is applied.

12 The sender unit is only available with the master cylinder reservoir filler cap. If faulty, the complete sender/cap assembly must be renewed.

13 To test the sender unit, remove it and use the equipment described in paragraph 3 to check that continuity exists between the unit's terminals only when the float is at the bottom of its travel.

Chapter 10
Suspension and steering

Contents

Degrees of difficulty

Easy, suitable for novice with little experience	**Fairly easy,** suitable for beginner with some experience	**Fairly difficult,** suitable for competent DIY mechanic	**Difficult,** suitable for experienced DIY mechanic	**Very difficult,** suitable for expert DIY or professional

Specifications

Front suspension

Type	Fully independent, with unequal-length upper (T-shaped) and lower (wishbone-type) transverse arms, Hydragas units providing (nitrogen) gas springing and fluid damping. Anti-roll bar on GTa and GTi 16v models. Telescopic, hydraulic dampers additional on GTi 16v models. Complete assembly rubber-mounted on subframe

Rear suspension

Type	Fully independent, with trailing arms, Hydragas units with helper springs providing (nitrogen) gas springing and fluid damping. Anti-roll bar on GTi 16v models. Complete assembly rubber-mounted on subframe

Hydragas suspension

System description	Front units mounted vertically, rear units horizontally. Units on each side connected front to rear through a plastic pipe; each side independent of the other
Nitrogen gas nominal pressure	2172 kN/m^2 ± 3% (315 lbf/in^2 ± 3%)
Ride height	Measured vertically from front hub centre to wheel arch underside, vehicle at kerb weight
Ride height - engine cold	341 ± 10 mm
Ride height - maximum permissible side-to-side difference	10 mm

Note: *Ride heights correct at nominal ambient temperature of 17°C above this temperature add 0.6 mm for every 1°C temperature difference, below it subtract 0.6 mm for every 1°C temperature difference*

10

Steering

Type	Rack and pinion
Turns lock-to-lock:	
GTa, GTi 16v	3.3
All other models	3.7

Wheel alignment and steering angles

Note: *All measurements are with car at kerb weight and at correct ride heights*

Toe-out in turns:	
GTa, GTi 16v	Inside roadwheel 31° 34', Outside roadwheel 28° 21'
All other models	Inside roadwheel 35° 18', Outside roadwheel 30° 40'
Camber angle:	
Front - GTa, GTi 16v	0° 10' ± 0° 37' positive
Front - all other models	0° 18' ± 0° 37' positive
Rear - all models	0° 0' ± 0° 30' negative
Castor angle:	
GTa, GTi 16v	2° 00' ± 0° 55' positive
All other models	0° 23' ± 0° 55' positive
Steering axis inclination/SAI - also known as kingpin inclination/KPI	10° 52'
Toe setting:	
Front	0° 00'/Parallel to 0° 50' (inclusive) toe-out
Rear	0° 10' to 0° 50' toe-in

Roadwheels

Type:	
1.1C, 1.1L, 1.1S, 1.4SL, 1.4GS	Steel
GTa	Steel (Alloy optional)
GTi 16v	Alloy
Size:	
1.1C, 1.1L, 1.1S, 1.4SL, 1.4GS	4.5J x 13
GTa - standard	5.5J x 13
GTa - optional, GTi 16v	5.5J x 13 x CH-52

Tyres

Type	Tubeless, steel-braced radial
Size:	
1.1C, 1.1L, 1.1S, 1.4SL, 1.4GS	155/65 R 13 73T
GTa, GTi 16v	185/55 R 13 77H
Pressures	See "*Weekly checks*" on page 0•16

Torque wrench settings

	Nm	lbf ft
Front suspension		
Lower arm pivot bolts	85	63
Lower balljoint:		
Balljoint-to-lower arm nuts and bolts - applicable to replacement parts only	40	30
Balljoint-to-hub carrier pinch-bolt and nut	60	44
Damper top mounting nut - GTi 16v	37	27
Upper balljoint:		
Balljoint-to-upper arm nut	55	40.5
Balljoint-to-hub carrier	105	78
Upper arm:		
Pivot shaft nuts	75	55
Pivot shaft retaining plate mounting bolts and nut	10	8
Damper bottom mounting/brake hose bracket bolt - GTi 16v	50	37
Brake hose bracket bolt - all other models	35	26
Anti-roll bar:		
Bar-to-suspension lower arm bolt and nut	25	19
Clamp bolts	45	33
Hydragas connecting pipe unions	20	15
Hydragas unit clamp plate bolts and nuts	25	19
Subframe fasteners:		
Mounting-to-body bolts or nuts	45	33
Engine/transmission support members-to-subframe bolts	45	33

Torque wrench settings (continued)

Torque wrench settings (continued)	Nm	lbf ft
Rear suspension		
Rear hub nut	90	66
Trailing arm:		
Pivot shaft nuts	75	55
Grease nipple	4	3
Pivot shaft retaining plate mounting bolts and nuts	25	19
Rear brake backplate nuts and bolts	25	19
Anti-roll bar:		
Clamp bolts	25	19
Bar-to-link bolts and nuts	25	19
Link-to-bracket bolts	25	19
Hydragas connecting pipe unions	20	15
Hydragas unit clamp plate bolts	25	19
Hydragas unit retaining strap nuts	7	5
Subframe fasteners:		
Mounting-to-body bolts	45	33
Mounting-to-subframe bolts	45	33
Steering		
Steering wheel nut:		
Without airbag	33	24
With airbag	45	33
Steering column:		
Mounting bolts and nut:		
Without airbag	25	19
With airbag	18	13
Universal joint pinch-bolt:		
Without airbag	30	22
With airbag	28	21
Column cover clamp bolt	11	8
Bulkhead aperture cover bolts or nuts	11	8
Steering lock/ignition switch shear-head bolts	Tighten until heads shear off - at least 19 Nm (14 lbf ft)	
Steering gear mounting nuts	25	19
Track rod:		
Balljoint locknuts	48	36
Balljoint-to-steering arm nuts	30	22
Roadwheels		
Roadwheel nuts	70	52

1 General information and precautions

General information

The suspension is fully independent at front and rear, with the principal suspension components being mounted on separate subframes. The subframes are rubber-mounted to the body.

The Hydragas suspension system is employed, using four suspension units (also known as displacers) each of which is connected by a knuckle joint to its respective upper arm (at the front) or trailing arm (at the rear). The units are basically sealed metal containers, divided into two chambers by a rubber diaphragm. The upper chamber contains dry nitrogen gas under pressure and thus forms a gas spring, whilst the lower contains a fluid (water-based, with alcohol to prevent freezing) and is further sub-divided by a damper valve through which the fluid must pass in either direction. The knuckle joints act on a tapered piston to bear against a second rubber diaphragm that seals the fluid in the unit's lower chamber. Thus when a roadwheel hits a bump, pressure is transmitted by the fluid to the gas spring formed in the upper chamber and also (through the fluid in the pipe connecting the pair of units on each side) to the remaining unit, thus levelling the vehicle and providing a smooth ride. When both units on one side are compressed together, as during cornering, the effect of the units acting together is to minimise roll. The damper valve orifices, the restrictor in each connecting pipe and the suspension lower arm pivot bushes are all carefully matched to provide the characteristics required; a helper spring is fitted to the rear unit to assist it in coping with various loads. The vehicle's ride heights are set and can be adjusted by pressurising the fluid in the system, via a Schrader-type valve located next to each rear unit.

The front suspension on each side comprises the hub carrier which is located, via upper and lower balljoints, by two transverse arms. The upper (T-shaped) arm pivots on needle roller bearings whilst the lower (wishbone-type) arm pivots on rubber bushes. The GTa and GTi 16v models are fitted with an anti-roll bar that is clamped to the underbody via rubber bushes and is attached at each end to the lower arms. The GTi 16v models are also fitted with a pair of telescopic, hydraulic dampers; one being mounted between each upper arm and the body. The hub rotates on a sealed, pre-adjusted and pre-lubricated, double-row tapered-roller bearing.

The rear suspension comprises two trailing arms that are pivoted on needle roller bearings and have the roadwheel stub axles pressed into their rear ends; each hub rotates on two ball-journal bearings. The GTi 16v models are fitted with an anti-roll bar clamped to the underbody via rubber bushes and attached at each end via links and brackets to the trailing arms.

The steering wheel is of the energy-absorbing type to protect the driver in the event of an accident and is attached by a deeply-recessed nut to the steering column, which is collapsible and is also of the energy-absorbing type. The steering column incorporates a rubber coupling to damp out road shocks and has a universal joint at its bottom end which is clamped to the steering gear pinion. The steering gear is clamped to the front subframe and is connected by two track rods, with balljoints at their outer ends, to the steering arms projecting rearwards from the hub carriers. The track rods ends are threaded to facilitate adjustment.

Precautions

Hydragas suspension

For the average DIY owner, most suspension removal, refitting and servicing procedures are complicated by the need to depressurise the Hydragas suspension before work starts and to evacuate air from it and to pressurise it (thus setting the ride heights) on completion. This can only be done by an experienced mechanic using the Hydragas Service Unit (Rover Service Tool Number 18G 703 V). Do not attempt to depressurise the suspension yourself.

Rover state that if the suspension is depressurised, then the car can be driven for repair at no more than 20 mph to the nearest dealer. Whilst obviously this is a "get-you-home" procedure for use in emergency only and is not intended as permission to drive the car in such a state at any other time, it does indicate a possible solution if you wish to carry out suspension repair work yourself. Before any work is attempted on the relevant parts of the suspension, you should check whether your local dealer is prepared to depressurise the suspension so that you can drive the car home, carry out the work yourself and then drive the car back to them for the suspension to be pressurised.

If the car is to be driven with the suspension depressurised (even if a leak is only suspected, or if either side's ride height is low), it must be loaded as lightly as possible and must be driven slowly and carefully over smooth roads for the minimum possible distance. Even apart from the effect on the car's handling and ride, driving it normally with the suspension depressurised will overload the Hydragas units and damage them.

Airbags (SRS)

A number of precautions must be observed when working on the steering components of vehicles equipped with airbags (SRS), these are listed in Section 1 of Chapter 12.

Wheels and tyres

On those models with 4.5J roadwheels and 155-section tyres (see Specifications), various suspension components differ from their counterparts fitted to GTa and GTi 16v models (5.5J roadwheels and 185-section tyres). The wider wheels and tyres must not be fitted to any of the other models.

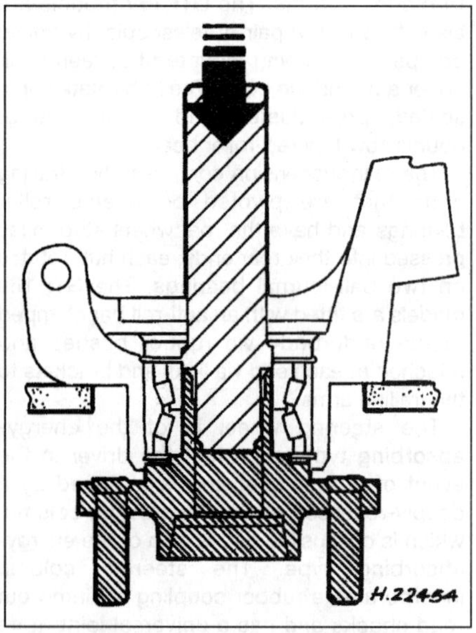

3.2 Pressing out hub from hub carrier

2 Front hub carrier - removal and refitting

Removal

1 Separate the hub carrier from the driveshaft as described in Chapter 8.

2 Unscrew the nut and fully remove the pinch-bolt securing the suspension lower balljoint to the hub carrier, then pull the hub carrier off the balljoint.

3 If the hub carrier is to be dismantled, remove the brake disc and its shield as described in Chapter 9.

4 If the steering arm is removed, note the two dowels locating the arm on the hub carrier. Ensure that the lockwasher is renewed and that the bolts are tightened securely and locked by bending up the lockwasher tabs against their flats on refitting.

Refitting

5 Refitting is the reverse of the removal procedure, referring for full details where necessary to the relevant Sections of this Chapter and of Chapters 8 and 9. Tighten all nuts and bolts to their specified torque wrench settings.

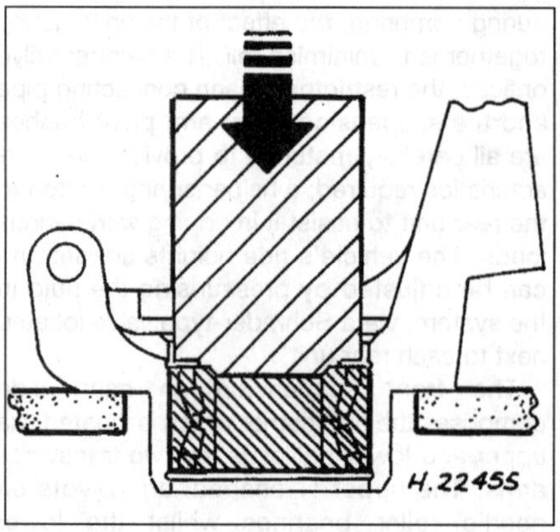

3.4 Pressing hub bearing out of hub carrier

3 Front hub and bearing - removal and refitting

Note: *The bearing is sealed, of the pre-adjusted and pre-lubricated, double-row tapered-roller type and is intended to last the entire service life of the vehicle without maintenance or attention. Do not attempt to remove the bearing unless absolutely necessary, as it will probably be damaged during the removal operation, and never overtighten the driveshaft nut beyond the specified torque wrench setting in an attempt to adjust the bearing.*

Note: *A press will be required to dismantle and rebuild the assembly. If such a tool is not available, a large bench vice and suitable spacers (such as large sockets) will serve as an adequate substitute. Also, the bearing's inner races are an interference fit on the hub. If the outboard inner race remains on the hub when it is pressed out of the hub carrier, a proprietary knife-edged bearing puller will be required to remove it*

Removal

1 Remove the hub carrier from the vehicle and remove the brake disc and its shield.

2 Press the hub out of the hub carrier **(see illustration)**. If the bearing's outboard inner race remains on the hub, remove it using the appropriate equipment.

3 Extract both circlips from the hub carrier and discard them; they should be renewed whenever they are disturbed.

4 Press the bearing out of the hub carrier **(see illustration)**.

5 Thoroughly clean the hub and hub carrier, removing all traces of dirt and grease and polishing away any burrs or raised edges which might hinder reassembly. Check both for cracks or any other signs of wear or damage and renew them if necessary. The bearing and its circlips must be renewed whenever they are disturbed.

6 Note that replacement bearings are available from Rover dealers, either as separate items or as part of a bearing kit which includes both circlips and the driveshaft nut. The purchase of the kit is advised because it will ensure that all replacement parts required are ready to hand on reassembly.

7 Check the condition of the roadwheel studs in the hub flange. If any are sheared off, stretched or have damaged threads, they can be pressed out of the hub providing that its flange is fully supported. On refitting, support the hub flange and press in the new stud until it seats fully.

Refitting

8 On reassembly, check (as far as is possible) that the new bearing is packed with grease and fit the new circlip to the hub carrier outboard groove. Apply a light film of oil to the bearing inner and outer races and to their matching surfaces in the hub and hub carrier to aid installation of the bearing.

9 Supporting the hub carrier outboard face and applying pressure only to the bearing's outer race, press in the new bearing until it seats against the circlip **(see illustration)**, then fit the second new circlip to the hub carrier's inboard groove.

10 Supporting the bearing's inner race fully, press the hub into the bearing and hub carrier until the hub shoulder seats against the bearing's inner race **(see illustration)**. Wipe off any surplus oil or grease.

11 Refit the brake disc shield and brake disc.

12 Refit the hub carrier assembly.

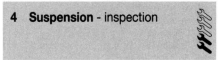

4 Suspension - inspection

1 Refer to Chapter 1, Sections 22 and 24 **(see illustrations)**.

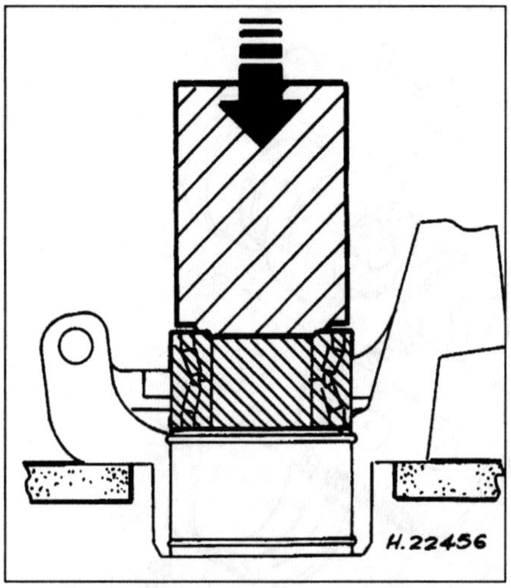

3.9 Pressing new hub bearing into hub carrier

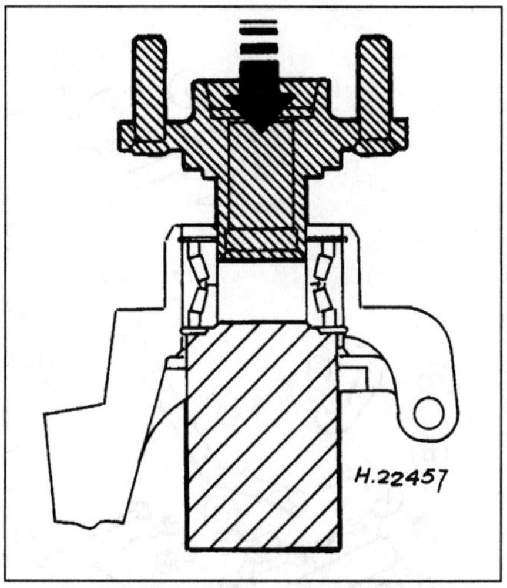

3.10 Pressing hub into hub carrier - note support for bearing inner race

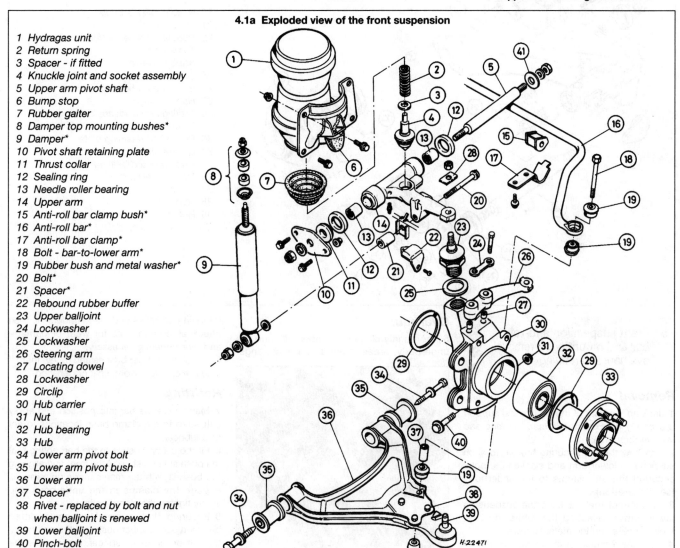

4.1a Exploded view of the front suspension

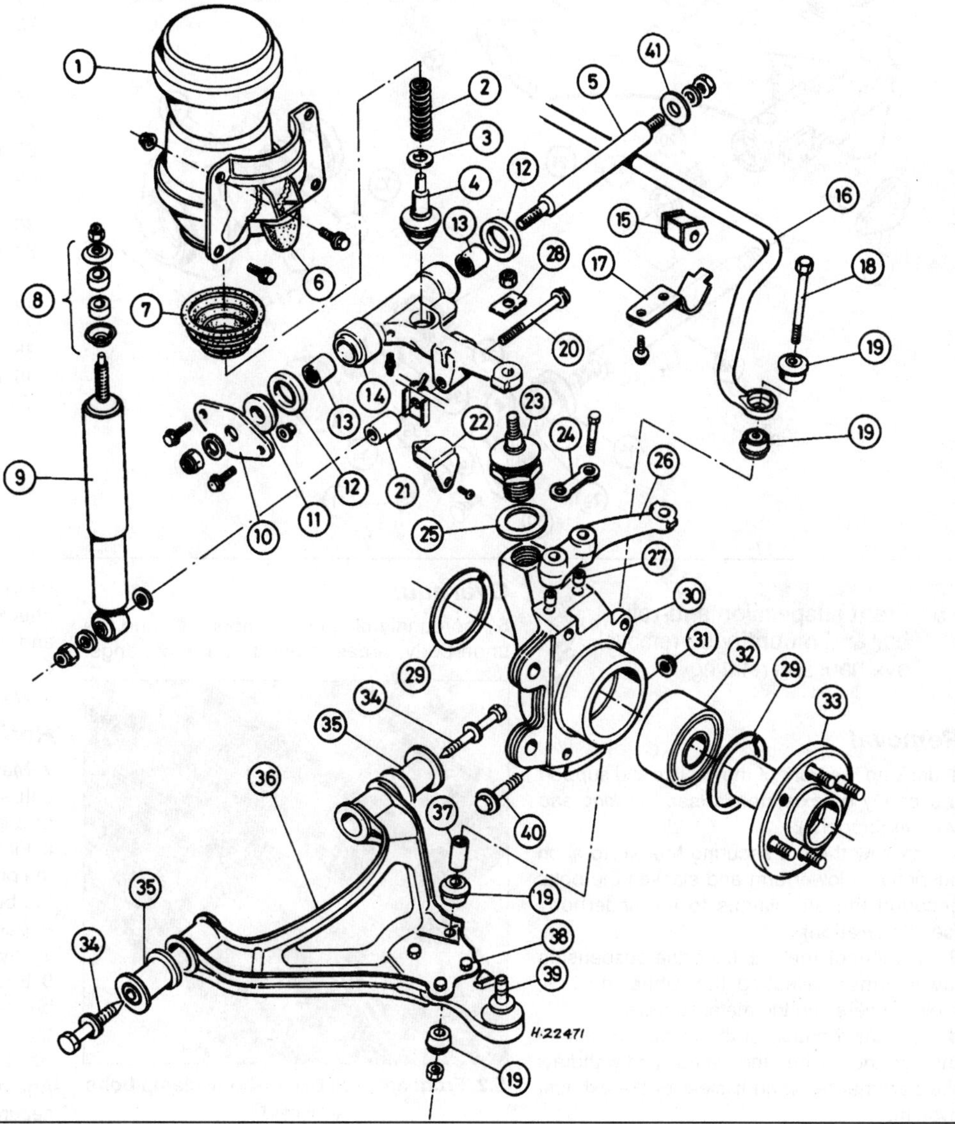

1 Hydragas unit
2 Return spring
3 Spacer - if fitted
4 Knuckle joint and socket assembly
5 Upper arm pivot shaft
6 Bump stop
7 Rubber gaiter
*8 Damper top mounting bushes**
*9 Damper**
10 Pivot shaft retaining plate
11 Thrust collar
12 Sealing ring
13 Needle roller bearing
14 Upper arm
*15 Anti-roll bar clamp bush**
*16 Anti-roll bar**
*17 Anti-roll bar clamp**
*18 Bolt - bar-to-lower arm**
*19 Rubber bush and metal washer**
*20 Bolt**
*21 Spacer**
22 Rebound rubber buffer
23 Upper balljoint
24 Lockwasher
25 Lockwasher
26 Steering arm
27 Locating dowel
28 Lockwasher
29 Circlip
30 Hub carrier
31 Nut
32 Hub bearing
33 Hub
34 Lower arm pivot bolt
35 Lower arm pivot bush
36 Lower arm
*37 Spacer**
38 Rivet - replaced by bolt and nut when balljoint is renewed
39 Lower balljoint
40 Pinch-bolt
41 Thrustwasher
**Not fitted to all models*

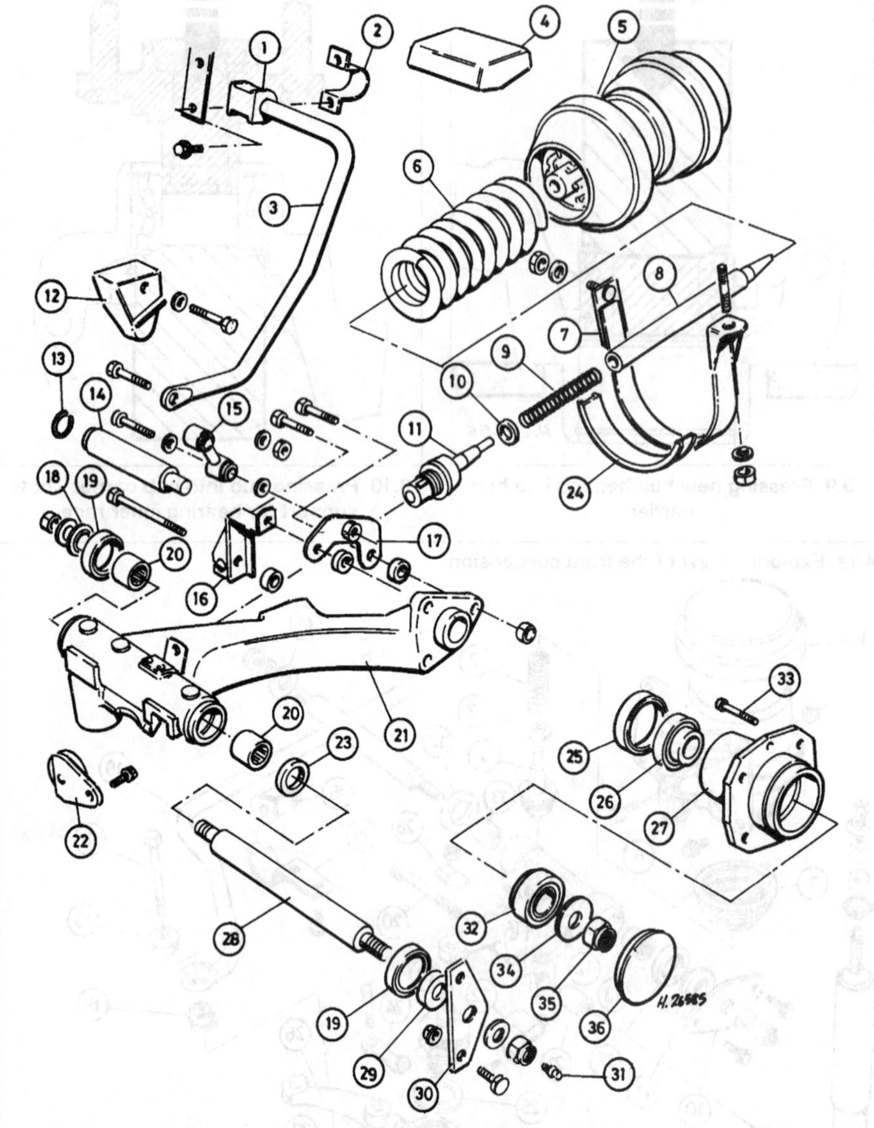

4.1b Exploded view of the rear suspension

1 *Anti-roll bar clamp bush**
2 *Anti-roll bar clamp**
3 *Anti-roll bar**
4 *Mounting pad*
5 *Hydragas unit*
6 *Helper spring*
7 *Hydragas unit retaining strap*
8 *Strut*
9 *Return spring*
10 *Spacer*
11 *Knuckle joint*
12 *Bump stop*
13 *Circlip*
14 *Stub axle*
15 *Anti-roll bar link**
16 *Handbrake cable bracket*
17 *Anti-roll bar link bracket**
18 *Thrustwasher*
19 *Seal*
20 *Needle roller bearing*
21 *Trailing arm*
22 *Rebound rubber buffer*
23 *Thrustwasher*
24 *Rubber sleeve*
25 *Oil seal*
26 *Hub inboard bearing*
27 *Hub*
28 *Trailing arm pivot shaft*
29 *Thrustwasher*
30 *Pivot shaft retaining plate*
31 *Grease nipple*
32 *Hub outboard bearing*
33 *Roadwheel stud*
34 *Washer*
35 *Hub nut*
36 *Hub cap*
**Not fitted to all models*

5 Front suspension anti-roll bar and mountings - removal, overhaul and refitting

Removal

1 Jack up the front of the vehicle and support it securely on axle stands (see "*Jacking and Vehicle Support*").

2 Unscrew the nut securing the bar to each suspension lower arm and slacken the bolts securing the bar clamps to the underbody **(see illustration)**.

3 Disconnect the bar from the suspension lower arms, collecting the rubber bushes, their washers and the metal spacers.

4 Mark the location of the clamp bushes on the bar, then unbolt the clamps and withdraw the bar, manoeuvring it clear of the exhaust system.

Overhaul

5 Thoroughly clean all components and the underbody areas around the mountings, removing all traces of dirt and underseal, then check all components for wear or damage and renew them if necessary.

5.2 Front anti-roll bar-to-body clamp bolts (arrowed)

6 Check the rubber bushes and renew them if they are cracked, worn, split or perished.

Refitting

7 Manoeuvre the bar into position and apply soft soap to the clamp bush locations to act as a lubricant.

8 Fit the clamp bushes to the bar, noting that the bush split must be at the front and aligning the bushes with the marks made on removal, engage the clamps in the underbody and lightly tighten the clamp bolts.

9 Ensuring that a metal washer is fitted between each rubber bush and the bolt head, the nut or the metal spacer, reassemble the bar-to-suspension lower arm mountings. Again tighten the nuts only by enough to secure the assembly **(see illustration)**.

5.9 Note location of metal washers on anti-roll bar-to-suspension lower arm mounting

10 With all bar mountings correctly installed, check that the bar is centred on the body and that all rubber bushes are seated without distortion.

11 Lower the vehicle to the ground. When all the weight is back on the wheels, rock it to settle the suspension, then tighten the bolts and nuts to their specified torque wrench settings.

6 Front suspension damper and mountings - removal, overhaul and refitting

Removal

1 Jack up the front of the vehicle and support it securely on axle stands (see "*Jacking and Vehicle Support*"), then turn the steering to full lock so that the damper bottom mounting can be reached. If better access is required, the roadwheel should be removed.

2 Open the bonnet and unscrew the nut securing the damper top mounting. On the right-hand side this will first require the removal of the washer system reservoir. Remove the nut, the metal washer and the top rubber bush **(see illustration)**.

3 Unscrew the nut and bolt securing the damper bottom mounting to the suspension upper arm and withdraw the damper, collecting the metal spacer and washers from the bottom mounting and the rubber bush and metal washer from the top mounting. Always store the damper in an upright position.

Overhaul

4 Check the damper's action by clamping it, by its bottom mounting eye, upright in a soft-jawed vice and moving the piston rod fully up and down. Firm, even resistance should be felt in both directions. If the damping is weak, if the unit shows signs of oil leaks at any point, or if the piston rod is bent, scored or damaged, the damper must be renewed. Note that it is good practice, if either damper requires renewal, to renew both together as a matched pair.

5 Check the damper's bottom mounting bush and renew it as follows if it is cracked, worn, split or perished.

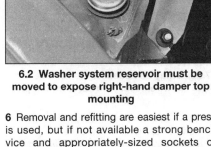

6.2 Washer system reservoir must be moved to expose right-hand damper top mounting

6 Removal and refitting are easiest if a press is used, but if not available a strong bench vice and appropriately-sized sockets or pieces of tubing will serve as an adequate substitute. Extract the bush's metal sleeve, then cut the rubber with a hacksaw or similar and remove it. Polish any burrs or raised edges from the damper bottom mounting eye, then lubricate the new bush components with liquid soap or petroleum jelly before pressing them into place. Ensure that both are located centrally in the mounting eye.

Refitting

7 If a new damper is being fitted, or if the original has been out of service for some time, the damper must be primed by clamping it, by its bottom mounting eye, upright in a soft-jawed vice and moving the piston rod fully up and down (through at least three full strokes) until full damping action is restored and there is no free play when changing direction at the end of each stroke.

8 First reassemble the top mounting, tightening the nut loosely, then align the damper bottom mounting eye with the upper arm and brake flexible hose bracket and refit the bolt with the spacer and washers, tightening the nut loosely **(see illustration)**.

9 Lower the vehicle to the ground. When all the vehicle's weight is back on its wheels, rock it to settle the suspension, then tighten the damper top mounting nut, followed by the bottom mounting nut and bolt, both to the specified torque wrench settings. Turn the

6.8 Note metal washer on each side of damper bottom mounting eye (arrowed)

steering to the full lock position required to reach the damper bottom mounting.

10 Refit the washer system reservoir if working on the right-hand damper.

7 Front suspension lower arm and pivot bushes - removal, overhaul and refitting

Removal

1 Jack up the front of the vehicle and support the body securely on axle stands (see "*Jacking and Vehicle Support*") then remove the roadwheel.

2 Relieve the pressure of the Hydragas system from the lower arm by using a trolley jack or similar (with a block of wood interposed to prevent damage) to jack up the suspension via the lower balljoint until it is just beginning to take the weight of the vehicle, then slip a wooden spacer between the suspension upper arm and the subframe and lower the jack **(see illustrations)**.

3 Where fitted, disconnect the anti-roll bar from the lower arm.

4 Unscrew the nut and fully remove the pinch-bolt securing the suspension lower balljoint to the hub carrier. Note that if the original balljoint has been replaced so that it is now secured by nuts and bolts rather than rivets, the balljoint can be unbolted from the lower arm instead, if required.

7.2a Jack up suspension under lower balljoint (arrowed) . . .

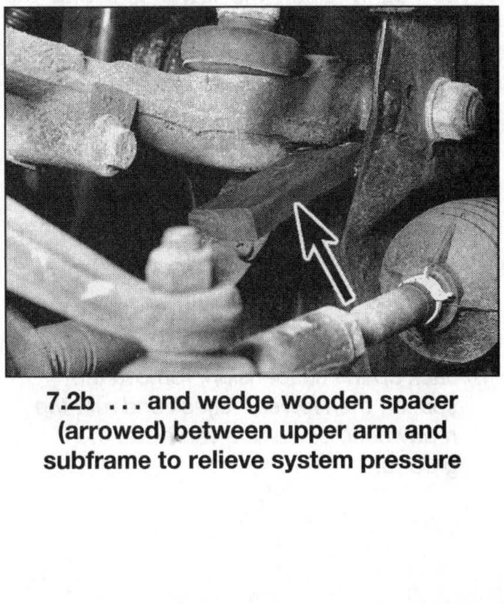

7.2b . . . and wedge wooden spacer (arrowed) between upper arm and subframe to relieve system pressure

7.5a Remove sealing grommet from subframe to reach lower arm front pivot bolt

5 Unscrew the lower arm front and rear pivot bolts. Prise out the sealing grommet from the front of the subframe to reach the front bolt. Note that it may be necessary to unscrew the front outboard mounting bolt from the subframe rear mounting to allow the rear pivot bolt to be removed **(see illustrations)**.

6 Withdraw the lower arm.

Overhaul

Note: *The suspension lower arm front and rear pivot bushes are different; if they are to be renewed, ensure that only the correct bush is fitted to each arm location*

7 Check the arm pivot bushes. If they are worn, cracked, split or perished they must be renewed. The renewal of these bushes is best left to a Rover dealer as a press is required with a bush removal/refitting mandrel, a support, a front bush fitting guide and a rear bush fitting guide (Rover Service Tool Numbers 18G 1612-1, 1612-4, 1612-3 and 1612-2 respectively). Whilst the old bushes can be extracted using a strong bench vice and suitable sockets, it is unlikely that new bushes can be installed successfully without the shaped mandrels.

8 For those owners with access to the required equipment, note that the rear bush must be fitted with its rounded flange to the rear of the arm and with the arrows on that face pointing outboard towards the lower balljoint. The front bush must be fitted with its flat flange to the front. Rover recommend the use of Marlene 148 rubber lubricant to aid installation.

9 Thoroughly clean the lower arm and the subframe around the arm mountings, removing all traces of dirt and of underseal if necessary, then check carefully for cracks, distortion or any other signs of wear or damage. Do not forget to check the pivot bolts.

Refitting

10 Refitting is the reverse of the removal procedure, noting the following points.

a) *Tighten only lightly at first the various nuts and bolts.*
b) *Jack up the suspension, remove the spacer, then lower the jack and refit the roadwheel. Lower the vehicle to the ground.*

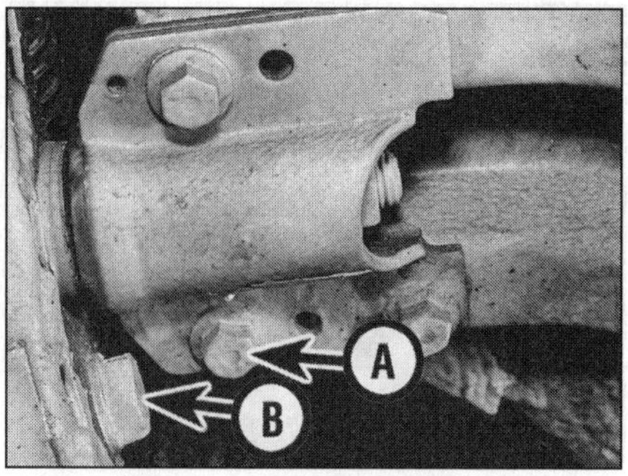

7.5b It may be necessary to remove bolt (A) to allow removal of lower arm rear pivot bolt (B)

c) *When all the vehicle's weight is back on its wheels, rock it to settle the suspension, then tighten all disturbed nuts and bolts to their specified torque wrench settings; refit the subframe sealing grommet.*
d) *Depending on the reason for the work, it may be advisable to check wheel alignment on completion.*

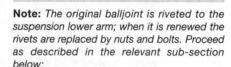

8 Front suspension lower balljoint - removal and refitting

Note: *The original balljoint is riveted to the suspension lower arm; when it is renewed the rivets are replaced by nuts and bolts. Proceed as described in the relevant sub-section below:*

Removal

Riveted (original) balljoint

1 Remove the suspension lower arm.

2 Extract the rivets. Rover recommend the use of a pedestal drill (for accuracy) to drill out the rivet heads so that a press can be used to remove the rivet studs.

3 Remove the old balljoint from the lower arm.

Bolted (replacement) balljoint

4 Jack up the front of the vehicle and support the body securely on axle stands (see "*Jacking and Vehicle Support*") then remove the roadwheel.

8.6a Fully remove pinch-bolt . . .

5 Relieve the pressure of the Hydragas system from the lower balljoint by using a trolley jack or similar (with a block of wood interposed to prevent damage) to jack up the suspension via the balljoint until it is just beginning to take the weight of the vehicle, then slip a wooden spacer between the suspension upper arm and the subframe and lower the jack.

6 Unscrew the nut and fully remove the pinch-bolt securing the lower balljoint to the hub carrier **(see illustrations)**.

7 Unbolt the balljoint from the lower arm and remove it. Note that it may be necessary to slacken the suspension lower arm pivot bolts and to disconnect the anti-roll bar (where fitted) from the lower arm so that the arm can be swung down far enough for the balljoint to be removed.

Refitting

8 Refitting is the reverse of the removal procedure, noting the following points.

a) *Tighten all disturbed nuts and bolts to their specified torque wrench settings. If the suspension lower arm pivot bolts and anti-roll bar mountings were slackened, tighten them when the weight of the car is back on its heels and the car has been rocked to settle the suspension components.*
b) *Depending on the reason for the work, it may be advisable to check wheel alignment on completion.*

9 Front suspension upper balljoint - removal and refitting

Note: *The upper balljoint is screwed into the hub carrier and will require a large spanner or socket to remove and refit it. The recommended Rover Service Tool is Number 18G 1341, but proprietary Metro balljoint sockets are available from any good motor accessory shop. These tools will make the job easier and will permit the balljoint to be tightened using a torque wrench. In addition, a universal balljoint separator tool may be required.*

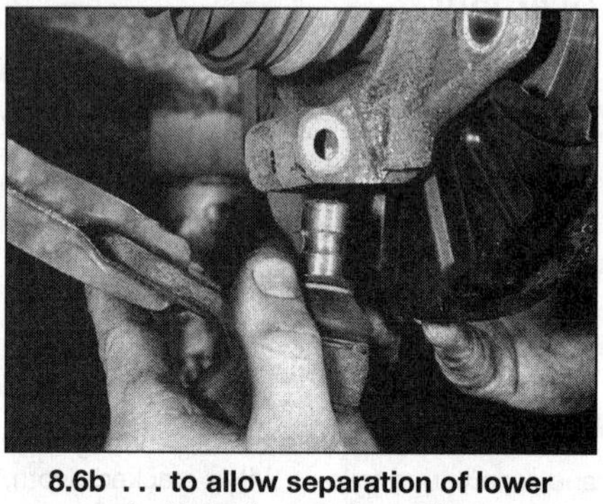

8.6b . . . to allow separation of lower balljoint from hub carrier

9.3 Push back lockwasher raised tab to unlock upper balljoint-to-upper arm nut - note also balljoint lockwasher tab (arrowed)

Removal

1 Jack up the front of the vehicle and support the body securely on axle stands then remove the roadwheel.

2 Relieve the pressure of the Hydragas system from the upper balljoint by using a trolley jack or similar (with a block of wood interposed to prevent damage) to jack up the suspension via the lower balljoint until it is just beginning to take the weight of the vehicle, then slip a wooden spacer between the suspension upper arm and the subframe to hold the suspension in that position.

3 Flatten back the lockwasher raised tabs from the balljoint-to-upper arm nut **(see illustration)** and from the balljoint itself. If a suitably-sized open-ended spanner is available, the balljoint can be slackened (or even unscrewed from the hub carrier) at this stage.

4 Unscrew the balljoint-to-upper arm nut and remove the lockwasher. Refit the nut so that it is flush with the end of the balljoint stud thread and disconnect the balljoint from the upper arm, if necessary using a universal balljoint separator tool **(see illustration)**.

5 Lower the hub carrier/suspension lower arm assembly on the jack, taking care that the brake flexible hose is not stretched or damaged, until the balljoint stud is clear of the upper arm. If necessary, unbolt the brake hose bracket (and damper bottom mounting, where fitted) from the upper arm.

6 Unscrew the balljoint from the hub carrier, if necessary, having an assistant hold the hub carrier steady. Discard the lockwashers, they must be renewed whenever disturbed.

Refitting

7 Check that the threads of the balljoint and of the hub carrier are clean, dry and undamaged and that the balljoint pin and upper arm tapers are undamaged and degreased. Always fit new lockwashers; note that these are included in the balljoint kit available from Rover dealers.

8 Screw the balljoint into the hub carrier and tighten it to the specified torque wrench setting, then secure it by bending a portion of the lockwasher up against one of its flats. If the lockwasher is not already secured to the hub carrier by a small tab, bend a portion of the lockwasher (opposite to that securing the balljoint) down against the hub carrier to secure the assembly.

9.4 Using a universal balljoint separator tool to release upper balljoint from upper arm

9 Jack up the hub carrier/suspension lower arm assembly until the balljoint taper is fully engaged with that of the upper arm, fit a new lockwasher and tighten the balljoint-to-upper arm nut to its specified torque wrench setting. Secure the nut by bending one of the lockwasher tabs up against one of its flats. If the lockwasher is not already secured to the upper arm by a small tab, bend down the lockwasher's other tab against the arm to secure the assembly.

10 Refit, if removed, the brake hose bracket bolt (and damper bottom mounting, where fitted). Tighten the bolt and nut to the specified torque wrench setting. Where a damper is fitted, the bolt and nut should be finally tightened only when the vehicle's weight is back on its wheels and the suspension components are settled in their normal working positions.

11 Jack up the suspension, remove the spacer, then lower the jack and refit the roadwheel. Lower the vehicle to the ground.

10 Front suspension upper arm and pivot bearings - removal, overhaul and refitting

Note: *This procedure requires the depressurisation of (the appropriate side of) the Hydragas suspension system. Refer to the precautions in Section 1 of this Chapter before starting work.*

Removal

1 Remove the Hydragas unit.

2 Remove the underwing shield.

3 Unbolt the brake hose bracket from the upper arm.

4 Support the weight of the hub carrier/suspension lower arm assembly using a block of wood or similar, then disconnect the upper balljoint from the arm end.

5 Remove the upper arm pivot shaft rear nut and washer, then undo the pivot shaft retaining plate bolts and nut. Withdraw the pivot shaft and retaining plate forwards.

6 Withdraw the upper arm, collecting the front and rear sealing rings and the rear thrustwasher.

Overhaul

7 Clamp the pivot shaft in a soft-jawed vice and unscrew the front nut and washer. Collect the retaining plate and thrust collar, noting which way round the collar is fitted.

8 Dismantle and check the knuckle joint.

9 Thoroughly clean all components and the subframe around the upper arm mountings. Check the subframe for signs of wear or damage to the upper arm pivot points and to the various threads, then check the rebound rubber buffer. Renew any component that shows signs of wear or damage.

10 If the pivot bearings are to be renewed, unscrew the grease nipple from the upper arm and extract the bearings using an internally-expanding bearing puller, or drive them out from the inside using a hammer and a slim metal drift passed through the arm pivot from the opposite end.

11 Carefully clean the pivot bore, polish away any burrs or raised edges that might damage the new bearings on installation and check that the grease nipple and the lubricant passage in the arm are clear.

12 Ensuring that they are fitted with their marked surfaces outwards and that they enter exactly squarely into the pivot bore, install the new bearings using either a press, a large bench vice or a length of studding, two large plain washers and nuts. Check that the bearings are installed correctly by passing the pivot shaft through them.

13 Pack the bearings with multi-purpose grease, refit the grease nipple and lubricate all other pivot components. Fit the rear thrustwasher to the arm (noting that its grooved surface must be against the bearing), grease it and fit the rear sealing ring to retain it. Fit the front sealing ring.

14 Refit the knuckle joint to the arm.

15 Clamp the pivot shaft in a soft-jawed vice and fit the thrust collar (noting that its grooved surface must be against the bearing), the retaining plate, the washer and the nut, tightening the nut to its specified torque wrench setting. Check that the shaft is clean and unmarked, then smear it with grease.

Refitting

16 Taking care not to displace the sealing rings or thrustwasher, refit the upper arm to the subframe, followed by the pivot shaft assembly. Tighten the retaining plate bolts and nut and the pivot shaft rear nut to their specified torque wrench settings, then check that the arm pivots smoothly but without free play.

17 Use a grease gun to pack the bearings until grease can be seen exuding from both ends of the pivot, then wipe off all surplus grease.

18 For the remainder of the refitting procedure, work as follows.

a) *Refit the Hydragas unit.*
b) *Refit the underwing shield.*
c) *Refit the brake hose bracket bolt (and damper bottom mounting, where fitted). Tighten the bolt and nut to the specified torque wrench setting. Where a damper is fitted, the bolt and nut should be finally tightened only when the vehicle's weight is back on its wheels and the suspension components are settled in their normal working positions.*
d) *Connect the upper balljoint to the upper arm.*
e) *Refit the roadwheel and lower the car to the ground.*
f) *Have any air evacuated from the Hydragas suspension and have it pressurised to the correct ride height.*

11 Front suspension Hydragas unit - removal and refitting

Note: *This procedure requires the depressurisation of (the appropriate side of) the Hydragas suspension system. Refer to the precautions in Section 1 of this Chapter before starting work.*

Removal

1 Have the Hydragas suspension depressurised on the relevant side.
2 Jack up the front of the vehicle and support it securely on axle stands (see "*Jacking and Vehicle Support*") then remove the roadwheel.
3 Uncouple the plastic connecting pipe from the Hydragas unit. Plug or cap the orifices immediately to prevent the entry of dirt.
4 Where a damper is fitted, unbolt the bottom mounting and slacken the top mounting so that the damper can be moved out of the way. Do not force it or its top mounting might be damaged.
5 Unbolt the unit's clamp plate from the subframe and withdraw the plate. Check the condition of the bump stop and renew it if worn or damaged **(see illustration)**.

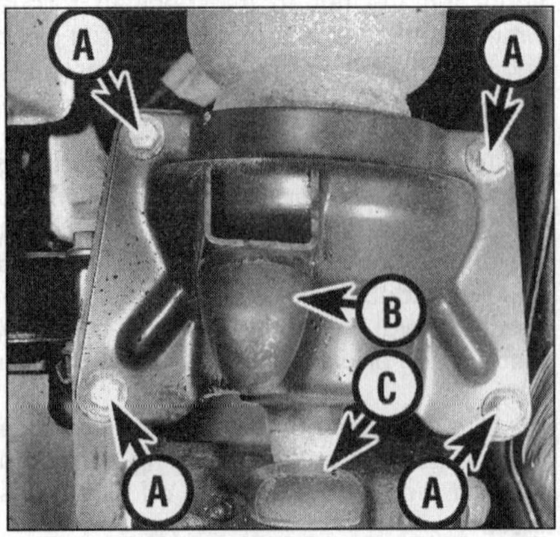

11.5 Front Hydragas unit clamp plate bolts (A) bump stop (B) and knuckle joint (C)

6 Withdraw the Hydragas unit, lifting it off the knuckle joint. Note the presence of the return spring and (where fitted) the spacer.
7 Whenever the unit is removed, the knuckle joint should be dismantled, checked for wear and greased.

Refitting

8 Clean carefully the mating surfaces of the unit and of the knuckle joint, then apply a smear of the recommended grease. Ensure that the spacer (if fitted) and return spring are in place.
9 Offer up the Hydragas unit, aligning it carefully on the knuckle joint, then refit the clamp plate and tighten the bolts and nuts to the specified torque wrench setting.
10 For the remainder of the refitting procedure, work as follows.

a) *Connect the plastic connecting pipe to the unit.*
b) *If applicable, reassemble the damper bottom mounting. The mounting bolt and nuts should be finally tightened (to their specified torque wrench settings) when the vehicle's weight is back on its wheels and the suspension components are settled in their normal working positions.*
c) *Refit the roadwheel and lower the vehicle to the ground.*
d) *Have any air evacuated from the Hydragas suspension and have it pressurised to the correct ride height.*

12 Front suspension knuckle joint - removal and refitting

Note: *This procedure requires the depressurisation of (the appropriate side of) the Hydragas suspension system. Refer to the precautions in Section 1 of this Chapter before starting work.*

Removal

1 Remove the Hydragas unit.
2 Withdraw the return spring and, where fitted, the spacer from the knuckle joint.
3 Carefully lift the rubber boot and remove the knuckle joint from the upper arm, then prise out the joint socket.
4 Thoroughly clean all components and check them for signs of wear or damage. Check particularly that the ball end of the knuckle joint is not corroded, worn or pitted and that the socket is not cracked or split.
5 Renew any worn or damaged components. Note that if the knuckle joint is to be renewed, it is available only as an assembly with the socket and the rubber boot, otherwise only the return spring, the spacer and the socket are available separately.

Refitting

6 On reassembly, clean the upper arm socket location and tap in the socket.
7 The recommended lubricant for the knuckle joint is Dextragrease Super GP (available from Rover dealers); apply a smear of this grease to all knuckle joint components before refitting.
8 Pack the socket with grease and press in the knuckle joint, then fill the space above the joint ball with grease and ensure that the rubber boot is correctly located over the socket lip so that no dirt or water can enter the joint.
9 Refit the spacer (if fitted) and the return spring, then wipe off any surplus grease.
10 Refit the Hydragas unit.

13 Front suspension subframe mountings - renewal

Note: *The subframe is secured at its four corners to the body, each mounting being secured by a bolt and nut (front) or three bolts (rear) to the body and by a through-bolt to the subframe. Removal and refitting is essentially the same for all mountings. Note that great care will be required in supporting the body securely while the subframe is disturbed.*

1 Jack up the front of the vehicle and support the body securely on axle stands (see "*Jacking and Vehicle Support*").
2 To dismantle one of the front mountings, first unscrew the through-bolt nut, then the mounting-to-body bolt and nut, then withdraw the mounting. It may be necessary carefully to prise down the subframe to allow the mounting to be removed **(see illustration)**.
3 The procedure is the same on the rear mountings, but where an anti-roll bar is fitted the bar-to-body clamps must be unbolted and the bar must be lowered so that the mounting can be removed.
4 Refitting is the reverse of the removal procedure. Tighten all disturbed nuts and bolts to their specified torque wrench settings (where given).

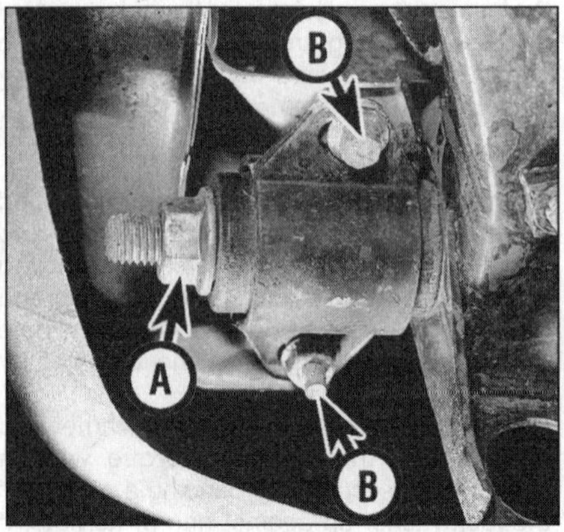

13.2 Front subframe front mounting through-bolt nut (A) and mountings (B)

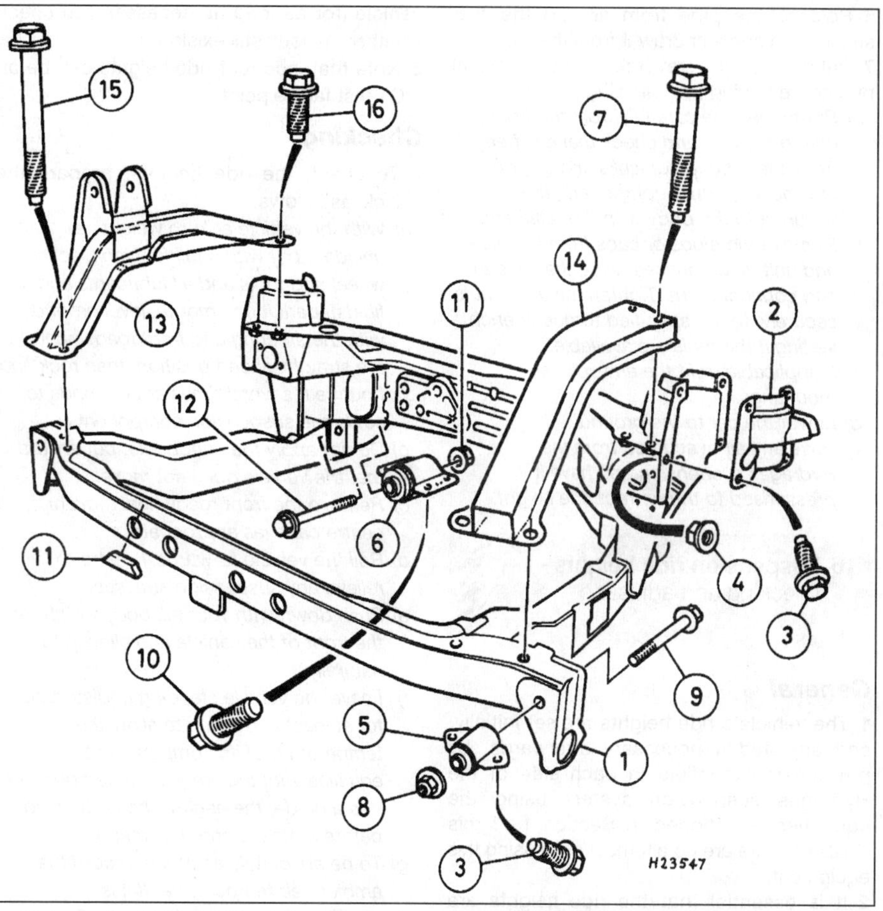

14.9 Front suspension subframe and mountings

1 Subframe
2 Hydragas unit clamp plate
3 Bolt
4 Nut
5 Subframe front mounting
6 Subframe rear mounting
7 Bolt - support member-to-subframe
8 Nut
9 Through-bolt - front mounting-to-subframe
10 Bolt - rear mounting-to-body
11 Sealing grommet
12 Through-bolt - rear mounting-to-subframe
13 Engine/transmission right-hand support member
14 Engine/transmission left-hand support member
15 Bolt - support member-to-subframe
16 Bolt - support member-to-subframe

14 Front suspension subframe - removal and refitting

Note: *This procedure requires the depressurisation of both sides of the Hydragas suspension system. Refer to the precautions in Section 1 of this Chapter before starting work.*

Removal

1 Remove the engine/transmission.
2 Remove the exhaust system front pipe.
3 Remove the gearchange linkage components from the subframe.
4 Either disconnect the plastic connecting pipes from the front Hydragas units or remove the units completely.
5 Remove the steering gear.
6 Disconnecting the brake flexible hoses from the metal hydraulic pipes if required. Ensure that both front brake calipers are separated from the subframe and suspension components.
7 Either completely remove the suspension damper and anti-roll bar (where fitted) and the upper and lower arms, or disconnect them from the body so that they can be removed with the subframe and subsequently dismantled. Refer to the relevant Sections of this Chapter.
8 Make a final check that all components have been removed or disconnected that are attached to the subframe or might prevent its removal.
9 Support the subframe, unbolt its mountings, then lower the subframe to the ground and remove it **(see illustration)**.

Refitting

10 Refitting is the reverse of the removal procedure. Tighten all disturbed nuts and bolts to their specified torque wrench settings (where given).

15 Hydragas suspension connecting pipes - renewal

Note: *This procedure requires the depressurisation of (the appropriate side of) the Hydragas suspension system. Refer to the precautions in Section 1 of this Chapter before starting work.*

1 Have the Hydragas suspension depressurised on the relevant side.
2 Jack the vehicle up, first at the front and support the body securely on an axle stand, then jack up the rear side and support the body securely on an axle stand.
3 Unscrew the union nut connecting each end of the pipe to the Hydragas front and rear units **(see illustration)**. To prevent the entry of dirt or other foreign matter into the system, immediately plug or cap both the pipe end and the unit orifice whenever they are disconnected.
4 Work from front to rear along the length of the (large-bore, plastic) pipe and release it from the retainers securing it to the underbody.
5 Carefully pull the pipe clear of the front suspension subframe. On models so equipped, it may be necessary to disconnect the anti-roll bar from the suspension lower arms and to unbolt the bar clamps from the underbody so that the pipe can be removed.

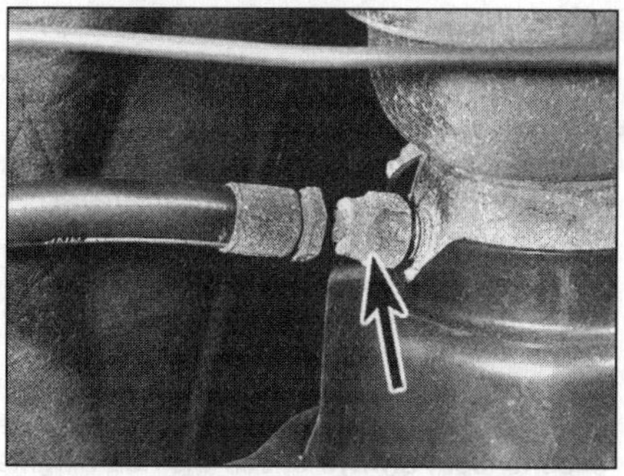

15.3 Hydragas connecting pipe union nut (arrowed) at front left-hand unit

6 Release the pipe from around the rear suspension and withdraw it from the car.

7 Refitting is the reverse of the removal procedure, noting the following points.

a) Route the pipe carefully from the front unit to the rear and check that it is free from sharp bends or kinks and clear of any moving or hot component, then secure it to the body with the retainers.

b) Remove the plugs or caps from the pipe and unit union orifices, wipe them clean and connect them. Tighten the union nuts securely, to the specified torque wrench setting if the tools are available.

c) If applicable, refit the anti-roll bar mountings.

d) Lower the car to the ground.

e) Have any air evacuated from the Hydragas suspension and have it pressurised to the correct ride height.

16 Suspension ride heights - checking and adjusting

General

1 The vehicle's ride heights are set initially, and adjusted if necessary afterwards, by pressurising the fluid in each side of the Hydragas suspension system using the equipment mentioned in Section 1 of this Chapter; there are no alternatives to using this equipment.

2 It is essential that the ride heights are checked at regular intervals and maintained at exactly the specified value. Whilst a permissible tolerance is given, the suspension and steering are designed to perform best with the ride heights as specified and the same on each side of the vehicle.

3 If the vehicle is used with incorrect ride heights, one or more of the following will happen.

a) The vehicle's ride and handling will deteriorate. The greater the variation from the specified value, the more marked will be the effect on the vehicle's comfort and stability.

b) The front suspension and steering geometry will alter, affecting the steering and causing exaggerated and uneven tyre wear.

c) As with vehicles with conventional suspension, braking performance will be affected and stopping distances increased if the suspension does not perform as the manufacturer intended.

d) If the ride heights are low (suspension pressure low) and the vehicle is driven over rough roads, heavily laden, or at high speeds, the Hydragas units may be overloaded and damaged.

4 If any of the above symptoms are experienced, always check the ride heights first before investigating further; have them set exactly if they are incorrect, then drive the vehicle (for as long as necessary) to check whether the fault still exists.

5 Note that incorrect ride heights can be an MOT test failure point.

Checking

6 To check the ride heights, prepare the vehicle as follows.

a) With the vehicle at kerb weight (ie, unladen, but with a full fuel tank, spare wheel and tools and all lubricants and fluids), park it on smooth, level ground with the steering and front roadwheels in the straight-ahead position, then rock and bounce it several times at both ends to settle the suspension components.

b) Do not apply the handbrake, but ensure that the vehicle does not move.

c) Remove the front roadwheel trims or centre caps (as appropriate).

d) Roll the vehicle forwards 1 metre to relieve any suspension stresses.

e) Push down with your full body weight on the front of the vehicle and allow it to rise naturally.

f) Leave the vehicle standing undisturbed for at least two hours to allow the temperature of its components to equalise with the ambient air temperature - as a guide, the engine should be cold before a measurement is made.

g) To be absolutely accurate, record the ambient air temperature. If it is significantly above or below 17°C, calculate a corrected ride height value according to the correction factor given in the Specifications Section of this Chapter.

7 Ensuring that the measurement is made exactly vertically (seen from the front of the vehicle, as well as from the side), use a straight-edged ruler to measure the distance from the front hub centre to the underside of the wheel arch.

8 Repeat the measurement on the opposite side of the vehicle; record both measurements and compare them with those specified.

9 If the ride heights recorded are outside the specified tolerances, or if one side differs significantly from the other, they must be adjusted as soon as possible.

10 If, for example, you are trying to establish the cause of uneven tyre wear it will be necessary to have the ride heights set to exactly the specified value; an experienced Rover mechanic should be able to do this without difficulty.

Adjusting

11 If the ride heights need adjustment, take the vehicle to a Rover dealer. Adjustment is made via a Schrader-type valve located next to each rear unit **(see illustration)**.

17 Hydragas suspension system - testing

1 If either suspension ride height is repeatedly found to be low, there is evidence of a leak in that side of the system.

2 Working from the front unit along the connecting pipe to the rear unit on the side affected, check the vehicle fully for any signs of fluid leakage. Raise and support the vehicle if better access is required.

3 If the leak is serious it may be revealed by damp patches, but in most cases all that will be visible is a slight residue left after the fluid has evaporated. If a leak is very difficult to spot, clean all Hydragas system components carefully, including those around them, and dust the suspect area with talcum powder; this should help to make the source of the leak more obvious.

4 If the leak is found to be from one of the connecting pipe unions, tighten the union carefully (but do not overtighten it) and have the ride heights adjusted. Check carefully that the leak is not from the Hydragas unit's valve.

5 If the leak is found to be in the connecting pipe or in one of the Hydragas units, renew the component concerned as described in the relevant Section of this Chapter.

6 If either ride height is low and there is no sign of a fluid leak from the system, it is possible that one of the Hydragas units is leaking nitrogen. If this is thought to be the case, the fault should be investigated by a Rover dealer.

18 Rear hub and bearings - removal and refitting

Note: *Do not attempt to remove a bearing from its hub unless absolutely necessary as it will probably be damaged during removal. Never overtighten the hub nut beyond the specified torque wrench setting in an attempt to "adjust" the bearings.*

Note: *A press will be required to rebuild the assembly. If one is not available, a large bench vice and suitable spacers (such as large*

16.11 Suspension ride height adjustment valve - right-hand side (arrowed)

18.2 Prising off rear hub cap

sockets) will serve as an adequate substitute. **Note:** *Depending on the equipment available, it may be easier for some owners to slacken and tighten the hub nut when the vehicle's weight is on its wheels. The nut is accessible once the roadwheel trim or centre cap (as appropriate) and the hub cap have been removed.*

Removal

1 Remove and check the brake drum.

2 Prise off the hub cap **(see illustration).**

3 Relieve the staking of the hub nut using a hammer and punch or (if necessary) an electric drill, then unscrew the hub nut and remove the washer.

4 Note that the left-hand side stub axle and nut have a left-hand thread; the nut is therefore unscrewed clockwise. The right-hand side components have a conventional right-hand thread and are unscrewed in the usual anti-clockwise direction. It is good practice to renew the hub nuts whenever they are disturbed.

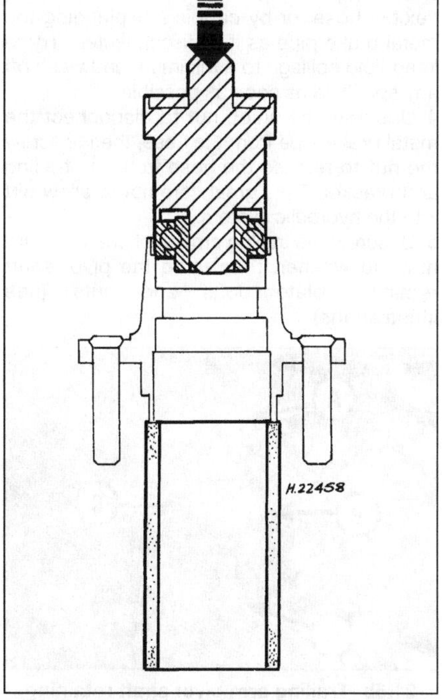

18.14 Pressing new inboard rear hub bearing into hub

18.5 Remove hub nut to permit removal of hub from stub axle

5 Withdraw the hub from the stub axle **(see illustration).**

6 If the stub axle is worn or damaged, it must be renewed using a press.

7 Taking care not to scratch or damage the seal housing, prise the oil seal out of the hub inboard end and discard it; the seal must be renewed whenever it is disturbed.

8 Drive the outboard bearing out of the hub, using a hammer and a suitable punch **(see illustration).**

9 Drive the inboard bearing out of the hub **(see illustration).**

10 Thoroughly clean the hub, removing all traces of dirt and grease and polishing away any burrs or raised edges which might hinder reassembly. Check it for cracks or any other signs of wear or damage and renew if necessary.

11 Note that replacement bearings are available from Rover dealers either as separate items or as part of a bearing kit which includes both bearings, the oil seal and the hub nut. The purchase of the kit is advised because it will ensure that all replacement parts required are readily to hand on reassembly.

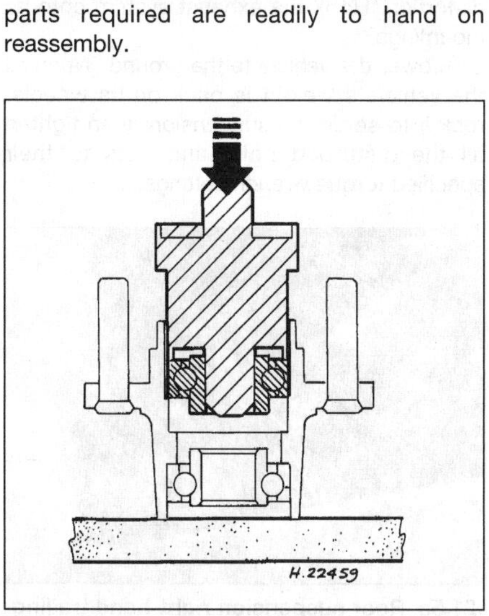

18.15 Pressing new outboard rear hub bearing into hub

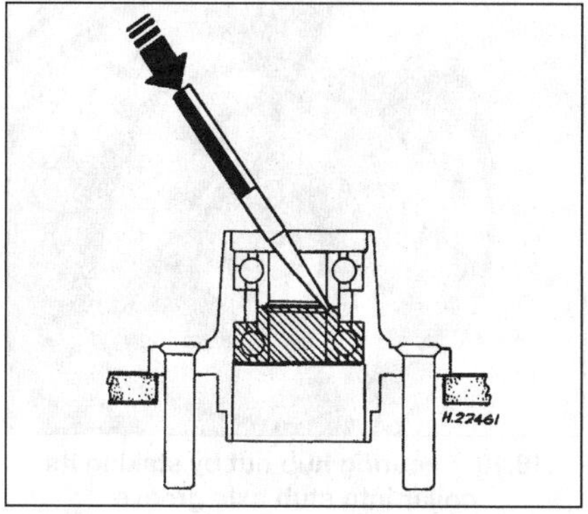

18.8 Driving outboard rear hub bearing out of hub

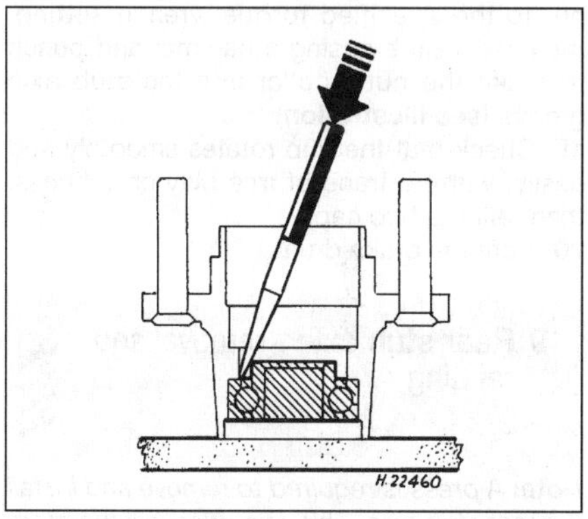

18.9 Driving inboard rear hub bearing out of hub

12 Check the condition of the roadwheel studs in the hub flange. If any are sheared off, stretched or have damaged threads, they can be pressed out of the hub providing that its flange is fully supported. On refitting, support the hub flange and press in the new stud until it seats fully.

Refitting

13 On reassembly, check (as far as is possible) that the new bearings are packed with grease. Apply a light film of oil to the bearing outer races and to the hub bores to aid bearing installation. Note that both bearings must be installed with their marked faces outwards (ie so that the inner races project towards each other).

14 Supporting the hub outboard end and applying pressure only to the bearing's outer race, press in the new inboard bearing until it seats against the shoulder **(see illustration).**

15 Similarly, support the hub inboard end and press in the new outboard bearing **(see illustration).**

16 Ensuring that it is fitted with its sealing lips pointing outboard (towards the bearings), press the new oil seal into the hub and apply a thin smear of grease to the seal lips. Wipe off any surplus oil or grease.

17 Refit the hub to the stub axle, followed by the washer and the new nut.

18.18 Securing hub nut by staking its collar into stub axle groove

18 Remembering that the left-hand nut must be tightened anti-clockwise, tighten the hub nut to the specified torque wrench setting, then secure it by using a hammer and punch to stake the nut's collar into the stub axle groove **(see illustration)**.

19 Check that the hub rotates smoothly and easily, with no trace of free play or stiffness, then refit the hub cap.

20 Refit the brake drum.

19 Rear stub axle - removal and refitting

Note: *A press is required to remove and install the rear stub axle. This operation will therefore require the removal of the relevant trailing arm which in turn involves the depressurisation of (the appropriate side of) the Hydragas suspension system. Refer to the information in Section 1 of this Chapter before starting work.*

Removal

1 Remove the trailing arm.

2 Remove the brake drum and backplate.

3 Press out the stub axle.

Refitting

4 Fitting a new circlip to locate it, press the new stub axle into the trailing arm, from the inboard side outwards.

5 Refit the brake components.

6 Refit the trailing arm.

20 Rear suspension anti-roll bar and mountings - removal, overhaul and refitting

Removal

1 Jack up the rear of the vehicle and support it securely on axle stands (see "*Jacking and Vehicle Support*").

2 Unscrew the bolt and nut securing the bar to each link and slacken the bolts securing the bar clamps to the underbody. Unbolt the links from their brackets if required **(see illustrations)**.

3 Unhook the exhaust system from its rubber mountings and lower it onto a support to take its weight without damaging or distorting it at the front.

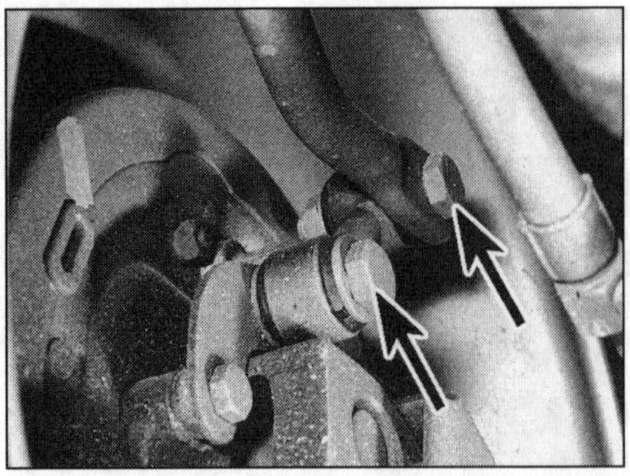

20.2a Anti-roll bar-to-suspension trailing arm link mounting bolts (arrowed)

4 Mark the location of the clamp bushes on the bar, then unbolt the clamps and withdraw the bar.

Overhaul

5 Thoroughly clean all components and the underbody areas around the mountings, removing all traces of dirt and underseal, then check all components for wear or damage and renew them if necessary.

6 Check the rubber bushes and renew them if they are cracked, worn, split or perished.

Refitting

7 Manoeuvre the bar into position and apply soft soap to the clamp bush locations to act as a lubricant.

8 Fit the clamp bushes to the bar, noting that the bush split must face downwards. Align the bushes with the marks made on removal, then refit the clamps and tighten the clamp bolts lightly.

9 Reassemble the bar-to-suspension trailing arm mountings; again tighten the bolts and nuts only by enough to secure the assembly.

10 With all bar mountings correctly installed, check that the bar is centred on the body and that all rubber bushes are seated without distortion. Hook the exhaust system onto its mountings.

11 Lower the vehicle to the ground. When all the vehicle's weight is back on its wheels, rock it to settle the suspension, then tighten all the disturbed bolts and nuts to their specified torque wrench settings.

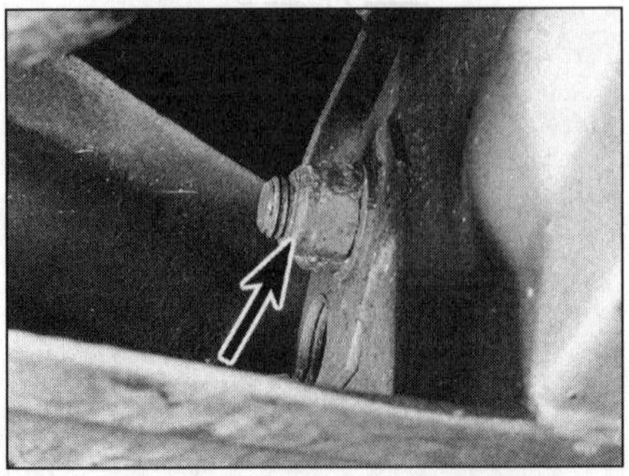

21.5a Rear suspension right-hand trailing arm inboard pivot shaft nut (arrowed) - seen from rear of subframe

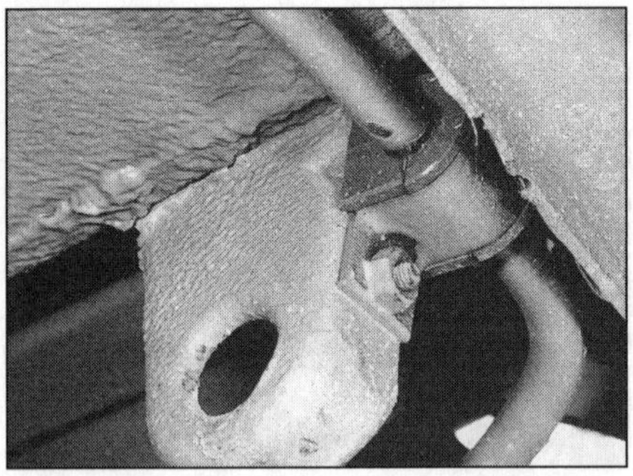

20.2b Rear anti-roll bar-to-body clamp

21 Rear suspension trailing arm and pivot bearings - removal, overhaul and refitting

Note: *This procedure requires the depressurisation of (the appropriate side of) the Hydragas suspension system. Refer to the precautions in Section 1 of this Chapter before starting work.*

Removal

1 Remove the Hydragas unit. Support the weight of the trailing arm, using a wooden block or similar.

2 Disconnect the handbrake cable from the rear brake lever assembly and release the cable from the cable-ties and bracket securing it to the trailing arm.

3 Minimise fluid loss by removing the master cylinder reservoir cap and then tightening it down onto a piece of polythene to obtain an airtight seal (taking care not to damage the sender unit), or by using a brake hose clamp, a G-clamp or a similar tool to clamp the flexible hose, or by capping or plugging the metal brake pipe as it is disconnected. Try to keep fluid spillage to a minimum and wash off any spilt fluid as soon as possible.

4 Unscrew the union nut to disconnect the metal brake pipe from the hose, then unscrew the nut to release the hose from the trailing arm bracket. Take great care not to allow dirt into the hydraulic system.

5 Unscrew the trailing arm pivot shaft inboard nut and washer, then undo the pivot shaft retaining plate bolts and nuts **(see illustrations)**.

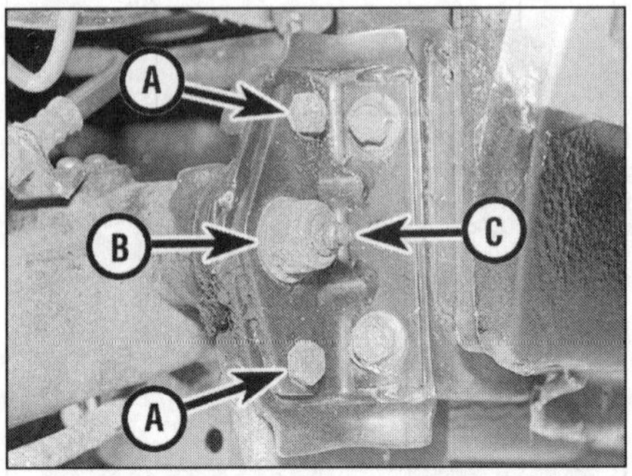

21.5b Trailing arm pivot shaft retaining plate bolts (A) outboard pivot shaft nut (B) and grease nipple (C)

6 Extract the pivot shaft with the retaining plate. If the pivot has been regularly greased the shaft will slide out easily. If, as is more likely, the shaft is stuck with corrosion, it must be driven out from its inboard end outwards using a hammer and a suitable drift. The only alternative is to grip the outboard nut with a self-locking wrench and to hammer the shaft out. In extreme cases, apply a liberal quantity of penetrating fluid to both ends of the pivot and allow time for it to "work", then break the shaft free by rotating it before attempting to remove it.

7 When the pivot shaft is removed withdraw the trailing arm, collecting the inboard and outboard seals and the thrustwasher(s). Check the condition of the rebound rubber buffer and renew it if worn or damaged.

8 Remove and check the helper spring, strut and knuckle joint.

9 Remove the rear brake drum and backplate, if required; removing the rear hub as described in the appropriate Section of this Chapter. If the stub axle is worn or damaged it must be renewed using a press but note that if the trailing arm is to be renewed, a stub axle will be supplied fitted to the new arm.

Overhaul

Note: *The trailing arm pivot needle roller bearings, the pivot shaft and the associated thrustwashers are available only as part of a repair kit and cannot be purchased separately. The pivot shaft nuts, washers, grease nipple and seal can be purchased separately if required, but are also part of the repair kit.*

10 Clamp the pivot shaft in a soft-jawed vice and unscrew the grease nipple, the outboard nut and its washer. Collect the retaining plate and thrustwasher, noting which way round the thrustwasher is fitted.

11 Thoroughly clean all components and the subframe around the trailing arm mountings. Check the subframe for signs of wear or damage to the trailing arm pivot points and to the various threads, then check the rebound rubber buffer and the bump stop **(see illustration)**. Renew any component that shows signs of wear or damage.

12 If the pivot bearings are to be renewed, first note the exact position of each in the arm pivot, measuring carefully the depth of each bearing's outer race from the arm's outer end. Extract them using an internally-expanding bearing puller or drive them out from the inside using a hammer and a slim metal drift passed through the arm pivot from the opposite end.

13 Carefully clean the pivot bore, polish away any burrs or raised edges that might damage the new bearings on installation and check that the grease nipple is clear.

14 Ensuring that they are fitted with their marked surfaces outwards and that they enter exactly squarely into the pivot bore, install the new bearings using either a press, or a large bench vice or a length of studding, two large plain washers and nuts. Press the bearings

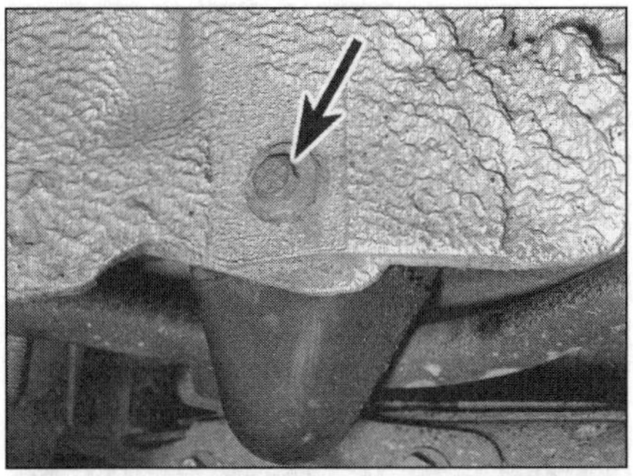

21.11 Rear suspension bump stop mounting bolt (arrowed)

into the positions noted on removal, then check that they are installed correctly by passing the pivot shaft through them.

15 Pack the bearings with multi-purpose grease and lubricate all other pivot components. Fit the thrustwashers and seals to the arm (noting that the thrustwasher grooved surfaces must be against their respective bearings), grease each as it is installed.

16 Clamp the pivot shaft in a soft-jawed vice and fit the thrustwasher (noting that the grooved surface must be against the bearing), the retaining plate, the washer and outboard nut and the grease nipple, tightening the nut and grease nipple to their respective specified torque wrench settings. Check that the shaft is clean and unmarked, then smear it with grease.

Refitting

17 Taking care not to displace the seals or thrustwashers, refit the trailing arm to the subframe, then use a wooden block or similar to support the weight of its rear end. Align the arm's pivot with the subframe holes and refit the pivot shaft assembly, taking care not to damage the shaft or the bearings. Tighten the retaining plate bolts and nuts and the pivot shaft inboard nut to their specified torque wrench settings, then check that the arm pivots smoothly but without free play.

18 Use a grease gun to pack the bearings until grease can be seen exuding from both ends of the pivot, then wipe off all surplus grease.

22.4a Rear Hydragas unit retaining strap nut (arrowed) in spare wheel compartment . . .

19 For the remainder of the refitting procedure, work as follows.

a) *Refit the helper spring, strut and knuckle joint to the arm.*
b) *Refit the Hydragas unit.*
c) *If they were removed, refit the brake backplate, the rear hub and the brake drum.*
d) *Connect the handbrake cable to the rear brake lever assembly, connect the brake flexible hose to the trailing arm bracket and the metal brake pipe, then bleed any air from the system. Adjust the rear brake shoes and the handbrake cable.*
e) *Refit the roadwheel and lower the vehicle to the ground.*
f) *Have any air evacuated from the Hydragas suspension and have it pressurised to the correct ride height.*

22 Rear suspension Hydragas unit - removal and refitting

Note: *This procedure requires the depressurisation of (the appropriate side of) the Hydragas suspension system. Refer to the precautions in Section 1 of this Chapter before starting work*

Removal

1 Have the Hydragas suspension depressurised on the relevant side.

2 Jack up the rear of the vehicle and support it securely on axle stands (see "*Jacking and Vehicle Support*") then remove the roadwheel.

3 Uncouple the plastic connecting pipe from the Hydragas unit. Plug or cap the orifices immediately to prevent the entry of dirt.

4 Open the tailgate and lift the luggage compartment floor covering and the spare wheel cover, then unscrew the retaining strap nut inside the vehicle. Working outside and underneath the vehicle, unscrew the second retaining strap nut, then withdraw the strap and its rubber sleeve **(see illustrations)**.

5 On models so equipped, unbolt the anti-roll bar from the link.

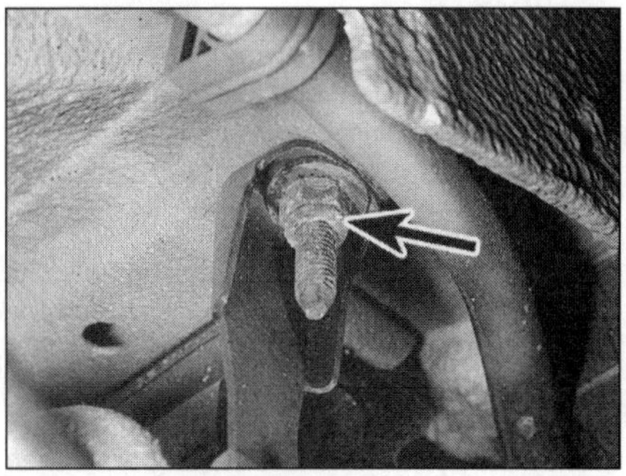

22.4b . . . and underneath body (arrowed)

6 Unbolt the Hydragas unit's clamp plate from the subframe and withdraw the plate **(see illustration)**.

7 Withdraw the Hydragas unit, lifting it off the helper spring, strut and knuckle joint; if these components come away with the unit, note how each is located and note the presence of the return spring and the spacer between the strut and knuckle joint.

8 Collect the unit's mounting pad. Check its condition, also that of the bump stop and renew either if worn or damaged.

9 Whenever the unit is removed, the strut and knuckle joint should be dismantled, checked for wear and grease.

Refitting

10 Clean carefully the mating surfaces of the unit and of the strut and knuckle joint, then apply a smear of the recommended grease. Ensure that the spacer and return spring are in place between the knuckle joint and strut and that the helper spring is correctly located on the trailing arm.

11 Offer up the Hydragas unit, aligning it carefully on the helper spring and ensuring that the strut fits into the centre hole in the unit, then refit the unit's mounting pad and its clamp plate, tightening the clamp plate bolts to the specified torque wrench setting.

12 Refit the retaining strap and its rubber sleeve, tightening the strap nuts to the specified torque wrench setting.

13 For the remainder of the refitting procedure, work as follows.

a) Connect the plastic connecting pipe to the unit.
b) Where fitted, connect the anti-roll bar to the link.
c) Refit the roadwheel and lower the car to the ground.
d) Have any air evacuated from the Hydragas suspension and have it pressurised to the correct ride height.

23 Rear suspension strut and knuckle joint - removal and refitting

Note: *This procedure requires the depressurisation of (the appropriate side of) the Hydragas suspension system. Refer to the precautions in Section 1 of this Chapter before starting work*

Removal

1 Remove the Hydragas unit.

2 Withdraw the helper spring, noting how it is located on the trailing arm, then remove the strut, return spring and spacer from the knuckle joint.

3 Carefully lift the rubber boot and remove the knuckle joint from the trailing arm, then prise out the joint socket.

4 Thoroughly clean all components and check them for any signs of wear or damage.

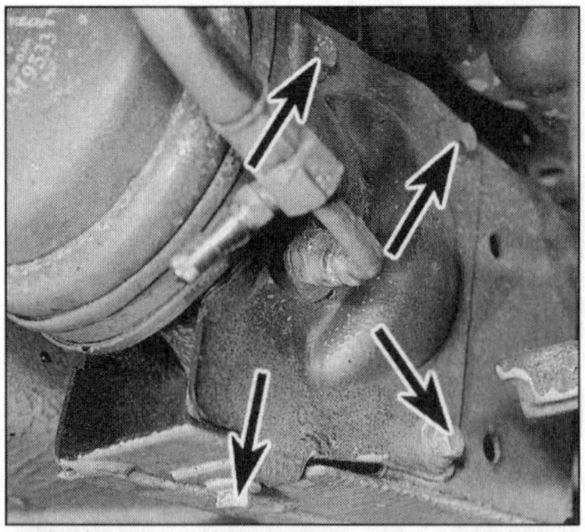

22.6 Rear Hydragas unit clamp plate bolts (arrowed)

Check particularly that the ball end of the knuckle joint is not corroded, worn or pitted and that the socket is not cracked or split.

5 Renew any worn or damaged components. Note that if the knuckle joint is to be renewed it is available only as an assembly with the socket and the rubber boot, otherwise only the return spring, the spacer and the strut are available separately.

Refitting

6 On reassembly, clean the trailing arm socket location and tap in the socket.

7 The recommended lubricant for the knuckle joint is Dextragrease Super GP (available from Rover dealers). Apply a smear of this grease to all knuckle joint components before refitting.

8 Pack the socket with grease and press in the knuckle joint, then fill the space above the joint ball with grease and ensure that the rubber boot is correctly located over the socket lip so that no dirt or water can enter the joint.

9 Refit the spacer and return spring to the knuckle joint, then refit the strut. Apply a smear of grease to all these components as they are refitted, then wipe off any surplus grease. Locate the helper spring on its trailing arm seat.

10 Refit the Hydragas unit.

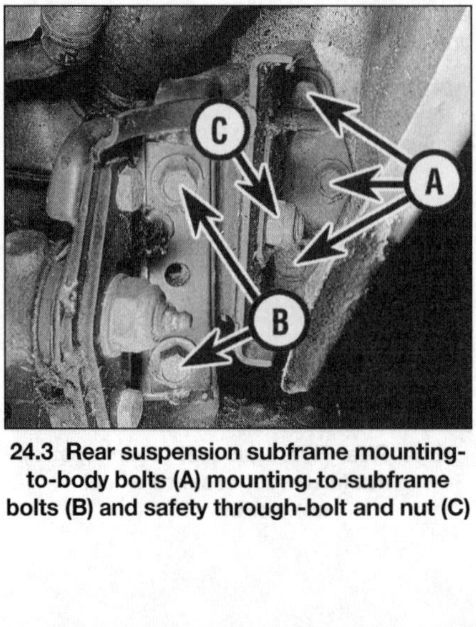

24.3 Rear suspension subframe mounting-to-body bolts (A) mounting-to-subframe bolts (B) and safety through-bolt and nut (C)

24 Rear suspension subframe (front) mountings - renewal

Note: *The subframe is fastened positively to the body only at its front corners; the rear ends being secured by the Hydragas units via their retaining straps and mounting pads. Each (front) mounting is secured by three bolts to the body and by two bolts to the subframe and comprises two metal plates sandwiching a bonded rubber layer. A safety through-bolt is provided to ensure that the rear suspension remains attached to the car if the bonding should shear. Great care will be required in supporting the body and subframe securely while the subframe is disturbed.*

1 Jack up the rear of the vehicle and support the body securely on axle stands (see "*Jacking and Vehicle Support*"), then remove the roadwheel. Where fitted, if better access is required to the various bolts, remove the side skirts/sill extensions.

2 Use a wooden block or similar to support the subframe securely in its correct position relative to the body, so that there is no strain on the mounting.

3 Unscrew the two mounting-to-subframe bolts, followed by the three mounting-to-body bolts. There is no need to disturb the safety through-bolt or its nut **(see illustration)**.

4 Withdraw the mounting. It may be necessary to prise down the subframe to allow the mounting to be removed. If so, take care not to stretch the brake flexible hose.

5 While the mounting is removed, check the condition of the threads in the body and of the body itself around the mounting points. Any signs of corrosion, wear or damage will mean that repairs must be carried out by an expert as soon as possible.

6 On reassembly, secure the mounting first to the body, then to the subframe; tighten the bolts and roadwheel nuts to their specified torque wrench settings.

25 Rear suspension subframe - removal and refitting

Note: *This procedure requires the depressurisation of both sides of the Hydragas suspension system. Refer to the remarks in Section 1 of this Chapter before starting work*

Removal

1 Jack up the rear of the vehicle and support the body securely on axle stands, then remove the roadwheels.

2 Disconnect the handbrake cable from the rear brake lever assemblies and release the cable from the cable-ties and bracket securing it to each trailing arm, then remove the cable from the subframe.

3 Minimise fluid loss by removing the master cylinder reservoir cap and then tightening it down onto a piece of polythene to obtain an airtight seal (taking care not to damage the sender unit), or by using brake hose clamps, G-clamps or similar tools to clamp the flexible hoses, or by capping or plugging the metal brake pipes as they are disconnected. Try to keep fluid spillage to a minimum and wash off any spilt fluid as soon as possible.
4 Unscrew the union nuts to disconnect the metal brake pipes from the hoses, then unscrew the nuts to release the hoses from the trailing arm brackets. Take great care not to allow dirt into the hydraulic system.
5 On models so equipped, unbolt the anti-roll bar from both links.
6 Unhook the exhaust system mounting from the subframe hook.
7 Uncouple the plastic connecting pipes from the Hydragas units. Plug or cap the orifices immediately to prevent the entry of dirt.
8 Make a final check that all components have been removed or disconnected that are attached to the subframe or might prevent its removal.
9 Support the subframe, unbolt its (front) mountings and remove the Hydragas unit retaining straps, then lower the subframe to the ground and remove it. The Hydragas units and trailing arms can then be removed, if required.
10 Thoroughly clean the subframe and the underbody areas around its mountings, removing all traces of dirt and underseal, then check it carefully for excessive corrosion, cracks, distortion or any other signs of wear or damage. Do not forget the pivot holes and the threads and check the (front) mountings for signs of the rubber deteriorating or separating from the metal outer plates. Renew any worn or damaged component.
11 If either the subframe or the underbody show signs of rusting, the affected area must be cleaned back to bare metal and treated before being repainted. If the underbody is seriously rusted or if any of the mounting bolt threads are damaged, seek professional advice.

Refitting

12 Refitting is the reverse of the removal procedure, noting the following points.

a) *Tighten all disturbed nuts and bolts to their specified torque wrench settings.*
b) *Connect the handbrake cable to the rear brake lever assemblies, connect the brake flexible hoses to the trailing arm brackets and the metal brake pipes, then bleed any air from the system. Adjust the rear brake shoes and the handbrake cable.*
c) *Have any air evacuated from the Hydragas suspension and have it pressurised to the correct ride height.*

26 Steering - inspection

Refer to Chapter 1, Section 23.

27 Steering wheel - removal and refitting

Models without SRS

Removal

1 With the vehicle parked on level ground, check that the roadwheels are in the straight-ahead position. The steering wheel spokes should be horizontal.
2 Prise off the wheel's centre cover.
3 Unscrew the steering wheel nut. If the nut is fitted with a separate cover, prise this off carefully **(see illustration)**.
4 Check for alignment marks between the steering wheel and the steering column; if none can be seen, make your own.
5 Grasp the steering wheel firmly and rock it to jar it free, then pull it off the steering column splines. It is permissible to thump the wheel from behind with the palms of the hands, but do not hammer the wheel or column, or use excessive force.

Refitting

6 On refitting, check that the steering column splines are clean. Refit the wheel, entering the projection on its lower surface with the direction indicator cancelling cam **(see illustration)** and aligning the marks made or noted on dismantling; this should leave the wheel positioned as described above.
7 Tighten the steering wheel nut to the specified torque wrench setting, then refit the nut cover (if fitted) and the wheel centre cover.

Models with SRS

Removal

8 Remove the ignition key and wait at least ten minutes to allow the SRS system backup circuit to fully discharge. Disconnect both battery leads, earth lead first, to avoid accidental detonation of the airbag.
9 Set the steering in the dead-ahead position.
10 Refer to Chapter 12 and remove the airbag unit. Disconnect the multiplug from the rotary contact unit.
11 Hold the steering wheel and unscrew its securing nut to the end of its thread but do not remove it.
12 Check for alignment marks between the steering wheel and the steering column; if none can be seen, make your own.
13 Grasp the steering wheel firmly and rock it to jar it free. It is permissible to thump the wheel from behind with the palms of the hands, but do not hammer the wheel or column, or use excessive force.
14 Remove and discard the nut and then remove the steering wheel.

Refitting

15 Refitting is the reverse of the removal procedure, noting the following points.

a) *Before refitting, check that the steering column splines are clean. Refit the wheel, entering the projection on its lower surface with the direction indicator cancelling cam and aligning the marks made or noted on dismantling. This should leave the wheel correctly positioned.*
b) *Fit and tighten the new steering wheel nut to the specified torque wrench setting.*
c) *Take care to ensure that all wiring is correctly routed and is not trapped between mating surfaces.*
d) *Check all wiring connectors are firmly fastened*
e) *On completion, reconnect the battery negative cable and turn the ignition switch to the "II" position. Check the condition of the system by observing the SRS warning light located in the steering wheel centre pad. The light should stay illuminated for 3 seconds whilst the system performs a self-diagnosis test. If the test is satisfactory, the light will extinguish. If the test is unsatisfactory, the light will remain on or fail to illuminate at all, denoting that the system must be serviced as soon as possible.*

27.3 Prise off steering wheel centre cover to reveal the steering wheel securing nut

27.6 When refitting steering wheel, ensure projecting tab engages with cam slot (arrowed)

10

28.2a Removing spring ring from steering column nacelle boss

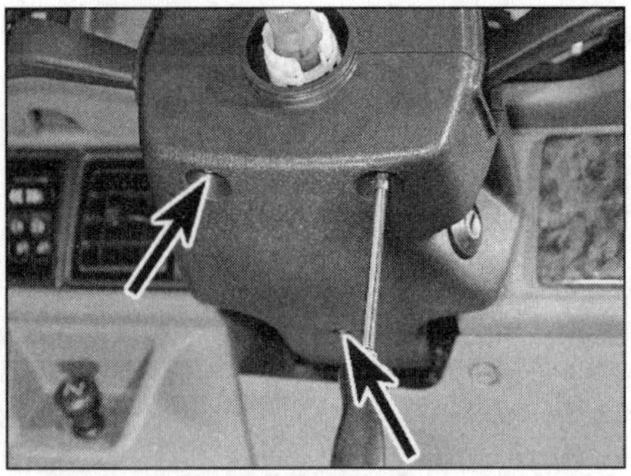

28.2b Nacelle lower half retained by three screws (arrowed) . . .

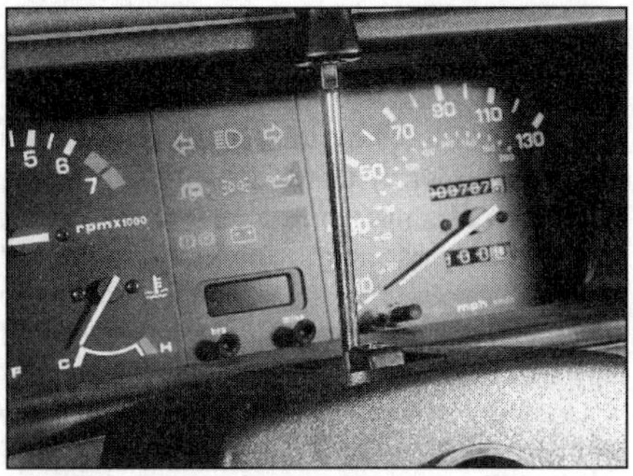

28.2c . . . and upper half by one screw

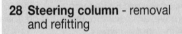

28 Steering column - removal and refitting

Models without SRS

Removal

1 Check that the steering is unlocked and remove the steering wheel.

2 Remove the spring ring from the nacelle boss then undo the retaining screws (one into the upper half, three into the lower half) and withdraw the steering column nacelle upper and lower halves **(see illustrations)**.

3 Disconnect the battery negative lead.

4 Disconnect the wiring of the multi-function switches and hazard warning switch by unplugging the three connectors. The switches and their centre housing need not be removed from the column unless required.

5 Release the retaining fasteners and remove the fusebox cover.

6 Remove its retaining screw and bolt and withdraw the steering column cover **(see illustration)**.

7 Unplug the ignition switch wiring connector plug (top row, left-hand connector, marked 'IGN') from the fusebox panel, then release the wiring from any clamps or ties securing it to the facia or its mountings.

8 Using a hammer and punch, white paint or similar, mark the exact relationship of the steering column universal joint to the steering gear pinion. Check first that the roadwheels are in the straight-ahead position. Unscrew and fully remove the pinch-bolt securing the joint to the pinion.

9 Unscrew the two remaining bolts and one nut securing the column to its mountings, then withdraw it from the car **(see illustration)**.

10 Note that the steering column is available only as a complete assembly. If there is any wear or damage to the column itself, to its jacket tube or mountings, to the rubber coupling or the universal joint, then the complete column assembly must be renewed.

Refitting

11 Refitting is the reverse of the removal procedure, noting the following points.

a) Loosely assemble the column mountings and universal joint ensuring that the joint is positioned on the steering gear pinion so that the pinch-bolt bore is aligned exactly with the pinion groove and the marks made on removal are aligned, then refit the pinch-bolt and tighten it to the specified torque wrench setting.

b) Check that the column is seated without stress on its mountings, then tighten the bolts and nut to the specified torque wrench setting.

c) When reconnecting the wiring, ensure that it is correctly routed and secured using any clamps or ties provided.

d) When refitting the steering wheel, ensure that the roadwheels are in the straight-ahead position and that the steering wheel and column are aligned as described.

e) Tighten the column cover clamp bolt and the steering wheel nut to their specified torque wrench settings.

f) When reassembly is complete, raise the front of the car and turn the steering from lock to lock to ensure that it is functioning correctly.

Models with SRS

Removal

12 Remove the ignition key and wait at least ten minutes to allow the SRS system backup circuit to fully discharge. Disconnect both battery leads, earth lead first, to avoid accidental detonation of the airbag.

13 Set the steering in the dead-ahead position.

14 Refer to Chapter 12 and remove the airbag unit.

15 Remove the steering wheel.

16 Refer to Chapter 12 and remove the airbag control unit and rotary contact unit.

17 Remove the indicator cancelling cam. Disconnect the wiring of the column switch assembly by unplugging the four multiplug connectors. Remove the two switch securing screws and remove the switch assembly from the column.

18 Detach the ignition/starter switch and airbag link harness multiplugs from the fusebox **(see illustration)**. Release the fuse holder from the fusebox.

19 Remove its retaining screw and bolt and withdraw the steering column cover.

20 Using a hammer and punch, white paint or similar, mark the exact relationship of the

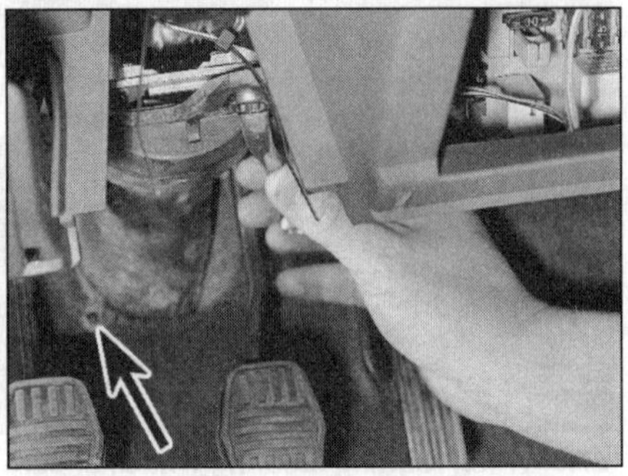

28.6 Unscrewing steering column cover clamp bolt - note screw (arrowed)

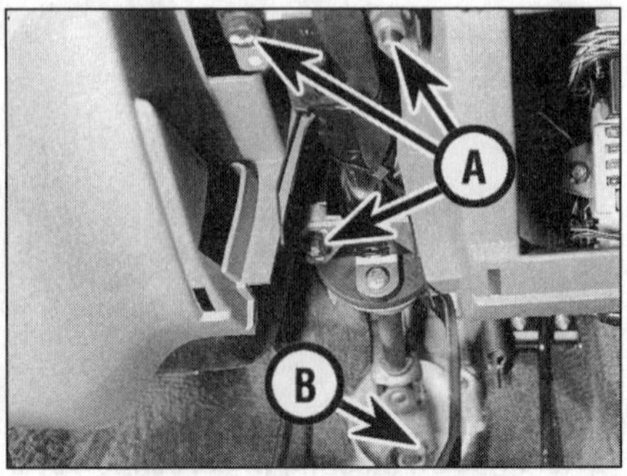

28.9 Steering column mountings (A) and universal joint pinch-bolt (B)

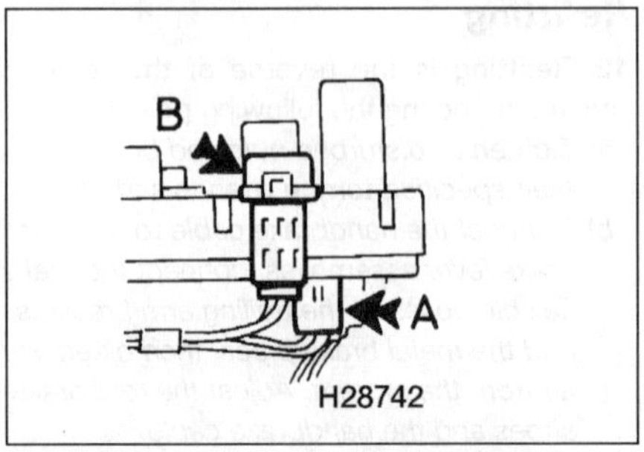

28.18 Detach the ignition/starter switch and airbag link harness multiplugs (A) and fuse holder (B) from the fusebox

steering column universal joint to the steering gear pinion. Unscrew and fully remove the pinch-bolt securing the joint to the pinion.

21 Unscrew the two remaining bolts and one nut securing the column to its mountings, then withdraw the column from the vehicle.

22 Remove the steering lock and ignition/starter switch from the column if it is to be renewed.

Refitting

23 Refitting is the reverse of the removal procedure, noting the points given in paragraph 11 above and in Chapter 12 for the fitting of the airbag unit, airbag control unit and rotary contact unit.

29 Steering lock/ignition switch - removal and refitting

Caution: Read the precautions listed in Section 1, Chapter 12, appertaining to vehicles equipped with airbags (SRS) before attempting removal of the ignition switch.

Note: *The steering lock/ignition switch is secured by two shear-head bolts. Although new bolts are supplied with replacement steering lock assemblies, always ensure that the bolts themselves are available before beginning work*

Removal

1 Check that the steering is unlocked and remove the steering wheel.

2 Remove the spring ring from the nacelle boss then undo the retaining screws (one into the upper half, three into the lower half) and withdraw the steering column nacelle upper and lower halves.

3 Release the retaining fasteners and remove the fusebox cover.

4 Remove its retaining screw and bolt and withdraw the steering column cover.

30.2 The steering gear rubber gaiter inboard clips are accessible through subframe apertures (arrowed)

5 Disconnect the battery negative lead.

6 Disconnect the wiring of the multi-function switches and hazard warning switch by unplugging the three connectors, then disconnect the ignition switch wiring by unplugging its connector plug (top row, left-hand connector, marked `IGN') from the fusebox panel, then release the wiring from any clamps or ties securing it to the column or to the facia or its mountings.

7 Unscrew the two remaining bolts and one nut securing the column to its mountings, then lower the column onto a support such as a wooden block

8 Centre-punch the shear-head bolts, then drill off the bolt heads. New bolts will be required on refitting.

9 Withdraw the steering lock/ignition switch, then unscrew the remains of the shear-head bolts using a self-locking wrench or similar on the exposed ends.

Refitting

10 On refitting, carefully align the assembly on the steering column, lightly tighten the bolts and check that the steering lock works smoothly.

11 Tighten the shear-head bolts evenly until their heads shear off.

12 The remainder of the reassembly procedure is the reverse of removal. Ensure that the wiring is correctly routed and that all disturbed fasteners are tightened to their specified torque wrench settings.

30 Steering gear rubber gaiters - renewal

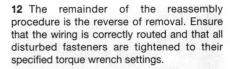

Note: *A balljoint separator tool will be required to separate the balljoint taper pin from the eye of the steering arm.*

1 Remove the track rod balljoint and locknut and release the gaiter outboard clip.

2 Working through the aperture in the front of the front suspension subframe, cut the gaiter inboard clip and slide the gaiter off the steering gear **(see illustration)**.

3 Check the gaiter for any signs of splits, tears or perishing. Renew it if any such damage is found or if it is not a tight fit on the steering gear or track rod. The clips should be renewed as a matter of course whenever they are disturbed.

4 Thoroughly clean the track rod and the steering gear housing, using fine abrasive paper to polish off any corrosion, burrs or sharp edges which might damage the new gaiter's sealing lips on installation.

5 On refitting, check that the steering gear components are correctly greased, grease the gaiter's lips and slide it on, then fasten the new inboard clip to secure it.

6 Settle the gaiter evenly on the track rod and fasten the outboard clip.

7 Refit the track rod balljoint and locknut.

8 When checking the steering's operation, ensure that the gaiter does not snag or bulge at any point in the steering gear travel. If necessary, unfasten the clip(s) and reposition the gaiter.

31 Steering gear - removal and refitting

Note: *The steering gear is available only as a complete assembly. If there is any wear or damage to the rack or pinion, to the housing or to either track rod, the complete assembly must be renewed* ***(see illustration).***

Removal

1 Working inside the car, remove the steering column, then unbolt the bulkhead aperture cover from the floor. Remove the cover and the seal.

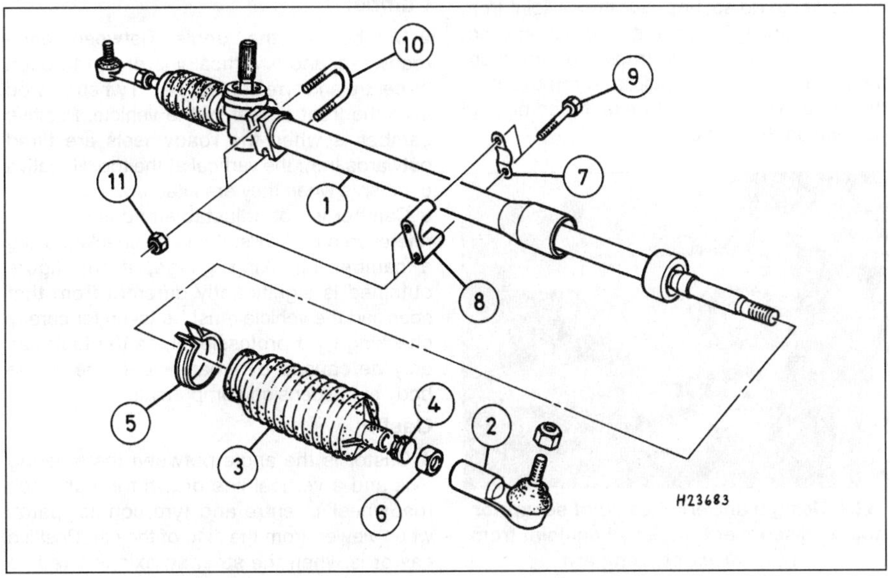

31.0 Steering gear components

1 Steering gear
2 Track rod balljoint
3 Steering gear rubber gaiter
4 Clip
5 Clip
6 Balljoint locknut
7 Mounting clamp
8 Mounting spacer
9 Bolts
10 U-bolt
11 Nuts

31.5a Steering gear mounting nuts - on right-hand side (arrowed) . . .

2 Jack up the front of the car and support the body securely on axle stands (see "*Jacking and Vehicle Support*"), then remove the roadwheels.
3 Disconnect the track rod balljoints from the hub carrier steering arms.
4 On models so equipped, slacken the anti-roll bar-to-suspension lower arm bolts and nuts, then unbolt the bar clamps from the underbody.
5 Unscrew the steering gear mounting nuts from the front of the front suspension subframe. Collect the mounting U-bolt, clamp, spacer and bolts **(see illustrations)**.
6 Unbolt the exhaust system front pipe from the intermediate pipe.
7 Support the subframe and engine/transmission on a trolley jack, using a metal girder or strong timber baulk placed across the subframe to take the weight evenly.
8 Unbolt the engine/transmission rear mounting tie-rod from the underbody and slacken the mounting bracket-to-tie-rod through-bolt. Unbolt the front suspension subframe rear mountings from the underbody.
9 Lower the jack until the subframe has dropped far enough to allow the removal of the steering gear. Manoeuvre the steering gear out to the right of the vehicle.

Refitting

10 On refitting, first ensure that the steering gear rack is at the exact mid-point of its travel, then refit the steering gear to the subframe, assemble the mounting components and lightly tighten the nuts.
11 Raise the subframe into position and tighten the mounting bolts to their specified torque wrench setting, then refit the engine/transmission rear mounting.
12 The remainder of the reassembly procedure is the reverse of removal, noting the following points.

a) Tighten all disturbed nuts and bolts to their specified torque wrench settings.
b) Connect the exhaust system.
c) When the steering gear is located correctly and is settled on its mountings, tighten its mounting nuts to the specified torque wrench setting, then connect the track rod balljoints to the hub carrier steering arms.

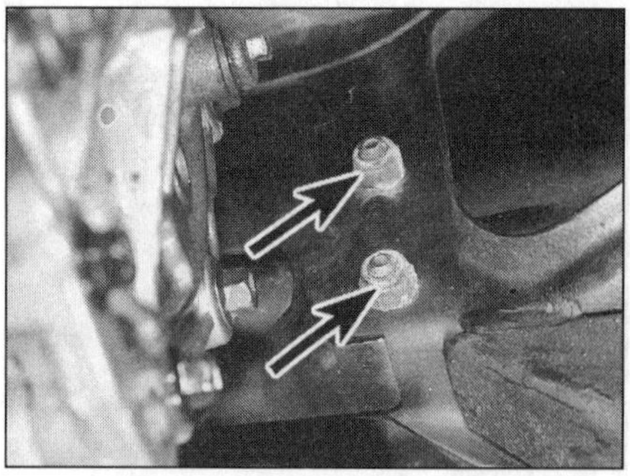

31.5b . . . and left-hand side of front suspension subframe (arrowed)

d) Reassemble the anti-roll bar (if fitted), but do not tighten its mountings until all the car's weight is back on its wheels.
e) Refit the roadwheels, lower the car to the ground and refit the steering column.
f) Have the wheel alignment checked as soon as possible.

32 Track rod balljoint - removal and refitting

Removal

1 Jack up the front of the vehicle and support it securely on axle stands (see "*Jacking and Vehicle Support*"), then remove the roadwheel.
2 If the balljoint is to be re-used, use a straight-edge and a scriber, or similar, to mark its relationship to the track rod.
3 Holding the balljoint, unscrew its locknut by one quarter of a turn.
4 Unscrew the balljoint-to-steering arm nut until it is flush with the end of its thread. Separate the balljoint from the hub carrier steering arm, using a universal balljoint separator tool if necessary **(see illustration)**.
5 Counting the exact number of turns necessary to do so, unscrew the balljoint from the track rod. If the locknut is to be removed, mark its position on the track rod and count the number of turns required to remove it so that it can be returned to exactly its original position on reassembly.

32.4 Using a universal balljoint separator tool to disconnect track rod balljoint from hub carrier steering arm

6 Carefully clean the balljoint and the threads. Renew the balljoint if its movement is sloppy or if it is too stiff, if it is excessively worn or if it is damaged in any way. Carefully check the stud taper and threads. No grease leakage should be visible. Renew the retaining nut as a matter of course whenever the balljoint is renewed; otherwise check that its locking action is still effective and renew it if necessary.

Refitting

7 On refitting, screw the balljoint onto the track rod by the number of turns noted on removal. This should, of course, bring the balljoint to within a quarter of a turn from the locknut, with the alignment marks that were made (if applicable) on removal lined up.
8 Degrease the tapers of the balljoint stud and of the hub carrier steering arm, then press the balljoint firmly into the steering arm while the nut is refitted and tightened to its specified torque wrench setting.
9 If the car is to be driven elsewhere in order to have the wheel alignment checked, hold the balljoint and tighten the locknut securely.
10 Where applicable, refit the roadwheel and lower the vehicle to the ground.

33 Wheel alignment and steering angles

Wheel alignment and steering angles

1 A vehicle's steering and suspension geometry is defined in five basic settings - all angles are expressed in degrees and the steering axis is defined as an imaginary line drawn through the centres of the front suspension upper and lower balljoints, extended where necessary to contact the ground **(see illustration)**.

Camber

2 Camber is the angle between each roadwheel and a vertical line drawn through its centre and tyre contact patch when viewed from the front or rear of the vehicle. Positive camber is when the roadwheels are tilted outwards from the vertical at the top. Negative camber is when they are tilted inwards.
3 Camber is not adjustable and is given for reference only. Whilst it can be checked using a camber checking gauge, if the figure obtained is significantly different from that specified the vehicle must be taken for careful checking by a professional, as the fault can only be caused by wear or damage to the body or suspension components.

Castor

4 Castor is the angle between the steering axis and a vertical line drawn through each roadwheel's centre and tyre contact patch when viewed from the side of the car. Positive castor is when the steering axis is tilted so that it contacts the ground ahead of the vertical. Negative castor is when it contacts the ground behind the vertical.

5 Castor is not adjustable and is given for reference only. Whilst it can be checked using a castor checking gauge, if the figure obtained is significantly different from that specified the car must be taken for careful checking by a professional, as the fault can only be caused by wear or damage to the body or suspension components.

Steering axis inclination/SAI

6 Steering axis inclination/SAI - also known as kingpin inclination/KPI - is the angle between the steering axis and a vertical line drawn through each roadwheel's centre and tyre contact patch when viewed from the front or rear of the vehicle.

7 SAI/KPI is not adjustable and is given for reference only.

Toe

8 Toe is the difference, viewed from above, between lines drawn through the roadwheel centres and the vehicle's centre-line. "Toe-in" is when the roadwheels point inwards, towards each other at the front, whilst "toe-out" is when they splay outwards from each other at the front.

9 At the front, the toe setting is adjusted by screwing the track rods in or out of their balljoints to alter the effective length of the track rod assemblies.

10 At the rear, the toe setting is not adjustable and is given for reference only. Whilst it can be checked as described below, if the figure obtained is significantly different from that specified the vehicle must be taken for careful checking by a professional, as the fault can only be caused by wear or damage to the body or suspension components.

Toe-out on turns

11 Toe-out on turns - also known as turning angles or Ackermann angles - is the difference, viewed from above, between the angles of rotation of the inside and outside front roadwheels when they have been turned through a given angle.

12 Toe-out on turns is set in production and is not adjustable as such but can be upset by altering the length of the track rods unequally. It is essential, therefore, to ensure that the track rod lengths are exactly the same and that they are turned by the same amount whenever the toe setting is altered.

General inspection

13 Due to the special measuring equipment necessary to check the wheel alignment and the skill required to use it properly, the checking and adjustment of these settings is best left to a Rover dealer or similar expert. Note that most tyre-fitting shops now possess sophisticated checking equipment.

14 For accurate checking, the vehicle must be.

a) At kerb weight.

b) At exactly the correct ride height.

15 Before starting work, always check first that the tyre sizes and types are as specified, then check the pressures and tread wear, the roadwheel run-out, the condition of the hub bearings, the steering wheel free play and the condition of the front suspension components. Correct any faults found.

16 Park the vehicle on level ground, check that the front roadwheels are in the straight-ahead position, then rock the rear and front ends to settle the suspension, release the handbrake and roll the vehicle backwards 1 metre, then forwards again to relieve any stresses in the steering and suspension components.

Toe-out on turns - checking and adjusting

17 As far as the home mechanic is concerned, this can be checked only using a pair of scuff plates.

18 Prepare the vehicle as described in paragraphs 14 to 16 above. Roll the vehicle backwards, check that the front roadwheels are in the straight-ahead position, then roll it forwards on to the scuff plates until each front roadwheel is seated squarely on the centre of each plate.

19 Turn the steering wheel first one way until the outside roadwheel is at the specified angle; record the angle of the inside roadwheel. Next turn the steering wheel back through the straight-ahead position and repeat the check on that side.

20 If, in either check, the inside roadwheel is not at the angle specified, check that both track rod assemblies are exactly the same length by counting the exposed threads inboard of the locknuts. If the lengths are different, this can be corrected by screwing the track rods in or out of the balljoints, but this will affect the toe setting and the steering wheel position.

21 If the angles are incorrect but the track rods are the same length and the steering mechanism components are known from the preliminary checks to be unworn, then there is damage to, or distortion of, part of the steering mechanism, the front suspension or the body itself. This will require careful checking, preferably by an expert such as a Rover dealer, as soon as possible.

Toe setting - checking and adjusting

22 The procedure given below refers specifically to the front toe setting. Whilst the rear toe setting can be checked, it is not adjustable and any variation from the specified setting must be caused by wear or damage of the suspension or body.

23 As far as the home mechanic is concerned, the toe setting can be checked only using a pair of scuff plates, in which the roadwheels are rolled across a moveable plate which records any deviation (or scuff) of the tyre relative to the straight-ahead position as it moves across the plate. Whilst such gauges are available in relatively inexpensive form from accessory outlets, only an individual owner can decide whether the expense is justified, in view of the small amount of use such equipment would normally receive.

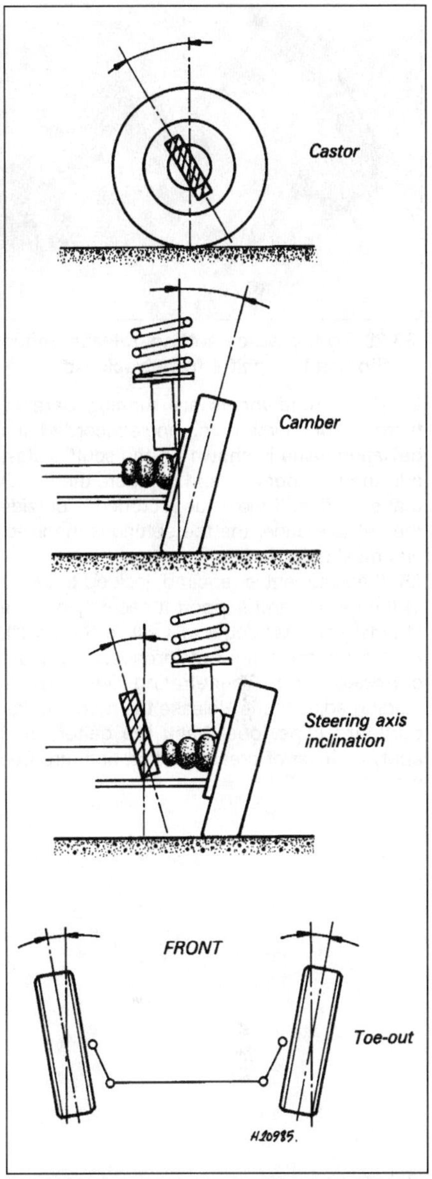

33.1 Wheel alignment and steering angles

24 Prepare the vehicle as described in paragraphs 14 to 16 above.

25 Roll the vehicle backwards, check that the roadwheels are in the straight-ahead position, then roll it across the scuff plates so that each roadwheel passes squarely over the centre of its respective plate. Note the angle recorded by the scuff plates.

26 To ensure accuracy, repeat the check three times and take the average of the three readings.

10

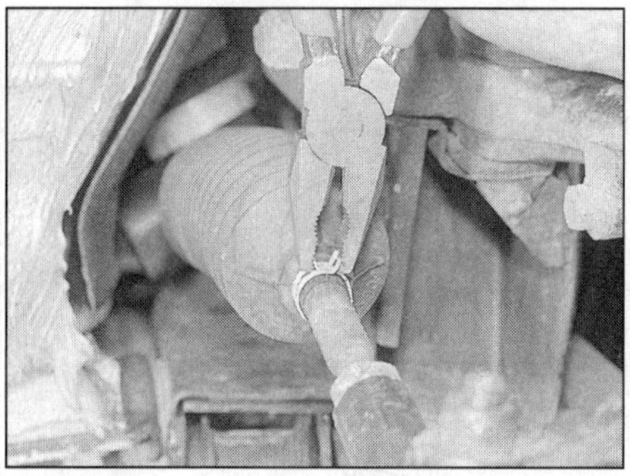

33.28 To adjust toe setting, release gaiter clip and free gaiter from track rod . . .

33.30 . . . then screw track rod into or out of balljoint until setting is correct

27 If the roadwheels are running parallel, there will of course be no angle recorded. If a deviation value is shown on the scuff plates, add the two together and compare them with that specified. If the value recorded is outside the set tolerance, the toe setting is incorrect and must be adjusted.

28 If adjustment is required, jack up the front of the vehicle and support it securely on axle stands (see "*Jacking and Vehicle Support*"). First clean the track rod threads; if they are corroded, apply penetrating fluid before starting adjustment. Release the rubber gaiter outboard clips, peel back the gaiters and apply a smear of grease so that both are free and will not be twisted or strained as their respective track rods are rotated **(see illustration)**.

29 Use a straight-edge and a scriber or similar to mark the relationship of each track rod to its balljoint then, holding each balljoint in turn, unscrew its locknut fully.

30 Alter the length of both track rods (by exactly the same amount) by screwing them into or out of the balljoints one-quarter of a turn at a time and rechecking the toe setting until it is correct. Shortening the track rods (screwing them into their balljoints) will reduce toe-in/increase toe-out. If the track rods are not provided with squared sections that permit the use of a spanner, they must be rotated using a self-locking wrench **(see illustration)**.

31 To ensure that the track rod lengths remain equal, always rotate them in the same direction (viewed from the centre of the vehicle).

32 When the setting is correct, hold the balljoints and tighten the locknuts securely. Check that the balljoints are seated correctly in their sockets and count the exposed threads to check the length of both track rods. If they are not the same, then the adjustment has not been made equally and problems will be encountered with tyre scrubbing in turns; also, the steering wheel will no longer be in the straight-ahead position.

33 If the track rod lengths are the same, check that the toe setting has been correctly adjusted by lowering the vehicle to the ground and preparing it (paragraph 16 above), then re-checking the toe setting. Re-adjust if necessary. If the setting is correct, ensure that the rubber gaiters are seated correctly and are not twisted or strained, then refit their clips to secure their outboard ends.

Chapter 11
Bodywork and fittings

Contents

Degrees of difficulty

Easy, suitable for novice with little experience	**Fairly easy,** suitable for beginner with some experience	**Fairly difficult,** suitable for competent DIY mechanic	**Difficult,** suitable for experienced DIY mechanic	**Very difficult,** suitable for expert DIY or professional

Specifications

Torque wrench setting	**Nm**	**lbf ft**
Bumper fasteners:		
Nuts - rear bumper only	22	16
Bolts - front and rear bumpers	10	8
Bonnet hinge mounting bolts	10	8
Bonnet lock mounting bolts	10	8
Underwing shield screws	9	7
Tailgate handle/number plate lamp housing nuts	6	5
Sunroof roof latch mounting bolts	6	5
Sunroof safety spring-to-roof nut	10	8
Tailgate hinge nuts	10	8
Tailgate striker Torx screws	10	8
Door hinge nuts and bolts	24	18
Door exterior handle mounting nuts	6	5
Door window regulator and motor nuts and bolts	6	5
Seat mounting Torx screws	25	19
Seat belt fasteners:		
Top anchorage bolts	25	19
All other anchorage bolts, retractor and stalk mounting bolts	32 to 35	24 to 26

1 General information

The bodyshell is made of pressed-steel sections in three-door and five-door Hatchback configurations. Most components are welded together but some use is made of structural adhesives. The front wings are bolted on. Childproof locks are fitted to the rear doors.

The bonnet, door, tailgate and some other vulnerable panels are made of zinc-coated metal. Once assembled, the entire body is given an eight-stage pre-treatment process including a high-pressure wash before painting. The first coat of primer is applied by cathodic electro-deposition, followed by four coats of paint and two of lacquer. An anti-stone chip coating (finished in matt black, where exposed) is applied to the outer faces of the sills and the corresponding surfaces of the front and rear wings. A PVC coating is applied to the underbody, followed by a coating of protective wax. All chassis members, box-sections and sills are injected with liquid cavity wax.

Extensive use is made of plastic materials, mainly on the interior but also in exterior components such as the (ABS) bonnet air inlets and the (modified polypropylene) bumper covers. The bumper covers are each fitted over a metal reinforcing member. Features such as the plastic front wheel arch liners are fitted to improve the body's resistance to corrosion.

2 Vehicle exterior and interior - maintenance and inspection

Vehicle exterior

The general condition of a vehicle's bodywork is the one thing that significantly affects its value. Maintenance is easy but needs to be regular. Neglect, particularly after minor damage, can lead quickly to further deterioration and costly repair bills. It is important also to keep watch on those parts of the car not immediately visible, for instance the underbody, inside all the wheel arches and the lower part of the engine compartment.

The basic maintenance routine for the bodywork is washing - preferably with a lot of water, from a hose. This will remove all the loose solids which may have stuck to the car. It is important to flush these off in such a way as to prevent grit from scratching the finish. The wheel arches and underbody need washing in the same way to remove any accumulated mud which will retain moisture and tend to encourage rust, particularly in winter when it is essential that any salt (from that put down on the roads) is washed off. Strangely enough, the best time to clean the underbody and wheel arches is in wet weather when the mud is thoroughly wet and soft. In very wet weather the underbody is usually cleaned automatically of large accumulations; this is therefore a good time for inspection.

If the car is very dirty, especially underneath or in the engine compartment, it is tempting to use one of the pressure washers or steam cleaners available on garage forecourts. Whilst these are quick and effective, especially for the removal of the accumulation of oily grime which sometimes is allowed to become thick in certain areas, their usage does have some disadvantages. If caked-on dirt is simply blasted off the paintwork, its finish soon becomes scratched and dull and the pressure can allow water to penetrate door and window seals and the lock mechanisms. If the full force of such a jet is directed at the vehicle's underbody, the wax-based protective coating can easily be damaged and water (with whatever cleaning solvent is used) could be forced into crevices or components that it would not normally reach. Similarly, if such equipment is used to clean the engine compartment, water can be forced into the components of the fuel and electrical systems and the protective coating can be removed that is applied to many small components during manufacture; this may therefore actually promote corrosion (especially inside electrical connectors) and initiate engine problems or other electrical faults. Also, if the jet is pointed directly at any of the oil seals, water can be forced past the seal lips and into the engine or transmission. Great care is required, therefore, if such equipment is used and, in general, regular cleaning by such methods should be avoided.

A much better solution in the long term is just to flush away as much loose dirt as possible using a hose alone, even if this leaves the engine compartment looking dirty. If an oil leak has developed, or if any other accumulation of oil or grease is to be removed, there are one or two excellent grease solvents available, which can be brush applied. The dirt can then be simply hosed off. Take care to replace the wax-based protective coat, if this was affected by the solvent.

Normal washing of the bodywork is best carried out using cold or warm water with a proprietary car shampoo. Remove dead insects etc; tar spots can be removed either by using white spirit, followed by soapy water to remove all traces of spirit, or by using a proprietary tar remover. Try to keep water out of the bonnet air inlets and check afterwards that the heater air inlet box drain tube is clear so that any water has drained out of the box.

After washing the paintwork, wipe off with a chamois leather to give an unspotted clear finish. A coat of clear protective wax polish, will give added protection against chemical pollutants in the air. If the paintwork sheen has dulled or oxidised, use a cleaner/polisher combination to restore the brilliance of the shine. This requires a little effort, but such dulling is usually caused because regular washing has been neglected. Care needs to be taken with metallic paintwork, as special non-abrasive cleaner/polisher is required to avoid damage to the finish.

Brightwork should be treated in the same way as paintwork.

Windscreens and windows can be kept clear of the smeary film which often appears, by the use of a proprietary glass cleaner. Never use any form of wax or other body or chromium polish on glass.

Vehicle interior

Mats and carpets should be brushed or vacuum cleaned regularly to keep them free of grit. If they are badly stained remove them from the car for scrubbing or sponging and make quite sure they are dry before refitting.

Where leather upholstery is fitted it should be cleaned only if necessary, using either a mild soap (such as saddle soap) or a proprietary leather cleaner; do not use strong soaps, detergents or chemical cleaners. If the leather is very stained, seek the advice of a Rover dealer. Fabric-trimmed seats and interior trim panels can be kept clean by wiping with a damp cloth and a proprietary cleaner. If they do become stained (which can be more apparent on light coloured upholstery) use a little liquid detergent and a soft nail brush to scour the grime out of the grain of the material. Do not forget to keep the headlining clean in the same way as the (fabric) upholstery.

When using liquid cleaners of any sort inside the car, do not over-wet the surfaces being cleaned. Excessive damp could get into the seams and padded interior causing stains, offensive odours or even rot. If the inside of the car gets wet accidentally it is worthwhile taking some trouble to dry it out properly, particularly where carpets are involved. *Do not leave oil or electric heaters inside the car for this purpose.*

3 Minor body damage - repair

Repair of minor scratches in bodywork

If the scratch is very superficial and does not penetrate to the metal of the bodywork, repair is very simple. Lightly rub the area of the scratch with a paintwork renovator, or a very fine cutting paste, to remove loose paint from the scratch and to clear the surrounding bodywork of wax polish. Rinse the area with clean water.

Apply touch-up paint, or a paint film, to the scratch using a fine paint brush. Continue to apply fine layers of paint until the surface of the paint in the scratch is level with the surrounding paintwork. Allow the new paint at least two weeks to harden, then blend it into the surrounding paintwork by rubbing the scratch area with a paintwork renovator, or a very fine cutting paste. Finally apply wax polish from one of the proprietary range of wax polishes.

Where the scratch has penetrated right through to the metal of the bodywork, causing the metal to rust, a different repair technique is required. Remove any loose rust from the bottom of the scratch with a penknife, then apply rust inhibiting paint, to prevent the formation of rust in the future. Using a rubber or nylon applicator fill the scratch with bodystopper paste. If required, this paste can be mixed with cellulose thinners, to provide a very thin paste which is ideal for filling narrow scratches. Before the stopper-paste in the scratch hardens, wrap a piece of smooth cotton rag around the top of a finger. Dip the finger in cellulose thinners, and quickly sweep it across the surface of the stopper-paste in the scratch; this will ensure that the surface of the stopper-paste is slightly hollowed. The scratch can now be painted over as described earlier in this Section.

Repair of dents in bodywork

When deep denting of the vehicle's bodywork has taken place, the first task is to pull the dent out, until the affected bodywork almost attains its original shape. There is little point in trying to restore the original shape completely, as the metal in the damaged area will have stretched on impact and cannot be reshaped fully to its original contour. It is better to bring the level of the dent up to a point which is about 3 mm below the level of the surrounding bodywork. In cases where the dent is very shallow anyway, it is not worth trying to pull it out at all. If the underside of the dent is accessible, it can be hammered out gently from behind, using a mallet with a wooden or plastic head. Whilst doing this, hold a suitable block of wood firmly against the outside of the panel to absorb the impact from the hammer blows and thus prevent a large area of the bodywork from being "belled-out".

Should the dent be in a section of the bodywork which has a double skin or some other factor making it inaccessible from behind, a different technique is called for. Drill several small holes through the metal inside the area - particularly in the deeper section. Then screw long self-tapping screws into the holes just sufficiently for them to gain a good purchase in the metal. Now the dent can be pulled out by pulling on the protruding heads of the screws with a pair of pliers.

The next stage of the repair is the removal of the paint from the damaged area and from an inch or so of the surrounding sound bodywork. This is accomplished most easily by using a wire brush or abrasive pad on a power drill, although it can be done just as effectively by hand using sheets of abrasive paper. To complete the preparation for filling, score the surface of the bare metal with a screwdriver or the tang of a file, or alternatively, drill small holes in the affected area. This will provide a really good key for the filler paste. To complete the repair see the Section on filling and respraying.

Repair of rust holes or gashes in bodywork

Remove all paint from the affected area and from an inch or so of the surrounding sound bodywork, using an abrasive pad or a wire brush on a power drill. If these are not available a few sheets of abrasive paper will do the job most effectively. With the paint removed you will be able to judge the severity of the corrosion and therefore decide whether to renew the whole panel (if this is possible) or to repair the affected area. New body panels are not as expensive as most people think and it is often quicker and more satisfactory to fit a new panel than to attempt to repair large areas of corrosion.

Remove all fittings from the affected area except those which will act as a guide to the original shape of the damaged bodywork (eg headlamp shells etc). Then, using tin snips or a hacksaw blade, remove all loose metal and any other metal badly affected by corrosion. Hammer the edges of the hole inwards in order to create a slight depression for the filler paste.

Wire brush the affected area to remove the powdery rust from the surface of the remaining metal. Paint the affected area with rust inhibiting paint, if the back of the rusted area is accessible treat this also.

Before filling can take place it will be necessary to block the hole in some way. This can be achieved by the use of aluminium or plastic mesh, or aluminium tape.

Aluminium or plastic mesh or glass-fibre matting, is probably the best material to use for a large hole. Cut a piece to the approximate size and shape of the hole to be filled, then position it in the hole so that its edges are below the level of the surrounding bodywork. It can be retained in position by several blobs of filler paste around its periphery.

Aluminium tape should be used for small or very narrow holes. Pull a piece off the roll and trim it to the approximate size and shape required, then pull off the backing paper (if used) and stick the tape over the hole; it can be overlapped if the thickness of one piece is insufficient. Burnish down the edges of the tape with the handle of a screwdriver or similar, to ensure that the tape is securely attached to the metal underneath.

Bodywork repairs - filling and respraying

Before using this Section, see the Sections on dent, deep scratch, rust holes and gash repairs.

Many types of bodyfiller are available, but generally speaking those proprietary kits are best for this type of repair which contain a tin of filler paste and a tube of resin hardener. A wide, flexible plastic or nylon applicator will be found invaluable for imparting a smooth and well contoured finish to the surface of the filler.

Mix up a little filler on a clean piece of card or board - measure the hardener carefully (follow the maker's instructions on the pack) otherwise the filler will set too rapidly or too slowly. Alternatively, a proprietary brand of no-mix filler can be used straight from the tube without mixing, but daylight is required to cure it. Using the applicator apply the filler paste to the prepared area; draw the applicator across the surface of the filler to achieve the correct contour and to level the surface. As soon as a contour that approximates to the correct one is achieved, stop working the paste - if you carry on too long the paste will become sticky and begin to pick-up on the applicator. Continue to add thin layers of filler paste at twenty minute intervals until the level of the filler is just proud of the surrounding bodywork.

Once the filler has hardened, excess can be removed using a metal plane or file. From then on, progressively finer grades of abrasive paper should be used, starting with a 40 grade production paper and finishing with a 400 grade wet-and-dry paper. Always wrap the abrasive paper around a flat rubber, cork, or wooden block - otherwise the surface of the filler will not be completely flat. During the smoothing of the filler surface the wet-and-dry paper should be periodically rinsed in water. This will ensure that a very smooth finish is imparted to the filler at the final stage.

At this stage, the dent should be surrounded by a ring of bare metal, which in turn should be encircled by the finely feathered edge of the good paintwork. Rinse the repair area with clean water, until all of the dust produced by the rubbing-down operation has gone.

Spray the whole area with a light coat of primer, - this will show up any imperfections in the surface of the filler. Repair these imperfections with fresh filler paste or bodystopper and once more smooth the surface with abrasive paper. If bodystopper is used, it can be mixed with cellulose thinners to form a really thin paste which is ideal for filling small holes. Repeat this spray and repair procedure until you are satisfied that the surface of the filler and the feathered edge of the paintwork are perfect. Clean the repair area with clean water and allow to dry fully.

The repair area is now ready for final spraying. Paint spraying must be carried out in a warm, dry, windless and dust free atmosphere. This condition can be created artificially if you have access to a large indoor working area, but if you are forced to work in the open, you will have to pick your day very carefully. If you are working indoors, dousing the floor in the work area with water will help to settle the dust which would otherwise be in the atmosphere. If the repair area is confined to one body panel, mask off the surrounding panels; this will help to minimise the effects of a slight mis-match in paint colours. Bodywork fittings (eg chrome strips, door handles etc) will also need to be masked off. Use genuine masking tape and several thicknesses of newspaper for the masking operations.

Before commencing to spray, agitate the aerosol can thoroughly, then spray a test area (an old tin, or similar) until the technique is mastered. Cover the repair area with a thick coat of primer; the thickness should be built up using several thin layers of paint rather than one thick one. Using 400 grade wet-and-dry paper, rub down the surface of the primer until it is really smooth. While doing this, the work area should be thoroughly doused with water and the wet-and-dry paper periodically rinsed in water. Allow to dry before spraying on more paint.

Spray on the top coat, again building up the thickness by using several thin layers of paint. Start spraying in the centre of the repair area and then, with a side-to-side motion, work outwards until the whole repair area and about 50 mm of the surrounding original paintwork is covered. Remove all masking material 10 to 15 minutes after spraying on the final coat of paint.

Allow the new paint at least two weeks to harden, then, using a paintwork renovator, or a very fine cutting paste, blend the edges of the paint into the existing paintwork. Finally, apply wax polish from one of the proprietary range of wax polishes.

Plastic components

With the use of more and more plastic body components by the vehicle manufacturers (eg bumpers, spoilers and in some cases major body panels), rectification of more serious damage to such items has become a matter of either entrusting repair work to a specialist in this field, or renewing complete components. Repair of such damage by the DIY owner is not really feasible owing to the cost of the equipment and materials required for effecting such repairs. The basic technique involves making a groove along the line of the crack in the plastic using a rotary burr in a power drill. The damaged part is then welded back together by using a hot air gun to heat up and fuse a plastic filler rod into the groove. Any excess plastic is then removed and the area rubbed down to a smooth finish. It is important that a filler rod of the correct plastic is used, as body components can be made of a variety of different types (eg polycarbonate, ABS, polypropylene).

Damage of a less serious nature (abrasions, minor cracks etc) can be repaired by the DIY owner using a two-part epoxy filler repair material. Once mixed in equal proportions, this is used in similar fashion to the bodywork filler used on metal panels. The filler is usually cured in twenty to thirty minutes, ready for sanding and painting.

If the owner is renewing a complete component himself, or if he has repaired it with epoxy filler, he will be left with the problem of finding a suitable paint for finishing which is compatible with the type of plastic used. At one time the use of a universal paint was not possible owing to the complex range of plastics encountered in body component applications. Standard paints, generally speaking, will not bond satisfactorily to plastic or rubber, but proprietary brands of paint to match any plastic or rubber finish can be obtained from dealers. However, it is now possible to obtain a plastic body parts finishing kit which consists of a pre-primer treatment, a primer and coloured top coat. Full instructions are normally supplied with a kit, but basically the method of use is to first apply the pre-primer to the component concerned and allow it to dry for up to 30 minutes. Then the primer is applied and left to dry for about an hour before finally applying the special coloured top coat. The result is a correctly-coloured component where the paint will flex with the plastic or rubber, a property that standard paint does not normally possess.

4 Major body damage - repair

Where serious damage has occurred, or large areas need renewal due to neglect, it means that complete new panels will need welding in. This is best left to professionals. If the damage is due to impact, it will also be necessary to check completely the alignment of the bodyshell. This can only be carried out accurately by a Rover dealer using special jigs. If the body is left misaligned, it is primarily dangerous as the car will not handle properly and secondly, uneven stresses will be imposed on the steering, suspension and possibly transmission, causing abnormal wear or complete failure, particularly to items such as the tyres.

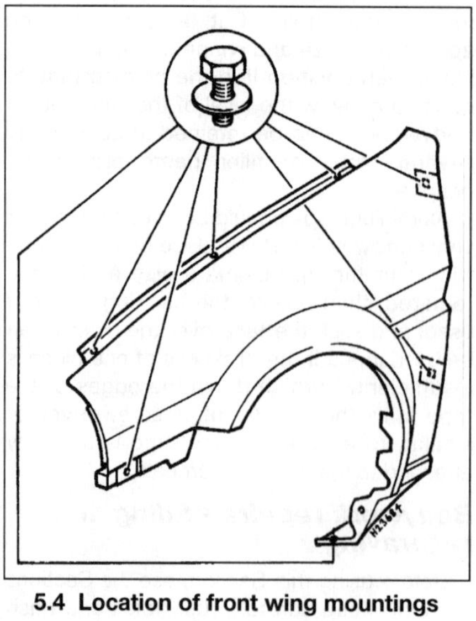

5.4 Location of front wing mountings

5 Front wings - removal and refitting

Removal

1 Remove the wheel arch liner and the side rubbing strip.

2 Remove the direction indicator side repeater lamp. Whilst not strictly necessary, it is advisable also to remove the front direction indicator lamp.

3 Remove the front bumper.

4 Open the bonnet and remove the (hex-head) screws securing the wing **(see illustration)**.

5 Cut along the joints and remove the wing.

Refitting

6 Before fitting the new wing, clean the body mating surfaces and apply new sealant.

7 Fit the wing and adjust its position before refitting the screws, then tighten them securely.

8 Apply protective coating under the wing and anti-stone chip coating to the bottom edge, then refinish the outer surface to match the body colour and paint the anti-stone chip coating matt black (if exposed).

9 Refit all remaining components using the reverse of the removal procedure.

6 Bumpers - removal and refitting

Metro type

Front

Note: *It is possible, with care, to prise the bumper cover's rear bottom edge off each wheel arch liner locating peg and to reach up inside the bumper cover to unscrew the top rear mounting bolts. Although difficult due to lack of visibility, this shorter procedure eliminates the steps described in paragraphs 1 and 2*

1 Jack up the front of the car and support it securely on axle stands (see "*Jacking and Vehicle Support*"), then remove the roadwheels.

2 Remove the front wheel arch liners.

3 Carefully prise the number plate off the self-adhesive pads. If either the bumper or the number plate is to be re-used, clean off all traces of adhesive with white spirit.

4 Carefully prise the covers off the two bumper front mounting bolts **(see illustration)**.

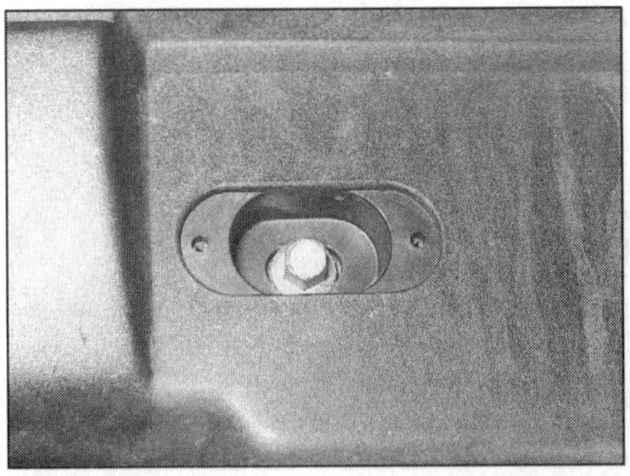

6.4 Front bumper front mounting bolts are concealed by covers under number plate

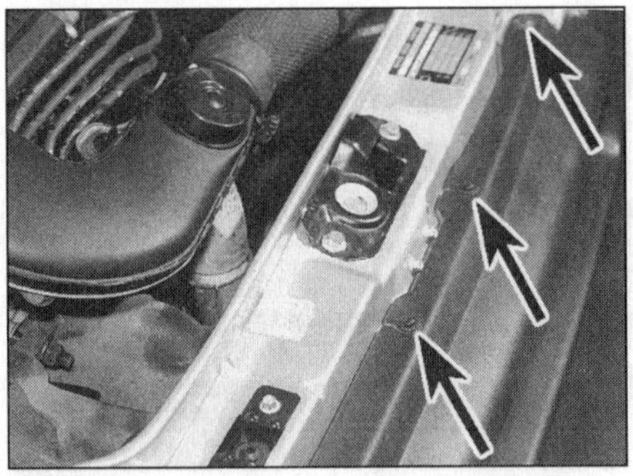

6.5 Front bumper cover-to-bonnet lock platform screws (arrowed) (three shown)

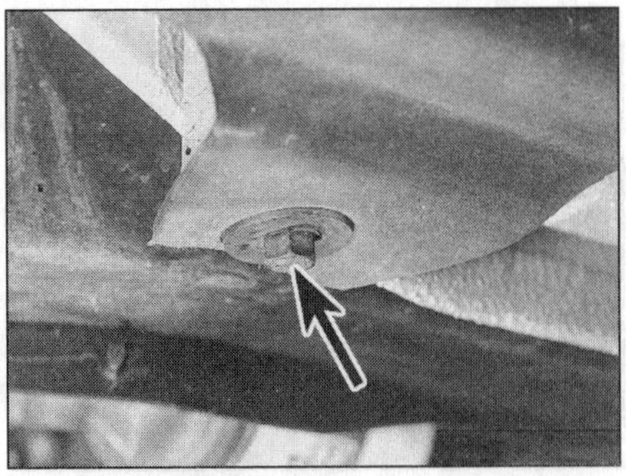

6.6a Front bumper cover-to-body lower mounting bolt (one arrowed)

5 Remove the four screws securing the bumper cover to the bonnet lock platform **(see illustration)**.

6 Being careful to support the bumper as necessary, unscrew the six mounting bolts, then remove the bumper assembly (including, where fitted, the front spoiler) **(see illustrations)**.

7 If required, the bumper cover can be unbolted from the reinforcing member, the brackets can be removed and the trim inserts (where fitted) can be detached from the cover by removing their retainer clips.

8 Refitting is the reverse of the removal procedure, noting the following points.

a) Tighten the mounting bolts to their specified torque wrench setting.

b) Ensure that the bumper cover is engaged correctly on the wheel arch liner peg.

c) Use four new self-adhesive pads to secure the number plate.

Rear

9 Open the tailgate and release the luggage compartment interior trim panels sufficiently to reach the bumper mounting bolts.

10 Release the rear foglamp wiring connector from its clip in the rear right-hand corner of the body, disconnect the wiring and press the sealing grommet out of the body **(see illustration)**.

11 Unscrew the bumper cover end mounting bolts **(see illustration)**. On 1.1C models fitted with the three-piece bumper, the bumper end caps can now be detached.

12 On all other models, fitted with the one-piece bumper cover, remove the retaining screws to release the cover from the lower mounting brackets **(see illustration)**.

13 Being careful to support the assembly as necessary, unscrew the two nuts from inside the luggage compartment **(see illustration)** then withdraw the bumper centre section (later 1.1C models) or the bumper assembly (all other models).

14 If required, remove the retaining screws, nuts or clips (as appropriate) to detach the rear foglamp, the reflector, the bumper cover (where fitted) and the trim inserts (where fitted).

15 Refitting is the reverse of the removal procedure. Tighten the nuts and bolts to their specified torque wrench settings, ensure that the sealing grommet is securely fixed in the body and check the operation of the foglamp.

100 series type

Front

16 Proceed as listed for the Metro type of bumper whilst noting the different positioning of the two upper bumper retaining screws and the need for the grille section to be detached before bumper removal can take place **(see illustration)**.

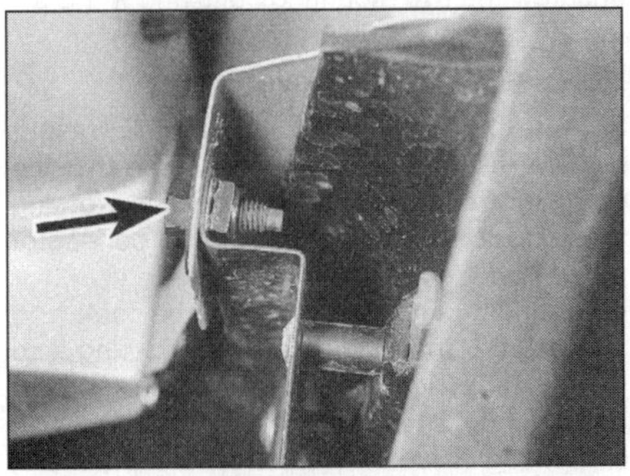

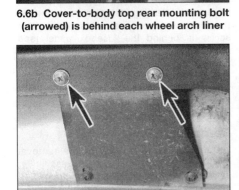

6.6b Cover-to-body top rear mounting bolt (arrowed) is behind each wheel arch liner

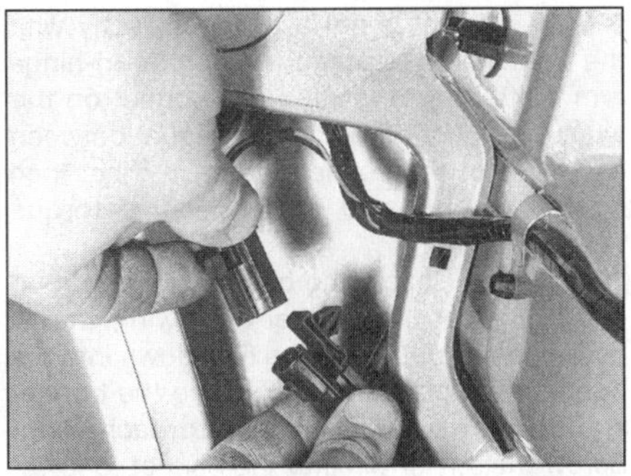

6.10 Disconnecting rear fog lamp wiring

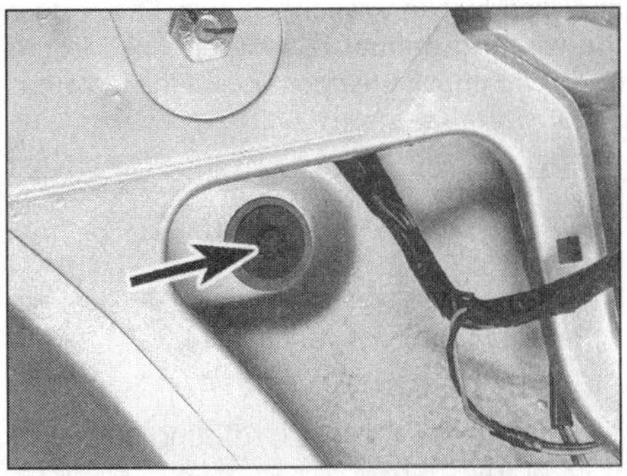

6.11 Rear bumper cover right-hand end mounting bolt (arrowed)

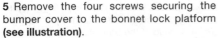

6.12 Cover-to-body mounting bracket screws (arrowed) on one-piece bumper

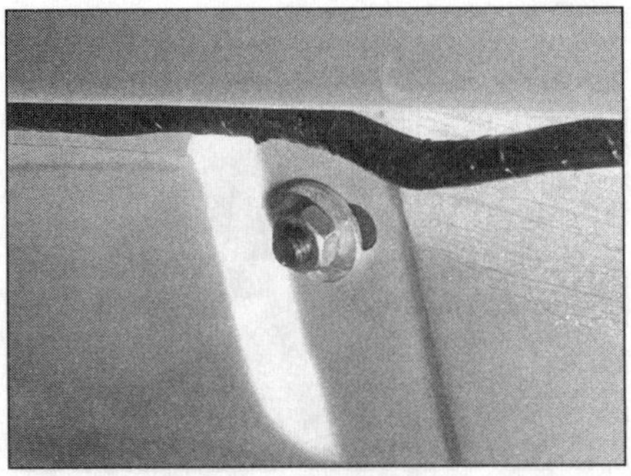

6.13 Rear bumper mounting nut inside luggage compartment

6.16 Rover 100 grille attachment screws (arrowed)

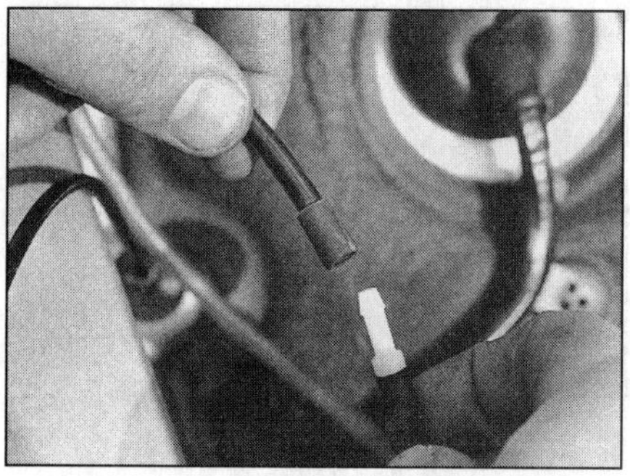

8.2 Disconnecting windscreen washer tubing

Rear

17 Open the tailgate and remove the four studs securing the luggage compartment side trim panels, releasing the panels sufficiently to gain access to the bumper securing bolts.
18 Remove the four screws securing the lower edge of the bumper to its retaining brackets.
19 Release the clip securing the foglamp wiring multiplug to the right-hand body panel inside the luggage compartment. Disconnect the multiplug and detach the wiring harness grommet from the body panel.
20 Remove the bolt securing each end of the bumper to the vehicle and the remaining two nuts and washers securing the centre of the bumper.
21 Carefully ease the bumper, together with the foglamp, clear of the vehicle.
22 Refitting is the reverse of the removal procedure. Tighten the nuts and bolts to their specified torque wrench settings. Ensure that the wiring grommet is securely fixed in the body and check the operation of the foglamp.

7 Hinges and locks - lubrication

Refer to Chapter 1, Section 14.

8 Bonnet - removal, refitting and adjustment

Removal

1 The help of an assistant will be required for these operations. First, with the bonnet propped open, place a thick pad of cloth beneath each rear corner of the bonnet to protect the paintwork.
2 Disconnect the windscreen washer tubing **(see illustration)**.
3 Mark with a pencil around the hinge arms where they meet the bonnet, then slacken the bonnet-to-hinge arm bolts.
4 Working with one person at each side **(see illustration)**, support the bonnet on the shoulders, lower the stay and unscrew the bolts. Remove the bonnet.

8.4 Always have an assistant to help with bonnet removal

5 The hinge arms are each retained by a single, shouldered pivot bolt. Check that these are greased and securely fastened whenever the bonnet is removed.
6 The bonnet stay can be removed by working it out of its locating rubber bush in the bonnet lock platform.

Refitting

7 Refitting is the reverse of the removal procedure. If the original bonnet is being refitted, align the marks made on removal. If a new bonnet is being fitted, centre the bolt holes on the hinge arms. Tighten the bonnet-to-hinge arm bolts only lightly at first, then gently close the bonnet and check that it aligns evenly with the surrounding bodywork.
8 When the fit of the bonnet is correctly adjusted (see below), tighten the bolts to the specified torque wrench setting.

Adjustment

9 If the bonnet is not aligned correctly with the front wings, slacken the bonnet-to-hinge arm bolts and reposition the bonnet on the hinge arms until the gaps are equal between each side of the bonnet and each wing, then tighten the bolts to their specified torque wrench setting.
10 If, when closed, the bonnet stands proud of, or is lower than, either front wing, screw both bonnet rubber buffers fully down into the bonnet lock platform, then close the bonnet and check its height relative to each wing. Screw the striker pin into the bonnet to lower its height, outwards to raise it. When the height is correct (ie. when closed, the bonnet is exactly flush with the adjacent wings) adjust the height of the buffers until they just contact the underside of the bonnet.

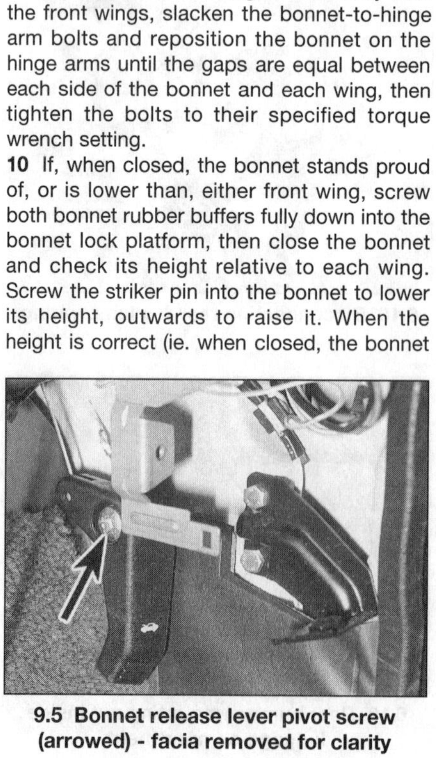

9.5 Bonnet release lever pivot screw (arrowed) - facia removed for clarity

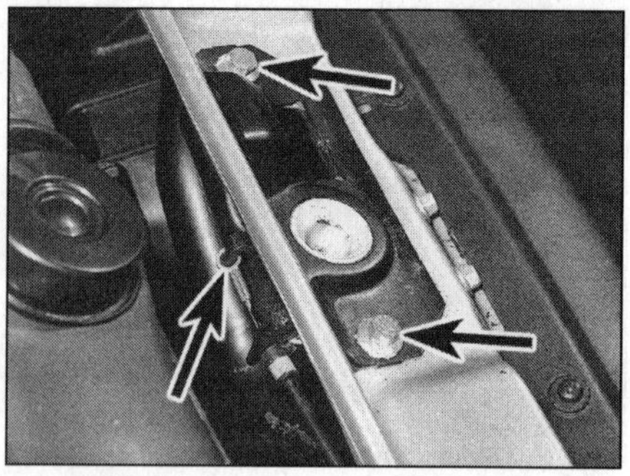

9.1 Bonnet lock mounting bolts and release cable connection (arrowed)

9 Bonnet lock and release cable - removal, refitting and adjustment

Removal

Lock

1 Open the bonnet and mark with a pencil around the bonnet lock, then unscrew the two mounting bolts and withdraw the lock and guide plate until the release cable can be disconnected **(see illustration)**.

Striker

2 Open the bonnet and mark with a pencil around the assembly's mounting plate, then unscrew the two mounting bolts and withdraw the striker and safety catch assembly.

Release cable and lever

3 Open the bonnet and remove the washer system reservoir retaining screws so that the reservoir can be moved clear of the working area. Disconnect the pump wiring connector plug(s) if the extra reach is required.
4 Disconnect the cable from the lock and release it from the clips or ties securing it to the body, then prise the cable sealing grommet out of the bulkhead aperture.
5 Working inside the passenger compartment, release the retaining fasteners and withdraw the fusebox cover. The release lever pivot screw is behind the fusebox panel **(see illustration)**. If the panel is removed to reach the lever screw, disconnect first the battery negative terminal. Remove the pivot screw, withdraw the lever and disconnect the cable.
6 Withdraw the cable into the engine compartment.

Refitting

7 Refitting is the reverse of the removal procedure, noting the following points.

a) Align (where applicable) the component on the marks made on removal. If a new bonnet or bonnet lock platform has been fitted, centre the component on its bolt holes.

b) Tighten the component's fasteners lightly, then check carefully the operation and adjustment of all disturbed components. If adjustment is required, proceed as described below.

c) Tighten the bolts securely, to the specified torque wrench settings (where given).

Adjustment

8 If the operation of any part of the bonnet release mechanism requires adjustment, check first the fit of the bonnet on the body. Whilst some adjustments are inter-dependent (the bonnet height adjustment being made using the lock's striker pin), the lock cannot function correctly if the bonnet is not aligned properly with the bodywork.

9 To adjust the lock and/or striker assembly, first slacken their mounting bolts, then move them as necessary until the striker pin and safety catch hook engage squarely in the centre of their respective lock apertures. Tighten the bolts securely, to the specified torque wrench settings (where given).

10 When the lock and striker are correctly aligned, check that the bonnet closes securely when dropped from a height of approximately 150 mm. There should be no trace of movement when attempting to lift the front edge of the bonnet.

11 If the bonnet does not lock when dropped, check first that the striker pin is properly lubricated. Some adjustment may be made by screwing the striker pin in or out, but take care that this does not alter the bonnet height. Renew the striker or the lock assembly as necessary if the fault is due to wear or damage of either component.

12 If there is any doubt about the safety catch's performance, the striker assembly must be renewed.

13 There is no adjustment as such of the release cable, but the cable outer stops can be bent slightly to effect minor alterations if required. Renew the cable if the bonnet release is ineffective.

10 Body exterior fittings - removal and refitting

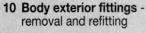

Removal

Front spoiler

1 The spoiler is in two halves, each secured to the bumper cover by five nuts and studs. The nuts can be unscrewed from behind the bumper cover. The spoiler can be removed with the bumper or separately, as required.

2 Always remove the left-hand half first, since it overlaps the right-hand half **(see illustration)**.

Underwing shields

3 Jack up the front of the car and support it securely on axle stands (see "*Jacking and Vehicle Support*"), then remove the roadwheel.

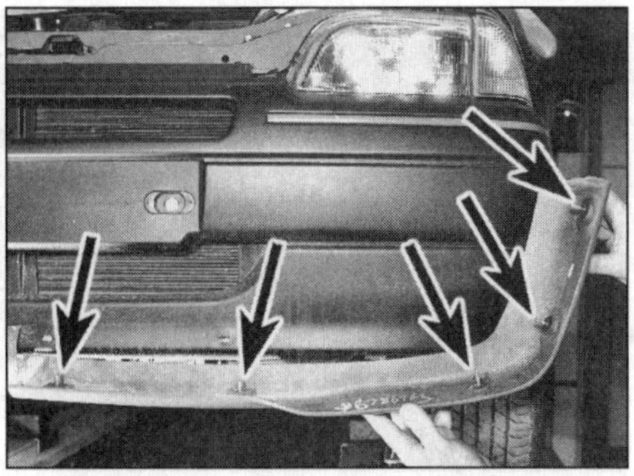

10.2 Removing front spoiler left-hand half - note mounting studs (arrowed)

4 Each shield is secured by three fasteners. Remove each fastener's screw and prise out its outer section to release it, then withdraw the panel **(see illustration)**.

Front wheel arch liners

5 Jack up the front of the car and support it securely on axle stands (see "*Jacking and Vehicle Support*"), then remove the roadwheel.

6 Remove the mudflap, if fitted.

7 Remove the three screws securing the liner to the rear of the wheel arch. Release the six fasteners by removing each fastener's screw and prising out its outer section **(see illustration)**. Remove the liner, releasing its locating peg from the bumper cover at its front and releasing the liner itself from the plastic clip (where fitted) at its rear inboard edge.

Mudflaps

8 The front mudflaps are each secured by three screws; the rear by two clips.

Bonnet air inlets

9 Each air inlet is secured by two small nuts or clips on the underside of the bonnet. Note that the unused inlet has a blanking plate fitted.

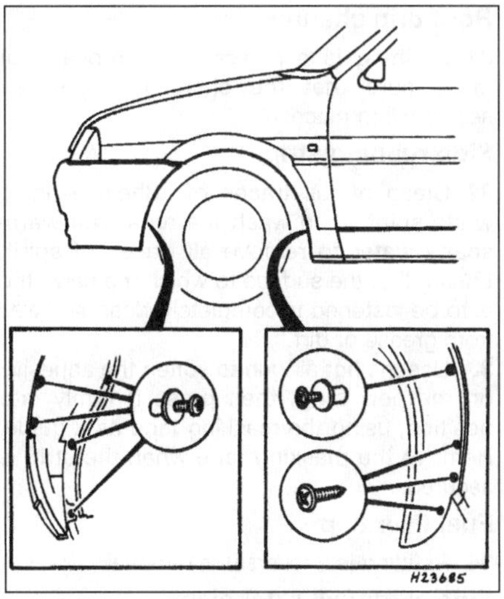

10.7 Location of front wheel arch liner mountings

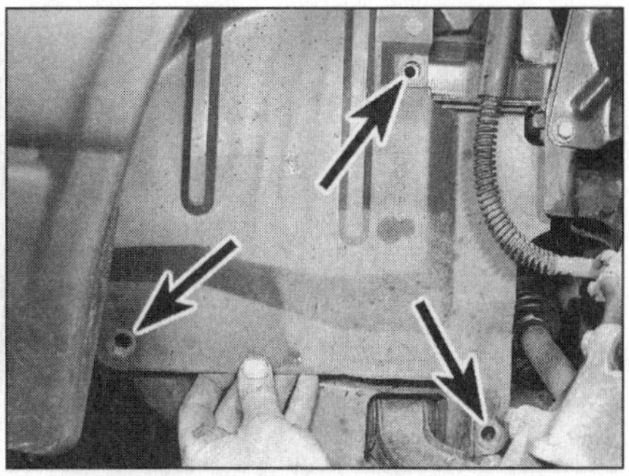

10.4 Location of underwing shield fasteners (arrowed)

Roof drip channel

10 The drip channel moulding along the roof edges is clipped in place and can be prised off if care is taken not to break it or to damage the paintwork.

Side rubbing strips

11 Apply masking tape along the edge of the strip to be removed, as an aid to correct location on refitting.

12 Using a hot air gun, heat the strip until the adhesive softens enough for the strip to be peeled off. Take care not to damage the surrounding paintwork with the hot air gun.

Fuel filler flap

13 The flap is secured by two screws.

Side skirts/sill extensions

14 These are in two sections. Since the front section overlaps the rear, always remove the front section first, as follows.

15 Remove the six screws securing the front section, then very carefully release the section from the clip securing its front upper edge to the wheel arch flare. Slide the section forwards to release it from the five locating pegs, then withdraw it **(see illustration)**.

16 Once the front section has been removed, the two screws which secure the rear section can be undone. Carefully release the rear section from its retainers to remove it, noting how the rear retainer hooks into the underbody.

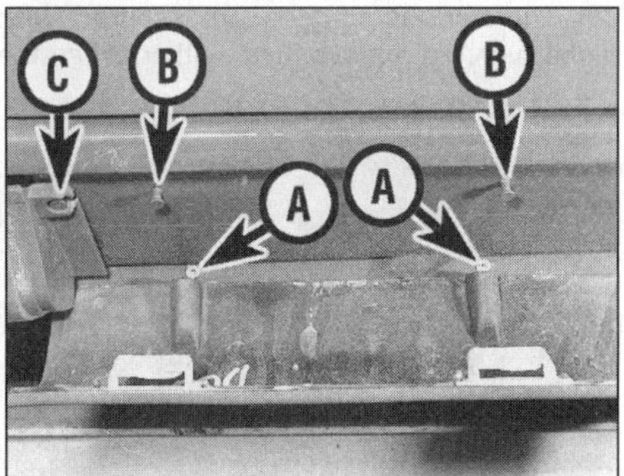

10.15 Side skirt/sill extension mountings - securing screws (A - two arrowed) locating pegs (B - two arrowed) and rear section retainer (C)

10.19 Rear spoiler (outside) top edge securing screws under cover plugs

Rear wheel arch flare moulding

17 Remove the rear bumper.

18 Remove the two retaining screws from inside the wheel arch (one being at the bumper lower mounting), then release the three clips to remove the moulding.

Rear spoiler

19 Taking care not to mark the spoiler, prise off the four cover plugs from the top outside surface of the spoiler **(see illustration)**, then undo the screws beneath each.

20 Open the tailgate and prise out the sealing grommet next to each of the rear window bottom corners. Unscrew the nut and remove the sealing washer beneath each **(see illustration)**.

21 Raise the wiper arm and very carefully remove the spoiler. It may also be secured by adhesive or (especially along the lower edge) trim clips.

Tailgate handle/number plate lamp housing

22 Remove the number plate lamp assemblies.

23 Open the tailgate and remove the interior trim panel.

24 Remove the clip securing the lock barrel to the handle/housing, then unscrew the four nuts securing the handle/housing to the tailgate. Withdraw the handle/housing, noting the gasket **(see illustration)**.

Badges

25 The various badges are secured with adhesives. To remove them, either soften the

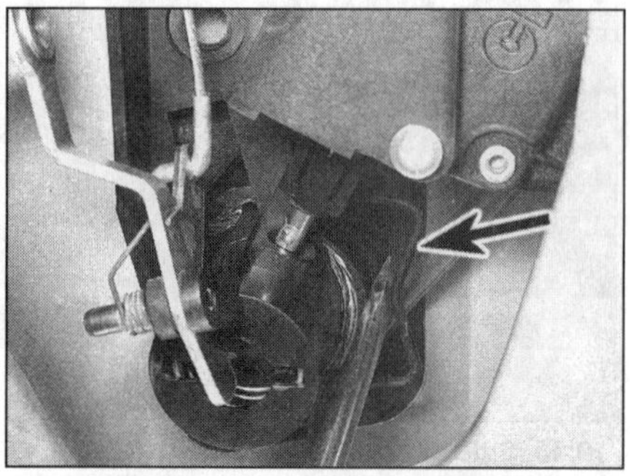

10.24 Removing clip (arrowed) securing tailgate lock barrel to tailgate handle/number plate lamp housing

10.20 Rear spoiler (inside) lower edge securing nuts under grommets

adhesive using a hot air gun (taking care to avoid damage to the paintwork) or separate the badge from the bodywork by sawing through the adhesive bond using a length of nylon cord.

Refitting

Front spoiler

26 Refitting is the reverse of the removal procedure.

Underwing shields

27 Refitting is the reverse of the removal procedure. Renew any damaged fasteners.

Front wheel arch liners

28 Refitting is the reverse of the removal procedure, noting the following points.

a) Ensure that the liner and the wheel arch interior are clean and dry before refitting the liner.

b) Locate the liner correctly on the front bumper cover and (if fitted) the plastic clip before refitting the fasteners.

c) Renew any damaged fasteners.

Mudflaps

29 Refitting is a reversal of removal.

Bonnet air inlets

30 Refitting is a reversal of removal.

Roof drip channel

31 Refitting is a reversal of removal, but make sure that the channel is pressed securely into place.

Side rubbing strips

32 Clean off all traces of adhesive using white spirit, then wash the area with warm soapy water to remove all traces of spirit. Ensure that the surface to which the new strip is to be fastened is completely clean and free from grease or dirt.

33 Use the hot air gun to soften the adhesive on the new strip, then press it firmly into position, using the masking tape as a guide. Remove the masking tape when the strip is secured.

Fuel filler flap

34 Refitting is a reversal of removal.

Side skirts/sill extensions

35 Refitting is a reversal of removal.

Rear wheel arch flare moulding

36 Refitting is a reversal of removal.

Rear spoiler

37 If adhesive was used, clean off all traces of adhesive using white spirit, then wash the area with warm soapy water to remove all traces of spirit.

38 Refitting is the reverse of the removal procedure.

Tailgate handle/number plate lamp housing

39 Refitting is the reverse of the removal procedure. Tighten the nuts to the specified torque wrench setting.

Badges

40 Clean off all traces of adhesive using white spirit, then wash the area with warm soapy water to remove all traces of spirit. Ensure that the surface to which the new badge is to be fastened is completely clean and free from grease or dirt.

41 Use the hot air gun to soften the adhesive on the new badge, then press it firmly into position.

11 Windscreen, fixed rear quarterlight and rear window - renewal

These areas of glass are secured by the tight fit of the weatherstrip in the body aperture. Although they are not fixed by the direct-bonding method used on many modern vehicles, the removal and refitting of these areas of fixed glass is still difficult, messy and time-consuming for the inexperienced. It is also difficult, unless one has plenty of practice, to obtain a secure, waterproof fit. Furthermore, the task carries a high risk of breakage; this applies especially to the laminated glass windscreen. In view of this, owners are strongly advised to have this sort of work carried out by one of the many specialist windscreen fitters.

12 Opening rear quarterlights - removal and refitting

Removal

1 Open the tailgate. Attach protective tape to the B pillar rear edge to prevent damage to the paintwork.

2 Open the rear quarterlight. Have an assistant support the quarterlight, then remove the two screws securing the catch, fully open the quarterlight and release its hinge tabs from their grommets.

Refitting

3 Refitting is the reverse of the removal procedure. Apply a smear of rubber lubricant to the grommets and check that the quarterlight seats correctly in its aperture before tightening the catch screws securely.

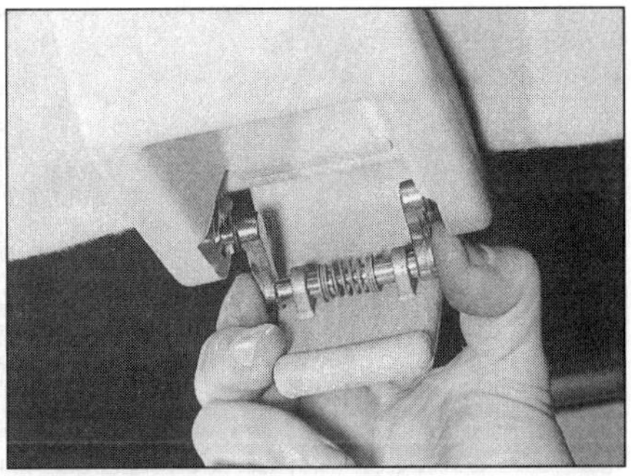

13.1a Disconnecting sunroof operating handle from roof latch (Metro models)

13 Sunroof - removal, refitting and adjustment

Removal

Glass panel

1 Open the sunroof. On Metro models, squeeze together the linkage arms of the operating handle to disconnect it from the roof latch **(see illustration).** On 100 series models, press the red catch to disconnect the handle from the latch **(see illustration).** From outside the car, unclip the safety spring from the hook on the panel's left-hand side (early models only), then withdraw the panel until its locating lugs are clear of their sockets.

2 Note that the glass panel should be stored carefully, wrapping it in a rug or blanket to prevent scratches. Each locating lug is fastened by two screws that are secured with Loctite. If either is removed, discard the gaskets and clean all traces of old thread-locking compound from the screw threads. Do not attempt to remove either the panel's seal or the safety hook. Rover state that the complete panel must be renewed if either of these are damaged. Note also that the locating lug sockets are bolted to the roof and concealed by the headlining; they should not, therefore, be disturbed except by those experienced in headlining removal and refitting.

Operating handle

3 Open the sunroof. On Metro models, squeeze together the linkage arms of the operating handle to disconnect it from the roof latch. On 100 series models, press the red catch to disconnect the handle from the latch.

4 Remove the two retaining screws, which are secured with Loctite, to release the handle from the roof. Discard any gaskets and clean all traces of old thread-locking compound from the screw threads.

Roof latch

5 Open the sunroof and disconnect the operating handle from the roof latch.

6 Removing its single retaining screw, withdraw the latch cover (where fitted) from the roof, then unbolt the latch.

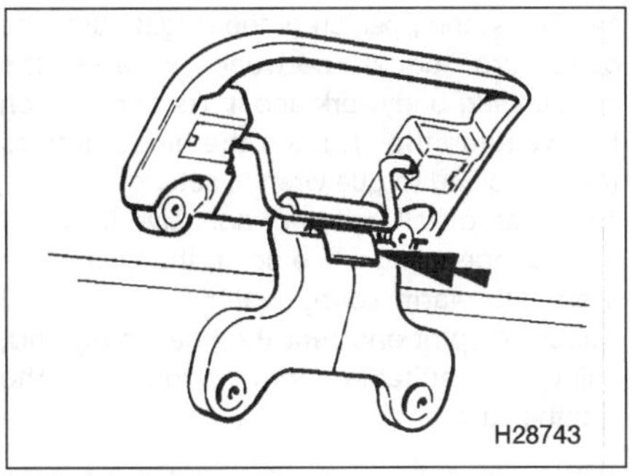

13.1b Disconnecting sunroof operating handle from roof latch (100 series models) - note red catch (arrowed)

Safety spring (early models)

7 Remove the glass panel. The spring is secured to the roof by a single nut.

Wind deflector (where fitted)

8 Remove the glass panel.

9 Remove the retaining screws and withdraw the deflector hinge covers **(see illustration).**

10 Remove the four screws and nuts securing the deflector hinges and detach the deflector from the headlining **(see illustration).** Note the sealing washer under each nut.

Refitting

11 Refitting is the reverse of the removal procedure, noting the following points:

a) *When refitting the locating lugs or the operating handle to the glass panel, apply a few drops of Loctite 222 to the screw threads and fit new gaskets. Check that the component is located correctly on the panel, then tighten the screws securely.*

b) *Tighten the nuts and bolts to the specified torque wrench settings (where given).*

c) *Ensure that the safety spring is engaged correctly around the hook* ***(see illustration).***

d) *Adjust the fit of the glass panel if necessary (see below).*

Adjustment

12 When the sunroof is closed, check that the glass panel sits squarely on its seal, with no sign of gaps.

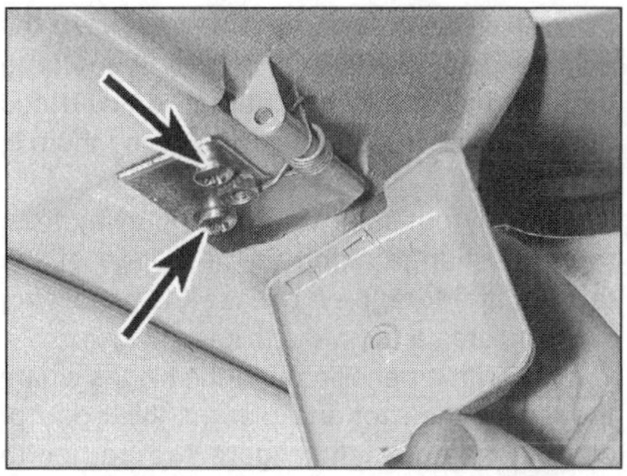

13.9 Remove cover to reach wind deflector hinge screws (arrowed) . . .

13 If the fit is not correct, remove the roof latch cover (see above), slacken the two roof latch mounting bolts and adjust the position of the latch until the panel closes fully and is in full contact with the seal. Tighten the two bolts to their specified torque wrench setting and refit the cover.

14 Tailgate - removal, refitting and adjustment

Removal

Note: *The aid of an assistant will be required for this operation*

1 Open the tailgate, detach the parcel shelf straps and remove the interior trim panel.

2 Disconnect (where fitted) the rear window wiper motor wiring and attach a drawstring to it.

3 Prise the heated rear window wire sealing grommet from each side of the tailgate, disconnect the wires and attach drawstrings to each.

4 Disconnect (where fitted) the washer system tube from the rear window wiper motor and plug it to prevent loss of water. Disconnect the wiring for the number plate lamps and (where fitted) the central locking motor. If a luggage compartment lamp is fitted, partially withdraw the latch until the two wires can be disconnected from it. Tape together the washer tube and wiring, then attach a drawstring to them.

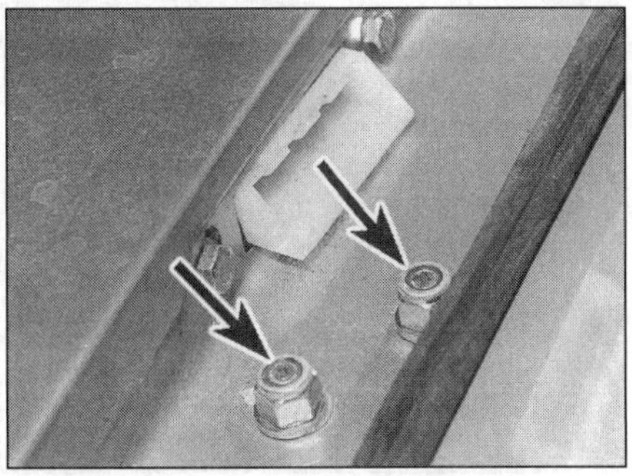

13.10 . . . noting sealing washers under securing nuts (arrowed)

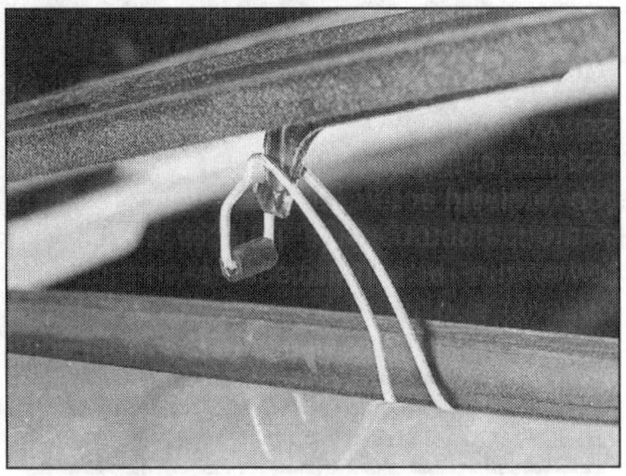

13.11 Ensure safety spring is engaged around hook as shown

5 Release the two harness sleeves from the tailgate top corners and pull the wiring through the apertures until the drawstrings appear. Untie the drawstrings, leaving them in the tailgate.

6 Carefully prise the weatherstrip away from the body flange along the top edge of the tailgate aperture, then release the headlining from the area around the tailgate hinges.

7 Mark with a pencil around the hinges where they meet the roof and place a thick pad of cloth beneath each tailgate top corner to protect the paintwork.

8 Support the tailgate and remove the struts.

9 Unscrew the four nuts securing the tailgate hinges to the roof, then remove the tailgate. Collect the two hinge plates from their studs so that they are not lost.

Refitting

10 Clean off all traces of adhesive from the body flange using white spirit, then wash the area with warm soapy water to remove all traces of spirit.

11 Refitting is the reverse of the removal procedure, noting the following points:

a) *If the original tailgate is being refitted, align the marks made on removal. If a new tailgate is being fitted, centre the hinges on the studs. Tighten the nuts only lightly at first, then gently close the tailgate and check that it fits correctly.*

b) *When the fit of the tailgate is correctly adjusted (see below), tighten the nuts to the specified torque wrench setting.*

c) *Use a suitable trim adhesive to secure the weatherstrip.*

Adjustment

12 When the tailgate is closed, check that it sits squarely on its weatherstrip, with no sign of gaps, also that it is aligned evenly with the surrounding bodywork.

13 If the fit is not correct, open the tailgate and carefully prise the weatherstrip away from the body flange along the top edge of the tailgate aperture, then release the headlining from the area around the tailgate hinges and slacken the hinge nuts.

14 Adjust the position of the tailgate until the gaps are equal between it and the surrounding bodywork and it sits correctly on the weatherstrip. Tighten the hinge nuts to their specified torque wrench setting.

15 Clean off all traces of adhesive from the body flange using white spirit, then wash the area with warm soapy water to remove all traces of spirit and refit the headlining and, using a suitable trim adhesive, the weatherstrip.

15 Tailgate support struts - removal and refitting

Removal

1 Open the tailgate and support it with a piece of wood.

2 Raise the spring clip and pull the strut off each of its mountings **(see illustration)**.

3 The struts are sealed, containing gas under pressure. Do not attempt to dismantle them or apply any heat. If failed or damaged, the struts must be renewed. Dispose of them safely.

Refitting

4 Refitting is the reverse of the removal procedure; ensure that each end of the strut snaps securely home on its mounting.

16 Tailgate lock components - removal and refitting

Removal

Lock

1 Open the tailgate and remove the interior trim panel.

2 Remove (where fitted) the rear window wiper motor.

3 Remove (where fitted) the plastic pin and separate the central locking motor from the lock.

15.2 Raising tailgate support strut spring clip to release mounting

4 Release the latch cable from the clip, release the cable outer from the lock abutment bracket and disconnect the cable inner from the lock lever **(see illustrations)**.

5 Remove the clip securing the lock barrel to the tailgate handle/number plate lamp housing, disconnect the number plate lamp wiring and unscrew the four nuts securing the handle/housing to the tailgate. Withdraw the handle/housing, noting the gasket, then remove the lock.

Latch

6 Open the tailgate and remove the interior trim panel.

7 Remove the two screws securing the latch to the tailgate and release the latch cable from the clip so that the latch can be withdrawn. If a luggage compartment lamp is fitted, disconnect the two wires from the latch **(see illustration)**.

8 Release the cable outer from the latch abutment bracket, then disconnect the cable inner from the latch and withdraw the latch.

Latch cable

9 Remove the latch.

10 Release the cable outer from the lock abutment bracket and disconnect the cable inner from the lock lever; withdraw the cable.

Striker

11 Open the tailgate and mark with a pencil around the striker, then undo the two Torx-type screws and withdraw the striker **(see illustration)**.

16.4a Release latch cable outer from lock abutment bracket (arrowed) . . .

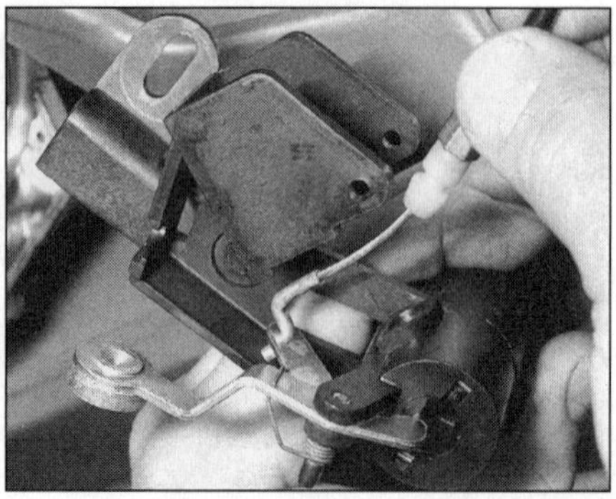

16.4b . . . and disconnect cable inner from lock lever

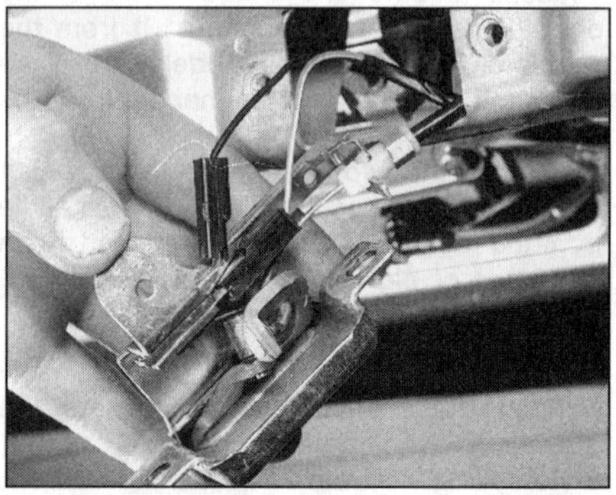

16.7 Tailgate latch partially removed to allow disconnection of wiring and cable

Central locking motor

12 Open the tailgate and remove the interior trim panel.

13 Remove the plastic pin and separate the motor from the lock, then disconnect the motor wiring and withdraw the motor **(see illustrations)**.

Refitting

Lock

14 Refitting is the reverse of the removal procedure. Tighten the tailgate handle/number plate lamp housing nuts to the specified torque wrench setting.

Latch

15 Refitting is the reverse of the removal procedure. Lubricate all moving parts and the striker.

Latch cable

16 Refitting is the reverse of the removal procedure.

Striker

17 On refitting, align the striker on the marks made on removal. If new components have been fitted, centre the striker on the screw holes, tighten the screws lightly and check the fit of the tailgate on the body (see below). When the fit is correct, tighten the screws to the specified torque wrench setting.

18 When the tailgate is closed, check that it sits squarely on its weatherstrip, with no sign of gaps, also that it is aligned evenly with the surrounding bodywork.

19 If the fit is not correct, open the tailgate and slacken the striker screws, then adjust the position of the striker until the tailgate aligns with the surrounding bodywork and the gaps are equal at all points between the tailgate and the body panels.

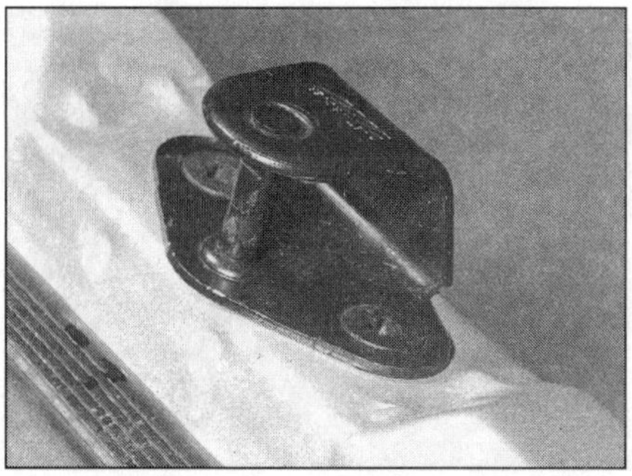

16.11 Tailgate striker

20 When the fit is correct, tighten the striker screws to the specified torque wrench setting and check the operation of the tailgate lock.

Central locking motor

21 Refitting is the reverse of the removal procedure.

17 Doors - removal, refitting and adjustment

Removal

Door

1 Remove the interior trim panel and peel back the plastic sheet.

2 Disconnect all door electrical components, referring for details to the relevant Sections of this Chapter. If removing a rear door from a car with central locking fitted, note that a considerable amount of preliminary dismantling is required to reach the motor's wiring connector. Prise the wiring harness gaiter out of the (front) door or the sealing grommet out of the (rear) door pillar and pull the wiring clear.

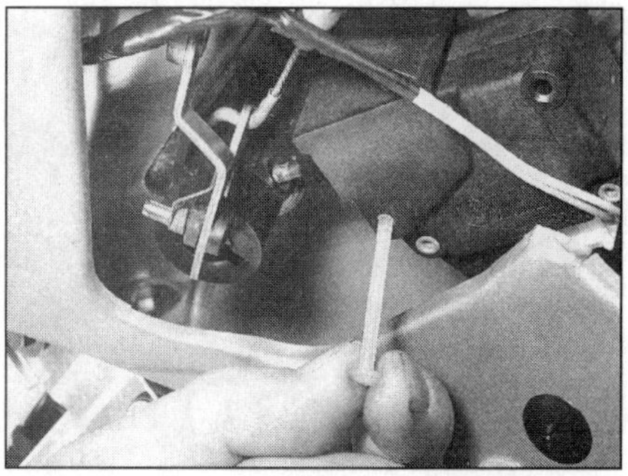

16.13a Removing plastic pin to release central locking motor from tailgate lock . . .

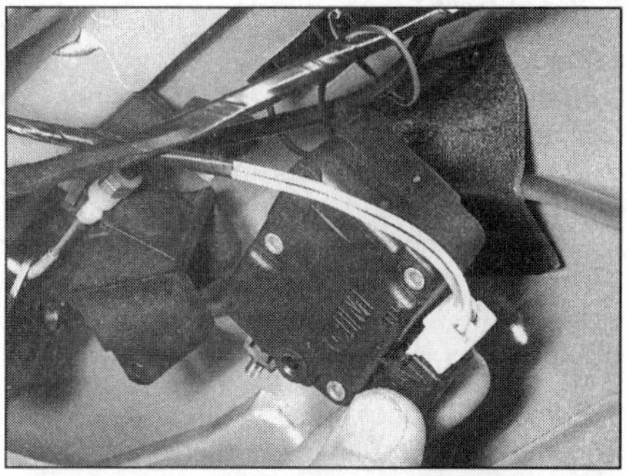

16.13b . . . so that motor wiring connector can be disconnected and motor removed

3 Support the door using a block of wood or a trolley jack. Ensure that the paintwork is protected with a wad of clean rag. Mark with a pencil around the hinges where they meet the door.

4 Unscrew the retaining nuts as shown in the appropriate illustration **(see illustrations)** and withdraw the door, collecting the two hinge plates.

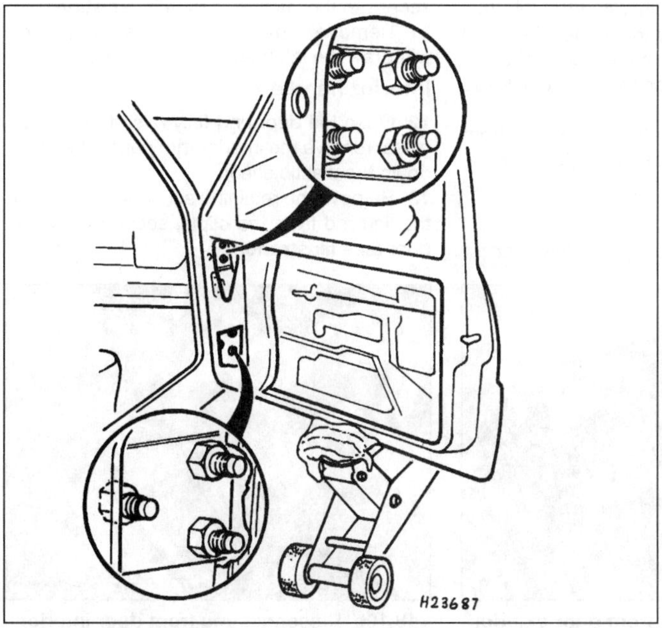

17.4a Location of front door-to-hinge retaining nuts

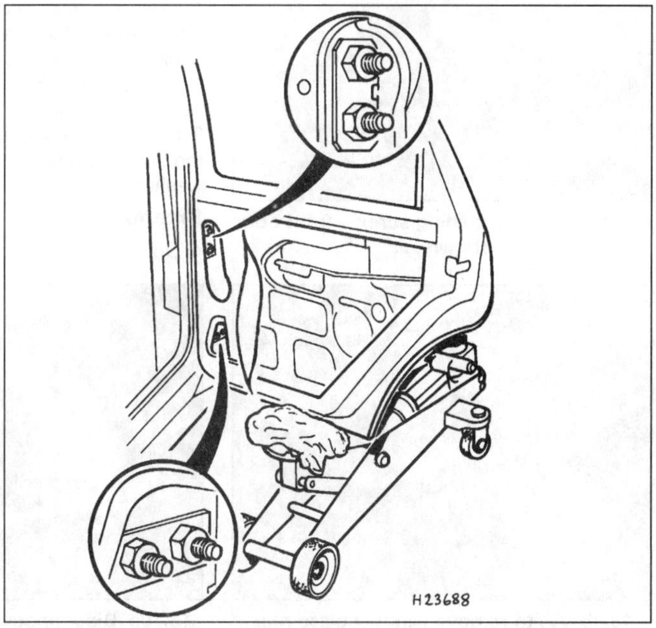

17.4b Location of rear door-to-hinge retaining nuts

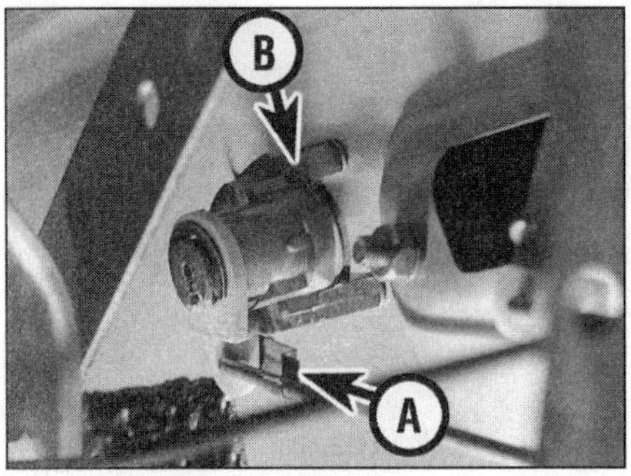

18.2 Front door lock link rod clip (A) and retaining clip (B)

Front door hinges

5 Remove the door.

6 Remove the front wheel arch liner to unscrew the bottom hinge-to-body bolt, then remove the A pillar lower interior trim panel and the foam insert behind to unscrew the two bottom hinge-to-body nuts.

7 Unscrew the two bolts to remove the top hinge.

Rear door hinges

8 Remove the door.

9 Remove the B pillar lower interior trim panel and unscrew the hinge-to-body nuts.

Refitting

10 Refitting is the reverse of the removal procedure, noting the following points:

a) *If the original door is being refitted, align the marks made on removal. If a new door is being fitted, centre it on the hinge studs. Tighten the nuts only lightly at first, then gently close the door and check that it fits correctly.*

b) *When the fit of the door is correctly adjusted, tighten the nuts and bolts to the specified torque wrench setting.*

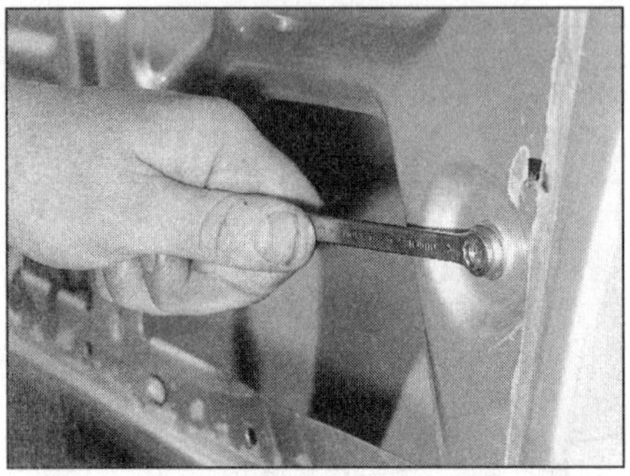
18.9a Remove retaining screw - front door shown . . .

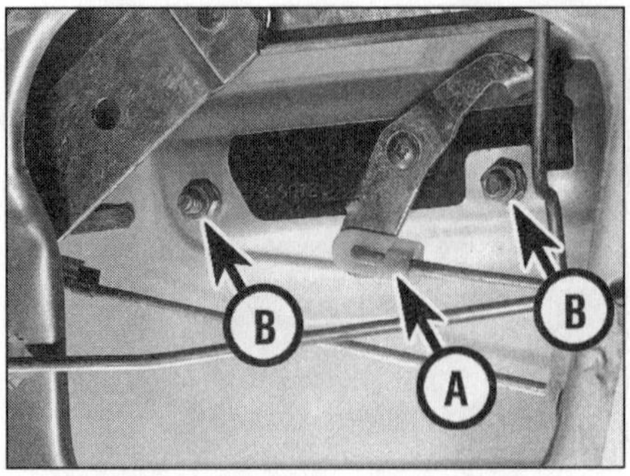

18.5 Front door exterior handle link rod clip (A) and mounting nuts (B)

Adjustment

11 When the door is closed, check that it fits flush with the surrounding bodywork and centrally in the body aperture.

12 If the fit is not correct, open the door, remove the interior trim panel and peel back the plastic sheet, then slacken the hinge nuts.

13 Adjust the position of the door until it fits correctly, then tighten the hinge nuts to their specified torque wrench setting.

18 Door lock and handle components - removal and refitting

Removal

Front door lock

1 Open the door and fully raise the window glass, remove the interior trim panel, then peel back the top rear corner of the plastic sheet.

2 Release the clip to disconnect the link rod from the lock **(see illustration)**.

3 Prise out the clip to release the lock from the door. Remove the lock, noting the seating washer.

Exterior handle

4 Open the door and fully raise the window glass, remove the interior trim panel, then peel back the top rear corner of the plastic sheet.

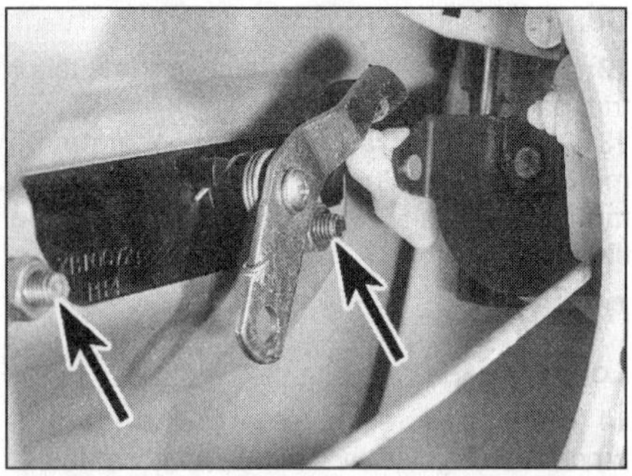
18.6 Rear door exterior handle mounting nuts

5 On the front door, release the clip to disconnect the link rod from the handle **(see illustration)**.

6 On the rear door, remove its retaining screw and move aside the window glass rear guide channel to reach the handle mounting nuts **(see illustration)**.

7 Unscrew the nuts and withdraw the handle. Note the sealing washers.

Latch

8 Open the door and fully raise the window glass, remove the interior trim panel, then peel back the rear half of the plastic sheet.

9 Remove its retaining screw and withdraw the window glass rear guide channel **(see illustrations)**.

10 Releasing their clips as necessary, disconnect the various link rods - at either end, whichever is convenient. It may prove necessary, for example, to detach the interior handle and to remove it with the latch so that the link rod can be disconnected off the car. On the rear door, note the rubber fillet which can be removed to improve visibility and access to the latch area **(see illustrations)**.

11 Remove the retaining screws and withdraw the latch **(see illustrations)**.

Interior handle

12 Open the door and fully raise the window glass, remove the interior trim panel, then peel down the plastic sheet.

13 Remove the retaining screw(s) and release the link rod from the clip(s) securing it to the door **(see illustration)**.

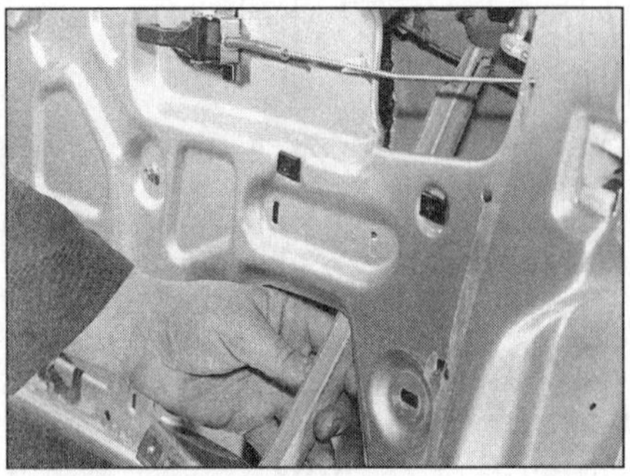
18.9b . . . to remove window glass rear guide channel

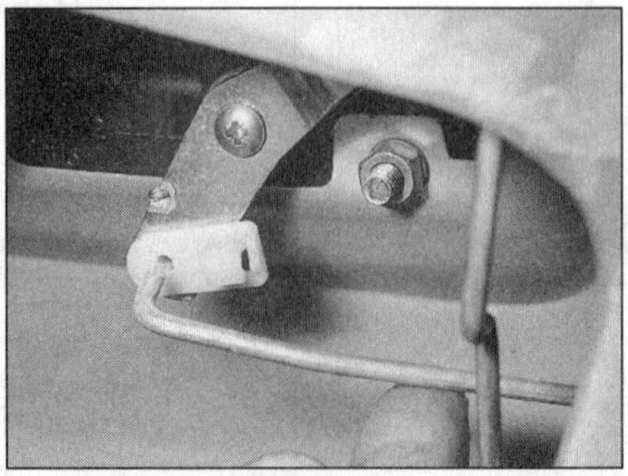
18.10a Disconnecting front door exterior handle link rod

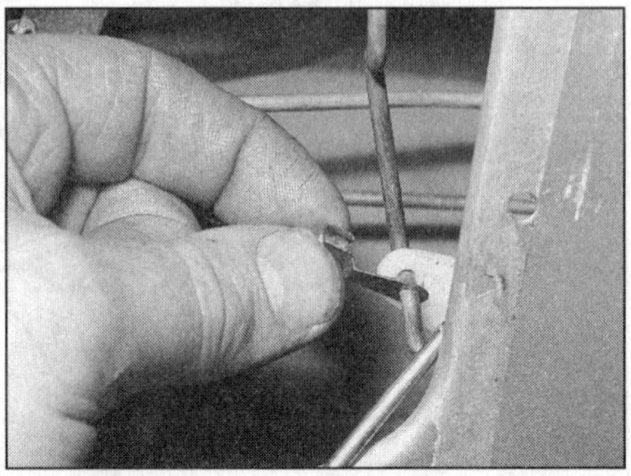
18.10b Disconnecting front door interior lock button link rod from latch

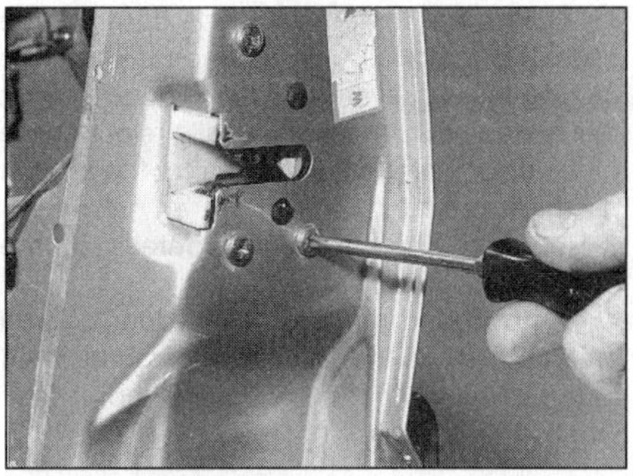

18.11a Remove latch retaining screws . . .

18.11b . . . and withdraw latch with link rods, if required

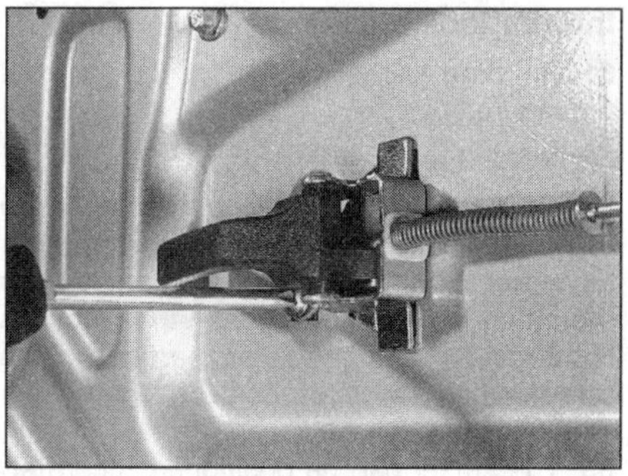

18.13 Removing interior handle retaining screw

14 Either remove the handle and link rod together, disconnecting them from the latch, or disconnect the handle from the link rod, as required. Compress the spring to disconnect the rod from the handle. Note the nylon bush and the washer.

Interior lock button

15 The button itself can be unscrewed from the top of its link rod with no prior dismantling being necessary.

16 If the link rod is to be removed, the door interior trim panel must be removed and the plastic sheet peeled back from the top rear corner (front door) or down as far as necessary (rear door).

17 On the front door, release the clip to disconnect the link rod from the latch.

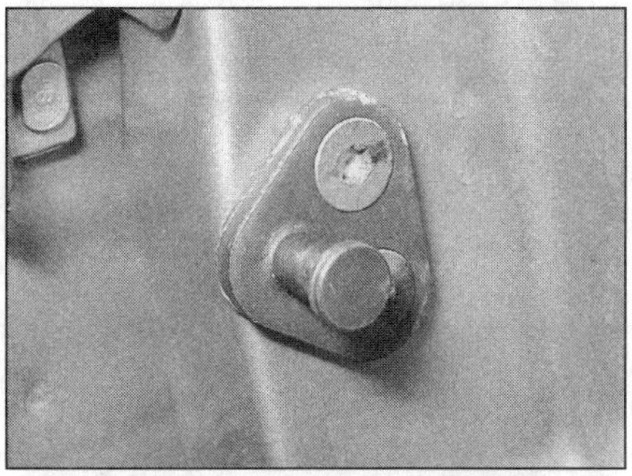

18.20 Door striker is either screwed into door pillar or secured by two screws (shown)

18 On the rear door, release the pin (immediately above and in front of the window regulator mounting bolts) securing the bellcrank to the door and (where fitted) release the snap-on connector to disconnect the central locking motor link rod. Disconnect the link rod from the latch and withdraw the assembly.

Striker

19 On five-door model rear doors and three-door models, the striker is screwed into the pillar. Do not overtighten the striker or its caged retaining nut might break free inside the pillar. Mark with a pencil around the striker before unscrewing it.

20 On five-door model front doors, open the door and mark with a pencil around the striker, then undo the two Torx-type screws and withdraw the striker **(see illustration)**.

Central locking control unit/motor - front door

21 Open the door and fully raise the window glass, remove the interior trim panel, then peel back the bottom rear corner of the plastic sheet.

22 Remove the two retaining screws, disconnect the control unit/motor from the link rod and withdraw it, then unplug the wiring connector to release the control unit/motor from the door **(see illustrations)**.

Central locking control unit/motor - rear door

23 Open the door and fully raise the window glass, remove the interior trim panel, then peel back the bottom front corner of the plastic sheet.

24 Remove the two retaining screws, then disconnect the motor from the link rod **(see illustration)**.

25 Prise both motor wiring sealing grommets out of the door and the B pillar, then remove the B pillar lower interior trim panel, unbolt the seat belt bottom anchorage and release the floor carpet from the door sill.

26 Disconnect the motor wiring by unplugging the connector from the floor behind the front seat rear mounting, attach a drawstring to the wiring and pull it up through the pillar and door until the motor can be removed. Leave the drawstring in place to assist with refitting.

Refitting

Front door lock

27 Refitting is the reverse of the removal procedure.

Exterior handle

28 Refitting is the reverse of the removal procedure. Tighten the nuts to the specified torque wrench setting.

Latch

29 Refitting is the reverse of the removal procedure. Check that the window glass slides easily up and down before tightening the guide channel screw securely.

Interior handle

30 Refitting is the reverse of the removal procedure.

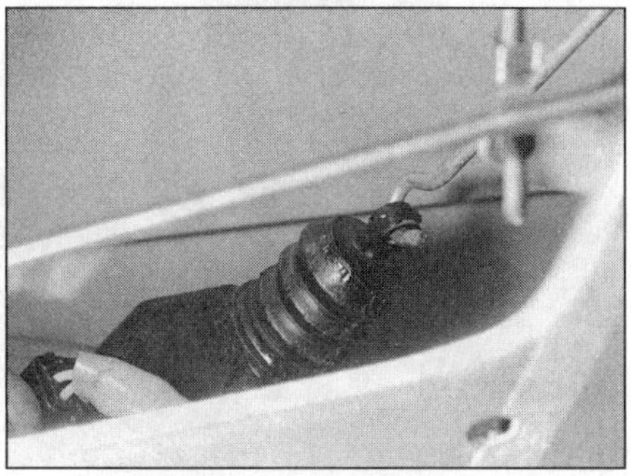

18.22a Remove retaining screws to release front door central locking control unit/motor from link rod . . .

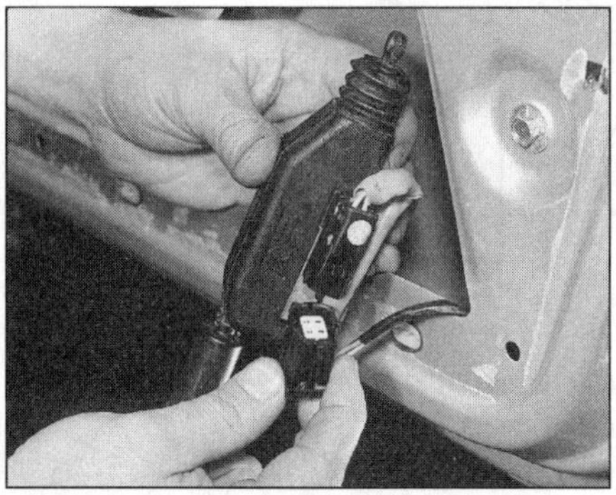

18.22b . . . and withdraw unit/motor until wiring can be disconnected

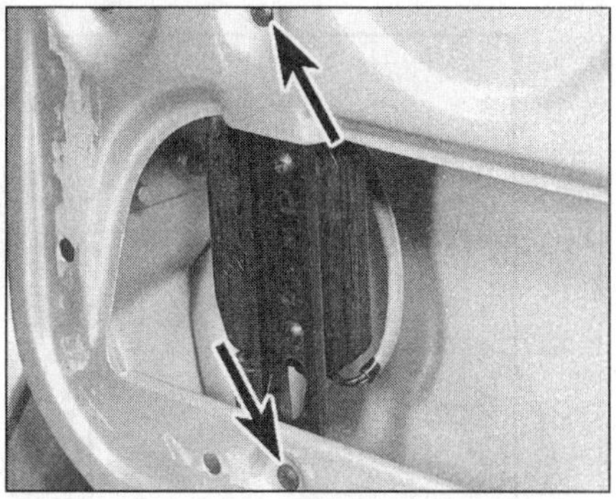

18.24 Rear door central locking motor retaining screws (arrowed)

11

Interior lock button

31 Refitting is the reverse of the removal procedure.

Striker

32 On refitting, align the striker with the marks made on removal. If new components have been fitted, centre the striker on its mounting hole(s), tighten the striker/screws lightly and check the fit of the door in the body. When the fit is correct, tighten the striker/screws securely.

33 The striker can be positioned accurately only when the door is properly located in its aperture.

34 When the door is closed, check that it sits squarely on its weatherstrip, with no sign of gaps, so that it is flush with the surrounding bodywork and so that the door lock closes securely, with no sign of rattles.

35 If the fit is not correct, open the door and slacken the striker/screws, then adjust the position of the striker by closing the door as gently as possible, then opening it again without disturbing the position of the striker.

36 When the fit is correct, tighten the striker/screws securely and check the operation of the door lock.

Central locking control unit/motor - front door

37 Refitting is the reverse of the removal procedure.

Central locking control unit/motor - rear door

38 Refitting is the reverse of the removal procedure.

19 Central locking system - operation and component renewal

1 The system allows the doors and tailgate to be locked or unlocked from a central point. Operating the driver's door lock, either from the outside with a key or from the inside using the interior lock button, will trigger the system.

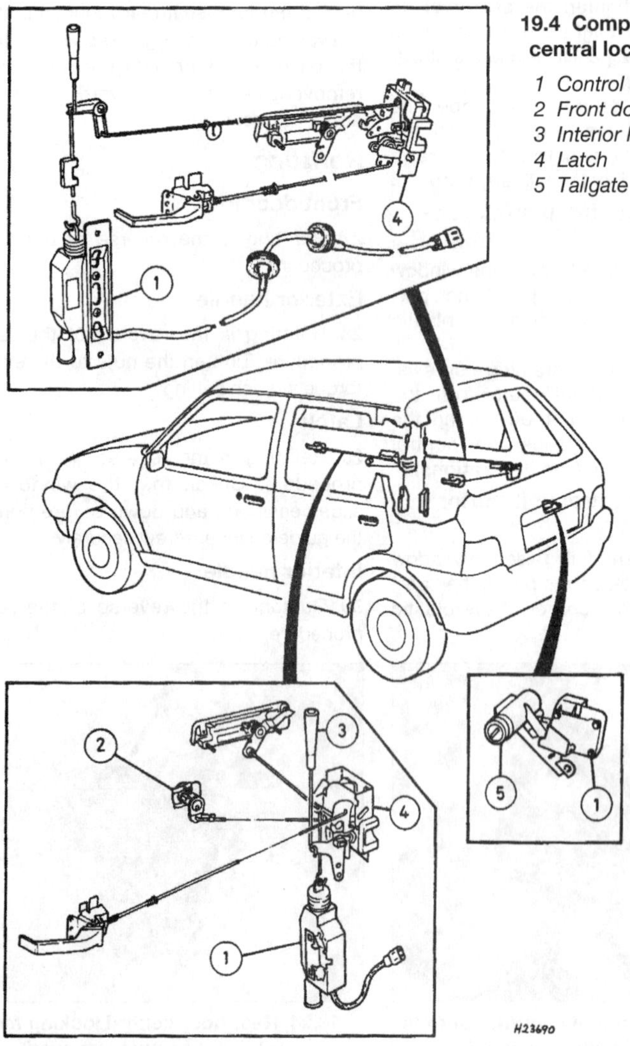

19.4 Components of the central locking system

1 Control unit/motor
2 Front door lock
3 Interior lock button
4 Latch
5 Tailgate lock

2 Locks other than the driver's door can be operated manually, independently of the central locking system. Note, however, that the system will not automatically relock these other locks if any is unlocked after the system has been operated.

3 Refer to Chapter 12 for details of the system's electrical components.

4 Removal and refitting of the door control unit/motors and the tailgate motor is covered in the relevant Sections of this Chapter **(see illustration)**.

20 Door window glass and regulator - removal and refitting

Removal

Window glass

1 Remove the regulator.

2 On a rear door only, remove the rubber fillet from the rear of the door, remove their retaining screws and withdraw both the front and rear guide channels **(see illustrations)**.

3 If not already done, support the glass and remove the two wedges.

4 Pull off the outside and inside weatherstrips **(see illustrations)**.

5 Manoeuvre the glass out of the door **(see illustration)**.

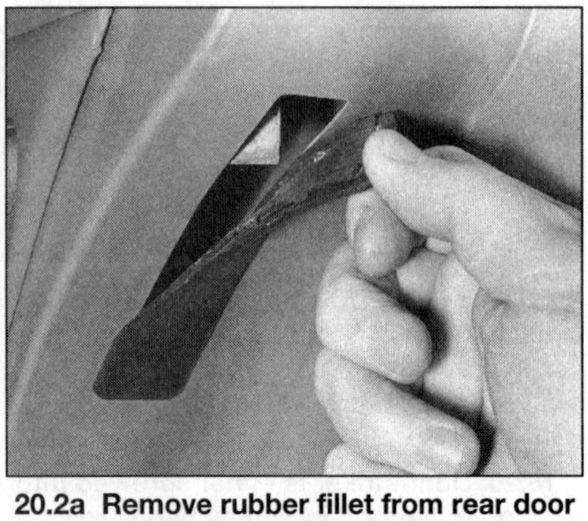

20.2a Remove rubber fillet from rear door to improve access . . .

20.2b . . . and remove screw (arrowed) to release window glass guide channel (rear shown, front similar)

20.4a Removing door outside . . .

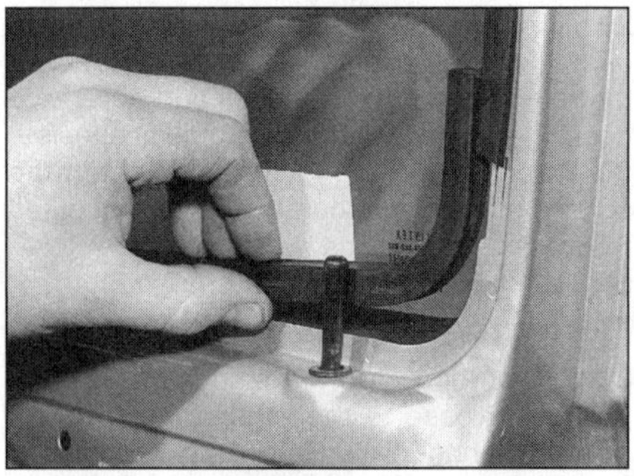

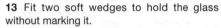

20.4b . . . and inside weatherstrips

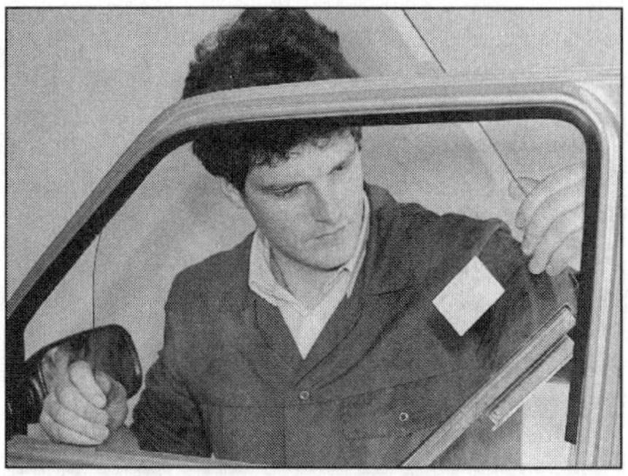

20.5 Manoeuvring window glass out of door

Manual regulator - front door

6 Open the door and fully raise the window glass, remove the interior trim panel, then peel down the plastic sheet.

7 Fit two soft wedges to hold the glass without marking it **(see illustration)**.

8 Unscrew the three bolts securing the regulator to the door.

9 Remove its retaining screw and withdraw the front guide channel from the door.

10 Unscrew the two nuts securing the regulator channel to the door inner panel, then remove the regulator channel.

11 Support the glass and remove the two wedges, lower the glass and release the regulator from the glass bottom channels, then manoeuvre the regulator out of the door.

Manual regulator - rear door

12 Open the door and fully raise the window glass, remove the interior trim panel, then peel down the plastic sheet.

13 Fit two soft wedges to hold the glass without marking it.

14 Unscrew the three bolts securing the regulator to the door, then gently push the regulator into the door to release it from the door inner panel **(see illustration)**.

15 Release the regulator top arms from the glass bottom channels, then manoeuvre the regulator out of the door.

Electric regulator

16 Open the door and fully raise the window glass, remove the interior trim panel, then peel down the plastic sheet.

17 Fit two soft wedges to hold the glass without marking it.

18 Remove its retaining screw and withdraw the front guide channel from the door **(see illustrations)**.

19 Release the connector from its clip, unplug the connector to disconnect the wiring, then unscrew the two motor mounting bolts **(see illustration)**.

20 Unscrew the two bolts securing the regulator to the door, then manoeuvre the motor and part of the cable out of the door **(see illustration)**.

21 Move the regulator towards the front of the door and release its top arms from the glass bottom channels, then manoeuvre the regulator out of the door **(see illustration)**.

Refitting

Window glass

22 On refitting, manoeuvre the glass into the door and support it in the fully-raised position while the regulator is greased and refitted. Where the front and rear guide channels were disturbed, refit them with their retaining screws, but do not fully tighten the screws until the operation of the complete assembly has been checked and adjusted as described later.

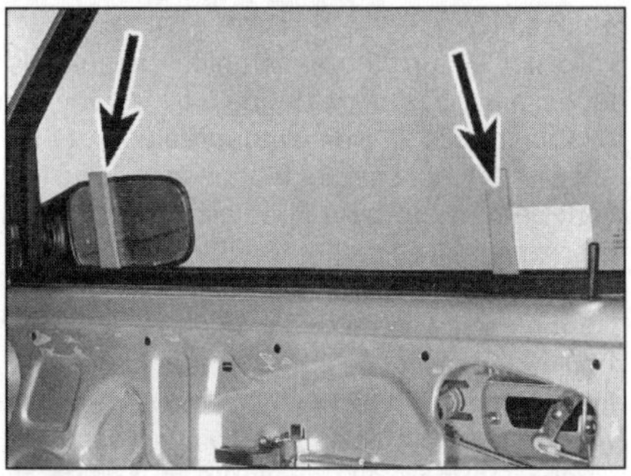

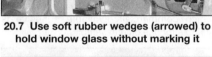

20.7 Use soft rubber wedges (arrowed) to hold window glass without marking it

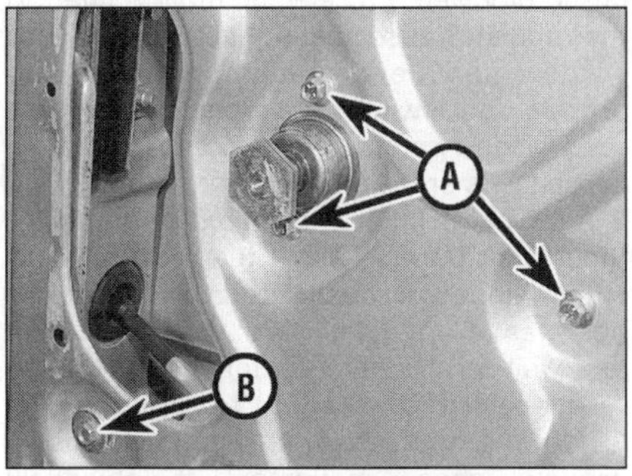

20.14 Regulator mounting bolts (A) and front guide channel screw (B)

20.18a Unscrewing window glass front guide channel screw . . .

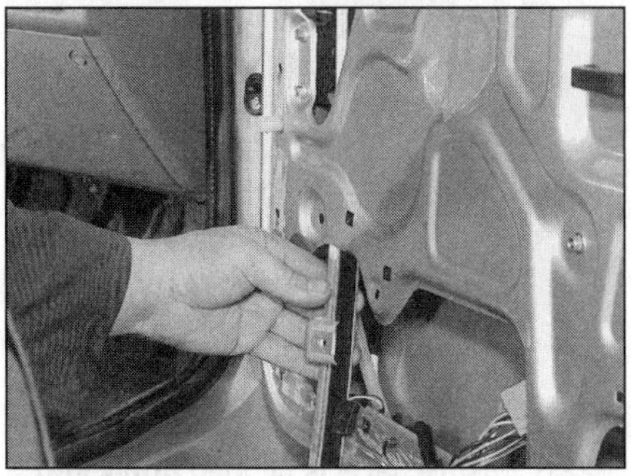

20.18b . . . to remove channel from front door

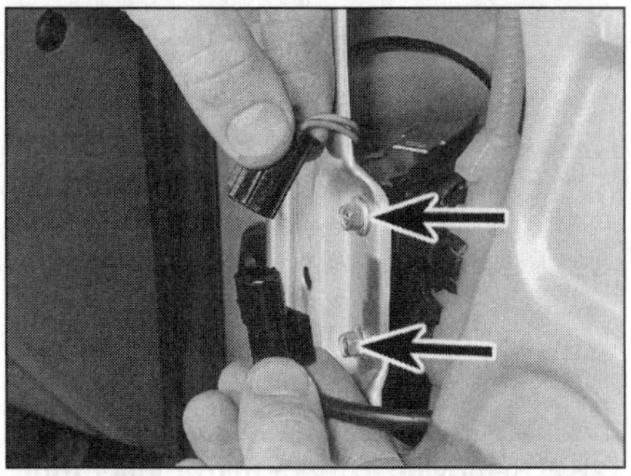

20.19 Disconnecting electric motor wiring - note motor mounting bolts (arrowed)

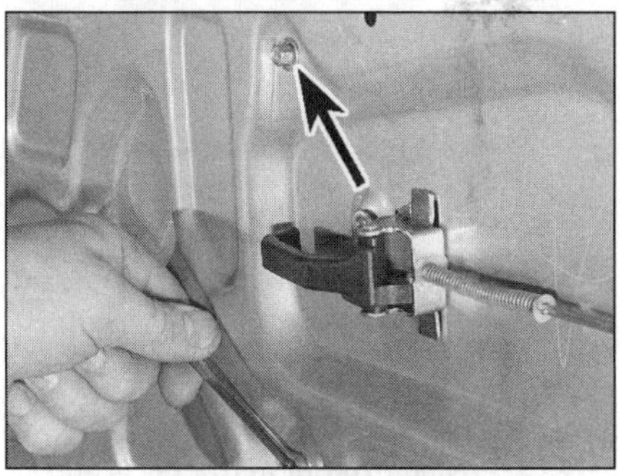

20.20 Unscrewing electric window regulator bolts (other bolt arrowed) . . .

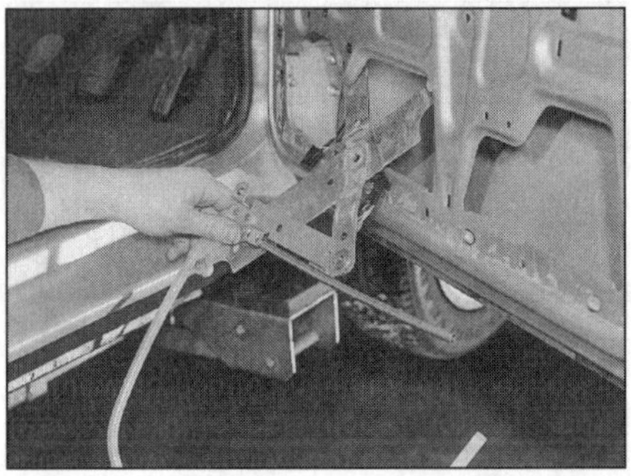

20.21 . . . to remove regulator and motor assembly from door

Manual regulator - front door

23 On refitting, apply a smear of general-purpose grease to the regulator and glass bottom channels, then refit the regulator and its bolts, raise the glass and secure it with the wedges. Engage the regulator top arms in the glass bottom channels and its lower arm in the regulator channel, then position the regulator channel on the door inner panel and tighten the nuts to their specified torque wrench setting.
24 Remove the wedges and wind the glass to the fully-raised position, refit the front guide channel and tighten its screw lightly, then lower and raise the glass several times to settle the components. If necessary, slacken the retaining screws and bolts and adjust the position of the guide channels.
25 When the setting is correct, tighten the screws and bolts securely, to their specified torque wrench settings, where given.
26 Refit the interior trim panel.

Manual regulator - rear door

27 On refitting, apply a smear of the general-purpose grease to the regulator and glass bottom channels, raise the glass and secure it with the wedges. Refit the regulator to the door inner panel, engage the regulator top arms in the glass bottom channels (lowering the glass if necessary) and refit the regulator top mounting bolt to secure the assembly; tighten the bolt only lightly.
28 Remove the wedges and wind the glass until the remaining two regulator mounting bolt holes align then refit the bolts, tightening them only lightly.
29 Raise and lower the glass several times to settle the components. If necessary, slacken the retaining screws and bolts and adjust the position of the regulator and guide channels.
30 When the setting is correct, tighten the screws and bolts securely to their specified torque wrench settings, where given.
31 Refit the interior trim panel.

Electric regulator

32 On refitting, apply a smear of general-purpose grease to the regulator and glass bottom channels. Refit the regulator, engaging its top arms in the glass bottom channels and its lower arm in the regulator channel attached to the door inner panel.
33 Align the bolt holes and refit the bolts, then refit the motor and its bolts. Refit the front guide channel and tighten its screw only lightly.
34 Connect the motor and switch wiring and remove the wedges, then lower and raise the glass several times to settle the components. If necessary, slacken the retaining screws and bolts and adjust the position of the guide channels.
35 When the setting is correct, tighten the screws and bolts securely to their specified torque wrench settings, where given.
36 Refit the interior trim panel.

21 Electric front windows - operation and component renewal

1 Where applicable, the front windows can be raised or lowered by electric motors fitted to the regulator assemblies. The driver's door window can be operated only from the driver's door switch, whilst the passenger's door window can be operated either from the passenger's or the driver's door switch.
2 A cut-out is fitted to each motor to protect them from burning-out if the movement of either window is obstructed. If the cut-out operates at any time, clear the obstruction and wait for 15 seconds for the cut-out to reset before attempting to operate the windows. Do not attempt to open or close a window whose movement is obviously obstructed, or if the window is frozen in place.
3 The regulator and motor assemblies are removed and refitted as described in this Chapter. Refer to Chapter 12 for details of the system's electrical components.

22 Mirrors - removal and refitting

Removal

Exterior mirror glass

1 Taking care not to mark the plastic and wearing gloves and suitable eye protection, carefully prise the mirror glass and bezel off the mirror casing **(see illustration)**.

Exterior mirror assembly

2 Pull off the adjusting knob (where fitted). Gently prise the inner trim panel off the retaining clip at its top corner and withdraw it, unhooking it at the bottom edge **(see illustration)**.
3 Remove the two retaining screws and withdraw the mirror and the outer trim panel. Remove and discard, if fitted, the sealing pad.
4 On some early models, note that the mirror may be secured by a retaining plate which uses screws and moulded tubes through the door. Note carefully how the components fit together on removal so that they can be correctly reassembled.

Interior rear view mirror

5 The mirror itself slides on to a base that is stuck to the windscreen; push upwards to remove.
6 Do not disturb the base unless absolutely necessary; it is very difficult to achieve a reliable bond. If the windscreen is to be renewed, this is a further reason for having the work carried out by a specialist windscreen fitter who will be well-versed in the removal and refitting of stick-on mirrors.
7 If the base is to be removed and is found to be glued in place, seek the advice of a Rover dealer. Find out how best to remove the base (without risking cracking the windscreen) and which commercially-available adhesive is suitable for use on reassembly.

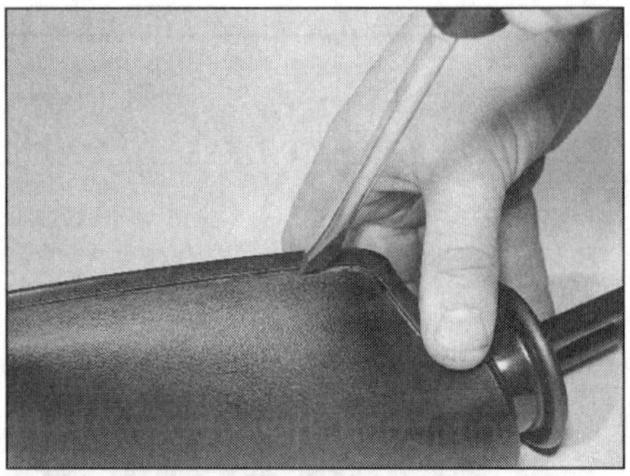

22.1 Prising exterior mirror glass and bezel from mirror casing

22.2 Removing exterior mirror inner trim panel to reveal mirror retaining screws (arrowed)

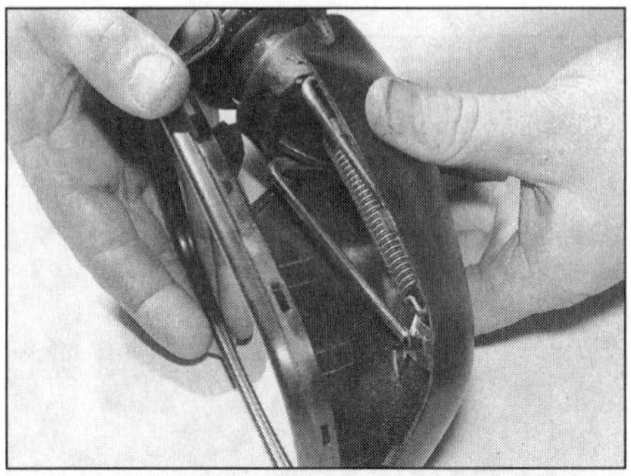

22.8 Ensure bezel is clipped firmly into casing on refitting

Refitting

Exterior mirror glass

8 Refitting is the reverse of the removal procedure. Ensure that the bezel is clipped securely into the casing **(see illustration)**.

Exterior mirror assembly

9 Refitting is the reverse of the removal procedure. Where applicable, fit a new sealing pad to the mirror.

Interior rear view mirror

10 Refitting is the reverse of removal.

23 Seats - removal and refitting

Removal

Front

1 Operate the adjuster and move the seat fully backwards, then undo the front mounting screws and remove the runner stops **(see illustration)**.

2 Move the seat fully forwards and undo the rear mounting screws **(see illustration)**.

3 Remove the seat.

Rear

4 Remove the parcel shelf. Release the seat belts from the seat, then fold the seat forwards.

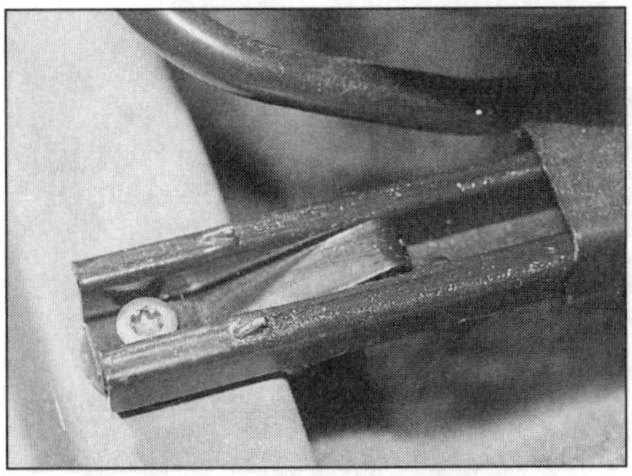

23.1 Front seat front mounting - note runner stop

23.2 Front seat rear mounting

23.5 Rear seat mounting points (arrowed)

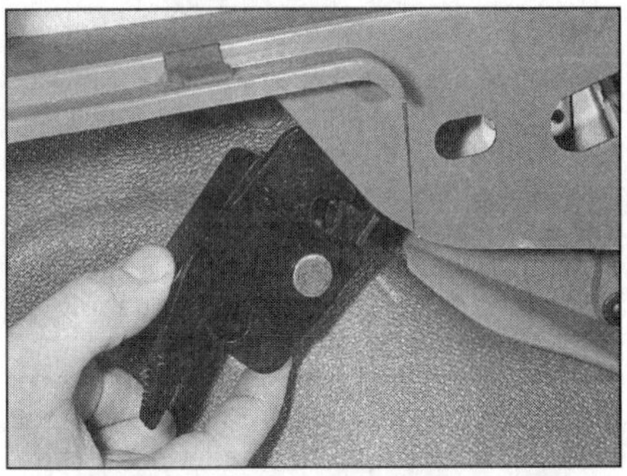

23.7 Removing rear seat backrest catch from parcel shelf side support

5 Undo the seat mounting screws and remove the seat, noting the spacer under each mounting point **(see illustration)**.

Refitting

Front and rear

6 Refitting is the reverse of the removal procedure. Tighten the screws to the specified torque wrench setting.

7 Note that the rear seat backrest catches are located under the parcel shelf side supports and can be removed once the mounting bolts have been unscrewed **(see illustration)**.

24 Seat belts - inspection

Refer to Chapter 1, Section 4.

25 Seat belts - removal and refitting

Removal

Front

1 Prise off the plastic cover and unbolt the belt top anchorage **(see illustration)**.

2 Unbolt the belt bottom anchorage **(see illustration)**.

3 Remove the rear quarter (three-door) or the B pillar lower (five-door) interior trim panel and unbolt the retractor from the body **(see illustration)**.

4 Prise out its retaining clip and withdraw the cover, then unbolt the stalks from the floor **(see illustration)**.

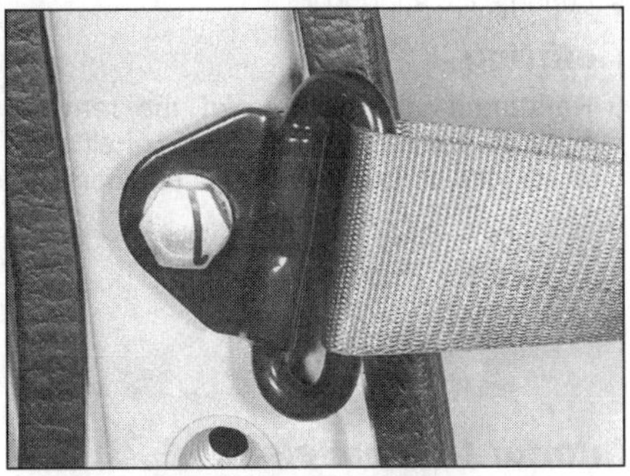

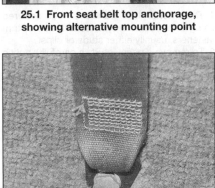

25.1 Front seat belt top anchorage, showing alternative mounting point

25.2 Front seat belt bottom anchorage - five-door models

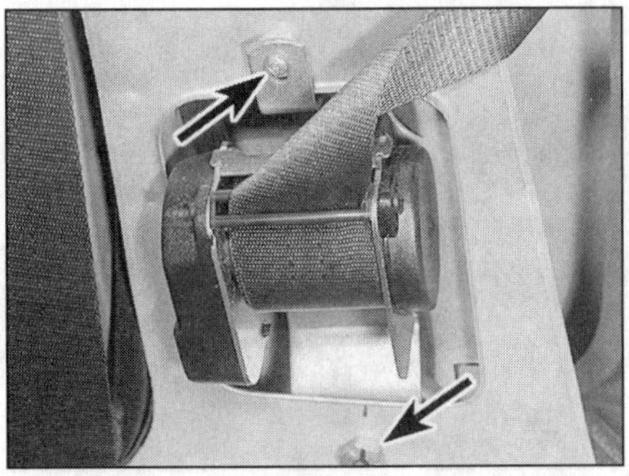

25.3 Retractor is secured by a bolt and screw (where fitted) (arrowed)

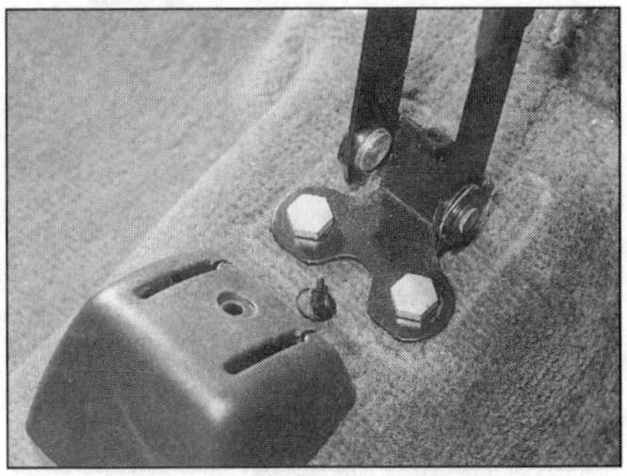

25.4 Front seat belt stalk mountings and cover

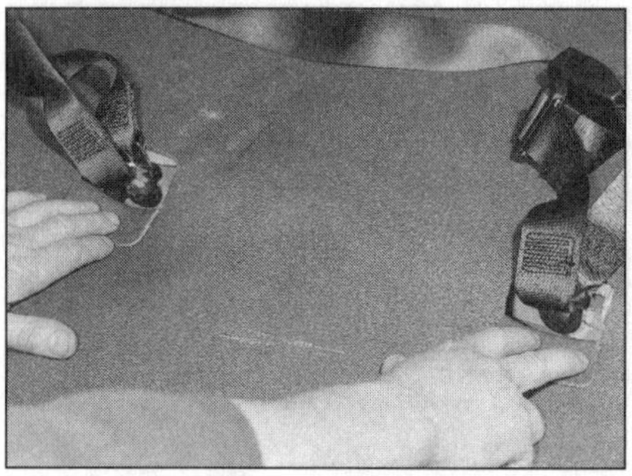

25.6a Rear centre seat belt mountings and side belt buckle mountings

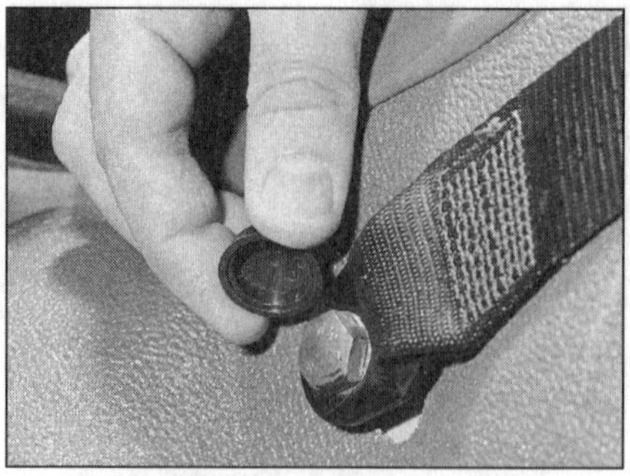

25.6b Rear side seat belt bottom anchorage

25.7 Rear side seat belt top anchorage

Rear

5 Remove the parcel shelf. Release the belts from the seat, then fold the seat forwards.

6 Unbolt the belt bottom anchorage and buckle from the floor **(see illustrations)**. Note that the centre two-point belt can be unbolted completely.

7 Prise off the plastic cover and unbolt the belt top anchorage **(see illustration)**.

8 Remove the luggage compartment interior trim panels as necessary to reach the belt retractor mountings. On the left-hand side, this will require the removal of the luggage compartment lamp (if fitted). Unbolt the retractor from the body **(see illustration)**.

9 Release the belt guide from the parcel shelf side support, remove the guide from the belt and feed the belt through the support until it can be removed.

Refitting

Front and rear

10 Refitting is the reverse of the removal procedure, but ensure that the anchorages are free to move when the bolts have been securely tightened, to their respective specified torque wrench settings.

26 Parcel shelf - removal and refitting

Removal

1 Open the tailgate, detach the parcel shelf straps and push the shelf to the right until the left-hand pivot pin is released from its retainer.

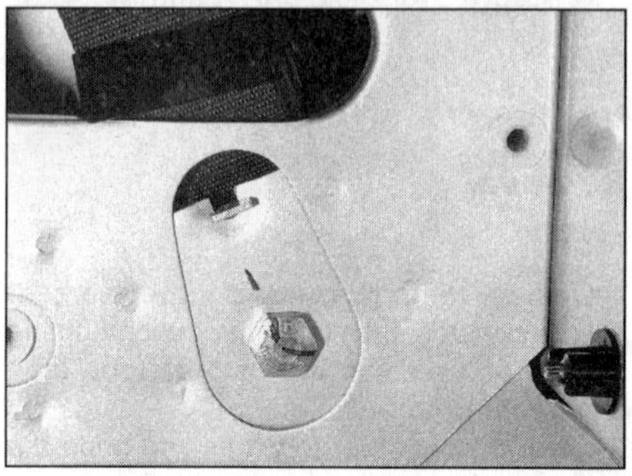

25.8 Remove luggage compartment interior trim panel to reach rear side seat belt retractor mounting bolt

2 To remove the parcel shelf side supports, remove the rear seat belt retractor, unbolt the rear seat catches, disconnect the loudspeaker wiring (if fitted) and remove the four screws securing each support.

Refitting

3 Refitting is the reverse of the removal procedure. Ensure that the parcel shelf pivot pins are located securely in their retainers.

27.2a Prise off armrest/door pull cover (where fitted) to reveal retaining screws

27.2b Prise out cover plug and remove screw . . .

27.2c . . . to release window regulator handle

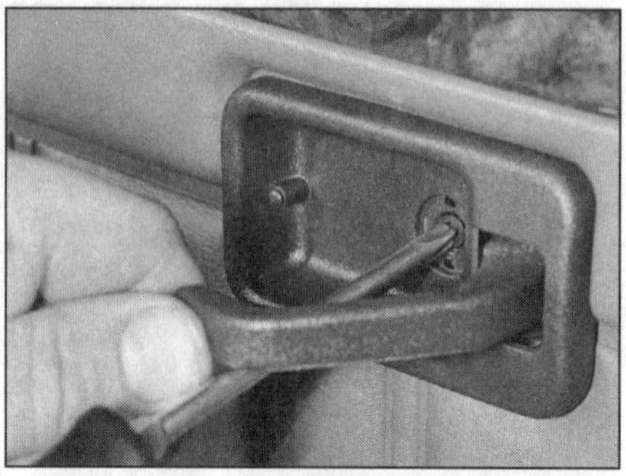

27.2d Prise out plug and remove screw to release door lock interior handle escutcheon

27 Interior trim - removal and refitting

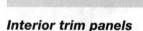

Interior trim panels

1 The interior trim panels are all secured using either screws or various types of trim fasteners, usually either studs or clips.

2 To remove a panel, study it carefully, noting how it is secured. Usually there are some ancillary components which must be removed first such as, on door trim panels, the front door pockets and loudspeakers, the armrests/door pulls, the manual window regulator handles and door lock interior handle escutcheons **(see illustrations)**.

3 Once any such components have been removed, check that there are no other panels overlapping the one to be removed. Usually there is a sequence that has to be followed that will become obvious on close inspection. For example, when removing two-piece door interior trim panels, the upper panel must be removed first.

4 Remove all obvious fasteners, such as screws. If the panel will not come free, it is held by hidden clips or fasteners. These are usually situated around the edge of the panel and can be prised up to release them. Note, however that they can break quite easily so replacements should be available. The best way of releasing such clips is to use the correct type of tool, an example of which is shown in some of the accompanying illustrations. If this is not available, an old, broad-bladed screwdriver with the edges rounded-off and wrapped in insulating tape will serve as a good substitute **(see illustrations)**.

5 The accompanying illustrations show typical examples of the location and number of fasteners securing most of the car's panels. Note in many cases that the adjacent weatherstrip must be prised back to release a panel.

6 When removing a panel, never use excessive force or the panel may be damaged. Always check carefully that all fasteners have been removed or released before attempting to withdraw a panel.

7 Refitting is the reverse of the removal procedure. Secure the fasteners by pressing them firmly into place and ensure that all disturbed components are correctly secured to prevent rattles. If adhesives were found at any point on removal, use white spirit to remove all traces of old adhesive, then wash off all traces of spirit using soapy water. Use a suitable trim adhesive (a Rover dealer should be able to recommend a proprietary product) on reassembly.

Carpets

8 The passenger compartment floor carpet is in one piece and is secured at its edges by screws or clips, usually the same fasteners used to secure the various adjoining trim panels.

9 Carpet removal and refitting is reasonably straightforward but very time-consuming due to the fact that all adjoining trim panels must be removed first, as must components such as the seats and their mountings, the gearchange lever gaiters, the cassette storage holder and seat belt lower anchorages.

Headlining

10 The headlining is clipped to the roof and can be withdrawn only once all fittings such as the grab handles, sun visors, roof console, sunroof (if fitted), windscreen and rear quarterlights and related trim panels have been removed and the door, tailgate and sunroof aperture weatherstrips have been prised clear.

11 Note that headlining removal requires considerable skill and experience if it is to be carried out without damage and is therefore best entrusted to an expert.

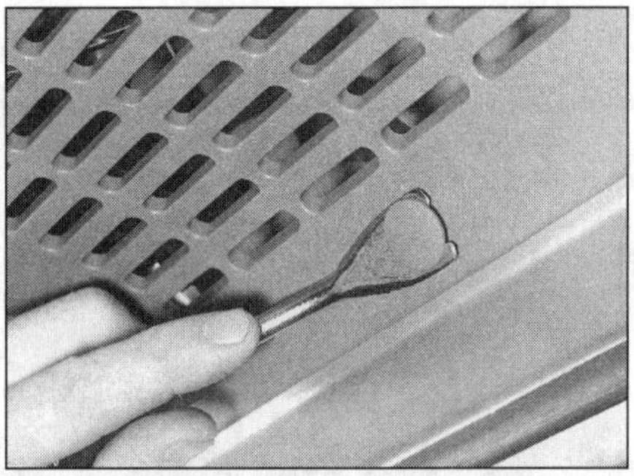

27.4a Remove obvious fasteners such as screws and trim clips to release trim panels

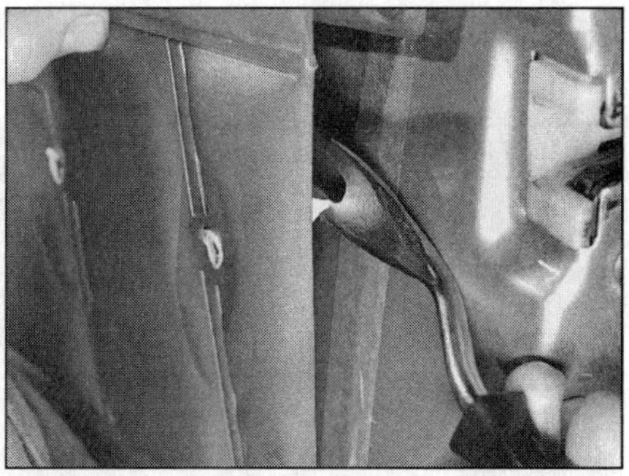

27.4b Removing a panel secured by hidden clips

28 Sun visor - removal and refitting

Removal

Unclip the visor and remove the two screws securing its pivot to the roof. Remove the visor. Each clip is secured by a single screw.

Refitting

Refitting is the reverse of the removal procedure.

29 Roof console - removal and refitting

Removal

1 Remove the interior lamp from the roof.

2 Release the four clips and withdraw the console.

Refitting

3 Refitting is the reverse of the removal procedure.

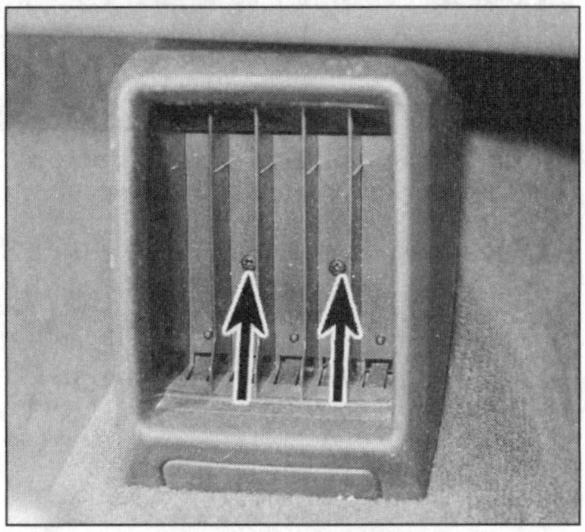

31.1 Cassette storage holder retaining screws (arrowed)

30 Grab handles - removal and refitting

Removal

Prise up the cover at each end of the handle, remove the retaining screws securing each end, then withdraw the handle.

Refitting

Refitting is the reverse of the removal procedure.

31 Cassette storage holder - removal and refitting

Removal

1 Remove the two retaining screws to release the holder **(see illustration)**.

2 The holder bracket is secured to the floor by two (hex-head) screws.

Refitting

3 Refitting is the reverse of the removal procedure.

32 Glovebox - removal and refitting

Removal

Lid

1 Open the lid and carefully lift the edge of the glovebox floor carpet, remove the four screws and withdraw the lid.

Lock

2 Open the glovebox lid and prise out the retaining clip to release the lock.

3 The striker is secured by two screws.

Glovebox

4 Open the glovebox lid (where fitted).

5 Where fitted, remove the glovebox lamp and switch.

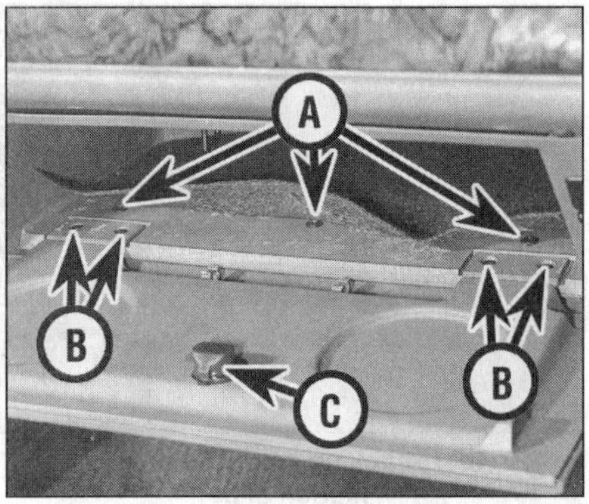

32.6 Glovebox floor securing screws (A) lid securing screws (B) and lock retaining clip (C)

6 Carefully lift the edge of the glovebox floor carpet and remove the three screws **(see illustration)**.

7 Remove the striker (if fitted) from the glovebox ceiling. Remove the four (ceiling) retaining screws and withdraw the glovebox from the facia. If required, remove the four remaining screws to release the glovebox support rail **(see illustration)**.

Refitting

Lid

8 Refitting is the reverse of the removal procedure. Use white spirit to remove the old adhesive, then wash off all traces of spirit using soapy water. Use a suitable trim adhesive to secure the carpet.

Lock

9 The striker's position can be altered on the slotted mounting holes until the lid closes securely and fits properly. Tighten the screws securely.

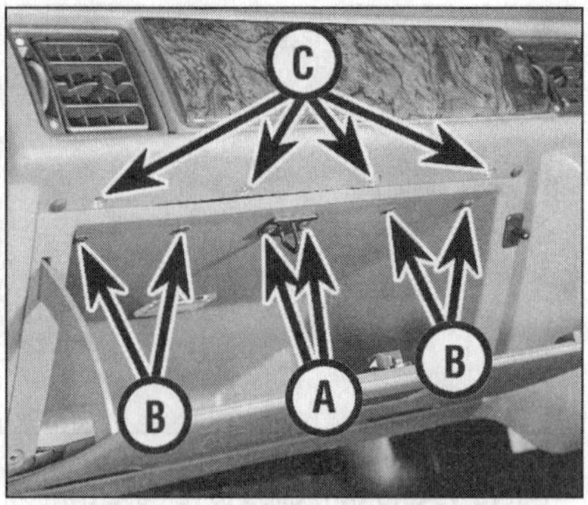

32.7 Glovebox striker screws (A) ceiling securing screws (B) and support rail screws (C)

Glovebox

10 Refitting is the reverse of the removal procedure; secure the floor carpet as described previously.

33 Facia - removal and refitting

Warning: Read carefully the precautions listed in Section 1, Chapter 12, appertaining to vehicles equipped with airbags (SRS) before attempting removal of the steering column.

Removal

1 Disconnect the battery negative lead.

2 On models with carburettor engines only, disconnect the choke cable from the facia.

3 Move both front seats as far as possible to the rear.

4 Lower the steering column onto a support such as a wooden block, referring to Chapter 10.

5 Reaching up inside the fusebox aperture, disconnect the speedometer drive cable from the rear of the instrument panel.

6 Disconnect the facia wiring by unplugging its connector plug (top row, right-hand connector, marked FACIA) from the fusebox panel and by unplugging the two connector plugs mounted on brackets at the left-hand end of the fusebox panel **(see illustration)**.

7 Remove the cassette storage holder.

8 Remove the nine screws securing the facia and pull it into the passenger compartment. Do not use excessive force; it is not necessary and may damage the plastic components. If difficulty is encountered at any point check carefully that all fasteners, electrical connections and other components have been removed or disconnected as required. Lower the facia to the floor; place wads of clean rag as necessary to protect the facia surfaces **(see illustrations)**.

9 Remove the heater control panel.

10 Disconnect, if fitted, the radio aerial and wiring.

11 Remove the facia from the car.

12 The facia components can be removed now if required.

Refitting

13 Refitting is the reverse of the removal procedure.

33.6 Disconnecting facia wiring

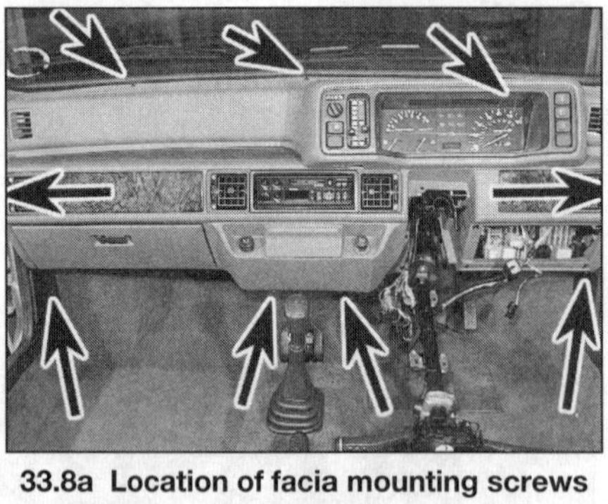
33.8a Location of facia mounting screws (front seats removed for clarity)

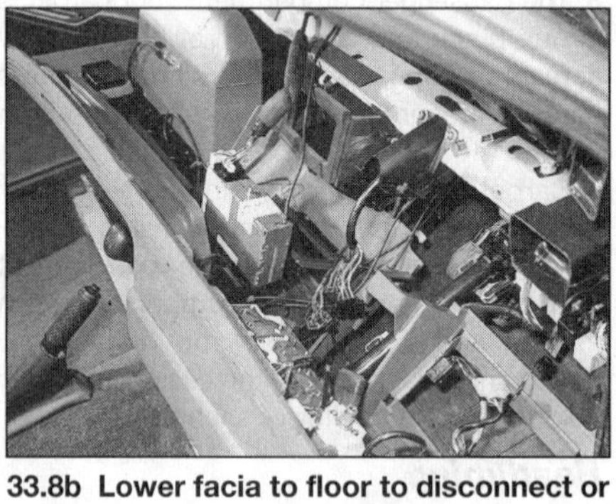
33.8b Lower facia to floor to disconnect or remove components

Chapter 12
Body electrical systems

Contents

Degrees of difficulty

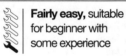

Easy, suitable for novice with little experience	**Fairly easy,** suitable for beginner with some experience	**Fairly difficult,** suitable for competent DIY mechanic	**Difficult,** suitable for experienced DIY mechanic	**Very difficult,** suitable for expert DIY or professional

Specifications

System

Type . 12 volt, negative earth

Fuses

Fuse	Rating (amps)	Circuit(s) protected
1	10	Engine (ignition HT coil, manifold pre-heater relay, carburettor idle bypass system, fuel pump relay)
2	10	Right-hand side and tail lamps, sidelamp warning lamp, number plate lamps, electric front window switch and instrument panel illumination
3	10	Instrument (panel) feed
4	15	Electric cooling fan
5	10	Right-hand headlamp main beam, main beam warning lamp
6	10	Stop-lamps
7	-	Unused
8	-	Unused
9	10	Direction indicators, reversing lamps, heated rear window relay
10	10	Rear foglamp
11	20	Heated rear window
12	15	Central locking system, radio/cassette memory, clock, interior lamp, luggage compartment lamp, interior lamp delay/lamps-on alarm unit
13	30	Electric front windows
14	15	Heater blower motor
15	15	Windscreen wipers and washer
16	15	Rear window wiper and washer
17	10	Fuel pump
18	10	Left-hand headlamp main beam
19	20	Headlamps, sidelamps
20	15	Dim-dip
21	20	Hazard warning lamps, horn
22	15	Radio/cassette feed, cigar lighter
23	-	Unused

Fuses (continued)

Fuse	Rating (amps)	Circuit(s) protected
24	10	Right-hand headlamp dip beam
25	10	Left-hand headlamp dip beam
26	10	Left-hand side and tail lamps, number plate lamps, illumination of instrument panel switches, cigar lighter and glovebox
Additional	3	Airbag (SRS)

Fusible links

Link	Rating (amps)	Circuit(s) protected
1 (Light blue)	60	Ignition switch, ignition relay
2 (Light blue)	60	Fusebox feed
3 (Light blue)	60	Fusebox feed
4 (Light green)	30	Manifold pre-heater and starter relay (carburettor engines), relay module (fuel-injected engines)

Relays and control units

Component	Location
Starter relay - carburettor engines	Engine compartment left-hand side, in front of heater air inlet box/blower motor assembly (front relay)
Inlet manifold pre-heater relay - carburettor engines	Engine compartment left-hand side, in front of heater air inlet box/blower motor assembly (rear relay)
Main relay, manifold heater relay, starter relay and fuel pump relay - fuel-injected engines	Part of relay module, in engine compartment between heater air inlet box and blower motor assembly and fuel-injection/ignition system ECU
Lambda sensor relay	Engine compartment left-hand side, next to heater air inlet box/blower motor assembly
Interior lamp delay/Lamps-on alarm unit	Fusebox panel (rear face)
Heated rear window relay	Fusebox panel (rear face)
Headlamp relay	Fusebox panel (rear face)
Ignition relay	Fusebox panel (rear face)
Electric front window/auxiliary relay	Fusebox panel (rear face)
Direction indicator/hazard warning relay	Fusebox panel (rear face)
Dim-dip unit	Fusebox panel (rear face)
Windscreen wiper relay	Fusebox panel (front face)
Rear window wiper relay	Fusebox panel (front face)

Bulbs

	Fitting	Wattage
Headlamps	H4	60/55
Front sidelamps	Capless	5
Direction indicator lamps	Bayonet	21
Direction indicator side repeater lamps	Capless	5
Interior lamp	Bayonet	10
Instrument panel warning and illumination	Integral with holder	14V 1.12, 1.4 or 2W
Hazard warning indicator lamp	Capless	1.2
Glovebox lamp	Festoon	5
Luggage compartment lamp	Bayonet	10
Reversing lamps	Bayonet	21
Stop/tail lamps	Bayonet (offset pin)	21/5
Rear foglamp	Bayonet	21
Number plate lamp	Festoon	5

Torque wrench settings

	Nm	lbf ft
Oil pressure switch	12	9
Speedometer drive upper-to-lower cable nut	9	6.5
Wiper arm-to-spindle nut	11	8
Windscreen wiper motor-to-mounting bracket (hex-head) screws	10	7.5
Windscreen wiper linkage spindle housing nuts	11	8
Rear window wiper motor-to-mounting bracket (hex-head) screws	10	7.5
Rear window wiper motor mounting bracket (hex-head) screws	5	3.5
Rear window wiper motor spindle housing nut	11	8
Airbag to steering wheel (Torx) screws	8	6
Airbag control unit to steering wheel (Torx) screws	3.5	2.5
Airbag rotary contact unit to column switch screws	1.5	0.7

1 General information and precautions

General information

The electrical system is of the 12-volt negative earth type and comprises a 12-volt battery, an alternator with integral voltage regulator, a starter motor and related electrical accessories, components and wiring. The battery is of the "maintenance-free" (sealed for life) type and is charged by the alternator, which is belt-driven from a crankshaft-mounted pulley.

Further details of the various systems are given in the relevant Sections of this Chapter. While some repair procedures are given, the usual course of action is to renew the component concerned. The owner whose interest extends beyond mere component renewal should obtain a copy of the *"Automobile Electrical & Electronic Systems Manual"*, available from the publishers of this manual.

Precautions

It is necessary to take extra care when working on the electrical system to avoid damage to semi-conductor devices (diodes and transistors), and to avoid the risk of personal injury. In addition to the precautions given in *Safety first!* at the beginning of this manual, observe the following when working on the system:

Always remove rings, watches, etc before working on the electrical system. Even with the battery disconnected, capacitive discharge could occur if a component"s live terminal is earthed through a metal object. This could cause a shock or nasty burn.

Do not reverse the battery connections. Components such as the alternator, fuel injection/ignition system ECU, or any other having semi-conductor circuitry could be irreparably damaged.

If the engine is being started using jump leads and a slave battery, connect the batteries *positive-to-positive* and *negative-to-negative*. This also applies when connecting a battery charger.

Never disconnect the battery terminals, the alternator, any electrical wiring or any test instruments when the engine is running.

Do not allow the engine to turn the alternator when the alternator is not connected.

Never "test" for alternator output by "flashing" the output lead to earth.

Never use an ohmmeter of the type incorporating a hand-cranked generator for circuit or continuity testing.

Always ensure that the battery negative lead is disconnected when working on the electrical system.

Before using electric-arc welding equipment on the car, disconnect the battery, alternator and components such as the fuel injection/ignition system ECU to protect them.

A number of additional precautions must be observed when working on vehicles equipped with airbags (SRS), they are as follows:

a) Before working on any part of the system, remove the ignition key and wait at least ten minutes to allow the system backup circuit to fully discharge. Disconnect both battery leads, earth lead first, to avoid accidental detonation of the airbag.

b) Make no attempt to splice into any of the electric cables in the SRS wiring harness as this may affect the operation of the SRS. Never fit electronic equipment such as mobile telephones, radios, etc. into the harness and ensure that the harness is routed so that it cannot be trapped.

c) Avoid hammering or causing any harsh vibration at the front of the vehicle , particularly in the engine bay, as this may trigger the crash sensors and activate the SRS.

d) Do not use ohmmeters or any other device capable of supplying current on any of the SRS components, as this may cause accidental detonation. Use only a digital circuit tester.

e) Always use new replacement parts. Never fit parts that are from another vehicle or show signs of damage through being dropped or improperly handled

f) Airbags are classed as pyrotechnical devices and must be stored and handled according to the relevant laws in the country concerned. In general, do not leave these components disconnected from their electrical cabling any longer than is absolutely necessary, in this state they are unstable and the risk of accidental detonation is introduced. Rest a disconnected airbag with the pad surface facing upwards and never rest anything on the pad. Store it on a secure flat surface, away from flammable materials, high heat sources, oils, grease, detergents or water, and never leave it unattended.

g) The SRS indicator light should extinguish 3 seconds after the ignition switch is turned to position "II". If this is not the case, check the electrical system connections as soon as possible.

h) The airbag control unit and rotary contact unit are non-serviceable components and no attempt should be made to carry out repairs or modifications to them.

i) Only use the recommended special bolts when fitting the airbag assembly. Do not use any other type of bolt.

j) Never invert the airbag unit.

k) Renew the airbag unit and rotary contact unit every ten years, regardless of condition.

l) Return an unwanted airbag unit to your Rover dealer for safe disposal. Do not endanger others by careless disposal of a unit.

2 Electrical fault-finding - general information

Warning: Always remove rings, watches, etc. before working on a vehicle electrical system. Even with the battery disconnected, capacitive discharge can occur if a component live terminal is earthed through a metal object, thereby causing a shock or burn.
Do not reverse the battery connections. The alternator or any other component having semi-conductor circuitry could be irreparably damaged.
The battery leads and alternator multi-plug must be disconnected before carrying out any electric welding on the vehicle if component damage is to be avoided.
Never disconnect the battery terminals or alternator multi-plug connector when the engine is running.
A short-circuit that occurs in the wiring between a circuit's battery supply and its fuse will not cause the fuse in that particular circuit to blow. This part of the circuit is unprotected - bear this in mind when fault-finding on the vehicle's electrical system.

1 A typical electrical circuit consists of an electrical component, any switches, relays, motors, fuses, fusible links or circuit breakers related to that component and the wiring and connectors that link the component to both the battery and the chassis. To help you pinpoint an electrical circuit problem, wiring diagrams are included at the end of this Chapter.

2 Before tackling any troublesome electrical circuit, first study the appropriate wiring diagram to get a complete understanding of what components are included in that individual circuit. Trouble spots, for instance, can be narrowed down by noting if other components related to the circuit are operating properly. If several components or circuits fail at one time, the problem is probably in a shared fuse or earth connection, as more than one circuit can be routed through the same connections.

3 Electrical problems usually stem from simple causes, such as loose or corroded connections, a faulty earth, a blown fuse, a melted fusible link or a faulty relay. Visually inspect the condition of all fuses, wires and connections in a problem circuit before testing the components. Use the diagrams to note which terminal connections will need to be checked in order to pinpoint the trouble spot.

4 The basic tools needed for electrical fault-finding include a circuit tester or voltmeter (a 12-volt bulb with a set of test leads can also be used), a continuity tester, a battery and set of test leads, and a jumper wire, preferably with a circuit breaker incorporated, which can be used to bypass electrical components. Before attempting to locate a problem with test instruments, use the wiring diagram to decide where to make the connections.

Voltage checks

5 Voltage checks should be performed if a circuit is not functioning properly. Connect one lead of a circuit tester to either the negative battery terminal or a known good earth. Connect the other lead to a connector in the circuit being tested, preferably nearest to the battery or fuse. If the tester bulb lights, voltage is present; this means that the part of the circuit between the connector and the battery is problem-free. Continue checking the rest of the circuit in the same fashion. When you reach a point at which no voltage is present the problem lies between that point and the last test point with voltage. Most problems can be traced to a loose connection. **Note:** *Bear in mind that some circuits are live only when the ignition switch is switched to a particular position.*

Finding a short circuit

6 One method of finding a short circuit is to remove the fuse and connect a test lamp or voltmeter to the fuse terminals with all the relevant electrical components switched off. There should be no voltage present in the circuit. Move the wiring from side to side while watching the test lamp. If the bulb lights there is a short to earth somewhere in that area, probably where the insulation has rubbed through. The same test can be performed on each component in the circuit, even a switch.

Earth check

7 To check whether a component is properly earthed, disconnect the battery and connect one lead of a self-powered test lamp (sometimes known as a continuity tester) to a known good earth point. Connect the other lead to the wire or earth connection being tested. If the lamp lights, the earth is sound; if not, it must be rectified.

8 The battery negative terminal is connected to "earth" - the metal of the car body - and most systems are wired so that they only receive a positive feed, the current returning via the metal of the car's body. This means that the component mounting and the body form part of that circuit and loose or corroded mountings, therefore, can cause a range of electrical faults; note that these may range from total failure of a circuit to a puzzling partial fault. In particular, lamps may shine dimly (especially when another circuit sharing the same earth point is in operation), motors (eg wiper motors or the radiator cooling fan motor) may run slowly and the operation of one circuit may have an apparently unrelated effect on another. **Note:** *A poor earth may not cause the circuit's fuse to blow; in fact it may reduce the load on the fuse.*

9 If an earth connection is thought to be faulty, dismantle the connection and clean back to bare metal both the bodyshell and the wire terminal or the component's earth connection mating surface. Be careful to remove all traces of dirt and corrosion, then use a knife to trim away any paint, so that a clean metal-to-metal joint is made. On reassembly, tighten the joint fasteners securely; if a wire terminal is being refitted, use serrated washers between the terminal and the bodyshell to ensure a clean and secure connection. When the connection is remade, prevent the onset of corrosion in the future by applying a coat of petroleum jelly or silicone-based grease or by spraying on (at regular intervals) a proprietary ignition sealer or a water dispersant lubricant.

10 The car's wiring harness has four multiple-earth connections referred to in the wiring diagrams as Earth Header joints. Each of these serves several circuits; their locations are as follows.

a) *Earth Header 1 - Attached to the front of the right-hand inner wing panel, next to the headlamp unit.*
b) *Earth Header 2 - Attached to the front of the left-hand inner wing panel, next to the headlamp unit.*
c) *Earth number 3 is the radio/cassette unit earth on the facia support rail.*
d) *Earth Header 4 - Attached to the luggage compartment left-hand side, below the seat belt retractor.*

11 All engine/transmission-mounted electrical components are earthed by the lead attached to the starter motor upper mounting bolt, which is connected to the battery negative terminal and the main earth point on the body front panel.

Continuity check

12 A continuity check is necessary to determine if there are any breaks in a circuit. With the circuit switched off (ie no power in the circuit), a self-powered test lamp (sometimes known as a continuity tester) can be used to check the circuit. Connect the test leads to both ends of the circuit (or to the positive end and a good earth); if the test lamp lights, the circuit is passing current properly. If the lamp does not light, there is a break somewhere in the circuit.

13 The same procedure can be used to test a switch, by connecting the continuity tester to the switch terminals. With the switch in the relevant position, the test lamp should light.

Finding an open circuit

14 When checking for possible open circuits, it is often difficult to locate them by sight because oxidation or terminal misalignment are hidden by the connectors; merely moving a connector on a sensor or in the wiring harness may correct the fault. Remember this if an open circuit is indicated when fault-finding in a circuit. Intermittent problems may also be caused by oxidised or loose connections.

General

15 Electrical fault-finding is simple if you keep in mind that all electrical circuits are basically electricity flowing from the battery, through the wires, switches, relays, fuses and fusible links to each electrical component (light bulb, motor, etc.) and to earth, from where it is passed back to the battery. Any electrical problem is an interruption in the flow of electricity from the battery.

3 Fuses, fusible links and relays - location and renewal

Fuses

1 The fusebox is located in the passenger compartment, on the right-hand end of the facia.

2 Access is gained by using a coin to turn the two fasteners through quarter of a turn, then unhooking the cover's bottom edge from the facia. Symbols on the reverse of the cover indicate the circuits protected by the fuses and four spare fuses are supplied together with plastic tweezers to remove and fit them. Further details on fuse ratings and circuits protected are given in the Specifications Section of this Chapter.

3 To remove a fuse, first switch off the circuit concerned (or the ignition), then fit the tweezers and pull the fuse out of its terminals **(see illustration)**. Slide the fuse sideways from the tweezers. The wire within the fuse is clearly visible; if the fuse is blown it will be broken or melted.

4 Always renew a fuse with one of an identical rating; never use a fuse with a different rating from the original or substitute anything else. Never renew a fuse more than once without tracing the source of the trouble. The fuse rating is stamped on top of the fuse; note that the fuses are also colour-coded for easy recognition.

5 If a new fuse blows immediately, find the cause before renewing it again; a short to earth as a result of faulty insulation is most likely. Where a fuse protects more than one circuit, try to isolate the defect by switching on each circuit in turn (if possible) until the fuse blows again.

3.3 Removing a fuse

6 If any of the spare fuses are used, always replace them immediately so that a spare of each rating is available.

Fusebox

7 To remove the fusebox, disconnect the battery negative lead, then remove the fusebox cover from the facia.

8 Unplug the two connector plugs from the top row of the fusebox panel (marked "IGN" and "FACIA") and unplug the two connector plugs clipped to brackets at the left-hand end of the panel.

9 Unscrew the two bolts securing the panel, then lower it until the eight connector plugs can be disconnected from the panel's reverse (front) face. The wiring is complex but the connector locations are clearly marked on the panel; make careful notes as to the connections before disconnecting any of the wires. Remove the panel.

10 Refitting is the reverse of the removal procedure; ensure that the wiring is correctly reconnected and routed.

Fusible links

11 The fusible link box is located in the engine compartment, on the body left-hand side member next to the battery; unclip the box cover to expose the links.

12 Details of link ratings and circuits protected are given in the Specifications Section of this Chapter; the links are numbered from front to rear.

13 Since the fusible links are almost identical to the fuses in form and function, refer to paragraphs 3 to 6 above for details of removal and refitting, noting that the links must be extracted and installed by hand, as a removal tool is not provided **(see illustration)**.

Note: *A blown fusible link indicates a serious wiring or system fault which must be diagnosed before the link is renewed.*

Relays

14 The Specifications Section of this Chapter gives full information on the location and function of the various relays fitted; refer to the relevant wiring diagram for details of wiring connections.

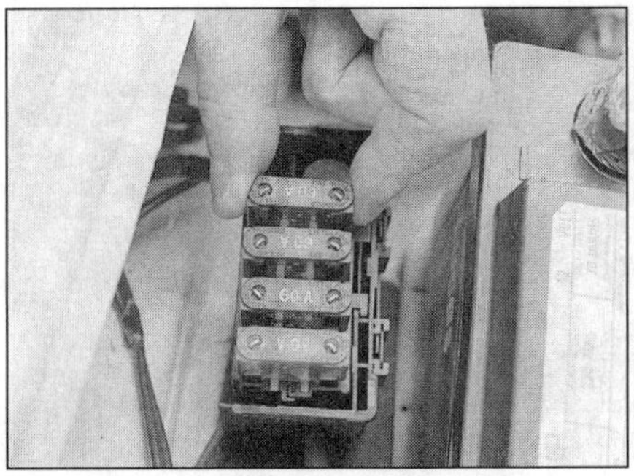

3.13 Removing a fusible link

15 A relay is an electrically operated switch that is used for the following reasons.

a) A relay can switch a heavy current at a distance, thus allowing the use of lighter gauge wiring and switch contacts.

b) A relay can receive more than one control input, unlike a mechanical switch.

c) A relay can have a "timer" function - eg the windscreen or rear window wiper relays.

16 If a circuit or system controlled by a relay develops a fault and the relay is suspect, operate the system; if the relay is functioning it should be possible to hear it click as it is energised. If this is the case the fault lies with the components or wiring of the system. If the relay is not being energised then either the relay is not receiving a main supply or a switching voltage or the relay itself is faulty. Testing is by the substitution of a known good unit but be careful; while some relays are identical in appearance and in operation, others look similar but perform different functions.

17 To renew a relay, disconnect the battery then simply pull direct from the socket and press in the new relay **(see illustrations)**. Reconnect the battery on completion.

18 On models with fuel-injected engines, certain relays are contained in the relay module attached to the fuel-injection/ignition system ECU. To remove this, disconnect its two connector plugs, release the clip and slide it back to withdraw it from the mounting bracket **(see illustrations)**. The complete module must be renewed, even if only one of the relays is faulty.

3.18a Unplug connectors (arrowed) to disconnect relay module wiring . . .

3.18b . . . and release clip (arrowed) to separate module from mounting bracket

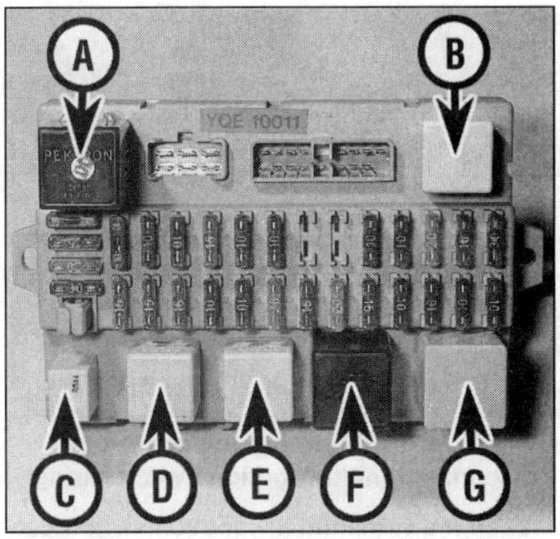

3.17a Relays on fusebox panel rear face

A Interior lamp delay/Lamps-on alarm unit
B Heated rear window relay
C Headlamp relay
D Ignition relay
E Electric front window/auxiliary relay
F Direction indicator/hazard warning relay
G Dim-dip unit

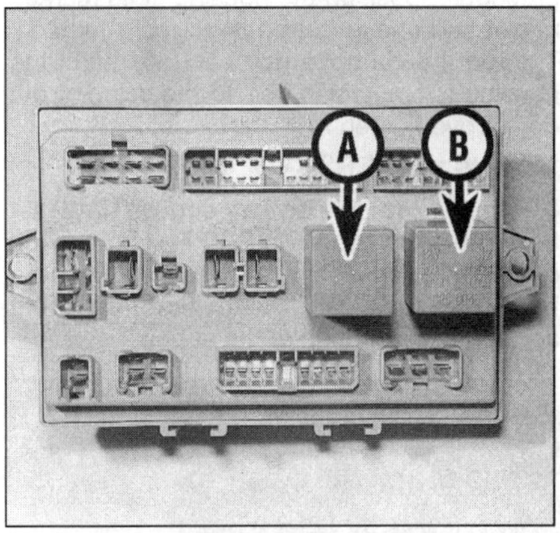

3.17b Relays on fusebox panel front (reverse) face

A Windscreen wiper relay
B Rear window wiper relay

4 Switches - removal and refitting

Note: *Disconnect the battery negative lead before removing any switch, and reconnect the lead after refitting the switch*

Ignition switch

1 Refer to Chapter 10 for details of switch removal and refitting. A Rover dealer will be able to tell you whether the switch can be obtained separately from the steering lock.

Steering column multi-function switches

Models without SRS

2 Remove the steering wheel and steering column nacelle. Disconnect the switch wiring as described in Chapter 10 **(see illustration)**.

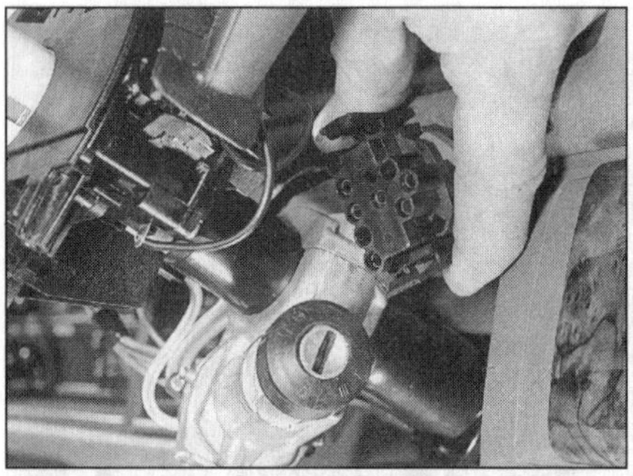

4.2 Press together locking tabs to disconnect multi-function switch wiring

3 Each individual multi-function switch can be removed by pressing together its retaining tongues and sliding the switch out of the housing **(see illustration)**.

4 To remove the complete assembly, mark the location on the column of the switch centre housing, then slacken (but do not remove) the housing clamp screw and withdraw the assembly **(see illustration)**.

5 Refitting is the reverse of the removal procedure; position the housing at its marked height and ensure that it is correctly located. Tighten the clamp screw securely, until the housing is firmly clamped to the column, but do not overtighten it.

Models with SRS

6 Remove the ignition key and wait at least ten minutes to allow the SRS system backup circuit to fully discharge. Disconnect both battery leads, earth lead first, to avoid accidental detonation of the airbag.

4.15 Removing a switch from the instrument panel cowl - showing locking tabs

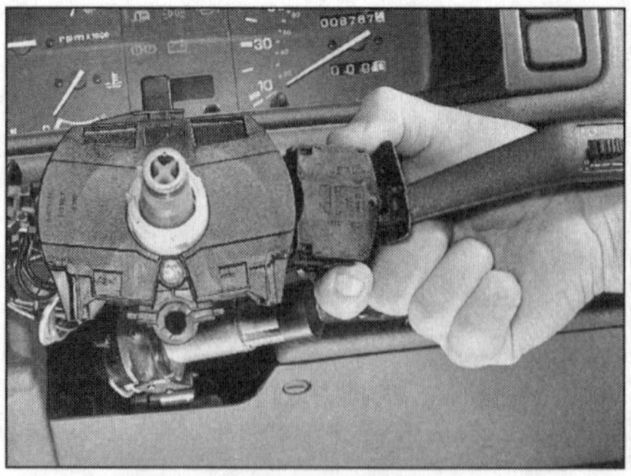

4.3 Multi-function switches can be removed individually . . .

7 Set the steering in the dead-ahead position.

8 Remove the airbag unit, followed by the airbag control unit and rotary contact unit.

9 Proceed as described in paragraphs 2 to 5, above.

10 Upon completion of refitting the airbag unit, reconnect the battery negative cable and turn the ignition switch to the "II" position. Check the condition of the system by observing the SRS warning light located in the steering wheel centre pad. The light should stay illuminated for 3 seconds whilst the system performs a self-diagnosis test. If the test is satisfactory, the light will extinguish. If the test is unsatisfactory, the light will remain on or fail to illuminate at all, denoting that the system must be serviced as soon as possible.

Horn push switch

11 Where the steering wheel has a horn push switch fitted to each of its arms, remove each switch by carefully using the flat blade of a small screwdriver to lever it from position.

12 Detach the two electrical connectors from the switch and remove it.

13 Refitting is the reversal of removal. Test the horn after refitting each switch.

Instrument panel switches

Removal

14 The rear foglamp, heated rear window, rear window wiper and rear window wash/wipe switches are removed as follows

15 Check that the switch is in the "off" position, then taking great care not to scratch or damage the switch or its surround, prise it out of the instrument panel cowl until the connector plug can be reached to disconnect it **(see illustration)**. **Note:** *If a switch cannot be removed without risk of damage, remove the instrument panel cowl, disconnect the switch wiring and push the switch out from behind; this latter method is preferred as it minimises the risk of damage.*

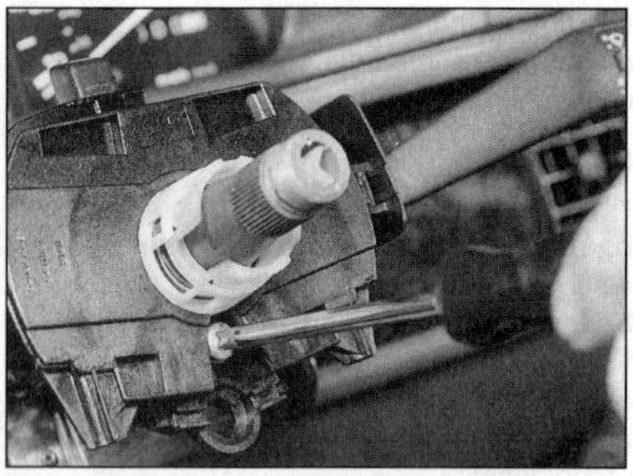

4.4 . . . or as a complete unit, by slackening clamp screw

16 To remove the heater blower switch, remove the instrument panel cowl and disconnect the switch wiring. Prise off the switch knob and unscrew the retaining nut to release the switch **(see illustration)**.

Refitting

17 Refitting is the reverse of the removal procedure.

Hazard warning switch

18 The switch is part of the left-hand multi-function switch **(see illustration)**.

Glovebox lamp switch

Removal

19 Open the glovebox lid.

20 Taking great care not to scratch or damage the switch or its surround, prise the switch out of the glovebox until the connectors can be removed to disconnect it **(see illustration)**.

Refitting

21 Refitting is the reverse of the removal procedure.

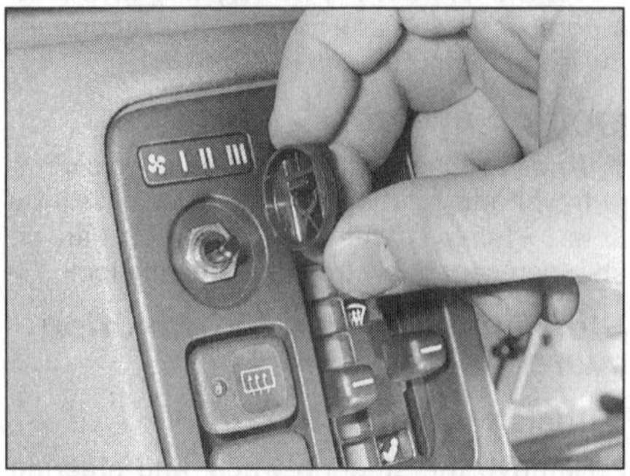

4.16 Prise off heater blower switch knob to expose switch retaining nut

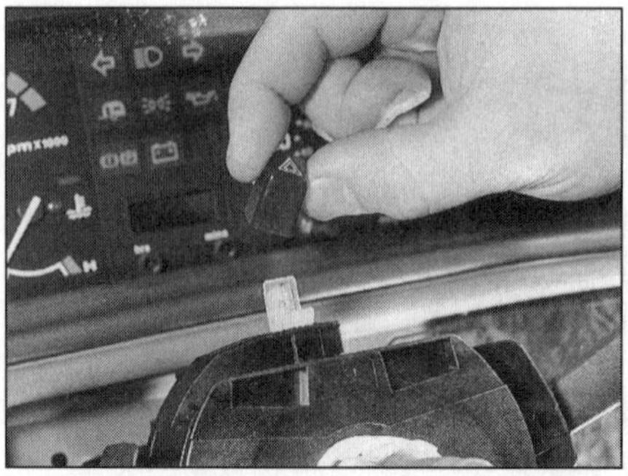

4.18 Hazard warning switch is part of multi-function switch assembly

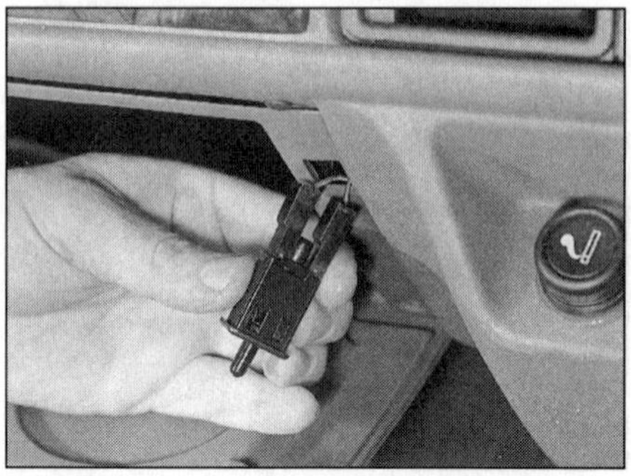

4.20 Removing glovebox lamp switch

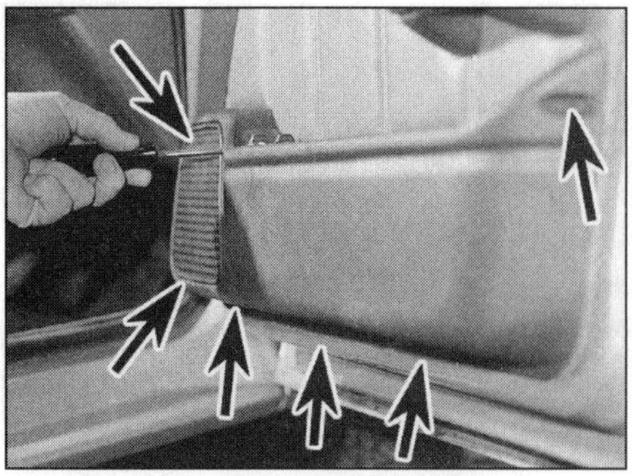

4.24a Door pocket retaining screw locations (arrowed)

Choke switch

Removal

22 Remove the ashtray and disconnect the switch wire from the choke cable, then prise out the clip securing the cable to the facia and withdraw the cable until the switch can be removed from it.

Refitting

23 Refitting is the reverse of the removal procedure.

Electric front window switches

Removal

24 Remove the seven screws securing the door pocket to the door and withdraw the pocket until the switch connectors can be unplugged to disconnect the wiring **(see illustrations)**.

25 Remove the two screws to release the switch bracket, then release the switch from the bracket.

Refitting

26 Refitting is the reverse of the removal procedure.

Interior lamp switches

27 The interior lamp is controlled by a switch mounted in each (front) door pillar and by a switch in the lamp assembly itself.

28 To remove a door pillar switch, remove its retaining screw **(see illustration)** and ease the switch out of the pillar, then disconnect the switch wire, taking care not to allow it to drop back into the pillar; refitting is the reverse of the removal procedure.

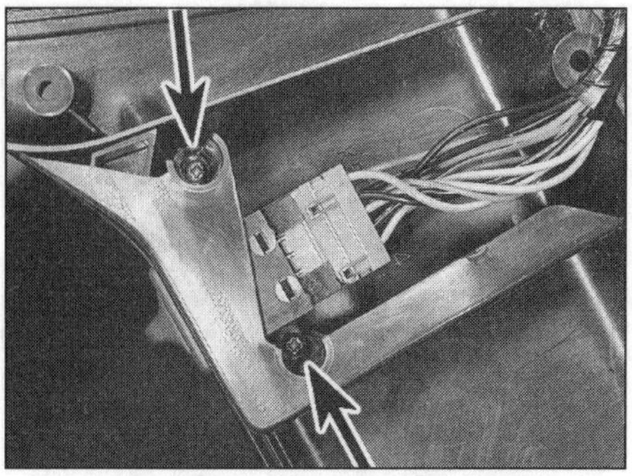

4.24b Electric front window switch mounting screws (arrowed)

29 The roof-mounted switch is part of the lamp assembly.

Luggage compartment lamp switch

30 The switch comprises two contacts which are part of the tailgate latch assembly. Refer to Chapter 11.

Oil pressure switch

Removal

31 The switch is screwed into the oil filter adapter **(see illustration)**. Access is extremely awkward. Either remove the switch working from underneath, with the car raised and supported on axle stands (see "*Jacking and Vehicle Support*"), or partially remove the alternator so that the switch can be removed from above.

32 Release the wire clip and disconnect the switch wiring connector plug, then unscrew the switch. Use clean rag to pack the opening in the adapter, to minimise the loss of oil.

Refitting

33 On refitting, clean the switch threads and renew the sealing washer if one is fitted. If a sealing washer is not fitted, apply a thin smear of suitable sealant to the threads.

34 Remove the packing rag and screw in the switch. Tighten it securely but do not overtighten it. Note the specified torque wrench setting.

Electric cooling fan thermostatic switch

35 Refer to Chapter 3 for details of switch removal, refitting and testing.

4.28 Removing an interior lamp door pillar switch

Throttle pedal switch

Removal

36 Remove the throttle pedal.

37 Disconnect the switch wiring by unplugging the connector and releasing it from its bracket, then unclip the wiring from its stud.

38 Prise out the C-clip securing the switch to its bracket, then withdraw the switch, noting the wave washer.

Refitting

39 Refitting is the reverse of the removal procedure. Ensure that the wiring is routed correctly and secured clear of the pedals **(see illustration)**.

Fuel cut-off inertia switch

Testing

40 If the switch is thought to be faulty, unplug its connector and bridge the connector's terminals on the wiring harness side, then switch on the ignition. If the fuel pump works, the switch is proven faulty and must be renewed **(see illustration)**.

Removal

41 Remove the two screws securing the switch to the body left-hand side member, withdraw the switch and unplug its connector to disconnect the wiring.

Refitting

42 Refitting is the reverse of the removal procedure. Ensure that the switch is set before attempting to start the engine.

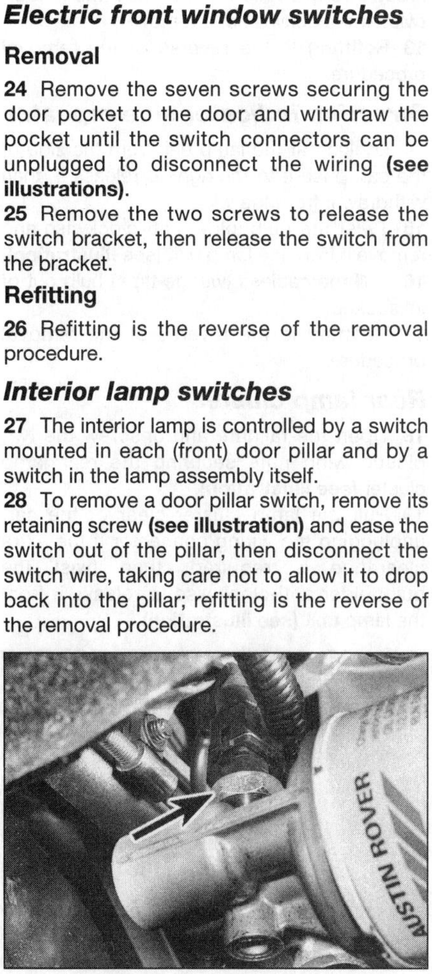

4.31 Oil pressure switch (arrowed)

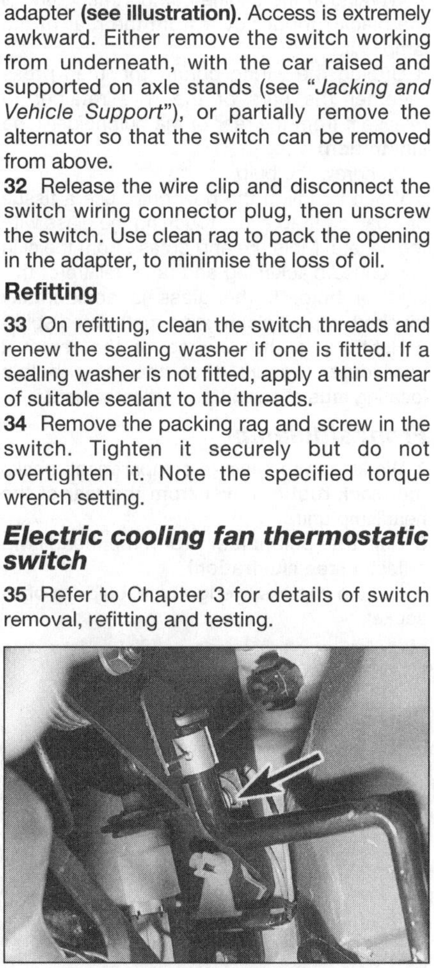

4.39 Location of throttle pedal switch (arrowed)

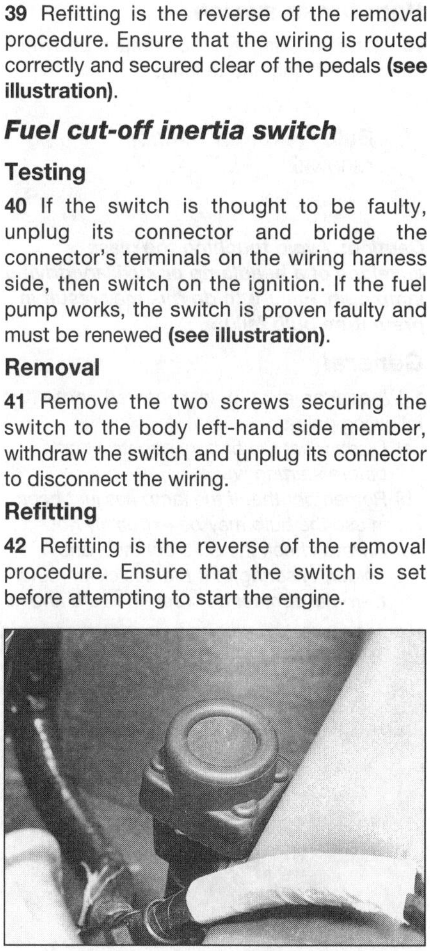

4.40 Fuel cut-off inertia switch is mounted on left-hand body side member

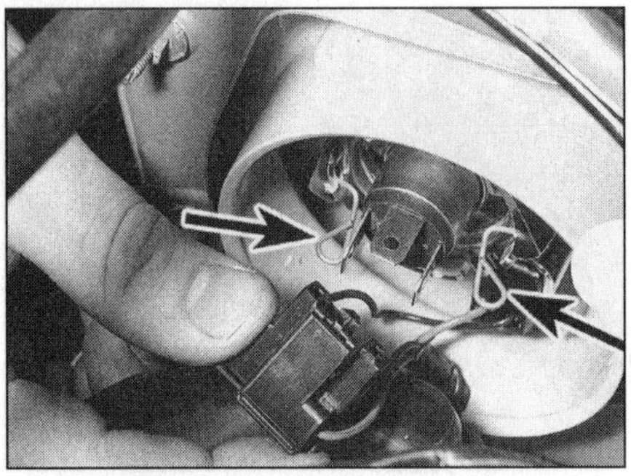

5.3 Release retainer (arrowed) to remove bulb

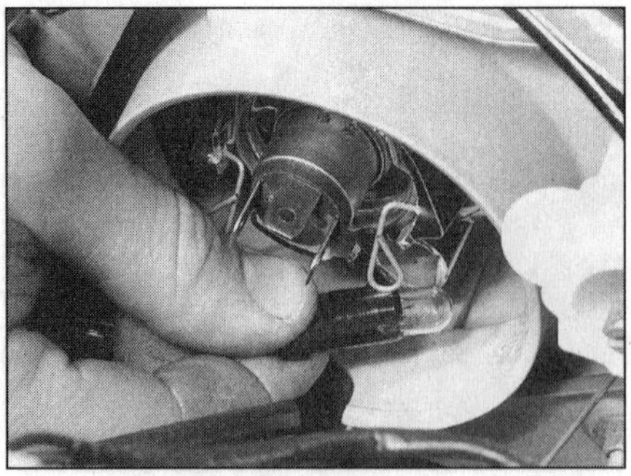

5.8 Removing front sidelamp bulbholder from headlamp unit

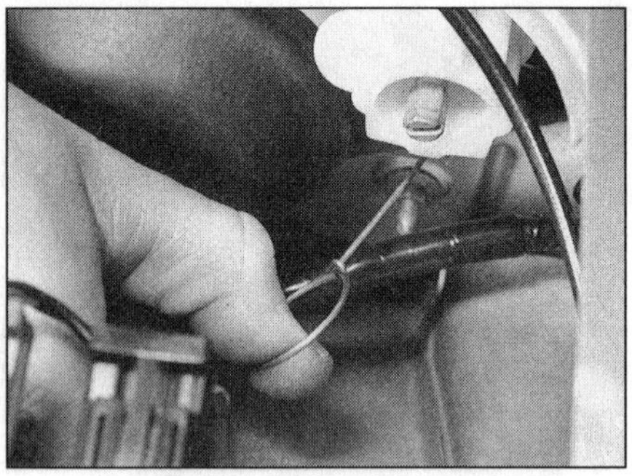

5.11 Pull wire ring to release spring clip . . .

Inlet manifold pre-heater temperature switch

43 Refer to Chapter 3 for details of switch removal, refitting and testing.

Reversing lamp switch

44 Refer to Chapter 7 for details of switch removal, refitting and testing.

Stop-lamp switch

45 Refer to Chapter 9 for details of switch removal, refitting and testing.

Handbrake switch

46 Refer to Chapter 9 for details of switch removal, refitting and testing.

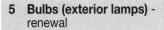

5 Bulbs (exterior lamps) - renewal

Caution: Avoid touching the glass envelope of a headlamp or auxiliary driving lamp bulb. Failure to do this may result in premature bulb failure.

General

1 Whenever a bulb is renewed, note the following points.

a) *Disconnect the battery negative lead before starting work.*
b) *Remember that if the lamp has just been in use the bulb may be extremely hot.*
c) *Always check the bulb contacts and holder, ensuring that there is clean metal-to-metal contact between the bulb and its live(s) and earth. Clean off any corrosion or dirt before fitting a new bulb.*
d) *Wherever bayonet-type bulbs are fitted (see Specifications) ensure that the live contact(s) bear firmly against the bulb contact.*
e) *Always ensure that the new bulb is of the correct rating and that it is completely clean before fitting it; this applies particularly to headlamp bulbs.*

Headlamp

2 Working in the engine compartment, unclip the black rubber cover from the rear of the lamp unit.
3 Unplug the wiring connector, then press together the ears of the wire retainer to release it from the rear of the bulbholder **(see illustration)**.
4 Withdraw the bulb.
5 When handling the new bulb, use a tissue or clean cloth to avoid touching the glass with the fingers. Moisture and grease from the skin can cause blackening and rapid failure of this type of bulb. If the glass is accidentally touched, wipe it clean using methylated spirit.
6 Refitting is the reverse of the removal procedure. Ensure that the new bulb's locating tabs align with the reflector slots.

Front sidelamp

7 Working in the engine compartment, unclip the black rubber cover from the rear of the headlamp unit.
8 Pull the bulbholder from the headlamp reflector **(see illustration)**.
9 Pull the capless (wedge-type) bulb out of its socket.
10 Refitting is the reverse of the removal procedure.

Front direction indicator

11 Working in the engine compartment next to the appropriate headlamp unit, pull the wire ring to release the indicator lamp unit, then pull it forwards, clear of the car **(see illustration)**.
12 Twist the bulbholder anti-clockwise to remove it from the rear of the lamp unit **(see illustration)**. Press the bulb into the holder, twist anti-clockwise and remove.
13 Refitting is the reverse of the removal procedure.

Direction indicator side repeater

14 Looking at the lamp unit from the side of the car, push it to the right to release it, then withdraw it from the wing.
15 Twist the bulbholder anti-clockwise and remove it from the lamp unit **(see illustration)**.
16 Pull the capless (wedge-type) bulb out of its socket.
17 Refitting is the reverse of the removal procedure.

Rear lamp cluster

18 Open the tailgate and unscrew the two plastic wing nuts securing the rear lamp cluster **(see illustration)**.
19 Pull the lamp cluster clear of the car, unplugging the wiring connector if the extra clearance is required, then twist the bulbholder anti-clockwise to release it from the lamp unit **(see illustration)**.

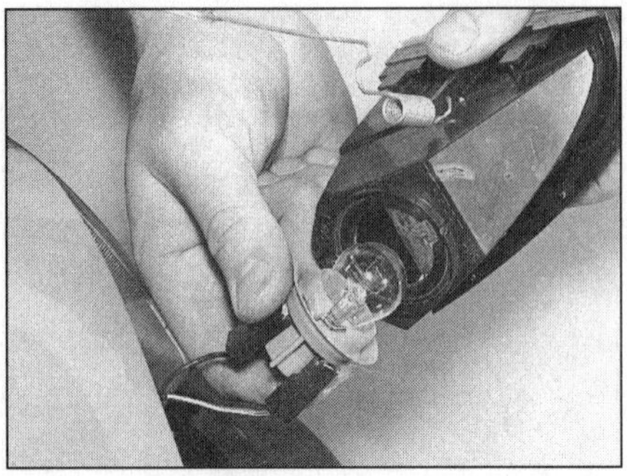

5.12 . . . so that lamp unit can be removed from car and bulbholder detached

5.15 Direction indicator side repeater lamp detached from front wing

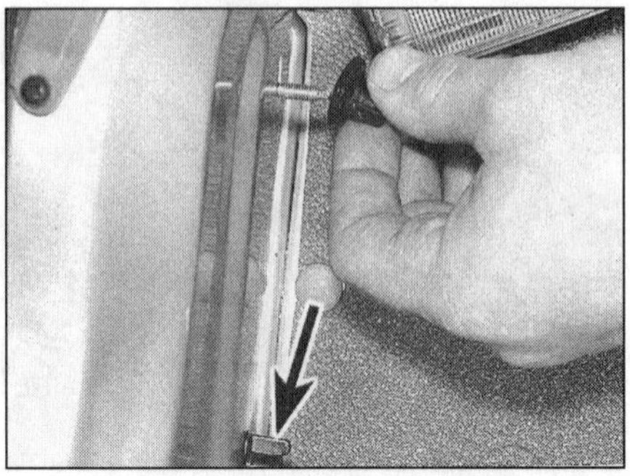

5.18 Unscrew plastic wing nuts (one arrowed) . . .

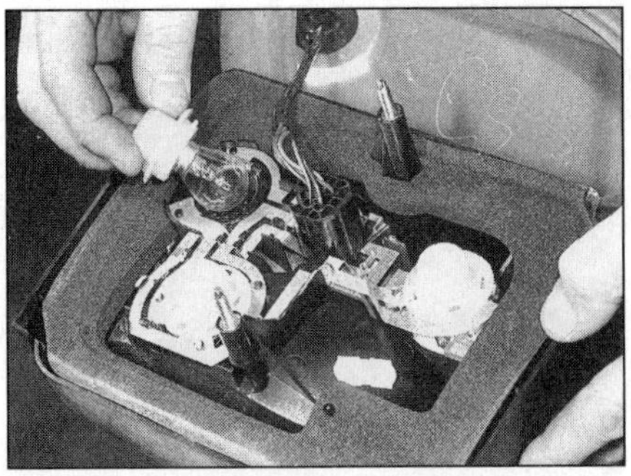

5.19 . . . so that rear lamp cluster can be detached from car and bulbholders removed

20 All bulbs are a bayonet-fitting; press the bulb into its holder, twist anti-clockwise and remove.

21 Refitting is the reverse of the removal procedure.

Rear foglamp

Note: *Only the right-hand foglamp unit contains a bulb and fittings; the other is a dummy that is clipped into the rear bumper cover.*

22 Remove the two screws securing the lamp lens, then withdraw the lens **(see illustration)**.

23 The bulb is bayonet-fitting; press the bulb into its holder, twist anti-clockwise and remove **(see illustration)**.

Number plate lamp

24 Remove the two screws securing the lamp unit, then withdraw the lamp unit **(see illustration)**.

25 The bulb is a festoon type which is prised out of its spring contacts.

26 Refitting is the reverse of the removal procedure, but ensure that the contacts are sufficiently tensioned to hold the bulb firmly.

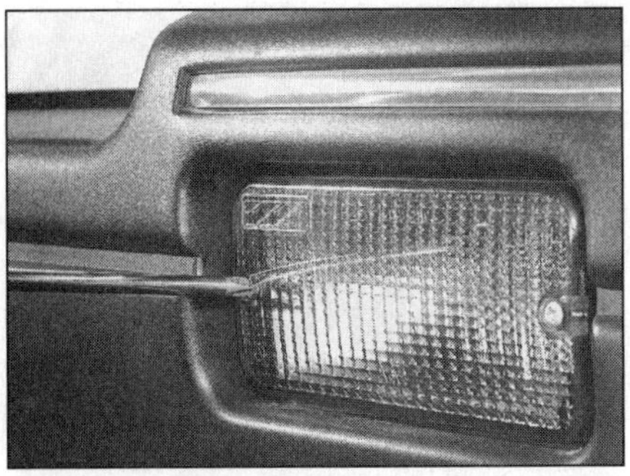

5.22 Remove two lens screws and withdraw lens . . .

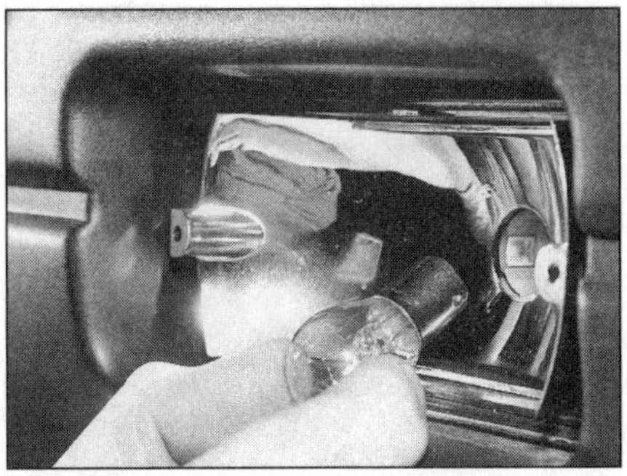

5.23 . . . to renew rear foglamp bulb

5.24 Number plate lamps are secured by two screws

6 Bulbs (interior lamps) - renewal

General

1 Refer to the information given for exterior lamp bulb renewal.

Interior lamp

2 Unclip the lamp unit by using a small flat-bladed screwdriver to prise it out of the roof console **(see illustration)**.

3 The bulb is a bayonet-fitting; press the bulb into its holder, twist anti-clockwise and remove.

4 Refitting is the reverse of the removal procedure.

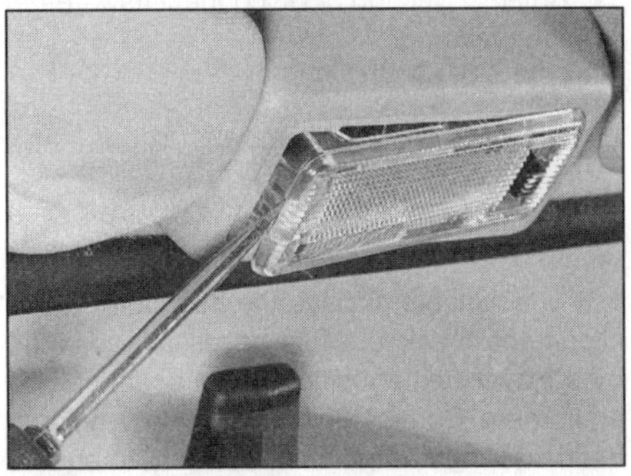

6.2 Removing interior lamp assembly from roof console

Glovebox lamp

5 Unclip the lamp unit by using a small flat-bladed screwdriver to prise it out of the ceiling of the glovebox **(see illustration)**.

6 The bulb is a festoon type which is prised out of its spring contacts.

7 Refitting is the reverse of the removal procedure, but ensure that the contacts are sufficiently tensioned to hold the bulb firmly.

Luggage compartment lamp

8 Disconnecting the lamps wiring if necessary to improve access, unclip the lamp unit from its mounting bracket **(see illustration)**.

9 The bulb is a bayonet-fitting; press the bulb into its holder, twist anti-clockwise and remove.

10 Refitting is the reverse of the removal procedure.

Instrument panel illumination and warning lamps

11 Remove the instrument panel.

12 Twist the bulbholder anti-clockwise and withdraw it from the rear of the panel **(see illustrations)**.

13 In some cases the bulbs are integral with their holders, but in others the bulbs can be renewed separately; seek the advice of a Rover dealer. Be very careful to ensure that

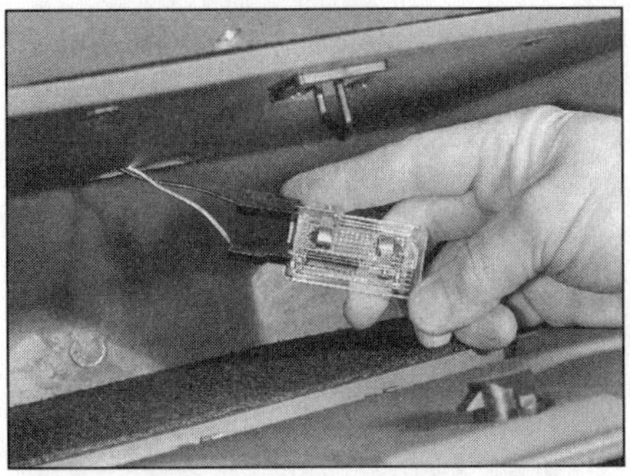

6.5 Glovebox lamp unit is clipped to glovebox ceiling

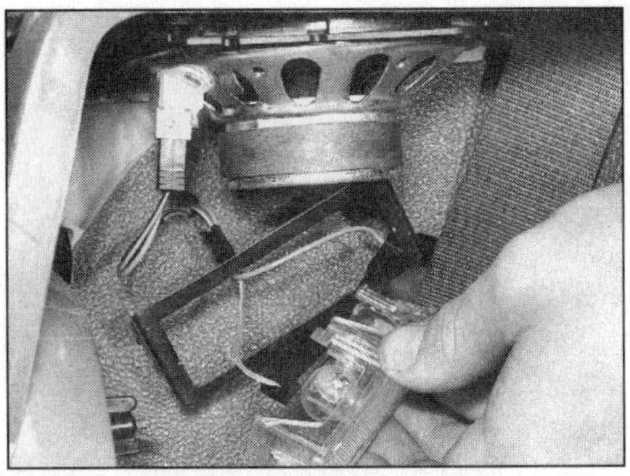

6.8 Unclip luggage compartment lamp unit to remove bulb

6.12a Removing a bulbholder from the rear of the instrument panel

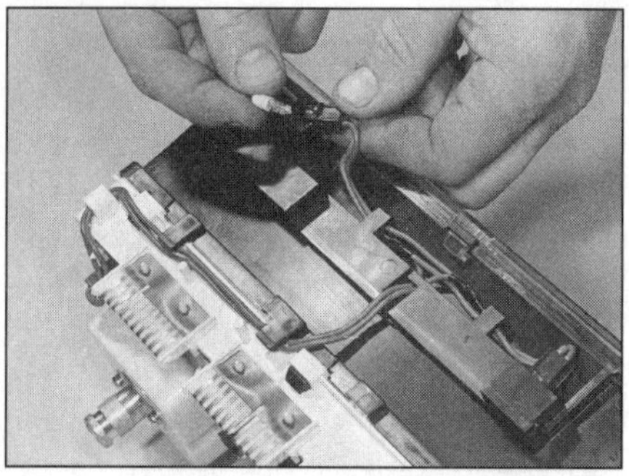
6.12b Removing a panel illuminating bulb from the instrument panel

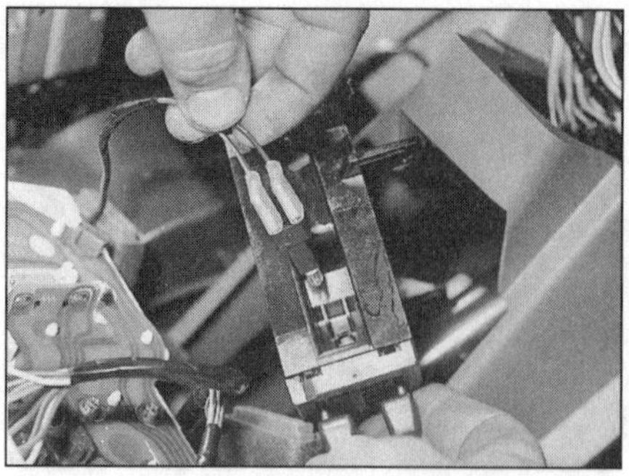
6.15 Heater control panel illuminating bulb

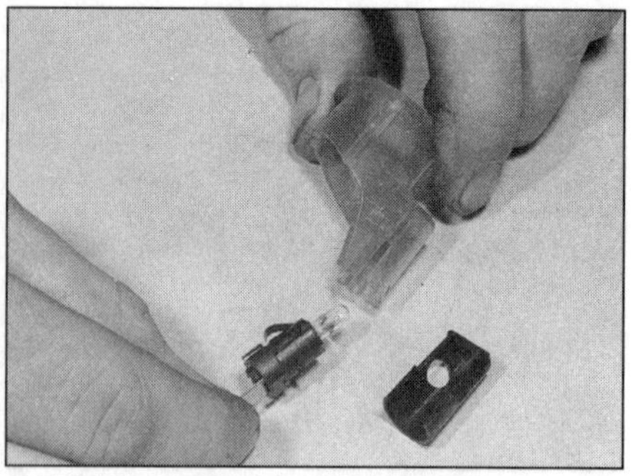
6.18 Cigar lighter illuminating bulb

the new bulbs are of the correct rating, the same as those removed; this is especially important in the case of the ignition/battery charging warning lamp.

14 Refitting is the reverse of the removal procedure.

Heater control panel illumination

15 Remove the control panel. The bulb can then be unplugged from the panel **(see illustration).**

16 Seek the advice of a Rover dealer as to the bulb's fitting or wattage.

17 Refitting is the reverse of the removal procedure.

Cigar lighter illumination

18 The bulb is secured in a container that is clipped to the side of the cigar lighter assembly **(see illustration).**

19 Remove the cigar lighter.

20 Unplug the bulbholder to remove it from the lighter body. Seek the advice of a Rover dealer as to the bulb's fitting or wattage.

21 Refitting is the reverse of the removal procedure.

Hazard warning indicator

22 Remove the red plastic cover and pull the capless (wedge-type) bulb out of its holder.

23 Refitting is the reverse of the removal procedure.

Switch illumination

24 The rear foglamp, heated rear window, heater blower, rear window wiper, rear window wash/wipe and electric window switches are fitted with an illuminating bulb; some are also fitted with warning bulbs to show when the circuit concerned is operating.

25 Seek the advice of a Rover dealer as to whether the bulb can be renewed separately from the switch or not.

7 Exterior lamp units - removal and refitting

Headlamp unit

Removal

1 Either unclip the black rubber cover from the rear of the lamp unit, pull off the headlamp bulb wiring connector and unplug the sidelamp bulbholder, or disconnect all lamp unit wiring by unplugging its connector.

2 Remove the direction indicator lamp unit.

3 Unscrew the three nuts securing the headlamp unit and remove it **(see illustration).**

4 Release the six retaining clips to remove the headlamp lens, if required **(see illustration).**

Refitting

5 Refitting is the reverse of the removal procedure. Check and adjust if necessary the headlamp alignment.

Front direction indicator

6 Refer to Section 5.

Direction indicator side repeater

7 Refer to Section 5.

Rear lamp cluster

8 Refer to Section 5.

Rear foglamp

Removal

9 Remove the rear bumper. Remove the two retaining screws to release the lamp unit from the bumper cover **(see illustration).**

Refitting

10 Refitting is the reverse of the removal procedure.

Number plate lamps

11 Refer to Section 5. Disconnect its wires to release the lamp.

8 Headlamps - beam alignment

1 It is advisable to have the headlamp beam alignment checked and if necessary adjusted by a Rover dealer using optical beam setting equipment. Correct alignment of the headlamp beams is most important, not only to ensure good vision for the driver but also to protect other drivers from being dazzled.

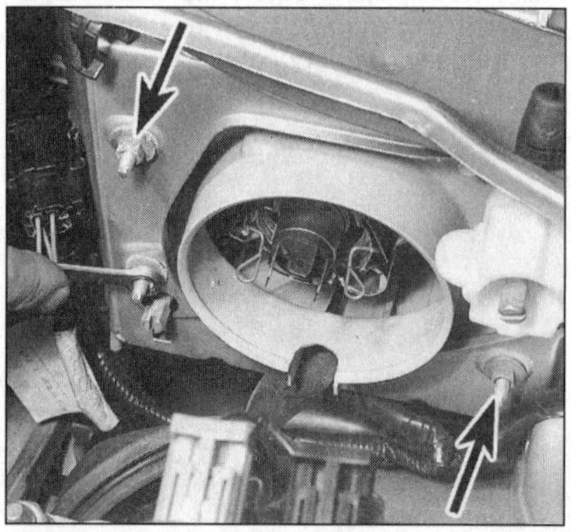
7.3 Removing headlamp unit securing nuts (other two arrowed)

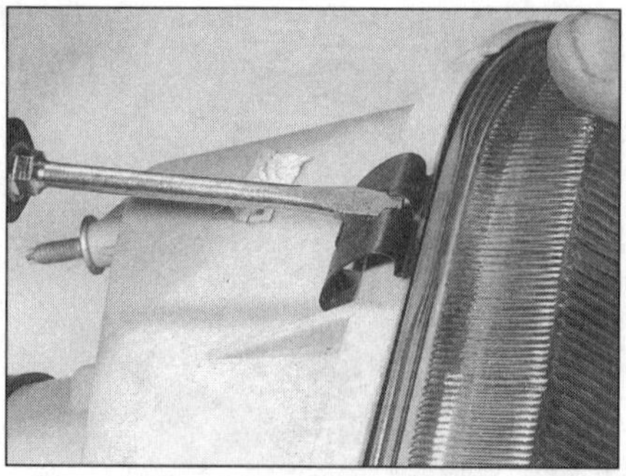
7.4 Headlamp lens is secured by clips - release as shown

7.9 Rear foglamp is secured by two screws (arrowed) to rear bumper cover

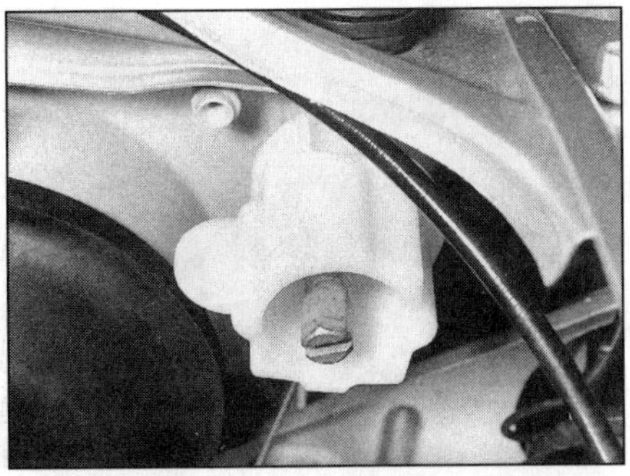

8.2 **Headlamp height-setting plastic knob (in normal-load position), with vertical alignment adjuster screw inside**

8.3 **Headlamp lateral alignment adjuster screw (arrowed)**

2 The headlamp beam height may be adjusted to compensate for the load being carried by turning the white plastic knob on the rear of each headlamp unit. The normal setting is with the knobs turned (anti-clockwise) to the left. If a heavy load is carried, the headlamp beams should be lowered to compensate by turning both knobs fully (clockwise) to the right. Ensure that both knobs are in the same position at all times and in the correct position for the load being carried **(see illustration).**

3 In an emergency, adjustment of the headlamps may be made by turning the adjuster screws on the rear of each headlamp unit. The upper screws (inside the plastic knobs) are for vertical adjustment and the lower screws for lateral adjustment **(see illustration).**

4 The car should be at kerb weight with the driver seated, the headlamp height-setting knobs in the normal-load position, the tyres correctly inflated and the suspension ride heights correctly set. Park the vehicle on level ground, approximately 5 metres in front of a flat wall or garage door and bounce it to settle the suspension.

5 Draw a vertical line on the wall or door corresponding to the centre-line of the car. (This can be determined by marking with crayon the centres of the windscreen and rear window, then viewing the wall or door from the rear of the car).

6 With the centre-line established, construct the other lines as shown **(see illustration).**

7 Switch the headlamps on to dipped beam. Cover one headlamp with cloth. Working on the other lamp, use its two adjuster screws to bring the centre of the beam to the point "C" on the appropriate side of the alignment chart.

8 Transfer the cloth to the adjusted headlamp and repeat the adjustment on the other.

9 While this will produce an acceptable setting, it is important to have accurate adjustments made at the earliest opportunity.

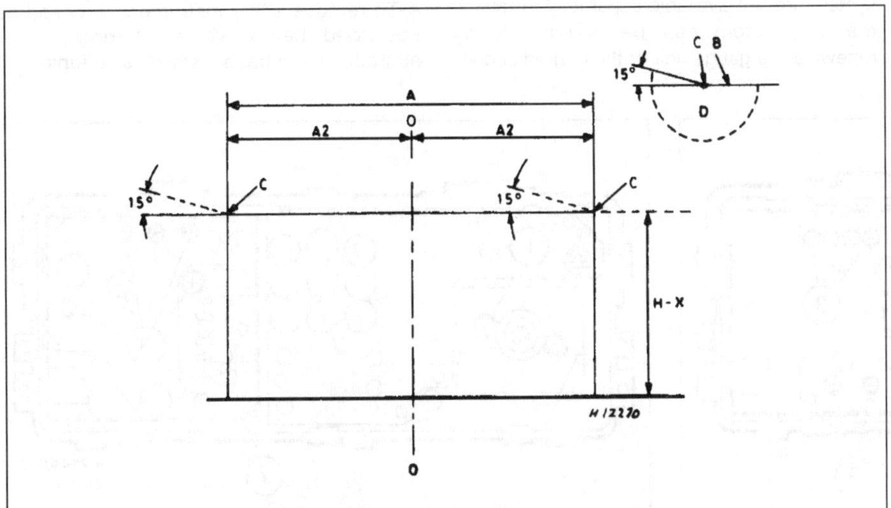

8.6 Headlamp beam alignment chart

A Distance between headlamp centres
B Light/dark boundary
C Dipped beam centre
D Dipped beam pattern
H Height from ground to headlamp centre
O Car's centre-line
X = 65 mm (2.5 in)

9 Dim-dip system - operation

The system comprises the dim-dip unit mounted on the fusebox panel and a resistor bolted to the right-hand inner wing panel. Remove the front wheel arch liner to reach the resistor **(see illustration).**

The dim-dip unit is supplied with current from the sidelamp circuit and energised by a feed from the ignition switch. When energised, the unit allows battery voltage to pass through a resistor to the fuses controlling the headlamp dipped-beam circuits. This lights the headlamps with approximately one-sixth of their normal power so that the car cannot be driven using sidelamps alone.

10 Interior lamp units - removal and refitting

Interior lamp

1 Refer to Section 6. Disconnect the switch and lamp wires to remove the lamp unit, having taken note of their connections.

Glovebox lamp

2 Refer to Section 6. Disconnect the wires to remove the lamp unit.

Luggage compartment lamp

3 Refer to Section 6. Peel back the interior trim panel and remove the two screws to release the lamp mounting bracket.

11 Instrument panel - removal and refitting

Removal

1 Disconnect the battery negative lead.

2 Remove the steering wheel.

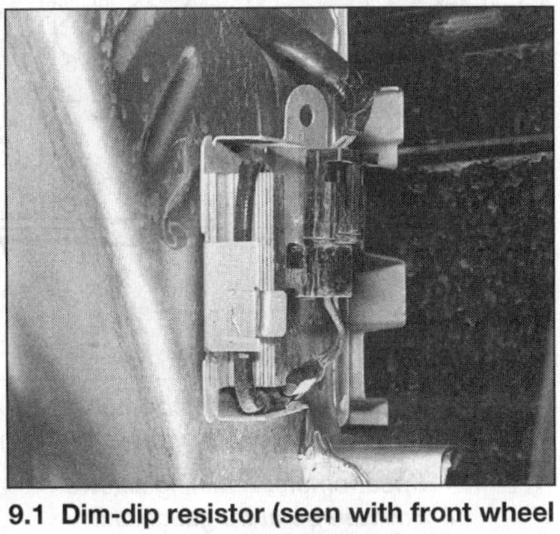

9.1 Dim-dip resistor (seen with front wheel arch liner removed)

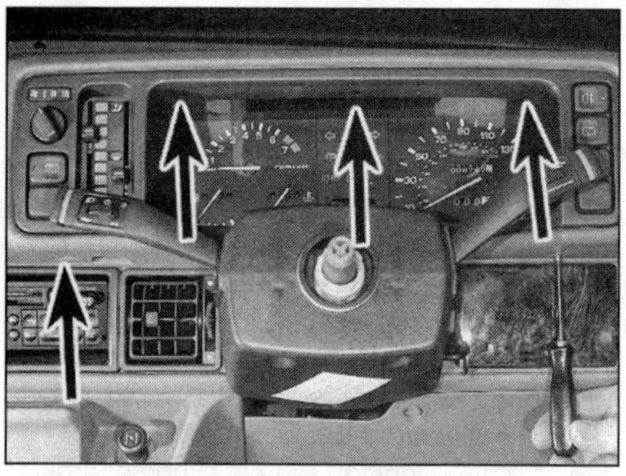

11.3a Location of instrument panel cowl retaining screws (arrowed)

11.3b Note connections before disconnecting switches to release cowl

11.4 Location of instrument panel retaining screws (arrowed)

3 Remove the five retaining screws and withdraw the instrument panel cowl. Take note of the various switch connections before disconnecting them. Remove the cowl **(see illustrations)**.

4 Remove the four screws securing the panel **(see illustration)**.

5 Disconnect the speedometer drive cable from the rear of the instrument panel **(see illustration)**.

6 Carefully pull the panel into the passenger compartment until the two connector plugs can be disconnected and the panel can be removed **(see illustration)**.

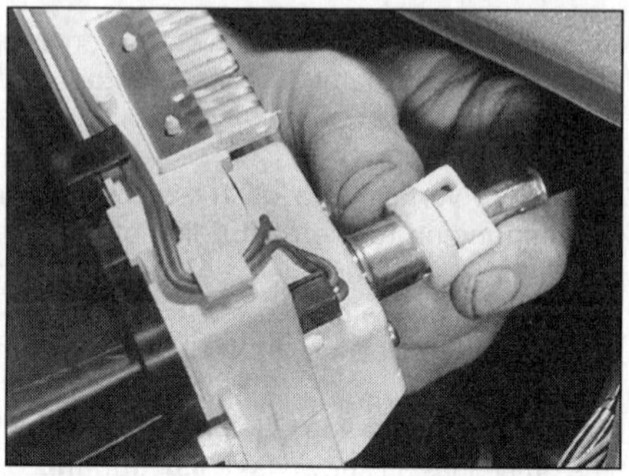

11.5 Disconnection of speedometer drive cable (panel partly removed for clarity)

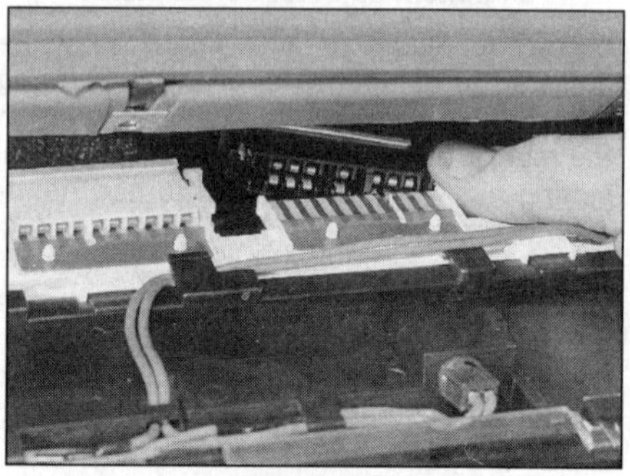

11.6 Disconnecting instrument panel wiring connectors

Refitting

7 Refitting is the reverse of the removal procedure.

12 Instrument panel components - removal and refitting

General

1 Remove the instrument panel, then proceed as described in the relevant sub-section following.

Instruments

Testing

2 Refer to Chapter 3 for details of tests of the coolant temperature gauge circuit. Some models are fitted with a high temperature warning lamp (actually an LED) to reinforce the warning if the coolant temperature rises to too high a level. The components of this sub-system are not available separately. A fault in the sub-system can be cured only by renewing the gauge unit or the printed circuit.

3 Refer to Chapter 4 for details of tests of the fuel gauge circuit. Some models are fitted with a low fuel warning lamp (actually an LED) to reinforce the warning if the fuel level falls to too low a point. The components of this sub-system are not available separately; a fault in the sub-system can be cured only by renewing the gauge unit or the printed circuit.

Removal

4 To remove either instrument, proceed as described below whilst referring to the appropriate illustration **(see illustrations)**.

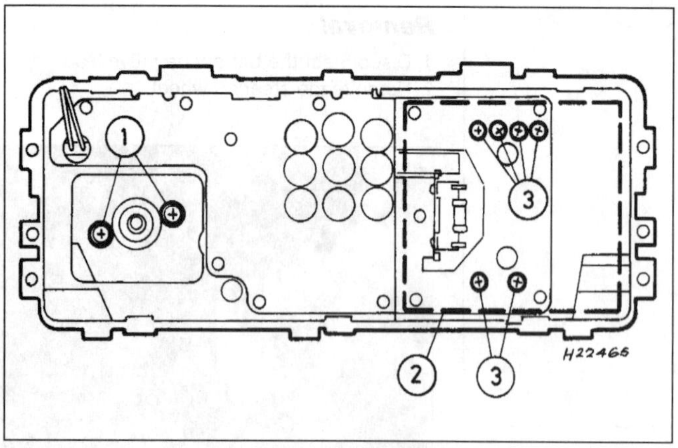

12.4a Speedometer and fuel/temperature gauge unit mountings - models without tachometer

1 Speedometer retaining screws
2 Fuel/temperature gauge unit
3 Fuel/temperature gauge unit retaining screws

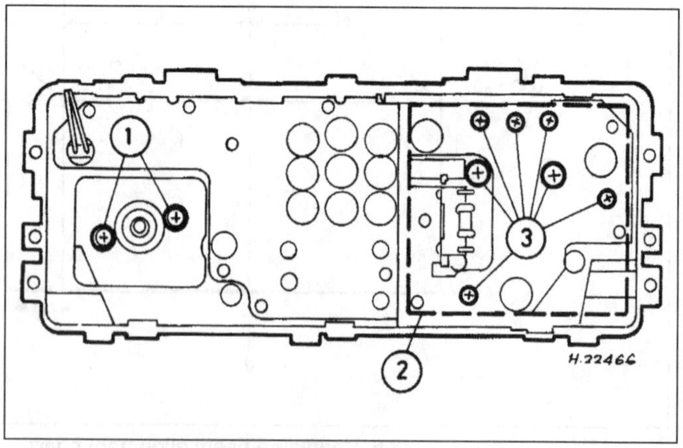

12.4b Speedometer and fuel/temperature gauge and tachometer unit mountings

1 Speedometer retaining screws
2 Fuel/temperature gauge and tachometer unit
3 Fuel/temperature gauge and tachometer unit retaining screws

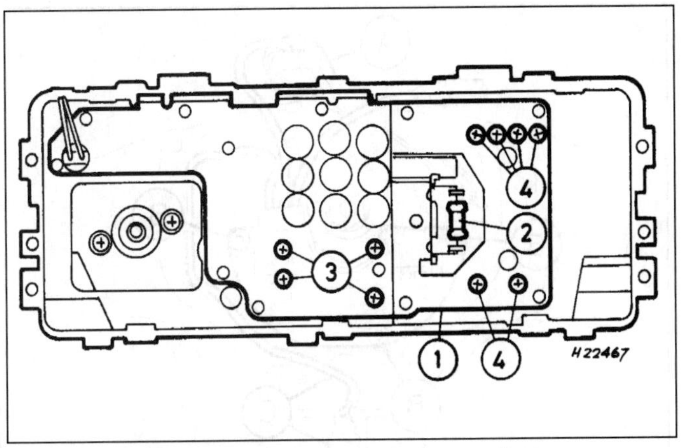

12.8a Printed circuit and clock mountings - models without tachometer

1 *Printed circuit*
2 *Ignition/battery charging warning lamp resistor*
3 *Clock retaining screws*
4 *Fuel/temperature gauge unit retaining screws*

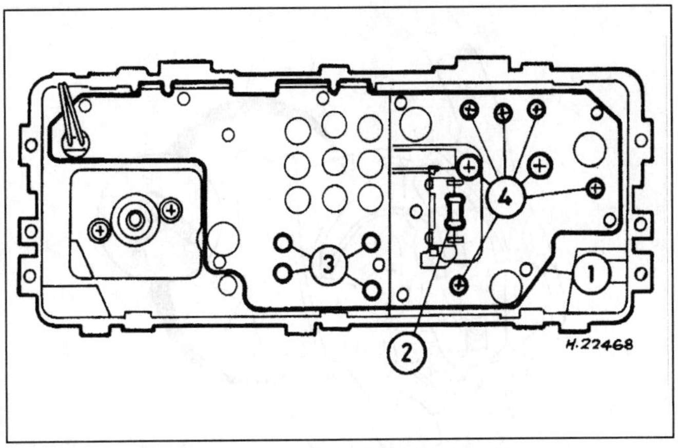

12.8b Printed circuit and clock mountings - models with tachometer

1 *Printed circuit*
2 *Ignition/battery charging warning lamp resistor*
3 *Clock retaining screws*
4 *Fuel/temperature gauge and tachometer unit retaining screws*

5 Remove the panel illuminating bulbs and unclip the illuminating bulb wiring harness from the panel housing, then release the six clips and separate the panel window and faceplate from the housing.
6 Remove the screws retaining the unit to be removed and withdraw it.

Refitting

7 Refitting is the reverse of the removal procedure.

Digital clock

Removal

8 Refer to the appropriate illustration **(see illustrations)**.
9 Remove the panel illuminating bulbs and unclip the illuminating bulb wiring harness from the panel housing, then release the six clips and separate the panel window and faceplate from the housing.
10 Remove the speedometer and the fuel/temperature gauge (and tachometer, where fitted) unit.
11 Remove the warning lamp panel.
12 Remove the retaining screws and withdraw the clock.

Refitting

13 Refitting is the reverse of the removal procedure.

Printed circuit

Removal

14 Refer to the appropriate illustration (see preceding sub Sections).
15 Remove all panel illuminating and warning lamp bulbs from the rear of the panel.
16 Remove the screws retaining the clock (where fitted) and the fuel/temperature gauge (and tachometer, where fitted) unit.
17 Release the ignition/battery charging warning lamp resistor.
18 Release the printed circuit from its locating pins and withdraw it.

Refitting

19 Refitting is the reverse of the removal procedure.

Voltage stabiliser

20 The voltage stabiliser is an integral part of the printed circuit.

13 Supplementary Restraint System (SRS) - operation

1 At vehicle start-up, a warning light located in the steering wheel centre pad will illuminate when the electrical circuits are activated by turning the ignition switch to position "II" and will stay illuminated for 3 seconds whilst the system performs a self-diagnosis test. If the test is satisfactory, the light will extinguish. If the test is unsatisfactory, the light will remain on or fail to illuminate at all, denoting that the system must be serviced as soon as possible. The sequence of operation is as follows:
2 Upon the vehicle suffering a frontal impact over a specified force, a sensor inside the airbag control unit, which is located in the steering wheel centre, activates the system. A safing sensor, fitted to discriminate between an actual impact and driving on rough road surfaces, etc. is also activated and power is supplied to the airbag ignitor from the battery or a backup circuit, causing the airbag to inflate within 30 milliseconds.
3 As the driver of the vehicle is thrown forward into the inflated airbag it immediately discharges its contents through a vent, thereby providing a progressive deceleration and reducing the risk of injury from contact with the steering wheel, facia or windscreen. The total time taken from the start of airbag inflation to its complete deflation is approximately 0.1 seconds.

14 Supplementary Restraint System (SRS) - component removal and refitting

Warning: Under no circumstances, attempt to diagnose problems with SRS components using standard workshop equipment.

Note: *For safety reasons, owners are strongly advised against attempting to diagnose problems with the SRS using standard workshop equipment. The information in this Section is therefore limited to those components in the SRS which must be removed to gain access to other components on the vehicle. Read carefully the precautions given in Section 1 of this Chapter before commencing work on any part of the system.*

Airbag unit

Removal

1 Remove the ignition key and wait at least ten minutes to allow the system backup circuit to fully discharge. Disconnect both battery leads, earth lead first, to avoid accidental detonation of the airbag.
2 Remove the two airbag unit retaining screws which are accessed from behind the steering wheel **(see illustration)**.
3 Carefully prise the airbag unit away from the steering wheel to gain access to the cabling behind. Do not allow the unit to hang from its wiring harness.
4 Unplug the cable connector from the rear of the airbag unit and carefully remove the unit from the vehicle, placing it in a safe storage area.

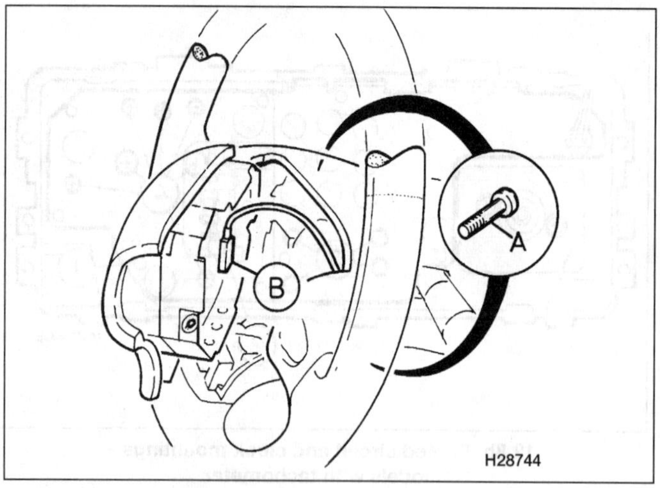

14.2 Removing the airbag unit

A Retaining screws *B Cable connector*

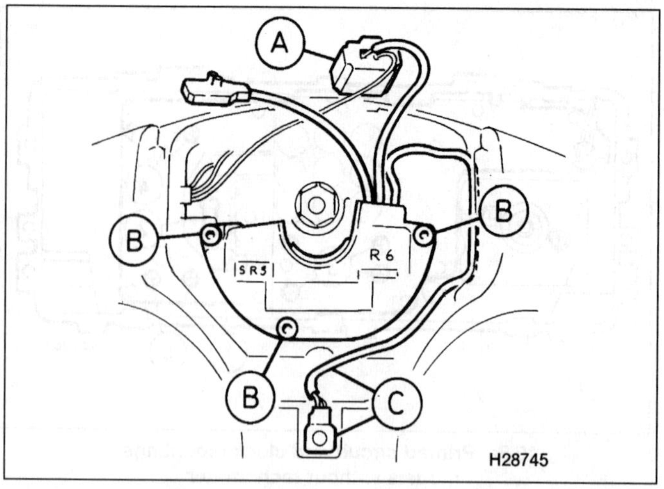

14.7 Removing the airbag control unit

A Control unit multiplug
B Securing screws
C Warning light wiring harness

Refitting

5 Refit the airbag unit by reversing the removal procedure whilst noting the following points:

a) The cable connector must face uppermost when refitted to the airbag unit.

b) Observe the specified torque wrench setting when tightening the airbag retaining screws (TX30 Torx type) and take care not to cross-thread them.

c) Reconnect the battery negative cable and turn the ignition switch to the "II" position. Check the condition of the system by observing the SRS warning light located in the steering wheel centre pad. The light should stay illuminated for 3 seconds whilst the system performs a self-diagnosis test. If the test is satisfactory, the light will extinguish. If the test is unsatisfactory, the light will remain on or fail to illuminate at all, denoting that the system must be serviced as soon as possible.

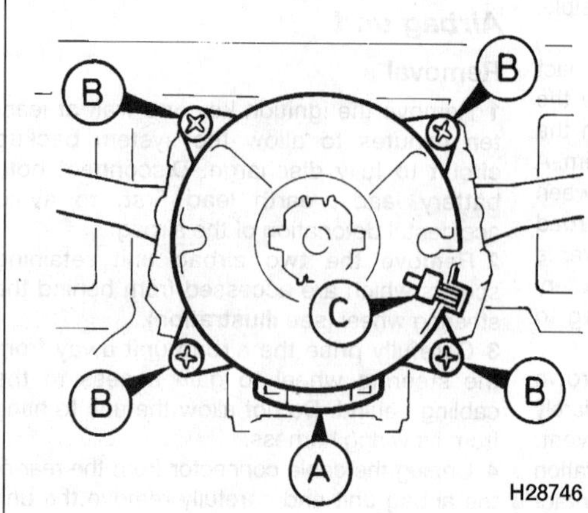

14.15 Removing the rotary contact unit

A Wiring harness multiplug
B Securing screws
C Locking peg (new unit)

Airbag control unit

Removal

6 Remove the airbag unit.

7 Release the control unit multiplug from the rotary contact unit **(see illustration).**

8 Remove the three screws which secure the control unit to the steering wheel and detach the SRS warning light wiring harness and the control unit from the wheel.

9 Release the control unit multiplug and remove the unit from the vehicle.

Refitting

10 Refit the control unit by reversing the removal procedure whilst noting the following points:

a) If the control unit is to be renewed, then the bar code on the new item must be recorded by your Rover dealer.

b) Take care to ensure that wiring is not trapped between mating surfaces.

c) Observe the specified torque wrench setting when tightening the control unit retaining screws (TX20 Torx type) and take care not to cross-thread them.

d) Refit the airbag unit, carrying out the system check.

Steering wheel rotary contact unit

Removal

11 Set the steering in the dead-ahead position.

12 Remove the airbag unit, followed by the airbag control unit.

13 Refer to Chapter 10 and remove the steering wheel, followed by the steering column nacelle.

14 If the rotary contact unit is to be reused, then put adhesive tape on its periphery to prevent it rotating.

15 Disconnect the airbag wiring harness multiplug from the underside of the contact unit **(see illustration).**

16 Remove the four screws which secure the unit to the column switch assembly and remove the unit from the vehicle.

Refitting

17 Refit the rotary contact unit by reversing the removal procedure whilst noting the following points:

a) If the unit is to be renewed, then the bar code on the new item must be recorded by your Rover dealer.

b) If a new unit is to be fitted, then the locking peg must be intact.

c) Take care to ensure that wiring is not trapped between mating surfaces.

d) Observe the specified torque wrench setting when tightening the unit retaining screws.

e) After reconnecting the multiplug, remove the adhesive tape or break off the locking peg.

f) Refit the airbag unit, carrying out the system check.

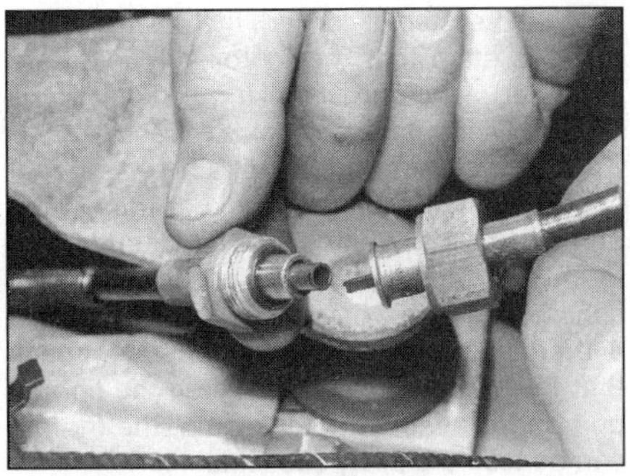

15.2 Unscrew nut to disconnect speedometer drive upper and lower cables

Airbag link harness

Removal

18 Set the steering in the dead-ahead position.

19 Remove the airbag unit, followed by the airbag control unit.

20 Refer to Chapter 10 and remove the steering wheel.

21 Release the fusebox cover fasteners and remove the cover.

22 Remove the three screws which secure the lower half of the steering column nacelle and remove the lower half of the nacelle.

23 Detach the harness multiplugs from the rotary contact unit and fusebox, and the link harness connector from the main wiring harness.

24 Release the SRS fuse from the underside of the fusebox and the two cable-ties which secure the harness to the steering column. Remove the harness from the vehicle.

Refitting

25 Refit the harness by reversing the removal procedure whilst noting the following points:

a) Take care to ensure that the wiring harness is correctly routed and is not trapped between mating surfaces.

b) Check all wiring connectors are firmly fastened

c) Refit the airbag unit, carrying out the system check.

15 Speedometer drive cable - removal and refitting

General

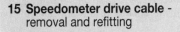

1 The drive cable is in two parts; the lower cable runs from the transmission to a point just in front of the clutch release lever, whilst the upper cable runs from that point to the rear of the instrument panel.

Upper cable

Removal

2 Open the bonnet and unscrew the nut securing the cable upper-to-lower sections, then release the upper cable from any clamps or ties securing it **(see illustration)**.

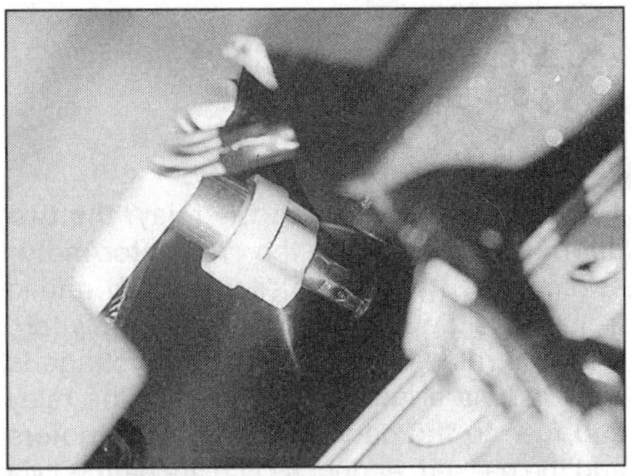

15.4 Upper cable attachment to speedometer - seen through fusebox aperture

3 Working inside the passenger compartment, release its retaining fasteners and withdraw the fusebox cover.

4 Reaching up inside the fusebox aperture, depress the locking prong to disconnect the cable from the speedometer **(see illustration)**.

5 Prise the sealing grommet out of the bulkhead and withdraw the cable into the engine compartment.

Refitting

6 Refitting is the reverse of the removal procedure. Press the cable upper end onto the speedometer boss to secure it. Do not overtighten the upper-to-lower cable nut and note the specified torque wrench setting.

Lower cable

Removal

7 Open the bonnet and unscrew the nut securing the cable upper-to-lower sections.

8 Jack up the front of the car and support it securely on axle stands (see *"Jacking and Vehicle Support"*).

9 Using a long-nosed pair of pliers, reach up above the right-hand side of the exhaust system front silencer and extract the rubber dowel retaining the cable lower end in the speedometer drive housing **(see illustration)**. Withdraw the cable from above.

Refitting

10 Refitting is the reverse of the removal procedure. Renew the sealing O-rings if they are worn or damaged, grease the cable lower end and ensure that the rubber dowel is fully engaged in the speedometer drive housing **(see illustration)**.

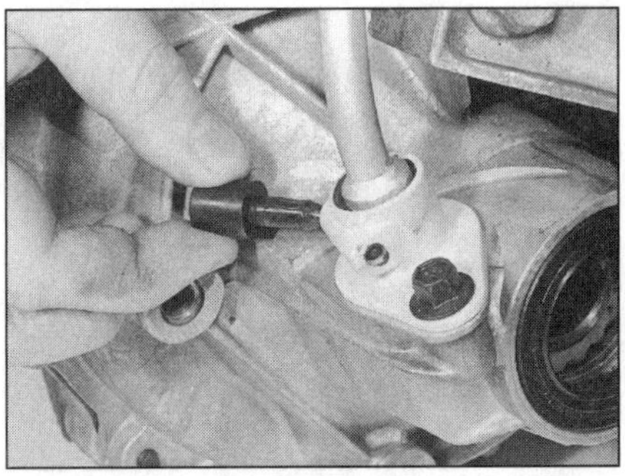

15.9 Speedometer drive cable lower end secured by rubber dowel

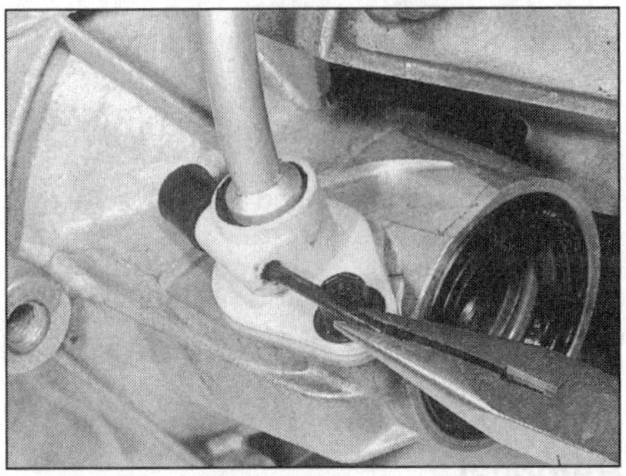

15.10 Ensure dowel is fully engaged on refitting

16 Cigar lighter - removal and refitting

Removal

1 Disconnect the battery negative lead.

2 Remove the lighter element, then release its clips and remove the metal surround, followed by the plastic body. Note the wiring connections before disconnecting and do not allow the wiring to fall back inside the facia once disconnected **(see illustrations)**.

Refitting

3 Refitting is the reverse of removal.

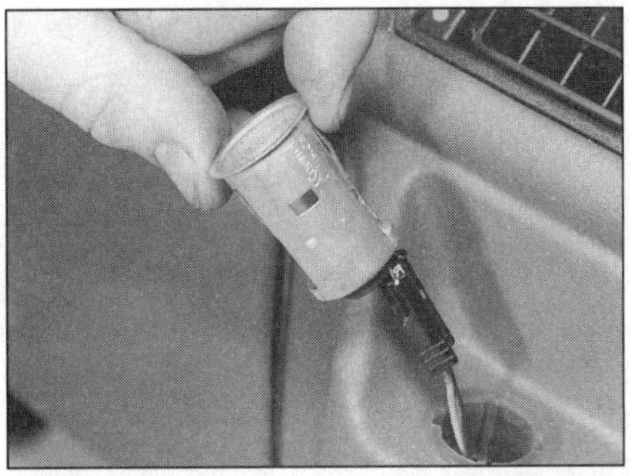

16.2a Release clips to extract cigar lighter metal surround . . .

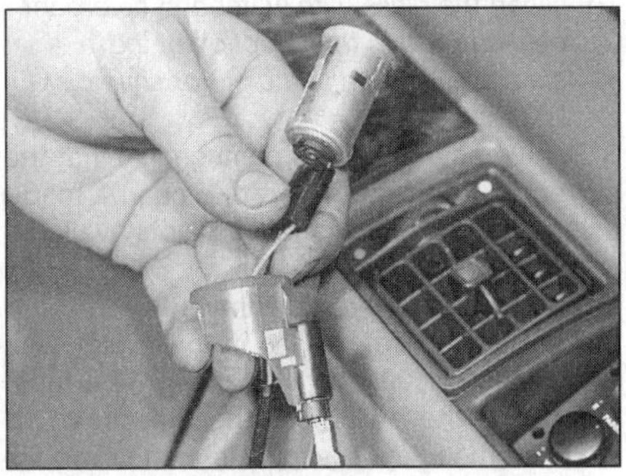

16.2b . . . then withdraw plastic body with illuminating bulb

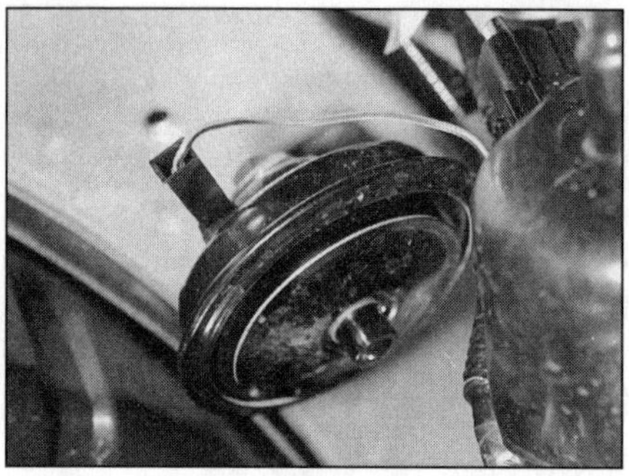

18.2 Location of horn

17 Clock - removal and refitting

Refer to Sections 11 and 12.

18 Horn - removal and refitting

Removal

1 Disconnect the battery negative lead.

2 Disconnect the horn wire and unbolt the horn from the body **(see illustration)**.

Refitting

3 Refitting is the reverse of the removal procedure.

19 Heated rear window - precautions and repair

1 The rear window is heated by passing current through a resistive grid bonded to the inside of the glass.

2 The heater elements are fragile and the following precautions should be observed.

a) Do not allow luggage or other items to rub against the inside surface of the glass.

b) Do not stick labels over the elements.

c) Avoid scratching the elements when cleaning with rings on the fingers.

d) Clean the glass with water and detergent only and rub in the direction of the elements using a soft cloth or chamois leather.

3 Should an element be damaged so that the current is interrupted, a repair can be made using one of the conductive paints available from motor accessory shops.

4 Note that the system draws a very high current and therefore has its own relay, the energising circuit of which is fed via a fuse. Operating the switch earths the circuit to energise the relay. A supply is then drawn via a fusible link and fuse to feed the element and the switch warning lamp.

20 Electric front windows - operation and repair

1 The system comprises the relay, the two door switches and the regulator/motor assemblies. The relay is energised by a feed from a fusible link and the ignition switch. With the relay energised, battery voltage is supplied via a fusible link, through the relay and fuse to the door switches. Both motors and the passenger door switch are earthed via the driver's door switch.

2 When a switch is pressed forwards to the down position, power is fed to the motor so that it rotates and operates the regulator to lower the window glass. When the switch is pressed rearwards to the up position, the feed's polarity is reversed so that the motor rotates in the opposite direction and the window glass is raised.

3 If the system fails completely, check the fuse, the fusible links and the feed to the relay, then check the driver's door switch earth return. If no fault is found, check the relay by substituting a new one.

4 If one window fails to operate and the above checks fail to cure the fault, check the feeds to both door switches, then check the motor feed and earth, first when the up switch is pressed, then when the down switch is pressed. If the switches and wiring prove sound, the motor is probably faulty and must be renewed with the regulator assembly; if the switches are suspect, check them by substitution.

21 Central locking system - operation and repair

1 This system is supplied with current via a fusible link and fuse to the control unit. Both the feed and earth return of the other motors in the system are through the control unit.

2 On operation of the driver's door lock, the system is triggered by the control unit mounted in the driver's door, which sends full battery voltage in the form of a short pulse, to the other door motor(s) and the tailgate motor. When the system is locked, the polarity of the pulse is such that the motor solenoids are extended, while on unlocking the polarity is reversed so that the solenoids retract.

3 If the system fails to work, check first that full battery voltage is available at the control unit and that the unit's earth is sound; if no fault is found, test the control unit by substituting a new component.

4 If an individual lock fails to operate, check that the wiring is sound between the control unit and the faulty motor; again, the motors can be tested only by substitution.

22 Lamps-on warning system - operation

If any exterior lamps are left on after the ignition has been switched off, a warning buzzer will sound as soon as either front door is opened. The buzzer will cease as soon as the door is closed or the lamps are switched off.

The system is fed via a fuse and is controlled, with the interior lamp door pillar switches, by the interior lamp delay/lamps-on alarm unit mounted in the fusebox panel.

23 Wiper arms - removal and refitting

Removal

1 Before removing a wiper arm, stick a piece of masking tape on the glass, along the blade, to aid arm alignment on refitting.

2 To remove a wiper arm, pull the arm fully away from the glass until it locks. Remove the blade only if required.

3 Flip up the cover to reveal the wiper-to-spindle nut. If removing the rear window wiper arm, withdraw the washer jet **(see illustration)**.

4 Unscrew the wiper arm-to-spindle nut and pull the arm from the spindle splines **(see illustration)**. If necessary use a large screwdriver blade to prise off the arm.

5 Clean the splines of the arm and of the spindle.

23.3 Remove washer jet (rear window only) to reach wiper arm nut . . .

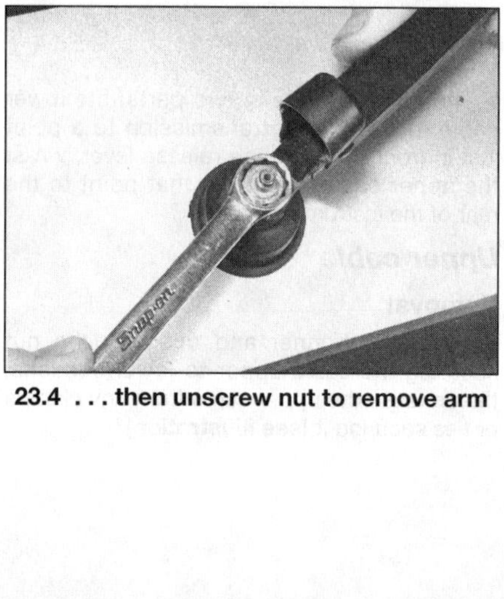

23.4 . . . then unscrew nut to remove arm

24.2 Remove clip (arrowed) to disconnect connecting rods from crank

24.3 Removing the crank from the windscreen wiper motor

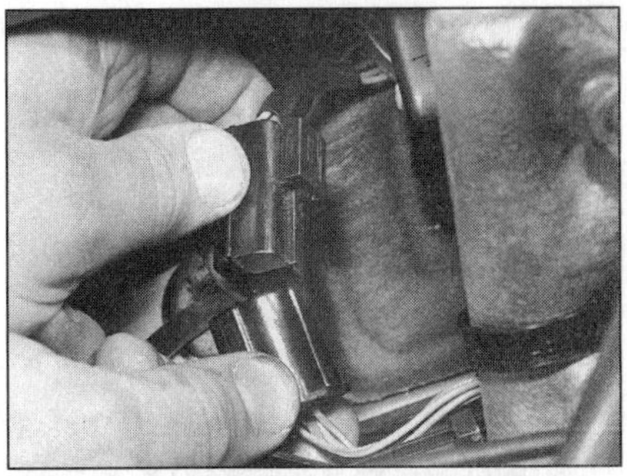

24.4 Disconnecting the windscreen wiper motor wiring

Refitting

6 Refitting is the reverse of the removal procedure. Use the masking tape to ensure that the arm is refitted in its original position and tighten the wiper arm-to-spindle nut to the specified torque wrench setting.

24 Windscreen wiper motor and linkage - removal and refitting

Motor

Removal

1 Operate the wipers, switching off the ignition to stop them when the crank/connecting rod joint is in sight.

2 Prise out the clip and disconnect the connecting rods from the crank **(see illustration)**. Remove the spacer washer and bushes, noting their positions.

3 Unscrew the nut and remove the washer and crank from the motor spindle **(see illustration)**.

4 Disconnect the battery negative lead. Unclip and separate the connector to disconnect the motor wiring **(see illustration)**.

5 Unbolt the motor from its mounting bracket and withdraw it **(see illustration)**.

Refitting

6 Refitting is the reverse of the removal procedure, noting the following points.

a) Tighten the motor mounting (hex-head) screws to the specified torque wrench setting.
b) Grease the motor spindle, the bushes and the spacer washers, then reconnect the motor wiring.
c) Switch the wipers on and off, allowing the motor to return to the park position. Check that the arms are in the park position.
d) Refit the crank, connect the connecting rods (do not forget the spacer washer and bushes) and secure the clip to retain them, then tighten the crank nut securely.
e) Connect the motor wiring and press the connector into its clip.
f) Check that the wipers operate correctly.

Motor and linkage

Removal

7 Remove both wiper arms.

8 Unscrew the linkage spindle housing nuts, then remove the washer and the upper rubber spacer under each.

9 Disconnect the battery negative lead. Unclip and separate the connector to disconnect the motor wiring.

10 Withdraw the motor and linkage assembly, removing if necessary the mounting bracket support rubber and collecting the lower rubber spacers **(see illustration)**.

11 The assembly can now be dismantled, if required.

Refitting

12 Refitting is the reverse of the removal procedure, noting the following points.

a) If the assembly was dismantled, refit the motor to the mounting bracket and position the crank so that it is parallel to the main length of the mounting bracket and pointing to the driver's side of the car.
b) Grease the bushes and spacer washers.
c) Ensure that the rubber spacers are correctly located.
d) Tighten all nuts and screws to their specified torque wrench settings.
e) Connect the motor wiring and press the connector into its clip.
f) Check that the wipers operate correctly.

25 Rear window wiper motor - removal and refitting

Removal

1 Remove the tailgate interior trim panel.

2 Disconnect the battery negative lead.

3 Remove the wiper arm and blade.

4 Remove the rubber cover and unscrew the spindle housing nut, then remove the washer and upper rubber spacer, noting their locations **(see illustration)**.

5 Disconnect the washer tube from the motor, then peel off the anti-rattle foam and separate the connector to disconnect the motor wiring **(see illustration)**.

6 Unbolt the motor and its mounting bracket, then remove the assembly **(see illustration)**.

7 The mounting bracket can be unbolted, if required. Note the arrangement of the ferrules and the mounting rubbers.

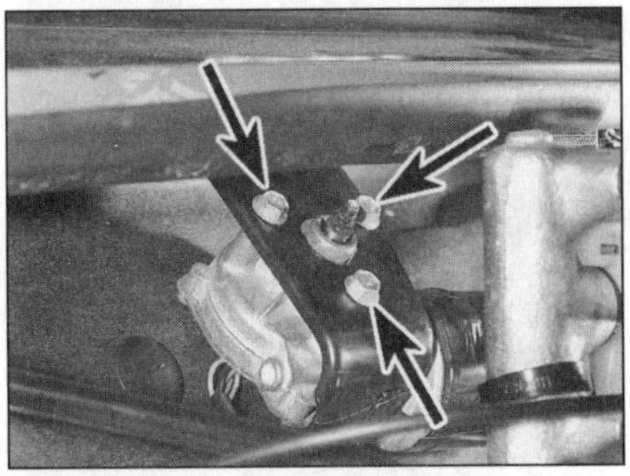

24.5 Undo three (hex-head) screws to remove motor from mounting bracket

24.10 Removing windscreen wiper motor and linkage assembly

25.4 Unscrew spindle housing nut, then remove washer and upper rubber spacer

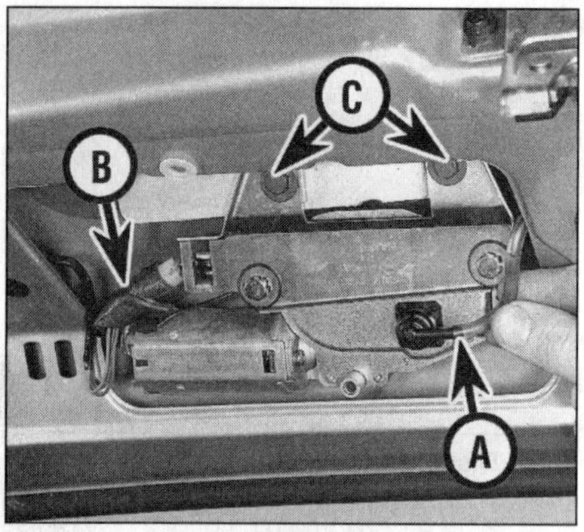

25.5 Rear window washer tube (A) motor wiring connector (B) and mounting bracket (hex-head) screws (C)

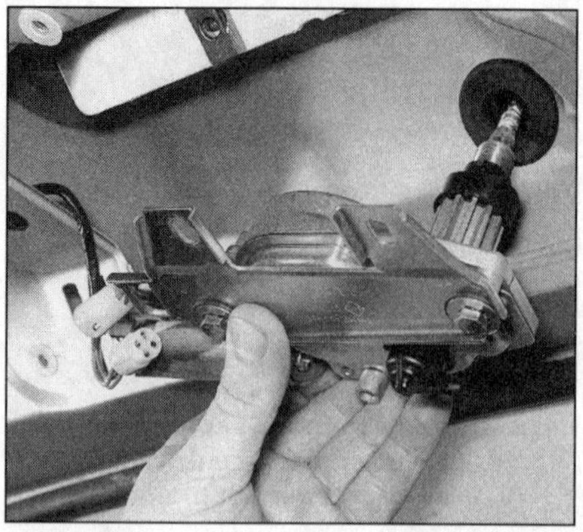

25.6 Removing the rear window wiper motor

Refitting

8 Refitting is the reverse of the removal procedure, noting the following points.

a) Tighten all nuts and screws to their specified torque wrench settings.

b) Connect the motor wiring and washer tube, then check that the wiper and washer operate correctly.

c) Ensure that the connector's wrapping is replaced to prevent rattles.

26 Washer system components - removal and refitting

1 Refer to Chapter 1 for details of maintenance requirements.

2 The system comprises the reservoir and a pump to direct flow to the windscreen and (if fitted) to the rear window, as required **(see illustration)**.

26.2 Washer system components

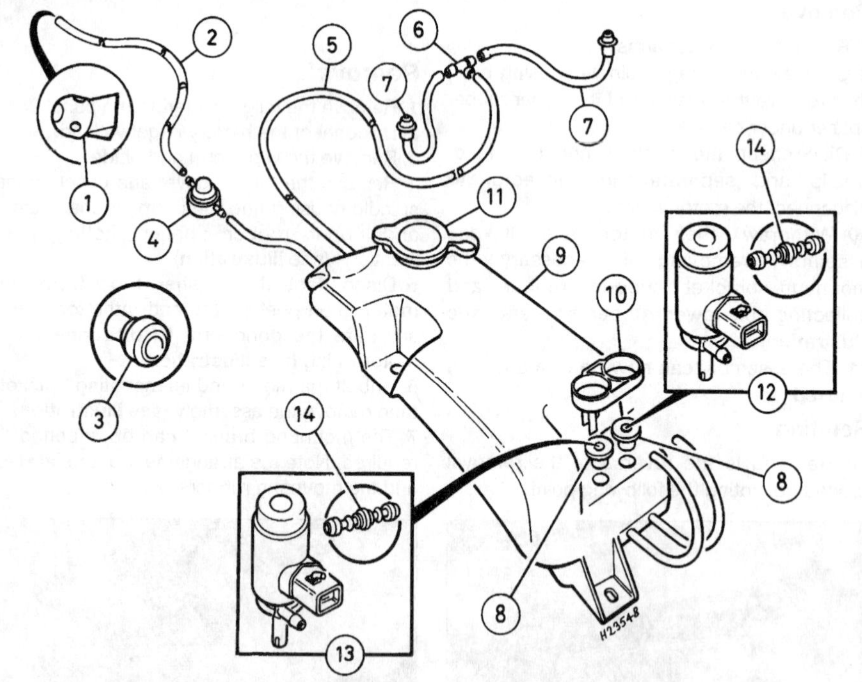

*1 Washer jet**
*2 Tube - non-return valve-to-rear window**
*3 Rubber grommet**
*4 Non-return valve - rear window washer only**
5 Tube - reservoir-to-bonnet
6 T-piece
7 Washer jet and tube
8 Grommet
9 Reservoir
10 Pump mounting bracket
11 Filler cap
12 Windscreen washer pump
*13 Rear window washer pump**
14 Connector
**Not fitted to all models*

3 The removal and refitting of all components is self-explanatory on examination. Ensure that the tubes are not trapped when refitting the reservoir and note that the connectors for the pumps are colour-coded to aid correct reconnection on reassembly.

4 If trouble is experienced at any time with the flow to the rear window washer, check that the non-return valve is not blocked; it is fitted in the tube next to the reservoir and should allow fluid to pass only outwards, to the jet.

27 Radio/cassette unit - removal and refitting

Removal

1 If the radio/cassette unit has a security code, de-activate the code temporarily and re-activate it when the battery is re-connected. Refer to the instructions and code supplied with the unit.

2 Disconnect the battery negative lead.

3 Actual removal and refitting procedures will vary according to the type of radio fitted, but one of the following will be a reasonably representative procedure:

a) If the unit has a finisher on each end of its faceplate, carefully prise these off and slacken the screw underneath each, then press the screws towards each other to release the unit's retaining clips. Reach behind the facia to push the unit out from behind. Disconnect the wiring plugs and aerial lead to remove the unit.

b) If the unit has two holes, one above the other, on each end of its faceplate, two standard DIN extraction tools are required to unlock and remove it ***(see illustration)****. The tools may possibly be obtained from a Rover dealer or any audio accessory outlet, or can be made out of 3 mm wire rod such as welding rod. Using the tools, push back the clamps on the left and right-hand sides, withdraw the unit and disconnect the wiring plugs and aerial.*

Refitting

4 Refitting is the reverse of the removal procedure.

27.3 Using DIN tools to remove radio/cassette unit

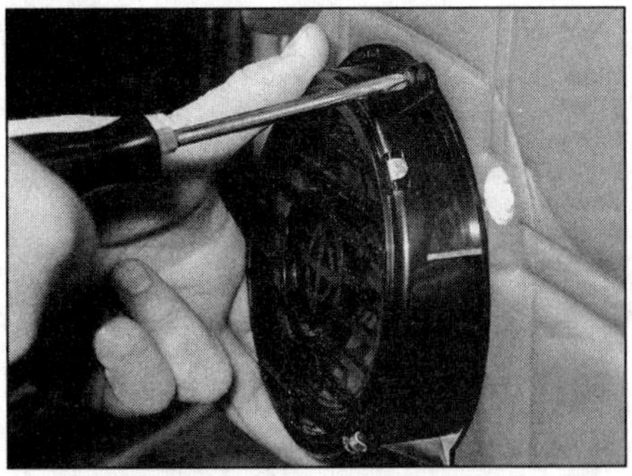

28.2 Front loudspeakers are mounted on door interior trim panels

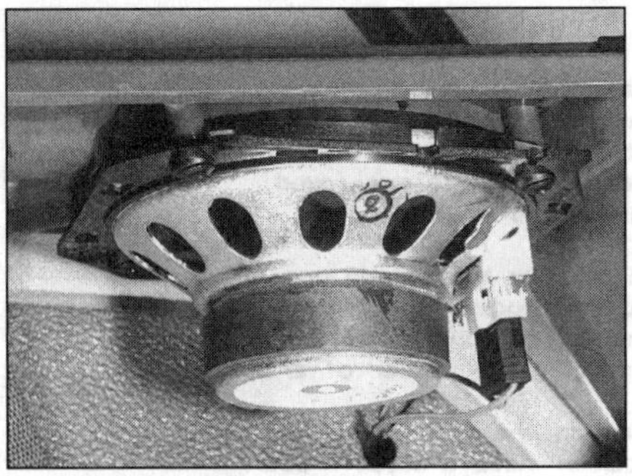

28.5 Rear loudspeakers are fastened under parcel shelf side supports

29.3 Remove interior lamp assembly to reach aerial base mounting screw

28 Loudspeakers - removal and refitting

Front

Removal

1 Remove the seven screws securing the door pocket to the door and withdraw the pocket. Disconnect the electric front window switch wiring if required.

2 Remove the three screws and withdraw the loudspeaker from the door, then disconnect its wiring **(see illustration)**.

Refitting

3 Refitting is the reverse of the removal procedure.

Rear

Removal

4 Open the tailgate. If removing the left-hand loudspeaker, remove first the luggage compartment lamp.

5 Remove the four screws and withdraw the loudspeaker from under the parcel shelf side support, then disconnect its wiring **(see illustration)**.

Refitting

6 Refitting is the reverse of the removal procedure.

29 Radio aerial - removal and refitting

Removal

1 Unscrew the aerial mast from the aerial base.

2 Remove the interior lamp assembly.

3 Prise off the anti-radio interference shield and undo the screw securing the aerial base, then remove the base **(see illustration)**.

4 Remove the radio/cassette unit and disconnect the aerial lead. Tie a long length of string to the aerial lead lower end, then pull the lead up through the bodywork. Untie the string when the end of the lead appears. Leave the string in place to aid refitting.

Refitting

5 Refitting is the reverse of the removal procedure. Use the string to draw the lead down into place.

30 Wiring diagrams - general information

Each wiring diagram covers a particular system of the appropriate vehicle; as indicated in each caption. Carefully read the Key to the diagrams before commencing work. The diagrams included are listed in the accompanying table.

Wiring diagrams

NOTES:

1. All diagrams are divided into numbered circuits depending on function e.g. Diagram 2: Exterior lighting.
2. Items are arranged in relation to a plan view of the vehicle.
3. Items may appear on more than one diagram so are found using a grid reference e.g. 2/A1 denotes an item on diagram 2 grid location A1.
4. Complex items appear on the diagrams as blocks and are expanded on the internal connections page.
5. Header joints represent a method of common connection of many different circuits whilst reducing the number of crimped or soldered joints.
6. Feed wire colour varies dependant on the circuit supplied but all earth wires are coloured black or have a black tracer.
7. Not all items are fitted to all models.

WIRE COLOURS

B	Blue	R	Red
Bk	Black	Rs	Pink
Bn	Brown	S	Grey
LGn	Light Green	V	Violet
Gn	Green	W	White
O	Orange	Y	Yellow
P	Purple		

KEY TO SYMBOLS

PLUG-IN CONNECTOR

EARTH

BULB

LINE CONNECTOR

DIODE

FUSE

ITEM	DESCRIPTION	DIAGRAM/ GRID REF.
1	Alternator	1/A3
2	Battery	1/C7, 1a/C7, 2/C6, 2a/B6, 3/B6, 3a/C6
3	Central Locking Control Unit	3a/J1
4	Central Locking Motor LH Front	3a/J8
5	Central Locking Motor LH Rear	3a/M8
6	Central Locking Motor RH Rear	3a/M1
7	Central Locking Motor Tailgate	3a/M4
8	Choke Switch	1/J6
9	Cigar Lighter	2a/J6, 3/H7
10	Coolant Temp. Gauge Sender Unit	1/C6
11	Coolant Temp. Sensor	1a/E4
12	Cooling Fan Motor	3/A5
13	Cooling Fan Switch	3/A4
14	Crank Sensor	1a/C5
15	Direction Indicator Flasher Relay	2/G2
16	Direction Indicator LH Front	2/A8
17	Direction Indicator RH Front	2/A1
18	Direction Indicator Side Repeater LH	2/C8
19	Direction Indicator Side Repeater RH	2/C1
20	Dim/Dip Resistor	2/A3
21	Dim/Dip Unit	2/G1
22	Distributor	1/A5, 1a/A5
23	Earth Header 1	1/A1, 2/B1, 2a/A1, 3/A1, 3a/A1
24	Earth Header 2	1a/A8, 2/B8, 2a/A8, 3/A8, 3a/A8
25	Earth Header 4	2/L8, 2a/L8, 3/L8
26	Electric Window/Auxiliary Relay	3a/F2
27	Electric Window Drivers Switch 1	2a/K1, 3a/G1
28	Electric Window Drivers Switch 2	2a/K2, 3a/G2
29	Electric Window Motor LH Front	3a/H8
30	Electric Window Motor RH Front	3a/H1
31	Electric Window Passengers Switch	2a/K8, 3a/G8
32	Foglamp Rear	2/M1
33	Foglamp Switch Rear	2/J3, 2a/G2
34	Fuel Gauge Sender Unit	1/L4
35	Fuel Injector	1a/D3

FUSE	RATING	CIRCUIT
1	10A	Engine - Ignition Coil
2	10A	RH Side, Tail, Number Plate Lamps
3	10A	Instruments
4	15A	Cooling Fan
5	10A	RH Headlamp Main Beam
6	10A	Stop-Lamps
9	10A	Heated Rear Window Relay, Flashers, Reversing Lamps
10	10A	Rear Foglamp
11	20A	Heated Rear Window
12	15A	Central Locking, Radio Memory, Clock, Interior Lamps
13	30A	Electric Windows
14	15A	Heater Blower Motor
15	15A	Windscreen Wash/Wipe
16	15A	Rear Wash/Wipe
17	10A	Fuel Pump
18	10A	LH Headlamp Main Beam
19	20A	Headlamps, Side Lamps
20	15A	Dim/dip
21	20A	Hazard, Horn
22	15A	Radio Cassette, Cigar Lighter
24	10A	RH Headlamp Dip Beam
25	10A	LH Headlamp Dip Beam
26	10A	LH Side, Tail, Number Plate Lamps

ITEM	DESCRIPTION	DIAGRAM/ GRID REF.
36	Fuel Pump	1a/M4
37	Fuel Pump Relay	1a/E8
38	Fusebox	1/G2, 1a/J2, 2/F3, 2a/E3, 3/C2, 3a/E2
39	Fusible Link Box	1/C8, 1a/C8, 2/C7, 2a/B7, 3/B7, 3a/C7
40	Glove Box Lamp	2a/G7
41	Glove Box Lamp Switch	2a/G6
42	Handbrake Warning Switch	1/K5
43	Header Joint 1	2a/G3, 3/H3

Notes, fuses, wire colours and key to wiring diagrams

ITEM	DESCRIPTION	DIAGRAM/ GRID REF.
44	Header Joint 2	2a/G5, 3/H4
45	Header Joint 3	2/J6, 2a/E6, 3/G6
46	Header Joint 4	1/H6, 2/G5, 2a/D5, 3/F5
47	Header Joint 5	1a/H2, 2a/B2, 3a/B3
48	Headlamp Relay	2/G3
49	Headlamp Unit LH	2/A7
50	Heahlamp Unit RH	2/A2
51	Heated Rear Window	3/L4
52	Heated Rear Window Relay	3/C1
53	Heated Rear Window Switch	2a/K5, 3/K6
54	Heater Blower Motor	3/G5
55	Heater Blower Switch	2a/J5, 3/H5
56	Heater Illumination	2a/J6
57	Horn	3/A7
58	Idle Solenoid	1/C5
59	Ignition Amplifier Module	1/A5
60	Ignition Coil	1/A6, 1a/A6
61	Ignition Relay	3/G3
62	Ignition Switch	1/K1, 1a/L1, 2/J1, 2a/F2, 3/G1, 3a/G3
63	Inertia Switch	1a/K7
64	Instrument Cluster	1/J4, 1a/L4, 2/H4, 2a/J4
65	Intake Air Temp. Sensor	1a/A3
66	Interior Lamp	2a/E5
67	Interior Lamp Door Switch LH Front	2a/D8
68	Interior Lamp Door Switch RH Front	2a/D1
69	Lamp Cluster LH Rear	2/M8
70	Lamp Cluster RH Rear	2/M1
71	Lamps On Alarm Unit	2a/C3
72	Low Brake Fluid Sender	1/E2
73	Luggage Comp. Lamp	2a/M7
74	Luggage Comp. Switch	2a/M4
75	Main Relay	1a/E6
76	Manifold Heater	1/D4, 1a/C4
77	Manifold Heater Relay	1/F7, 1a/F6
78	Manifold Temp. Switch	1/D5
79	MEMS Unit	1a/J6
80	Multi-Function Switch	2/J4, 2a/K4, 3/K3
81	Number Plate Lamp	2/M4, 2/M5
82	Oil Pressure Switch	1/C2
83	Radio/Cassette Unit	3a/H6
84	Reversing Lamp Switch	2/B5
85	Relay Module	1a/F6
86	Spark Plugs	1/B4, 1a/B4
87	Speaker LH Front	3a/H7
88	Speaker LH Rear	3a/M7
89	Speaker RH Front	3a/H2
90	Speaker RH Rear	3a/M2
91	Starter Motor	1/A7
92	Starter Relay	1/E7, 1a/F8
93	Stepper Motor	1a/E3
94	Stop-Lamp Switch	2/E5
95	Throttle Pedal Switch	1/F4, 1a/J4
96	Throttle Potentiometer	1a/B3
97	Washer Pump Front	3/E1
98	Washer Pump Rear	3/D1
99	Washer Switch Rear	2a/H2, 3/K2
100	Wiper Motor Front	3/C3
101	Wiper Motor Rear	3/M4
102	Wiper Relay Front	3/D3
103	Wiper Relay Rear	3/E3
104	Wiper Switch Front	3/L4
105	Wiper Switch Rear	2a/H2, 3/J2

INTERNAL CONNECTION DETAILS

KEY TO INSTRUMENT CLUSTER (ITEM 64)

a = Ignition Warning Lamp
b = Oil Pressure Warning Lamp
c = Brake Warning Lamp
d = Choke Warning Lamp
e = Tachometer
f = Coolant Temp. Gauge
g = Fuel Gauge
h = Low Fuel Warning Lamp
i = High Temp. Warning Lamp
j = Clock
k = General Illumination
l = Sidelamp Warning Lamp
m = Main Beam Warning Lamp
n = LH Direction Indicator Lamp
p = RH Direction Indicator Lamp
q = Trailer Warning Lamp

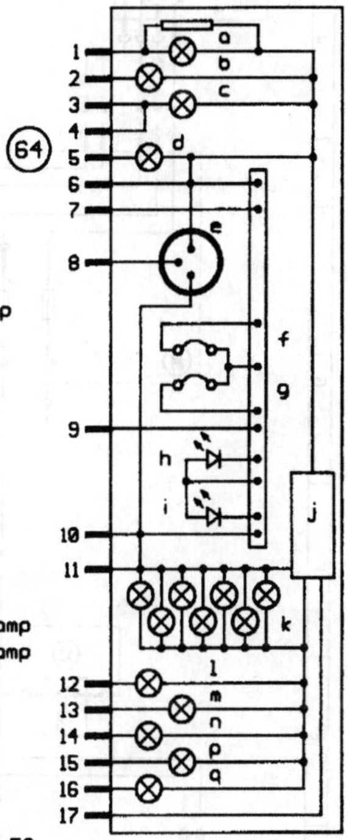

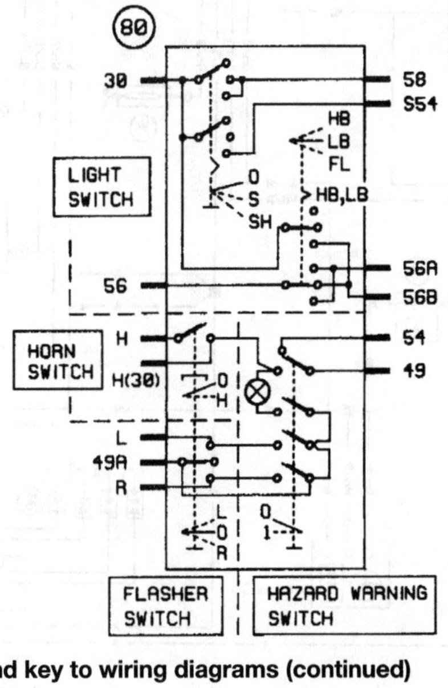

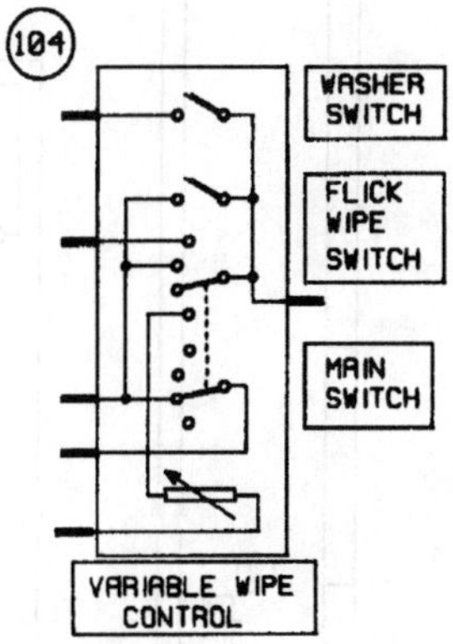

Internal connection details and key to wiring diagrams (continued)

H24085
T.M.MARKE

12

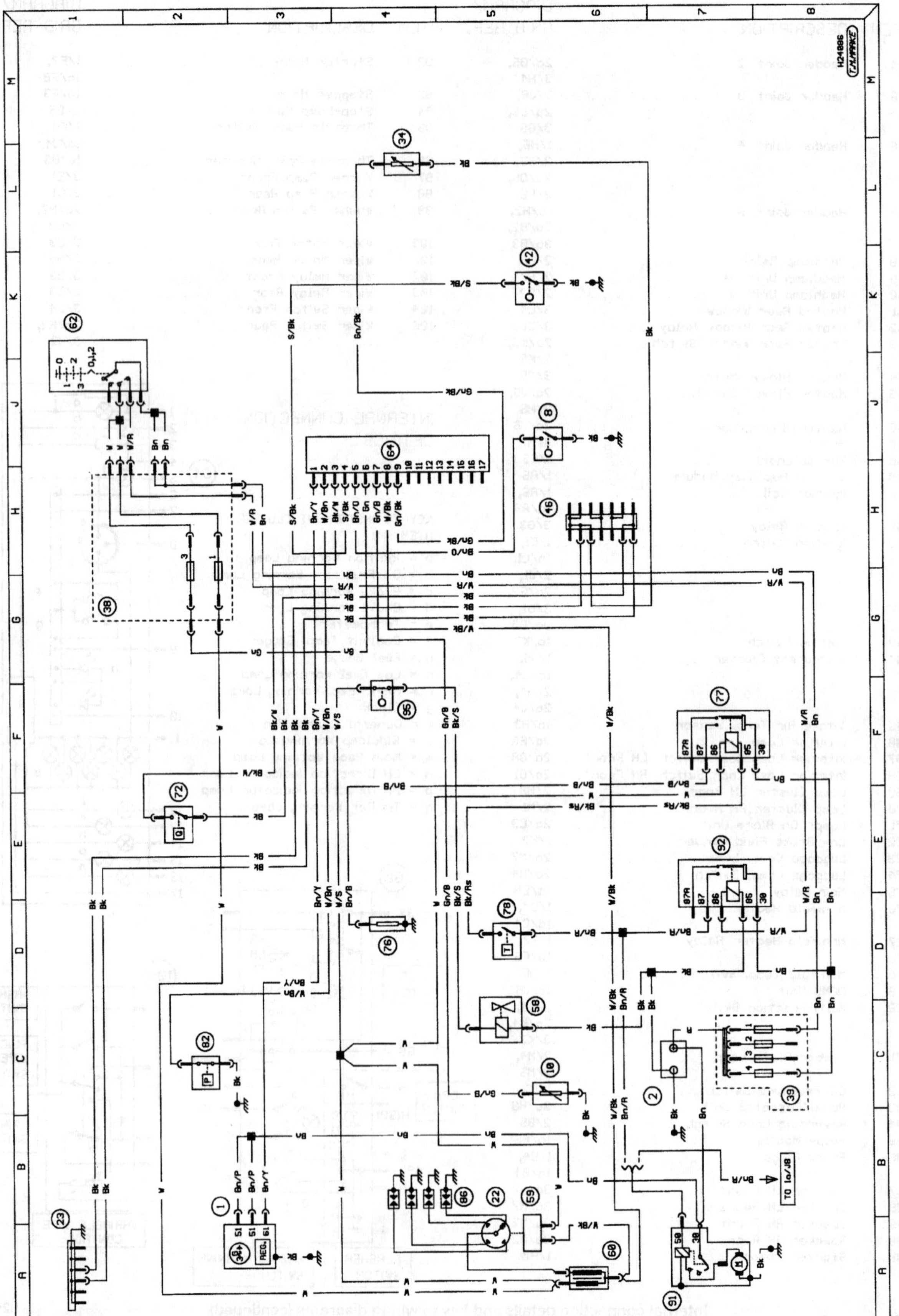

Diagram 1: Starting, charging, ignition (carburettor models), warning lamps and gauges

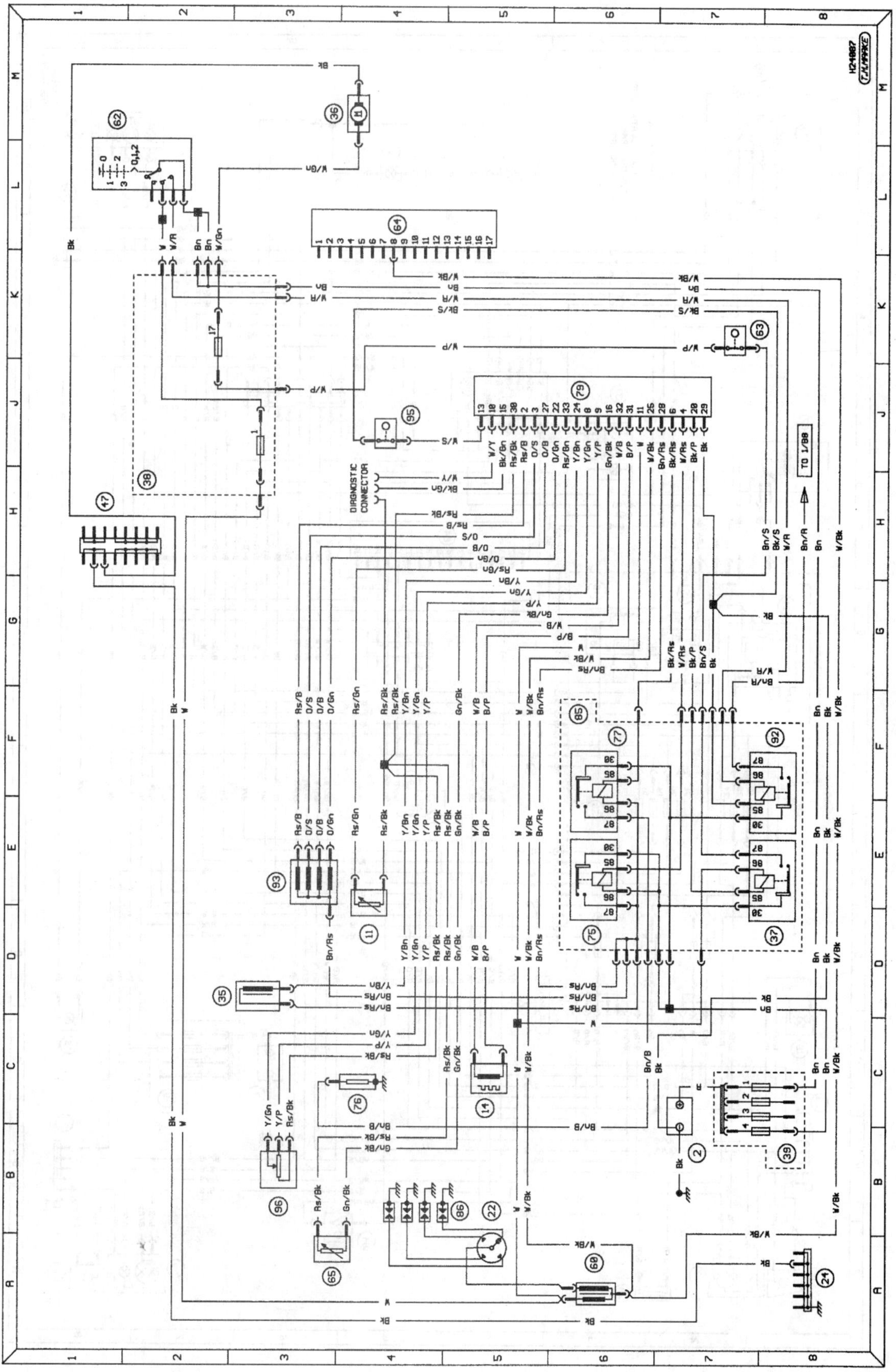

Diagram 1a: Modular engine management - single-point injection

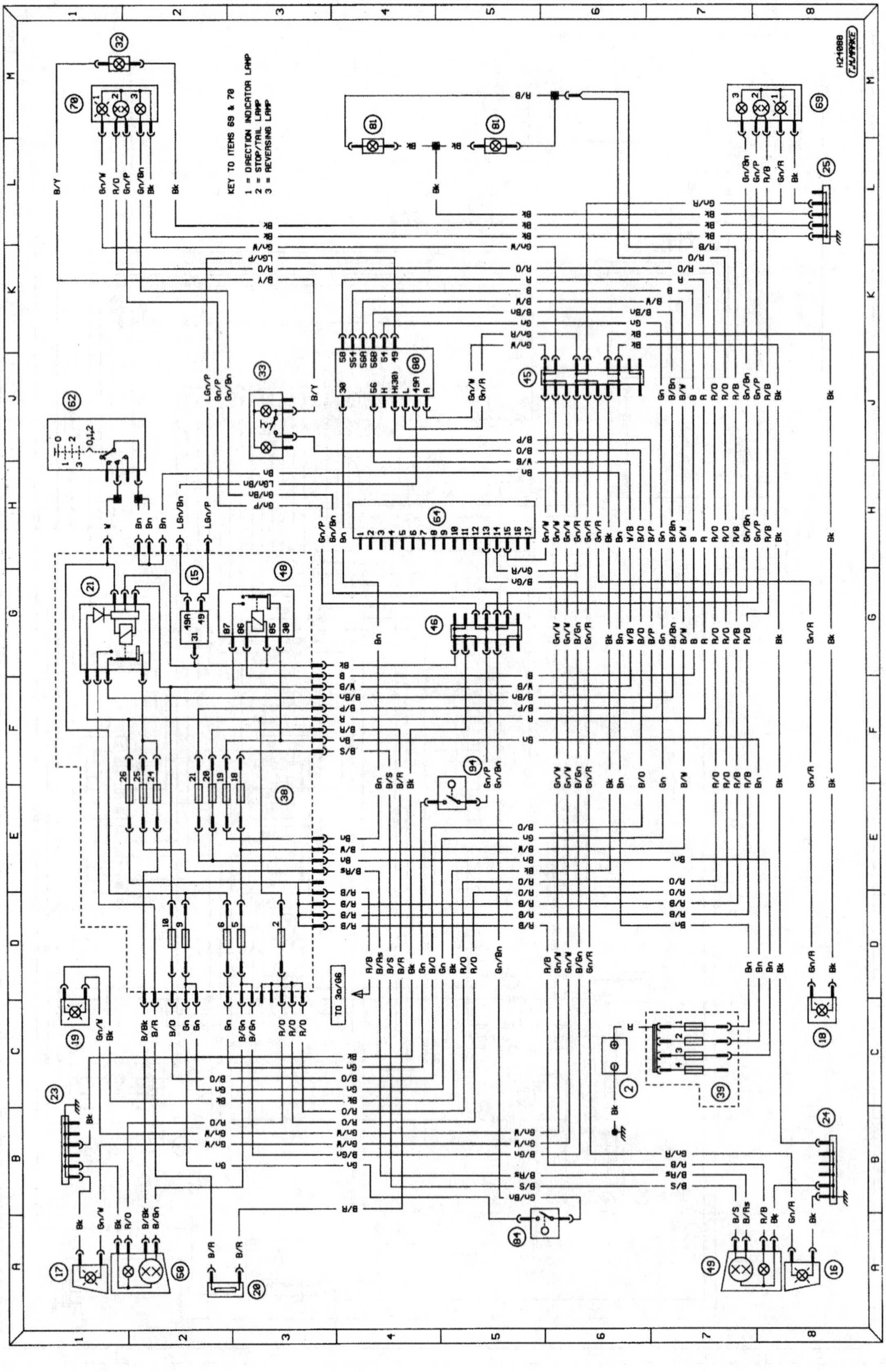

Diagram 2: Exterior lighting

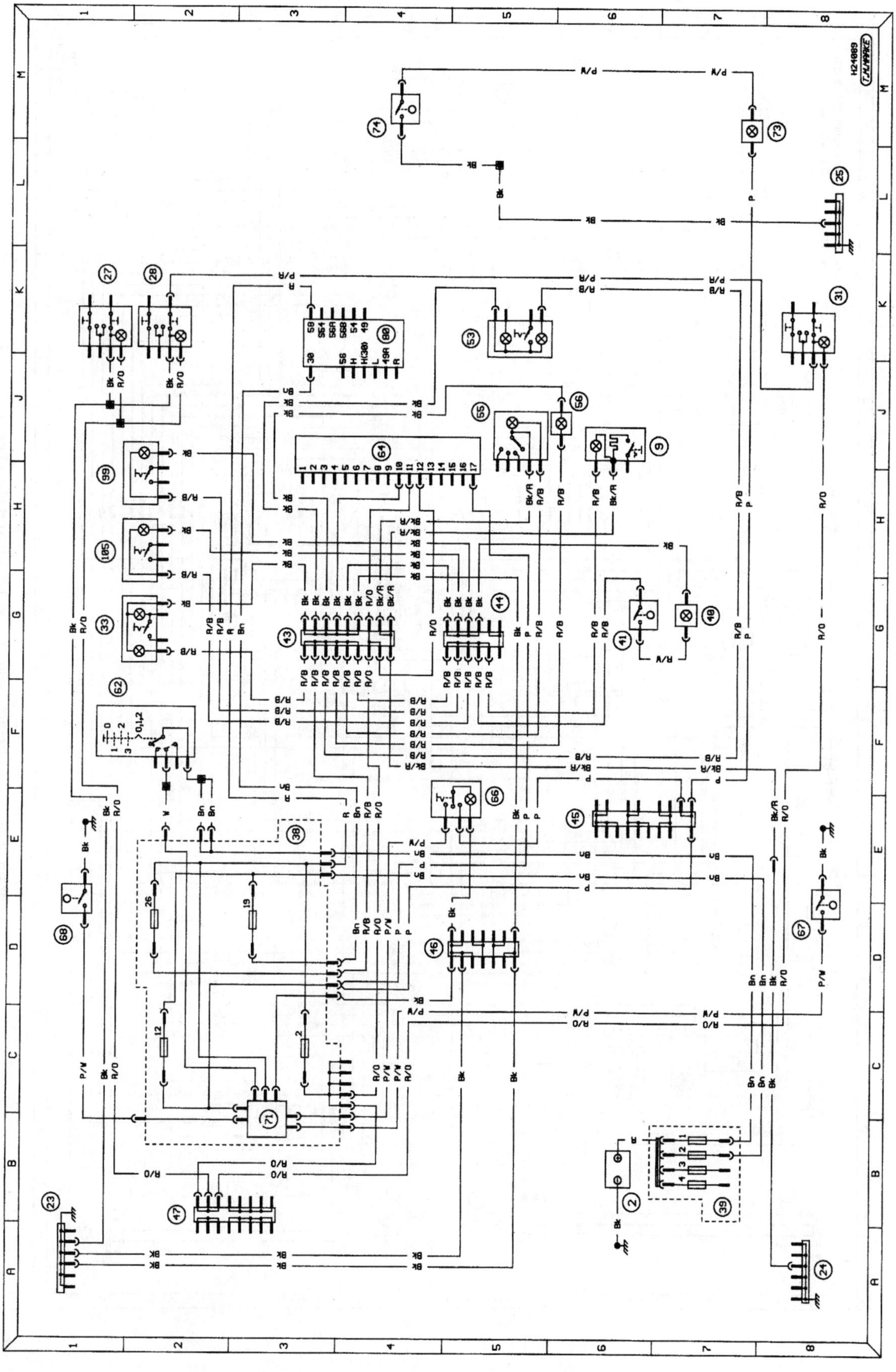

Diagram 2a: Interior lighting

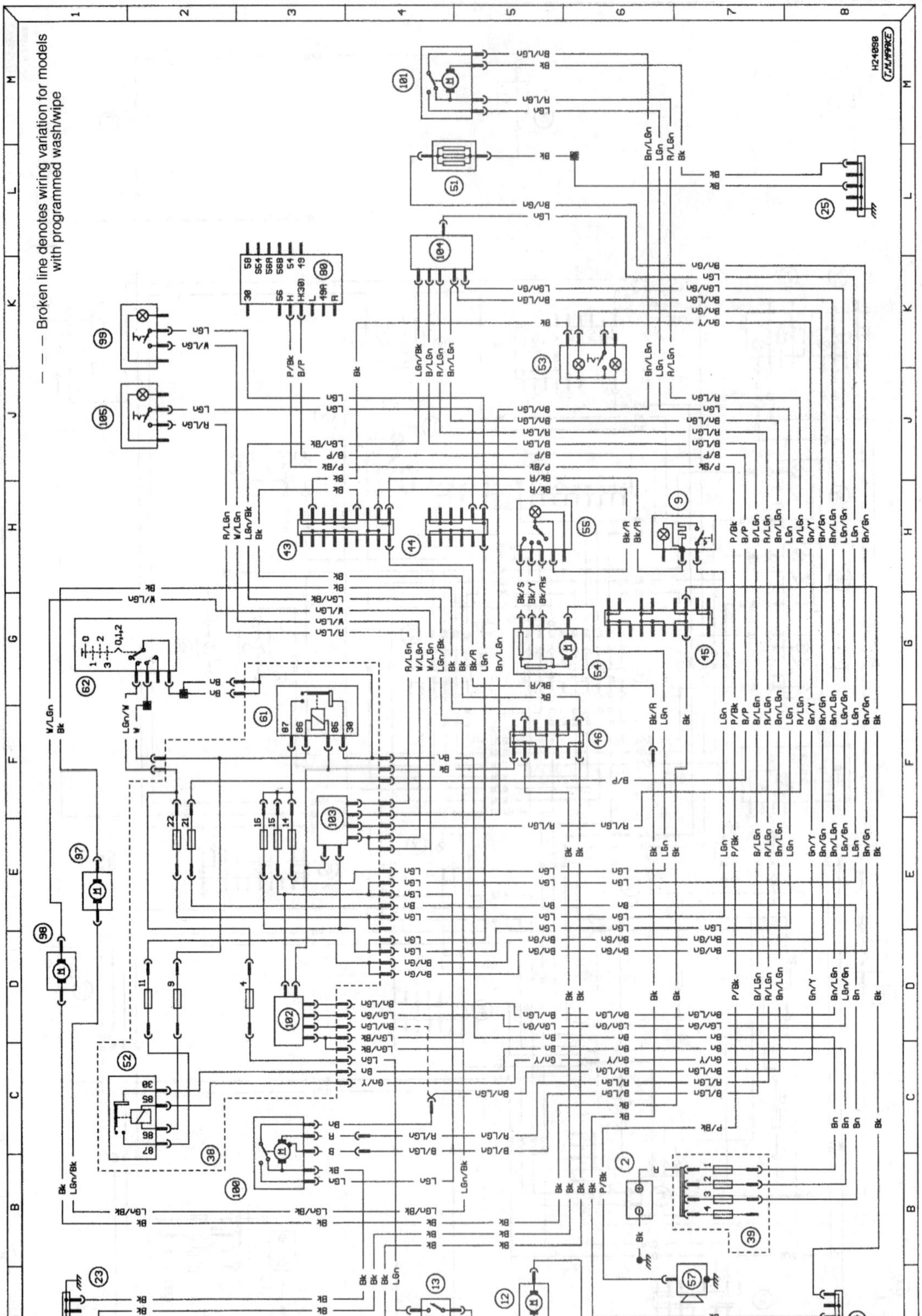
Broken line denotes wiring variation for models with programmed wash/wipe
H24098

Diagram 3: Ancillary circuits - wash/wipe, heater and cigar lighter

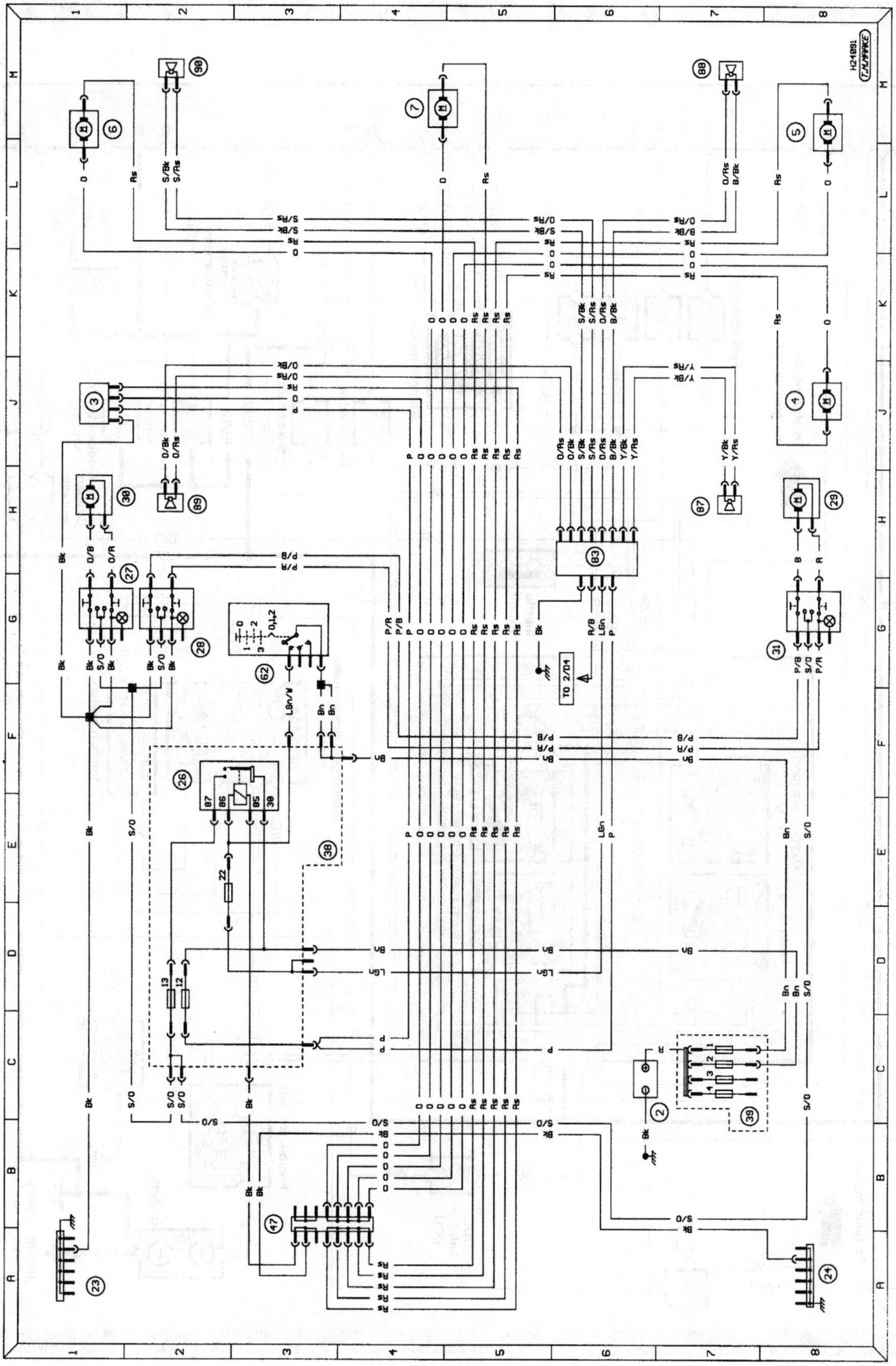

Diagram 3a: Ancillary circuits - electric windows, central locking and radio cassette

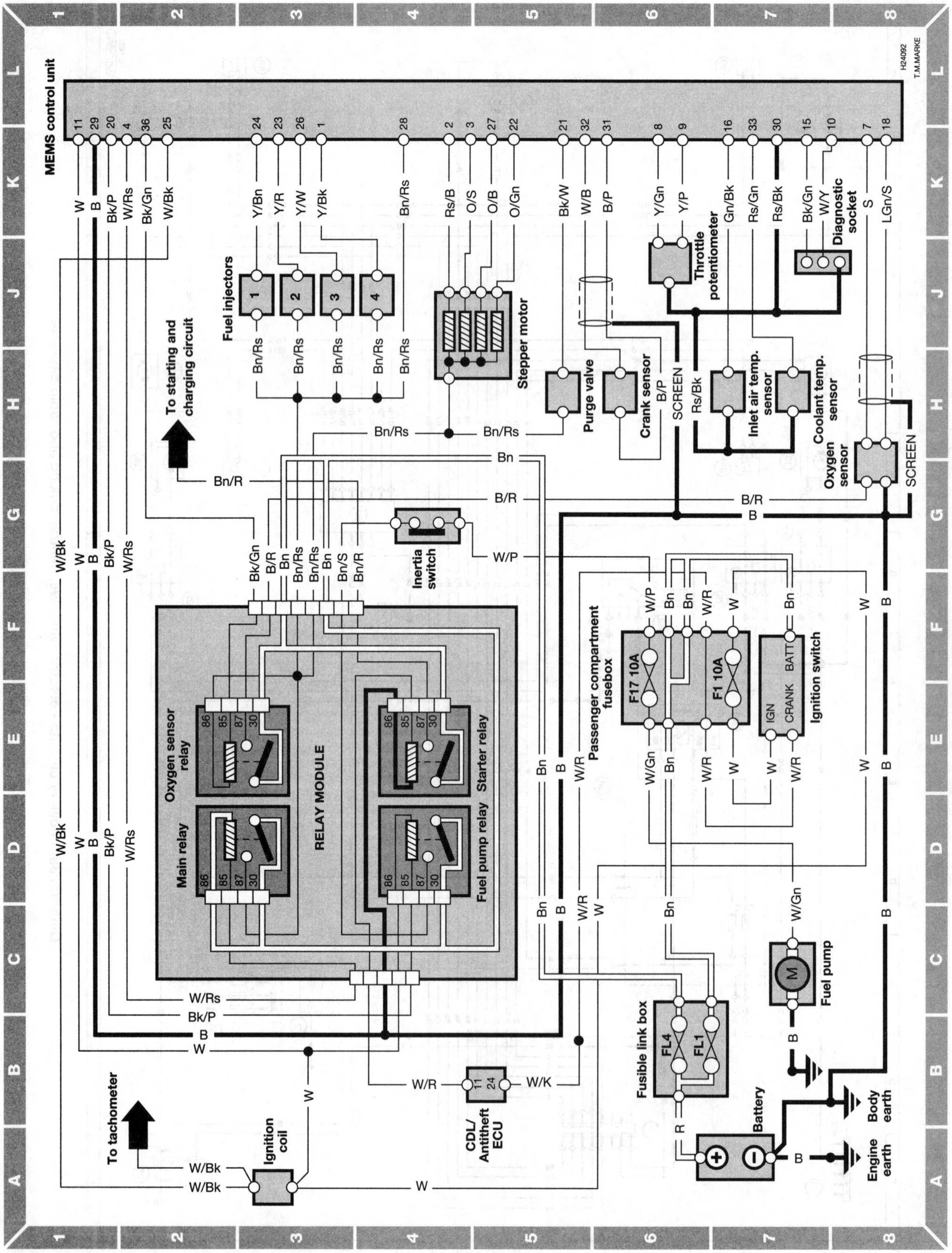

Supplementary diagram for multi-point fuel injection

Dimensions and Weights

Note: *All figures are approximate, and may vary according to model. Refer to manufacturer's data for exact figures.*

Dimensions

Overall length	3521 mm
Overall width (including mirrors)	1775 mm
Overall height (at kerb weight and specified ride height)	1377 mm
Wheelbase	2269 mm
Front track	1475 mm
Rear track	1470 mm
Turning circle:	
GTa, GTi 16v	10710 mm
All other models	9890 mm

Weights

Kerb weight - car unladen, less options, but with full fuel tank, coolant and all fluids, tools and spare wheel:	
1.1C - three-door	815 kg
1.1L - three-door	820 kg
1.1S - three-door	825 kg
1.1C - five-door	830 kg
1.1L - five-door, 1.4SL - three-door	835 kg
1.1S - five-door	840 kg
GTa - three-door	845 kg
1.4SL - five-door	850 kg
1.4GS, GTa - five-door	860 kg
GTi 16v	875 kg
Note: *Add 5 kg if a catalytic converter is fitted.*	
Maximum gross vehicle weight	1290 kg
Maximum roof rack load	50 kg
Maximum towing weight - with braked trailer:	
1.1 models	700 kg
1.4 models	800 kg
Towing hitch downward load	50 kg

Conversion Factors

Length (distance)

Inches (in)	25.4	=	Millimetres (mm)	x 0.0394	=	Inches (in)
Feet (ft)	0.305	=	Metres (m)	x 3.281	=	Feet (ft)
Miles	1.609	=	Kilometres (km)	x 0.621	=	Miles

Volume (capacity)

Cubic inches (cu in; in³)	x 16.387	=	Cubic centimetres (cc; cm³)	x 0.061	=	Cubic inches (cu in; in³)
Imperial pints (Imp pt)	x 0.568	=	Litres (l)	x 1.76	=	Imperial pints (Imp pt)
Imperial quarts (Imp qt)	x 1.137	=	Litres (l)	x 0.88	=	Imperial quarts (Imp qt)
Imperial quarts (Imp qt)	x 1.201	=	US quarts (US qt)	x 0.833	=	Imperial quarts (Imp qt)
US quarts (US qt)	x 0.946	=	Litres (l)	x 1.057	=	US quarts (US qt)
Imperial gallons (Imp gal)	x 4.546	=	Litres (l)	x 0.22	=	Imperial gallons (Imp gal)
Imperial gallons (Imp gal)	x 1.201	=	US gallons (US gal)	x 0.833	=	Imperial gallons (Imp gal)
US gallons (US gal)	x 3.785	=	Litres (l)	x 0.264	=	US gallons (US gal)

Mass (weight)

Ounces (oz)	x 28.35	=	Grams (g)	x 0.035	=	Ounces (oz)
Pounds (lb)	x 0.454	=	Kilograms (kg)	x 2.205	=	Pounds (lb)

Force

Ounces-force (ozf; oz)	x 0.278	=	Newtons (N)	x 3.6	=	Ounces-force (ozf; oz)
Pounds-force (lbf; lb)	x 4.448	=	Newtons (N)	x 0.225	=	Pounds-force (lbf; lb)
Newtons (N)	x 0.1	=	Kilograms-force (kgf; kg)	x 9.81	=	Newtons (N)

Pressure

Pounds-force per square inch (psi; lbf/in²; lb/in²)	x 0.070	=	Kilograms-force per square centimetre (kgf/cm²; kg/cm²)	x 14.223	=	Pounds-force per square inch (psi; lbf/in²; lb/in²)
Pounds-force per square inch (psi; lbf/in²; lb/in²)	x 0.068	=	Atmospheres (atm)	x 14.696	=	Pounds-force per square inch (psi; lbf/in²; lb/in²)
Pounds-force per square inch (psi; lbf/in²; lb/in²)	x 0.069	=	Bars	x 14.5	=	Pounds-force per square inch (psi; lbf/in²; lb/in²)
Pounds-force per square inch (psi; lbf/in²; lb/in²)	x 6.895	=	Kilopascals (kPa)	x 0.145	=	Pounds-force per square inch (psi; lbf/in²; lb/in²)
Kilopascals (kPa)	x 0.01	=	Kilograms-force per square centimetre (kgf/cm²; kg/cm²)	x 98.1	=	Kilopascals (kPa)
Millibar (mbar)	x 100	=	Pascals (Pa)	x 0.01	=	Millibar (mbar)
Millibar (mbar)	x 0.0145	=	Pounds-force per square inch (psi; lbf/in²; lb/in²)	x 68.947	=	Millibar (mbar)
Millibar (mbar)	x 0.75	=	Millimetres of mercury (mmHg)	x 1.333	=	Millibar (mbar)
Millibar (mbar)	x 0.401	=	Inches of water (inH_2O)	x 2.491	=	Millibar (mbar)
Millimetres of mercury (mmHg)	x 0.535	=	Inches of water (inH_2O)	x 1.868	=	Millimetres of mercury (mmHg)
Inches of water (inH_2O)	x 0.036	=	Pounds-force per square inch (psi; lbf/in²; lb/in²)	x 27.68	=	Inches of water (inH_2O)

Torque (moment of force)

Pounds-force inches (lbf in; lb in)	x 1.152	=	Kilograms-force centimetre (kgf cm; kg cm)	x 0.868	=	Pounds-force inches (lbf in; lb in)
Pounds-force inches (lbf in; lb in)	x 0.113	=	Newton metres (Nm)	x 8.85	=	Pounds-force inches (lbf in; lb in)
Pounds-force inches (lbf in; lb in)	x 0.083	=	Pounds-force feet (lbf ft; lb ft)	x 12	=	Pounds-force inches (lbf in; lb in)
Pounds-force feet (lbf ft; lb ft)	x 0.138	=	Kilograms-force metres (kgf m; kg m)	x 7.233	=	Pounds-force feet (lbf ft; lb ft)
Pounds-force feet (lbf ft; lb ft)	x 1.356	=	Newton metres (Nm)	x 0.738	=	Pounds-force feet (lbf ft; lb ft)
Newton metres (Nm)	x 0.102	=	Kilograms-force metres (kgf m; kg m)	x 9.804	=	Newton metres (Nm)

Power

Horsepower (hp)	x 745.7	=	Watts (W)	x 0.0013	=	Horsepower (hp)

Velocity (speed)

Miles per hour (miles/hr; mph)	x 1.609	=	Kilometres per hour (km/hr; kph)	x 0.621	=	Miles per hour (miles/hr; mph)

Fuel consumption*

Miles per gallon (mpg)	x 0.354	=	Kilometres per litre (km/l)	x 2.825	=	Miles per gallon (mpg)

** It is common practice to convert from miles per gallon (mpg) to litres/100 kilometres (l/100km), where mpg x l/100 km = 282*

Temperature

Degrees Fahrenheit = (°C x 1.8) + 32

Degrees Celsius (Degrees Centigrade; °C) = (°F - 32) x 0.56

Buying Spare Parts

Spare parts are available from many sources, including maker's appointed garages, accessory shops, and motor factors. To be sure of obtaining the correct parts, it will sometimes be necessary to quote the vehicle identification number. If possible, it can also be useful to take the old parts along for positive identification. Items such as starter motors and alternators may be available under a service exchange scheme - any parts returned should always be clean.

Our advice regarding spare part sources is as follows.

Officially-appointed garages

This is the best source of parts which are peculiar to your car, and which are not otherwise generally available (eg badges, interior trim, certain body panels, etc). It is also the only place at which you should buy parts if the vehicle is still under warranty.

Accessory shops

These are very good places to buy materials and components needed for the maintenance of your car (oil, air and fuel filters, spark plugs, light bulbs, drivebelts, oils and greases, brake pads, touch-up paint, etc). Components of this nature sold by a reputable shop are of the same standard as those used by the car manufacturer.

Besides components, these shops also sell tools and general accessories, usually have convenient opening hours, charge lower prices, and can often be found not far from home. Some accessory shops have parts counters where the components needed for almost any repair job can be purchased or ordered.

Motor factors

Good factors will stock all the more important components which wear out comparatively quickly, and can sometimes supply individual components needed for the overhaul of a larger assembly (eg brake seals and hydraulic parts, bearing shells, pistons, valves, alternator brushes). They may also handle work such as cylinder block reboring, crankshaft regrinding and balancing, etc.

Tyre and exhaust specialists

These outlets may be independent, or members of a local or national chain. They frequently offer competitive prices when compared with a main dealer or local garage, but it will pay to obtain several quotes before making a decision. When researching prices, also ask what "extras" may be added - for instance, fitting a new valve and balancing the wheel are both commonly charged on top of the price of a new tyre.

Other sources

Beware of parts or materials obtained from market stalls, car boot sales or similar outlets. Such items are not invariably sub-standard, but there is little chance of compensation if they do prove unsatisfactory. In the case of safety-critical components such as brake pads, there is the risk not only of financial loss but also of an accident causing injury or death.

Second-hand components or assemblies obtained from a car breaker can be a good buy in some circumstances, but this sort of purchase is best made by the experienced DIY mechanic.

Vehicle Identification

Modifications are a continuing and unpublicised process in vehicle manufacture, quite apart from major model changes. Spare parts manuals and lists are compiled upon a numerical basis, the individual vehicle identification numbers being essential to correct identification of the component concerned.

When ordering spare parts, always give as much information as possible. Quote the car model, year of manufacture, body and engine numbers as appropriate.

The *vehicle identification plate* is located on the bonnet lock platform **(see illustration)**. It gives the VIN (vehicle identification number), vehicle weight information and paint and trim colour codes. The VIN is also stamped into the drain channel at the rear edge of the bonnet, above the braking system master cylinder.

The *body number* is stamped into a plate fixed to the right-hand lip of the spare wheel well, in the luggage compartment **(see illustration)**.

The *engine number* is stamped into a raised pad on the front left-hand end of the cylinder block/crankcase, next to the transmission **(see illustration)**.

Other identification numbers or codes are stamped on major items such as the gearbox, final drive housing, distributor etc. These numbers are unlikely to be needed by the home mechanic.

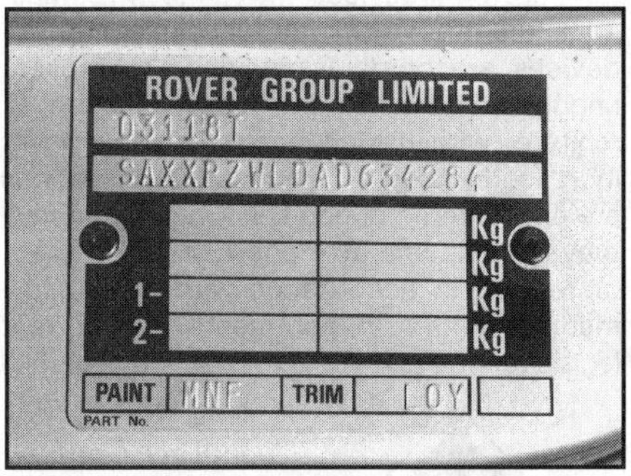

Vehicle identification plate on bonnet lock platform

Vehicle body number on right-hand lip of spare wheel well

Engine number on front of cylinder block/crankcase

Whenever servicing, repair or overhaul work is carried out on the car or its components, it is necessary to observe the following procedures and instructions. This will assist in carrying out the operation efficiently and to a professional standard of workmanship.

Joint mating faces and gaskets

When separating components at their mating faces, never insert screwdrivers or similar implements into the joint between the faces in order to prise them apart. This can cause severe damage which results in oil leaks, coolant leaks, etc upon reassembly. Separation is usually achieved by tapping along the joint with a soft-faced hammer in order to break the seal. However, note that this method may not be suitable where dowels are used for component location.

Where a gasket is used between the mating faces of two components, ensure that it is renewed on reassembly, and fit it dry unless otherwise stated in the repair procedure. Make sure that the mating faces are clean and dry, with all traces of old gasket removed. When cleaning a joint face, use a tool which is not likely to score or damage the face, and remove any burrs or nicks with an oilstone or fine file.

Make sure that tapped holes are cleaned with a pipe cleaner, and keep them free of jointing compound, if this is being used, unless specifically instructed otherwise.

Ensure that all orifices, channels or pipes are clear, and blow through them, preferably using compressed air.

Oil seals

Oil seals can be removed by levering them out with a wide flat-bladed screwdriver or similar tool. Alternatively, a number of self-tapping screws may be screwed into the seal, and these used as a purchase for pliers or similar in order to pull the seal free.

Whenever an oil seal is removed from its working location, either individually or as part of an assembly, it should be renewed.

The very fine sealing lip of the seal is easily damaged, and will not seal if the surface it contacts is not completely clean and free from scratches, nicks or grooves. If the original sealing surface of the component cannot be restored, and the manufacturer has not made provision for slight relocation of the seal relative to the sealing surface, the component should be renewed.

Protect the lips of the seal from any surface which may damage them in the course of fitting. Use tape or a conical sleeve where possible. Lubricate the seal lips with oil before fitting and, on dual-lipped seals, fill the space between the lips with grease.

Unless otherwise stated, oil seals must be fitted with their sealing lips toward the lubricant to be sealed.

Use a tubular drift or block of wood of the appropriate size to install the seal and, if the seal housing is shouldered, drive the seal down to the shoulder. If the seal housing is unshouldered, the seal should be fitted with its face flush with the housing top face (unless otherwise instructed).

Screw threads and fastenings

Seized nuts, bolts and screws are quite a common occurrence where corrosion has set in, and the use of penetrating oil or releasing fluid will often overcome this problem if the offending item is soaked for a while before attempting to release it. The use of an impact driver may also provide a means of releasing such stubborn fastening devices, when used in conjunction with the appropriate screwdriver bit or socket. If none of these methods works, it may be necessary to resort to the careful application of heat, or the use of a hacksaw or nut splitter device.

Studs are usually removed by locking two nuts together on the threaded part, and then using a spanner on the lower nut to unscrew the stud. Studs or bolts which have broken off below the surface of the component in which they are mounted can sometimes be removed using a stud extractor. Always ensure that a blind tapped hole is completely free from oil, grease, water or other fluid before installing the bolt or stud. Failure to do this could cause the housing to crack due to the hydraulic action of the bolt or stud as it is screwed in.

When tightening a castellated nut to accept a split pin, tighten the nut to the specified torque, where applicable, and then tighten further to the next split pin hole. Never slacken the nut to align the split pin hole, unless stated in the repair procedure.

When checking or retightening a nut or bolt to a specified torque setting, slacken the nut or bolt by a quarter of a turn, and then retighten to the specified setting. However, this should not be attempted where angular tightening has been used.

For some screw fastenings, notably cylinder head bolts or nuts, torque wrench settings are no longer specified for the latter stages of tightening, "angle-tightening" being called up instead. Typically, a fairly low torque wrench setting will be applied to the bolts/nuts in the correct sequence, followed by one or more stages of tightening through specified angles.

Locknuts, locktabs and washers

Any fastening which will rotate against a component or housing during tightening should always have a washer between it and the relevant component or housing.

Spring or split washers should always be renewed when they are used to lock a critical component such as a big-end bearing retaining bolt or nut. Locktabs which are folded over to retain a nut or bolt should always be renewed.

Self-locking nuts can be re-used in non-critical areas, providing resistance can be felt when the locking portion passes over the bolt or stud thread. However, it should be noted that self-locking stiffnuts tend to lose their effectiveness after long periods of use, and should be renewed as a matter of course.

Split pins must always be replaced with new ones of the correct size for the hole.

When thread-locking compound is found on the threads of a fastener which is to be re-used, it should be cleaned off with a wire brush and solvent, and fresh compound applied on reassembly.

Special tools

Some repair procedures in this manual entail the use of special tools such as a press, two or three-legged pullers, spring compressors, etc. Wherever possible, suitable readily-available alternatives to the manufacturer's special tools are described, and are shown in use. In some instances, where no alternative is possible, it has been necessary to resort to the use of a manufacturer's tool, and this has been done for reasons of safety as well as the efficient completion of the repair operation. Unless you are highly-skilled and have a thorough understanding of the procedures described, never attempt to bypass the use of any special tool when the procedure described specifies its use. Not only is there a very great risk of personal injury, but expensive damage could be caused to the components involved.

Environmental considerations

When disposing of used engine oil, brake fluid, antifreeze, etc, give due consideration to any detrimental environmental effects. Do not, for instance, pour any of the above liquids down drains into the general sewage system, or onto the ground to soak away. Many local council refuse tips provide a facility for waste oil disposal, as do some garages. If none of these facilities are available, consult your local Environmental Health Department, or the National Rivers Authority, for further advice.

With the universal tightening-up of legislation regarding the emission of environmentally-harmful substances from motor vehicles, most current vehicles have tamperproof devices fitted to the main adjustment points of the fuel system. These devices are primarily designed to prevent unqualified persons from adjusting the fuel/air mixture, with the chance of a consequent increase in toxic emissions. If such devices are encountered during servicing or overhaul, they should, wherever possible, be renewed or refitted in accordance with the vehicle manufacturer's requirements or current legislation.

OIL CARE
FOLLOW THE CODE
OIL BANK LINE
0800 66 33 66

Note: It is antisocial and illegal to dump oil down the drain. To find the location of your local oil recycling bank, call this number free.

Jacking and Vehicle Support

The jack supplied with the vehicle tool kit should only be used for changing the roadwheels - see *"Wheel changing"* at the front of this Manual. When using the jack, position it on firm ground and locate its head in the relevant vehicle jacking point **(see illustrations)**.

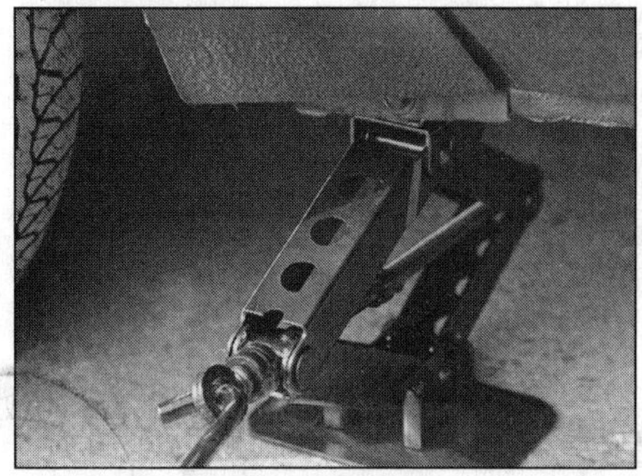

With jack base on firm ground . . .

. . . locate jack head into vehicle jacking point (arrowed)

When carrying out any other kind of work, raise the vehicle using a hydraulic (or "trolley") jack, and always supplement the jack with axle stands positioned under the vehicle jacking points.

Always use the recommended jacking, support and towing points **(see illustration)** and refer to the following instructions:

If the front of the vehicle is to be raised, place the jack head under point 1 or on a jacking beam placed across points 2. Axle stands should be placed at points 3 and 4 or points 7.

To raise the rear of the vehicle, place the jack head on a jacking beam placed across points 8. Axle stands should be placed at points 5 and 6 or points 9.

To raise the side of the vehicle, place the jack head under point 3 or 4 at the front, point 9 at the rear, with axle stands at points 5, 6 or 7, as appropriate.

Never work under, around or near a raised vehicle unless it is adequately supported in at least two places.

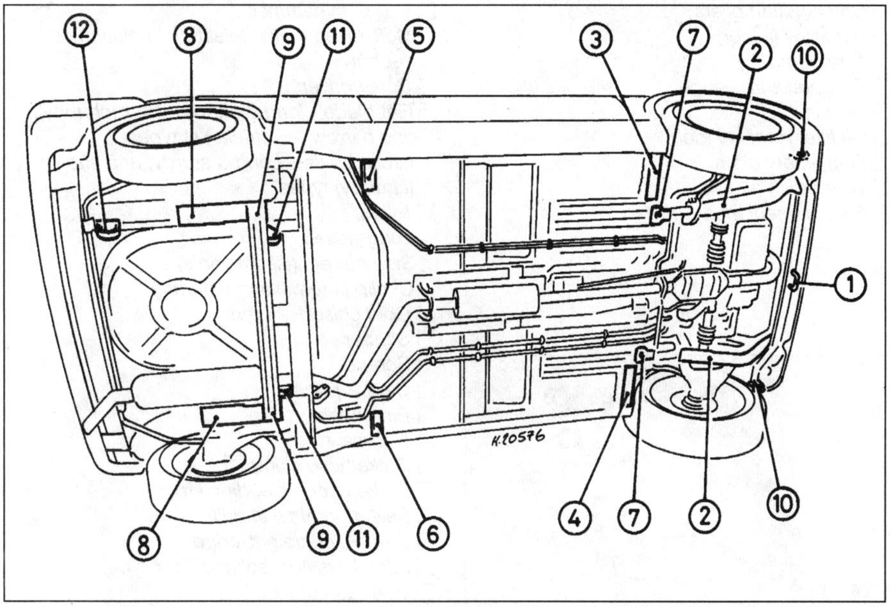

Jacking, supporting and towing points

1 *Central jack location pad*
2 *Front suspension subframe longitudinals*
3 *Jacking/support point*
4 *Jacking/support point*
5 *Jacking/support point*
6 *Jacking/support point*
7 *Underbody longitudinal sections*
8 *Rear suspension subframe bolts*
9 *Rear suspension subframe reinforced areas*
10 *Front towing eyes*
11 *Transporter lashing points*
12 *Rear towing eye*

Radio/cassette Anti-theft system - precaution

The radio/cassette unit fitted as standard equipment by Rover is equipped with a built-in security code, to deter thieves. If the power source to the unit is cut, the anti-theft system will activate. Even if the power source is immediately reconnected, the radio/cassette unit will not function until the security code has been entered. Therefore if you do not know the correct security code for the unit, **do not** disconnect the battery negative lead, or remove the radio/cassette unit from the vehicle.

The procedure for reprogramming a unit that has been disconnected from its power supply varies from model to model - consult the handbook supplied with the unit for specific details or refer to your Rover dealer.

Tools and Working Facilities

Introduction

A selection of good tools is a fundamental requirement for anyone contemplating the maintenance and repair of a motor vehicle. For the owner who does not possess any, their purchase will prove a considerable expense, offsetting some of the savings made by doing-it-yourself. However, provided that the tools purchased meet the relevant national safety standards and are of good quality, they will last for many years and prove an extremely worthwhile investment.

To help the average owner to decide which tools are needed to carry out the various tasks detailed in this manual, we have compiled three lists of tools under the following headings: *Maintenance and minor repair*, *Repair and overhaul*, and *Special*. Newcomers to practical mechanics should start off with the *Maintenance and minor repair* tool kit, and confine themselves to the simpler jobs around the vehicle. Then, as confidence and experience grow, more difficult tasks can be undertaken, with extra tools being purchased as, and when, they are needed. In this way, a *Maintenance and minor repair* tool kit can be built up into a *Repair and overhaul* tool kit over a considerable period of time, without any major cash outlays. The experienced do-it-yourselfer will have a tool kit good enough for most repair and overhaul procedures, and will add tools from the *Special* category when it is felt that the expense is justified by the amount of use to which these tools will be put.

Maintenance and minor repair tool kit

The tools given in this list should be considered as a minimum requirement if routine maintenance, servicing and minor repair operations are to be undertaken. We recommend the purchase of combination spanners (ring one end, open-ended the other); although more expensive than open-ended ones, they do give the advantages of both types of spanner.

- ☐ *Combination spanners:*
  Metric - 8 to 19 mm inclusive
- ☐ *Adjustable spanner - 35 mm jaw (approx.)*
- ☐ *Spark plug spanner (with rubber insert) - petrol models*
- ☐ *Spark plug gap adjustment tool - petrol models*
- ☐ *Set of feeler gauges*
- ☐ *Brake bleed nipple spanner*
- ☐ *Screwdrivers:*
  Flat blade - 100 mm long x 6 mm dia
  Cross blade - 100 mm long x 6 mm dia
- ☐ *Combination pliers*
- ☐ *Hacksaw (junior)*
- ☐ *Tyre pump*
- ☐ *Tyre pressure gauge*
- ☐ *Oil can*
- ☐ *Oil filter removal tool*
- ☐ *Fine emery cloth*
- ☐ *Wire brush (small)*
- ☐ *Funnel (medium size)*

Repair and overhaul tool kit

These tools are virtually essential for anyone undertaking any major repairs to a motor vehicle, and are additional to those given in the *Maintenance and minor repair* list. Included in this list is a comprehensive set of sockets. Although these are expensive, they will be found invaluable as they are so versatile - particularly if various drives are included in the set. We recommend the half-inch square-drive type, as this can be used with most proprietary torque wrenches.

The tools in this list will sometimes need to be supplemented by tools from the *Special* list:

- ☐ *Sockets (or box spanners) to cover range in previous list (including Torx sockets)*
- ☐ *Reversible ratchet drive (for use with sockets)*
- ☐ *Extension piece, 250 mm (for use with sockets)*
- ☐ *Universal joint (for use with sockets)*
- ☐ *Torque wrench (for use with sockets)*
- ☐ *Self-locking grips*
- ☐ *Ball pein hammer*
- ☐ *Soft-faced mallet (plastic/aluminium or rubber)*
- ☐ *Screwdrivers:*
  Flat blade - long & sturdy, short (chubby), and narrow (electrician's) types
  Cross blade – Long & sturdy, and short (chubby) types
- ☐ *Pliers:*
  Long-nosed
  Side cutters (electrician's)
  Circlip (internal and external)
- ☐ *Cold chisel - 25 mm*
- ☐ *Scriber*
- ☐ *Scraper*
- ☐ *Centre-punch*
- ☐ *Pin punch*
- ☐ *Hacksaw*
- ☐ *Brake hose clamp*
- ☐ *Brake/clutch bleeding kit*
- ☐ *Selection of twist drills*
- ☐ *Steel rule/straight-edge*
- ☐ *Allen keys (inc. splined/Torx type)*
- ☐ *Selection of files*
- ☐ *Wire brush*
- ☐ *Axle stands*
- ☐ *Jack (strong trolley or hydraulic type)*
- ☐ *Light with extension lead*

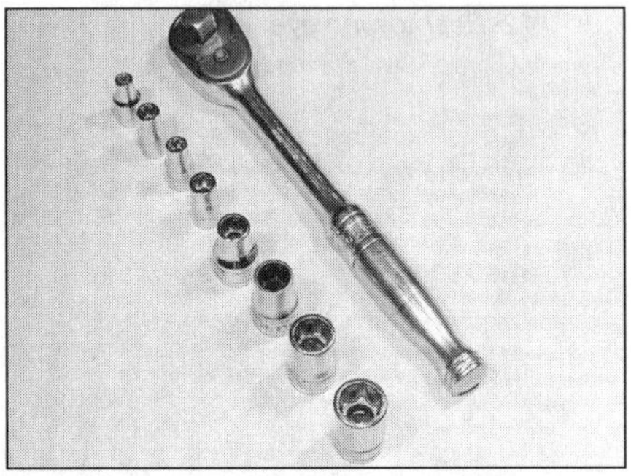

Sockets and reversible ratchet drive

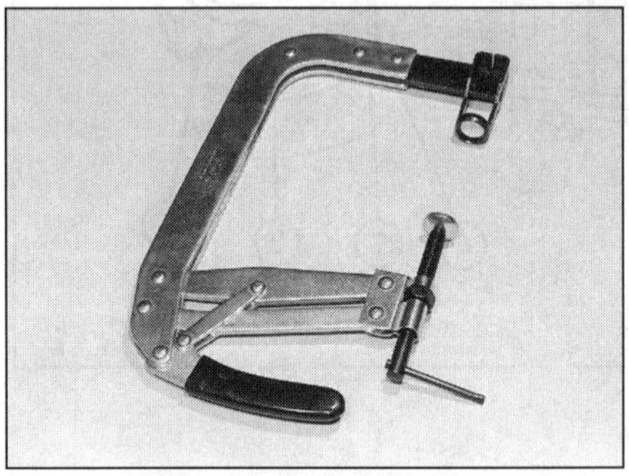

Valve spring compressor

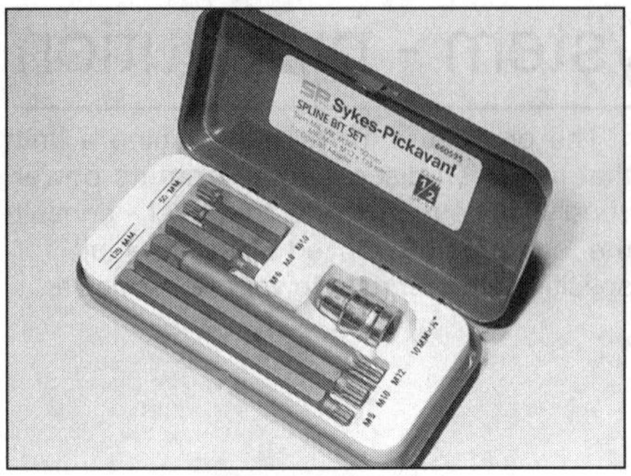

Spline bit set

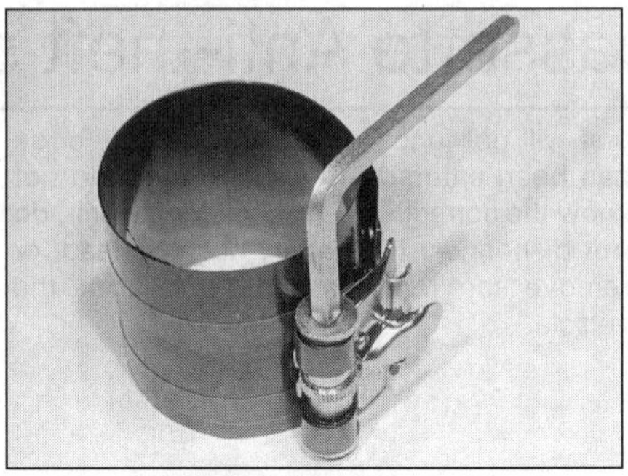

Piston ring compressor

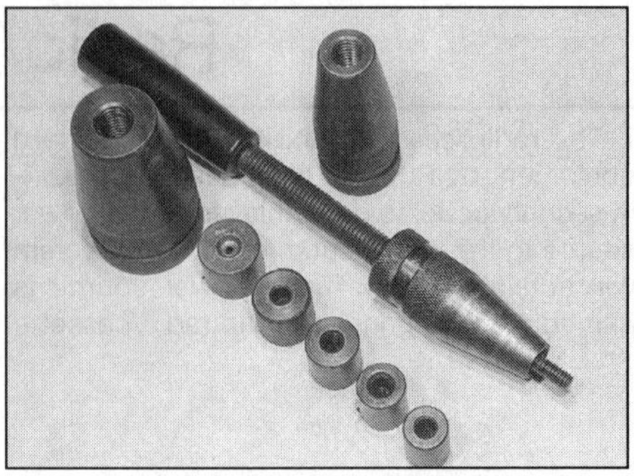

Clutch plate alignment set

Special tools

The tools in this list are those which are not used regularly, are expensive to buy, or which need to be used in accordance with their manufacturers' instructions. Unless relatively difficult mechanical jobs are undertaken frequently, it will not be economic to buy many of these tools. Where this is the case, you could consider clubbing together with friends (or joining a motorists' club) to make a joint purchase, or borrowing the tools against a deposit from a local garage or tool hire specialist. It is worth noting that many of the larger DIY superstores now carry a large range of special tools for hire at modest rates.

The following list contains only those tools and instruments freely available to the public, and not those special tools produced by the vehicle manufacturer specifically for its dealer network. You will find occasional references to these manufacturers' special tools in the text of this manual. Generally, an alternative method of doing the job without the vehicle manufacturers' special tool is given. However, sometimes there is no alternative to using them. Where this is the case and the relevant tool cannot be bought or borrowed, you will have to entrust the work to a dealer.

☐ *Valve spring compressor*
☐ *Valve grinding tool*
☐ *Piston ring compressor*
☐ *Piston ring removal/installation tool*
☐ *Cylinder bore hone*
☐ *Balljoint separator*
☐ *Coil spring compressors (where applicable)*
☐ *Two/three-legged hub and bearing puller*
☐ *Impact screwdriver*
☐ *Micrometer and/or vernier calipers*
☐ *Dial gauge*
☐ *Stroboscopic timing light*
☐ *Dwell angle meter/tachometer*
☐ *Universal electrical multi-meter*
☐ *Cylinder compression gauge*
☐ *Hand-operated vacuum pump and gauge*
☐ *Clutch plate alignment set*
☐ *Brake shoe steady spring cup removal tool*
☐ *Bush and bearing removal/installation set*
☐ *Stud extractors*
☐ *Tap and die set*
☐ *Lifting tackle*
☐ *Trolley jack*

Buying tools

Reputable motor accessory shops and superstores often offer excellent quality tools at discount prices, so it pays to shop around.

Remember, you don't have to buy the most expensive items on the shelf, but it is always advisable to steer clear of the very cheap tools. Beware of 'bargains' offered on market stalls or at car boot sales. There are plenty of good tools around at reasonable prices, but always aim to purchase items which meet the relevant national safety standards. If in doubt, ask the proprietor or manager of the shop for advice before making a purchase.

Care and maintenance of tools

Having purchased a reasonable tool kit, it is necessary to keep the tools in a clean and serviceable condition. After use, always wipe off any dirt, grease and metal particles using a clean, dry cloth, before putting the tools away. Never leave them lying around after they have been used. A simple tool rack on the garage or workshop wall for items such as screwdrivers and pliers is a good idea. Store all normal spanners and sockets in a metal box. Any measuring instruments, gauges, meters, etc, must be carefully stored where they cannot be damaged or become rusty.

Take a little care when tools are used. Hammer heads inevitably become marked, and screwdrivers lose the keen edge on their blades from time to time. A little timely attention with emery cloth or a file will soon restore items like this to a good finish.

Working facilities

Not to be forgotten when discussing tools is the workshop itself. If anything more than routine maintenance is to be carried out, a suitable working area becomes essential.

It is appreciated that many an owner-mechanic is forced by circumstances to remove an engine or similar item without the benefit of a garage or workshop. Having done this, any repairs should always be done under the cover of a roof.

Wherever possible, any dismantling should be done on a clean, flat workbench or table at a suitable working height.

Any workbench needs a vice; one with a jaw opening of 100 mm is suitable for most jobs. As mentioned previously, some clean dry storage space is also required for tools, as well as for any lubricants, cleaning fluids, touch-up paints etc, which become necessary.

Another item which may be required, and which has a much more general usage, is an electric drill with a chuck capacity of at least 8 mm. This, together with a good range of twist drills, is virtually essential for fitting accessories.

Last, but not least, always keep a supply of old newspapers and clean, lint-free rags available, and try to keep any working area as clean as possible.

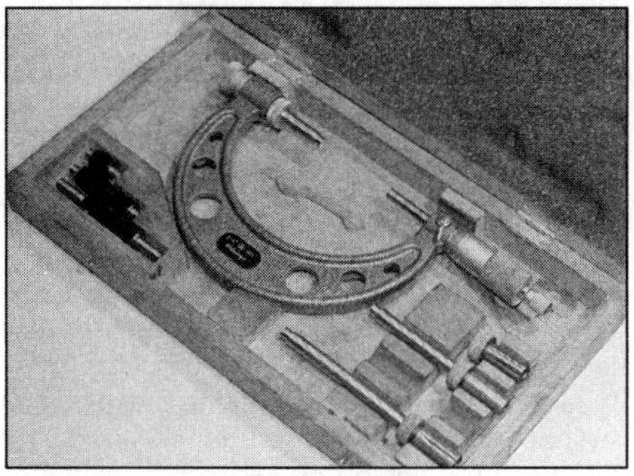

Micrometer set

Dial test indicator ("dial gauge")

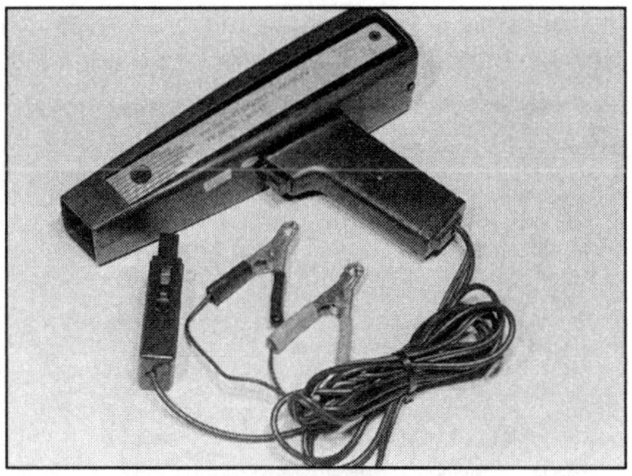

Stroboscopic timing light

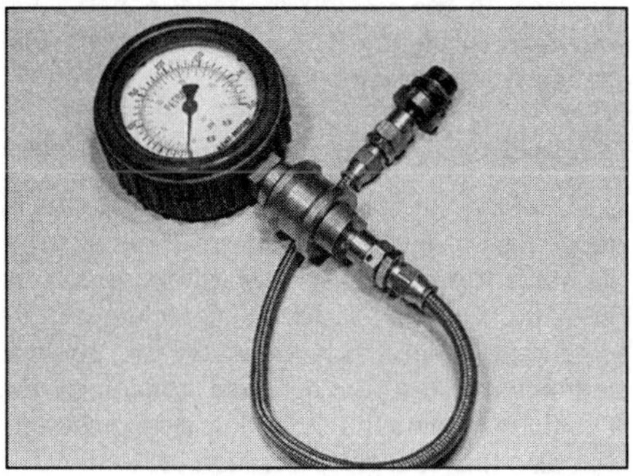

Compression tester

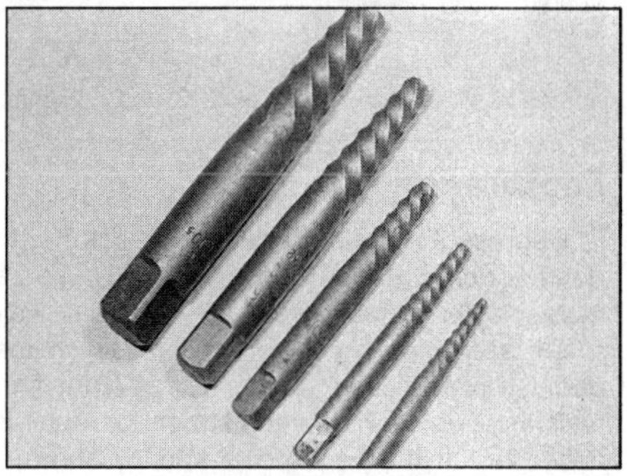

Stud extractor set

This is a guide to getting your vehicle through the MOT test. Obviously it will not be possible to examine the vehicle to the same standard as the professional MOT tester. However, working through the following checks will enable you to identify any problem areas before submitting the vehicle for the test.

Where a testable component is in borderline condition, the tester has discretion in deciding whether to pass or fail it. The basis of such discretion is whether the tester would be happy for a close relative or friend to use the vehicle with the component in that condition. If the vehicle presented is clean and evidently well cared for, the tester may be more inclined to pass a borderline component than if the vehicle is scruffy and apparently neglected.

It has only been possible to summarise the test requirements here, based on the regulations in force at the time of printing. Test standards are becoming increasingly stringent, although there are some exemptions for older vehicles. For full details obtain a copy of the Haynes publication Pass the MOT! (available from stockists of Haynes manuals).

An assistant will be needed to help carry out some of these checks.

The checks have been sub-divided into four categories, as follows:

1 Checks carried out **FROM THE DRIVER'S SEAT**

2 Checks carried out **WITH THE VEHICLE ON THE GROUND**

3 Checks carried out **WITH THE VEHICLE RAISED AND THE WHEELS FREE TO TURN**

4 Checks carried out on **YOUR VEHICLE'S EXHAUST EMISSION SYSTEM**

1 Checks carried out FROM THE DRIVER'S SEAT

Handbrake

☐ Test the operation of the handbrake. Excessive travel (too many clicks) indicates incorrect brake or cable adjustment.

☐ Check that the handbrake cannot be released by tapping the lever sideways. Check the security of the lever mountings.

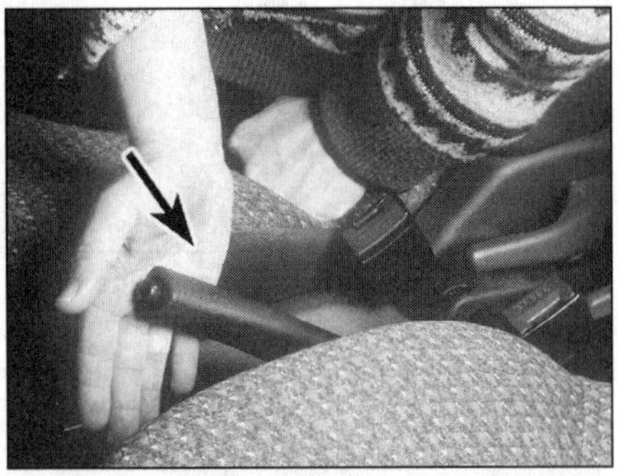

Footbrake

☐ Depress the brake pedal and check that it does not creep down to the floor, indicating a master cylinder fault. Release the pedal, wait a few seconds, then depress it again. If the pedal travels nearly to the floor before firm resistance is felt, brake adjustment or repair is necessary. If the pedal feels spongy, there is air in the hydraulic system which must be removed by bleeding.

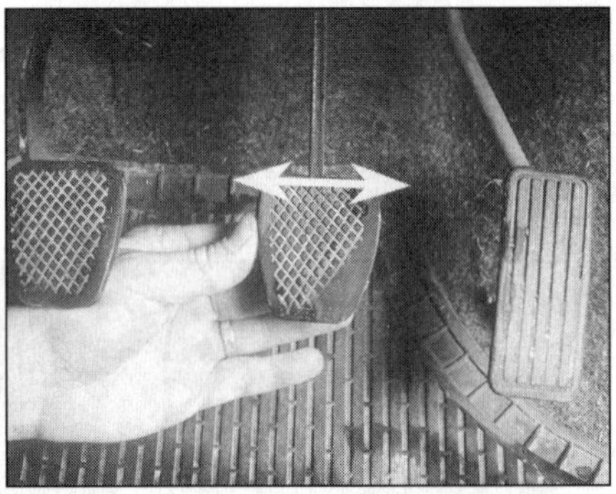

☐ Check that the brake pedal is secure and in good condition. Check also for signs of fluid leaks on the pedal, floor or carpets, which would indicate failed seals in the brake master cylinder.

☐ Check the servo unit (when applicable) by operating the brake pedal several times, then keeping the pedal depressed and starting the engine. As the engine starts, the pedal will move down slightly. If not, the vacuum hose or the servo itself may be faulty.

Steering wheel and column

☐ Examine the steering wheel for fractures or looseness of the hub, spokes or rim.

☐ Move the steering wheel from side to side and then up and down. Check that the steering wheel is not loose on the column, indicating wear or a loose retaining nut. Continue moving the steering wheel as before, but also turn it slightly from left to right.

☐ Check that the steering wheel is not loose on the column, and that there is no abnormal

movement of the steering wheel, indicating wear in the column support bearings or couplings.

Windscreen and mirrors

☐ The windscreen must be free of cracks or other significant damage within the driver's field of view. (Small stone chips are acceptable.) Rear view mirrors must be secure, intact, and capable of being adjusted.

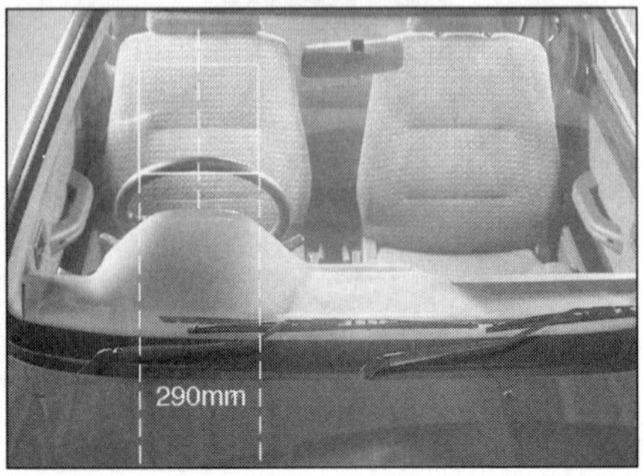

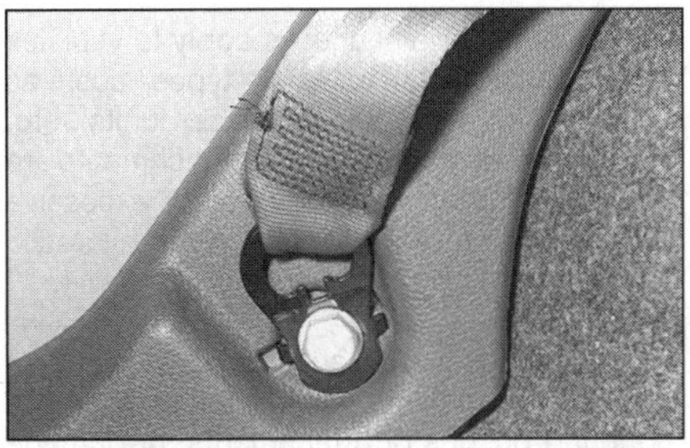

Seat belts and seats

Note: *The following checks are applicable to all seat belts, front and rear.*

☐ Examine the webbing of all the belts (including rear belts if fitted) for cuts, serious fraying or deterioration. Fasten and unfasten each belt to check the buckles. If applicable, check the retracting mechanism. Check the security of all seat belt mountings accessible from inside the vehicle.

☐ The front seats themselves must be securely attached and the backrests must lock in the upright position.

Doors

☐ Both front doors must be able to be opened and closed from outside and inside, and must latch securely when closed.

2 Checks carried out WITH THE VEHICLE ON THE GROUND

Vehicle identification

☐ Number plates must be in good condition, secure and legible, with letters and numbers correctly spaced – spacing at (A) should be twice that at (B).

☐ The VIN plate and/or homologation plate must be legible.

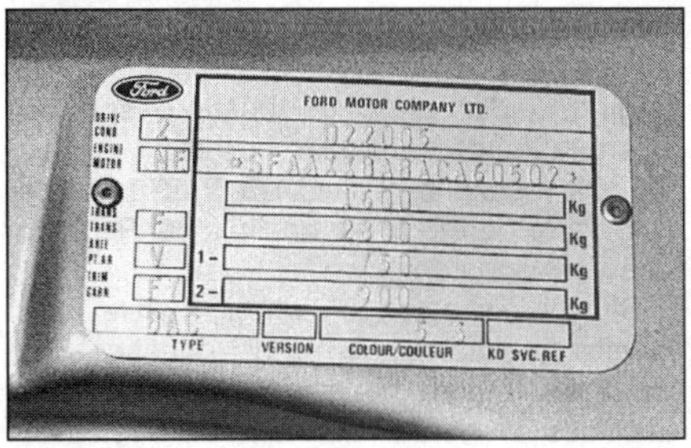

Electrical equipment

☐ Switch on the ignition and check the operation of the horn.

☐ Check the windscreen washers and wipers, examining the wiper blades; renew damaged or perished blades. Also check the operation of the stop-lights.

☐ Check the operation of the sidelights and number plate lights. The lenses and reflectors must be secure, clean and undamaged.

☐ Check the operation and alignment of the headlights. The headlight reflectors must not be tarnished and the lenses must be undamaged.

☐ Switch on the ignition and check the operation of the direction indicators (including the instrument panel tell-tale) and the hazard warning lights. Operation of the sidelights and stop-lights must not affect the indicators - if it does, the cause is usually a bad earth at the rear light cluster.

☐ Check the operation of the rear foglight(s), including the warning light on the instrument panel or in the switch.

Footbrake

☐ Examine the master cylinder, brake pipes and servo unit for leaks, loose mountings, corrosion or other damage.

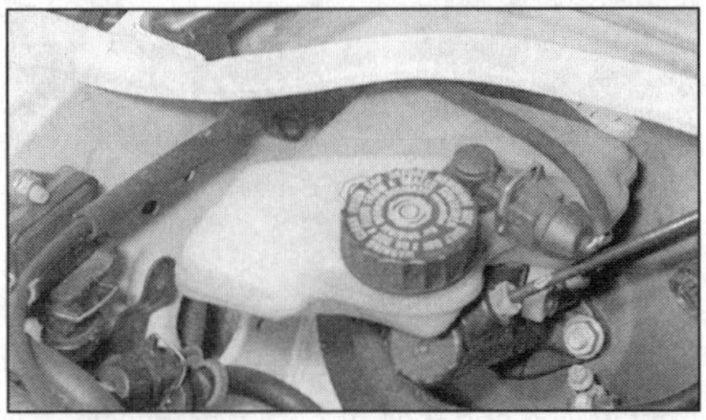

☐ The fluid reservoir must be secure and the fluid level must be between the upper (**A**) and lower (**B**) markings.

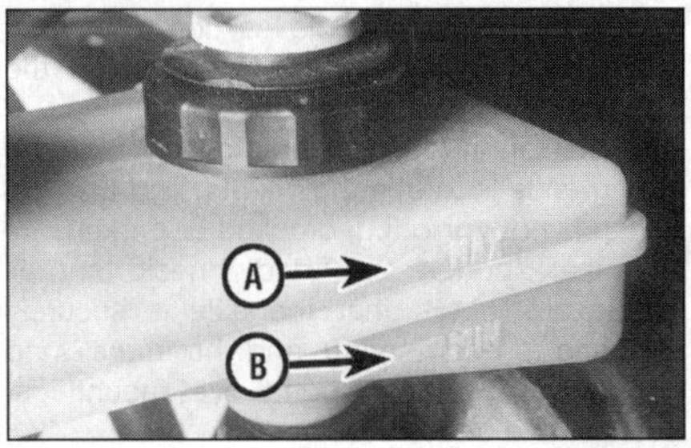

☐ Inspect both front brake flexible hoses for cracks or deterioration of the rubber. Turn the steering from lock to lock, and ensure that the hoses do not contact the wheel, tyre, or any part of the steering or suspension mechanism. With the brake pedal firmly depressed, check the hoses for bulges or leaks under pressure.

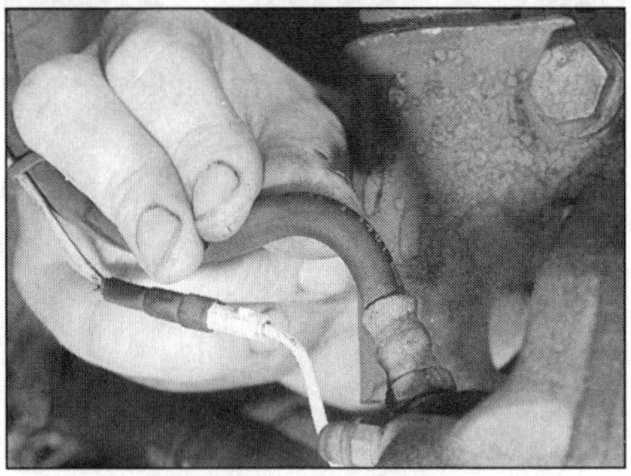

Steering and suspension

☐ Have your assistant turn the steering wheel from side to side slightly, up to the point where the steering gear just begins to transmit this movement to the roadwheels. Check for excessive free play between the steering wheel and the steering gear, indicating wear or insecurity of the steering column joints, the column-to-steering gear coupling, or the steering gear itself.

☐ Have your assistant turn the steering wheel more vigorously in each direction, so that the roadwheels just begin to turn. As this is done, examine all the steering joints, linkages, fittings and attachments. Renew any component that shows signs of wear or damage. On vehicles with power steering, check the security and condition of the steering pump, drivebelt and hoses.

☐ Check that the vehicle is standing level, and at approximately the correct ride height.

Shock absorbers

☐ Depress each corner of the vehicle in turn, then release it. The vehicle should rise and then settle in its normal position. If the vehicle continues to rise and fall, the shock absorber is defective. A shock absorber which has seized will also cause the vehicle to fail.

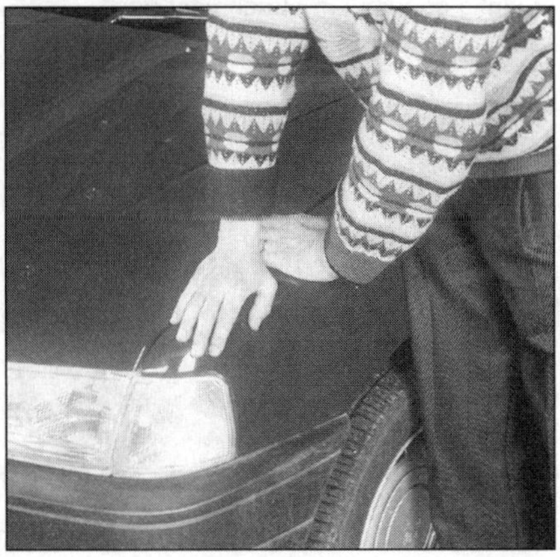

Exhaust system

☐ Start the engine. With your assistant holding a rag over the tailpipe, check the entire system for leaks. Repair or renew leaking sections.

3 Checks carried out **WITH THE VEHICLE RAISED AND THE WHEELS FREE TO TURN**

Jack up the front and rear of the vehicle, and securely support it on axle stands. Position the stands clear of the suspension assemblies. Ensure that the wheels are clear of the ground and that the steering can be turned from lock to lock.

Steering mechanism

☐ Have your assistant turn the steering from lock to lock. Check that the steering turns smoothly, and that no part of the steering mechanism, including a wheel or tyre, fouls any brake hose or pipe or any part of the body structure.

☐ Examine the steering rack rubber gaiters for damage or insecurity of the retaining clips. If power steering is fitted, check for signs of damage or leakage of the fluid hoses, pipes or connections. Also check for excessive stiffness or binding of the steering, a missing split pin or locking device, or severe corrosion of the body structure within 30 cm of any steering component attachment point.

Front and rear suspension and wheel bearings

☐ Starting at the front right-hand side, grasp the roadwheel at the 3 o'clock and 9 o'clock positions and shake it vigorously. Check for free play or insecurity at the wheel bearings, suspension balljoints, or suspension mountings, pivots and attachments.

☐ Now grasp the wheel at the 12 o'clock and 6 o'clock positions and repeat the previous inspection. Spin the wheel, and check for roughness or tightness of the front wheel bearing.

☐ If excess free play is suspected at a component pivot point, this can be confirmed by using a large screwdriver or similar tool and levering between the mounting and the component attachment. This will confirm whether the wear is in the pivot bush, its retaining bolt, or in the mounting itself (the bolt holes can often become elongated).

☐ Carry out all the above checks at the other front wheel, and then at both rear wheels.

Springs and shock absorbers

☐ Examine the suspension struts (when applicable) for serious fluid leakage, corrosion, or damage to the casing. Also check the security of the mounting points.

☐ If coil springs are fitted, check that the spring ends locate in their seats, and that the spring is not corroded, cracked or broken.

☐ If leaf springs are fitted, check that all leaves are intact, that the axle is securely attached to each spring, and that there is no deterioration of the spring eye mountings, bushes, and shackles.

☐ The same general checks apply to vehicles fitted with other suspension types, such as torsion bars, hydraulic displacer units, etc. Ensure that all mountings and attachments are secure, that there are no signs of excessive wear, corrosion or damage, and (on hydraulic types) that there are no fluid leaks or damaged pipes.

☐ Inspect the shock absorbers for signs of serious fluid leakage. Check for wear of the mounting bushes or attachments, or damage to the body of the unit.

Driveshafts (fwd vehicles only)

☐ Rotate each front wheel in turn and inspect the constant velocity joint gaiters for splits or damage. Also check that each driveshaft is straight and undamaged.

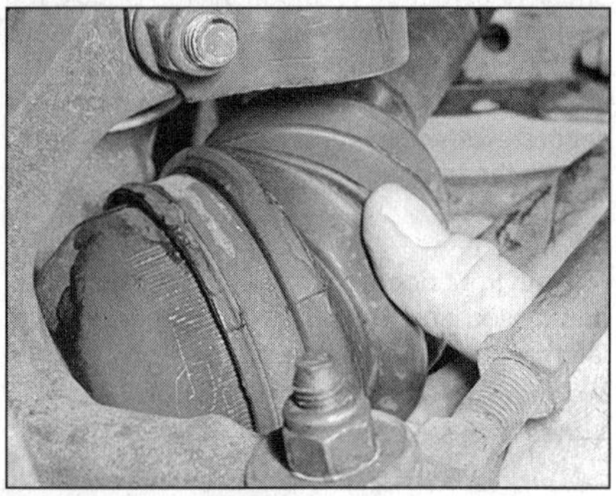

Braking system

☐ If possible without dismantling, check brake pad wear and disc condition. Ensure that the friction lining material has not worn excessively, (A) and that the discs are not fractured, pitted, scored or badly worn (B).

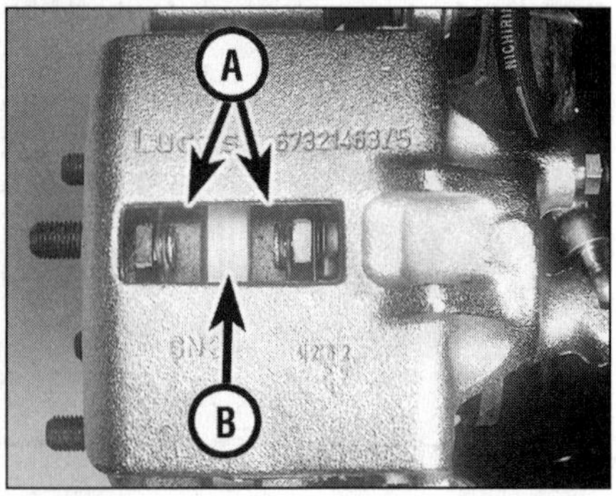

☐ Examine all the rigid brake pipes underneath the vehicle, and the flexible hose(s) at the rear. Look for corrosion, chafing or insecurity of the pipes, and for signs of bulging under pressure, chafing, splits or deterioration of the flexible hoses.

☐ Look for signs of fluid leaks at the brake calipers or on the brake backplates. Repair or renew leaking components.

☐ Slowly spin each wheel, while your assistant depresses and releases the footbrake. Ensure that each brake is operating and does not bind when the pedal is released.

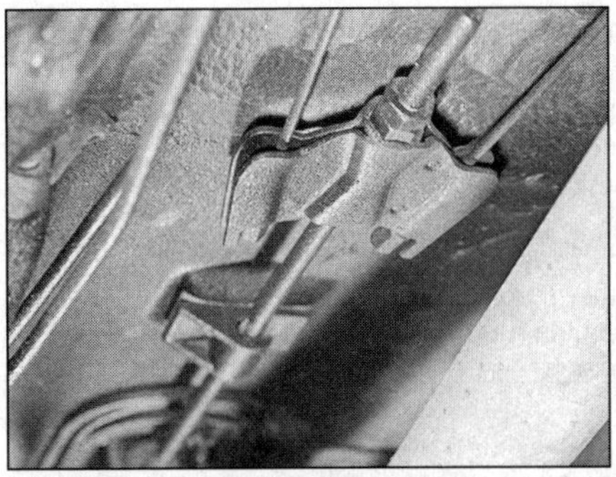

☐ Examine the handbrake mechanism, checking for frayed or broken cables, excessive corrosion, or wear or insecurity of the linkage. Check that the mechanism works on each relevant wheel, and releases fully, without binding.

☐ It is not possible to test brake efficiency without special equipment, but a road test can be carried out later to check that the vehicle pulls up in a straight line.

Fuel and exhaust systems

☐ Inspect the fuel tank (including the filler cap), fuel pipes, hoses and unions. All components must be secure and free from leaks.

☐ Examine the exhaust system over its entire length, checking for any damaged, broken or missing mountings, security of the retaining clamps and rust or corrosion.

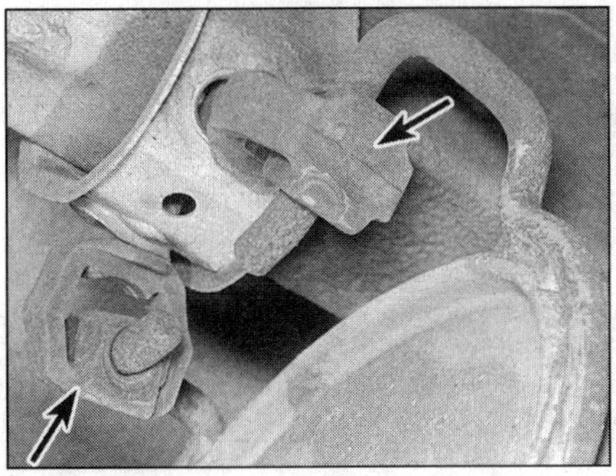

Wheels and tyres

☐ Examine the sidewalls and tread area of each tyre in turn. Check for cuts, tears, lumps, bulges, separation of the tread, and exposure of the ply or cord due to wear or damage. Check that the tyre bead is correctly seated on the wheel rim, that the valve is sound and

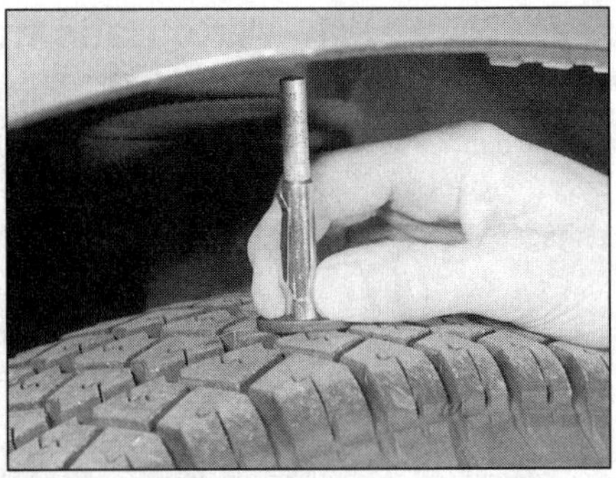

properly seated, and that the wheel is not distorted or damaged.

☐ Check that the tyres are of the correct size for the vehicle, that they are of the same size and type on each axle, and that the pressures are correct.

☐ Check the tyre tread depth. The legal minimum at the time of writing is 1.6 mm over at least three-quarters of the tread width. Abnormal tread wear may indicate incorrect front wheel alignment.

Body corrosion

☐ Check the condition of the entire vehicle structure for signs of corrosion in load-bearing areas. (These include chassis box sections, side sills, cross-members, pillars, and all suspension, steering, braking system and seat belt mountings and anchorages.) Any corrosion which has seriously reduced the thickness of a load-bearing area is likely to cause the vehicle to fail. In this case professional repairs are likely to be needed.

☐ Damage or corrosion which causes sharp or otherwise dangerous edges to be exposed will also cause the vehicle to fail.

4 Checks carried out on **YOUR VEHICLE'S EXHAUST EMISSION SYSTEM**

Petrol models

☐ Have the engine at normal operating temperature, and make sure that it is in good tune (ignition system in good order, air filter element clean, etc).

☐ Before any measurements are carried out, raise the engine speed to around 2500 rpm, and hold it at this speed for 20 seconds. Allow the engine speed to return to idle, and watch for smoke emissions from the exhaust tailpipe. If the idle speed is obviously much too high, or if dense blue or clearly-visible black smoke comes from the tailpipe for more than 5 seconds, the vehicle will fail. As a rule of thumb, blue smoke signifies oil being burnt (engine wear) while black smoke signifies unburnt fuel (dirty air cleaner element, or other carburettor or fuel system fault).

☐ An exhaust gas analyser capable of measuring carbon monoxide (CO) and hydrocarbons (HC) is now needed. If such an instrument cannot be hired or borrowed, a local garage may agree to perform the check for a small fee.

CO emissions (mixture)

☐ At the time of writing, the maximum CO level at idle is 3.5% for vehicles first used after August 1986 and 4.5% for older vehicles. From January 1996 a much tighter limit (around 0.5%) applies to catalyst-equipped vehicles first used from August 1992. If the CO level cannot be reduced far enough to pass the test (and the fuel and ignition systems are otherwise in good condition) then the carburettor is badly worn, or there is some problem in the fuel injection system or catalytic converter (as applicable).

HC emissions

☐ With the CO emissions within limits, HC emissions must be no more than 1200 ppm (parts per million). If the vehicle fails this test at idle, it can be re-tested at around 2000 rpm; if the HC level is then 1200 ppm or less, this counts as a pass.

☐ Excessive HC emissions can be caused by oil being burnt, but they are more likely to be due to unburnt fuel.

Diesel models

☐ The only emission test applicable to Diesel engines is the measuring of exhaust smoke density. The test involves accelerating the engine several times to its maximum unloaded speed.

Note: *It is of the utmost importance that the engine timing belt is in good condition before the test is carried out.*

☐ Excessive smoke can be caused by a dirty air cleaner element. Otherwise, professional advice may be needed to find the cause.

Introduction

The vehicle owner who does his or her own maintenance according to the recommended service schedules should not have to use this section of the manual very often. Modern component reliability is such that, provided those items subject to wear or deterioration are inspected or renewed at the specified intervals, sudden failure is comparatively rare. Faults do not usually just happen as a result of sudden failure, but develop over a period of time. Major mechanical failures in particular are usually preceded by characteristic symptoms over hundreds or even thousands of miles. Those components which do occasionally fail without warning are often small and easily carried in the vehicle.

With any fault finding, the first step is to decide where to begin investigations. Sometimes this is obvious, but on other occasions a little detective work will be necessary. The owner who makes half a dozen haphazard adjustments or replacements may be successful in curing a fault (or its symptoms), but will be none the wiser if the fault recurs and ultimately may have spent more time and money than was necessary. A calm and logical approach will be found to be more satisfactory in the long run. Always take into account any warning signs or abnormalities that may have been noticed in the period preceding the fault - power loss, high or low gauge readings, unusual smells, etc - and remember that failure of components such as fuses or spark plugs may only be pointers to some underlying fault.

The pages which follow provide an easy reference guide to the more common problems which may occur during the operation of the vehicle. These problems and their possible causes are grouped under headings denoting various components or systems, such as Engine, Cooling system, etc. The Chapter and/or Section which deals with the problem is also shown in brackets. Whatever the fault, certain basic principles apply. These are as follows:

Verify the fault. This is simply a matter of being sure that you know what the symptoms are before starting work. This is particularly important if you are investigating a fault for someone else who may not have described it very accurately.

Don't overlook the obvious. For example, if the vehicle won't start, is there petrol in the tank? (Don't take anyone else's word on this particular point, and don't trust the fuel gauge either!) If an electrical fault is indicated, look for loose or broken wires before digging out the test gear.

Cure the disease, not the symptom. Substituting a flat battery with a fully charged one will get you off the hard shoulder, but if the underlying cause is not attended to, the new battery will go the same way. Similarly, changing oil-fouled spark plugs for a new set will get you moving again, but remember that the reason for the fouling (if it wasn't simply an incorrect grade of plug) will have to be established and corrected.

Don't take anything for granted. Particularly, don't forget that a 'new' component may itself be defective (especially if it's been rattling around in the boot for months), and don't leave components out of a fault diagnosis sequence just because they are new or recently fitted. When you do finally diagnose a difficult fault, you'll probably realise that all the evidence was there from the start.

1 Engine

Engine fails to rotate when attempting to start

- ☐ Battery terminal connections loose or corroded *(Weekly checks)*.
- ☐ Battery discharged or faulty (Chapter 5).
- ☐ Broken, loose or disconnected wiring in the starting circuit (Chapter 5).
- ☐ Defective starter solenoid or switch (Chapter 5).
- ☐ Defective starter motor (Chapter 5).
- ☐ Starter pinion or flywheel ring gear teeth loose or broken (Chapters 2 and 5).
- ☐ Engine earth strap broken or disconnected (Chapter 5).

Engine rotates but will not start

- ☐ Fuel tank empty.
- ☐ Battery discharged (engine rotates slowly) (Chapter 5).
- ☐ Battery terminal connections loose or corroded *(Weekly checks)*.
- ☐ Ignition components damp or damaged (Chapters 1 and 5).
- ☐ Broken, loose or disconnected wiring in the ignition circuit (Chapters 1 and 5).
- ☐ Worn, faulty or incorrectly gapped spark plugs (Chapter 1).
- ☐ Choke mechanism sticking, incorrectly adjusted, or faulty (Chapter 4).
- ☐ Major mechanical failure (eg camshaft drive) (Chapter 2).

Engine difficult to start when cold

- ☐ Battery discharged (Chapter 5).
- ☐ Battery terminal connections loose or corroded *(Weekly checks)*.
- ☐ Worn, faulty or incorrectly gapped spark plugs (Chapter 1).
- ☐ Choke mechanism sticking, incorrectly adjusted, or faulty (Chapter 4).
- ☐ Other ignition system fault (Chapters 1 and 5).
- ☐ Low cylinder compressions (Chapter 2).

Engine difficult to start when hot

- ☐ Air filter element dirty or clogged (Chapter 1).
- ☐ Choke mechanism sticking, incorrectly adjusted, or faulty (Chapter 4).
- ☐ Carburettor float chamber flooding (Chapter 4).
- ☐ Low cylinder compressions (Chapter 2).

Starter motor noisy or excessively rough in engagement

- ☐ Starter pinion or flywheel ring gear teeth loose or broken (Chapters 2 and 5).
- ☐ Starter motor mounting bolts loose or missing (Chapter 5).
- ☐ Starter motor internal components worn or damaged (Chapter 5).

Engine starts but stops immediately

- ☐ Insufficient fuel reaching carburettor (Chapter 4).
- ☐ Loose or faulty electrical connections in the ignition circuit (Chapters 1 and 5).
- ☐ Vacuum leak at the carburettor or inlet manifold (Chapter 4).
- ☐ Blocked carburettor jet(s) or internal passages (Chapter 4).

Engine idles erratically

- ☐ Incorrectly adjusted idle speed and/or mixture settings (Chapter 1).
- ☐ Air filter element clogged (Chapter 1).
- ☐ Vacuum leak at the carburettor, inlet manifold or associated hoses (Chapter 4).
- ☐ Worn, faulty or incorrectly gapped spark plugs (Chapter 1).
- ☐ Uneven or low cylinder compressions (Chapter 2).
- ☐ Camshaft lobes worn (Chapter 2).
- ☐ Timing belt incorrectly tensioned (Chapter 2).

Engine misfires at idle speed

- ☐ Worn, faulty or incorrectly gapped spark plugs (Chapter 1).
- ☐ Faulty spark plug HT leads (Chapter 1).
- ☐ Incorrectly adjusted idle mixture settings (Chapter 1).
- ☐ Incorrect ignition timing (Chapter 1).
- ☐ Vacuum leak at the carburettor, inlet manifold or associated hoses (Chapter 4).
- ☐ Distributor cap cracked or tracking internally (Chapter 1).
- ☐ Uneven or low cylinder compressions (Chapter 2).
- ☐ Disconnected, leaking or perished crankcase ventilation hoses (Chapters 1 and 4).

Engine misfires throughout the driving speed range

- ☐ Blocked carburettor jet(s) or internal passages (Chapter 4).
- ☐ Carburettor worn or incorrectly adjusted (Chapters 1 and 4).
- ☐ Fuel filter choked (Chapter 1).
- ☐ Fuel pump faulty or delivery pressure low (Chapter 4).
- ☐ Fuel tank vent blocked or fuel pipes restricted (Chapter 4).
- ☐ Vacuum leak at the carburettor, inlet manifold or associated hoses (Chapter 4).
- ☐ Worn, faulty or incorrectly gapped spark plugs (Chapter 1).
- ☐ Faulty spark plug HT leads (Chapter 1).
- ☐ Distributor cap cracked or tracking internally (Chapter 1).
- ☐ Faulty ignition coil (Chapter 5).
- ☐ Uneven or low cylinder compressions (Chapter 2).

Engine hesitates on acceleration

- ☐ Worn, faulty or incorrectly gapped spark plugs (Chapter 1).
- ☐ Carburettor accelerator pump faulty (Chapter 4).
- ☐ Blocked carburettor jets or internal passages (Chapter 4).
- ☐ Vacuum leak at the carburettor, inlet manifold or associated hoses (Chapter 4).
- ☐ Carburettor worn or incorrectly adjusted (Chapters 1 and 4).

1 Engine (continued)

Engine stalls

- ☐ Incorrectly adjusted idle speed and/or mixture settings (Chapter 1).
- ☐ Blocked carburettor jet(s) or internal passages (Chapter 4).
- ☐ Vacuum leak at the carburettor, inlet manifold or associated hoses (Chapter 4).
- ☐ Fuel filter choked (Chapter 1).
- ☐ Fuel pump faulty or delivery pressure low (Chapter 4).
- ☐ Fuel tank vent blocked or fuel pipes restricted (Chapter 4).

Engine lacks power

- ☐ Incorrect ignition timing (Chapter 1).
- ☐ Carburettor worn or incorrectly adjusted (Chapter 1).
- ☐ Timing belt incorrectly fitted or tensioned (Chapter 2).
- ☐ Fuel filter choked (Chapter 1).
- ☐ Fuel pump faulty or delivery pressure low (Chapter 4).
- ☐ Uneven or low cylinder compressions (Chapter 2).
- ☐ Worn, faulty or incorrectly gapped spark plugs (Chapter 1).
- ☐ Vacuum leak at the carburettor, inlet manifold or associated hoses (Chapter 4).
- ☐ Brakes binding (Chapters 1 and 9).
- ☐ Clutch slipping (Chapter 6).

Engine backfires

- ☐ Ignition timing incorrect (Chapter 1).
- ☐ Timing belt incorrectly fitted or tensioned (Chapter 2).
- ☐ Carburettor worn or incorrectly adjusted (Chapter 1).
- ☐ Vacuum leak at the carburettor, inlet manifold or associated hoses (Chapter 4).

Oil pressure warning light illuminated with engine running

- ☐ Low oil level or incorrect grade (*Weekly checks*).
- ☐ Faulty oil pressure switch (Chapter 12).
- ☐ Worn engine bearings and/or oil pump (Chapter 2).
- ☐ High engine operating temperature (Chapter 3).
- ☐ Oil pressure relief valve defective (Chapter 2).
- ☐ Oil pick-up strainer clogged (Chapter 2).

Engine runs-on after switching off

- ☐ Idle speed excessively high (Chapter 1).
- ☐ Faulty anti-run-on solenoid (Chapter 4).
- ☐ Excessive carbon build-up in engine (Chapter 2).
- ☐ High engine operating temperature (Chapter 3).

Engine noises

Pre-ignition (pinking) or knocking during acceleration or under load

- ☐ Ignition timing incorrect (Chapter 1).
- ☐ Incorrect grade of fuel (Chapter 4).
- ☐ Vacuum leak at the carburettor, inlet manifold or associated hoses (Chapter 4).
- ☐ Excessive carbon build-up in engine (Chapter 2).
- ☐ Worn or damaged distributor or other ignition system component (Chapter 5).
- ☐ Carburettor worn or incorrectly adjusted (Chapter 1).

Whistling or wheezing noises

- ☐ Leaking inlet manifold or carburettor gasket (Chapter 4).
- ☐ Leaking exhaust manifold gasket or pipe to manifold joint (Chapter 1).
- ☐ Leaking vacuum hose (Chapters 4, 5 and 9).
- ☐ Blowing cylinder head gasket (Chapter 2).

Tapping or rattling noises

- ☐ Faulty hydraulic tappets (Chapter 1 or 2).
- ☐ Worn valve gear or camshaft (Chapter 2).
- ☐ Worn timing belt or tensioner (Chapter 2).
- ☐ Ancillary component fault (water pump, alternator etc) (Chapters 3 and 5).

Knocking or thumping noises

- ☐ Worn big-end bearings (regular heavy knocking, perhaps less under load) (Chapter 2).
- ☐ Worn main bearings (rumbling and knocking, perhaps worsening under load) (Chapter 2).
- ☐ Piston slap (most noticeable when cold) (Chapter 2).
- ☐ Ancillary component fault (alternator, water pump etc) (Chapters 3 and 5).

2 Cooling system

Overheating

- ☐ Insufficient coolant in system (*Weekly checks*).
- ☐ Thermostat faulty (Chapter 3).
- ☐ Radiator core blocked or grille restricted (Chapter 3).
- ☐ Electric cooling fan or thermostatic switch faulty (Chapter 3).
- ☐ Pressure cap faulty (Chapter 3).
- ☐ Timing belt worn, or incorrectly tensioned (Chapter 2).
- ☐ Ignition timing incorrect (Chapter 1).
- ☐ Inaccurate temperature gauge sender unit (Chapter 3).
- ☐ Air lock in cooling system (Chapter 1).

Overcooling

- ☐ Thermostat faulty (Chapter 3).
- ☐ Inaccurate temperature gauge sender unit (Chapter 3).

External coolant leakage

- ☐ Deteriorated or damaged hoses or hose clips (Chapter 1).
- ☐ Radiator core or heater matrix leaking (Chapter 3).
- ☐ Pressure cap faulty (Chapter 3).
- ☐ Water pump seal leaking (Chapter 3).
- ☐ Boiling due to overheating (Chapter 3).
- ☐ Core plug leaking (Chapter 2).

Internal coolant leakage

- ☐ Leaking cylinder head gasket (Chapter 2).
- ☐ Cracked cylinder head or cylinder bore (Chapter 2).

Corrosion

- ☐ Infrequent draining and flushing (Chapter 1).
- ☐ Incorrect antifreeze mixture or inappropriate type (Chapter 1).

3 Fuel and exhaust systems

Excessive fuel consumption

- ☐ Air filter element dirty or clogged (Chapter 1).
- ☐ Carburettor worn or incorrectly adjusted (Chapter 4).
- ☐ Choke cable incorrectly adjusted or choke sticking (Chapter 4).
- ☐ Ignition timing incorrect (Chapter 1).
- ☐ Tyres under-inflated *(Weekly checks).*

Fuel leakage and/or fuel odour

- ☐ Damaged or corroded fuel tank, pipes or connections (Chapter 1).
- ☐ Carburettor float chamber flooding (Chapter 4).

Excessive noise or fumes from exhaust system

- ☐ Leaking exhaust system or manifold joints (Chapter 1).
- ☐ Leaking, corroded or damaged silencers or pipe (Chapter 1).
- ☐ Broken mountings causing body or suspension contact (Chapter 1).

4 Clutch

Pedal travels to floor - no pressure or very little resistance

- ☐ Broken clutch cable (Chapter 6).
- ☐ Faulty clutch pedal self-adjust mechanism (Chapter 6).
- ☐ Broken clutch release bearing or fork (Chapter 6).
- ☐ Broken diaphragm spring in clutch pressure plate (Chapter 6).

Clutch fails to disengage (unable to select gears)

- ☐ Faulty clutch pedal self-adjust mechanism (Chapter 6).
- ☐ Clutch friction plate sticking on transmission input shaft splines (Chapter 6).
- ☐ Clutch friction plate sticking to flywheel or pressure plate (Chapter 6).
- ☐ Faulty pressure plate assembly (Chapter 6).
- ☐ Transmission input shaft seized in crankshaft spigot bearing (Chapter 2).
- ☐ Clutch release mechanism worn or incorrectly assembled (Chapter 6).

Clutch slips (engine speed increases with no increase in vehicle speed)

- ☐ Faulty clutch pedal self-adjust mechanism (Chapter 6).
- ☐ Clutch friction plate friction material excessively worn (Chapter 6).
- ☐ Clutch friction plate friction material contaminated with oil or grease (Chapter 6).
- ☐ Faulty pressure plate or weak diaphragm spring (Chapter 6).

Judder as clutch is engaged

- ☐ Clutch friction plate friction material contaminated with oil or grease (Chapter 6).
- ☐ Clutch friction plate friction material excessively worn (Chapter 6).
- ☐ Clutch cable sticking or frayed (Chapter 6).
- ☐ Faulty or distorted pressure plate or diaphragm spring (Chapter 6).
- ☐ Worn or loose engine or gearbox mountings (Chapter 2).
- ☐ Clutch friction plate hub or transmission input shaft splines worn (Chapter 6).

Noise when depressing or releasing clutch pedal

- ☐ Worn clutch release bearing (Chapter 6).
- ☐ Worn or dry clutch pedal bushes (Chapter 6).
- ☐ Faulty pressure plate assembly (Chapter 6).
- ☐ Pressure plate diaphragm spring broken (Chapter 6).
- ☐ Broken clutch friction plate cushioning springs (Chapter 6).

5 Manual gearbox

Noisy in neutral with engine running

- ☐ Input shaft bearings worn (noise apparent with clutch pedal released but not when depressed) (Chapter 7).*
- ☐ Clutch release bearing worn (noise apparent with clutch pedal depressed, possibly less when released) (Chapter 6).

Noisy in one particular gear

- ☐ Worn, damaged or chipped gear teeth (Chapter 7).*

Difficulty engaging gears

- ☐ Clutch fault (Chapter 6).
- ☐ Worn or damaged gear linkage (Chapter 7).
- ☐ Incorrectly adjusted gear linkage (Chapter 7).
- ☐ Worn synchroniser units (Chapter 7).*

Jumps out of gear

- ☐ Worn or damaged gear linkage (Chapter 7).
- ☐ Incorrectly adjusted gear linkage (Chapter 7).
- ☐ Worn synchroniser units (Chapter 7).*
- ☐ Worn selector forks (Chapter 7).*

Vibration

- ☐ Lack of oil (Chapter 1).
- ☐ Worn bearings (Chapter 7).*

Lubricant leaks

- ☐ Leaking driveshaft oil seal (Chapter 7).
- ☐ Leaking housing joint (Chapter 7).*
- ☐ Leaking input shaft oil seal (Chapter 7).*

**Although the corrective action necessary to remedy the symptoms described is beyond the scope of the home mechanic, the above information should be helpful in isolating the cause of the condition so that the owner can communicate clearly with a professional mechanic*

6 Automatic transmission

Note: *Due to the complexity of the automatic transmission, it is difficult for the home mechanic to properly diagnose and service this unit. For problems other than the following, the vehicle should be taken to a dealer service department or automatic transmission specialist.*

Fluid leakage

☐ Automatic transmission fluid is usually deep red in colour. Fluid leaks should not be confused with engine oil, which can easily be blown onto the transmission by air flow.

☐ To determine the source of a leak, first remove all built-up dirt and grime from the transmission housing and surrounding areas, using a degreasing agent or by steam-cleaning. Drive the vehicle at low speed, so that air flow will not blow the leak far from its source. Raise and support the vehicle, and determine where the leak is coming from. The following are common areas of leakage:

a) Fluid pan (transmission sump).
b) Dipstick tube (Chapter 7).
c) Transmission-to-fluid cooler fluid pipes/unions (Chapter 7).

Transmission fluid brown, or has burned smell

☐ Transmission fluid level low, or fluid in need of renewal (Chapter 1).

General gear selection problems

☐ The most likely cause of gear selection problems is a faulty or poorly-adjusted gear selector mechanism. The following are common problems associated with a faulty selector mechanism:

a) Engine starting in gears other than Park or Neutral.
b) Indicator on gear selector lever pointing to a gear other than the one actually being used.
c) Vehicle moves when in Park or Neutral.
d) Poor gear shift quality, or erratic gear changes.

☐ Refer any problems to a Rover dealer, or an automatic transmission specialist.

Transmission will not downshift (kickdown) with accelerator pedal fully depressed

☐ Low transmission fluid level (Chapter 1).
☐ Incorrect selector adjustment (Chapter 7).

Engine will not start in any gear, or starts in gears other than Park or Neutral

☐ Faulty starter inhibitor switch (Chapter 7).
☐ Incorrect selector adjustment (Chapter 7).

Transmission slips, shifts roughly, is noisy, or has no drive in forward or reverse gears

☐ There are many probable causes for the above problems, but the home mechanic should be concerned with only one possibility - fluid level. Before taking the vehicle to a dealer or transmission specialist, check the fluid level and condition of the fluid as described in Chapter 1. Correct the fluid level as necessary, or change the fluid and filter if needed. If the problem persists, professional help will be necessary.

7 Driveshafts

Clicking or knocking noise on turns (at slow speed on full lock)

☐ Lack of constant velocity joint lubricant (Chapter 8).
☐ Worn outer constant velocity joint (Chapter 8).

Vibration when accelerating or decelerating

☐ Worn inner constant velocity joint (Chapter 8).
☐ Bent or distorted driveshaft (Chapter 8).

8 Braking system

Note: *Before assuming that a brake problem exists, make sure that the tyres are in good condition and correctly inflated, the front wheel alignment is correct and the vehicle is not loaded with weight in an unequal manner*

Vehicle pulls to one side under braking

☐ Worn, defective, damaged or contaminated front or rear brake pads/shoes on one side (Chapter 1).
☐ Seized or partially seized front or rear brake caliper/wheel cylinder piston (Chapter 9).
☐ A mixture of brake pad/shoe lining materials fitted between sides (Chapter 1).
☐ Brake caliper mounting bolts loose (Chapter 9).
☐ Rear brake backplate mounting bolts loose (Chapter 9).
☐ Worn or damaged steering or suspension components (Chapter 10).

Noise (grinding or high-pitched squeal) when brakes applied

☐ Brake pad or shoe friction lining material worn down to metal backing (Chapter 1).
☐ Excessive corrosion of brake disc or drum, especially if the vehicle has been standing for some time (Chapter 1).
☐ Foreign object (stone chipping etc) trapped between brake disc and splash shield (Chapter 1).

Excessive brake pedal travel

☐ Faulty master cylinder (Chapter 9).
☐ Air in hydraulic system (Chapter 9).

Brake pedal feels spongy when depressed

☐ Air in hydraulic system (Chapter 9).
☐ Deteriorated flexible rubber brake hoses (Chapter 1 or 9).
☐ Master cylinder mounting nuts loose (Chapter 9).
☐ Faulty master cylinder (Chapter 9).

Excessive brake pedal effort required to stop vehicle

☐ Faulty vacuum servo unit (Chapter 9).
☐ Disconnected, damaged or insecure brake servo vacuum hose (Chapter 9).
☐ Primary or secondary hydraulic circuit failure (Chapter 9).
☐ Seized brake caliper or wheel cylinder piston(s) (Chapter 9).
☐ Brake pads or brake shoes incorrectly fitted (Chapter 1).
☐ Incorrect grade of brake pads or brake shoes fitted (Chapter 1).
☐ Brake pads or brake shoe linings contaminated (Chapter 1).

8 Braking system (continued)

Judder felt through brake pedal or steering wheel when braking

- ☐ Excessive run-out or distortion of front discs or rear drums (Chapter 9).
- ☐ Brake pad or brake shoe linings worn (Chapter 1).
- ☐ Brake caliper or rear brake backplate mounting bolts loose (Chapter 9).
- ☐ Wear in suspension, steering components or mountings (Chapter 9).

Brakes binding

- ☐ Seized brake caliper or wheel cylinder piston(s) (Chapter 9).
- ☐ Incorrectly adjusted handbrake mechanism or linkage (Chapter 1).
- ☐ Faulty master cylinder (Chapter 9).

Rear wheels locking under normal braking

- ☐ Rear brake shoe linings contaminated (Chapter 1).
- ☐ Faulty brake pressure regulator (Chapter 9).

9 Suspension and steering

Note: *Before diagnosing suspension or steering faults, be sure that the trouble is not due to incorrect tyre pressures, mixtures of tyre types or binding brakes*

Vehicle pulls to one side

- ☐ Defective tyre *(Weekly checks)*.
- ☐ Excessive wear in suspension or steering components (Chapter 10).
- ☐ Incorrect front wheel alignment (Chapter 10).
- ☐ Accident damage to steering or suspension components (Chapter 10).

Wheel wobble and vibration

- ☐ Front roadwheels out of balance (vibration felt mainly through the steering wheel) (Chapter 10).
- ☐ Rear roadwheels out of balance (vibration felt throughout the vehicle) (Chapter 10).
- ☐ Roadwheels damaged or distorted (Chapter 10).
- ☐ Faulty or damaged tyre (Chapter 10).
- ☐ Worn steering or suspension joints, bushes or components (Chapter 10).
- ☐ Wheel nuts loose (Chapter 1).

Excessive pitching and/or rolling around corners or when braking

- ☐ Defective Hydragas units and/or dampers (where fitted) (Chapter 10).
- ☐ Broken or weak suspension component (Chapter 10).
- ☐ Worn or damaged anti-roll bar or mountings (Chapter 10).

Wandering or general instability

- ☐ Incorrect front wheel alignment (Chapter 10).
- ☐ Worn steering or suspension joints, bushes or components (Chapter 10).
- ☐ Roadwheels out of balance (Chapter 10).
- ☐ Faulty or damaged tyre (Chapter 10).
- ☐ Wheel nuts loose (Chapter 1).
- ☐ Defective Hydragas units and/or dampers (where fitted) (Chapter 10).

Excessively stiff steering

- ☐ Lack of steering gear lubricant (Chapter 10).
- ☐ Seized track rod balljoint or suspension balljoint (Chapter 10).
- ☐ Incorrect front wheel alignment (Chapter 10).
- ☐ Steering rack or column bent or damaged (Chapter 10).

Excessive play in steering

- ☐ Worn steering column universal joint(s) or intermediate coupling (Chapter 10).
- ☐ Worn steering track rod balljoints (Chapter 10).
- ☐ Worn steering gear (Chapter 10).
- ☐ Worn steering or suspension joints, bushes or components (Chapter 10).

Tyre wear excessive

Tyres worn on inside or outside edges

- ☐ Tyres under-inflated (wear on both edges) *(Weekly checks)*.
- ☐ Incorrect camber or castor angles (wear on one edge only) (Chapter 10).
- ☐ Worn steering or suspension joints, bushes or components (Chapter 10).
- ☐ Excessively hard cornering.
- ☐ Accident damage.

Tyre treads exhibit feathered edges

- ☐ Incorrect toe setting (Chapter 10).

Tyres worn in centre of tread

- ☐ Tyres over-inflated *(Weekly checks)*.

Tyres worn on inside and outside edges

- ☐ Tyres under-inflated *(Weekly checks)*.

Tyres worn unevenly

- ☐ Tyres out of balance *(Weekly checks)*.
- ☐ Excessive wheel or tyre run-out *(Weekly checks)*.
- ☐ Defective Hydragas units and/or worn dampers (where fitted) (Chapter 10).
- ☐ Faulty tyre *(Weekly checks)*.

10 Electrical system

Note: *For problems associated with the starting system, refer to the faults listed under "Engine" earlier in this Section*

Battery will not hold a charge for more than a few days

- ☐ Battery defective internally (Chapter 5).
- ☐ Battery electrolyte level low (Chapter 1).
- ☐ Battery terminal connections loose or corroded *(Weekly checks)*.
- ☐ Alternator drivebelt worn or incorrectly adjusted (Chapter 1).
- ☐ Alternator not charging at correct output (Chapter 5).
- ☐ Alternator or voltage regulator faulty (Chapter 5).
- ☐ Short-circuit causing continual battery drain (Chapter 5).

10 Electrical system (continued)

Ignition warning light remains illuminated with engine running

- ☐ Alternator drivebelt broken, worn, or incorrectly adjusted (Chapter 1).
- ☐ Alternator brushes worn, sticking, or dirty (Chapter 5).
- ☐ Alternator brush springs weak or broken (Chapter 5).
- ☐ Internal fault in alternator or voltage regulator (Chapter 5).
- ☐ Broken, disconnected, or loose wiring in charging circuit (Chapter 12).

Ignition warning light fails to come on

- ☐ Warning light bulb blown (Chapter 12).
- ☐ Broken, disconnected, or loose wiring in warning light circuit (Chapter 12).
- ☐ Alternator faulty (Chapter 5).

Lights inoperative

- ☐ Bulb blown (Chapter 12).
- ☐ Corrosion of bulb or bulbholder contacts (Chapter 12).
- ☐ Blown fuse (Chapter 12).
- ☐ Faulty relay (Chapter 12).
- ☐ Broken, loose, or disconnected wiring (Chapter 12).
- ☐ Faulty switch (Chapter 12).

Instrument readings inaccurate or erratic

Instrument readings increase with engine speed

- ☐ Faulty voltage regulator (Chapter 5).

Fuel or temperature gauge give no reading

- ☐ Faulty gauge sender unit (Chapters 3 or 4).
- ☐ Wiring open circuit (Chapter 12).
- ☐ Faulty gauge (Chapter 12).

Fuel or temperature gauges give continuous maximum reading

- ☐ Faulty gauge sender unit (Chapters 3 or 4).
- ☐ Wiring short-circuit (Chapter 12).
- ☐ Faulty gauge (Chapter 12).

Horn inoperative or unsatisfactory in operation

Horn operates all the time

- ☐ Horn push either earthed or stuck down (Chapter 12).
- ☐ Horn cable to horn push earthed (Chapter 12).

Horn fails to operate

- ☐ Blown fuse (Chapter 12).
- ☐ Cable or cable connections loose, broken or disconnected (Chapter 12).
- ☐ Faulty horn (Chapter 12).

Horn emits intermittent or unsatisfactory sound

- ☐ Cable connections loose (Chapter 12).
- ☐ Horn mountings loose (Chapter 12).
- ☐ Faulty horn (Chapter 12).

Windscreen/tailgate wipers inoperative or unsatisfactory in operation

Wipers fail to operate or operate very slowly

- ☐ Wiper blades stuck to screen, or linkage seized or binding (Chapter 12).
- ☐ Blown fuse (Chapter 12).
- ☐ Cable or cable connections loose, broken or disconnected (Chapter 12).
- ☐ Faulty relay (Chapter 12).
- ☐ Faulty wiper motor (Chapter 12).

Wiper blades sweep over too large or too small an area of the glass

- ☐ Wiper arms incorrectly positioned on spindles (Chapter 12).
- ☐ Excessive wear of wiper linkage (Chapter 12).
- ☐ Wiper motor or linkage mountings loose or insecure (Chapter 12).

Wiper blades fail to clean the glass effectively

- ☐ Wiper blade rubbers worn or perished *(Weekly checks).*
- ☐ Wiper arm tension springs broken or arm pivots seized (Chapter 12).
- ☐ Insufficient windscreen washer additive to adequately remove road dirt film *(Weekly checks).*

Windscreen/tailgate washers inoperative or unsatisfactory in operation

One or more washer jets inoperative

- ☐ Blocked washer jet (Chapter 12).
- ☐ Disconnected, kinked or restricted fluid hose (Chapter 12).
- ☐ Insufficient fluid in washer reservoir *(Weekly checks).*

Washer pump fails to operate

- ☐ Broken or disconnected wiring or connections (Chapter 12).
- ☐ Blown fuse (Chapter 12).
- ☐ Faulty washer switch (Chapter 12).
- ☐ Faulty washer pump (Chapter 12).

Washer pump runs for some time before fluid is emitted from jets

- ☐ Faulty one-way valve in fluid supply hose (Chapter 12).

Electric windows inoperative or unsatisfactory in operation

Window glass will only move in one direction

- ☐ Faulty switch (Chapter 12).

Window glass slow to move

- ☐ Incorrectly adjusted door glass guide channels (Chapter 11).
- ☐ Regulator seized or damaged, or in need of lubrication (Chapter 11).
- ☐ Door internal components or trim fouling regulator (Chapter 11).
- ☐ Faulty motor (Chapter 12).

Window glass fails to move

- ☐ Incorrectly adjusted door glass guide channels (Chapter 11).
- ☐ Blown fuse (Chapter 12).
- ☐ Faulty relay (Chapter 12).
- ☐ Broken or disconnected wiring or connections (Chapter 12).
- ☐ Faulty motor (Chapter 12).

Central locking system inoperative or unsatisfactory in operation

Complete system failure

- ☐ Blown fuse (Chapter 12).
- ☐ Faulty relay (Chapter 12).
- ☐ Broken or disconnected wiring or connections (Chapter 12).

Latch locks but will not unlock, or unlocks but will not lock

- ☐ Faulty master switch (Chapter 12).
- ☐ Broken or disconnected latch operating rods or levers (Chapter 11).
- ☐ Faulty relay (Chapter 12).

One motor fails to operate

- ☐ Broken or disconnected wiring or connections (Chapter 12).
- ☐ Faulty motor (Chapter 12).
- ☐ Broken, binding or disconnected latch operating rods or levers (Chapter 11).
- ☐ Fault in door latch (Chapter 11).

A

ABS (Anti-lock brake system) A system, usually electronically controlled, that senses incipient wheel lockup during braking and relieves hydraulic pressure at wheels that are about to skid.

Air bag An inflatable bag hidden in the steering wheel (driver's side) or the dash or glovebox (passenger side). In a head-on collision, the bags inflate, preventing the driver and front passenger from being thrown forward into the steering wheel or windscreen.

Air cleaner A metal or plastic housing, containing a filter element, which removes dust and dirt from the air being drawn into the engine.

Air filter element The actual filter in an air cleaner system, usually manufactured from pleated paper and requiring renewal at regular intervals.

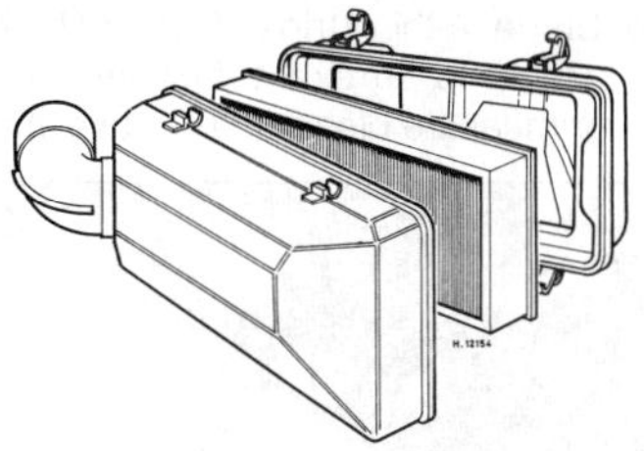

Air filter

Allen key A hexagonal wrench which fits into a recessed hexagonal hole.

Alligator clip A long-nosed spring-loaded metal clip with meshing teeth. Used to make temporary electrical connections.

Alternator A component in the electrical system which converts mechanical energy from a drivebelt into electrical energy to charge the battery and to operate the starting system, ignition system and electrical accessories.

Ampere (amp) A unit of measurement for the flow of electric current. One amp is the amount of current produced by one volt acting through a resistance of one ohm.

Anaerobic sealer A substance used to prevent bolts and screws from loosening. Anaerobic means that it does not require oxygen for activation. The Loctite brand is widely used.

Antifreeze A substance (usually ethylene glycol) mixed with water, and added to a vehicle's cooling system, to prevent freezing of the coolant in winter. Antifreeze also contains chemicals to inhibit corrosion and the formation of rust and other deposits that would tend to clog the radiator and coolant passages and reduce cooling efficiency.

Anti-seize compound A coating that reduces the risk of seizing on fasteners that are subjected to high temperatures, such as exhaust manifold bolts and nuts.

Asbestos A natural fibrous mineral with great heat resistance, commonly used in the composition of brake friction materials. Asbestos is a health hazard and the dust created by brake systems should never be inhaled or ingested.

Axle A shaft on which a wheel revolves, or which revolves with a wheel. Also, a solid beam that connects the two wheels at one end of the vehicle. An axle which also transmits power to the wheels is known as a live axle.

Axleshaft A single rotating shaft, on either side of the differential, which delivers power from the final drive assembly to the drive wheels. Also called a driveshaft or a halfshaft.

B

Ball bearing An anti-friction bearing consisting of a hardened inner and outer race with hardened steel balls between two races.

Bearing The curved surface on a shaft or in a bore, or the part assembled into either, that permits relative motion between them with minimum wear and friction.

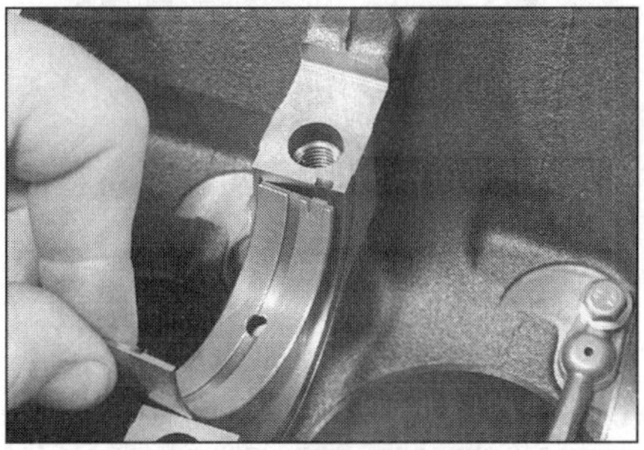

Bearing

Big-end bearing The bearing in the end of the connecting rod that's attached to the crankshaft.

Bleed nipple A valve on a brake wheel cylinder, caliper or other hydraulic component that is opened to purge the hydraulic system of air. Also called a bleed screw.

Brake bleeding Procedure for removing air from lines of a hydraulic brake system.

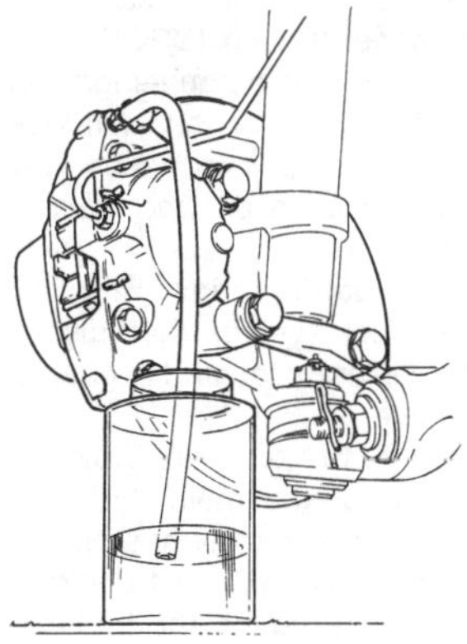

Brake bleeding

Brake disc The component of a disc brake that rotates with the wheels.

Brake drum The component of a drum brake that rotates with the wheels.

Brake linings The friction material which contacts the brake disc or drum to retard the vehicle's speed. The linings are bonded or riveted to the brake pads or shoes.

Brake pads The replaceable friction pads that pinch the brake disc when the brakes are applied. Brake pads consist of a friction material bonded or riveted to a rigid backing plate.

Brake shoe The crescent-shaped carrier to which the brake linings are mounted and which forces the lining against the rotating drum during braking.

Braking systems For more information on braking systems, consult the *Haynes Automotive Brake Manual*.

Breaker bar A long socket wrench handle providing greater leverage.

Bulkhead The insulated partition between the engine and the passenger compartment.

C

Caliper The non-rotating part of a disc-brake assembly that straddles the disc and carries the brake pads. The caliper also contains the hydraulic components that cause the pads to pinch the disc when the brakes are applied. A caliper is also a measuring tool that can be set to measure inside or outside dimensions of an object.

Camshaft A rotating shaft on which a series of cam lobes operate the valve mechanisms. The camshaft may be driven by gears, by sprockets and chain or by sprockets and a belt.

Canister A container in an evaporative emission control system; contains activated charcoal granules to trap vapours from the fuel system.

Canister

Carburettor A device which mixes fuel with air in the proper proportions to provide a desired power output from a spark ignition internal combustion engine.

Castellated Resembling the parapets along the top of a castle wall. For example, a castellated balljoint stud nut.

Castor In wheel alignment, the backward or forward tilt of the steering axis. Castor is positive when the steering axis is inclined rearward at the top.

Catalytic converter A silencer-like device in the exhaust system which converts certain pollutants in the exhaust gases into less harmful substances.

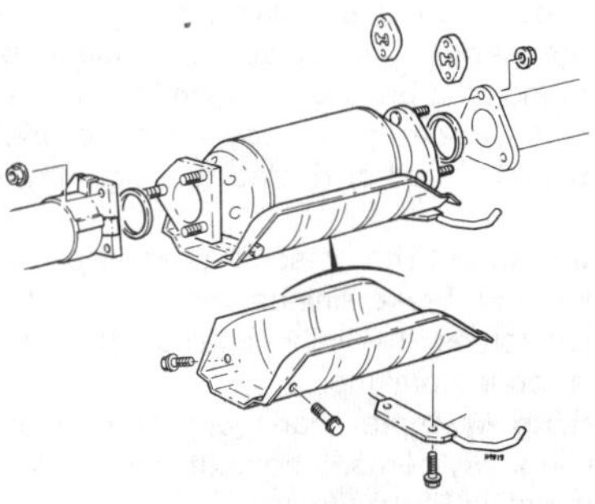

Catalytic converter

Circlip A ring-shaped clip used to prevent endwise movement of cylindrical parts and shafts. An internal circlip is installed in a groove in a housing; an external circlip fits into a groove on the outside of a cylindrical piece such as a shaft.

Clearance The amount of space between two parts. For example, between a piston and a cylinder, between a bearing and a journal, etc.

Coil spring A spiral of elastic steel found in various sizes throughout a vehicle, for example as a springing medium in the suspension and in the valve train.

Compression Reduction in volume, and increase in pressure and temperature, of a gas, caused by squeezing it into a smaller space.

Compression ratio The relationship between cylinder volume when the piston is at top dead centre and cylinder volume when the piston is at bottom dead centre.

Constant velocity (CV) joint A type of universal joint that cancels out vibrations caused by driving power being transmitted through an angle.

Core plug A disc or cup-shaped metal device inserted in a hole in a casting through which core was removed when the casting was formed. Also known as a freeze plug or expansion plug.

Crankcase The lower part of the engine block in which the crankshaft rotates.

Crankshaft The main rotating member, or shaft, running the length of the crankcase, with offset "throws" to which the connecting rods are attached.

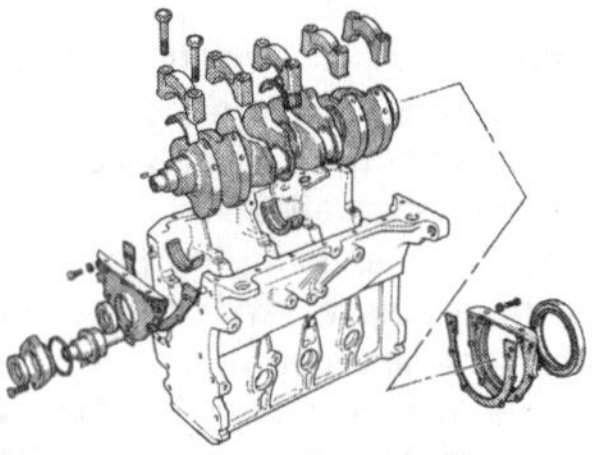

Crankshaft assembly

Crocodile clip See Alligator clip

D

Diagnostic code Code numbers obtained by accessing the diagnostic mode of an engine management computer. This code can be used to determine the area in the system where a malfunction may be located.

Disc brake A brake design incorporating a rotating disc onto which brake pads are squeezed. The resulting friction converts the energy of a moving vehicle into heat.

Double-overhead cam (DOHC) An engine that uses two overhead camshafts, usually one for the intake valves and one for the exhaust valves.

Drivebelt(s) The belt(s) used to drive accessories such as the alternator, water pump, power steering pump, air conditioning compressor, etc. off the crankshaft pulley.

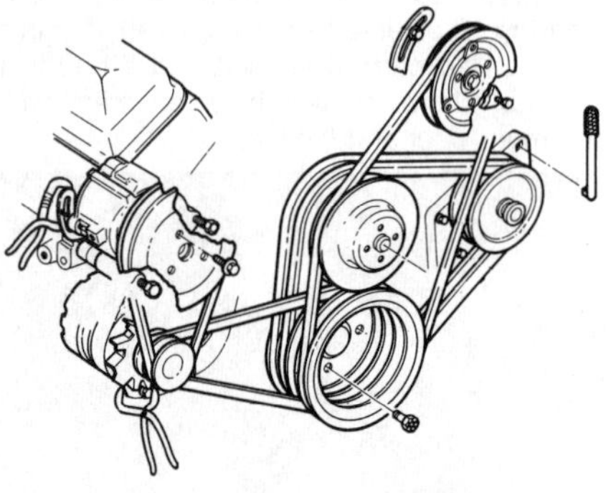

Accessory drivebelts

Driveshaft Any shaft used to transmit motion. Commonly used when referring to the axleshafts on a front wheel drive vehicle.

Drum brake A type of brake using a drum-shaped metal cylinder attached to the inner surface of the wheel. When the brake pedal is pressed, curved brake shoes with friction linings press against the inside of the drum to slow or stop the vehicle.

E

EGR valve A valve used to introduce exhaust gases into the intake air stream.

Electronic control unit (ECU) A computer which controls (for instance) ignition and fuel injection systems, or an anti-lock braking system. For more information refer to the *Haynes Automotive Electrical and Electronic Systems Manual.*

Electronic Fuel Injection (EFI) A computer controlled fuel system that distributes fuel through an injector located in each intake port of the engine.

Emergency brake A braking system, independent of the main hydraulic system, that can be used to slow or stop the vehicle if the primary brakes fail, or to hold the vehicle stationary even though the brake pedal isn't depressed. It usually consists of a hand lever that actuates either front or rear brakes mechanically through a series of cables and linkages. Also known as a handbrake or parking brake.

Endfloat The amount of lengthwise movement between two parts. As applied to a crankshaft, the distance that the crankshaft can move forward and back in the cylinder block.

Engine management system (EMS) A computer controlled system which manages the fuel injection and the ignition systems in an integrated fashion.

Exhaust manifold A part with several passages through which exhaust gases leave the engine combustion chambers and enter the exhaust pipe.

F

Fan clutch A viscous (fluid) drive coupling device which permits variable engine fan speeds in relation to engine speeds.

Feeler blade A thin strip or blade of hardened steel, ground to an exact thickness, used to check or measure clearances between parts.

Feeler blade

Firing order The order in which the engine cylinders fire, or deliver their power strokes, beginning with the number one cylinder.

Flywheel A heavy spinning wheel in which energy is absorbed and stored by means of momentum. On cars, the flywheel is attached to the crankshaft to smooth out firing impulses.

Free play The amount of travel before any action takes place. The "looseness" in a linkage, or an assembly of parts, between the initial application of force and actual movement. For example, the distance the brake pedal moves before the pistons in the master cylinder are actuated.

Fuse An electrical device which protects a circuit against accidental overload. The typical fuse contains a soft piece of metal which is calibrated to melt at a predetermined current flow (expressed as amps) and break the circuit.

Fusible link A circuit protection device consisting of a conductor surrounded by heat-resistant insulation. The conductor is smaller than the wire it protects, so it acts as the weakest link in the circuit. Unlike a blown fuse, a failed fusible link must frequently be cut from the wire for replacement.

G

Gap The distance the spark must travel in jumping from the centre electrode to the side electrode in a spark plug. Also refers to the spacing between the points in a contact breaker assembly in a conventional points-type ignition, or to the distance between the reluctor or rotor and the pickup coil in an electronic ignition.

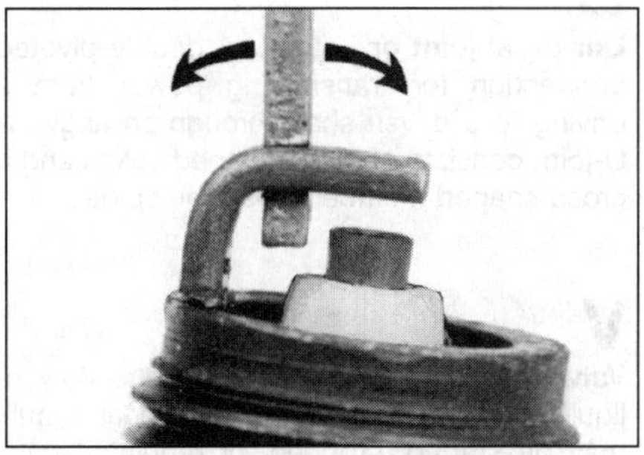

Adjusting spark plug gap

Gasket Any thin, soft material - usually cork, cardboard, asbestos or soft metal - installed between two metal surfaces to ensure a good seal. For instance, the cylinder head gasket seals the joint between the block and the cylinder head.

Gasket

Gauge An instrument panel display used to monitor engine conditions. A gauge with a movable pointer on a dial or a fixed scale is an analogue gauge. A gauge with a numerical readout is called a digital gauge.

H

Halfshaft A rotating shaft that transmits power from the final drive unit to a drive wheel, usually when referring to a live rear axle.

Harmonic balancer A device designed to reduce torsion or twisting vibration in the crankshaft. May be incorporated in the crankshaft pulley. Also known as a vibration damper.

Hone An abrasive tool for correcting small irregularities or differences in diameter in an engine cylinder, brake cylinder, etc.

Hydraulic tappet A tappet that utilises hydraulic pressure from the engine's lubrication system to maintain zero clearance (constant contact with both camshaft and valve stem). Automatically adjusts to variation in valve stem length. Hydraulic tappets also reduce valve noise.

I

Ignition timing The moment at which the spark plug fires, usually expressed in the number of crankshaft degrees before the piston reaches the top of its stroke.

Inlet manifold A tube or housing with passages through which flows the air-fuel mixture (carburettor vehicles and vehicles with throttle body injection) or air only (port fuel-injected vehicles) to the port openings in the cylinder head.

J

Jump start Starting the engine of a vehicle with a discharged or weak battery by attaching jump leads from the weak battery to a charged or helper battery.

L

Load Sensing Proportioning Valve (LSPV) A brake hydraulic system control valve that works like a proportioning valve, but also takes into consideration the amount of weight carried by the rear axle.

Locknut A nut used to lock an adjustment nut, or other threaded component, in place. For example, a locknut is employed to keep the adjusting nut on the rocker arm in position.

Lockwasher A form of washer designed to prevent an attaching nut from working loose.

M

MacPherson strut A type of front suspension system devised by Earle MacPherson at Ford of England. In its original form, a simple lateral link with the anti-roll bar creates the lower control arm. A long strut - an integral coil spring and shock absorber - is mounted between the body and the steering knuckle. Many modern so-called MacPherson strut systems use a conventional lower A-arm and don't rely on the anti-roll bar for location.

Multimeter An electrical test instrument with the capability to measure voltage, current and resistance.

N

NOx Oxides of Nitrogen. A common toxic pollutant emitted by petrol and diesel engines at higher temperatures.

O

Ohm The unit of electrical resistance. One volt applied to a resistance of one ohm will produce a current of one amp.

Ohmmeter An instrument for measuring electrical resistance.

O-ring A type of sealing ring made of a special rubber-like material; in use, the O-ring is compressed into a groove to provide the sealing action.

Overhead cam (ohc) engine An engine with the camshaft(s) located on top of the cylinder head(s).

Overhead valve (ohv) engine An engine with the valves located in the cylinder head, but with the camshaft located in the engine block.

Oxygen sensor A device installed in the engine exhaust manifold, which senses the oxygen content in the exhaust and converts this information into an electric current. Also called a Lambda sensor.

P

Phillips screw A type of screw head having a cross instead of a slot for a corresponding type of screwdriver.

Plastigage A thin strip of plastic thread, available in different sizes, used for measuring clearances. For example, a strip of Plastigage is laid across a bearing journal. The parts are assembled and dismantled; the width of the crushed strip indicates the clearance between journal and bearing.

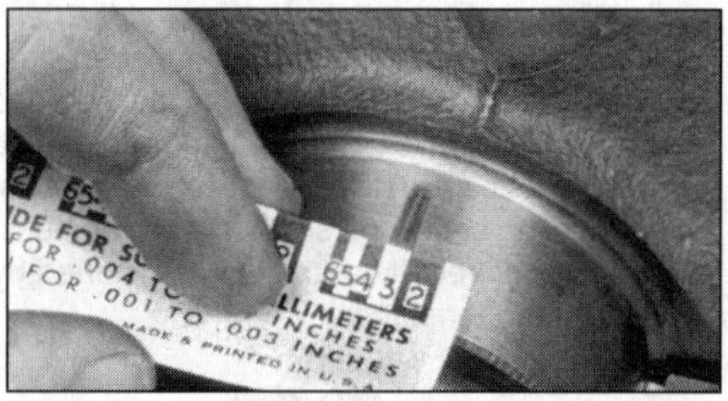

Plastigage

Propeller shaft The long hollow tube with universal joints at both ends that carries power from the transmission to the differential on front-engined rear wheel drive vehicles.

Proportioning valve A hydraulic control valve which limits the amount of pressure to the rear brakes during panic stops to prevent wheel lock-up.

R

Rack-and-pinion steering A steering system with a pinion gear on the end of the steering shaft that mates with a rack (think of a geared wheel opened up and laid flat). When the steering wheel is turned, the pinion turns, moving the rack to the left or right. This movement is transmitted through the track rods to the steering arms at the wheels.

Radiator A liquid-to-air heat transfer device designed to reduce the temperature of the coolant in an internal combustion engine cooling system.

Refrigerant Any substance used as a heat transfer agent in an air-conditioning system. R-12 has been the principle refrigerant for many years; recently, however, manufacturers have begun using R-134a, a non-CFC substance that is considered less harmful to the ozone in the upper atmosphere.

Rocker arm A lever arm that rocks on a shaft or pivots on a stud. In an overhead valve engine, the rocker arm converts the upward movement of the pushrod into a downward movement to open a valve.

Rotor In a distributor, the rotating device inside the cap that connects the centre electrode and the outer terminals as it turns, distributing the high voltage from the coil secondary winding to the proper spark plug. Also, that part of an alternator which rotates inside the stator. Also, the rotating assembly of a turbocharger, including the compressor wheel, shaft and turbine wheel.

Runout The amount of wobble (in-and-out movement) of a gear or wheel as it's rotated. The amount a shaft rotates "out-of-true." The out-of-round condition of a rotating part.

S

Sealant A liquid or paste used to prevent leakage at a joint. Sometimes used in conjunction with a gasket.

Sealed beam lamp An older headlight design which integrates the reflector, lens and filaments into a hermetically-sealed one-piece unit. When a filament burns out or the lens cracks, the entire unit is simply replaced.

Serpentine drivebelt A single, long, wide accessory drivebelt that's used on some newer vehicles to drive all the accessories, instead of a series of smaller, shorter belts. Serpentine drivebelts are usually tensioned by an automatic tensioner.

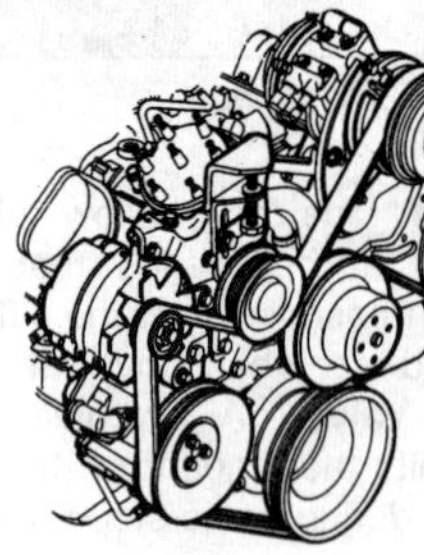

Serpentine drivebelt

Shim Thin spacer, commonly used to adjust the clearance or relative positions between two parts. For example, shims inserted into or under bucket tappets control valve clearances. Clearance is adjusted by changing the thickness of the shim.

Slide hammer A special puller that screws into or hooks onto a component such as a shaft or bearing; a heavy sliding handle on the shaft bottoms against the end of the shaft to knock the component free.

Sprocket A tooth or projection on the periphery of a wheel, shaped to engage with a chain or drivebelt. Commonly used to refer to the sprocket wheel itself.

Starter inhibitor switch On vehicles with an automatic transmission, a switch that prevents starting if the vehicle is not in Neutral or Park.

Strut See MacPherson strut.

T

Tappet A cylindrical component which transmits motion from the cam to the valve stem, either directly or via a pushrod and rocker arm. Also called a cam follower.

Thermostat A heat-controlled valve that regulates the flow of coolant between the cylinder block and the radiator, so maintaining optimum engine operating temperature. A thermostat is also used in some air cleaners in which the temperature is regulated.

Thrust bearing The bearing in the clutch assembly that is moved in to the release levers by clutch pedal action to disengage the clutch. Also referred to as a release bearing.

Timing belt A toothed belt which drives the camshaft. Serious engine damage may result if it breaks in service.

Timing chain A chain which drives the camshaft.

Toe-in The amount the front wheels are closer together at the front than at the rear. On rear wheel drive vehicles, a slight amount of toe-in is usually specified to keep the front wheels running parallel on the road by offsetting other forces that tend to spread the wheels apart.

Toe-out The amount the front wheels are closer together at the rear than at the front. On front wheel drive vehicles, a slight amount of toe-out is usually specified.

Tools For full information on choosing and using tools, refer to the *Haynes Automotive Tools Manual.*

Tracer A stripe of a second colour applied to a wire insulator to distinguish that wire from another one with the same colour insulator.

Tune-up A process of accurate and careful adjustments and parts replacement to obtain the best possible engine performance.

Turbocharger A centrifugal device, driven by exhaust gases, that pressurises the intake air. Normally used to increase the power output from a given engine displacement, but can also be used primarily to reduce exhaust emissions (as on VW's "Umwelt" Diesel engine).

U

Universal joint or U-joint A double-pivoted connection for transmitting power from a driving to a driven shaft through an angle. A U-joint consists of two Y-shaped yokes and a cross-shaped member called the spider.

V

Valve A device through which the flow of liquid, gas, vacuum, or loose material in bulk may be started, stopped, or regulated by a movable part that opens, shuts, or partially obstructs one or more ports or passageways. A valve is also the movable part of such a device.

Valve clearance The clearance between the valve tip (the end of the valve stem) and the rocker arm or tappet. The valve clearance is measured when the valve is closed.

Vernier caliper A precision measuring instrument that measures inside and outside dimensions. Not quite as accurate as a micrometer, but more convenient.

Viscosity The thickness of a liquid or its resistance to flow.

Volt A unit for expressing electrical "pressure" in a circuit. One volt that will produce a current of one ampere through a resistance of one ohm.

W

Welding Various processes used to join metal items by heating the areas to be joined to a molten state and fusing them together. For more information refer to the *Haynes Automotive Welding Manual.*

Wiring diagram A drawing portraying the components and wires in a vehicle's electrical system, using standardised symbols. For more information refer to the *Haynes Automotive Electrical and Electronic Systems Manual.*

Note: *References throughout this index are in the form - "Chapter number" • "page number"*

Haynes Manuals - The Complete List

Title	Book No.
ALFA ROMEO	
Alfa Romeo Alfasud/Sprint (74 - 88)	**0292**
Alfa Romeo Alfetta (73 - 87)	**0531**
AUDI	
Audi 80 (72 - Feb 79)	**0207**
Audi 80, 90 (79 - Oct 86) & Coupe (81 - Nov 88)	**0605**
Audi 80, 90 (Oct 86 - 90) & Coupe (Nov 88 - 90)	**1491**
Audi 100 (Oct 82 - 90) & 200 (Feb 84 - Oct 89)	**0907**
Audi 100/A6 (May 91 - May 97)	**3504**
AUSTIN	
Austin/MG Maestro 1.3 & 1.6 (83 - 95)	**0922**
Austin/MG Metro (80 - May 90)	**0718**
Austin Montego 1.3 & 1.6 (84 - 94)	**1066**
Austin/MG Montego 2.0 (84 - 95)	**1067**
Mini (59 - 69)	**0527**
Mini (69 - Oct 96)	**0646**
Austin/Rover 2.0 litre Diesel Engine (86 - 93)	**1857**
BEDFORD	
Bedford CF (69 - 87)	**0163**
Bedford Rascal (86 - 93)	**3015**
BMW	
BMW 316, 320 & 320i (4-cyl) (75 - Feb 83)	**0276**
BMW 320, 320i, 323i & 325i (6-cyl) (Oct 77 - Sept 87)	**0815**
BMW 3-Series (Apr 91 - 96)	**3210**
BMW 3-Series (sohc) (83 - 91)	**1948**
BMW 520i & 525e (Oct 81 - June 88)	**1560**
BMW 525, 528 & 528i (73 - Sept 81)	**0632**
BMW 5-Series (sohc) (81 - 91)	**1948**
BMW 1500, 1502, 1600, 1602, 2000 & 2002 (59 - 77)	**0240**
CITROËN	
Citroën 2CV, Ami & Dyane (67 - 90)	**0196**
Citroën AX Petrol & Diesel (87 - 94)	**3014**
Citroën BX (83 - 94)	**0908**
Citroën C15 Van Petrol & Diesel (89 - 98)	**3509**
Citroën CX (75 - 88)	**0528**
Citroën Saxo Petrol & Diesel (96 - 98)	**3506**
Citroën Visa (79 - 88)	**0620**
Citroën Xantia Petrol & Diesel (93 - 98)	**3082**
Citroën XM Petrol & Diesel (89 - 98)	**3451**
Citroën ZX Diesel (91 - 93)	**1922**
Citroën ZX Petrol (91 - 94)	**1881**
Citroën 1.7 & 1.9 litre Diesel Engine (84 - 96)	**1379**
COLT	
Colt 1200, 1250 & 1400 (79 - May 84)	**0600**
DAIMLER	
Daimler Sovereign (68 - Oct 86)	**0242**
Daimler Double Six (72 - 88)	**0478**
FIAT	
Fiat 126 (73 - 87)	**0305**
Fiat 127 (71 - 83)	**0193**
Fiat 500 (57 - 73)	**0090**
Fiat Cinquecento (June 93 - 98)	**3501**
Fiat Panda (81 - 95)	**0793**
Fiat Punto (94 - 96)	**3251**
Fiat Regata (84 - 88)	**1167**
Fiat Strada (79 - 88)	**0479**

Title	Book No.
Fiat Tipo (88 - 91)	**1625**
Fiat Uno (83 - 95)	**0923**
Fiat X1/9 (74 - 89)	**0273**
FORD	
Ford Capri II (& III) 1.6 & 2.0 (74 - 87)	**0283**
Ford Capri II (& III) 2.8 & 3.0 (74 - 87)	**1309**
Ford Cortina Mk IV (& V) 1.6 & 2.0 (76 - 83)	**0343**
Ford Escort (75 - Aug 80)	**0280**
Ford Escort (Sept 80 - Sept 90)	**0686**
Ford Escort (Sept 90 - 97)	**1737**
Ford Escort Mk II Mexico, RS 1600 & RS 2000 (75 - 80)	**0735**
Ford Fiesta (inc. XR2) (76 - Aug 83)	**0334**
Ford Fiesta (inc. XR2) (Aug 83 - Feb 89)	**1030**
Ford Fiesta (Feb 89 - Oct 95)	**1595**
Ford Fiesta Petrol & Diesel (Oct 95 - 97)	**3397**
Ford Granada (Sept 77 - Feb 85)	**0481**
Ford Granada (Mar 85 - 94)	**1245**
Ford Mondeo (93 - 99)	**1923**
Ford Mondeo Diesel (93 - 96)	**3465**
Ford Orion (83 - Sept 90)	**1009**
Ford Orion (Sept 90 - 93)	**1737**
Ford Sierra 1.3, 1.6, 1.8 & 2.0 (82 - 93)	**0903**
Ford Sierra 2.3, 2.8 & 2.9 (82 - 91)	**0904**
Ford Scorpio (Mar 85 - 94)	**1245**
Ford Transit Petrol (Mk 2) (78 - Jan 86)	**0719**
Ford Transit Petrol (Mk 3) (Feb 86 - 89)	**1468**
Ford Transit Diesel (Feb 86 - 95)	**3019**
Ford 1.6 & 1.8 litre Diesel Engine (84 - 96)	**1172**
Ford 2.1, 2.3 & 2.5 litre Diesel Engine (77 - 90)	**1606**
FREIGHT ROVER	
Freight Rover Sherpa (74 - 87)	**0463**
HILLMAN	
Hillman Avenger (70 - 82)	**0037**
HONDA	
Honda Accord (76 - Feb 84)	**0351**
Honda Accord (Feb 84 - Oct 85)	**1177**
Honda Civic (Feb 84 - Oct 87)	**1226**
Honda Civic (Nov 91 - 96)	**3199**
HYUNDAI	
Hyundai Pony (85 - 94)	**3398**
JAGUAR	
Jaguar E Type (61 - 72)	**0140**
Jaguar MkI & II, 240 & 340 (55 - 69)	**0098**
Jaguar XJ6, XJ & Sovereign (68 - Oct 86)	**0242**
Jaguar XJ6 & Sovereign (Oct 86 - Sept 94)	**3261**
Jaguar XJ12, XJS & Sovereign (72 - 88)	**0478**
JEEP	
Jeep Cherokee Petrol (93 - 96)	**1943**
LADA	
Lada 1200, 1300, 1500 & 1600 (74 - 91)	**0413**
Lada Samara (87 - 91)	**1610**
LAND ROVER	
Land Rover 90, 110 & Defender Diesel (83 - 95)	**3017**
Land Rover Discovery Diesel (89 - 95)	**3016**
Land Rover Series IIA & III Diesel (58 - 85)	**0529**
Land Rover Series II, IIA & III Petrol (58 - 85)	**0314**

Title	Book No.
MAZDA	
Mazda 323 fwd (Mar 81 - Oct 89)	**1608**
Mazda 323 (Oct 89 - 98)	**3455**
Mazda 626 fwd (May 83 - Sept 87)	**0929**
Mazda B-1600, B-1800 & B-2000 Pick-up (72 - 88)	**0267**
MERCEDES-BENZ	
Mercedes-Benz 190, 190E & 190D Petrol & Diesel (83 - 93)	**3450**
Mercedes-Benz 200, 240, 300 Diesel (Oct 76 - 85)	**1114**
Mercedes-Benz 250 & 280 (68 - 72)	**0346**
Mercedes-Benz 250 & 280 (123 Series) (Oct 76 - 84)	**0677**
Mercedes-Benz 124 Series (85 - Aug 93)	**3253**
MG	
MGB (62 - 80)	**0111**
MG Maestro 1.3 & 1.6 (83 - 95)	**0922**
MG Metro (80 - May 90)	**0718**
MG Midget & AH Sprite (58 - 80)	**0265**
MG Montego 2.0 (84 - 95)	**1067**
MITSUBISHI	
Mitsubishi 1200, 1250 & 1400 (79 - May 84)	**0600**
Mitsubishi Shogun & L200 Pick-Ups (83 - 94)	**1944**
MORRIS	
Morris Ital 1.3 (80 - 84)	**0705**
Morris Minor 1000 (56 - 71)	**0024**
NISSAN	
Nissan Bluebird fwd (May 84 - Mar 86)	**1223**
Nissan Bluebird (T12 & T72) (Mar 86 - 90)	**1473**
Nissan Cherry (N12) (Sept 82 - 86)	**1031**
Nissan Micra (K10) (83 - Jan 93)	**0931**
Nissan Micra (93 - 96)	**3254**
Nissan Primera (90 - Oct 96)	**1851**
Nissan Stanza (82 - 86)	**0824**
Nissan Sunny (B11) (May 82 - Oct 86)	**0895**
Nissan Sunny (Oct 86 - Mar 91)	**1378**
Nissan Sunny (Apr 91 - 95)	**3219**
OPEL	
Opel Ascona & Manta (B Series) (Sept 75 - 88)	**0316**
Opel Ascona (81 - 88) (Not available in UK see Vauxhall Cavalier 0812)	**3215**
Opel Astra (Oct 91 - 96) (Not available in UK see Vauxhall Astra 1832)	**3156**
Opel Calibra (90 - 98) (See Vauxhall/Opel Calibra Book No. 3502)	
Opel Corsa (83 - Mar 93) (Not available in UK see Vauxhall Nova 0909)	**3160**
Opel Corsa (Mar 93 - 97) (Not available in UK see Vauxhall Corsa 1985)	**3159**
Opel Frontera Petrol & Diesel (91 - 98) (See Vauxhall/Opel Frontera Book No. 1985)	
Opel Kadett (Nov 79 - Oct 84)	**0634**
Opel Kadett (Oct 84 - Oct 91) (Not available in UK see Vauxhall Astra & Belmont 1136)	**3196**
Opel Omega & Senator (86 - 94) (Not available in UK see Vauxhall Carlton & Senator 1469)	**3157**
Opel Omega Petrol & Diesel (94 - 98) (See Vauxhall/Opel Omega Book No. 3510)	